MW01485773

República del Perú

**Embassy of Peru
in the U.S.A.**

| If this item is found, please return it to the Embassy of Peru in the United States. | Phone number: (202)-833-9860 |
| | Address: 1700 Massachusetts Ave NW, Washington, DC, 20036 |

WESLEYAN POETRY

publication of this book is funded by the

BEATRICE FOX AUERBACH FOUNDATION FUND

at the Hartford Foundation for Public Giving

Selected Writings of
CÉSAR VALLEJO

Edited by JOSEPH MULLIGAN

WESLEYAN

UNIVERSITY

PRESS

Middletown,

Connecticut

\

Wesleyan University Press
Middletown, CT 06459
www.wesleyan.edu/wespress
© 2015 Wesleyan University Press
All rights reserved
Manufactured in the United States of America
Designed by Richard Hendel
Typeset in Arnhem by Tseng Information Systems, Inc.

Wesleyan University Press is a member of the
Green Press Initiative. The paper used in this book
meets their minimum requirement for recycled paper.

Library of Congress Cataloging-in-Publication Data
Vallejo, César, 1892–1938.
[Works. Selections. English]
Selected writings of César Vallejo / edited [and translated]
by Joseph Mulligan.
    pages cm.—(Wesleyan poetry series)
Includes bibliographical references and index.
Summary: "Selected Writings of César Vallejo has all the best writing
of a major Spanish modernist"—provided by publisher.
ISBN 978-0-8195-7484-8 (cloth: alk. paper)—ISBN 978-0-8195-7525-8 (ebook)
1. Vallejo, César, 1892–1938—Translations into English. I. Mulligan,
Joseph W., 1981– editor, translator. II. Title.
PQ8497.V35A2 2015
861'.62—dc23   2014048342

5 4 3 2 1

publication of this book is funded by the
BEATRICE FOX AUERBACH FOUNDATION FUND
at the Hartford Foundation for Public Giving

CONTENTS

ACKNOWLEDGMENTS

The materialization of this book would never have been possible without the dedicated work of the contributing translators: Clayton Eshleman, Pierre Joris, Suzanne Jill Levine, Nicole Peyrafitte, Michael Lee Rattigan, William Rowe, Eliot Weinberger, and Jason Weiss. Without their good will and expertise, this publication of so many pages of previously untranslated texts and the compilation of preexisting translations would still exist only as an idea. My deep gratitude to them for sharing this vision and making it a reality.

Special thanks are due to Clayton Eshleman, who suggested I take on this project. He was its first supporter and provided crucial suggestions regarding the structure of the book. My thanks as well go to Pierre Joris, who, for the past ten years, has been my mentor and an invaluable guide in my search for an understanding of poetics and translation.

I am grateful to Suzanne Jill Levine, who was an adviser on this project and, in addition to translating, provided feedback on the structure of the book and helped facilitate a collaborative review of the selection by Jorge Luis Castillo, Michelle Clayton, Efraín Kristal, José Antonio Mazzotti, Eliot Weinberger, and Jason Weiss, all of whom deserve my utmost thanks for their work toward developing a balanced range of writings.

I should also express my gratitude to Ernesto Livon Grossman, whose views on the Latin American experimental tradition—in a conversation that has lasted over a decade—have profoundly shaped the way I've come to frame Vallejo's writings. My thanks are also due to James Sherry, who edited my translation *Against Professional Secrets* (Roof Books) and helped me see the trajectory of Vallejo's previously untranslated prose.

A thousand thanks to Stephen Hart, who generously reviewed the biographical material of the introduction; Gustavo Faverón Patriau, whom I consulted on several occasions about problems in interpretation; Cory Merril, who helped determine the transliteration of Vallejo's Russian vocabulary; and Odi Gonzáles, who analyzed and commented on Vallejo's Quechua vocabulary, offering modern standard spellings.

Michael Lee Rattigan also deserves singular recognition for the magnitude of his contribution of previously untranslated magazine articles and letters and for his constant support and selfless dedication in our collaborative translation process. I must also thank poet and translator Mario Domínguez Parra, who, over the past three years, has weighed in extensively on some of the most intricate translation problems that arise in the texts presented here. His dedication to helping preserve the idiosyncrasy of Vallejo's writing contributed in a major way to these translations and the notes that follow them. Finally, this volume would never have been possible without the support of my wife, Beatriz Sosa Matta, who has enthusiastically encouraged my work and shared in the discovery entailed by retracing Vallejo's steps down his many winding roads.

Some of my translations have appeared in *Literal Magazine*, Jerome Rothenberg's *Poems and Poetics*, and *Asymptote Magazine*. Some early versions of Michael Lee Rattigan's translations appeared in the *Black Herald*. Eliot Weinberger's contribution was first published in *Sulfur*. Clayton Eshleman's translations have been widely published over the past fifty years, in magazines, journals, and a trove of books. We are grateful to the University of California Press for allowing us to reprint his most recent versions in *The Complete Poetry* (2007).

INTRODUCTION

César Vallejo is by far the most well-known Peruvian writer, yet he's also the most obscure. Since his rise to fame in the mid-twentieth century, hundreds of books, essays, academic theses, and dissertations have been written on his poetry and literary persona. Numerous editions of his poems have appeared in the original Castilian and in translation, as comprehensive volumes and as anthologies.[1] With the stamp of his name, a line from his poems, or the titles of his books, magazines have been launched, conferences have been held, publishing houses have been formed, high schools have been created, and even soccer clubs have taken to the field. A survey of Vallejo's complete writings, however, shows us that the poetry accounts for only one-sixth of the whole. For the past fifty years, Hispanic scholars, such as Jorge Puccinelli, whose argument I paraphrase, have embarked on the heuristic work of "tracing down and recovering the *disjecta membra* of a vast literary corpus," which proved vital, since "to cut off the limb of a tree is to deprive it of life, which resides in the unity of the organism—it is to isolate a fragment from the whole to which it is inextricably bound."[2]

More often than not, Vallejo's readers in English translation sever the tree limb and, onto an already truncated representation, they graft a contrived avant-garde branch, which they're convinced belongs there because they've already seen it in his contemporaries. But can we blame these readers for this confusion, or must we, his translators, assume responsibility, since we're the ones who've known enough to shudder at his poetry's intensity, but out of professional interest or genric prejudice have consciously or unconsciously ignored the rest of his oeuvre? Few times in the history of Western literature has the representation of such a multifaceted figure been so one-dimensional.

The following compendium reconfigures César Vallejo's oeuvre. It's an opportunity to reformulate an understanding of the writings and persona of one of the most important literary figures of the twentieth century. In the following introduction, I sketch out Vallejo's biography to show where and in whose company he was during specific historical moments and during the composition of certain texts, before moving on to characterize the works or collections of writings from which the selections have been drawn, with the aim of elucidating the oeuvre, specifying its publication history in relation to the author's writing process, and synthesizing predominant aesthetic features that let us better understand his ideas.

Finally, by way of conclusion, I offer some brief remarks on the English translation work that lies ahead.

1

High in the Andes of northern Peru, where the cordillera rises ten thousand feet above sea level in a distance of about 350 miles, in the Department of La Libertad there's a place called Santiago de Chuco. On March 16, 1892, on Calle Colón 96 in that town, a forty-two-year-old mestiza named María de los Santos Mendoza Gurrionero (1850–1918), wife of Francisco de Paula Vallejo Benítez (1840–1924) and mother of eleven, gave birth to her twelfth and final child, whom she named César Abraham.[3]

Santiago de Chuco doesn't only mark César Vallejo's birthplace but also exposes his outlier status ab initio. Both his parents were born and raised in Santiago, and before it became the provincial capital (when it was still a district in the province of Huamachuco), his father had been governor. Additionally, his paternal grandparents were the Galician priest José Rufo Vallejo and his Chimú concubine Justa Benítez; and his maternal grandparents, the Galician priest Joaquín de Mendez and his Chimú concubine Natividad Gurrionero, placing young César in a typical context of mestizaje in the Andes.

Perched on the limb of the new millennium, many of us in North America or Western Europe struggle to imagine what it must have been like to live in Santiago de Chuco a century ago. Even a journey today to that highland town is likely to be misleading; for eyes accustomed to the comfort, commodities, and technologies of developed cities and countries, a journey to Santiago will feel like a trip back in time. But the truth is that this little mountain town has already modernized extensively. According to the 1940 census, in Santiago de Chuco many houses were still lacking utilities that had started to become mainstays in other less remote homes—utilities as basic as electricity and potable water. If we take into account that as late as 1940, out of 957 households, as few as 147 had running water, 130 had drainage, and a mere 2 had electricity, then we must imagine a Santiago in 1892 when Vallejo was born there quite a bit less modern.[4]

We must also be careful not to assume that La Libertad at large had dodged the European influence that so radically changed so much of South America. Out of the approximately forty-eight thousand people in the department, as many as forty-six thousand were mestizos, and about forty thousand over the age of five were proficient only in the Castilian language, while a mere seventy or so individuals knew Castilian and Quechua; no one in the census is said to have known only Quechua or any other indigenous language. Therefore, the Santiago where César Vallejo was born and raised, as Luis Monguío suggests, contained "biological, linguistic, and Indo-Hispanic cultural fusion that extends to the majority . . . [He] was born in neither the Andalusian nor the indigenous Peru, but in the mestizo, *cholo* Peru."[5]

So here we have Vallejo's early stomping ground, a rural town of the Andes where the process of modernization seemed to lurk on the horizon but not fully arrive. Although there's a lack of sufficient information to determine his early childhood education with detail and certainty, we do know that he was largely inspired by his grandfathers and, at an early age, is said to have wanted to follow in their footsteps and become a priest. We also know that he attended secondary school in Huamachuco, as Santiago didn't have one, but apparently only in 1905 and 1906 and thereafter sporadically, probably coming in only to take exams, since his family couldn't afford to send him full-time.

Nevertheless, when 1910 rolled around, the horizons of a now eighteen-year-old César began to widen as he moved from his highland hometown to the coastal city of Trujillo on April 2. There he enrolled in the Department of Humanities at La Universidad de La Libertad but didn't even finish his first year on account of economic hardship, which led him to work for a stint in the Quiruvilca mines instead—an experience that eventually received literary expression in his novel *Tungsten* and his play *Brothers Colacho*. Desperately trying to carry out his studies, on April 11, 1911, he enrolled in the Department of Science at the same university but again dropped out for financial reasons, and this time found work from May to December tutoring the children of a wealthy land owner, Domingo Sotil.

César continued to live as a sort of rogue intellectual for the next few years, looking for a vocation. In 1912, for example, he took a job on a sugar plantation called Roma, nor far from Trujillo in the Chicama valley, which was "owned by the Larco Herreras, one of the two big families (the other being the Gildemeisters) who had come to monopolize the sugar industry in Peru after the war of the Pacific." It's not hard to imagine how strongly impacted the future champion of social justice would've been when he saw "hundreds of peons arriving at the sugar estate at the crack of dawn and working until nightfall in the fields, with only a fistful of rice to live on."[6] Vallejo was horrified by the way those workers' lives "were dominated by alcohol sold to them on credit," creating debts that rapidly accrued to the point that they'd surely outlive their debtors, and it was this "hideous process [that] devastated him and lit a fuse that burned until 1928, the year he suffered the implosion that resulted in his inability to conform with social conditions for the rest of his life."[7] We should also point out that Vallejo's direct contact with these workers, who would've been native speakers of Quechua, can help explain where some of his surprisingly large Quechua vocabulary may have come from.

In 1913–14, Vallejo managed to reenroll in the Department of Humanities with the money he was earning from a job he'd landed teaching botany and anatomy at Centro Escolar de Varones in Trujillo. This proved to be a formative period in his life, since this return to the university also placed him in a literary environment that fostered his creative endeavors and shaped his artistic theories. The following year, he was adopted by Grupo Norte in the Trujillo counterculture, his "bohemia" as he referred to it fondly over the years. The group consisted of Eulogio Garrido, whose house was the central meeting place; Antenor Orrego Espinoza; Alcides Spelucín; Juan Espejo; Óscar Imaña; Macedonio de la Torre; Eloy Espinosa; Federico Esquerre; Leoncio Muñoz; Alfonso Sánchez Arteaga; Francisco Sandoval; Juan Sotero; and Víctor Raúl Haya de la Torre. During this time Vallejo started taking courses in law and switched jobs, giving preference to a position at Colegio Nacional de San Juan, where, as it turns out, he ended up teaching a young man by the name of Ciro Alegría.[8] Complicating this adventure into Trujillo's literary underworld was the terrible loss of César's brother Miguel, who died in Santiago.[9]

Later that year Vallejo earned his *licenciatura* in philosophy and letters at La Universidad de La Libertad with his thesis "Romanticism in Castilian Poetry," a sweeping survey that demonstrates remarkable critical skill and foresight. In the thesis Vallejo saw José Manuel Quintana as "the father of revolutionary poets," praised José María de Heredia for his innovative "Galician vocabulary and natural pomp," and disputed the claim that in the work of José Zorrilla romantic poetry reached its apogee, because it was in José de Espronceda's *El diablo mundo* that "the robust poetic temperament . . . exploded in a blast of asphyxia, thirsty for light and space." With the thesis out of the way, over the next couple of years Vallejo started publishing poems from *The Black Heralds* in magazines and had an affair with María Rosa Sandoval, who inspired several of his early love poems. This was when he started reading magazines like *Cervantes*, *Colónida*, *La Esfera*, and *España*, which were crucial resources that fostered his production of experimental poetry.

From July to December 1917 Vallejo had a love affair with Zoila Rosa Cuadra, whom he nicknamed "Mirtho"—a name that resurfaced as the title of a short story in *Scales* published five years later. In the midst of this relationship, on September 22, 1917, to be precise, the Lima magazine

Variedades took interest in one of his poems. Like many young writers who emerge from the peripheries, Vallejo had initially been ignored, and when the professional critics of Lima deemed it unfashionable to disregard his youthful voice, they acknowledged his presence by using him as a punching bag. "The Poet to His Lover," which he'd submitted to *Variedades* and simply initialed, was published, accompanied by a rather unflattering cartoon and the following note from Clemente Palma:

> Mr. C. A. V. Trujillo. You too belong to the lot that comes whistling the ditty which we attribute to everyone who keeps trying to tune their lyrical wind bags, i.e., the youth that has been dealt a hand to write kitsch poetic rubbish. And said ditty should let you rest assured that we shall publish your monstrosity. You have sent us a sonnet titled "The Poet to His Lover" which, in all honesty, would be more appropriate for the accordion or the ocarina than for poetry. Your verses are noxious twaddle and, until you remove your piece of junk from the wastepaper basket, we shall see nothing else than the dishonor you have done to the people of Trujillo, and if one day your neighbors discover your name, they will find a rope and bind you to the tracks like a tie on the Malabrigo railroad.[10]

By 1918 Vallejo's situation started to change dramatically. After moving to Lima, he began graduate studies in January in the Humanities Department of La Universidad Nacional Mayor de San Marcos. The following month he met the visionary poet and founder of *Colónida*, Abraham Valdelomar, whom he came to see as one of the few guides for the literary youth of Peru. Since Vallejo was preparing for the upcoming publication of *The Black Heralds*, Valdelomar offered to write a foreword, but while visiting Ayacucho he tragically fell, broke his back, and died before he could do so. Vallejo delayed the release a few more months and printed the book with the biblical epigraph *qui potest capere capiat* (Matthew 9:12). In the brief time that the two men knew each other personally, Valdelomar managed to leave the kind of impression on Vallejo that only a mentor can and, aside from framing questions on the future of Peruvian poetry, one day in Lima Valdelomar introduced César to a young man by the name of Pablo Abril de Vivero, whose future in international diplomacy awaited him in Europe. No one could've imagined that this introduction would end up turning into the strongest of friendships (recorded in more than two hundred moving letters).

That May Vallejo's spirits must have been high when he secured a teaching position at the prestigious Colegio Barrós. Yet here again we see the unfortunate pattern of hope and devastation continue to unfold: on August 8, 1918, María de los Santos Mendoza died of angina in Santiago. The death of his mother marked César for the rest of his life and became the inspiration of many compositions.[11] It's difficult to emphasize enough the weight of this event on his writings. The mother figure seems to haunt the texts with absence, almost always appearing in spectral form, leading the author to contemplate union from divorce, to view wholeness from the fragment, and to conceive of being from the existential standpoint of orphanhood.

In October 1918 Vallejo rebounded from the tragedy and became romantically involved with a young woman named Otilia Villanueva, who appears to be the subject of many love poems in *Trilce*. According to Espejo, who was close to Vallejo during those years, the relationship lasted until August 1920. As it turns out, Otilia was the sister-in-law of one of Vallejo's colleagues at Colegio Barrós, and when she was looking for commitment but he refused to marry her, he was scorned by the administration, since, in the eyes of aristocratic Lima, his failure to formalize the relationship diminished the dignity and social status of the young woman and her family. Vallejo was ultimately forced to resign in May 1919.

Yet, only a couple of months later, César saw his first major publication in print, *The Black Heralds*, released by Souza Ferreira in Lima on July 23, 1919. This forerunner of literary indigenism received a warm reception for its originality of style and thematic treatments of rural Peruvian life. Vallejo's satisfaction with the monograph is reflected in two small but revealing documents: a dedicated copy of the book to his "brothers" in Trujillo (July 1919) and a second dedicated copy sent to his father in Santiago.[12] *The Black Heralds* was the crowning achievement of Vallejo's literary youth, and after its release he lost his innocence, demolishing the limits of Hispanic literature rather than securing a place for his writing within those boundaries.

The sweetness of this literary success, however, didn't last long, and on August 1, 1920, when Vallejo went to visit his brother in Santiago on the last day of the festival of Saint James, he got caught up in a town feud that had been fueled by the last elections. The general store of Carlos Santa María went up in flames, a bystander was shot, and two police officers were killed. Despite the fact that Vallejo had been helping the subprefect write up the legal report of the shooting, the Santa María family indicted him, Héctor M. Vásquez, Pedro Lozada, and fifteen others. Vallejo fled to Mansiche (on the outskirts of Trujillo), where he stayed with his friend Antenor Orrego. After being pursued for nearly two months, in a letter to Óscar Imaña from October 26, 1920, Vallejo started to recognize what was awaiting him: "Maybe in a few days the case will be solved, and will be solved in my favor. I find it hard to believe. But, maybe . . ." In that same letter he expressed his plans to travel abroad. On November 6 he was captured and imprisoned in Trujillo Central Jail, where he was held for the next three and a half months. In the dehumanizing conditions of that provincial prison—a dungeon that haunted him for years to come and saturated his next two books with the excruciating anguish of incarceration, the feeling of condemnation, and the imagery of confinement—Vallejo wrote some of his most celebrated experimental poetry.[13] On February 26, 1921, with the help of his attorney, Carlos Godoy, in addition to a publicity campaign mounted by students at La Universidad de La Libertad and influential figures like poet Percy Gibson, César was released on bail.

Whether Vallejo was innocent or guilty remains to be proven with certainty, and several important factors must be taken into consideration. As Stephen Hart explains, "Legal accounts show that—despite an adroit campaign mounted by the Trujillo intelligentsia in defense of the poet—Vallejo was directly involved in the events leading up to the destruction of the Santa María premises." In his reading of El proceso Vallejo by Patrón Candela, Hart reports that the proceedings "indicate that Vallejo was at the front of the crowd that gathered in the main square that afternoon and was heard inciting others to take part in the mayhem. He was seen holding a revolver, and in much of the evidence for the prosecution, he is mentioned as the instigator."[14]

This new reading contradicts the traditional claim of his innocence and seems plausible, given Vallejo's later commitment to social revolution; however, we must be careful not to confuse official records for irrefutable truth, since there's certainly the possibility of bias in a case like this. For example, in a rural setting like Santiago de Chuco circa 1920, authorities would've sought a scapegoat at any cost (especially a bohemian cholo like Vallejo) to appease a member of the mercantile class or send a message to other bothersome miscreants of that irreverent counterculture. Furthermore, Vallejo had already started to garner renown as an emerging poet; so in the eyes of his provincial prosecutors, his move to the capital could've been perceived as class betrayal. Vallejo alluded to this prejudice in a letter to Gastón Roger, where he claimed he'd been indicted because he came "from the heartland," and that in "this provincial environment" there was no way he'd receive a fair trial.

After his 1921 release, Vallejo returned to Lima and was appointed to a teaching position at Colegio Nacional de Nuestra Señora de Guadalupe. Leaving the prison experience behind him as best he could, he managed to publish a surprising number of important texts in a remarkably brief span. On November 15, 1921, his short story "Beyond Life and Death" won first prize in a competition organized by *Entre Nous*—a text subsequently published in the magazine *Variedades* on June 17, 1922, and finally placed in *Scales*. Then, in October 1922 César delivered a poetry manuscript to Talleres Tipográficos de la Penitenciaría in Lima, with a prologue by Antenor Orrego. The book was titled *Bronze Skulls* and, at the last minute, Vallejo slipped a correction sheet into the galley to change the title to *Trilce*, a word that he'd invented. Despite the great anticipation, in the months following the book's publication, as Vallejo himself remarked in a letter to Orrego, "only a handful of young still-unknown writers and several college kids have shuddered at its message." To put it bluntly, the book initially went unnoticed. Five months later, in March 1923, César delivered another manuscript to the same publisher, this time a collection of prose poems and short stories that had been composed during the same period as the texts of *Trilce*. This book was titled *Scales* and—never one to miss out on an opportunity to flaunt his youthful flair and so thematically rhyme this book with its predecessor—these *Scales* were to be "Melographed by César Vallejo." Almost immediately after the publication of *Scales*, Vallejo's other early prose fiction, *Savage Lore*, was included in *La Novela Peruana*, a biweekly edited by Pedro Barrantes Castro in Lima.

By the time this flurry of literary success was outlining an aura around the now thirty-one-year-old, his days in Peru were numbered, and his sights were set on the City of Light. Before he left, he signed on as a correspondent for the magazine *El Norte*, which his Trujillo friends were about to launch. He communicated with Enrique Casterot, also from Trujillo, who gave him the address of a Peruvian musician who, at that time, was living in Paris and going by the name Alfonso de Silva.[15] Vallejo didn't have the money for a grand European vacation, even if he intended on working while abroad, and he was only able to take the trip thanks to Julio Gálvez (Antenor Orrego's nephew), who exchanged his own first-class ticket on the steamship *Oroya* for two third-class tickets, keeping one and giving the other to his friend.[16] In the days preceding his departure, Vallejo was visited by his brother Néstor, who said good-bye in Lima. The day before leaving for Europe, César wrote to Carlos Godoy and said that he "would've liked to stop in Salaverry" to visit him in person, but the boat unfortunately didn't pass through that port. He also asked his attorney to oversee the development of the case from August while he was out of the country and to mind the well-being of his family. Joined by the selfless Gálvez, Vallejo boarded the *Oroya* on June 17, 1923, and headed up the western coast of South America toward the Panama Canal, where the ship was to reach Atlantic waters and take its eastbound course.

* * *

A little less than one month later, on July 13, 1923, to be exact, Vallejo arrived in Paris at 7 a.m. on the express train from La Rochelle. Filled with unreal expectations and a somewhat incomprehensible naivety regarding his personal finances, César tested the waters of Parisian intellectual life. Although most of his later poems didn't reach the public until after his death, it was at this time that he started to write "extremely somber, straightforward, and deeply felt works [that] form a bridge between *Trilce* and the poetry Vallejo would write in the thirties when, having committed himself to Marxist ideology, he forced the teeth of the revolution into the gums of his personal life."[17] His first steps took him from rue d'Odessa, where he was lodged in the Odessa Hotel, near the Gare de Montparnasse, over to Montmartre. A few days later he attended the Paris premiere of Maeterlink's play *The Blue Bird*, produced by Cora Laparcerie, and to his dismay the warm response it received, as he says in *El Norte*, was the result of "undeniable decadence in the sensibility, a consistent decadence, no longer the Byzantine hyperesthesia, but rather an alarming anesthesia" (February 1, 1924). Vallejo also went to and wrote in *El Norte* about la Rotonde, where he gawked at that "ambiguous hypogeum . . . a boisterous alveolus of cosmopolitan mange" (February 22, 1924), a polyglot crowd that filled the salons, where he saw Japanese painter Tsuguharu Foujita, Belgian poet and playwright Maurice Maeterlinck, and Guatemalan critic Enrique Gómez Carillo, plus Tristan Tzara, Max Jacob, and Pierre Reverdy.

A couple of weeks after his arrival in Paris, Vallejo made use of the contact information that Casterot had given him back in Peru, and on July 28 (Peruvian Independence Day), he and Gálvez strode into the Peruvian Embassy looking for a man by the name of Alfonso de Silva. This, of course, was the first of many meetings between César and Alfonso, whose friendship during 1923 was essential to Vallejo's adjustment to life in Paris as a young insolvent foreigner. In a letter to Carlos Raygada, Silva describes this initial encounter:

Having only previously known each other by sight and like-mindedness (which is, after all, the most important), we shook hands and began to chat. I offered to guide him around and help him out with whatever I could, and so we decided to get together the following day, not without having shared some champagne to toast to the "missing Country." . . .

The next day we met up as we had planned and took a stroll around Paris.[18]

In the short time they spent together, Silva taught Vallejo how to be poor in Paris, and Vallejo, whose spiritual genealogy can be traced back to Dostoevsky, became intimately acquainted with suffering. Eventually, César recognized how poverty had worn down his friend, and on September 15, 1923, he wrote to Raygada, begging him to purchase Alfonso a ticket so that he could return to Peru. "Europe is like this," he explains. "Sometimes it can give and other times it crumbles your soul from which it repossesses something that it gave and something it did not. Alfonso no longer has anything to take away from here. He must return."[19]

Watching Silva's mental and physical health decline must have weighed heavily on Vallejo, whose conviction to support himself was tested by a brutal interwar economy and his own contumacious ideals. His letters to Pablo Abril de Vivero, which spanned the 1924–34 period, attest to the constant financial hardship that befell Vallejo in Europe. This, no doubt, explains part of what motivated Abril, around that time, to start pushing the paperwork to get César a grant to study law in Madrid.

When Vallejo reached Europe, he hit the ground not running but scrambling, working anyway as a correspondent with *El Norte*.[20] His first years in Paris, precisely the period least known in his biography (after his early childhood education), are punctually registered in his chronicles published in that paper launched only five months earlier by his Trujillan brethren. To the surface rose figures of Peruvian literature and history that proved capital in that century: Antenor Orrego, Víctor Raúl and José Agustín Haya de la Torre, Alcides Spelucín, Juan Asturrizaga, Eloy B. Espinosa, Óscar Imaña, and Macedonio de la Torre. *El Norte* was well received for its opinion columns, unusual in journalism of that era, and it was distinguished by its courageous editors and their commentary on national and international affairs and their campaigns in defense of the interests of the country and the department of La Libertad.

At the time when Vallejo entered the world of journalism, it had become fashionable to follow a model of light, frivolous, impressionist reading, whose formal expression was epitomized by the articles of Enrique Gómez Carrillo and Ventura García Calderón.[21] Contrary to this decadent aesthetic sauna, Vallejo's chronicles are more closely relegated to those of Alejandro Sux, Manuel Ugarte, José Carlos Mariátegui, and J. J. Soiza Reilly. In the early chronicles his writing still bears traces of *Trilce* and *Scales*, where the text includes a metanarration of its own creation and the author looks for the perfect turn of phrase, the unimaginable expressions that would aston-ish his unsuspecting readers. This, of course, changed considerably as Va-llejo became more comfortable with the genre and started to take stronger stances and embrace the directness of his extraliterary prose.

The article "Peruvian Literature: The Latest Generation," published just a couple of months after his arrival to Paris, is early proof of his lucid gen-erational awareness that he reveals throughout his European chronicles, without becoming smitten by a false devotion to a system that attempts to explain everything in function of age.[22] The search for generational identity and the identification of worthy role models emerged in multiple articles and chronicles in which Vallejo distinguished two key concepts in his work: "indigenist will" and "indigenous sensibility." It's by distin-guishing these two tendencies that, five years later, he reformulated the question of the "New" in terms of autochthony that, in the proclamatory article "Against Professional Secrets," he so eloquently laid out: "Autoch-thony does not consist in saying that one is autochthonous but precisely in being so, even when not saying so."[23] Perhaps this authenticity is what he sensed in the then recently deceased Abraham Valdelomar, whose leader-ship he clearly recognized for his generation. Although it isn't celebrated internationally to the same degree that it is in Peru, Valdelomar's work paved the way for an entire generation to explore new literary modalities and to salvage from the past what was still useful.

In September 1924, around the time Vallejo was introduced to Vicente Huidobro and Juan Larrea, Costa Rican sculptor Max Jiménez generously allowed him to stay in his studio at 3, rue Vercingétorix, where César posed for Spanish sculptor José de Creeft, whose bust of the Peruvian has be-come iconic. Vallejo wrote about the sculpture and whether or not portrai-ture truly exists. "I'm afraid you may say it does," he chides. "I'm afraid you may say it doesn't, that the portrait is already an extinct artistic genre, an aesthetic species that, like the milodon in zoology or like the bone *pfeil-strecker* in Barbarian sculpture, now belongs to archaeology." But he uses the debate to wage a critique against ambivalence, since he's most suspi-cious of those who lack the resolve to tell him whether "the portrait does or doesn't exist in art."[24]

The following month, out of the blue, Vallejo suffered an intestinal hemorrhage and was hospitalized in la Charité hospital. Fifteen months in Paris and suddenly his life was flashing before his eyes. His stay in the hospital was long and drawn out, and during the fourth week, in a letter to Abril a fatalist Vallejo confessed his terrible suffering and confrontation with mortality:

There are hours more, perhaps much more sinister and terrible than the tomb itself. I didn't know what they were until this hospital showed me, and now I'll never forget them. In the process of recovery, I often cry for any reason at all. An infantile facility for tears keeps me saturated in an immense mercy for things. I often remember my house, my parents, and lost loves. One day I'll be able to die, in the course of this hazardous life that has befallen me to live, and so I shall see myself, then just as now, an orphan of all family encouragement and even of love. But my luck has already landed. It's written. I'm a fatalist. I think everything has been written.[25]

A couple of weeks later, after the operation, César suffered a second hemorrhage, and this disturbing news he related to Abril in a letter written with a tone that testifies to the intensity of the spiritual challenge he was facing. With his life in peril, he claimed to believe in Jesus Christ again and insisted that he had rediscovered his religion, "taking religion as the supreme consolation in life. Yes. Yes. There must be another world of refuge for the many on earth who suffer" (November 5, 1924).[26] But neither two intestinal hemorrhages nor his recently rediscovered religion prevented him from discussing finances in that same letter. Vallejo explains that Mariano H. Cornejo, Peruvian minister to France in the 1920s, had begun a process to purchase him a ticket from Paris to Lima, but he wasn't seriously considering a return to Peru, since Abril had all but secured his grant to study law in Madrid. Naturally, Vallejo didn't want the ticket, but its cash value, on which he could survive until the grant came through—and this miraculously happened on March 16, 1925. It was three hundred pesetas per month and, although he never carried out formal studies, he diligently traveled to Spain in October 1925, July 1926, and June 1927 to collect his modest funds.

In 1925 Vallejo experienced a brief period of semistability when he started working in the Bureau des Grands Journaux Ibéroaméricains, a vast publicity organization directed by Alejandro Sux. Right around the time he took this job, he also began writing for the Lima magazine *Mundial*, headed by Andrés Avelino Aramburú.[27] All of a sudden Vallejo was no longer going to be writing articles for his bohemian friends in Trujillo, but for a vaster, more diverse readership. "For this new audience," Puccinelli explains, Vallejo continued "to mold the new writing of his chronicles and articles," allowing himself to explore the journalistic form only to "imperceptibly enter the same literary space as his prose poems and *Human*

Poems, to which the articles and chronicles count as parallel texts." Thus, we see how the modality of journalism played a central role in the maturity of Vallejo's later writings: "[His] youthful concern for finding *le mot rare* is replaced by the search for *le mot juste*," and this transformation was organically "impacted by his readings of Joseph Conrad."[28]

As it turns out, Joseph Conrad had passed away one year after César Vallejo arrived in Paris. An extraordinary homage to Conrad appeared in the *Nouvelle Revue Française* (December 1, 1924), which, aside from a series of testimonies and critical studies, presented a selection of his works in French translation under the title "L'art et la morale de Conrad éclairés par quelques citations." Over the course of his years in Paris, Vallejo gleaned this miniature anthology, translated his favorite phrases from French to Castilian, and scattered them throughout his own writings, allowing us to situate Conrad as one of Vallejo's literary heroes.

In May 1926 César met a woman by the name of Henriette Maisse, and they became lovers in a relationship that lasted for about a year and a half. Soon after they moved in together at Hôtel Richelieu (20, rue Molière), the High Court of Trujillo issued a warrant for Vallejo's arrest, making a return to Peru all the less likely. Later that year he took a brief trip to Spain to collect his grant money and, with coeditor Juan Larrea, he also launched the short-lived literary magazine *Favorables-París-Poema*. They put out the first of two volumes in July 1926. With a knack for agitation and a biting sense of humor, inside the cover of each copy they slipped a business card that read, "In the event of a discrepancy with our attitude, Juan Larrea and César Vallejo request your most resolved hostility."

Aside from texts by the coeditors, *Favorables-París-Poema* contained contributions from Gerardo Diego and Tristan Tzara and even poems by Pierre Reverdy, translated by none other than Vallejo. Yet we must be careful not to imagine Vallejo completely integrated into European life with barely a foggy memory of his South American past. From Madrid in the middle of 1926, he made sure to stay in touch with Alejandro Peralta, a seminal figure of early twentieth-century Peruvian literature; Alcides Spelucín, Vallejo's longtime friend from Trujillo who'd written *El libro de la nave dorada*; and even a young poet by the name of Emilio Armaza, who'd written a volume called *Falo*.[29] Additionally, the letters he wrote to Abril circa 1926–28 reveal "a total change that starts operating in Vallejo's conception of art, literature, and the function of the artist. This conceptualization would take a hard left, which is why in his writings one will find a tone that is more political than literary."[30]

Back in Paris, in the winter of 1926, César Vallejo met Georgette Philippart, his future wife. The young girl's mother, Mme Marie Travers, is said to have disapproved of the relationship. The following year, on March 10, Vallejo traveled again to Spain and again stayed for only a brief visit, which was also a parting of ways for him and Henriette, who moved out of Hôtel Richelieu. This was when César's relationship with Georgette began to develop; however, on May 5, 1927, they got into an argument that sent him running back to Henriette with the hopes that she would forgive him, and she did. He left Hôtel Richelieu and went to live with her in Hôtel Mary. One month later he took yet another trip to Spain, where he was put up by Xavier Abril in his apartment on Calle de la Aduana in Madrid. There he met Juan Domingo Córdoba, who ended up traveling with him back to Paris just a few months later and whose accounts of their time together in Europe have proved to be essential material for the biographical study of our author.[31]

Vallejo's health again declined in July 1928, and this time his doctor in Paris advised him to take a vacation in the country to recuperate. Accompanied by Henriette and Domingo Córdoba, he stayed at the house of Monsieur Nauty in Ris Orangis (Seine-et-Oise).[32] He'd been in Paris for five years only to live a life of poverty and frustration. His success in literary publishing had been stunted by his open rejection of the prevailing trends. At a time when life was hard, his stubborn ideals made it harder. Yet, if the letters reveal sentiments of self-pity, nowhere in the writings of César Vallejo do we find a defeated attitude; a robust vivacity dominates his oeuvre—a gritty willingness to live and perhaps a perverse desire to suffer.

By the end of 1928, the ethical dilemma that had taken hold of Vallejo erupted into an all-out crisis. Change had become a necessity—radical change: revolution! In a letter to Abril written on October 19, Vallejo explained that he was leaving that day for Russia. Although his health had improved and he'd recovered his strength, his sense of purpose in life had become turbid with doubt, and it was this desire for clarity that drove him to the land of the Soviet:

> I feel (perhaps more than ever) tormented by the problem of my future, and it's precisely with the drive to resolve this problem that I'm setting off on this journey. I realize what my role in life is not. I haven't found my path yet, but I want to find it, and perhaps in Russia I will, since on this other side of the world where I live, things move on springs similar to the rusty wing nuts of America. I'll never do anything in Paris. Perhaps in Moscow I'll find better shelter from the future.

* * *

On October 19, 1928, César Vallejo stepped off a Paris platform and onto a train headed for Moscow. This was the first of three trips that he took in the next few years. Despite his high hopes for finding a long-term solution to the worsening crisis tearing him apart, none of his trips to that young USSR lasted very long and, on this first occasion, he was back in Paris as early as November 13, 1928. Yet it's astounding how many people he managed to interview and how many locations he visited in what turned out to be just under one month's time. These raw materials transformed into a trove of new articles, a political report, and two books of thoughts.

The highlight of this trip took place in Leningrad, in late October, when Vallejo attended a meeting of Bolshevik writers, which became the central topic of chapter 8 of *Russia in 1931*. Two of the writers there (Sergei Kolbasiev and Vissarion Sayanov) were mentioned in the Peruvian's oft-contended article "The Mayakovsky Case" from *Art and Revolution*:

> At a gathering of Bolshevik writers in Leningrad, Kolbasiev said to me, "Contrary to what's presumed abroad, Mayakovsky isn't the greatest Soviet poet or anything of the sort. Mayakovsky is nothing more than a thespian hyperbolist. Before him are Pasternak, Biedny, Sayanov, and many others . . ."
>
> I knew Mayakovsky's work, and my opinion was in absolute agreement with Kolbasiev's. And, a few days later, when I spoke in Moscow with the author of *150,000,000*, our conversation confirmed Kolbasiev's judgment for all of eternity. In reality, Mayakovsky isn't the greatest Soviet poet. He's merely the most published. If one read more of Pasternak, Kaziin, Gastev, Sayanov, Viesimiensky, the name Mayakovsky would vanish from many radio waves.

For years, questions surrounding this meeting riddled Vallejo's readers; however, thanks to Alexander Batrakov, director of the Centro Cultural Ruso in Lima, and the late Manuel Miguel de Priego, we know quite a bit about this meeting that, for Vallejo, proved quite important. It took place in the house of Sergei Adamovich Kolbasiev (1898–1937), a Russian writer on maritime topics and member of the literary group Ostrovityane (Islanders). In his autobiographical novels he recounts experiences of his service in the Red Fleet. He was the author of the poetry collection *The Open Sea* (1922) and numerous narratives: *The Rules of Group Navigation* (1935) and *Tales of the Wartime Seascape* (1936), inter alia. He was arrested in 1937 and died in jail that same year. Also at the meeting was Vissarion

Mikhailovich Sayanov (1903–59), born in the village of Ivanushkinskaia, in modern-day Kirensk Raion, Irkutsk Oblast, author of the poetry collection *Komsomol Poetry* (1928), *Contemporaries* (1929), and *The Golden Olyokma* (1934), as well as the novels *Heaven and Earth, I–IV* (1935–54) and *The Lena, I–II* (1953–55). During World War II he was a frontline correspondent and wrote *In the Battles for Leningrad* (1943) and then *The Nuremberg Diaries* (1948).

In addition to Kolbasiev and Sayanov, the other writers at this meeting included Boris Viktorovich Lipatov, Wolf Yosifovich Ehrlich, and Ilya Ivanovich Sadofiev.[33] Lipatov (1905–54), born in Yekaterinburg, participated in the civil war, and from 1926 he wrote for the stage and the screen. Among his screenplays is *Tri Soldata*, which he adapted with Aleksandr Ivanov from John Dos Passos's realist novel *Three Soldiers* (1920). He also wrote the screenplay *Treasure of the Wrecked Vessel* (1935), inter alia. Ehrlich (1902–37) was a Russian-Jewish poet who authored the collection *Wolf Song* and others that glorify the revolutionary orthodoxy. For his part, Sadofiev (1889–1965) began to publish his poems in *Pravda* during the pre-revolutionary period. Then in 1917 he became an activist in Protekult: in the second half of the 1920s he became the president of the Association of Leningrad Poets (a position he held when Vallejo was visiting). He's the author of the poetry collections *Dynamo Verses* (1918) and *Simpler Than Simplicity* (1925), as well as the short story collection *The Bloody Staircase* (1925), which is saturated with heavy revolutionary dramatics.

From this meeting in Leningrad, Vallejo seems to have confirmed a suspicion he'd been contemplating in an array of magazine articles, namely, that the prevailing schools of poetry—such as dadaism, futurism, surrealism, ultraism, and creationism—all contained a similar, if not identical, contradiction. They wanted to patent a technique by which new art was to be created. Vallejo recognized the problematic of aesthetic secularism and exposed the sociopolitical underpinnings of those avant-garde platforms that, by dint of excluding themselves from the problems they were addressing, actually reinforced the kinds of divisions that writers like Kolbasiev, Sayanov, Lipatov, Ehrlich, and Sadofiev were fighting to destroy. In the Peruvian's eyes, the European avant-garde appeared as a cult of decadence, the sign of decrepitude, whereas the Latin American avant-garde was imported posture, the sign of insincerity and self-deceit; and just like the romantics had surged out of the worn-out neoclassical mentality, so too did the moderns need to eschew the personally amusing fin de siècle parlor games and produce socially responsible art to get out from under the rubble left by decades of war. The Leningrad writers confirmed Vallejo's hypothesis that, at a time when modernism was fully coming into itself, there was a viable alternative to the avant-garde.

Upon his return to Paris, during this socialist shift that soon became evident in his writings circa 1928, Vallejo took special interest in the performing arts, first as critic and then as creator. His affinity for the stage and screen is unambiguous with just a glance at such articles as "Avant-Garde Religions," "Contribution to Film Studies," "Vanguard and Rearguard," and of course his unforgettable homage to and defense of one of his major inspirations in the genre, "The Passion of Charles Chaplin." This last article in particular was centered on *The Gold Rush* and explained how misunderstood the U.S. film pioneer was at that time. Russians exited cinemas teary-eyed with the belief that he was a realist; Germans considered him from an intellectual perspective; the English thought he was a clown; the French were sure he was a comedian; and, as for Chaplin's compatriots,

> [they have not] perceived, even at a distance, the profound and tacitly revolutionary spirit of *The Gold Rush*. I'm lying. In a subconscious way, perhaps, the gringos have teamed up with Lita Grey to stone Chaplin, just like the other Philistines stoned Our Lord, equally unconscious of the historical meaning of their hatred.[34]

Vallejo valued screen and stage performance for its effectiveness at transmitting to the masses the representation of human struggle and perseverance, shining the spotlight on social injustice and pressing a finger on an untreated wound so that even people who'd rather ignore it could no longer deny its existence. This was possible, according to the Peruvian, only in truly revolutionary works, since these don't fall into the usual ideological traps of exploiting preestablished aesthetics and jumping on the bandwagon, which prohibits the production of sincere artistic expression. As an authentic visionary in an emerging field, Chaplin embodied the perfect revolutionary artist, because he didn't require political propaganda to condemn systemic corruption, and the fact that he was wealthy and championed the poor proved that human solidarity could outrank class loyalty:

> So it is, without a cheap protest against subprefects or ministers; without even uttering the words "bourgeois" or "exploitation"; without political adages or maxims; without childish messianics, Charles Chaplin, millionaire and gentleman, has created a marvelous work of revolution. This is the role of the creator.

Over time, unsuspected political platforms and economic doctrines will be yanked out of *The Gold Rush*. That will be the work of second-rate artists and imitators, propagandists, university professors, and candidates for the government of the people.[35]

The Peruvian's first stabs at writing for the performing arts (stage plays written in French: *Mampar*, *Les Toups*, and *Lock-Out*) fell flat on their face and made clear that drama wasn't going to come as easily to the natural-born poet as verse had, but this didn't stop him from trying and, in the last months of his life, he achieved astounding success.

In late December, as 1928 was winding down, Armando Bazán, Juan Paiva, Eudocio Ravines, Jorge Seoane, Demetrio Tello, and César Vallejo formed a Peruvian Socialist Party cell in Paris and soon thereafter informed José Carlos Mariátegui, who had founded the Peruvian Socialist Party in Lima on October 7, 1928. It was also around that time that César reunited with Georgette, and in January 1929 the couple rented an apartment together at 11, avenue de l'Ópera, in Paris—a street not far from where Vallejo internalized massive Parisian traffic jams in rue de Rivoli, which he interpreted as "the picturesque and, at once, tragic peripeteia of the political scene of history," since the chauffeurs defended their fare-paying passengers (the "higher-ups") instead of the pedestrians (the "underdogs"), and the pedestrians berated the chauffeurs, who were underdogs without realizing it, instead of seeking solidarity with them. "These two errors," he concludes, "are the blunders and irony inherent in the drama, and they make it all the more bloody and painful."[36]

No matter how hard the left was that Vallejo took around 1928, it would be an error to dub him a "grammatical Marxist" and lay the issue to rest. A close reading of his articles and chronicles shows that he saw Marx's ideas as essential developments in the transformation of philosophical thought, but that by no means did Marx represent a final solution to the problems that challenge humanity. Suffice a review of "The Lessons of Marxism" to drive this point home:

> What a pitiful orgy of parroting eunuchs the traitors of Marxism get in on. Based on the conviction that Marx is the only philosopher of the past, present, and future, who has scientifically explained social motion and who, as a consequence, has once and for all hit the nail on the head of the laws governing the human spirit, their first vital disgrace consists of amputating their own creative possibilities at the root, relegating them to the condition of panegyrist parrots and parrots of *Das Kapital*.[37]

For Vallejo, Marxian philosophy offered the promise of perpetual transformation, a concept visible in the Peruvian's writings not only on a theoretical register, as is laid out in his articles and chronicles, but also in praxis throughout the pages of his poetry, fiction, and plays. For example, Vallejo satirizes this error of imposing a finalist nature on Marx's transformative function of thought in act 1, scene 3, of *The River Flows between Two Shores*, where the young revolutionary, Ilitch, challenges his older conservative brother, Vladimir, to a reading duel, in which the former recites passages from his Marxist reader at the top of his lungs while the latter tries to drown him out by reading passages from one of his mother's religious books.

In February 1929, at the age of thirty-seven, Vallejo started writing articles for *El Comercio* of Lima. Certain that he wanted to visit the Soviet Union again after he'd returned to Paris in mid-November 1928, Vallejo kept in contact with the Union of Soviet Societies for Friendship and Cultural Relations with Foreign Countries (VOKS), and thanks to this organization he was able to organize a second trip in the fall of 1929. This time, he and Georgette traveled together, planning a sort of Europe-by-rail tour that had the following itinerary: Paris–Berlin–Moscow–Leningrad–Prague–Cologne–Vienna–Budapest–Trieste–Venice–Florence–Rome–Pisa–Genoa–Nice–Paris. Despite the apparent grandeur of this journey, it lasted only slightly longer than the first.

Akin to his first trip to Russia, on this tour, short as it was, Vallejo obtained a wealth of information and interviewed many people, this time in factories, on farms, at industrial centers, in laboratories, on the street, in their homes—we're talking about hundreds of people! The direct observations, the in situ reflections, and a great majority of the material he recorded ended up receiving concrete expression in magazine articles and the report *Russia in 1931*—a best seller in Spain and the most successful publication in the author's lifetime.

One sequence of interviews occurred while Vallejo recorded a day in the life of a stonemason, observing the man's family, workmates, workplace, his eating habits, his research at the Workers' Club, and his view on sports. The Peruvian even joined him at a theater where the large diverse audience admired and was moved by the conflict in Vladimir Kirshon's play *The Rails Are Humming*. With the objective voice of a journalist, Vallejo vividly recounted the experience in chapter 9 of that report as well as in an article called "New Russian Theater."

Another momentous meeting transpired when the father of Russian futurism, Vladimir Mayakovsky, introduced César Vallejo to Sergei Eisenstein at a preliminary screening of *The General Line*. In that film, Eisenstein's radical celebration of collective labor and mechanized agriculture along with the dramatization of the exploitation suffered by prerevolutionary workers was light-years ahead of what passed as cutting edge in Parisian cinemas. Next to Conrad and Chaplin, Russian film pioneer Sergei Eisenstein undoubtedly stands as one of Vallejo's great contemporary inspirations, and his films received rigorous treatment by the enthused Peruvian in chapter 4, "Russia Inaugurates a New Era on the Silver Screen," in *Russia in 1931*. "Labor is the father of human society," he proclaims, after viewing *The General Line*, and he can't help recognize "how far we are here from Hollywood and all its schmaltzy, decadent dressing rooms!"[38]

Soon after César and Georgette had left Moscow, not without first visiting Lenin's tomb in Red Square, Abril started placing Vallejo's new chronicles in his biweekly review called *Bolívar*. The column was titled "A Report from Russia" and essentially constituted early iterations of chapters that later became *Russia in 1931*. In addition to his reportage and with the generous logistical support of Gerardo Diego, the second edition of *Trilce* was published on April 9, 1930, by José Bergamín, who wrote an insightful prologue at the author's request. A letter from Vallejo to Diego (January 6, 1930) informs us that Peruvian placed his complete trust in the sensibility and skill of his Spanish colleagues and didn't directly take the manuscript to press for the second edition.

The month after *Trilce* came out, César and Georgette traveled from Paris to Spain. We know that while they were there, Vallejo met with Gerardo Diego, Rafael Alberti, and Pedro Salinas in Café de Recoletos and also that he received 15,000 pesos in front-end royalties for the second edition of *Trilce*. It was also during this excursion that the Peruvian went to Salamanca with Domingo Córdoba to meet with Miguel de Unamuno, but the interview never happened. No matter what the reason may have been, it's hard not to think that Vallejo must've seen this absence, at least in part, as confirmation of the harsh evaluation he'd dealt the Spaniard four years prior: it was just further "proof of his mediocrity."[39]

After a few weeks in Spain, César and Georgette returned to France, where they stayed until the end of the year, when they were hit with a disturbing surprise. On December 2, 1930, Vallejo received notification that he was being expulsed from France for his political activities and had until January 29 of the following year to leave the country. He and Georgette were out of France by December 29 and on their way back to Madrid. They arrived on New Year's Eve and stayed at a modest home on Calle del Acuerdo. "When he left Paris," Meneses explains, "despite the curse that city had cast on him, he seems to have shown optimism toward his future"—optimism that surpassed the realm of literature:

The possibilities of publishing in Spain and finding work with a fair wage became strong incentives. But four months later, the fundamental reason for residing in the Spanish capital had other motives. The monarchy had fallen and the Republic had been established. Vallejo began to see this new chapter in the pages of Spanish history as the Castilian translation of the rise of the Soviet Union.[40]

Without the stigma of exile, Vallejo moved to Madrid and kept the company of Spanish intellectuals and artists, like Rafael Alberti, Federico García Lorca, Fernando Ibáñez, Damaso Alonso, Pedro Salinas, Leopoldo Panero, Corpus Barga, José Bergamín, and Gerardo Diego. He joined the Spanish Communist Party and began teaching in clandestine cells. He also started writing for *La Voz* and was commissioned to translate two novels from French to Castilian, one by Henri Barbusse, which he titled *Elevación*, and the other by Marcel Aymé, which he titled *La calle sin nombre*.[41] Since these works have been disregarded because they were carried out *pro panis lucrando* and because of their sensitive political thematics, Vallejo's translation methodology has virtually gone unstudied, which is an oversight that must be addressed because an analysis of this modality, among other things, could reconcile the contradiction that arises out of his own translations and the contentious position he took against the practice of literary translation just two years earlier.[42]

On March 7, 1931, Vallejo's social realist novel *Tungsten* was published by Editorial Cenit in Madrid just over a month before King Alfonso XIII abdicated and the Spanish Republicans came to power. According to Georgette, César said to her that a revolution that spills no blood isn't a real revolution.[43] In July 1931 Vallejo's report *Russia in 1931* was published by Ulises in Madrid, and despite being reprinted twice in four months and attaining best-seller status, the author didn't see much of the revenue it brought in, although it was enough to mobilize again, and again he returned to Eastern Europe.

Vallejo took his third trip to Russia in the autumn of 1931. He departed from Madrid on October 11 and, after crossing Europe by rail, reached the Polish-Russian border five days later. Starting from Moscow, he began an impressive southbound journey, through present-day Russia, Ukraine, and Georgia, with the following itinerary: Tula–Kiev–Kharkov–Dnieprostroi–Donetsk–Rostov–Tiflis–Elista–Volgograd–Voronezh. The delegation he was with continued toward the Caucasus region, but Vallejo split off and returned to Moscow on the twenty-seventh and to Madrid at the beginning of November.

During this third and final trip to the Soviet Union, Vallejo was pleased to find that the infrastructural development he'd witnessed two years earlier had already made significant progress. The social organization of the Soviet seemed to be on the upswing, and what progress he saw was aggrandized by his own hopes for its success. Nor was the Peruvian the sole intellectual from the Americas to think that the Soviet socialist structure could overtake the capitalist system of the West with its bottomed-out economies and to suspect that the news reaching Western Europe and the Americas propagandized Soviet reality.[44] On this trip he visited a Workers' Club and transcribed discussions on a host of topics, from salaries to working conditions, literature, theater, music, food, living quarters, and so on. Without any other recording devices than his notebook, Vallejo annotated his travels and registered as many conversations as he could in preparation for his next book on Russia.

Back in 1928, and then again in 1931, César visited numerous Russian prisons and, after that three-year lapse, he confirmed an astounding decrease in criminality: a 70 percent drop according to his figures. He was also fascinated by Zernograd (literally, City of Grain), a then entirely socialist population of ten thousand inhabitants, covering an area of 463 square miles. There, mechanized agriculture had taken hold in 1929 and, as Priego explains, in this process Vallejo had great dreams of a massive population where hunger would no longer exist:

> In terms of the rise of production, Vallejo's dreams, incarnated in his lyric poetry, rest on this: the mechanization of agriculture and, consequently, socialist rationalization, which could end up flooding the universe with wheat in only a few years; yet, unfortunately, this did not happen, because that most powerful country of hopes ended up purchasing almost all the wheat it needed from abroad."[45]

So, as 1931 was nearing its end, there was César Vallejo, standing in the Soviet countryside, fathoming the future of many cities of grain and marveling at the feats of modern agriculture. Filled perhaps with the optimism that this very kind of collective labor would soon spread throughout the world or perhaps with a memory of the poverty he'd seen in his own highland region of the Andes in what must've seemed like another lifetime— and without the historical vantage point from which he might glimpse the imminent failure of the socialist experiment and Stalin's heinous purges— there he stood, gazing into the vast fertile landscape between the Black and Caspian Seas, as he took inventory of livestock and, with notebook in hand, carefully counted out those "225 oxen, 325 cows, 220 calves, 2000 rams, and 4000 hogs, raised to feed the population."[46]

* * *

Vallejo's return from the Soviet Union placed him back in Spain, where he began writing his second book of reports, *Russia Facing the Second Five-Year Plan*, which unfortunately wasn't published until more than thirty years later. Yet, in addition to his reportage and with still kindled admiration for his Soviet heroes—Eisenstein on-screen and Kirshon onstage— Vallejo further developed his dramatic writing and actively tried to stage his plays. In January 1932 Federico García Lorca took him to see Camila Quiroga about staging *Moscow vs. Moscow*, but she turned it down. Lorca insisted that heavy editing would be in order before they could offer it elsewhere, in response to which Vallejo agreed and complained that he lacked the skills to edit his work to suit the taste of the general public.[47]

On January 25, 1932, when Georgette returned to Paris to arrange for César's return, she discovered that her apartment had been sacked by the police.[48] The Peruvian stayed in Madrid until February 12, when he crossed the border illegally and reunited with her in Paris. He was told that they could stay in France as long as he refrained from participating in political activities and reported to the prefecture on a monthly basis. Despite showing up at the prefecture only a couple of times, he regained legal status in France in August 1933, but his political activity didn't wane. For example, just the following year, on February 6, 1934, he attended a leftist demonstration against Croix de Feux in Paris.[49] This antifascist thread became increasingly pronounced in the later years of the author's life when the theme of social justice saturated all his poems and plays.

In 1934 César and Georgette got married in Paris, eight years after they first met. This was also the year that he went back to *Tungsten* and adapted that novel into a full-length farce, *Brothers Colacho*, which he continued to edit through 1936. The drastic changes that occurred through three versions attest to Vallejo's struggle with playwriting, but also to his perseverance, since the last (so as not to call it the *final*) version indeed contains outstanding improvements that produce striking social and ethical critiques through the mode of farce. In addition to the play, he also worked on the poems that eventually were collected in *Human Poems*.[50]

For the first few years of his marriage to Georgette (1934–36), César scaled back his journalistic contributions and communicated less frequently with his faraway friends, or at least that's what his surviving writings lead us to believe. Of those that have been preserved, less than ten letters were written in this three-year lapse. He wrote no articles in 1934 and, in 1935–36, he wrote only five. Yet, curiously, in these few articles we observe the resurgence of Vallejo's interest in Peruvian politics, society, history, and, especially, the prehistory of Latin America. For sure, he was distancing himself from the world of journalism and reportage, giving priority to his growing body of poetry, of which he was trying to publish a third volume. On Christmas Day of 1935, he wrote to Larrea and, among other things, asked him whether José Bergamín had received, via Rafael Alberti, poems that he wanted him to publish—likely some of the undated prose pieces that found their way into *Human Poems*.

In Spain of 1936, political tensions were reaching their boiling point. On July 12 Falange members murdered Lt. José Castillo of the Assault Guards Police Force and Socialist Party. The following day leading Spanish monarchist and prominent parliament member José Calvo Sotelo was arrested by the Assault Guards and shot without a trial. Five days later uprisings rocked Spanish Morocco and, soon thereafter, reached mainland Spain. Before the planned coup of 1936 had even been completed, the Popular Front, the National Confederation of Labor, and the International Workers Association armed the people. The Spanish civil war had broken out.

Over the next months, through a series of letters and telegrams with Juan Larrea and Juan Luis Velázquez, a deeply troubled Vallejo, who was by no means well off, discussed the ethical complexity of being so committed to Republican Spain from the comfort of his Parisian armchair: "Never have I measured my human smallness as I do now. Never have I been so aware of how little an individual can do alone. This crushes me." Having witnessed the aftermath of the October Revolution and the Russian civil war, it was evident to Vallejo that "at moments like this, each person has his role, no matter how humble, and our gears must shift and submit to the collective cog."[51]

Presumably it was for that reason that Vallejo left Paris on December 15, 1936, to visit Barcelona and Madrid, and why, while in Madrid, he reached the frontlines of the war, where he interviewed volunteers for the Republic. As a staunch supporter of the Republicans, Vallejo was interested in publicizing their heroic feats; but to his surprise, one volunteer explained in good socialist fashion that "no one knows the names of the heroes" and, more important, "no one cares too much about them." Each volunteer of the Republic "does what he can, without concern for glory . . . in the army of the people. Either they're all heroes, or there are no heroes left."[52] This notion that no individual can be more valuable than the whole pervades

Vallejo's writings across genres and modalities and was accentuated in the poetry he started writing upon his return to Paris, on December 31, which crowned his poetic corpus with *Spain, Take This Cup from Me*, composed in an astonishing sermonic lyrical mode, as we see in "Hymn to the Volunteers for the Republic," which carries all the weight of his poetic maturity:

> The same shoes will fit whoever climbs
> without trails to his body
> and whoever descends to the form of his soul!
> Entwining each other the mutes will speak, the paralyzed will walk!
> The blind, now returning, will see
> and throbbing the deaf will hear!
> The ignorant will know, the wise will not!
> Kisses will be given that you could not give!
> Only death will die! The ant
> will bring morsels of bread to the elephant chained
> to his brutal gentleness; aborted children
> will be born again perfect, spatial
> and all men will work,
> all men will beget,
> all men will understand!

Just over three decades after it had begun, Vallejo's literary production was reaching its peak in 1937, while he was back in Paris. He continued to work on *Human Poems* and in a frenzy had embarked on *Spain, Take This Cup from Me*, which incarnated his political commitment to Republican Spain, whose destiny in his eyes was also the destiny of the world. "At this point," Clayton Eshleman suggests, "it is possible to watch Vallejo build what might be called a 'popular poetry,' incorporating war reportage, while at the same time another branch of his poetry was becoming more hermetic than ever before."[53] It was also around this time that the Peruvian revisited that novella he'd written more than ten years earlier—*Toward the Reign of the Sciris*—and transformed it into the three-act tragedy, *The Tired Stone*. Writing in a creolized Castilian-Quechua tongue, he saturated the language with an exalted tone and socialist themes that crystalized in an unprecedented poetic creation.

On June 26, 1937, Vallejo wrote to his compatriot, Luis Alberto Sánchez, regarding his participation in the Second International Congress of Writers in Defense of Culture.[54] Sánchez was unable to attend, and Vallejo jumped at the chance to take his place as the sole Peruvian delegate. Shortly thereafter, he took his last trip to Spain to visit the frontlines of the war again and to attend the congress in mass protest against fascism. The 1937 congress was held in Valencia (July 4), Madrid (July 5–8), and Barcelona (July 11), with closing ceremonies in Paris (July 16–17). More than one hundred antifascist writers from all over the world participated. While Vallejo was there, he delivered the speech "The Writer's Responsibility," in which, ghosting Conrad's famous lines, he criticized his contemporaries for being ashamed of what they do, since it is precisely writers who are "responsible for what happens in the world, because we have the most formidable weapon—the word."[55]

After leaving Spain and returning to Paris, Vallejo produced an astonishing amount of work in a very short period. From September 4 to December 8, 1937, he wrote the dated poems of *Human Poems* and *Spain, Take This Cup from Me*, which he typed on René Mossisson's typewriter in Ernesto More's hotel room on rue Daguerre.[56] As if that weren't enough, he also submitted *The Tired Stone* to a rigorous revision, drastically modifying the structure of the play, which resulted in a more cogent plot and a more coherent premise. The Vallejo writings that come down to us from this 1937–38 period bear unmistakable pathos, the poet's most exalted tone, linguistic originality that doesn't get hung up searching for *le mot rare*, and an autochthonous sensibility in praxis that the Peruvian had been demanding for fifteen years. Aside from the sheer volume of that production, the consistency and quality of those works continue to make his readers shudder, from aspiring writers who've recently discovered them to professional critics and translators who've pored over them for decades.

In early March 1938 "the years of strain and deprivation, compounded by heartbreak over Spain, as well as exhaustion from the pace of the previous year, finally took their toll," and César Vallejo started experiencing abdominal pain so acute it kept him in bed.[57] As days went by, the gravity of the situation started to sink in. The pain was persistent, the symptoms, worsening. "A terrible *surmenage* has laid me up in bed for the past two weeks," he explained to Luis José de Orbegoso in a tone of desperation: "The doctors don't know yet how long I'll continue like this." The reality was that he was going to need a "lengthy treatment," which he simply couldn't afford.[58] On March 24, 1938, the Peruvian Embassy had Vallejo transferred to the Clinique Générale de Chirugie (Villa Arago). The team of doctors, which included renowned specialist Dr. Lemiére, ran various tests but couldn't find a way to effectively treat the illness or, perhaps, identify what the problem truly was. On April 15, 1938, which turned out to be a Good Friday, the fascists swept down the Ebro Valley in Spain and cut the loyalist army in two, right around the time that in the Villa Arago clinic of

Paris, César Vallejo cried out in delirium, "I am going to Spain! I want to go to Spain!" and at 9:20 a.m. he died.[59] The death certificate states that the cause of death was acute intestinal infection.

The following day Georgette had a death mask made, and two days later Vallejo was buried in the Cimetière Montrouge, the communist cemetery of Paris. At the service, homilies were given by Louis Aragon, Antonio Ruiz Viliplana, and Gonzalo More. For someone like Vallejo, who could never seem to catch a break in life, it's sadly fitting that his headstone erroneously listed his birthdate as 1893. Additionally, in 1970, when a new generation of scholars, poets, and translators had begun to formally analyze Vallejo's controversial politics and aesthetics, Georgette had his remains transferred from Montrouge to his final resting place in the noble Cimetière Montparnasse (division 12, line 4 north, no. 7), not far from Baudelaire's grave, where, according to the widow, her husband wished to be buried. The engraving on the headstone corrected his birthdate, states his name, and, without mentioning that he was a poet or writer, displays the anomalous epitaph that she had written: "J'ai tant neigé / pour que tu dormes / Georgette."[60]

2

We now turn our attention to Vallejo's writings themselves to specify details of their publication history with the aim of elucidating the breadth and depth of his oeuvre. We also highlight predominant aesthetic features in each of the works and in the compilations of letters, notebooks, articles, and chronicles from which the translations have been drawn, to give the reader a sense of the whole that we aim to synthesize in this anthology. It should be noted that neither in the following characterizations nor in the translations themselves do we cover absolutely all of Vallejo's writings. For a rigorous registry of the writings in toto and a wealth of research sources, readers are encouraged to reference critical bibliographies.[61] Our agenda here is to analyze Vallejo's writings in condensed form and establish an essential overview for readers facing these texts for the first time. Although Vallejo's writings are generally not easy to access, they are by no means inaccessible, and the presumption that they are, as he might argue, is more revealing of a strategic problem with the reading than of a technical problem with the writing.

* * *

César Vallejo's first complete work was *Romanticism in Castilian Poetry*, completed in and published in Trujillo by Tipografía Olaya (1915). With this undergraduate thesis, he obtained his *licenciatura* in philosophy and letters at La Universidad de La Libertad under the advisory of Eleazar Boloña, to whom he dedicated the volume. In his analysis Vallejo sounds the roots of the Spanish romantic movement and locates foreign influences from Dante, Petrarch, Shakespeare, Milton, Byron, Walter Scott, Goethe, Schiller, Andrés Chenier, Germaine de Staël, Alphonse de Lamartine, Victor Hugo, and Alfred de Musset. Inspired by the notion that poetry must not only *reflect* but *refract* questions that stir the human spirit, Vallejo sees Spanish romanticism as a vital response to neoclassical satire—the sure sign of decrepitude—which Juan Pablo Forner, José Francisco de Isla, Tomás de Iriarte, Félix María Samaniego, and Nicasio Álvarez de Cienfuegos breathed through their works with bitterness and irony.

For Vallejo, Spanish romanticism began with José Manuel Quintana, whose poetry "hoists up above his philosophically sweet and penetrating lines, as from the bow of daydream's golden ships, the flag of his race and his century." José María de Heredia, in turn, had a tendency to "exteriorize his inner life"—as when his heart is broken by a thunderstorm—since "this lugubrious preoccupation that roused in his soul the beautiful, the great, the ineffable, which does not fit into pseudo-realist, reasoned and serene poetry of the neoclassical period," forged a space for romantic poets to project new philosophical ideas and possibilities for social change.[62]

In the poetry of José de Espronceda, Vallejo admires the poet's sincerity, the absence of "a personality to engage his surroundings, as in the French romanticism of Victor Hugo," and the presence of "the firm gaze with which the poet pierces himself [which] engendered the instability that was throbbing through all spheres of activity in his century, thereby giving origin to doubt and skepticism." Espronceda is the figurehead of Spanish romanticism not because he inaugurated an intellectual movement (he did not) but because he acknowledged his predecessors, and when his time came he took the flag of the rebellion, "raising himself up with it to a height he had not reached before." Espronceda's technical ability in *El diablo mundo* and his willingness to break from the hendecasyllable that had become the romantic go-to meter (along with the *romance*) was proof of the poet's authenticity and confidence in his creations.

The case of José Zorrilla is different, since the author of *Don Juan Tenorio*, working within the realm of legend, incorporated popular motifs and phraseological expressions rooted in contemporary Spanish society. Vallejo suggests that this was a main reason for the resounding reception of his work and the popularity it still preserved in the early twentieth century, since those expressions were recognizable by Zorrilla's readers who, in this way, were also authors. Thus, the Peruvian had no choice but to dispute Spanish critic Alberto Lista's claim—that in Zorrilla "an incorrect expression, an improper word, an impossible Gallicism or neologism warns us that we are stuck in the mud"—by explaining that "to the chagrin of the Aristarchuses of the world . . . , rather than being transgressions . . . , those breaks with the academic rules of language have become the greatest merits of his work." Zorrilla's nonconformity was justified by the fact that morphology, "the true legislator and motor for the transformation or disappearance of words is not the fanciful will of writers but of society."[63]

Romanticism in Castilian Poetry shows Vallejo's early generational awareness; his ability to perceive the intimate relation between philosophies and aesthetic trends through the course of major historical transitions; his affinity for the idiosyncratic writer, the authentic outlier detested by traditionalists; and the autonomous exaltation of deeply felt poetry. The bitterness and irony of neoclassical poetry revealed the decay of that era and the romantics' need for new modalities of thought and art. This notion of salvaging from the past only what is essential and discarding dead weight in the name of transformation crosscuts Vallejo's oeuvre and becomes the principle axis of his eventual critique of the European and Latin American avant-garde.

This brings us to Vallejo's first book of poems, *The Black Heralds*, which was written in 1916–18 during the high tide of the Trujillo bohemia and stands as a testament to the hybridity of the author's cultural identity and the autochthony of his poetic voice that dominates this early collection. Published in Lima by Souza Ferreira in 1918 and released on July 23, 1919, it's divided into six sections: "Agile Soffits," "Divers," "Of the Earth," "Imperial Nostaligas," "Thunderclaps," and "Songs of Home." *The Black Heralds* is generally celebrated for its linguistic originality, tonic authenticity, treatment of Andean reality, and the potent emblem of *nostos* that resurfaces in multiple forms throughout the poetic movement.

Vallejo inherits from the romantic tradition the dark side, inspired by the Satanism and Cainism of Byron and Espronceda, which would later manifest itself as a feeling of accursedness, as seen in Baudelaire.[64] The Peruvian's early poetics are of this genealogy and, while it's true that he seems to pay homage to Darío with impressively composed Alexandrine sonnets, silvas, and an overall mastery of very complex meter and rhyme, he also breaks away from this and uses it as a springboard to produce a poetic form that would accommodate his thematic content: crisis. This subversion of traditional form is a function of the expulsion of authority. "Vallejo projects his inner struggles onto an order that exceeds his individuality but cannot save him: 'I was born on a day / when God was sick.' . . . The omnipotent deity has been purged from Vallejo's poetry."[65]

In *The Black Heralds* Vallejo dramatizes individual experience and elevates it to the category of myth, now with moral guilt before a cruel and vengeful God—"There are blows in life, so powerful . . . I don't know! / Blows as from the hatred of God" ("The Black Heralds")—now with the curse of unintelligibility and the threat of a meaningless existence—"So life goes, a vast orchestra of Sphinxes / belching out its funeral march into the Void" ("The Voice in the Mirror")—now looking for lucidity in pain—"I am the blind corequenque / who sees through the lens of a wound" ("Huaco").

The linguistic originality of *The Black Heralds*, which indigenists saw as a forerunner of their movement, plays out through Vallejo's incorporation of a Quechua vocabulary within his Castilian verse. Since he was not a native speaker of Quechua, but probably acquired it through reading and being in proximity to native speakers into his twenties, his employment of Quechua and pre-Incan words and phrases signals a unique synthetic feature of his writing—one that summons forth the native voice as a deliberate project. Thus, "Imperial Nostalgias" takes us to "a lake soldering crude mirrors / where shipwrecked Manco Capac weeps," and in "Ebony Leaves" we find "the mood of ancient camphors / that hold vigil *tahuashando* down the path," or in his "Autochthonous Tercet" the sounds of a "yaraví" and "[q]uenaing deep sighs [of] the Pallas" evoke the hybridity through sound. Perhaps this trademark feature appears most clearly in "Huaco," where the poet proclaims that he is "Incan grace, gnawing at itself / in golden coricanchas baptized / with phosphates of error and hemlock."

The Quechua voice in *The Black Heralds* counts as Vallejo's first step toward a poetics of *mestizaje*, a project he continued to modify through the development of later works, such as *Toward the Reign of the Sciris* and *The Tired Stone*. This sign of miscegenation is indicative of the direction Vallejo's writing would take and of the optics through which he would cast his critical eye on European culture in the years to come. By inscribing Andean reality into the symbolist literary tradition, in *The Black Heralds* Vallejo stakes out a poetic space on the peripheries of a literature suffering the symptoms of cultural homogeny, thus foreshadowing the proliferation of a new *sensibility*, grounded fundamentally in Marxist dialectics.

Vallejo's second book of poems, *Trilce*, was first published in 1922 in Lima by Talleres Tipográficos de la Penitenciaría with a prologue by Antenor Orrego and then again in 1930 in Madrid by Compañía Iberoamericana de Publicaciones with a prologue by José Bergamín. It collects seventy-seven poems composed 1918–22, each titled with a roman numeral. Prior to its 1922 publication—that golden year of high modernism—no book had been written in Castilian that was so obsessed with the arbitration of poetic inflection as was *Trilce*, with its bizarre mixture of traditional form and poetic subversion, its technical acrobatics, its view beyond the then prevailing symbolist trends, and an unabashed sentimentality toward the loss of the poet's mother, which clashes with his anguish from being incarcerated in Trujillo Central Jail, where about one-third of the collection was written.[66]

It's hard to imagine where Hispanic literature would be today had Vallejo not written *Trilce*, a book that bears all the bravado of European avant-garde literature but refuses to adopt a consistent aesthetic and even goes so far as to mock the stylistically obsessed. So great has this book's impact been on twentieth-century Hispanic poetry that when we consider any other modern literary work of radical innovation, we're forced to ask if it came before or after Vallejo's great poetic adventure. To put it frankly, even though Vicente Huidobro had already published *El espejo de agua* as early as 1916, Vallejo's *Trilce* is the indisputable catalyst of the Latin American experimental tradition and "the most radical book in the Castilian language."[67]

Unlike Vallejo's first and last collections, the poems of *Trilce* aren't neatly packaged into a thematic sequence but appear more like a boiling kettle of great obsessions with the Origin, Incompletion, Imperfection, Orphanhood, and Death, which the poet stirs with masochistic perversity. In *Trilce* Vallejo evokes "a world whose two poles are immediate sensation and memory, the perception of incoherent diversity and the closed space of the irremediable."[68] Armed with uncanny technical abilities and dizzying poetic intensity, Vallejo is determined to work within these two poles without placing his emotional content inside any imported form, and the strength of his conviction transforms into exhortations, rejections, repudiations, and even mockery. Thus, the opening line of the book—"Who's making all that racket"—takes aim at the prolific hackneyed aesthetes of an imported French symbolist school and, in so doing, celebrates autochthonous expression and ushers in a new era of Hispanic poetry.

The drama of *Trilce* arises through webs of inner tensions in which disparate themes and figures are bonded by unorthodox techniques (hence, the famous "union of contraries"). The search for harmony is possible only because of the presence of dissonance that saturates the poems, and in that dissonance resides the fear that harmony may not be reached, that it may not be reachable or, as in poem LXX, that we may not be able to know if it has been reached or is reachable, since "we shudder to step forth, for we know not whether / we knock into the pendulum, or already have crossed it." Poem XVIII, in turn, reconfigures the bildungsroman narrative to reveal adulthood itself as incomplete, which is why the narrator goes "in search of a tertiary arm / that must pupilate, between my where and when, / this stunted adulthood of man." In poem XXXVI, considered by some to be the manifesto of the book, Vallejo's absurd description of human existence, in which "[w]e struggle to thread ourselves through a needle's eye," leads him to evoke the Venus de Milo, the symbol of perfection that's missing one arm, because this is the contradiction he sees "enwombed in the plenary arms / of existence, / of this existence that neverthelessez / perpetual imperfection." As if he had taken Camus's advice and imagined Sisyphus happy, at the end of the poem he proclaims, "Make way for the new odd number / potent with orphanhood!"

In a similar thread to *Trilce* is Vallejo's first book of narrative prose titled *Scales*. Composed in 1919–22 and published in 1923 by Talleres Tipográficos de la Penitenciaría, *Scales* belongs to Vallejo's most experimental period and, like its predecessor, it teeters between gushing sentimentalism and radical innovation. It's divided into two sections: *Cuneiforms*, which contains six brief narrative prose poems—the unforgettable "walls" that link *Scales* to *Trilce*—and *Wind Choir*, a section of short stories: "Beyond Life and Death," "The Release," "The Caynas," "The Only Child," "Mirtho," and "Wax."[69]

Continuing the experimental thread with all the exuberance of the poetic and now-narrative adventure, *Cuneiforms* might as well be an appendix on *Trilce*, with its brutal descriptions of existence in prison and desperate encounters with mortality recounted in bold lines soldered by syntax that obeys the author's meandering ruminations: "Some cartilaginous breath of an invisible death appears to mix with mine, descending perhaps from a pulmonary system of Suns and then, with its sweaty self, permeating the first of the earth's pores."[70] And in the asphyxiating space of the prison cell, nostalgia insufflates the writing by projecting memories onto the silver screen of the walls: "[A]ll this domestic morning-time aroma reminds me of my family's house, my childhood in Santiago de Chuco, those breakfasts of eight to ten siblings from the oldest to youngest, like the reeds of an antara" ("Windowsill").

Wind Choir enters the gothic world of fantasy and madness, of existential predicaments and nauseating feelings of responsibility. In "Wax," for example, Vallejo places his protagonist Chalé under the Sword of Damocles at a craps table in a boozy Lima. In "The Release" (which could also be translated as "Liberation") the convict Solís inadvertently drives to madness his dear fellow inmate Palomino, who's sure he's being stalked by the family of the man he is accused of killing, and Solís does so by excessively warning the paranoid man to beware of his paranoia. In "Beyond Life and Death" the anonymous narrator journeys home to the rugged countryside to join his family in mourning the loss of his mother, when he comes across a woman who's convinced that he's her son who'd died and has come back to life.

The characters of *Scales* find themselves in unbelievable situations, tempted to interpret their predicaments with supernatural justifications that are rivaled by dry pragmatic rationale. In these early fictions we see Vallejo's romantic inheritance take on strange new life as it morphs into a fantastic world described with the dissident, bizarre language of his most radical poetic voice. In the thematics of *Scales* we perceive the influence of Edgar Allan Poe, but the language is shockingly innovative, light-years beyond Poe, and often tests the ability of the narrative mode to bear the weight of its poetic overhaul.

Not long after *Scales* had come off the press, Vallejo's other early prose fiction, *Savage Lore*, appeared in *La Novela Peruana*, an illustrated bi-weekly edited by Pedro Barrantes Castro. Relegated to the first experimental phase of his writing, this ambitious novella takes place in a Santiago de Chuco that's as gothic as it is Andean, a rural place where the unknown is master, an environment filled with inexplicable mysteries and bad omens that shimmer in the reflections of mirrors and pools of water. Like many of these writings, *Savage Lore* blurs the lines of genre: as fantasy fiction, it narrates the breakdown of the marriage of two peasants and the demise of the husband, Balta Espinar, at the hands of the unknown; as realist fiction, the story recounts the self-destruction of a deranged psychopath.[71]

Set in the sierra of northern Peru, a pastoral landscape of fields tilled by plows driven by the force of oxen, the heart of this fantasy narration shows a sort of superstition that's not uncommon in that region. A hen crows, a mirror breaks, the sure sign of imminent catastrophe. Then a stranger appears, at first as a fleeting image. Balta wonders if his mind is playing tricks on him, but no. The stranger is implacable, and his presence is haunting. In drawn-out frenzied moments of suspicion, Balta starts to demonstrate (excessively) peculiar jealousy toward his wife, Adelaida. This drive toward self-destruction is either a symptom of Balta's psychopathology or a portentous sign of imminent ruin.

With this gesture, as Ricardo Silva-Santisteban explains, Vallejo inscribes *Salvage Lore* in the literary tradition of the Double, among the works of E. A. Hoffmann, Edgar Allan Poe, Guy de Maupassant, Robert

Louis Stevenson, Henry James, and so on. "The figure of the double, which Vallejo has undoubtedly borrowed," he says, "fits all the criteria of the prototype whose own will leads him to try to destroy the character on whom he depends . . . The sinister scenario that Vallejo paints in *Savage Lore* is framed by the resonance of superstition which he integrates into fantasy fiction. He links a literary tradition (of the Double) . . . with oral culture of the northern Peruvian highlands, as is the superstitious element of the crowing hen that foretells the demise of the marriage."[72]

Vallejo's interest in madness had already shown itself in *Scales* and, in the wake of *Trilce*, reveals that genealogy. *Savage Lore*, on the other hand, prefigures a new thread of narrative that is further developed in "Individual and Society" and "Reputation Theory" of *Against Professional Secrets*, giving us a glimpse at where the writing is headed. With regard to the theme, this early exploration of superstition would be superseded by an examination of ritual belief in a historical context, as occurred in his next work of prose fiction, *Toward the Reign of the Sciris*, and the later stage transcreation that it inspired, *The Tired Stone*.

Even though *Toward the Reign of the Sciris* wouldn't be published until after the author's death—in *Nuestro Tiempo*—Vallejo did extract some passages and place them in *La Voz* of Madrid: "An Incan Chronicle" and "The Dance of the Situa." Set in the Inca Empire prior to the arrival of the Spaniards, this historical fiction was probably first drafted out in 1923, during the Lima–Paris journey, and then edited in 1924–28. As Vallejo himself admitted to Abril, he'd targeted the prevailing symbolist tastes of a wide readership, hoping the exotic aesthetic of pre-Hispanic America would garner mass appeal and lead to more lucrative work. It didn't.

Although it's one of the simplest narrations Vallejo wrote with respect to plot and character development, this novella showcases a hybrid language of Castilian and Quechua—a feature he'd only gestured at five years earlier in his indigenist forerunner *The Black Heralds*—which led him to implement extensive research into his shoot-from-the-hip narrative strategy. The bravado of the creolized Castilian-Quechua tongue is visible, at just a glance, in chapter 1. As the defeated Army of the Sun returns to Cuzco, Vallejo narrates the somber procession of "*rumancha* masters," the unfurled rainbow standard "with holes left by a *suntupáucar* spike," and angular heroes who carried on their "shoulders the dense mass of *queschuar*," behind whom limped "lancers with enormous dangling arms wearing *guayacán* headpieces with tassels" and "an old *apusquepay*, with a protruding chin and serene eyes, wearing his yellow turban, tied by a piece of stretched bow string and feathers."[73]

Although Vallejo failed to crystalize the conflict of the novella, in chapter 3 we find the central (if underdeveloped) question that, in *The Tired Stone*, he transformed into masterful drama: is society more fruitful in times of war or peace? Once the Inca's son and heir-apparent retreated from the north, the Inca called off the conquest because he now "yearned for peace and labor . . . [that] the sky unfurrow the brows of farmhands and herders; [that] the husband kiss his wife . . . The Inca now yearned for love, meditation, the seed, leisure, great ideas, eternal images."[74] But pulling out of the war unleashes a series of foreboding events: a gigantic stone crushes scores of stonemasons, thunder rumbles during the *quipuchica* of the enigmatic Kusikayar, and during a ritual sacrifice an eviscerated llama leaps off the altar and scampers away. These events signal the anger of the gods, forcing the Inca to resume the war.

Our discussion now turns to Vallejo's journalistic production, the evaluation of which has thus far largely been reduced to a finalist concept of work carried out strictly as a means of survival. This sort of finalist reduction, for which Vallejo himself held so much contempt, is a convenient way to ignore an entire genre en bloc without attempting to engage its complexity or the intertextuality of the articles and chronicles in relation to the rest of the oeuvre. The articles and chronicles don't represent slag but the transformational process of absorbing raw material and recasting it in a way that necessarily modifies the original. Again, we are reminded of the principle: not *reflection*, but *refraction*. The articles and chronicles reveal the "con-text, inter-text, and sometimes pre-text" of other writings and help us understand the author in a much broader literary and historical framework.[75] Although in his lifetime Vallejo published in nearly forty magazines and newspapers worldwide, the majority of these texts appeared in four primary outlets: *El Norte* (1923–30), *Mundial* (1925–30), *Variedades* (1926–30), and *El Comercio* (1929–30). This journalistic work accounted for most of his earned income during the Paris years, which were grueling, as his letters to Abril and Larrea show, but the circumstance of their creation doesn't preclude them from literary value. Quite the contrary, in his articles and chronicles—and in his books of thoughts—Vallejo employed a method of emulation that allowed him to level an integral critique of social norms, artistic trends, and political theories without falling into the trap of oppositional polemics. Before the eyes of unsuspecting readers, a chameleonic Vallejo entered the modality and composed highly poetic and critical texts about whatever topics he was assigned.[76]

In synthetic nonsecular fashion, Vallejo wonders if it's possible or even advisable for a poet like Paul Valéry to accept an invitation to clarity from a distinguished historiographer. He refuses to do battle with Vicente Huidobro's superintelligence because his vote is for sensibility. He's hopeful of inventor Georges Claude's idea to harness the power of the sea but pragmatically encourages us to be patient since nature takes no leaps. He distrusts André Breton's aesthetic proclamations, rejects Diego Rivera's call for propagandistic art, and denounces Jean Cocteau's artistic catechism, his pure angelic poets, and all professional secrets. In his articles and chronicles Vallejo lends an ear to the wheezing tombs and fine mummies of Lord Carnavon and the Carnegie Institute. He sees the sporting match as the sign of capitalist competition and exposes the record-holding faster, smoker, philatelist, bride, groom, divorcee, singer, laugher, do-gooder, and killer in whom the malice of man mixes together with the good sweat of the beast. He soberly wonders what laws and instincts drove the Incas—in times of war and peace—to manifest a destiny whose historical significance is marked by highly developed social organization. He immortalizes Charlie Chaplin's supreme creations and insists that the United States is blind to their revolutionary meaning. He sings accolades to Sergei Eisenstein and Vladimir Kirshon for their daring screen and stage aesthetics and yet vituperates Marxist ideologues who have forgotten that even their own messiah's brilliance must one day be synthesized into higher forms of thought.

Through a host of critical readings of contemporary sculpture, painting, music, film, literature, architecture, history, politics, archaeology, anthropology, sociology, and sports, in his articles and chronicles Vallejo seeks a way out of artistic secularism by revolutionizing the journalistic form as a poetic space where he emulates the writing of other modalities and absorbs contents that he transforms and recasts as a species all their own. This innovative strategy, as poetic as it is critical, becomes visible only when we read his journalism.

In addition to the massive compilation of articles and chronicles that has shed so much light on Vallejo's biography, his political orientation, and his literary production in genres other than journalism, over the past fifty years enormous gains have been made in the recovery of his epistolary documents. The compilation of letters, telegrams, and postcards between Vallejo and his family, friends, and colleagues began in 1960 with the work of Manuel Castañón, who compiled a series of letters dated between May 26, 1924, and December 27, 1928, documents delivered to him by Pablo Abril de Vivero, who explained that they had been part of a larger cache that burned during a Francoist bombing. After this initial publication, several compilations appeared as more epistolary documents surfaced and critical interest grew, fostered by Juan Larrea, who collected, rigorously dated, and published letters in *Aula Vallejo*, starting in 1961. This continued for the next forty years until 2002, when Jesús Cabel edited the *Correspondencia Completa* for the Pontificia Universidad Católica del Perú, amassing a total of 281 epistolary documents.

Although Vallejo wrote to about forty-five different people, his main correspondents, in order of the frequency with which he communicated to them, were Pablo Abril de Vivero (117), Juan Larrea (39), Gerardo Diego (14), Juan Domingo Córdoba (12), Victor Clemente Vallejo (8), Ricardo Vegas García (8), Carlos Godoy (8), and Luis Varela Orbegoso (8). As for Vallejo's family, there are only seventeen letters registered to date, eight of which correspond to 1912–22, and the remaining nine, to 1923–29. It's clear that there must have been more addressed to his relatives, since he makes reference to documents that we don't have: "Tell Mom, Dad, and Agüedita that I'll write to them on Wednesday" (May 2, 1915); "I wrote to Dad during one of my worst bouts of fear" (December 2, 1918); and "I'll write to Dad tomorrow" (July 14, 1923).

In the letters between Vallejo and Abril, which begin on January 31, 1924, and end on or around February 4, 1934, we learn about the extremity of Vallejo's financial hardship and the resulting frustration and anguish.[77] It's through this correspondence that he organized his entrance into mass-publication journalism as a means of cobbling together a living and diversifying the modality of his writing. In his letters from France, there's an undercurrent of resentment in his feelings toward Peru; however, there's also a tone of solidarity, especially when he speaks with marginal writers who hadn't fallen into the grips of Lima's aesthetic aristocracy or the importers of literary fads.

The letters from the Trujillo Central Jail are especially disturbing. There, Vallejo wrote an appeal to Gastón Roger, a journalist who immediately published it in *La Prensa* on December 29, 1920, along with another appeal, signed by Víctor Raúl Haya de la Torre. Vallejo kept correspondence with Juan Larrea from January 19, 1925, to February 14, 1938. These letters reveal an endearing friendship, reiterate Vallejo's need for economic support, and give insight into his vision of Spain, highlighting his torturous ethical struggle leading up to and during the Spanish civil war.

One hundred years after Vallejo's birth, his final letter was published in the magazine *Oiga*.[78] It was addressed to Luis José de Orbegoso precisely one month before Vallejo passed away. It's a heart-wrenching plea for funds to cover the cost of a lengthy medical treatment. It turns out that Orbegoso, the excellent friend that he was, did in fact reply on March 25,

1938, wishing Vallejo a quick and complete recovery and including a check for the one thousand francs he'd requested. But neither the letter nor the check arrived in time and, what's worse, Georgette was unable to receive the funds, since they'd been returned to Lima by the time she tried to collect them.

We now turn to *Tungsten*, first published in March 1930 by Cenit in Madrid. It counts as Vallejo's only full-length novel and one of the five monographs published in his lifetime. Demonstrative of his political commitment, as evinced in his articles and chronicles from this period, *Tungsten* reveals Vallejo submitting his literary writing to the service of ideological propaganda in support of the Communist Party. Since literature was one of the most efficient means of ideological dissemination in the heat of 1930, it is understandable that Vallejo's *Tungsten* riffed on Feodor Gladkov's hit novel, *Cement*, which had been translated to Castilian by José Viana and published by Cenit in two editions in 1928 and 1929.

In view of Vallejo's financial hardship, it seems plausible to suppose that, in addition to his ideological motivations, he's likely to have wanted to capitalize on the aura of Gladkov's immensely popular novel by situating *Tungsten* in the same marketplace and targeting its impassioned Spanish readers. We cannot underestimate the influence that social realism still had in 1930, and when we add to that the decade-long robust surge of Russian fiction in the era of the new political economy—*The Naked Year* (1922) by Boris Pasternak, *Cities and Years* (1924) by Konstantin Fedin, *Red Cavalry* (1926) by Isaac Babel, *The Thief* (1927) by Leonid Leonov, *The Rout* (1927) by Alexander Fadeyev, and *We* (1929) by Yevgeny Zamyatin—it's no wonder why Vallejo allowed himself to commit what critical consensus calls a literary sin.[79]

Whereas *Cement* celebrates postwar reconstruction in Russia, *Tungsten* scandalizes collusion in the exploitation of Andean workers: the Peruvian denounces U.S. Mining Incorporated for exploiting the indigenous Soras, abusing the workers in the mines, and creating a system of forced labor for their own profits and as a contribution to the U.S. war effort in Europe. The other side of this critique satirizes the servility of Peruvian bourgeoisdom, which generously lends its hand to the wealthy Yanks with hopes of winning their favor. In this way, with a forehand *Tungsten* smacks down the foreign imperialists who greedily exploit the naive indigenous workers and with a backhand hits the self-serving Peruvian upstarts who remain indifferent to the consequence of their vertical social aspirations. Their ascent to high society comes at the cost of their compatriots' descent into misery. Such is the case with the protagonist Leónides Benites: as long as he's under the spell of capital, he's self-absorbed, and only when faced with his own mortality does he realize that no individual is worth more than the collective, which leaves him no choice but to join the revolution.

Following up *Tungsten* chronologically and also in the narrative thread is a text written in 1931—though not published until 1951—called *Paco Yunque*, the only children's story Vallejo wrote. Oddly enough, it's also couched in political ideology. It appears to have been written upon request of the Spanish publisher Cenit, which had just published *Tungsten*, but the manuscript was rejected on account of the violence with which the characters (most of them children) treat one another. *Paco Yunque* is easily the most formulaic text out of all Vallejo's writings.

Although this children's story was judged too violent for Iberian tastes in the early 1930s and has been disregarded by many readers for ideological reasons, it has nonetheless formed part of the national curriculum in Peruvian public schools since the early 1970s, while Juan Francisco Velasco headed the military dictatorship in 1968–75, after the coup d'état against President Fernando Belaunde. Under Velasco, an education reform was launched that made Quechua an official language and aimed to provide bilingual education to the indigenous peoples of the Andes and the Amazon (nearly half of the country's population at the time). Although the increasingly intolerant dictator had his censors exile all newspaper publishers in 1974, he incorporated into the national curriculum works that championed the peasants' struggle, and, in a strange turn of events, *Paco Yunque* became a perfect match for the dictatorship's ideology.

The story's protagonist is a poor country boy named Paco Yunque, who lives with his mother in the home of the Grieves, wealthy English landowners, whose son Humberto abuses Paco at school while revealing his own stupidity. Since Paco Yunque is afraid to stand up to Humberto, Paco Fariña, another boy whom Yunque just met, intervenes in an act of solidarity. The characters are easily recognizable figures that Vallejo uses to prove the premise that the rich are the blight of the poor; the poor don't stand up for themselves out of fear and ignorance; and this cycle can be broken only by people who have the courage to intervene.

This brings us to *Russia in 1931: Reflections at the Foot of the Kremlin*, which was composed in 1928–31 from materials Vallejo collected during his first two trips to the Soviet Union. This political report was published in 1931 by Ulises in Madrid and quickly became a best seller. Many sections of it had been placed in *El Comercio* in 1929 and then in *Bolivar* in 1930 as a series of ten chronicles that bore the headline "A Report on Russia." The book was press-ready in the first quarter of 1931, which is when the phrase

"Russia in 1931" was added to the title to give it a greater sense of currency. The lengthy sixteen chapters aimed to provide contemporary readers a demystified description of Soviet reality, without filtering the author's perception through the tinted filters of a partisan newspaper or magazine. In this terrain Vallejo's *Russia in 1931* is a forerunner of *A Russian Journal* (1948) by John Steinbeck.

As early as August 1927, Vallejo had revealed the method of the survey abroad employed by French journalists. Large-scale Parisian newspapers and magazines used to send their most famous journalists to foreign countries to report on events and interview officials, but well before they arrived those reporters already knew what they wanted to find; it was just a matter of locating the right person to prove their hypothesis. Vallejo's objective was different, since he wasn't interested in simply regurgitating more propaganda or even going to Moscow to smoke cigarettes with Anatoly Lunacharsky. He wanted to provide a technical interpretation of social organization in Soviet Russia by stripping his accounts of bias so that he could transparently record whom and what he saw and then carry out a nonpartisan analysis. Whether he achieved this or not is another question, but this was his agenda, as he laid it out in the introduction. The Russia Vallejo saw still lay under the rubble left by the October Revolution, which had been described by another best-selling American author of the same genre, John Reed, in his book *Ten Days That Shook the World* (1919). But whereas Reed narrated the destructive period of social upheaval during the end of the tzarist regime, Vallejo optimistically studied the peaceful construction of a new society at the beginning of the socialist experiment.

The Peruvian's approach to evaluating the state of Russian social organization was the cross-sector interview, in which he recorded accounts of people from as many sectors of society as possible with the aim of achieving a sample representative of the whole. This method led him to speak with Boris Pessis, secretary of VOKS; Maria Schlossberg, a candy factory worker on the outskirts of Moscow; a German worker from Bremen, who showed him that no worker in Russia could be considered a foreigner; the director of the Commercial Textile Union, who explained defects, setbacks, and gaps in Russian technology; Aleksei Gastev, director and founder of the Central Institute of Labor (CIT); Valerian Muraviev, editor of the organization's journal; a professor of the Academy of Social Sciences in Moscow, who explained the system of salaries; and then with the director of a metallurgic facility, who put the Peruvian in contact with workers. After only the first five chapters, Vallejo crosses from the economic plane to infrastructure, production, labor, until finally reaching morality, and there he lingers for the remainder of the book.

Chapter 8 recounts Vallejo's meeting in Leningrad with a group of Bolshevik writers: Sergei Adamovich Kolbasiev, Vissarion Mikhailovich Sayanov, Boris Viktorovich Lipatov, Wolf Yosifovich Ehrlich, and Ilya Ivanovich Sadofiev, inter alia. In chapter 9 he follows a stonemason around for a day only to end up at a theater, where he sees Kirshon's play *The Rails Are Humming*. Vallejo marvels at the scenery with those larger-than-life sprockets and gears of a half-built locomotive, the socially diverse audience, and the revolutionary resolutions: A disenchanted worker is about to commit suicide, but "he's still fighting. It's time to sweat blood and 'take this cup from me.' As he lifts up the jar, a small hand suddenly stops him. It's the hand of his son, who wasn't sleeping. The boy's action is of far-reaching historical significance." The awakening son as hero crystallizes the revolutionary premise that the new generation will be the savior of the old. Finally, in the no less remarkable chapter 14, which is centered on film, Vallejo extols the achievements of Sergei Eisenstein's *The General Line*, in whose collaged scenes of exploitation, labor, and mechanized agriculture he perceives the future of revolutionary art in Russia as well as his own growing oeuvre.

Not long after finishing *Russia in 1931*, Vallejo began work on *Russia Facing the Second Five-Year Plan*, which was composed in 1931–32, though not published until as late as 1965 by Gráfica Labor in Lima. In a sense, it can be read as a sequel to *Russia in 1931* with regard to its thematic concerns and methodology, but only to the extent that the first report focuses on Russian social organization during the socialist experiment, whereas the second studies the lifestyle such organization could afford. Vallejo divided this book of thoughts into two large sections, the first, consisting of thirty-two chapters, and the second, twenty-seven, all of which run considerably shorter than those from the first report.

The narrative device of this interwar Eurasian tour is the guide, a man named Yerko, the "servant"—a delicate term that Vallejo has us understand in the widest of senses, from the porter, to the waiter, to a political official. Obedience is the universal code here, and everyone obeys everyone else. Therefore, when Vallejo asks, "Has the revolution wiped out the servants?" the only possible response is "yes and no." In Russia everyone is a servant, or no one is a servant to anyone. On their tour Vallejo and Yerko are accompanied by an anonymous Austrian Social Democrat, whose anti-socialist perspective produces the conflicts necessary for lively dialectical debate.

Gathered in the Workers' Club, Yerko and other comrades attend a night of the arts. A choir sings the "Internationale," applauds the classical dances of an artist from the Moscow Opera, listens to musical pieces by Tchaikovsky and Liszt on the balalaika and piano, ballads played by Red Army veterans and a scene from another play by Kirshon. The discussion then turns to the topic of an article in *Izvestia* by the former commissioner of enlightenment, Anatoly Lunacharsky, which gives rise to a debate about the newly formed French literary school, populism, and how it may or may not be relevant to current affairs in Russia.

As proof of Vallejo's attempt at writing unbiased accounts of the socialist experiment, the chapter "Accidents on a Socialist Job" exposes some of the shortcomings of Soviet modernization. Among a group of trudging workers, Vallejo and his travel companion cross the bridge over the Dnieper, and when they reach the other shore, they find a woman unconscious on the ground. It's unclear whether she's dead or alive, and the other workers pass by without even noticing her, let alone stopping to see if she needs help. That same day the Peruvian sees a giant steel plate fall not far from him and flatten two workers. The delayed response to the accidents reveals the lack of infrastructure and the emotional detachment of the workers.

From climactic changes to the notion of comfort; from fashion to family life; from cuisine to social gatherings; from the role of passions to the role of reason; from religion to architecture; from hygiene to locomotion and sports, in *Russia Facing the Second Five-Year Plan* Vallejo reports on the quality of life and the progress of social organization during the early Stalin years. Rather than withdrawing from the less-than-perfect outcome of the revolution, falling into dissolution and then further dissolution, as a bitter anarchist might, Vallejo saw Russians in the early 1930s as the pioneers of a world they were making with their own hands.[80]

In addition to his formal reportage, Vallejo wrote a book of thoughts in 1926–32, *Art and Revolution*, and, like so many of his works, it was published only posthumously, in 1973 by Mosca Azul Editores in Lima. Some of these texts, however, were published in newspapers and magazines as early as 1926. In this book we see Vallejo reconcile his literary aspirations with his commitment to the socialist revolution. He explores the revolutionary writer's role in and to the benefit of society, and he decides that this writer is no longer the romantic poet worn out from heartfelt sighs in the privacy of his study; nor is he the lackadaisical bohemian dreamer ignorant to the consequence of his apathy; nor is he the avant-garde sectarian who seeks the "New" by exclusion and change by opposition. The revolutionary writer is open to all sectors of life and to these he goes boldly in search of concrete contact with social reality.

Given their thematic concerns and the context of their composition, the texts of *Art and Revolution* deliberately or coincidentally evoke certain essays of Anatoly Lunacharsky (1875–1933). For example, when we read through such texts by the Russian as "Taneyev and Scriabin" (1925), "Chernyshevsky's Ethics and Aesthetics" (1928), or "Theses on the Problem of Marxist Criticism" (1928), we get the sense that Vallejo is emulating his contemporary while exposing the political underpinnings of the aesthetics of prevailing writers in the late 1920s and early 1930s. If Lunacharsky's *Revolutionary Silhouettes* (1923) reflects on the collective efforts of individuals who gave rise to the October Revolution, Vallejo's *Art and Revolution* attacks intellectual puppets for declaring that artistic innovation comes from fixed doctrine rather than perpetual transformation.

In "Tell Me How You Write and I'll Tell You What You Write," Vallejo clarifies that artistic technique must be used not as a disguise but as an instrument of transparency. The technical problem that he locates in the schools of dadaism, futurism, surrealism, and populism is rooted to their attempt to critique the traditional (romantic, realist, symbolist) methodology of artistic production by opposing it with doctrine written as a bellicose manifesto established by an exclusive tribe of specialists. Vallejo doesn't necessarily disagree with the vanguards in their social or aesthetic critiques, but in their approach toward developing on the flaws they found. He foresees the pitfalls of oppositional doctrine and demands self-inclusive solutions. In this sense, César Vallejo is far too cosmic to be considered avant-garde and proves to be an alternative to it.

Perhaps the two most disconcerting texts from *Art and Revolution* are "The Mayakovsky Case" and "Autopsy of Surrealism." In the former Vallejo relates one of the interactions he had in Leningrad with Kolbasiev, who claims that Mayakovsky isn't the best, but merely the most published, Soviet poet. Vallejo had already taken the same position as Kolbasiev in 1927, but now he enters precarious territory and offers an explanation of the Russian's suicide: the result of a tragic disagreement between what he was saying in his poetry and what he was truly feeling and thinking.[81] Mayakovsky was a highly skilled poet, who suffered not from an inability to craft good poetry but from denying himself the opportunity to do so with sincerity.

"Autopsy of Surrealism," in turn, follows the debate between André Breton, specifically in his *Second Manifesto of Surrealism*, and Georges Ribemont-Dessaignes, who'd published a polemical pamphlet titled

A Corpse that included essays by Desnos, Queneau, Leiris, Carpentier, Baron, Prévert, Vitrac, Morise, and Boiffard countering Breton's initial attacks. In his *Autopsy* Vallejo describes how that movement's critical and revolutionary spirit transitioned to anarchism and then, once the surrealists noticed that Marxian methodology seemed as interesting as that crisis of consciousness they'd been promoting, they went out, bought new clothes, and became communists. It was surrealism's feigned adoption of Marxism that led to the movement's atrophy and eventual demise. It realized that it couldn't embody the truly revolutionary spirit of the age and, once it had lost its social prestige—its only raison d'être—the agony commenced, there was some gasping, and the death knells tolled.

Also straddling poetic and critical modalities is another book of thoughts, composed in 1923–24 while Vallejo was taking his first steps in Paris, and then in 1928–29 when he took the hard left toward Marxism: *Against Professional Secrets*. In step with his poor publication record, this gem was released only in 1973 by Mosca Azul. Essential to this book is Vallejo's reportage, which sent him interviewing scores of people across interwar Russia, attending theatrical and musical performances in Paris, looking at society as a complex conglomeration of sectors that are irremediably bound, and noticing the tendency of prevailing avant-garde writers to create innovative literature behind closed doors. Many of the texts in *Against Professional Secrets* were early drafts of longer pieces the author had placed in magazines.

The phrase "Contra el secreto professional" first appeared as the title of a 1927 magazine article that Vallejo published in *Variedades* and seems to be his way of rebuking the idea of sectarian literature, which he saw epitomized in Jean Cocteau's *Le secret professionnel* (1922). In that article Vallejo levels an attack on avant-garde literature and enumerates several formulas that Latin American poets were appropriating from the European tradition. As an alternative to this, he invokes a new attitude, a "new sensibility," one that denounces the gross plagiarists of literary trends, because "their plagiarism prevents them from expressing and realizing themselves humanly and highly" and because they imitate foreign aesthetics about which they gloat with insolent rhetoric that they create out of autochthonous inspiration. The closer we read this book, the more apparent it becomes that Vallejo modulates styles to demonstrate a chameleonic strategy that allows him to adopt romantic, symbolist, surrealist, socialist, realist, scientific, and even existentialist modalities. What makes this tactic so compelling is that, by emulating these literary tendencies, he implicates himself in his own critique, widens the scope of his project, and shapes a collaborative poetics instead of the usual oppositional polemics.

From "The Motion Inherent in Matter," a scientific description of the phenomenon of parallelism; to the gothic account "Individual and Society," which resembles the tales of Poe; to the surrealist fragments in "Negations of Negations"; to the Kafkaesque "Reputation Theory" and the Borgesian "Masterful Demonstration of Public Health"; to the desperate romantic confessions in "Languidly His Liqueur" and even the Biblical parable in "Vocation of Death," *Against Professional Secrets* takes us on an aesthetic journey through nineteenth- and early twentieth-century Europe, only to reveal that the poetic vehicles that have transported us are as arbitrary as they are exploitative. These meditations are at once an attack on the European avant-garde and an appeal to Latin American writers to quit the practice of aesthetic importation. By moving art from the realm of aesthetics to that of ethics, passing through the political economy, Vallejo lays the foundation for a poetics of human solidarity.[82]

Our discussion on Vallejo's books of thoughts has organically led us his notebooks, which contain entries from 1926 to 1938, with the author's final dictation. According to Vallejo, many of the entries were supposed to be appended to *Art and Revolution* or *Against Professional Secrets* and, in some cases, to both. The notebooks cover a wide range of topics and rarely contain lyricism like that which we find in the poetry and sometimes the articles; instead, they are more of a meditative nature, more conceptual and fragmented, and many of these philosophical kernels emerge in subsequent magazine articles, reports, poems, and plays.

It's fascinating to see how a simple concept from one entry—"The mercy and compassion of men for men. If at a man's moment of death, all the mercy of all the men were mustered up to keep him from dying, that man wouldn't die"—eventually grew into "Mass," the crowning poem of *Spain, Take This Cup from Me*; or how notes on a film premiere in Moscow—"the foundation for a new aesthetic: the *aesthetic of labor*"—could give rise to such sizable endeavors as the plays *Brothers Colacho* and *The Tired Stone*; or how an ironic contradiction—"the revolutionary intellectual who, under a pseudonym, secretly contributes to reactionary magazines"—could transform into dialogue in the chapter "Workers Discuss Literature" from *Russia Facing the Second Five-Year Plan*.

This list could go on and on, but we'll limit ourselves to these few examples, holding onto the belief that the pleasure of reading these fragments derives from discovering their permutations throughout the oeuvre.

The intertextuality disclosed by the notebooks reveals a series of beginnings in Vallejo's iterative writing process across the modalities of poetry, fiction, drama, reportage, and journalism. Although some entries are characterized by the cleverness of ludic puns and quips, which has led one translator to go so far as to publish them under the banner of "aphorisms," the greater value seems to reside in their relation to the whole and in what can be learned about Vallejo's writing process by patiently examining that relation.[83]

Now, we switch gears to briefly discuss what is arguably Vallejo's most polished performance piece, *The Final Judgment*, a short one-scene play that the author extracted from *Moscow vs. Moscow*, which itself was an early draft of *The River Flows between Two Shores*. It was probably written in or around 1930 but not published until 1979.[84] A review of the early drafts reveals that Vallejo first planned this scene as a prologue to the full-length play, but as he reworked the longer text (apparently to lock the characters into the conflict and give the tragedy a stronger foundation), the prologue seemed to hold up on its own. The scene acquires its dramatic strength through agony. Atovov lies on his deathbed and Father Rulak has come to hear his last confession: prior to the October Revolution, he killed Rada Pobadich, who was about to assassinate Lenin at a rally.

The priest is beside himself with rage. "So you saved the life of a man who brought misfortune to Russia and atheism to its souls? . . . You wretch! You heinous man! The true culprit of the Russian disaster!" Yet, Atovov, just before giving up the ghost, explains to his confessor that this same Pobadich had an affair with the priest's concubine. Rulak is doubly destroyed and from this destruction his character transforms to offer the socialist message that Vallejo has planted from the beginning: "Lord God," appeals the priest, "with the same mercy reap every soul, large or small, that has fallen into sin." Thus, *The Final Judgment* is Vallejo's most lucid stage script and demonstrates the form of self-implication he deemed necessary to engage the most complex socioeconomic problems of the era.

Much like in *The Final Judgment*, Vallejo drafted out his one-act tragedy *Death* in or around 1930 and extracted it from the full-length play called *Moscow vs. Moscow*, which, after rigorous rewrites, eventually became *The River Flows between Two Shores*. The script wasn't published until 1979 in *Teatro Completo*, and the play was never staged in the author's lifetime. Since Vallejo revised this text in Castilian and French, an update in one language doesn't always appear in another. Such is the case with *La Mort*, originally written in French. *Death* is a well-crafted one-act tragedy set in the early days of Soviet Russia that examines the role of the Russian Orthodox Church in relation to the civil war and the ideological chasms it left between generations within a single family. In a sense, *Death* is the fall of the Polianovs, a once-wealthy royal family whose life has undergone a radical revision since the political tumult of the preceding years. Osip has abandoned the house and family, drowning his anguish in vodka and women, while Vara, his wife, suffers the loss of her husband and is destroyed by her children's enthusiasm for the Bolsheviki and the ideals of the new society.

Against this backdrop of the Polianovs's crisis, Vallejo stages a debate between Fathers Sakrov, Sovarch, and Rolanski, who agree that Osip's soul is in peril but disagree on how it must be saved. Sakrov is convinced that his only hope for escape from moral and intellectual decadence is manual labor in the countryside with the workers. He thinks that Osip should once and for all leave his wife to go work on a kolkhoz outside Moscow. For a man of Osip's stature, such a decision would be unprecedented, which is why Sakrov must insist, "history, my brothers, never repeats itself"—insistence that's countered by Rolanski's skeptical rebuttal: "But it spirals up, dear friend. Here's the proof: we, here, in Soviet Russia, are already witnessing a similar revenge of human sentiment against Marxist rationalism." Thus, Vallejo allows the dialectic to unfold, on the one side, with the forward-thinking Sakrov, who's committed to collectively building the future in that land of hopes, and on the other side, with Rolinski, who's wary of radical change and still clings on to a past he knows even if it no longer exists.

When the other priests go outside to beg, Sakrov stays behind, since begging isn't in his nature (here again Vallejo accentuates his commitment to labor), thus allowing him to talk to Osip, who has entered the scene, on the verge of a breakdown, caused by the inner turmoil of his moral tailspin. "I have told you," Sakrov says, that "it is given to man to rise up to God only if he leans on the shoulders of other men." For Vallejo, an individual cannot achieve spiritual well-being without working to improve the well-being of society. The kolkhoz, the collective farm, perfectly embodies this image and is in keeping with his concentric relation of the individual and society—the self and the world. The isolation of medieval hermits no longer suits modern man, who knows that "God can be discovered only in the midst of the great human gatherings, amid the crowds. This is the religious statement of our times!" When the fate of Osip's soul dangles on the question of whether or not to eschew individual love and embrace the collective, Vara suddenly enters the scene, and Osip's dilemma acquires its full dramatic weight. The strength of his character is his moral weakness, and his tragedy stems from his inability to leave her, even though it's evident to him, her, and everyone else that their relationship is doomed and that reuniting will end only in disgrace, misfortune, death.

With *The Final Judgment* and *Death* at arm's reach, we turn our attention to *The River Flows between Two Shores*, first drafted in or around 1930 and edited as late as 1936. During the author's lifetime, it was never staged, and the script never published.[85] This was Vallejo's first full-length play, a tragedy with a prologue, three acts, and five scenes—and it was work that did not come easily. He struggled with the title of the play and, over the course of multiple drafts, changed it from *Vera Polianova* to *The Game of Love and Hatred*, then to *The Game of Love, Hatred, and Death*, and then to *The Game of Life and Death*, mimicking Romain Rolland's *The Game of Love and Death* (1925). The play then went on to be called *Moscow vs. Moscow*, only to finally be given the title it bears today, *The River Flows between Two Shores*.

The title Vallejo finally chose perfectly captures the conflict: the generational antagonism established on the two shores (the parents and older children represent the old aristocracy; and the younger children, the new social order). Between these shores runs the unstoppable river, where water serves as the figure of historical transformation, tacitly evoking Heraclitus of Ephesus. The drama of the play surges out of the implacable flow of history, indifferent to whatever gets in its way. Although the tension arises from the conflict among Vera and her husband, Vallejo's point of attack comes through Vera's attempt to stop her younger children from embracing the new social order. Her downfall results not from the revolution, but from her inability to accept social reality in the wake of the revolution, and it's precisely this state of denial that leads to her daughter's tragedy, with unmistakable resonance of the early generational insight of *Trilce* LVI, which complains about the grown-ups who "understood themselves even as creators / and loved us even to doing us harm."[86]

The River Flows between Two Shores isn't Vallejo's best play, but it has redeeming qualities, and these he fought for tooth and nail. Such an ambitious endeavor for our Andean author—a full-length play set in Moscow about the generational conflict after the Russian civil war—bled into melodrama, and we get the sense that Vallejo recognized this, since he had the mind to salvage the successful shorts, *The Final Judgment* and *Death*. Additionally, we mustn't forget that, contrary to his more mature stage writing (*Brothers Colacho* and *The Tired Stone*), *The River Flows between Two Shores* is the only full-length play that wasn't adapted from a novel he'd previously written, thus revealing his absolute fearlessness as a writer willing to venture into unknown waters of genre and explore extremely complicated, controversial topics.

The case is different with *Brothers Colacho*. In 1932 Vallejo adapted his novel *Tungsten* into this full-length farce and edited it thoroughly thereafter, even imagining one of the revisions, *Presidents of America*, as a screenplay. None of the iterations was ever produced in the author's lifetime, and the script, never published. Although Vallejo has the tendency of pouring salt on the wound of social conflict in all his plays, in *Brothers Colacho* it stings the most. The play is about two poor merchants, Acidal and Mordel Colacho, who rise from their humble beginnings into social and political positions of power and, through this transition, they're quick to exploit members of the working class as they once were exploited. Here, exploitation occurs as a result of the lack of education, specifically the basic skills of mathematics and spelling. Acidal and Mordel are able to cheat the indigenous patrons of their store because these astute store owners know how to calculate and spell and their humble clients don't. What makes their characters ruthless (and the play hysterical) is their sanctimony and ignorance. While gloating about their intelligence, they reveal their own stupidity.

Whereas *Tungsten* can be read as Vallejo's nod at Gladkov's *Cement* (1925), when we imagine what a production of *Brothers Colacho* would look like, *The Gold Rush* (1925) of Chaplin appears before our eyes. Like the novel that gave rise to it, Vallejo's farce formulates a systemic critique of Peruvian government, which in 1930 was suffering grave problems brought on by the administration of Augusto B. Leguía and then several other fleeting administrations that ensued, a period when infamous deals were struck with the governments of imperialist countries. And Vallejo's foresight must be recognized, since in *Brothers Colacho* he predicts that Peru would end with a dictatorship, which it did, led by Gen. Óscar R. Benevides.

At the heart of the play is a critique of collusion, since Vallejo isn't against only U.S. imperialism but exploitation of all kinds, and he goes to great lengths to show that corruption, like that which occurred in the mining industry of the Peruvian Andes, was fostered by native power brokers. The self-inclusive feature of this argumentation is precisely what makes the Colacho brothers so despicable and the premise of the play so universal. Driven by personal greed, they sell out their own people behind a facade of sanctimony. Their malice—with its self-serving logic and part-time morality—makes their sociopolitical success detestable and drives the farce to hilarity.

Now, we turn our attention to what is considered one of Vallejo's greatest literary accomplishments: *Human Poems*. The first edition was published in Paris in 1939, by Georgette de Vallejo and Raúl Porras Barrenchea (Les Editions des Presses Modernes), with an epilogue by Luis Alberto Sánchez and Jean Cassou. Composed in 1923–38 and comprising a cache of 108 texts, half of which were dated in the autumn of 1937 and half undated, the collection doesn't appear to have a deliberate order, except for the final fifteen poems titled *España, aparta de mí este cáliz*. It's safe to say that had Vallejo lived longer, these poems would've received further editing, and the collection a title, since critical consensus affirms that the phrase *Poemas humanos* was not Vallejo's invention.

Human Poems counts as the first of two major works of a poet who has reached maturity. No longer obsessed with the convoluted syntax and idiosyncratic morphology which he had flaunted in *Trilce* with that artistic perversion and love for the cryptic, in this collection Vallejo has a much more universal and far-reaching agenda, transitioning from "multiplicity to integration."[87] Through a complex system of historical references and toponyms in tune with the currents of high modernism, Vallejo's poetry—interchangeably in verse and prose at this stage—refuses to forego its sentimentality and confessional mode that had defined him from the start. Now, saturated with pathos, not unlike the tragicomic aesthetic of Chaplin, the poetic voice begins its outward turn and starts to express a cosmic vision through the experienced lens of a man in his prime.

Whereas it was the *nostos* that drove the poetic of *The Black Heralds* and the *kryptikos* that created tension in *Trilce*, we perceive in *Human Poems* the poet yearning for the world to become a *kosmos* in which fields of maize transmute into human fields, and these into the "[s]olar and nutritious absence of the sea, / and oceanic feeling for everything!" as we read in the poem "Telluric and Magnetic." In this quest for a complex orderly self-inclusive system, the manifestation of the poet's desire for completion takes the form of complaints that he has only ever been given life and never once death; yet this feeling is frustrated by the very language that expresses it, as we see in the poem "Today I like life much less," where he writes, "I almost touched the part of my whole and restrained myself / with a shot in the tongue behind my word."

This notion of language as an obstruction from reaching cosmic totality was prefigured in the image of the Venus de Milo from poem XXXVI of *Trilce*, but in *Human Poems* the poet doesn't appear to have only accepted his "orphanhood." Instead, he starts acquiring a quasi-Whitmanian everythingist vision; although contrary to his democratic forebear, Vallejo's gaze is set on the promise of socialism. Thus, in "The peace, the wausp, the shoe heel, the slopes," he seeks to fraternize with "[t]he horrible, the sumptuous, the slowest, / the august, the fruitless, / the ominous, the convulsive, the wet, the fatal, / the whole, the purest, the lugubrious, / the bitter, the satanic, the tactile, the profound."

From the experimental poetics of *Trilce* and *Scales* to the compositions we find in *Human Poems*, the direction of the poetic voice begins its outward turn, and the thematics shift from the existential concerns of the individual to the universal crises of the species. This can be explained by Vallejo's adoption of a sort of Marxism that, as Ricardo González Vigil shows, "was 'critical' and 'creative,' loyal in this regard to Marx and not to the dogmas fabricated by his disciples." In *Human Poems* Vallejo's fundamental *sensibility* underlies his Marxism, formed during his childhood years with its Andean household background, his Christian and pantheistic upbringing, and his early awareness of injustice and sociocultural marginalization. These are poems seeking Peruvian roots and the origin of being, leading the poet "to accept the Revolution as the (dialectically superior) return trip to the paradise of the origin, the communal model of the Indian (cf. 'Telluric and Magnetic' and *Tungsten*) galvanized by the Bolsheviks ('Angelic Salutation,' *Russia in 1931*, and *Reflections at the Foot of the Kremlin*) and the militiamen of the Spanish Civil War (*Spain, Take This Cup from Me*)."[88]

The time has come for us to linger on Vallejo's last and most accomplished book of poems, *Spain, Take This Cup from Me*, composed and revised in 1937–38. Published in 1939 with a prologue by Juan Larrea, with the editorial support of Manuel Altolaguirre and a drawing by Pablo Picasso designed especially for the cover, it was printed at the Montserrat monastery near the end of the Spanish civil war. As we've recently learned from the first edition, discovered in the Montserrat library by Julio Vélez and Antonio Merino and subsequently published in facsimile at the hands of Alan Smith Soto, the government of the Generalitat had transformed the monastery into a hospital and printing center. Created in the fourteenth century by direct descendants of Guttenberg and then under the direction of Altolaguirre, the press was operated by soldiers of the Aragon front and published the imprint Ediciones Literarias del Comisariado, Ejército del Este, which, in addition to Vallejo's book, produced editions of Pablo Neruda's *España en el corazón: Himno a las glorias del pueblo en la guerra* and Emilio Prados's *Cancionero menor de los combatientes*. In February 1939 Francoist forces destroyed virtually all Republican publications no sooner than it occupied the monastery.[89]

In the heat of 1937 Vallejo was tormented more than ever by the tragedy taking shape in the Spanish landscape and by the hidden designs of evil incarnated by imperialist powers, which is why, when many people wavered, he marched down the socialist path and produced politically committed art in response to the threat of fascism.[90] The profound inspiration that he found in the selflessness of Spanish militiamen is recorded in "Popular Statements of the Spanish Civil War," which might as well have been a preface to *Spain, Take This Cup from Me*, since there, writing as what in today's lingo would be called an "embedded reporter," Vallejo profiled the heroic feats of anonymous Republican soldiers who ended up resurfacing in the opening hymn of his last book of poems.

Comparative readings of Vallejo's edited typescripts reveal a reordering of the poetic sequence, which resulted in a remarkable sense of continuity. The anguished editing of the texts from *Spain, Take This Cup from Me* and, in some cases, the existence of labyrinthine originals, attest to Vallejo's rare ability to assimilate the experience of the war while it was happening with a seemingly supernatural drive toward completion. Reordered, the poem moves like a play, with an opening act that depicts the war as a panorama in which impassioned soldiers march off to battle (I); the succession of different battles (II); funeral songs for the anonymous heroes and the emblematic contemplation of death (III–VII); the poet's meditations on death and destruction alongside corpses (IX–XI); resurrection triggered by universal solidarity and the transfiguration of the universe raised by the dust of the dead (XII–XIII); and the final warning to Mother Spain of her potential defeat and the prophesy of her fall (XIV–XV).[91]

If in his earlier poetry Vallejo's voice aims inward and in *Human Poems* it begins its outward turn, in *Spain, Take This Cup from Me*, it's directed completely outward to address the masses, crowds, and soldiers, against a backdrop of "the world of twentieth-century man, at the center of which Vallejo portrays himself as conceiving his own death. By the time the *España* manuscript was completed, the elitist tradition of many of the Modernist and Postmodernist poets had been turned inside out."[92] When these poems reach their emotive heights, the poetry "obtains the grandeur and potency of an epinikion," as is the case with the opening "Hymn to the Volunteers for the Republic," where the poet frames the entire poetic sequence in just a couple of lines: "Battles? No! Passions. And passions preceded / by aches with bars of hopes, / by aches of the people with hopes of men! / Death and passion for peace, of common people!"[93] With Marxian ideology and a sermonic drive reminiscent of Whitman, Vallejo's "Hymn" can be read as "an overture of the entire collection of poems. It becomes a microcosm of almost all the themes and issues that we find in the compositions that follow it." [94]

Further on in that same "Hymn," when Vallejo gives the order to "kill / death" and the reassuring exclamation that "[o]nly death will die!" he's alluding to the prophecies of Isaiah (25:6–8, 26:19, and 28:15, 18, with clear echoes of Saint Paul: "For he must reign until he has put all his enemies under his feet. The last enemy to be destroyed is death" (1 Cor. 15:25–26). But, Vallejo's biblical allusions are more auditory than visual, and this line is also the revolutionary response to the infamous motto of Gen. Millán Astray: "¡Viva la muerte!" Nor can we forget that this was the motto of the Legión de los Tercios Españoles, who sinisterly called themselves the Volunteers of Death and used to sing the hymn "El novio de la muerte." [95]

The resurrection we see in poem III, dedicated to Pedro Rojas, who "after being dead, / got up, kissed his blood-smeared casket [and] / wept for Spain"—reveals his act of martyrdom as the saving grace of not only the side he's fighting for but all of humanity, which is why "[h]is corpse was full of world." He has accepted death voluntarily out of love for humanity to create a better world, and he is not dead as long as his ideals live on. [96] The invincibility of these ideals acquires more potent meanings toward the end of the collection, when the poet addresses the "[c]hildren of the world" and "sons of fighters," warning them that if Mother Spain ends up falling, it will be their duty to "go look for her!"

In late 1937, around the time that he was writing *Spain, Take This Cup from Me*, Vallejo transformed his novella *Toward the Reign of the Sciris* into a three-act tragedy called *The Tired Stone*. He wrote this piece in an exalted poetic language saturated with a Quechua vocabulary, an element that returns this late composition to pre-Columbian Peru, where he depicts a hero hiding in a stonemason of the Inca Empire as the archetype of proletarian man. In January 1938 he submitted the play to radical revisions that yielded outstanding results. The first published edition, included in *Teatro completo* (1979), misconstrues the structure of the play as the author had envisioned it and renders that version unreadable. The most accurate version, *Teatro completo III* (1999), edited by Ricardo Silva-Santisteban and Cecilia Moreano, incorporates Vallejo's handwritten changes and restores the integrity of the text.

In *The Tired Stone*, a stonemason named Tolpor falls in love with Kaura, a *ñusta* (princess), which is a sin, and this sets the tragedy in motion. When he realizes that he can neither have nor deny his love and that he has angered the gods, in response to which the Conquest is resumed in an attempt to pacify them, Tolpor selflessly heads off to war. But when he fights his enemies to save his people in search of Death instead of Glory, Fame ends up claiming him and, by popular demand, he ascends to the throne, without Kaura, who was displaced during the battles. No sooner does he receive the sacred tassel, than Tolpor renounces it, blinds himself, and goes to the countryside to live the life of a beggar, where years later he runs into Kaura. But, on account of his blindness, he can't tell that it's she, and because he's transformed into a beggar, she doesn't realize it's he.

The confluence of the aesthetic and political visions—that the poor ensure the well-being of the people and that individual love is inferior to the love of a collective—epitomizes Vallejo's late writings in which his ideals of indigenism fuse with those of socialism.[97] The central axis of *The Tired Stone* is the protagonist's ethically negative concept of hubris, which arises from the dynamic of his destructive passions. The paradox that unites determinism and free will drives the tragic climax of his actions off a cliff and sends him falling into the traps of Fate and the world of Fault, where he demands his own punishment, giving way to the path of self-sacrifice and expiation.[98]

Two years before he wrote the play, Vallejo was already wondering, "What laws and interests, what instincts or ideals, moved [the Incas]—in war and peace—to manifest a destiny whose historical essence and meaning seem to contain extraordinary kernels of wisdom and organization?"[99] Resources that the author appears to have used in response to those questions and in the creation of the play include the essay "Saycuscca-Rumi: Tradición cusqueña" by Eleazar Boloña (his thesis advisor at La Universidad de La Libertad) and the chapter "Tres torreones, los maestros mayores y las piedra cansada" from the *Comentarios reales de los Incas* by the Inca Garcilaso de la Vega, as well as the anonymous classical Quechua play *Ollantay*. Moreover, Sacsayhuaman, one of the primary settings and symbols of Vallejo's play—that architectonic structure under construction and being built by collective labor—can be read as an Andean translation of Vladimir Kirshon's half-assembled locomotive in *The Rails Are Humming*, which we know Vallejo deeply admired.[100]

But aside from these sources, certain themes and movements of *The Tired Stone* seem to have been inspired by the writings of Sophocles, for example, in act 1, scene 5. There Tolpor, who has committed the sin of falling in love with a princess and, entranced by that love, wanders in front of the sacred Coricancha temple without removing his shoes, which clearly echoes the opening scene of *Oedipus at Colonus*, where Oedipus and Antigone wander into the sacred bronze gateway to Athens owned by the revered god Poseidon. Where the Greek and the Peruvian diverge is in the trajectory of their tragic heroes. For Sophocles, the king falls into disgrace for the sake of his people; for Vallejo, the serf ascends to the throne involuntarily and when he realizes that this power has cost him his love he renounces the throne and blinds himself, which prevents him from seeing that love at the end. Thus, the blindness of Oedipus (for his ignorance) and Tolpor (for his hubris) is their final punishment and revelation—what they know but can't see is the ironic consequence of expiation.[101]

3

Despite the apparent breadth of the present volume, these *Selected Writings* paint César Vallejo's oeuvre with very broad brushstrokes. One need only consult the fourteen volumes of the *Obras completas* published by the PUCP (1997–2002), which amasses approximately six thousand pages, to realize just how much of this writer's work there really is left to translate. For years, one major problem translators faced was finding trustworthy sources on which to base their work, but the scholarship that has been carried out, especially in the past fifteen years, has resolved this and created an immense foundation of newly set texts informed by an expansive field of investigation.

In the English-speaking world, Vallejo's poetry initially appealed to the poets and readers of the Deep Image movement and later on attained certain resonance with L=A=N=G=U=A=G=E poets and critics. Moreover, the dedication with which Clayton Eshleman has worked and reworked his versions, compiling his notes and presenting bilingual versions, has not only given Anglo readers an excellent point of entry to Vallejo's poetic world, but has also provided future translators with a solid foundation for the creation of new versions. The most difficult poetry requires continual retranslation, which becomes ever more urgent over the passing of time. Does Vallejo's poetry still need to be translated? Of course it does, but not nearly as urgently as the rest of his oeuvre.

Beyond the genre of poetry the field is wide open. The two most pressing tasks are the translation of *Scales* and *The Tired Stone*. The short stories of *Scales* and the tragic drama of *The Tired Stone* are essential to Vallejo's oeuvre, and, beyond the field of bilingual specialists, they have stayed under the radar of most Anglo readers. Their linguistic complexity and poetic intensity—the exuberance and exaltation of the early and late aesthetics, respectively—mark pinnacles in Vallejo's narrative prose and writing for the stage. Added to this, there are multiple Castilian versions of both works, and a comparative reading, as Eshleman showed us with the poetry, is sure to illuminate the author's compositional strategies.

With these short but essential volumes in translation, we'll be in a position to compile and publish complete editions, akin to the series released by the PUCP. The order of urgency for these compendia would be *Complete Plays*, *Complete Articles and Chronicles*, *Complete Narratives*, *Complete Reportage and Books of Thoughts*, and *Complete Letters*. On account of the size of these volumes and the availability of the Castilian versions, these English editions need not be bilingual but will require annotations and commentaries to catalog translation problems, historical references, and Vallejo's idiosyncrasies that may otherwise be presumed errors.

Complete editions of Vallejo's writings will help us better understand his poetry, but they will also relocate the oeuvre of one of the most influential twentieth-century writers to a more mainstream sphere, which seems appropriate in view of the author's lifelong endeavor to avoid artistic secularism. The dark corner of modern literature that Vallejo's writings have inhabited is the consequence of our having focused so much attention on his poetry alone, without opening our eyes as enthusiastically to his writings in other genres, or without opening our eyes to them at all. The lack of translations from these modalities has seduced readers into seeing him as an aggregate of (rather than alternative to) the European avant-garde, by representing him solely as a poet, as a poet of poets, when the breadth of his writings clearly shows us that he was a complete intellectual, a blue-collar journalist, an incisive critic, a masterful emulator, a ruthless humorist, a fearless dramatist, a passionate socialist, and a devout antifascist. The reconfiguration of Vallejo's writings doesn't diminish his poetry, which is his greatest literary accomplishment, but it does allow us to evaluate him in a new light, since it's one thing to write that poetry and that poetry alone, but it's something quite different to write brilliantly and prolifically in other genres in addition to writing that poetry.

Joseph Mulligan
New Paltz, NY

NOTE ON THIS EDITION

The translations presented in this volume have been based on the *Obras completas* published by the Pontificia Universidad Católica del Perú: *Poesía completa I–IV* (1997), edited by Ricardo Silva-Santisteban; *Narrativa completa* (1999) and *Teatro completo I–III* (1999), edited by Silva-Santisteban and Moreano; *Correspondencia completa* (2002), edited by Jesús Cabel; *Ensayos y reportajes completos* (2002), edited by Manuel Miguel de Priego; and *Artículos y crónicas completos I–II* (2002), edited by Jorge Puccinelli; as well as the *Obras completas* published by Banco de Crédito: *Obra poética* (1991), edited by Ricardo González Vigil, and *Artículos y crónicas (1918–1939) desde Europa* (1997), edited by Jorge Puccinelli.

The poems translated by Clayton Eshleman have been drawn from *The Complete Poetry* published in 2007 by the University of California Press, which contains translations that supersede the translator's many previous versions that have appeared in print over the past fifty years. Due to the large number of discrepancies over the setting of many of Vallejo's poems, this work is carefully cataloged by editors, as is the case with Eshleman's versions. Readers are encouraged to reference his notes and commentary in *The Complete Poetry*.

The formatting and style of the source text, including abnormalities such as irregular capitalization, have been replicated—to the extent possible—in the following translations, except for the thesis, plays, and letters. In *Romanticism in Castilian Poetry* we adhere to basic norms in the presentation of analytic prose by not italicizing quoted poems, as the author did, and by offering block quotes for larger portions of text. These conventions are designed to increase the readability of the text and not to lead the reader into believing that the author was revolutionizing the form in Castilian when he was not. This is always a risk with Vallejo, since in many other places, he is in fact formally subversive.

Due to the unfinished state in which all the theatrical works remained at the time of Vallejo's death, certain editorial decisions are required (even to set the Castilian version). As evinced by the facsimiles reproduced in *Teatro completo III*, where we find typescripts of *La piedra cansada* that Vallejo himself edited by hand, we observe that he left-aligned the play and in parentheses placed stage directions, which he could not italicize, since this function wasn't available in his typewriter technology.

The editions of the plays edited by Silva-Santisteban and Moreano justify the dialogue and stage directions, and center-align the name of the speaker on the line preceding the dialogue. Moreover, in those editions the stage directions have been italicized. We've preferred to set the text flush left throughout (character names, dialogue, and stage directions) and place the stage directions in italics. In an attempt to elucidate certain portions of the dramatic movement, we've blocked out stage directions that don't pertain to the speaker of that same line. This format, as in Bertold Brecht's *Mother Courage and Her Children* (1939)—as translated by Eric Bentley for Grove Press in 1966—has been used to clarify how the plays are intended to be performed.

Regarding *Brothers Colacho*, three editions have been identified: a Castilian edition edited by Georgette de Vallejo and Enrique Ballón Aguirre, *Teatro completo* (1979), published by PUCP; a French typescript held by the PUCP Library; and a Castilian typescript held by the Biblioteca Nacional del Perú. A comparative reading of the three documents and the explanations offered by Silva-Santisteban lead us to believe that, while the latter two are very similar in terms of their content and stage of development, the Castilian version at the Biblioteca Nacional can be considered the most finished product and is the source of the translation we present. It's divided into three acts, five scenes, and fifteen movements. Through the transformation of the three versions, if this supposition holds true, we see Vallejo improve the composition not only by editing but also by translating.

Although Georgette de Vallejo has stated that *The Tired Stone* was written in its entirety in December 1937, Silva-Santisteban has identified dubious modifications to scenes in the typescript that obstruct the plot of the play. At the end of act 2, a page is cut in half and another is pasted on top of it, such that page 20 repeats itself; on page 25 there's the handwritten note "Cuadro onceavo" and on page 29, the note "Cuadro doceavo." These notes contain egregious morphological errors—"onceavo" for "undécimo" (eleventh) and "doceavo" for "duodécimo" (twelfth)—which Vallejo simply could not have made. His wife Georgette, a native French speaker and infamous meddler in Vallejo's papers, is the primary suspect. When we compare the version published by Georgette in *Teatro completo* (1979) against the versions published in *Visión del Perú*, edited by Washington Delgado, where he presents pages from the typescript with handwritten corrections, it appears that Georgette deliberately omitted Vallejo's revisions, which most likely were made during January 1938. Silva-Santisteban has incorporated Vallejo's handwritten changes, and the present translation is based on his version, as it appears in *Teatro Completo III* (1999).

Moreover, the plays *Death* and *The Final Judgment* were originally written in French and then translated to Castilian by Georgette de Vallejo. Over the years the French version of *The Final Judgment* went missing, which has forced us to render our English version from her Castilian. *Death*, on the other hand, has been translated from the original French version, as it appears in *César Vallejo, su estética teatral*, by Guido Podestá.

The epistolary documents present the double difficulty of their tone and multiform layout. Vallejo's tone in his letters is overtly cordial and strikingly affectionate, yet a literal translation into English tends to turn this into saccharine verbosity. A more interpretative approach, like the one we've taken here, can modulate the tonality to produce a similar effect but to a different degree. Bearing in mind that the most loyal translation is never the most literal, we've deliberately attenuated Vallejo's tone in his letters so that it's evidently affectionate and noticeably intimate, but not distractingly so. With regard to the format, the PUCP's compendium of the letters reproduces the manuscripts and typescripts exactly as the texts appear in the originals, including, when available, facsimiles. We, on the other hand, have standardized basic elements of the letters, such as greetings, salutations, and the placement of the date, location, and signature, in an attempt to increase their readability, recognizing that the heteroclite nature of the present anthology already presents the reader with considerable challenges.

Moreover, we should clarify that Castilian was Vallejo's default language; while living in Paris, he gained proficiency in French to the extent that he successfully translated from French, published some of his own articles in French, and drafted some of his plays in French. Although he didn't know Quechua or Russian, this didn't stop him from scattering words from those languages (the spelling and transliteration of which he often imagined) throughout his writings as he saw fit. In the following translations, French words have been left in French, with a note for the first instance of a word or expression that's not generally understood among modern readers of literature in English. In a few cases, we've corrected the French spelling to avoid confusion.

Although one may be tempted to think that César Vallejo, this native Andean, imbued a text like *The Tired Stone* with authentic Quechua while living in Paris, recent scholarship has confirmed that his Quechua is relegated to a modernist imagination, far from demonstrating accurate usage and correct modern spelling. Rather than updating these Quechua words, we've copied them verbatim, and for the first instance of words or phrases identifiable to modern Quechua scholars, we have included an endnote with a corrected spelling and definition. In addressing the Quechua vocabulary, I sought the assistance of NYU Professor Odi Gonzales and asked him to comment on a vocabulary I had selected, which admittedly doesn't encompass every instance of Quechua in these translations. With regard to the usage of Russian words, since the transliteration of the Cyrillic alphabet to the Latin differs orthographically when it comes into the Castilian and English languages, we've offered new English transliterations of the Russian words and names in Vallejo's vocabulary. The first instance of a loan word or phrase is accompanied by an annotated explanation.

Finally, we've included endnotes in which we offer commentaries on the translation of neologisms, obscure historical references, deliberate misspellings, drastically nonliteral renderings, and any idiosyncrasy that might otherwise be presumed a typographical error in the process of printing or an overlooked mistake in the translated composition. The notes and commentaries are meant as a reminder to the reader that the text is, in fact, a translation and as encouragement to seek out the original Castilian versions we've chosen to omit in order to present the reader with a wider selection.

TRANSLATORS

[CE]   Clayton Eshleman

[PJ]   Pierre Joris

[SJL]   Suzanne Jill Levine

[JM]   Joseph Mulligan

[NP]   Nicole Peyrafitte

[MLR]   Michael Lee Rattigan

[WR]   William Rowe

[EW]   Eliot Weinberger

[JW]   Jason Weiss

BOOK ONE 1915–1919

FROM *Romanticism in Castilian Poetry*

INTRODUCTION

More than a century ago, German thought laid the groundwork for critical science in art. The Schlegel brothers,[1] who indisputably represent this epiphany, share the glory of having founded the best instrument thus far for scientifically registering the diverse manifestations of fine arts in our times. Since then, art criticism has stopped limiting itself to a superficial analysis of form and a more or less incomplete consideration of a specific technique to become the profound, wide-reaching judgment that stems from a scientific vision seen through a prism, the multiple facets of which direct many lights toward a central, high, and vigorous conclusion in harmonious theory. That is to say, the critic of today is the master who corrects, the chisel that files down the works of other activities, but who corrects and files in accordance with the models that he has come to obtain as ideals by dint of an eager drive toward perfection. And it will not be hyperbole to attribute this elevated, integrating mission of improvement to contemporary criticism, if at the outset we disinherit the belief of certain didactic publicists that art criticism has no transformative bearing on the work of art that it considers.

Every science like every man, every thought like every device, can stand a bit more sunlight or some possibility of progressive force so that life may advance down the road of civilization toward ever brighter horizons. On the contrary, it is also possible that they may constitute a negative element of progress, which in the final analysis is a reactionary tendency at the heart of their apparently ecstatic temerity. And under the laws of existence, it is necessary to evaluate in fair terms exactly what in every work concerns the interests of the common endeavor in one way or another. Thus values in the spirit exist as the need to place human labor in plain sight, with the objective of specifying the degree to which and the sense in which it impacts on the great universal work—and herein lies the essential role of the critic.

There was therefore a need for the charitable action of truly scientific criticism, since the analytic spirit in the century of Luis XIV was, as Le Bon states in *The Psychology of Revolution*,[2] nothing more than a storm that razed and destroyed, whose fertilizing action would bear fruit only at a much later date, when humanity, revitalized under the archway of peace in the wake of the neoplatonic epic, began to live again, and science, philosophy, and art took to truer courses; when the spirit started to think about the fate of the people and all that has been done over centuries past in favor of their well-being and progress. Romantic autonomy in art was thus thrust forward, elevating, as a logical consequence, the critic to his corresponding place in literature. [JM]

CRITIQUE OF ROMANTICISM[3]

This brings us to José de Espronceda, "the typical man of romanticism." The poetry of this brother of Byron is the loyal image, the eminently precise spirit of Spanish romanticism. Since his verse sinks into the reader's soul like fantastic tears of darkness and acrimony, bores through the tranquil sky of faith like the crackling embers of an entire people—perhaps of an entire epoch—and shakes in the torturous flames of a pessimistic philosophy on the brink of skepticism, we see the romantic doctrine fulfilled in a broad and definitive way. To begin with the orientation of Espronceda's influences, the personal reference is the essential motif in all his cantos, and this positive element of artistic subjectivism, the life and color to his cantos, as the Englishman Fitzmaurice-Kelly says, undoubtedly makes him the most distinguished Spanish poet of his century.

Espronceda presents himself with complete sincerity in his poetry, that is, exactly as he is in himself, and no longer assumes a personality to engage his surroundings, as in the French romanticism of Victor Hugo, which came later to give origin to objective thinking and naturalism, whereupon the romantic school reached its end. Espronceda, on the other hand, was none of that; the firm gaze with which the poet pierces himself engendered the instability that was throbbing through all spheres of activity in his century, thereby giving origin to doubt and skepticism. And thus, José Martí, has said,

> Poets of today can be neither epic nor lyric with naturalness and serenity; there is no room for more lyric poetry except the kind that one pulls out of oneself, as if out of one's own being whose existence cannot be doubted, or as if the problem of human life had been undertaken so courageously and investigated so fervently, that there could be no better motive more stimulating or more prone to profundity and greatness than the study of oneself. Today, no one is certain of his faith. True believers have fallen into self-deceit. All have been kissed by the same sorceress. Men may tear their innermost selves to shreds, but in the calmest recesses there remains famished furious Unrest, some Vague Hope, and the Secret Vision. An immense pale man, with a gaunt face, weepy

eyes and a dry mouth, dressed in black, traverses the earth with serious strides without stopping to sleep; and he has sat down in every home and placed his trembling hand on all the bedsteads—Oh, what blows to the brain! What a shock to the breast! To demand what never comes! To know not what one desires! To feel delight and nausea equally in the spirit, nausea of the day that dies and delight in the dawn![4]

Espronceda is this man who lives and will live for centuries to come, breathing life into the poetry of *El diablo mundo*. This poet's philosophy also belongs to Byron, and the kinship is so evident that there is no shortage of people who believe that they see in his poetry imitations of the author of *Cain*. But there can be no greater foolishness than this kind of imposture. If Espronceda were not who he is, an original personality, an unmistakably distinct genius, with a trademark all his own, perhaps that claim could hold some weight. In the Spanish poet the soul of his race is latent; it is the genuine expression of the Iberian Latinity of the century, which was debated in fights of all kinds—social, political, philosophical—and this more than anything else distinguishes his arduous impassioned sentimentalism, that subjugator of the brain, and the creative power of his dreaming mind, the docile instrument of his Castilian heart. In his most sublime intonations, the genius of Espronceda bears no likeness to Byron, and it is precisely at those moments that the originally Latin tendency is highlighted by the strong emotive exaltation, the thrilling ferocity of blistering heat and the rogue flight of the impossible ideal giving in to vague fractures that open up to the night of nothingness and disillusion. With waveringly unreligious abstraction—an attitude like someone who retires from the symposium of the world headed toward the occult with his eyes fixed on what he abandons—he furrows a contemptuous brow of protest and rises into the air to make contact with the shadows before vanishing among them. Instead, an influence from Goethe may be perceptible, but only because of what he touched on in his plan for and execution of *El diablo mundo* and because of the spiritualism of his metaphysics. The rest is proper to nineteenth-century Spanish psychology, as seen in these lines by Espronceda:

¡Dicha es soñar, y el riguroso seño
no ver jamás de la verdad impía!

His principle poem, *El diablo mundo*, is the battle of vanity and ephemerality in the world against the eternal ideal of immortality, the childish reality of life—"a la que tanto nuestro afán se adhiere"—against the eternal destinies, which may have created the spirit of man by dint of his intellectualizing the instinctive feeling of perpetuity. Thus, this is the battle of the spirit of the century and of Spain: the poet did not try to paint the objective aspect of his work deliberately, with the preconceived notion that his lyre was to be the diapason on which he would shudder a sublime tumultuous breath of human life, in order to catch, in some formidable clash, the echo that would return to the shores of history as the complaint of a century fleetingly passing through the mute bosom of Nature.

Espronceda did not think of this, just as the Cripple of Lepanto did not think that the core of *Don Quixote* was going to reflect two opposite modes of perceiving life for all of eternity. His psyche was the poem, and the poetry of Espronceda, let us add, existed from the moment that the poet began to live.

In *El diablo mundo*, on one hand the world throbs with its objects that reach their end, that are born and die like fatuous fires, and on the other hand there is a distant, magical, diffuse, and mysterious chimera that comes from beyond the grave. Might this otherworldly vision be grounded in reality? And if it is, could this be the paradise that the Nazarene spoke of at Golgotha?

This epopoeia that lived in the soul of Espronceda is his own. It is his idiosyncrasy, his artistic personality, his philosophical brilliance, and this is what legitimizes it and why the particular concrete physiognomy of one sole man characterizes the metaphysical concern of an epoch of humanity—a consistent concern for knowing where to locate the eternal, absolute core of all revolutions of thought, expressions of society, and evolutionary progress of Nature. This romantic in heart and soul, obsessed with the not-too-distant memory and devastating analysis of the previous century and with contemplating the uncertainty and revolt swaying the society of his time, in the absence of a strong, firm metaphysics, José de Espronceda wondered, if everything (including the work of reason and human freedom) is torn to shreds and pulverized, dies and is replaced by another formula, then where is invariable eternal certainty? And this thought of the poet is made tangible in the energetic painting of the "man overwhelmed by his age, embittered by painful useless experience, who hopelessly closes a book he was reading sadly convinced of the sterility of science."[5]

Espronceda's other poems respond to the same spirit of *El diablo mundo*, although to varying degrees. For a new thought, a new eternal universal question, he was to demand a new elocution, a new mode of expression. The artistic manifestation of the social spirit that speaks in these terms to all men, who in turn grow enthused by it and love it, as a father loves his babe in whom the soul of the life giver is sweetly transformed, is the ideal of art—and this is what Espronceda achieved.

Under the law of evolution, the Castilian language transformed by the power of the romantic poets' innovative spirit, like the French language, evolved in its richness and flexibility at the price of breaking off with the dictatorial, inclement, and erroneous grammar of its neoclassical past. Without altering the individuality of the Castilian lexicon, many gaps were filled that had stymied the manifestation of ideas which could not pass through the diction as long as the voices that uttered them were previously consecrated by the intransigent despotic academy; in a word, the language was enriched. So, Espronceda did just this and broke the laws governing poetic language, fatally, irresistibly, with the blind force of his psyche— that tough precept of poetry, as one feels in his breast this man's robust poetic temperament, exploded in a gasp of asphyxia, thirsty for light and space. Ros de Olano said that "while our poet was aspiring to condense humanity into a book, the first thing he did was break all the established precepts, except for the logical unity."[6]

Suffice a reading of *El diablo mundo* to recognize the metrical variety, the marvelous sensationalist rhythmic play, no less impressive than the well-understood freedom with which he has handled the rhyme in such an intensely profound musical way. But again, we repeat, he did not create this poetic voluntarily, reflectively, and, if he did, it would not have resulted in poetry of emotion, feeling, and enthusiastic rhythmical vitality: Espronceda is not the Parnassian who sacrifices the tones of life to the ingenuous games of color and harmony, which is what Hugo's successors resorted to in the end; nor is he the Greek or Hellenistic pasticheur of cold pulchritude and symmetry from some previous pseudoclassic of his in a Spanish Parnassus. His poetry is none of this, but rather the frank, uncovered, tumultuously melodious canto whipped out, the image of emotion, the intense palpitation of great beautiful thoughts, like a burning touch of sunlight inside the transparent crystal of the word, which trembles and glimmers; a canto that is heard reverberating in the innermost core of the heart, like the orchestra of universal life in which every note of the human heart's scale rings from silent tears all the way to the garrulous laughter of joy. For such a sublime lyric the music could not have been otherwise.

The stanzas deemed of lesser art—being frivolous, light, and childish—offered themselves to him and, for reasons of fidelity, he accepted and used them to orchestrate ideas that were ordinary because of their lack of importance or to play with errant breezes in which he would exteriorize the vanities of the world. With variable euphony, due to the proper nature of their prosodic organisms, these forms of meter had no need for improvement beneath the chisel of Espronceda, after all that had been achieved by the instructive poets of the eighteenth century. The image of beings, who wander the world in pursuit of frivolous pleasures, without experiencing the disconcerting lofty idea of the reason of things, we see in this short stanza:

Allá va la nave,
bogad sin temor,
ya el aura la arrulle,
ya silve Aquilón.

Yet that severe, olympic, inflexible, and majestic hendecasyllable of the Argensolas took on an infinite variety of attitudes and intensities, along with a determined number of tonic accents in a slow duration or swift parade, as when he says,

Los siglos a los siglos se atropellan,
los hombres a los hombres se suceden . . .

In explosions such lines let out a piercing scream of anguish, pain, or anger, which nails a profound sustained accent into the word that has been expressed, even though the total cadence of the verse gets dislocated and its prosodic sound gets altered. The hendecasyllable is the verse par excellence, preferred not only by Espronceda but by all Spanish romantic poets. It seems that the Alexandrine of Berceo and the dodecasyllable of Juan de Mena, which are also meters favored by the Castilian muse, were not to Espronceda's liking or in accordance with his poetic sense of organization, since he hardly worked in these.

The laws of poetry, no doubt, like the laws of language in general, are based on the psychophysiological laws of man. Each people has its poetry, just as each individual has his own voice, a special timber in his words: each form of meter and rhythm could be considered the special timber of the poetry of a people, just as rhyme is the note of distinction of phrasing in music. For that reason, just as French romanticism's favorite expression was the eighteenth-century Alexandrine modified by Hugo, the Spanish romantic period crystalized its exteriorization in the *romance* and the hendecasyllable, by making these malleable and adorning them with rich, opulent rhyme. This is why we can say that it's logical and rational, without fear of being mistaken, that a single metrical form corresponding to a determined sociability is susceptible to transformation and even abandon over the course of time and with the evolution of said sociability. And this is the legitimacy of the revolution that Espronceda put in effect, since he was the voice of his people and the moment.

From our perspective, José de Espronceda is the head of romanticism in Castilian poetry, not because he is the leader of an intellectual or physical movement who for the first time raises the revolutionary flag and unleashes the nacent vision of a new activity but rather because he is the one who, though serving after other predecessors in the already-formed ranks, grabs ahold of the standard of the rebellion and, raising himself up with it to a height he had not reached before, waves it next to the sun, like a victorious eagle, and leaves it nailed on high while he flies off to Glory.

* * *

Behind Espronceda, who completed his mission in the progress of humanity by the age of thirty-three, the eminent José Zorrilla appears, in whose literary figure, according to the critics, romanticism displays its most outstanding mark. Yet here we are wont to resolve a question of great importance for the principles of the school in question and its history. The author of *Don Juan Tenorio* does not represent the apogee of romanticism for well-founded reasons.

Far above the legends into which Zorrilla has injected the genuinely Spanish note, whose poetry is driven by the rancid perfume of the traditions of the race tacked together beneath the burning meridianal sun, far above the legends is the polyphonic canto of *El diablo mundo*, that grandiose poem, engendered by humanity's innermost core, which rises out of the century that came before it and thus spontaneously surpasses Goethe's *Faust* in its motivation and Christian sentiment. If these legends indeed draw from their source of inspiration, insofar as this is the history of the Spanish people—with all its war-riddled episodes and fanaticism, with all its effervescence and fragile ideals—in a word, if these poems "are written in the dust and ruins of the ancient monuments and castles" and are the voice of their race, then they might respond to one of the characters of romantic poetry, but their intrinsic importance does not fulfill the ideal of romanticism in relation to society and human evolution. "Zorrilla is not outstanding for his familiarity with the modern philosophical systems that form the superior feature in the stories of Goethe," Camacho Roldán explains. "Before all else he is a poet, a poet of nature, a poet of the music of language, a poet whose amenable expression imitates the roaring thrust of the harsh wind."[7] Zorrilla, a contemporary of Espronceda, had a longer life to bring his artistic ideals to reality, and so he did.

In the literary oeuvre of Zorrilla there are two perfectly distinct genres:

drama and legend. Corresponding to the first are the so very popular *Don Juan Tenorio* and *El puñal del godo*, among other dramas; and to the second, *Más vale llegar a tiempo que rondar un año* and *Ganar perdiendo* among his comedies. The grand tribunal of posterity has already handed down its ruling on these works, and the critics have said so much about them that there is no need for us here to engage them again, except insofar as these poems respond in one way or another to the school we are studying.

From our perspective, *Don Juan Tenorio* is clearly the most popular drama of all theatrical works to have been written in Castilian, and this deep sincere prestige that it enjoys among its readers can be explained by two main reasons: the water sources of inspiration Zorrilla drank from to elaborate the broad thought of this work and the form he used to embody his ideas. *Don Juan Tenorio* is not a figure created by Zorrilla, dispensing with a vision of society, as an a priori consequence of his astonishing fantasy, which, along with much else, was well within Zorrilla's capabilities. Rather, *Don Juan* is a character who corresponds to the tradition of the Spanish people and to the spirit of its sociability. Moreover, the protagonist of this drama is a genuine model of human idiosyncrasy. To be precise, he is the passionately erotic, unreligious, and courageous personification of romantic man, and as the image of these ideas and feelings of the spirit, he has risen from society to the stage, like a natural flower, obeying one of Guyau's laws which says that, just as in the towering mountains there exists some corner where nature's polyrhythm goes to echo and all the voices of the region convene, so too from human activity does a man emerge who encapsulates the tumultuous palpitations of the heart in his superior psychic vitality. Hence, *Don Juan Tenorio*. He undoubtedly corresponds to the simple basic essence of this figure of art, the real existence of a man, whom the people knew and tradition embellished with fantastic features and painted with the stunning lines of a rare psychological composition. Tirso took him to stage and, in this sense, Tirso was romantic.[8] But Zorrilla modified him, because aside from presenting us with this figure onstage, with this universal character to whom we have alluded, he infused him with a vigorous spirit of Spanish Latinity; it is in this way that *Don Juan Tenorio* is the pure and loyal image of Spanish man, and this is why the work's widespread reception has been so favorable. With regard to the formal art of the dramatic development, this is another powerful strength that has made the author's thought ineradicable in the astonished imagination of all who speak Castilian. Everywhere someone is heard delightfully reciting portions of the verses from *Don Juan Tenorio*, due to the sublime simplicity of style, the familiar phraseological elocutions, and the trademark usage of the *romance* and hendecasyllable meters, which the Spanish hold so dear, as if those bits of harmony are themselves the beating of the Castilian breast.

And what can we say about *El puñal del godo* that we haven't said already? The organizing dramatic idea of this poem does not have a different origin than that of *Don Juan*; it too is a flower of Spanish blood and sentiment; it too is the faithful representation of the social spirit of the epoch in which it was written, and this is why its genuine inspiration is the people, informed as it is by the legendary memories of medieval times.

In the second genre, Zorrilla maintains the romantic temperament of the motifs from his dramatic works. One could say that, with the miracle of his portentous genius in the legends, he has brought us the living breath of ancient platonic love from the grave, melancholic burial ground of medieval Spain, from the remote gothic monasteries, and from the burning, mystical, patriotic enthusiasm of the *Cids* and *Pelayos*. Never before did Spanish lyricism know how to gain momentum so energetically from the heated breath of the Iberian soul; never in its creations did it unfurl so completely the net of its distant glorious memories, nor did it endow such lucid beauty of local color and architectonic forms. Other poets might have created something better with regard to highbrow ideas, lineal perfection, and beauty in the visual tonalities, but no one has managed to copy with such fidelity the mysterious majestic mansions from the Middle Ages, full of unnerving penumbras and monastic abstractions, the dark stormy nights that plunge the rugged sierras of Spain into mourning, where the wind howls and a religious tone of spiritual sadness reigns. Finally, no one has managed to show us so clearly the ephemeral nuances of the race—the wild impetuses of falconry, the mildest winged swooning of tenderness, blind Christian fanaticism, vulgarity, violence, irreligiousness, criminal blood, and the martyr's purple heart. Admire here a brushstroke of quintessential beauty in the execution of such idealization, when he paints the vision of Margarita la Tornera in the convent:

> Pero con fulgor tan puro,
> tan fosfórico y tan tenue,
> que el templo seguía oscuro
> y en silencio y soledad.

> Solo de la monja en torno
> se notaba vaporosa
> teñida de azul y rosa
> una extraña claridad.

Although some critics suggest that his traditions lack research with regard to philosophical speculations, this defect is completely nonexistent in the author's lyric, no matter what portion of text one cites from his immense oeuvre. This contra is mistaken and unjust. Let he who says otherwise say so when Zorrilla pontificates and sings that

> . . . la hermosa
> es prenda que con envidia
> el cielo dio, y con perfidia
> por castigo a la mujer.
>
> Y que quien cifra sobre ella
> el bien del amor ajeno,
> no acierto más que veneno
> en su delicia verter.

It is easy to see in the literary endeavor of Zorrilla a common character identifiable in all his poetry—the dramatic form—no matter how imperceptible the perpetual dialogue may be, a circumstance that can be explained by the intense zest for life that the author wished to communicate and did communicate in all his works, the reason for which concurs so strongly with the dramatization of thought to the benefit of the clarity and vigor of his ideas.

> No aspiro a más laurel ni a más hazaña,
> que a una sonrisa a mi dulce España.

This is what the poet sang in his prelude, when he was inviting the reader to a tasting of his poetry:

> las sabrosas historias de otros días.

In effect, whereas Espronceda lost himself in the national meaning of his inspirational themes, throwing himself into the world to harvest from the activity of the human spirit the eternal concerns, the perpetual agitation that makes him thirst for a solution to the metaphysical problems; while this colossus of spiritualist thought, confronting the odyssey of the century on his way toward the conquest of his ideals, was singing all the disillusions and all the doubts in a free, robust, burning, and booming intonation, like the thrust of life itself; Zorrilla, nostalgic for the infancy of his race, dreaming of legendary times of his people's past, more Spanish than human, more patriotic than universal, put on the chords of his lyre the old fibers of the Castilian heart. That is why in his poetry, as we have already said, there prevails the ardent fantasy of the low latitudes, gold-plated melancholy of the meridian, fierce heroic impetuosity, consoling theology, and the instinctive sadness of the soul of Spain. In this sense, the oeuvre of the author of *Don Juan* marks the resurgence of Spanish classicism, insofar as all the arguments of his works are so genuinely portrayed from social reality that they resemble, as we have already said, projections of actuality, repetitions of events, ideas and feelings that have transpired on the stage of life.

Just look at the vital breath with which he is penetrating a thought that, exposed in another way, would have become figurative:

¿No es verdad que cuando a solas
hablo con vos, Don Rodrigo,
va vuestra alma en lo que os digo
como nave entre las olas,

esperando de un momento
a otro, verse sumergida
por la mar embravecida
de mi airado pensamiento?

And the energetic image of an attitude:

¿No es verdad que cuando clavo
mis ojos en vuestro rostro,
os hielo el alma y os postro
a mis pies como un esclavo?

And as for his technique? When we were speaking about Espronceda, we said that the preferred verse of romanticism in Spain has been the hendecasyllable, and Zorrilla shows us just this. For the most part his dramatic poems are developed in this metrical form, and in the secular assonant *romance*, which, as Piñeiro puts quite well, only on the Zorrillesque plectrum does the natural charm and untamed music thrive as it does in the Spanish *cantares* of heroic feats.

With regard to what of Zorrilla's is relegated to the traditionalist genre, including the poems *Granada* and *Al Hamar*, there prevails almost exclusively the same combination of primitive measure, sometimes adorned with consonant rhyme that may diminish its value of spontaneity and finesse like the popular heroic meter, but it also enables it to gain auditory and melodic force, as well as a visual effect.

Therefore, without denying the guiding influence of Lamartine and Musset,[9] given the preponderance that French romanticism exercises on all European literatures, one can say that José Zorrilla was a genius whose works are the exclusive fruit of his own artistic organization and philosophical temperament. This is confirmed by the fact that no poet of his rank has become the representative voice of his race and epoch to the point of reaching his level or rising above him, which is clearly manifest not only in the content but also in the formal technique of his works, and this has incited Alberto Lista—a classicist through and through—to read the grandiose creations of this author and then exclaim in a scathing critique of the liberty of Zorrilla's executive manner,

> [W]hen on the wings of the idea our fantasy wants to fly to the empire, an incorrect expression, an improper word, an impossible Gallicism or neologism warns us that we are stuck in the mud of the earth . . . We cannot attribute this defect to the school of contemporary romanticism, first because its leaders in France have never managed to remove the yolk of their grammar, which is one thousand times more burdensome in French than in Spanish, and second because there are many poets among us who belong to the same school and who despite the liberty that they take during their raptures of imagination, still do not dare trespass the limits that preformulated poetic language has imposed on the license of genius.[10]

As for his technique, there is no doubt that Zorrilla left many of his contemporaries in the dust, with his autonomous exaltation and profound knowledge of the science of the belles lettres, which is why to the chagrin of the Aristarchuses of the world[11] and the rulings of prescribed science, rather than being transgressions, as the professor of the University of Madrid suggests, those breaks with the academic rules of language have become the greatest merits of his work. With regard to morphology, the true legislator and motor for the transformation or disappearance of words is not the fanciful will of writers but of society, which thus fulfills one of the various projections of the evolution of the human spirit. That is why, when Zorrilla had penetrated this truth, placing in his poetry all the feeling, desire, and action of his people, he knew better than anyone where it was going, following the impulses of his own original artistic orientation. Today in his diction society sees words and phrases heard every day in different situations of life among the Spanish people. For this reason, one author says,

[I]n Zorrilla one does not find reminiscences of Homer's grandiosity or Virgil's delicate tenderness or Horace's cultured philosophical expression: in his poetry one does not sense the exotic yet enjoyable flavor that reading the works of foreign writers transmits, but of him one can say what Michelet said of Alexander Dumas: he was a force of Nature.[12]

[JM]

FROM *The Black Heralds*

THE BLACK HERALDS

There are blows in life, so powerful . . . I don't know!
Blows as from the hatred of God; as if, facing them,
the undertow of everything suffered
welled up in the soul . . . I don't know!

They are few; but they are . . . They open dark trenches
in the fiercest face and in the strongest back.
Perhaps they are the colts of barbaric Attilas;
or the black heralds sent to us by Death.

They are the deep falls of the Christs of the soul,
of some adored faith blasphemed by Destiny.
Those bloodstained blows are the crackling of
bread burning us at the oven door.

And man . . . Poor . . . poor! He turns his eyes, as
when a slap on the shoulder summons us;
turns his crazed eyes, and everything lived
wells up, like a pool of guilt, in his look.

There are blows in life, so powerful . . . I don't know!

[CE]

THE SPIDER

It is an enormous spider that now cannot move;
a colorless spider, whose body,
a head and an abdomen, bleeds.

Today I watched it up close. With what effort
toward every side
it extended its innumerable legs.
And I have thought about its invisible eyes,
the spider's fatal pilots.

It is a spider that tremored caught
on the edge of a rock;
abdomen on one side,
head on the other.

With so many legs the poor thing, and still unable
to free itself. And, on seeing it
confounded by its fix
today, I have felt such sorrow for that traveler.

It is an enormous spider, impeded by
its abdomen from following its head.
And I have thought about its eyes
and about its numerous legs . . .
And I have felt such sorrow for that traveler!

[CE]

THE POET TO HIS LOVER

My love, on this night you have been crucified on
the two curved beams of my kiss;
your torment has told me that Jesus wept,
that there is a goodfriday sweeter than that kiss.

On this strange night when you looked at me so,
Death was happy and sang in his bone.
On this September night my second fall
and the most human kiss have been presided over.

My love, we two will die together, close together;
our sublime bitterness will slowly dry up;
and our defunct lips will have touched in shadow.

There will be no more reproach in your holy eyes;
nor will I offend you ever again. In one grave
we two will sleep, as two siblings.

[CE]

DREGS

This afternoon it is raining, as never before; and I
have no desire to live, my heart.

This afternoon is sweet. Why should it not be?
Dressed in grace and pain; dressed like a woman.

This afternoon in Lima it is raining. And I recall
the cruel caverns of my ingratitude;
my block of ice over her poppy,
stronger than her "Don't be this way!"

My violent black flowers; and the barbaric
and terrible stoning; and the glacial distance.
And the silence of her dignity
with burning holy oils will put an end to it.

So this afternoon, as never before, I am
with this owl, with this heart.

Other women go by; and seeing me so sad,
they take on a bit of you
in the abrupt wrinkle of my deep remorse.

This afternoon it is raining, raining hard. And I
have no desire to live, my heart!

[CE]

THE BLACK CUP

Night is a cup of evil. Shrilly a police
whistle pierces it, like a vibrating pin.
Listen, bitch, how come if you are gone now
the flicker is still black and still makes me burn?

The Earth has coffinesque edges in the dark.
Listen, bitch, don't come back.

My flesh swims, swims
in the cup of darkness still aching me;
my flesh swims in her,
in the marshy heart of woman.

Astral ember . . . I have felt
dry scrapes of clay
fall upon my diaphanous lotus.
Ah, woman! Flesh formed of instinct
exists because of you. Ah, woman!

That is why—oh, black chalice! even after you left
I am choking on dust,
and more urges to drink paw at my flesh!

[CE]

IMPERIAL NOSTALGIAS

I

In the landscapes of Mansiche the twilight
fashions imperial nostalgias;
and the race takes shape in my word,
a star of blood on the surface of muscle.

The bell tower tolls . . . There is no one to open
the chapel . . . One could say that
a biblical opuscule died in the words of
this twilight's Asiatic emotion.

A stone bench with three gourd pots, is an altarpiece
on which a chorus of lips have just raised
the Eucharist of golden chicha.

Beyond, smoke smelling of sleep and stable
rises on the wind from the farms,
as if a firmament were being exhumed.

II

Like a relief on a pre-Incan block,
the pensive old woman spins and spins;
in her Mama fingers the thin spindle
shears the gray wool of her old age.

A blind, unlit sun guards and mutilates
her sclerotic snowy eyes . . . !
Her mouth is scornful, and with a deceptive calm
her imperial weariness perhaps holds vigil.

There are meditating ficuses, routed
shaggy Incan troubadours,
the rancid pain of this idiotic cross,

in the shameful hour that now escapes,
and is a lake soldering crude mirrors
where shipwrecked Manco Capac weeps.

III

Like old caciques the oxen walk
the road to Trujillo, meditating . . .
And in the iron of the evening, they feign kings
who wander dead domains sobbing.

Standing on the wall, I ponder the laws
happiness and anguish keep exchanging:
already in the oxen's widowed pupils
dreams that have no when are rotting.

The village, as they pass, is dressed in
harsh gray, where a cow's mooing
is oiled with dreams and huaca emotion.

And in the banquet of the blue iodized sky
an ancient exiled corequenque[13] moans in
the chalice of a melancholy cattle-bell.

IV

La Grama—gloomy, secluded, unadorned—
stifled I don't know what unknown protest:
it resembles the exhausted soul of a poet,
withdrawn in an expression of defeat.

La Ramada[14] has carved its silhouette,
a cadaverous cage, alone and broken,
where my sick heart calms itself in
a statuesque tedium of terra-cotta.

The song saltlessly arrives from the sea
fitted out in the farcical mask of a thug
who drools and staggers, hanged!

The fog weaves a bandage about the lilac hill
enwalled with milliary dreams,
like a gigantic huaco holding vigil.

[CE]

EBONY LEAVES

My cigarette sparkles;
its light cleansed by gunpowder alerts.
And to its yellow wink
a little shepherd intones
the tamarind of his dead shadow.

The whole ramshackle house drowns in
an energetic blackness
the faded distinction of its whiteness.
A delicate odor of downpour lingers.

All the doors are very old,
and a sleepless piety of a thousand hollow eyes
sickens in their worm-eaten Havana brown.
I left them robust;
today spiderwebs have already woven into
the very heart of their wood,
clots of shadow smelling of neglect.
The day the woman by the road
saw me arrive, she shrieked
as if crying for joy, tremulous and sad,
while half-opening her two arms.
For in every fiber there dwells,
for the loving eye, a sleeping
bridal pearl, a hidden tear.

My anxious heart
whispers with I don't know what recollection.
—Señora? . . . —Yes, señor; she died in the village;
I still see her wrapped in her shawl . . .

And the grandmotherly bitterness
of an outcast's neurasthenic song
—oh defeated legendary muse!—
sharpens its melodious outpouring
under the dark night;
as if below, below,
in an open grave's
muddy gravel eye,
celebrating perpetual funerals,
fantastic daggers were shattering.

It's raining . . . raining . . . The downpour condenses,
reducing itself to funereal odors,
the mood of ancient camphors
that hold vigil *tahuashando*[15] down the path
with their ponchos of ice and no sombreros.

[CE]

AUTOCHTHONOUS TERCET

I

The laborer fist velvetizes
and outlines itself as a cross on every lip.
It's feast day! The plow's rhythm takes wing;
and every cowbell is a bronze precentor.

What's crude is sharpened. Talk pouched . . .
In indigenous veins gleams
a yaraví[16] of blood filtered
through pupils into nostalgias of sun.

Quenaing[17] deep sighs, the Pallas,[18]
as in rare century-old prints, enrosarize
a symbol in their gyrations.

On his throne the Apostle shines, then;
and he is, amid incense, tapers, and songs,
a modern sun-god for the peasant.

II

  The sad Indian is living it up.
The crowd heads toward the resplendent altar.
The eye of twilight desists
from watching the hamlet burned alive.

  The shepherdess wears wool and sandals,
with pleats of candor in her finery;
and in her humbleness of sad and heroic wool,
her feral white heart is a tuft of flax.

  Amid the music, Bengal lights,
an accordion sol-fas! A shopkeeper
shouts to the wind: "Nobody can match that!"

  The floating sparks—lovely and charming—
are wheats of audacious gold sown by
the farmer in the skies and in the nebulae.

III

  Daybreak. The chicha finally explodes
into sobs, lust, fistfights;
amid the odors of urine and pepper
a wandering drunk traces a thousand scrawls.

  "Tomorrow when I go away . . ." a rural
Romeo bewails, singing at times.
Now there is early-riser soup for sale;
and an aperitive sound of clinking plates.

  Three women go by . . . an urchin whistles . . . Distantly
the river flows along drunkenly, singing and weeping
prehistories of water, olden times.

  And as a *caja* from Tayanga[19] sounds,
as if initiating a blue *huaino*,[20] Dawn
tucks up her saffron-colored calves.

[CE]

HUACO

I am the blind corequenque
who sees through the lens of a wound,
and who is bound to the Globe
as to a stupendous huaco spinning.

I am the llama, whose hostile stupidity
is only grasped when sheared by
volutes of a bugle,
volutes of a bugle glittering with disgust
and bronzed with an old yaraví.

I am the fledgling condor plucked
by a Latin harquebus;
and flush with humanity I float in the Andes
like an everlasting Lazarus of light.

I am Incan grace, gnawing at itself
in golden coricanchas[21] baptized
with phosphates of error and hemlock.
At times the shattered nerves of an extinct puma
rear up in my stones.

A ferment of Sun;
year of darkness and the heart!

[CE]

DEAD IDYLL

What would she be doing now, my sweet Andean Rita
of rush and tawny berry;
now when Byzantium asphyxiates me, and my blood
dozes, like thin cognac, inside of me.

Where would her hands, that showing contrition
ironed in the afternoon whitenesses yet to come,
be now, in this rain that deprives me of
my desire to live.

What has become of her flannel skirt; of her
toil; of her walk;
of her taste of homemade May rum.

She must be at the door watching some cloudscape,
and at length she'll say, trembling: "Jesus . . . it's so cold!"
And on the roof tiles a wild bird will cry.

[CE]

AGAPE

Today no one has come to inquire;
nor have they asked me for anything this afternoon.

I have not seen a single cemetery flower
in such a happy procession of lights.
Forgive me, Lord: how little I have died!

On this afternoon everybody, everybody passes by
without inquiring or asking me for anything.

And I do not know what they forget and feels
wrong in my hands, like something that is not mine.

I have gone to the door,
and feel like shouting at everybody:
If you are missing something, here it is!

Because in all the afternoons of this life,
I do not know what doors they slam in a face,
and my soul is seized by someone else's thing.

Today no one has come;
and today I have died so little this afternoon!

[CE]

THE VOICE IN THE MIRROR

So life goes, like a bizarre mirage.
The blue rose that sheds light, giving the thistle its being!
Together with the dogma of the murderous
burden, the sophism of Good and Reason!

What the hand grazed, by chance, has been grasped;
perfumes drifted, and among them the scent of
mold that halfway down the path has grown
on the withered apple tree of dead Illusion.

From *The Black Heralds* 25

So life goes,
with the treacherous canticles of a shriveled bacchante.
Completely rattled, I push onward . . . onward,
growling my funeral march.

Walking at the feet of royal Brahacmanic[22] elephants
and to the sordid buzzing of a mercurial boiling,
couples raise toasts sculpted in rock,
and forgotten twilights a cross to their lips.

So life goes, a vast orchestra of Sphinxes
belching out its funeral march into the Void.

[CE]

OUR BREAD

For Alejandro Gamboa

One drinks one's breakfast . . . The damp graveyard
earth smells of beloved blood.
City of winter . . . Mordant crusade
of a cart that seems to drag along
a feeling of fasting in chains!

One wants to knock on each door
and ask for who knows who; and then
see to the poor, and, crying softly,
give morsels of bread to everybody.
And to strip the rich of their vineyards
with the two saintly hands
that with a blast of light
flew off unnailed from the Cross!

Matinal eyelash, don't raise up!
Our daily bread—give it to us,
Lord . . . !

All my bones belong to others;
maybe I stole them!
I took for my own what was perhaps
meant for another;
and I think that, had I not been born,

another poor man would be drinking this coffee!
I'm a lousy thief . . . Where will I go?

And in this cold hour, when the earth
smells of human dust and is so sad,
I want to knock on every door
and beg who knows who, forgive me,
and bake him morsels of fresh bread
here, in the oven of my heart . . . !

[CE]

THE MISERABLE SUPPER

How long will we have to wait for what is
not owed to us . . . And in what corner will
we kick our poor sponge[23] forever! How long before
the cross that inspires us does not rest its oars.

How long before Doubt toasts our nobility for
having suffered . . .
                        We have already sat so
long at this table, with the bitterness of a child
who at midnight, cries from hunger, wide awake . . .

And when will we join all the others, at the brink
of an eternal morning, everybody breakfasted.
For just how long this vale of tears, into which
I never asked to be led.
                        Resting on my elbows,
all bathed in tears, I repeat head bowed
and defeated: how much longer will this supper last.

There's someone who has drunk too much, and he mocks us,
and offers and withdraws from us—like a black spoonful
of bitter human essence—the tomb . . .
                        And this abstruse one knows
even less how much longer this supper will last!

[CE]

THE ETERNAL DICE

FOR MANUEL GONZÁLEZ PRADA,
this wild, choice emotion, one for
which the great master has most
enthusiastically applauded me.

My God, I am crying over the being I live;
it grieves me to have taken your bread;
but this poor thinking clay
is no scab fermented in your side:
you do not have Marys who leave you!

My God, had you been a man,
today you would know how to be God;
but you, who were always fine,
feel nothing for your own creation.
Indeed, man suffers you; God is he!

Today there are candles in my sorcerer eyes,
as in those of a condemned man—
my God, you will light all of your candles
and we will play with the old die . . .
Perhaps, oh gambler, throwing for the fate of
the whole universe,
Death's dark-circled eyes will come up,
like two funereal snake eyes of mud.

My God, and this deaf, gloomy night,
you will not be able to gamble, for the Earth
is a worn die now rounded from
rolling at random,
it cannot stop but in a hollow,
the hollow of an immense tomb.

[CE]

DISTANT FOOTSTEPS

My father is asleep. His august face
expresses a peaceful heart;
he is now so sweet . . .
if there is anything bitter in him, it must be me.

There is loneliness in the house; there is prayer;
and no news of the children today.
My father stirs, sounding
the flight into Egypt, the styptic farewell.
He is now so near;
if there is anything distant in him, it must be me.

My mother walks in the orchard,
savoring a savor now without savor.
She is so soft,
so wing, so gone, so love.

There is loneliness in the house with no bustle,
no news, no green, no childhood.
And if there is something broken this afternoon,
something that descends and that creaks,
it is two old white, curved roads.
Down them my heart makes its way on foot.

[CE]

TO MY BROTHER MIGUEL

In memoriam

Brother, today I am on the stone bench by the door,
where we miss you terribly!
I recall how we would play at this hour, and Mama
would caress us: "Now, boys . . ."

Now I go hide,
as before, all those evening
prayers, and hope you do not find me.
Through the living room, the hall, the corridors.
Then, you hide, and I cannot find you.
I recall that we made each other cry,
brother, with that game.

Miguel, you hid
one night in August, at dawn;
but, instead of hiding laughing, you were sad.
And your twin heart of those extinct
evenings has grown weary from not finding you. And now
shadow falls into the soul.

Hey, brother, don't take so long
to come out. Okay? Mama might get worried.

[CE]

———————

JANUNEID[24]

My father can hardly,
in the bird-borne morning, get
his seventy-eight years, his seventy-eight
winter branches, out into the sunlight.
The Santiago graveyard, anointed
with Happy New Year, is in view.
How many times his footsteps have cut over toward it,
then returned from some humble burial.

Today it's a long time since my father went out!
A hubbub of kids breaks up.

Other times he would talk to my mother
about city life, politics;
today, supported by his distinguished cane
(which sounded better during his years in office),
my father is unknown, frail,
my father is a vesper.   ·
He carries, brings, absentmindedly, relics, things,
memories, suggestions.
The placid morning accompanies him
with its white Sister of Charity wings.

This is an eternal day, an ingenuous, childlike,
choral, prayerful day;
time is crowned with doves
and the future is filled with
caravans of immortal roses.
Father, yet everything is still awakening;
it is January that sings, it is your love
that keeps resonating in Eternity.
You will laugh with your little ones,
and there will be a triumphant racket in the Void.

It will still be New Year. There will be empanadas;
and I will be hungry, when Mass is rung

in the pious bell tower by
the kind melic blind man with whom
my fresh schoolboy syllables, my rotund
innocence, chatted.
And when the morning full of grace,
from its breasts of time,
which are two renunciations, two advances of love
which stretch out and plead for infinity, eternal life,
sings, and lets fly plural Words,
tatters of your being,
at the edge of its white
Sister of Charity wings, oh! my father!

[CE]

EPEXEGESIS[25]

   I was born on a day
when God was sick.

   Everybody knows that I am alive,
that I am bad; and they do not know
about the December of that January.
For I was born on a day
when God was sick.

   There is a void
in my metaphysical air
that no one is going to touch:
the cloister of a silence
that spoke flush with fire.

   I was born on a day
when God was sick.

   Brother, listen, listen . . . .
Okay. And do not let me leave
without bringing Decembers,
without leaving Januaries.
For I was born on a day
when God was sick.

Everybody knows that I am alive,
that I chew . . . And they do not know
why in my poetry galled winds,
untwisted from the inquisitive
Sphinx of the Desert,
screech an obscure
coffin anxiety.

Everybody knows . . . And they do not know
that the Light is consumptive,
and the Shadow fat . . . .
And they do not know how the Mystery synthesizes . . . .
how it is the sad musical
humpback who denounces from afar
the meridional step from the limits to the Limits.

I was born on a day
when God was sick,
gravely.

[CE]

Articles and Chronicles

WITH MANUEL GONZÁLEZ PRADA

Lima, March 1918

The reading room of the library, as always, jam-packed.

Its peace, abstractive. One hand after another that impatiently thumbs through pages. The delayed footsteps of some conservative, scouring the stacks. Oil paintings of illustrious Peruvians on the walls get damaged by the light of the large old windows.

We walk in. To the board room. With a fine welcoming attitude, seated softly on the couch, as if he were auscultating the spiritual moment, the maestro drops words I never dreamed I'd hear.

His vigorous sentimental dynamism, captivating and absorbing; the fresh expression of his venerable continent's spring, has something of soft winged marble in which the pagan Hellas used to incarnate divine gestures, the superhuman energy of its gods. I don't know why, before this man, an extraordinary reverberation, a breath of centuries, an idea of synthesis, one like an emotion of unity comes together between my fibers. One could say his shoulders fly that legendary flight of an entire race, and on his snowy apostolic crown, the maximum spiritual prowess of one hemisphere bursts in beams of inextinguishable white light.

Moved, I look upon him; my heart beating faster than ever; my greatest mental energies shooting out and flying toward every horizon in a thousand shimmering sparks, as if some diligent flogging were suddenly given with a million invisible arms for some miraculous job, beyond the cell . . . Because González Prada, by hypnotic virtue that in a normal state is only peculiar to genius, imposes himself, sequesters us, takes possession of our spirit, and ends up altering our course.

During this visit, as in the prior ones, Prada speaks of art. He doesn't lavish us with his words. Rather, they are lapped with emotion and optimism, but not solemnity.

What a way to detox in front of this immense mountain of thought!

"But the professors say no," I reply. "They say symbolist literature is nonsense."

"The professors . . . always the professors!" He smiles mercifully.

Not even in his sentences does he expend pontifical solemnity. The

33

line of his noble silhouette forever vibrates in a thirsty fervor for truth. He doesn't have that pause of senescence; he feels life right in the meridian, yearning, restless, renewing. No mild wing passes though him to swoop away horizontally, but instead it's the wing in accelerated rhythm of a flight that eternally rises. That's why he's not solemn, why he doesn't look old. He's a rare, perennial, equatorial flower of prolific rebellion.

I ask him about Peruvian poetry.

"There's the influence of contemporary French decadents," he says, and, savoring a proclamation feigning complacence, he adds, "and Maeterlinck."

A broad pause of conviction ensues at the end of his every phrase that, after being uttered, seems to consolidate their substantial value into blood, powerfully stuffing our veins with their ideal melody.

So I fervently beg the great Renán commentator, "As Valdelomar remarked to me the other day, Peru will never know how to express the immense gratitude it owes to Maeterlinck."

The hue of his face enlivens in a smile that flutters, through the silence of forgotten summits far from here.

"And the youth of today," he says, as if enthusiastically hammering out a warm applause with his lips, "is the offspring of his sublime liberating work. Yes, indeed," he continues, "one must go against the shackles, against academics." A founding diamond twinkles in his visionary eyes. And I remember that steel bible called *Páginas libres*. And I feel enveloped in the incense of a modern altarpiece without effigies.

"In literature," he goes on, "the shortcomings of technique, the incongruities of manner, are unimportant."

"And the grammatical errors?" I ask. "And the boldness of expression?"

He smiles at my naivety. "Those errors go unnoticed," he replies with an expression of patriarchal tolerance. "And the boldness, in particular, is to my liking."

I lower my head.

In the grave distinction of his demeanor, the splenetic opaque clarity of the room blows out and withers. At his feet a tongue of humble sunshine crawls, which forms a delicate flame of opal woolens that had arrived from afar out of breath on the run.

As I hear these last words from the philosopher, I think about so many hostile hands already in the distance, and I look forward to the morning when there will be a dawn.

With a slight smile that curves in subtle interrogation, sounding and studying, González Prada talks, thus lengthening the moments of his intellectual acceptance, and he introduces me with an unexpected enthusiastic eulogy.

He invites me to visit him again. This master of the continent, this orator who's pulverized so much of the deformed organ of our republican life, whose work is not of dried-out leaves, of simply speaking well, but of incorruptible immortal bronze, like that of Plato and Nietzsche; this egregious captain of generations, always brilliant, whom the youth arms and of whom it thinks and will keep on thinking; this gentle man, enemy of all formalism, and likewise of all farce, shakes my hand in the doorway of the Biblioteca Nacional in a most personal expression of intelligence and courtesy.

I leave trembling. In view of what I've been told by the author of *Horas de lucha*, *Minúsculas*, and *Exóticas*, I feel my nerves ineffably stiffen like spears recently sharpened for combat.

Amid the gravelly noises of people who come and go, a beggar's flute is weeping, played by the weak panting of his fast; and turning onto San Pedro, I discern that his sobbing is directed in supplication at the doors of the church. Could that blind man not know that those doors lead to the church and, since no one lives inside, no one will open them for him on this Friday afternoon of the poor?

[Taken from Antenor Orrego's personal files, without date or place of its first publication]   [JM]

WITH JOSÉ MARÍA EGUREN

With certain bitterness, the great symbolist of *El Dios de la centella* says to me, "Oh, there's so much to fight, so much that's combated me! When I was starting out, friends with some authority in these matters would always discourage me. And I, as you understand, ended up believing that I was making a mistake. Only a good while later did González Prada celebrate my verse."

While his agile, cordial, and deeply sinuous voice dissolves, his stunningly dark eyes seem to search for memories and wander slowly through the room. Eguren the poet is of a medium build. On his face, of a noble, somewhat toasted white tone, his thirty-six years already babble some lines of autumn. His spontaneous manners, cut up in distinction and fluidity, inspire devotion and sympathy at the outset. The explanations he gives for some of his symbols suggest the rarest of illusions. He resembles an oriental prince who travels in pursuit of impossible sacred berry bushes.

"Has your approach always been the same as it is now?" I ask him.

"Yes," he replies, lively and joyful, "with a short romantic parenthesis. Many of Rubén Darío's skills," he adds, "I had too, before they became known over here. It's just that, until very recently, no newspaper wanted to publish my poems. Of course, I never exposed myself to rejection, but as you already know, no one would accept them."

Then, he recalls for me his long years of literary isolation, which proved to be fertile for American letters.

"Symbolism has now prevailed in America," he says with a polished accent. Symbolism of the phrase, that is, French symbolism, has already been consolidated on the continent; as for the symbolism of thought, this has been too, but with rather diverse nuances. For example, my tendency is different from any other, according to González Prada. It's in this way that, as you see, it's impossible to specify the compendious physiognomy of contemporary American poetry."

Eguren is enthused and visibly takes pleasure in his discussions about art. He offers me an aromatic English cigarette and, between one and the next puff of smoke, through our lips pass the names of Goncourt, Flaubert, and Lecont de Lisle, along with some American and Peruvian writers, mixed into some divine eternal verse.

"You and I have to fight so much," he says, with a gesture of mild resignation.

"But you have already enjoyed success all over America," I argue. "What news do you have from abroad?"

"In Argentina, Chile, Ecuador, and Colombia, they know of me and publish my poems enthusiastically. And I have numerous relationships with the intellectuals from those countries. Beyond that, we shall see, we shall see, not just yet . . ." (The pain and genius of Verlaine, Poe, and Baudelaire, unrecognized by their century, passes through my mind.) "And in Trujillo?" Eguren asks me with lively interest.

I'm caught off guard by this question and, without a way out, I shuffle and reposition myself on the divan, until finally, as if suddenly pushed forward by a memory, I reply, "In Trujillo—" Eguren interrupts and talks about those writers, friends of mine, to whom he dedicates phrases of enthusiastic praise.

"What's more," he rounds off his words with fine gallantry, "Trujillo is a comely city in my opinion, and I believe it possesses quite a bit of culture. I'm fond of it."

When I said good-bye, the day had flown by.

On the way home, I look at Barranco, with its straight streets, lined with poplars, arborescent ferns, and pines. The chalets, in the most varied of styles, flaunt gardens of beautiful elegance, and vestibules open to the evening breeze—luxurious residences of bourgeois comfort.

The hour virgilian, turquoise, energetic green. And the sea rich in silver.

[*La Semana* (Trujillo), no. 2, March 30, 1918]   [JM]

ABRAHAM VALDELOMAR HAS DIED

"Abraham Valdelomar has died," it says on the chalkboard of *La Prensa*.

At four in the afternoon I read these incomprehensible syllables, and even right now they refuse to stay in my heart. Gastón Roger has said it too and can't resign to accepting such news. Weeping, however, I cross the street where I walked so many times with Abraham, and overwhelmed by anguish and desperation, I reach my house and quickly sit down to write these lines like a madman.

Abraham Valdelomar has died. By this time the news is flying. But can it be? Oh, this is terrible!

"Brother in pain and beauty, brother in God," Abraham, you cannot have left forever; it's impossible, only "like when you were traveling, brother, you're missing."[26] Yes, that's all, you've been missing since the rainy morning when you left on a train that will bring you back. Yes, you're traveling, brother, that's all. And you'll come back, Abraham, very soon. Your mother awaits you; we your brothers await you too. You'll come back to realize all your dreams of love, beauty, bounty in life, and because you have so much pain that you've gathered on your latest sojourns from the land which you'll immortalize by dint of and thanks to your immense heart of a brilliant creator and artist. That's why you'll come back, my dear friend. Thus I feel and desire in this spring twilight with the sad pink ink that I use to write this now. And I shall see you again and wrap my arms around you, like always, with all my soul, with all my heart. Isn't that right? At supper tonight, at the family table, when your mother, who might wish to say a word, sees the empty seat and bursts into tears . . . at supper tonight, we'll tell her that you'll come back soon, very soon, to the arms of your mother, that they'll sing the tender and melancholic a-rro-rrO of your early poems.

But what's come over me? Am I weeping? Why is my chest so tight? Oh, detestable chalkboard of *La Prensa*.

Abraham Valdelomar has died.

[*La Prensa* (Lima), November 4, 1919]   [JM]

Letters

TO ÓSCAR IMAÑA

Lima, January 29, 1918
Dear Óscar,

Only today have I been able to reply to your affectionate card. I've already told you: here, I don't know why, the hours and days go by so quickly. Excuse me. Well? . . . You already know how much I care for you and how many reasons I have to remember you every instant.

Seemingly or effectively, there's a peculiar yet powerful pain in all the letters you guys write to me. Every time I read one, my heart aches mysteriously. It might be that our missing bohemian brothers are more bohemian by the day, or it might be that I love you more from a distance. One month has passed since I embraced you on board the *Ucayali*, where we parted ways, and in my spirit I feel that an unknown sentimental construction has been built, one that I never foresaw. Now, I'm living my life—what can I say! I don't know how to pin it down into any expression, but what I do know is that I'm very peaceful, filled with laughter. The sentimentality of bygone days shall never again return. I feel beautiful, lucid, crystal clear, strong, upright, olympic—come on! What do you say? Are you happy I feel this way? Very well. Such is my kingdom within!

And you? As I write this morning, I recall so many faraway things we shared. The unhealthy, stupid days of December, full of tedium; the arrogant idiotic examinations, with our bloodshot eyes, anointed with ether and pain; the Vegas Zanabrias, the Chavarrys . . . Oh, the horror! . . . I wish I didn't remember! My tooth is going to ache, and I'm going fall into disgrace for staining this whole brotherly-love-lit letter with such dark and fateful shadows . . . I'd better not! As I was saying, this pleasant morning, I recall our most recent emotions from Trujillo. But, come on! Some detestable image always must surface, some heroic silhouette of Hoyos and Vinent, some deluxe memory of blind flesh that comes at a price!

As I was saying, all those long nights the two of us spent endlessly talking, all those expressions of complete, noble, spiritual comprehension between two friends, two brothers, they flow through this hour in which I'm far away from so many evil people. And, in a shirt, worked up, my mane now longer, my solitary room, full of suffering, I seem to see you approach me, affectionate, solicitous, startled, nervous, like in the good ole days, and I believe that I see you start to sigh, to smile, telling me, No, man! Go on, and you believe that! . . . And then, you lie down on your bed with your old coat and start reading in silence some marvelous line of French poetry . . . But, shoo! . . . Here in Lima, far from you, I revive another César, another unrest, another kind of anxiety, another life, another warmth of friendship, less spontaneous, less true, less lyrical, less great, less blue! And it makes me want to cry . . . What do you have to tell me about the state of your soul? Your loves, your nervous crisis, your metaphysical tortures, your lesser concerns, your urbane sensations, and the countless idiots there are in life.

Tell me, Osquitar, don't stay silent, don't keep quiet. I wish that your confidence, your emotions, your heartbeats always were my own.

Your little girl by now must be big and intelligent and pretty, with her select expression of goodness and spiritual distinction. Even though I haven't made her acquaintance, you know how much sympathy your affection for her fostered in me. Give her my regards with my most devoted sign of respect. I likewise send my best for your younger sister, María.

And the two-bit girls? Lolita always with restrained desires? Marina always frivolously passionate and never without a man? Zoila Rosa, they write to me, already has another guy, blond haired and a very good friend of mine! Is it true? Will she then be suffering again that sweet desire to cry over what Benavente is telling us? Is Isabel still obviously smitten by Clark and his fox trots? And Virginia? Nice and smooth, always smooth and always nice? (Hold on . . . who else? who else? Hold on . . . Ah . . .) How is poor María getting on? Poor little thing, no?

Send Concepción my highest regards; and to all the girls I've mentioned, a fond memory.

And Muñoz? And Benjamín? And Espejo? And Federico? And? . . . A stupendous, immortal, noisy, troglodytic, buffoon's embrace, without limits, without shame . . . (Come on, by dint of not and not and not knotting a shameless note).[27] Well. It doesn't matter. Now you see, terrible nonsense. So what?

Over here, Lima. What can I say? Valdelomar, González Prada, Eguren, Mariátegui, Félix del Valle, Belmonte, Camacho, Zapata López, Julio Hernández, Góngora.

All just literary pouting. Because you must know that the phenomenon is also of letters or rather of the man of letters. You'll see what will become of this false, tacky stuff. I've not yet become friends with Clemente Palma, much less Gálvez. Do you guys know yet about *Sudamérica*? That newspaper is truly scandalous. What trash-talking drivel. I don't know even by sight this Pérez Cánepa. I just know that he's an animal and his woman is loaded. And that Raúl Porras gave him a beating the other day at the door to *Excelsior.* That's Lima for you. It's about running around with hat in hand, looking for a way out. There is More, in La Paz, the editor in chief of the best newspaper of the city: *El Fígaro.* Fernán Cisneros in New York. Gibson and Rodríguez in Arequipa. Behold, the intellectual generation of the present. According to the consideration of Lima, Belaúndes, Gálvez, Miró Quesadas, Riva Agüeros, Lavalles, and Barretos have been kept out of sight for a while now, that is, as intellectuals.

Beingolea went to an unknown corner to sell jewelry, lace, and who knows what other monstrosities with a group of Turks, and nothing else is known of him.

Carlos Parra is also in La Paz; Juan is still in Buenos Aires. Rivero Falconí, Falcón, Luis Rivero, Meza, broke!

As for me . . . frightened; and like a bird who descends to an unknown land and hops around, flutters and perches once again, and rehearses the propitious point at which he must fold his wings and cease the flight, I keep spending my days with one, and another, and I've not yet made contact with anyone! I think I've reached a deeper understanding with the count,[28] and I spend more time with him and feel better around him.

Women? There are many a beaut. Fortunately, I feel like I'm in a coffin. And perhaps . . .

Send my highest regards to Dr. Puga and his wife.

And my affection to Poyito and your other nieces.

What's the word on my trip among those Trujillano fools? Good-bye. With a strong embrace and with my heart so that you never forget me.

César   [JM]

TO ÓSCAR IMAÑA

Lima, August 2, 1918

Dear Óscar,

It's two o'clock in the morning, and I'm writing to you. Could you know how I'm doing at this very moment? Can you guess what's transpiring in my soul? Let's see if you can.

I'm all alone. At a desk you never touched. With a light you never saw. Everything unknown. Everything for you to imagine. In front of me strange pieces of furniture await a stranger. A housefly does laps with a thick, raspy, lazy, nauseating voice. It fights another fly in the air. They emit a sound like celluloid that burns. Then I see several envelopes with the addresses of other people. Then various winter hats hanging in peeping chorus. I scratch the top of my right calf: some pesky, fleeting, nocturnal bug. A rooster crows in mathematically equal periods; the fly again swoops over my filthy hair. Explain yourself. I sigh, grow tired. The snoring of a neighbor brings me the fat heavy breathing of pork-filled slumber, and that man is far away.

A booming alert. It's a car that passes preaching that one must take caution on the roads . . . Two beats of my "tell-tale heart" echo throughout the house.

I have a cold, and sometimes my nostrils wheeze and anguish. Another sigh. A slight pause, barely long enough to measure. Gone.

I don't have any cigarettes. I'm going to smoke my recidivist butt. This humble little hick isn't guilty of anything but having spent the night mysteriously on guard with God knows what tiny invisible sort of subhuman force. My poor friend. No one will save him. For sure . . . Now I'm burning it down, and, what's worse, I've used my last match too.

In this house there are familiar, recognizable dreams. Poor things. Let them sleep. Men and women. Or let them make . . . whatever they feel like. In waking life, one suffers greatly. Poor things. And my butt has gone out.

I contemplate a calendar figure: one broad man punching another who writhes and winces on his feet. This murder lasts twenty-four hours. So strange.

Someone has vanished before my eyes. He left worried, after asking me for money. I told him no, to pull himself together, to stop worrying. Now, affected, I remember him and pray to God for his well-being. Let him sleep deeply, without being frightened.

There is a rope hanging. Hanging toward tomorrow night. And it shakes intensely.

Good-bye.

César   [JM]

TO MANUEL NATIVIDAD VALLEJO

December 2, 1918
My dear little brother Manuel,
Santiago de Chuco.
I've finally had the pleasure of receiving a letter from you, after the numerous letters I've written you since March 1917, when I left home. I've

taken pleasure and wept upon reading your sad, tender, and moving words. I've taken painful, horrible pleasure. Oh, how much I remember and how much happiness is gone forever. Oh, my dear Manuelito! What a dark fate was awaiting me; far forever from our beloved mother! Oh my dear, dear little brother. The horror!

114 days have passed since the unforgettable eighth of August, and I'll always live in the faith of God, sure that mom is alive, over there in our house, and that tomorrow or some day when I return, she'll be waiting for me with open arms, bawling her eyes out. Yes . . . I can't accept that God has taken her so early, given the love and hope of her children who've fought to conquer a future that was to be placed at the feet of our blessed mother! Oh, my Manuelito, my dear brother!

So I'm writing to you with my heart torn to shreds. I hope that Néstor comes at the end of this month, and we'll see each other then to resolve our matters for good. We'll let you know immediately. And in the meantime, don't lose your cool, and I beg you, in the name of our brotherly love, to have patience for a few more months. Patience, a bit of patience. Oh, my brother! I've fought so much, and so much have I learned never to fall into despair. And, oh, how I've learned to believe that there's always a future ahead that's not completely bleak. We'll contact you soon. What's important is that you don't lose yourself to silence and that we stay in touch, to see how we should move on.

I wrote to Dad on one of the steamships I took, and to Víctor so that he'd have a letter of his own and to tell him that I'd write on the next ship.

Give my best to Augustito. How is he? And where is he? Let me know about him, since his silence makes him seem buried to me.

This month it will be a year since I've been in Lima.

Take good care of Dad. Needless to say, he's the only treasure we have remaining in the world. There, the love and affection of you who live with the support of his gentle company.

Don't lose yourself to silence. And with my best for Juanita and for you, I'll say good-bye. Your brother, who loves and misses you dearly.

César   [JM]

DEDICATION OF A COPY OF *THE BLACK HERALDS* TO FRIENDS IN TRUJILLO

[Lima, July 1919]

Brothers,

The black heralds have just arrived. And they will head to the North, their native land. Speckled, they proclaim: someone's crossing all the himalayas and circumstantial andes. Behind such stunned panting monsters, an absolutely shrill *Solo of Blades* rings in the aurora's writhing . . . Let our ears perk up—Confession: And on the other side: the good friendly guy, the long-suffering Korriskoso[29] of yesteryear, the trembling expression at life. And if I am to make some offering out of this book with all my heart, this one's for my brothers in Trujillo.

César   [JM]

BOOK TWO 1920-1923

FROM *Trilce*

I

   Who's making all that racket,[1] and not even letting
the islands that linger make a will.

   A little more consideration
as it will be late, early,
and easier to assay
the guano,[2] the simple fecapital[3] ponk[4]
a brackish gannet
toasts unintentionally,
in the insular heart, to each hyaloid
     squall.

   A little more consideration,
and liquid muck, six in the evening
    OF THE MOST GRANDIOSE B-FLATS

   And the peninsula raises up
from behind, muzziled,[5] imperturbable
on the fatal balance line.

[CE]

II

      Time Time.

   Noon clogged up nighttime fog.[6]
Boring pump of the cellblock backwashes
time time time time.

      Was Was.

   Roosters songsing[7] scratching in vain.
Clear day's mouth that conjugates
was was was was.

      Tomorrow Tomorrow.

47

The warm repose of being though.
The present thinks hold on to me for
tomorrow tomorrow tomorrow tomorrow.

      Name Name.

   What calls all that puts on hedge us?[8]
It's called Thesame that suffers
name name name namE.[9]

                                       [JM]

IV

   Two carts grind our eardrums down
three-pwronged[10] to our tear ducts, when
we never did anything to them.
To that other yes, unloved,
embitternessed[11] in tunnel unsheltered
by the one, and over tough aljid[12]
spiritizing   tests.

   I stretched out like a third party,
but the evening—whatta whe to do—
rings around my head, furiously
not wanting two dose up on mother.[13] They are
           the rings.
They're the already chawed nuptial tropics.
The withdrawal, best of all,
shatters the Crucible.

   That not having discolored
at all. Side by side with fate and cries
and cries. The whole song
squared into three silences.

   Heat. Ovary. Nearly transparency.
All's been mourned.   Vigil's been utterly kept
in deep left.

                                         [JM]

VI

   The suit that tomorrow I wore
my laundress has not washed:

she used to wash it in her otilian[14] veins,
at the brook of her heart, and I need today
not ask myself if I've left the suit
tinged with injustice.

   At this our[15] when no one's going to the water,
the fabric for feathering
fledges on my guidelines, and everything
on the nightstand of so much what'll become of me[16]
is not all mine
at my side.

                        They stayed put in her possession,
bonded, sealed up with her flaxen goodness.

   And if I knew that she would return;
and if I knew what morning she'd walk in
to deliver me cleaned the clothes, that soul
laundress of mine. What a morning she'd walk in,
satisfied, a goldenberry of labor, delighted
to prove that yes she does know, that yes she can
      HOW COULD SHE NOT!
dye blue and iron out all the chaoses.

[JM]

IX

   I sdrive to dddeflect at a blow the blow.
Her two broad leaves, her valve
opening in succulent reception
from multiplicand to multiplier,
her condition excellent for pleasure,
all readies truth.[17]

   I strive to ddeflect at a blow the blow.
To her flattery, I transasfixiate[18] Bolivarian asperities
at thirty-two cables and their multiples,
hair for hair majestic thick lips,
the two tomes of the Work, constringe,
and I do not live absence then,
            not even by touch.

I fail to teflect at a blow the blow.
We will never saddle the torose Trool
of egotism or of that mortal chafe
of the bedsheet,
since this here woman
        —how she weighs being general!

And female is the soul of the absent-she.
And female is my own soul.

[CE]

X

Primary and final stone of groundless
chance, has soul and all
just died, October bedroom and pregnant.
From three months of absent and ten of sweet.
How fate,
the mitred monodactyl, laughs.

How unions of contraries
despair behind. How always the digit emerges
beneath all avatar lineage.

How whales go dutch with doves.[19]
How these in turn abandon their beak
cubed up in third wing.
How we saddlebow,[20] facing monotonous haunches.

Toward the tenth are ten months towed,
toward another beyond.
At least two are still in diapers.
And the three months of absence.
And the nine of gestation.

There's not even any violence.
The patient props himself up,
and seated smears on the soothing salfe.[21]

[JM]

XIII

I think about your sex.
My heart simplified, I think about your sex,

before the ripe daughterloin[22] of day.
I touch the bud of joy, it is in season.
And an ancient sentiment dies
degenerated into brains.

I think about your sex, furrow more prolific
and harmonious than the belly of the Shadow,
though Death conceives and bears
from God himself.
Oh Conscience,
I am thinking, yes, about the free beast
who takes pleasure where he wants, where he can.

Oh, scandal of the honey of twilights.
Oh mute thunder.

Rednuhtetum!

[CE]

XVII

This 2 distills in a single batch,
and together we'll finish it off.
No one'd heard me. Striate urent
civil abracadabra.

The morning doesn't touch like the first,
like the last stone ovulatable[23]
by force of secrecy. The barefoot morning.
The clay halfway
between gray matters, more and less.

Faces do not know of the face, nor of the
walk to the encounters.
And without a toward the exergue may nod.
The tip of fervor wanders.

June, you're ours. June, and on your shoulders
I stand up to guffaw, drying
my meter and my pockets
on your 21 seasonal fingernails.

Good! Good!

[CE]

XVIII

Oh the four walls of the cell.
Ah the four whitening walls
that irrefutably face the same number.

Breeding ground of nerves, evil breach,
through its four corners how it snaps
apart daily shackled extremities.

Loving keeper of innumerable keys,
if you were here, if you could see
unto what hour these walls are four.
Against them we'd be with you, just the two,
more two than ever. And you wouldn't even cry,
speak, liberator!

Ah the four walls of the cell.
Meanwhile as for those that hurt me, most
the two lengthy ones that tonight
have something of mothers who now
deceased each lead through bromined slides,[24]
a child by the hand.

And only will I keep my hold,
with my right hand, that makes do for both,
upraised, in search of a tertiary arm
that must pupilate, between my where and when,
this stunted adulthood of man.[25]

[JM]

XX

Flush with the beaten froth bulwarked
by ideal stone. Thus I barely
render 1 near 1 so as not to fall.

That mustachioed man. The sun,
his only wheel iron-rimmed, fifth and perfect,
and upwardly from it.
Clamor of crotch buttons
                    free,
clamor that reprehends A vertical subordinate.
Juridical drainage. Pleasant prank.

But I suffer. Hereabouts I suffer. Thereabouts I suffer.

And here I am doting, I am
one beautiful person, when
williamthesecondary man
toils and sweats happiness
in gushes, putting a shine on the shoe
of his little three-year-old girl.

Shaggy cocks his head and rubs one side.
The girl meanwhile sticks her forefinger
on her tongue which starts spelling
the tangles of tangles of the tangles,
and she daubs the other shoe, secretly,
with an itty bit of silyba and dirt,[26]
                  but only with,
                  an itty bi-
                  .t.

[JM]

XXIII

Estuous oven of those my sweet rolls
pure infantile innumerable yolk, mother.

Oh your four gorges, astoundingly
mislamented, mother: your beggars.
The two youngest sisters, Miguel who has died
and me still pulling
one braid for each letter in the primer.

In the room upstairs you handed out to us
in the morning, in the evening, from a dual stowage,
those delicious hosts of time, so
that now we'd have more than enough
clock husks in flexion of 24 hours
stopped on the dot.

Mother, and now! Now, in which alveolus
might remain, on what capillary sprout,
a certain crumb that today perplexed in my throat
doesn't want to go down. Today when even
your pure bones might be flour

with nowhere to knead
—tender confectioner of love,
even in raw shade, even in the great molar
whose gum throbs on that lacteal dimple
which unseen builds and abounds—you saw it so often!
in closed hands newborn.

So the earth will hear in your silencing,
how they keep charging us all
rent on the world in which you leave us
and the cost of that interminable bread.
And they charge us for it, when, being only
children then, as you could see,
we couldn't have snatched it
from anyone; when you gave it to us,
no, mama?

[CE]

XXV

Chess bishops upthrust to stick[27]
to lute, down deep, to napes,
to upright numerators' undersides.
Bishops and burs from lupine piles.

As the lee of each unraveled
carabel snorts, without amerecanizing,[28]
blighting ploughtails in spasm slacken,
with the scanty pulse improperly prone
to blowing its nose on the back of its wrist.
And the sharpest sopranancy
gets tonsured, ensnared, and at length
imnazaled[29] near icicles
of infinite pity.

Biggity haunches huff hard
to bear, pendent on musty breast plates
standards with their seven colors
under zero, from guano islands
to guano islands.
Hence the honey harvests in the wide open of bad

faith.
Hence the time of the rounds. Hence the man of the back
roads onward to future planes,
when innanimous gryphion only reports
blundered mute-due crusades.[30]

So then bishops come even to stick
to trapdoors and to rough drafts.

[JM]

XXVIII

I've had lunch alone now, and without any
mother, or may I have, or help yourself, or water,
or father who, over the eloquent offertory
of ears of corn, asks for his postponed
image, between the greater clasps of sound.

How could I have had lunch. How served myself
these things from such distant plates,
when my own home will have broken up,
when not even mother appears at my lips.
How could I have had a nothing lunch.

At the table of a good friend I've had lunch
with his father just arrived from the world,
with his white-haired aunts who speak
in dapple-gray tinkle of porcelain,
mumbling through all their widow alveoli;
and with generous place settings of lively tootlings,
because they're in their own home. What a snap!
And the knives on this table
have hurt me all over my palate.

Viandry[31] at such tables, where one tastes
someone else's love instead of one's own,
turns into earth the mouthful not offered by
            MOTHER,
makes the hard degllusion[32] a blow; the dessert,
bile; the coffee, funereal oil.

Now when my own home has broken up,
and the maternal help yourself does not leave the
tomb,
the kitchen in darkness, the misery of love.

[CE]

XXX

Burn of the second
in all of yearning's tender carnage,
platter of vigrant[33] chilies,
at two in the immoral afternoon.

Warrant of edges edge to edge.
Heady truth tapped alive, upon hooking up
our sexual antenna
to what we're being unawares.

Dishwater of maximum ablution.
Voyaging crocks
that collide and spatter from fresh unanimous
shadow, the color, fraction, enduring life,
    the eternal enduring life.
Don't fret. Such is Death.

The sex blood of the Beloved, who all sweetnessed-up[34]
bemoans such lugging around *so* much
for such a ridiculous reason.
And the circuit
between our poor day and the big night,
at two in the immoral afternoon.

[JM]

XXXI

Hope between cotton bawls.[35]

Uniform husky arris
of magnificent spore woven threats
and with porter buttons inborn.
Are six rubbed out by sun?
Nativity. Shut up, fear.

Christian I hope, ever hope
kneeling down upon the circular stone
that on this chance's hundred corners
is so vague where I appear.

And God overwhelmed subdues
our pulse, silent, grave,
and as father to his babe
      barely,
but barely, half-opens up bloody cotton balls
and takes hold of hope between his fingers.

Lord, it's I who want it . . .
And that's enough!

                         [JM]

XXXVI

We struggle to thread ourselves through a needle's eye,
face to face, hell-bent on winning.[36]
The fourth angle of the circle ammoniafies[37] almost.
Female is continued the male, on the basis
of probable breasts, and precisely
on the basis of how much does not flower.

Are you that way, Venus de Milo?
You hardly act crippled, pullulating
enwombed in the plenary arms
of existence,
of this existence that neverthelessez[38]
perpetual imperfection.
Venus de Milo, whose cut-off, increate
arm swings round and tries to elbow
across greening stuttering pebbles,
ortive nautili, recently crawling
evens, immortal on the eves of.
Lassoer of imminences, lassoer
of the parenthesis.

Refuse, all of you, to set foot
on the double security of Harmony.
Truly refuse symmetry.

Intervene in the conflict
of points that contend
in the most rutty of jousts
for the leap through the needle's eye!

So now I feel my little finger
in excess on my left. I see it and think
it shouldn't be me, or at least that it's
in a place where it shouldn't be.
And it inspires me with rage and alarms me
and there is no way out of it, except by
imagining that today is Thursday.

Make way for the new odd number
                          potent with orphanhood!

[CE]

XXXVIII

This crystal waits to be sipped
in the rough by a future mouth
without teeth. Not toothless.
This crystal is bread yet to come.

It wounds when they force it
and no longer shows animal affection.
But if it gets excited, it could deposit honey
and become a sugar mold for nouns
which adjectivize in self-offerings.

Those who see it there a sad colorless
individual, could dispatch it for love,
through the past and at most into the future:
if it does not surrender any of its sides;
if it waits to be sipped in a gulp
and as transparence, by a future mouth at will no longer have teeth.

This crystal has passed from animal,
and now goes off to form lefts,
the new Minuses.
Just leave it alone.

[CE]

XLII

Wait, all of you. Now I'm going to tell you
everything. All of you wait this headache
may subsside. Wait.

Where have you left yourselves
that you're never needed?

No one's needed! Very good.

Rosa, entering from the top floor.
I feel like a child. And again rosa:
you don't even know where I'm going.

Is the death star reeling?
Or are strange sewing machines
inside the left side.
All of you wait one moment more.   .

No one has seen us. Pure one
search for your waist.
Where have your eyes popped!

Enter reincarnated the parlors
of western crystal. Exact
music plays almost a pity.

I feel better. Without fever, and fervent.
Spring. Peru. I open my eyes.
Ave! Don't leave. God, as if suspecting
some ebbless flow ay.

A facial shovelful, the curtain sweeps
nigh to the prompt boxes.

Acrisia. Tilia, go to bed.

[CE]

XLIV

This piano journeys within,
it journeys in merry leaps.
Then meditates in iron-plated repose,
nailed into ten horizons.

Onward it goes. Down into tunnels it stoops,
yonder, down into tunnels of pain,
down into vertebrae that naturally fugue.

Other times its tubes go,
lingering asias yellow from living,
enter eclipse,
and delouse do insectile nightmares,
now dead from thunder, the herald of geneses.

Dark piano, on whom do you spy
with your deafness that hears me,
with your muteness that deafens me?

Oh mysterious pulse.

[JM]

XLV

I lose contact with the sea
when the waters come to me.

Let us always depart. Let us savor
the stupendous song, the song expressed
by the lower lips of desire.
Oh prodigious maidenhood.
The saltless breeze passes.

In the distance I scent the pith
listening to the deep sounding, in search
of undertow keys.

And if in this way we bang head-on
into the absurd,
we'll cover ourselves with the gold of having nothing,
and will hatch the yet unborn wing
of night, the sister
of this orphan wing of day,
that by dint of being one no longer is a wing.

[CE]

XLIX

Murmured in restlessness, I cross,
my long suit of feeling, the Mondays
        of truth.
Nobody seeks or recognizes me,
and even I have forgotten
        from whom I might be.

    A certain wardrobe, only she, will know
us all in the white leaves
        of certificates.
That wardrobe, she alone,
while returning from each faction,
        of each candelabrum
        blind from birth.

    Nor do I come upon anyone, beneath
this humus that iridesends[39] the Mondays
        of reason;
and I no more than smile at each spike
of the gratings, in the mad search
        for the known.

    Good wardrobe, open up for me
your white leaves;
I want at least to recognize 1,
I want the fulcrum, I at least
        want to know of being.

    Offstage where we dress,
there's not, there Is no one: only leaves
        opened up wide.
And always the suits letting go
by themselves, from the hangers
like ghastly guiding pointers,
and departing without bodies, vacant,
        even to the prudent hint
of a grand wing stock with causes
and limits fried deep.
Right down to the bone!

                                        [JM]

L

    Cerberus four times
per day his padlock wields, opening
closing our sternums, with winks
we comprehend perfectly.

    With astounded melancholic breeches,
childish in transcendental disarray,
standing, the poor ole man is adorable.
He jokes with the prisoners, chockfull
the groins with jabs. And lunkhead even
gnaws on some crust for them; but always
just doing his job.

    In between the bars he sticks the fiscal
point, unseen, hoisting up the phalanx
of his pinky,
on the trail of what I say,
what I eat,
what I dream.
The raven wants there nevermore be insides,
and how we ache from this that Cerberus wants.

    In a clockwork system, the imminent,
pythagorean! ole man plays
breadthwise in the aortas. And only
from time to night, by night
he somewhat skirts his exception from metal.
But, naturally,
always just doing his job.

                                [JM]

LII

    And we'll get up when we feel
like it, even though mama all luminosity
rouses us with melodious
and charming maternal anger.
We'll laugh in secret about this,
biting the edge of the warm vicuña
quilts—and don't do that to me!

Fumes from thatched huts—ah bunch
of scamps!—rising early to play
with bluish, bluing kites,
and, copping grinders and stones, they'd
pungently incite us with cow dung,
                    to draw us out
into the baby air that doesn't know its letters yet,
to struggle over the strings.

   Another time you'll want to pasture
between your omphaloid hollows
                    avid caverns,
               ninth months,
                    my drop curtains.
Or you'll want to accompany the elders
to unplug the tap of a dusk,
so that all the water slipping away by night
surges during the day.

   And you arrive dying of laughter,
and at the musical lunch,
popped roasted corn, flour with lard,
with lard,
you tease the decubital peasant
who today once again forgets to say buenos días,
those días of his, buenos with the b of barrens,
that keep backfiring for the poor guy
through the dentilabial
v that holds vigil in him.

[CE]

LV

   Samain would say[40] the air is calm and of a contained sadness.

   Vallejo says today Death is soldering each limit to each strand of lost
hair, from the bucket of a frontal, where there is seaweed, lemon balm
that sings of divine seedbeds on the alert, and antiseptic verses with no
master.

Wednesday, with dethroned fingernails peels back its own nails
of camphor, and instills through dusty sieves, echoes, turned pages,
incrustations,
                    the buzzings of flies
when there is corpse, and clear spongy suffering and some hope.

A sickman reads La Prensa,[41] as if at a lectern.
Another is laid out palpitating, longirostrine,
about to be buried.
And I notice a shoulder is still in place
and almost stays ready behind this one, the other side.

The afternoon has now passed sixteen times through the
empatrolled[42] subsoil,
and is almost absent
in the yellow wood number
on the bed that's been unoccupied for so long
                    over there . . . .
                                        in front.

                                                    [CE]

LVI

Every day I wake blindly
to work so as to live; and I eat breakfast,
not tasting a bit of it, every morning.
Not knowing if I have achieved, or even more, never,
something that explodes with flavor
or is merely the heart and that returned now, will lament
to what extent this is the least.

A child could grow up bloated with happiness
                    oh dawns,
before the grief of parents unable to avoid
wrenching us from their dreams of love into this world;
before those who, like God, from so much love
understood themselves even as creators
and loved us even to doing us harm.

Fringes of a invisible weft,
teeth that ferret from neuter emotion,
pillars
free of base and crown,
in the great mouth that has lost speech.

Match after match in the blackness,
tear after tear in clouds of dust.

[CE]

LVII

The highest points craterized, the points
of love, of capital being, I drink, I fast, I absorb heroin for the sorrow, for the languid
throb and against all correction.

Can I say that they've betrayed us? No.
That all were good? Neither. But
good will exists there, no doubt,
and above all, being so.

And so what who loves himself so! I seek myself
in my own design which was to be a work
of mine, in vain: nothing managed to be free.

And yet, who pushes me.
I bet I don't dare shut the fifth window.
And the role of loving oneself and persisting, close to the
hours and to what is undue.

And this and that.

[CE]

LVIII

In the cell, in what's solid, the
corners are huddling too.

I straighten up the nudes that're crumpling,
doubling over, stripshredding.[43]

I dismount the panting horse, snorting
lines of slaps and horizons;
lathered foot against three hoofs.
And I help him along: Move, animal!

Less could be taken, always less, from what
I'm obliged to distribute,
in the cell, in what's liquid.

The prison mate used to eat wheat
from the hills, with my spoon,
when, at my parents' table, a child,
I'd fall asleep chewing.

I whisper to the other:
Come back, go out by the other corner;
hurry up . . . hurry . . . hasten!

And unnoticed I adduce, I plan,
nigh to the broken-down makeshift bed, pious:
Don't think so. That doctor was a healthy man.

I'll no longer laugh when my mother prays
in childhood and on Sunday, at four o'clock
in the morning, for travelers,
the imprisoned,
the sick
and the poor.

In the sheepfold of children, I'll no longer aim
punches at anyone, who, afterward,
still bleeding, might whimper: Next Saturday
I'll give you some of my lunch meat, but
don't hit me!
Now I won't tell him OK.

In the cell, in the gas boundless
until balling in condensation,
who's stumbling outside?

[CE]

LXI

Tonight I get down from my horse,
before the door of the house, where
I said farewell with the cock's crowing.
It is shut and no one responds.

The stone bench on which mama gave birth
to my older brother, so he could saddle
backs I had ridden bare,
through lanes, past hedges, a village boy;
the bench on which I left my heartsick childhood
yellowing in the sun . . . And this mourning
that frames the portal?

God in alien peace,
the beast sneezes, as if calling too;
noses about, prodding the cobbles. Then doubts,
whinnies,
his ears all ears.

Papa must be up praying, and perhaps
he will think I am late.
My sisters, humming their simple,
bubblish[44] illusions,
preparing for the approaching holy day,
and now it's almost here.
I wait, I wait, my heart
an egg in its moment, that gets blocked.

Large family that we left
not long ago, no one awake now, and not even a candle
placed on the altar so that we might return.

I call again, and nothing.
We fall silent and begin to sob, and the animal
whinnies, keeps on whinnying.

They're all sleeping forever,
and so nicely, that at last
my horse dead-tired starts nodding
in his turn, and half-asleep, with each pardon, says
it's all right, everything is quite all right.

[CE]

From *Trilce* 67

LXIII

    Dawn cracks raining. Well combed
the morning pours forth its fine hair.
Melancholy's bound;
and on the Hindu-furnished ill-paved oxident,[45]
it veers, destiny hardly settles down.

    Heavens of puna disheartened
by great love, heavens of platinum, dizmal[46]
with impossible.

    The sheepfold chews its cud
and is underscored by an Andean whinny.

    I remember myself. But the wind staves
suffice, the rudders so still
until becoming one,
and the tedium cricket and unbreakable gibbous elbow.

    Morning suffices with free natty manes
of precious, highland tar,
when I leave to look for eleven
and it's not but untimely twelve.

[JM]

LXV

    Mother, tomorrow I am going to Santiago,
to dip myself in your blessing and in your tears.
I am taking on my disillusions and the rosy
sore of my pointless tasks.

    Your arch of astonishment will await me,
the tonsured columns of your longings
that exhaust life. The patio will await me,
the downstairs corridor with its tori[47] and festive
pie edgings. My tutorial armchair will await me,
that solid bigjawed piece of dynastic
leather, forever grumbling to the great-great-grandchild
rumps, from strap to strand.

    I am sifting my purest affections.
I am axling[48]—don't you hear the plummet gasping?

          —don't you hear the reveilles champing?[49]
I am molding your love formula
for all the hollows of this ground.
Oh if only tacit volantes were available
for all the most distant ribbons,
for all the most diverse appointments.

    There, there, immortal dead one. There, there.
Under the double arches of your blood, where
one can only pass on tiptoes, even my father
to go through there,
humblest[50] himself until less than half a man,
until being the first child that you had.

    There, there, immortal dead one.
In the colonnade of your bones
which not even sobs can topple,
and in whose side not even Destiny could intrude
even one of his fingers.

    There, there, immortal dead one.
There, there.

                                    [CE]

LXVIII

    We're at the fourteenth of July.
It's five in the evening. It rains all throughout
some third corner of blotting paper.
And more it rains from below aye it does upward.

    The hands two lagoons come forth
from ten at bottom,
of a murky Tuesday that for six days
has been frozen in lachrymals.

    A week was beheaded
with the sharpest of drops; all's been done
to make miserable swell
in great railingless bar. Now we are
okay, with this rain that cleanses
and pleases and graces us with subtlety.

We have at gross weight trudged, and, in sole
                    defiance,
our animal pureness whitened.
And we ask for eternal love,
for the absolute encounter,
for all that passes from here to there.

    And we respond from where mine are not yours
from what an hour the coda, being carried on,
sustains and isn't sustained. (Net.)

    And it was black, hung in a corner,
without even uttering an iota, my paletot,
a
t
f
u
l
m
a
s
T[51]

[JM]

LXX

    Everyone smiles at the nonchalance with which I sub-
merge[52] to the bottom, cellular from foods aplenty and drinks ga-
lore.

    Do suns get on bereft of viands? Or is there someone
who feeds them grain as if to birdies? Frankly,
I hardly know anything about this.

    Oh stone, benefactory pillow at last. Let us the living
love the living, since it will for good dead things be
afterwards. So much must we love them
and pull them in, so much. Let us love the actuali-
ties, for we shan't ever again be as we are.
For there aren't interim Barrancos[53] in essential
cemeteries.

The payload goes in the upsurge, beak first. The journey clouts
us in the core, with its dozen stairways, scal-
ed, in the horizontifying[54] frustration of feet, in dread-
ed empty sandals.

And we shudder to step forth, for we know not whether
we knock into the pendulum, or already have crossed it.

[JM]

LXXI

Coils the sun does in your cool hand
and cautiously spills into your curiosity.

Quiet you. Nobody knows you're in me
all throughout. Quiet you. Don't breathe. Nobody
knows my succulent snack of unity:
legion of obscurities, Amazonians in tears.

Off go the wagons whippt[55] through evening,
and between them mine, facing back, at the fatal
reins of your fingers.
Your hands and my hands reciprocal offer
poles on guard, practicing depressions,
and temples and sides.

You too be quiet, Oh future twilight, pull yourself
together to laugh inwardly, at this rut
of red pepper gamecocks,
blinged out with cupola
blades, with cerulean widow halves.
Rejoice, orphan; drink your cup of water
at the bodega on any corner whatsoever.

[JM]

LXXIII

Another ay has triumphed. The truth is there.
And whoever acts that way, won't he know
how to train excellent dijitigrades
for the mouse Yes . . . No . . . ?

Another ay has triumphed and against no one.
Oh exosmosis of water chemically pure.
Ah my southerns. Oh our divines.
                    I have the right then
to be green and happy and dangerous, and to be
the chisel, what the coarse colossal block fears;
to make a false step and to my laughter.

Absurdity, only you are pure.
Absurdity, only facing you does this excess sweat golden pleasure.

[CE]

LXXV

You are dead.

What a weird way of being dead.
Anybody would say you're not. But, really, you be
Dead.

You voidly float behind that membrane
which tick-tocking from zenith to nadir
journeys from sunset to sunset, throbbing before
the music box of a painless wound. I tell you,
then, that life is in the mirror, and that you are
Death. The original.

While the wave goes, while the wave comes,
with impunity one is dead. Only when
the waters burst upon the facing shores
curling and churning do you then transfigure
and, believing you're dying, sense the sixth chord
that's no longer yours.

You are dead, not having ever lived before.
Anyone would say, not being now, in another time
you were. But, really, you are the cadavers
come from a life that never was. Sad fate.
Not having been anything but dead, always.
To be a dry leaf, without ever having been green.
Orphanhood of orphanhoods.

And nonetheless the dead are not, cannot be
cadavers of a life they've not yet lived.
They died of life.

You are dead.

[SJL]

LXXVII

It hails *so* hard, as if to remind me
and increase the pearls
I've gathered from the same snout
of every tempest.

May this rain not dry up.
At least allow me now
to fall for her, or be buried
soaked in water
that will surge from all the fires.

How far until this rain will hit me?
I'm afraid of being left with one side dry;
afraid that she may leave, without having tasted me
in the droughts of incredible vocal chords,
through which,
to reach harmony,
one must always arise—never descend!
Don't we in fact arise downward?

Rain, sing, on the coast still without a sea!

[JM]

FROM *Scales*

NORTHWESTERN WALL

Penumbra.

The only cell mate left now sits down to eat in front of the horizontal window of our dungeon, a barred little opening in the upper half of the cell door, where he takes refuge in the orange anguish of evening's full bloom.

I turn toward him.

"Shall we?"

"Let's. Please be served," he replies with a smile.

While looking at his bullish profile thrown against the folded bright red leaf of the open window, my gaze locks onto an almost aerial spider, seemingly made of smoke, emerging in absolute stillness on the wood, a half meter above the man's head. The westerly wind wafts an ocher glitter upon the tranquil weaver, as if to bring her into focus. She has undoubtedly felt the warm solar breeze, as she stretches out some of her limbs with drowsy lackadaisical languor, and then she starts taking fitful downward steps, until stopping flush with the man's beard so that, while he chews, it appears as if he were gobbling up the tiny beast.

And as he finally finishes eating, the animal flanks out in a sprint for the door hinges, just as the man swings the door shut. Something has happened. I go up and reopen the door, examine the hinges, and find the body of the poor wanderer, mashed and transformed into scattered filaments.

"You've killed a spider," I say to him with evident enthusiasm.

"Have I?" he asks with indifference. "All the better: this place is roach motel anyway."

And as if nothing had happened, he begins to pace the length of the cell, picking food from his teeth and spitting it out profusely.

Justice! This idea comes to mind.

I know that this man has just harmed an anonymous, yet existing and real being. And the spider, on the other hand, has inadvertently pushed the poor innocent man to the point of murder. Don't both, then, deserve to be judged for their actions? Or is such a means of justice foreign to the human spirit? When is man the judge of man?

He who's unaware of the temperature, the sufficiency with which he finishes one thing or begins another; who's unaware of the nuance by which what's white is white and the degree to which it's white; who is and will be unaware of the moment when we begin to live, the moment when we begin to die, when we cry, when we laugh, when sound limits with form the lips that say: *I* . . . he won't figure out, nor can he, the degree of truth to which a fact qualified as criminal IS criminal. He who's unaware of the instant when 1 stops being 1 and starts being 2, who even within mathematical exactitude lacks wisdom's unconquerable plenitude—how could he ever manage to establish the fundamental and criminal moment of any action, through the warp of fate's whims, within the great powered gears that move beings and things in front of things and beings?

Justice is not a human function. Nor can it be. Justice operates tacitly, deeper inside than all insides, in the courts and the prisoners. Justice— listen up, men of all latitudes!—is carried out in subterranean harmony, on the flipside of the senses and in the cerebral swings of street fairs. Hone down your hearts! Justice passes beneath every surface, behind everyone's backs. Lend subtler an ear to its fatal drumroll, and you will hear its only vigrant cymbal that, by the power of love, is smashed in two—its cymbal as vague and uncertain as the traces of the crime itself or of what is generally called crime.

Only in this way is justice infallible: when it's not seen through the tinted enticements of the judges, when it's not written in the codes, when there's no longer a need for jails or guards.

Therefore, justice is not, cannot be, carried out by men, not even before the eyes of men.

No one is ever a criminal. Or we all are always criminals. [JM]

ANTARCTIC WALL

Desire magnetizes us.

She, at my side, in the bedchamber, charges and charges the mysterious circuit with volts by the thousand per second. There's an unimaginable drop that drips and pools and burns wherever I turn, trying to escape; a drop that's nowhere and trembles, sings, cries, wails through all five senses and my heart, and then finally flows like electrical current to the tips . . .

I quickly sit up, leap toward the fallen woman, who kindly confided in me her warm welcome, and then . . . a warm drop that splashes on my skin, separates me from my sister, who stays back in the environs of the dream that I wake up from overwhelmed.

Gasping for breath, confused, bullish my temples, it pierces my heart with pain.

Two . . . Three . . . Foooooouuuuur! . . . Only the angry guards' voices reach the dungeon's sepulchral gloom. The cathedral clock tolls two in the morning.

Why with my sister? Why with her, who now must surely be sleeping in a mild innocent calm? Why did it have to be her?

I roll over in bed. Strange perspectives resume their movements in the darkness, fuzzy specters. I hear the rain begin to fall.

Why with my sister? I think I'm running a fever. I'm suffering.

And now I hear my own breathing rise, fall, collide, and graze the pillow. Is it my breathing? Some cartilaginous breath of an invisible death appears to mix with mine, descending perhaps from a pulmonary system of Suns and then, with its sweaty self, permeating the first of the earth's pores. And that old-timer who suddenly stops yelling? What's he going to do? Ah! He turns toward a young Franciscan who rises up from his imperial dawn-ward genuflection, as if facing a crumbling altar. The old man walks up to him and, with an angry expression, tears off the wide-cut sacred habit that the priest was wearing . . . I turn my head. Ah, immense palpitating cone of darkness, at whose distant nebulous vortex, at whose final frontier, a naked woman in the living flesh is glowing! . . .

Oh woman! Let us love each other to the nth degree. Let us be scorched by every crucible. Let us be cleansed by all the storms. Let us unite in body and soul. Let us love each other absolutely, through every death.

Oh flesh of my flesh and bone of my bone! Do you recall those budding passions, those bandaged anxieties of our eight years? Remember that spring morning warmed by the sierra's spontaneous sun, when, having played so late the night before, we, in our shared bed sleeping late, awoke in each other's arms and, after realizing that we were alone, shared a nude kiss on our virgin lips. Remember that your flesh and mine were mag-netized, our friction course and blind; and also remember that we were thenceforth still good and pure and that ours was the impalpable pure-ness of animals . . .

Oneself the end of our departure; oneself the alvine equator of our mis-chief, you in the front, I behind. We have loved each other—don't you re-call?—when the minute had yet to become a lifetime. In the world we've come to see ourselves through lovers' eyes after the bleakness of an ab-sence.

Oh, Lady Supreme! Wipe from your bona fide eyes the blinding dust kicked up on winding roads and tergiversate your concrete climb. And rise higher even still! Be the complete woman, the entire chord! Oh flesh of my flesh and bone of my bone! . . . Oh my sister, my wife, my mother!

And I break down into tears until dawn.

"Good morning, Mr. Mayor . . ." [JM]

EAST WALL

Wait. I can't figure out how to get this going. Wait. Now.

Aim here, right where the tip of my left hand's longest finger is touching. Don't back down, don't be afraid. Just aim here. Now!

Vrrrooommm . . .

So, now a projectile bathes in the waters of the four pumps that have just combusted in my chest. The recoil sears and burns. Thirst ominously saharangues my throat and devours my gut . . .

Yet I hear three lonely sounds bombard and completely dominate two ports and their three-boned piers that, oh, are always just a hair shy of sinking. I perceive those tragic and thricey sounds quite distinctively, almost one by one.

The first comes from one errant strand of hair still mincing upon the thick tongue of night.

The second sound is a bud, an eternal self-revelation, an endless announcement. It's a herald. It constantly circles a tender ovoid waist like a hand carved from a shell. Thus it always appears and can never blow past the last wind. So it's ever-beginning, the sound of all humanity.

The final sound. The one final sound watches over with precision, pedestyled in the clearing of those communicating vessels. In this final blow of harmony, thirst dissipates (one of threat's little windows slams shut) and acquires a different sensation, becomes what it was not, until it reaches the counter key.

And the projectile in the blood of my stranded heart
used to sing
to make plumes
in vain has forced its way in order to put me to death.

"And so?"

"This is the one I've got to sign twice, Mr. Scribe. Is it in duplicate?"

[SJL/JM]

On this swelter of a night, one of my inmates tells me the story of his trial. He finishes the abstruse narration, stretches out on his soiled cot, and hums a *yaraví*.

I now possess the truth of his conduct.

This man is a criminal. His mask of innocence transparent, the criminal has been arrested. Through the course of his prattle, my soul has followed him, step-by-step, through his unlawful act. Between us we've festered through days and nights of idleness, garnished with arrogant alcohol, chuckling dentures, aching guitar strings, razor blades on guard, drunken bouts of sweat and disgust. We've disputed with the defenseless companion who cries for her man to quit drinking, to work and earn some dough for the kids, so that God sees . . . And then, with our dried-out guts thriving on booze, each dawn we'd take the brutal plunge into the street, slamming the door on the groaning offspring's own fat lips.

I've suffered with him the fleeting calls to dignity and regeneration; I've confronted both sides of the coin; I've doubted and even felt the crunching of the heel that insinuated a one-eighty. One morning this barfly, in great pain, thought about going on the straight and narrow, left to look for a job, then ran into an old friend and took a turn for the worse. In the end, he stole out of necessity. And now, given what his legal representative is saying, his sentence isn't far off.

This man is a thief.

But he's also a killer.

One night, during the most boisterous of benders, he strolls through bloody intersections of the ghetto, while at the same time, an old-timer who, then holding down an honest job, is on his way home from work. Walking up next to him, the drinker takes him by the arm, invites him in, gets him to share in his adventure, and the upright man accepts, though much to his regret.

Fording the earth ten elbows deep, they return after midnight through dark allies. The irreproachable man with alarming diphthongs brings the drinker to a halt; he takes him by the side, stands him up, and berates the shameless scum, "Come on! This is what you like. You don't have a choice anymore."

And suddenly a sentence bursts forth in flames and emerges from the darkness: "Hold it right there! . . ."

An assault of anonymous knives. Botched, the target of the attack, the blade doesn't pierce the flesh of the drunkard but mistakenly and fatally punctures the good worker.

Therefore, this man is also a killer. But the courts, naturally, do not suspect, nor will they ever, the third hand of the thief.

Meanwhile, he keeps doing pushups on that suspicious cot of his, while humming his sad yaraví.   [JM]

WINDOWSILL

I'm pasty. While I comb my hair, in the mirror I notice that the bags under my eyes have grown even blacker and bluer and that the hue of my shaved face's angular copper has scathingly jaundiced.

I'm old. I wipe my brow with the towel, and a horizontal stripe highlighted by abundant pleats is highlighted therein like a cue of an implacable funeral march . . . I'm dead.

My cell mate has gotten up early and is making the dark tea that we customarily take in the morning, with the stale bread of a new hopeless sun.

We sit down afterward at the bare table, where the melancholic breakfast steams, within two teacups that have no saucers. And these cups afoot, white as ever and so clean, this bread still warm on the small rolled tablecloth from Damascus, all this domestic morning-time aroma reminds me of my family's house, my childhood in Santiago de Chuco, those breakfasts of eight to ten siblings from the oldest to youngest, like the reeds of an *antara*,[56] among them me, the last of all, glued to the side of the dining room table, with the flowing hair that one of my younger sisters has just endeavored to comb, in my left hand a whole piece of sweet roll—it had to be whole!—and with my right hand's rosy fingers, crouching down to hide the sugar granule by granule . . .

Ah! The little boy that took the sugar from his good mother, who, after finding our hideout, sat down to snuggle with us, putting in timeout the couple of fleabags up to no good.

"My poor little son. Some day he won't have anyone to hide the sugar from, when he's all grown up, and his mother has died."

And the first meal of the day was coming to an end, while mother's two blazing tears were soaking her Nazarene braids.   [JM]

Hackneyed rockrose of July; wind belted around each of the great grain's one-armed petioles that gravitate inside it; dead lust upon omphaloid hillsides of the summertime sierra. Wait. This can't be. Let's sing again. Oh, how sweet a dream!

My horse trotted that away. After being out of town for eleven years, that day I finally drew near to Santiago, where I was born. The poor irrational thing pushed on, and from all my being to my tired fingers that held onto the reins, through the attentive ears of the quadruped and returning though the trotting of the hooves that mimicked a stationary jig, in the mysterious score-keeping trial of the road and the unknown, I wept for my mother who, dead for two years now, would no longer be waiting the return of her wandering wayward son. The whole region, its mild climate, the color of harvest in the lime afternoon, and also a farmhouse around here that recognized my soul, stirred up in me a nostalgic filial ecstasy, and my lips grew almost completely chapped from suckling the eternal nipple, the ever lactating nipple of my mother; yes, ever lactating, even beyond death.

As a boy I had surely passed by there with her. Yes. For sure. But, no. It wasn't with me that she'd crossed those fields. Back then I was too young. It was with my father—how long ago must that have been! Ah . . . It was also in July, with the Saint James festival not far off. Father and mother rode atop their mules; he in the lead. The royal path. Perhaps my father who had just dodged a crash with a wandering maguey:

"Señora . . . Watch out! . . ."

My poor mother didn't have enough time and was thrown from her saddle onto the stones of the path. They took her back to town on a stretcher. I cried a lot for my mother, and they didn't tell me what had happened. She recovered. The night before the festival, she was cheerful and smiling, no longer in bed, and everything was fine. I didn't even cry for my mother.

But now I was crying more, remembering her as she was sick, laid out, when she loved me more and showed me more affection and also gave me more sweetbread from underneath her cushions and from the nightstand drawer. Now I was crying more, drawing near to Santiago, where I'd only find her dead, buried beneath the ripe fragrant mustard plants of a poor cemetery.

My mother had passed away two years earlier. The news of her death first reached me in Lima, where I also learned that my father and siblings had set out on a trip to a faraway plantation owned by an uncle of ours, to ease the pain, as best one can, of such a terrible loss. The country estate was located in the most remote region on the mountain, on the far side of the Río Marañón. From Santiago I'd head that way, devouring unending trails of precipitous puna and unknown blistering jungles.

My animal suddenly started huffing. Fine dust kicked up abundantly with a gentle breeze, blinding me nearly. A pile of barley. And then, Santiago came into view, on its jagged plateau, with its dark brown rooftops facing the already horizontal sun. And still, toward the east, on the ledge of a brazil-yellow promontory stood the pantheon carved at that hour by the 6:00 p.m. tincture; and I couldn't go any farther, as an atrocious sorrow had seized me.

I reached the town just as night did. I made the last turn, and as I entered the street that my house was on, I saw someone sitting alone on the bench in front of the door. He was alone. Very alone. So much so that, choking on my soul's mystical grief, I was frightened by him. It must've also been due to the almost inert peace with which, stuck by the penumbra's half strength, his silhouette was leaning against the whitewashed face of the wall. A particular bluster of nerves dried my tears. I moved on. From the bench jumped my older brother, Ángel, and he gave me a helpless hug. He'd come from the plantation on business only a few days earlier.

That night, after a frugal meal, we stayed up until dawn. I walked through the rooms, hallways, and patios of the house; even while making a visible effort to skirt that desire of mine to go through our dear ole house, Ángel also seemed to take pleasure in the torture of someone who ventures through the phantasmal domain of life's only past.

During his few days in Santiago, Ángel did not leave home, where, according to him, everything lay just as it was left after Mom's death. He also told me about the state of her health during the days preceding the fatal pain and what her agony was like. Oh, the brotherly embrace scratched at our guts and suctioned out new tears of frozen tenderness and mourning!

"Ah, this bread box, where I used to ask Mom for bread, with big crocodile tears!" And I opened a little door with plain dilapidated panels.

As in all rustic constructions of the Peruvian sierra, where each doorway is almost always accompanied by a bench, alongside the threshold I'd just crossed, there sat the same one from my boyhood, without a doubt, repaired and shined countless times. With the rickety door open, we each took a seat on the bench, and there we lit the sad-eyed lantern that we were carrying. Its firelight went in full gallop onto Ángel's face, which grew more tired from one moment to the next, while night ran its course and we pressed on the wound some more, until it almost seemed transparent. As I noticed his state, I hugged him and, with kisses, covered his severe bearded cheeks that once again got soaked in tears.

A flash in the sky, without any thunder, the kind that comes from far away, during the highland summer, emptied the guts of night. I kept wiping Ángel's eyelids. And neither he nor the lantern, nor the bench, nor anything else was there. I couldn't hear. I felt like I was in a tomb.

Then I could see again: my brother, the lantern, the bench. But I thought I saw in Ángel a refreshed complexion now, mild and perhaps I was mistaken—let's say he looked as though he'd overcome his previous affliction and gauntness. Perhaps, I repeat, this was a visual error on my part, since such a change is inconceivable.

"I feel like I still see her," I continued weeping, "without the poor thing knowing what to do about that gift, she keeps scolding me, 'I caught you, you little liar; you pretend you're crying when you're secretly laughing!' And she kissed me more than all of you, since I was the youngest!"

After the vigil, Ángel again seemed broken up and, as before the flash of light, shockingly emaciated. I'd surely suffered a momentary loss of sight, brought on by the strike of the meteor's light, when I found in his physiognomy relief and freshness that, naturally, couldn't have been there.

The dawn had yet to crack the following day when I mounted up and left for the plantation, bidding farewell to Ángel, who'd stay a few days more for the matters that had motivated his arrival to Santiago.

With the first leg of the journey behind me, an inexplicable event took place. At an inn I was leaning back, resting on a bench, when from the hut an old woman suddenly stared at me with an alarmed expression.

"What happened to your face?" she asked out of pity. "Good God! It's covered in blood . . ."

I jumped up from the bench and, in the mirror, confirmed that my face was speckled with dried bloodstains. A giant shudder gripped me, and I wanted to run from myself. Blood? From where? I had touched my face to Ángel's, who was crying . . . But . . . No. No. Where was that blood from? One will understand the terror and shock that knotted my chest with a thousand thoughts. Nothing is comparable with that jolt of my heart. There are no words to express it now, nor will there ever be. And today, in the solitary room where I write, there's that aged blood and my face smeared with it and the old woman from the wayside inn and the journey and my brother who cries and whom I don't kiss and my dead mother and . . .

. . . After tracing the lines on my face, I fled onto the balcony, panting in a cold sweat. So frightening and overwhelming is the memory of that scarlet mystery . . .

Oh nightmarish night in that unforgettable shack, where the image of my mother, between struggles of strange endless threads that later snapped just from being seen, became the image of Ángel, who wept glowing rubies, for ever and never![57]

I kept to the road, and, finally, after a week on horseback through the high peaks, temperate mountain terrain, and crossing the Marañón, one morning I reached the outskirts of the plantation. The overcast space intermittently reverberated with claps of thunder and fleeting sun showers.

I dismounted alongside the post of the gate to the house near the driveway. Some dogs barked in the mild sad calm of the sooty mountain. After so long I now returned to that solitary mansion, buried deep in the ravines of the jungle!

Between the garrulous alarm of riled up domesticated birds, a voice that called and contained the mastiffs inside seemed to be strangely whiffed by the weary trembling soliped who several times sneezed, perked his ears forward almost horizontally, and by bucking tried to get the reins out of my hands in an attempt to escape. The enormous door was locked. I knocked on it mechanically. Yet the voice kept trilling from inside the walls, and, as the gigantic doors opened with a frightening creak, that oral doorbell rose over all sixteen of my years and handed me Eternity blade first. Both doors had swung open.

Meditate briefly on this incredible event that breaks the laws of life and death and surpasses all possibility; word of hope and faith between absurdity and infinity, undeniable nebulous disconnect of time and space that brings on tears of unknowable inharmonious harmonies!

My mother appeared and wrapped me in her arms!

"My son," she exclaimed in astonishment. "You're alive? You've come to life? What's this I see before me, Lord Almighty?"

My mother! My mother in body and soul. Alive! And with so much life that today I think I felt in her presence two desolate hailstones of decrepitude suddenly emerge in my nostrils and then fall and weigh on my heart until making me hunch over in senility, as if, by dint of a fantastic trick of fate, my mother had just been born and I, on the other hand, had come from times so remote that I experienced a paternal feeling toward her. Yes. My mother was there. Dressed in unanimous black. Alive. No longer dead. Could it be? No. Impossible. There's no way. That woman wasn't my mother. She couldn't be. And what did she say when she saw me? She thought I was dead . . . ?

"Oh my son!" my mother said, bursting into tears, and she ran to pull me close to her breasts, in that frenzy and with those tears of joy that she would always use to protect me during my arrivals and departures.

I had turned to stone. I saw her wrap her lovely arms around my neck, kiss me avidly, as though she wanted to devour me, and weep her affection that will never again rain down in my guts. She then coarsely took my impassive face between her hands, looked at me head on, asking question after question. A few seconds later, I started to cry too, but without changing my expression or attitude: my tears were pure water that poured from a statue's two pupils.

I finally focused all the diffused lights of my spirit. I took a few steps back and stood before—oh my God!—that maternity that my heart didn't want to receive, that it didn't know, that it feared; I made them appear before the mysterious holiest of whens, till then unbeknown to me, and I let out a mute double-edged scream in her presence, with the same beat of the hammer that comes close and then withdraws from the anvil, the same that the child lets out with his first groan, when he's pulled from his mother's womb, indicating to her that he's going to live in the world and, at once, that he's giving her a signal by which they can recognize each other for centuries on end. And I groaned beside myself.

"Never! Never! My mother died long ago. This can't be . . ."

She sat up, startled by my words, as if she doubted whether it was me. She pulled me in again between her arms, and we both continued to cry tears that no living being has ever cried or will ever cry again.

"Yes," I repeated to her. My mother already died. My brother Ángel knows this too."

And here the bloodstains she'd noticed on my face passed through my mind as signs of another world.

"But my dear son!" she whispered almost effortlessly. "Are you my dead son that I myself saw in the casket? Yes! It's you! I believe in God! Come to my arms! But, what? . . . Can't you see that I'm your mother? Look at me! Look at me! Touch me, my son! What, don't you think it's me?"

I beheld her again, touched her adorable salt-and-pepper head, but nothing. I didn't believe her one bit.

"Yes, I see you," I replied. "I'm touching you, but I don't believe it. Such impossibilities just can't happen."

And I laughed with all my strength!   [JM]

THE RELEASE

Yesterday I was at the Panopticon print shops to correct a set of page proofs.

The shop manager is a convict, a good guy, like all the criminals of the world. Young, smart, very polite, Solís, that's his name, he's whipped together excellent intelligence and told me his story, revealed his complaints, unveiled his pain.

"Out of the five hundred prisoners here," he says, "only as many as a third deserve to be punished like this. The others don't; the others are as or more moral than the judges who sentenced them."

His eyes scope out[58] the trim of who knows what invisible bitter plate. Eternal injustice! One of the workers comes up to me. Tall, broadshouldered, he walks up jubilantly.

"Good afternoon," he says. "How are you?" And he shakes my hand with lively effusion.

I don't recognize him, so I ask him his name.

"You don't remember me? I'm Lozano. We did time together in the Trujillo penitentiary. I was so glad to hear that the court acquitted you."

Just like that. I remember him. Poor guy. He was sentenced to nine years in prison for conspiring in a murder.

The thoughtful man walks away.

"What!" Solís inquires with surprise. "You were in prison too?"

"I was," I reply. "Indeed I was, my friend."

And I in turn explain the circumstances of my imprisonment in Trujillo, charged with frustrated arson, robbery, and sedition . . .

"If you've done time in Trujillo," he says smilingly, "then you ought to have met Jesús Palomino, who's from that department. He drained away twelve years in this prison."

I remember.

"There you go," he adds. "That man was an innocent victim of the poor organization of the justice system." He falls silent for a few moments and, after looking me in the face with a piercing gaze, decisively breaks out, "I'm going to tell you off the cuff what happened to Palomino here."

The afternoon is gray and rainy. Metallic machinery and linotypes painfully hang clanging in the damp, dark air. I turn my eyes and in the distance notice the chubby face of a prisoner who smiles kindly among the black steel bits in movement. He's my worker, the one who's paginating my book. This bastard won't stop smiling. It's as though he's lost the true feeling of his misfortune or has become an idiot.

Solís coughs and, with a toilsome inflection, begins his tale: "Palomino was a good man. It turns out that he was swindled in a cynical, insulting way by a hardened criminal never convicted by the courts, since he was from an upper-class family. Verging on misery, as Palomino was, and as a result of a violent altercation between these two, the unforeseeable occurred: a gunshot, a dead body, the Panopticon. After being locked up in here, the poor man endured sinister nightmares. It was horrendous. Even those of us who used to watch him were forced to suffer his hellish contagion! It was awful! Death would've been better. Yes, indeed. Death would've been better! . . ."

The tranquil narrator wants to weep. He noticeably relives his past with clarity, since his eyes moisten and he has to pause in silence for a moment, so as not to show in his voice that he's started to sob in his soul.

"When I think about it," he adds, "I don't know how Palomino resisted so much. His was a torment beyond words. I don't know through which channels he was informed that someone was plotting to poison him inside the prison and had been doing so even prior to his incarceration. The family of the man he killed prosecuted him far beyond his misfortune. They weren't satisfied with his fifteen-year sentence or with the way it dragged his family into clamorous ruin: they carried their thirst for revenge even lower. And then they would hide behind the cellar doorjambs and between one spore and the next of the lichens that grow on incarcerated fingers, in search of the most secret passageways of the prison; and so they would move around here, with more freedom than before in the light of day for this unjust sentence, and they would flutter their infamous ambushy eyelashes in the air that the prisoner had no choice but to breathe. Being notified of that, Palomino, as you'll imagine, suffered a terrible shock; he knew it and could do nothing from then on to make it disappear. A man of good stature, like him, feared such a death, not for himself, of course, but for her and for them, the innocent offspring skewered with stigma and orphanhood. Hence, the minute-by-minute anxiety and fright in the everyday fight for his life. Ten years had passed like this when I saw him for the first time. In his soul there awoke that tormented, not pity and compassion, but religious and almost inexplicable beatific transformation. He didn't evoke pity. His heart was filled with something perhaps milder and calmer and nearly sweet. When I looked at him, I no longer felt compelled to unlock his shackles or dress the blackish-green wounds that were open at the end of all his ends. I wouldn't have done any of that. In the face of such a plea, such a superhuman attitude of dread, I always wanted to leave him as he was, to march out step-by-step, startled, with pauses, line-by-line, toward the fatal crossroads, toward death under oath, so much has time revealed. Back then Palomino no longer sought help. He only filled his heart with something more vague and ideal, more serene and sweet; and it was pleasant, a merciful pleasure, to let him climb his hill, to let him walk through the hallways in the dark, entering and exiting the cold cells, in his horrendous game of shaky trapezes, agonizingly flying toward fate, with no fixed point for him to catch. With his fleecy red beard and eyes polar algae green, tattered uniform, skittish, abashed, he always seemed to see everything. An obstinate gesture of disbelief bounced off his dreadful just man lips, his vermilion hair, his mended pants and even his handicapped fingers that sought, in the full extent of his prisoner chapel, a safe place to lean and rest, without ever being able to find one. How many times I saw him at death's door! During work one day, he came to the print shop. Silent, pensive, taciturn, Palomino was cleaning some black rubber belts in a corner of the shop, and from time to time, he'd shoot a most watchful glance at his surroundings, making his eyeballs furtively roll, with the visionary air of a nocturnal bird that catches sight of dreadful ghosts. He suddenly jerked back. On repeated occasions I had caught one of his coworkers casting, from one landmark to the next, noticeable expressions and uttering strange words of subtle aversion, perhaps without a reason, on the other side of the shop. Since their intention couldn't have been pleasing to my friend, given the background story I've already mentioned, such behavior caused him to experience an awkward jolt and a sharp stinging sensation that frayed his every nerve. The gratuitous hater, in turn, was surprised when he noticed this and, serenity now lost, poured out a few drops from a glass carafe with rather meaningful clumsiness and alarm; the color and density of the liquid was almost completely enveloped and veiled by a winged spiral of smoke coming from over by the motors. I don't know how to describe where those long mysterious tears ending up falling, but the man who shed them continued rifling through his work tools, each time with more visible alarm until he couldn't possibly have been aware of what he was doing. Palomino observed him without moving, overwhelmed by thought, with his eyes fixed, hanging on that maneuver that caused in him intense expectation and distressing anxiety. Then the worker's hands proceeded to assemble a lead ingot between other bars resting on the workbench. Palomino took his eyes off him and, dumbfounded, absorbed, downcast, he superimposed circles on the wounded fantasy of suspicion, released affinities, discovered more knots, reharnessed fatal intentions and summited sinister staircases . . . Another day a mysterious guest came in off the street. She went up to the typesetter and spoke to him at length: their words were indecipherable with all the noise of the shop. Palomino jumped up, stared at her carefully, studying her from head to toe, pale with fear . . . 'Look, Palomino!' I consoled him. 'Just forget about it; there's no way.' And he, in every response, rested his forehead on his hands, stained from being shut in and abandoned, defeated, powerless. Only a few months after they brought me here, he was the closest, most loyal and righteous friend I had."

Solís becomes visibly emotional and so do I.

"Are you cold?" he asks with sudden tenderness.

For a while the large room has been filled with a dense fog that turns blue in strange veils around the hourglasses of red light. Through the high-reaching windows one can see that it's still raining. It really is quite cold.

Notes dispersed from distant sight-singing, as if from between compacted cotton impregnated by swarfs of ice. It's the penitentiary band rehearsing the Peruvian national anthem. Those notes resound, and in my spirit they exert an unexpected suggestion, to the extent that I almost feel the very lyrics of the song, syllable after syllable, set in, nailed with gigantic spikes into each of the wayward sounds. The notes crisscross, iterate, stamp, squeal, reiterate, and destroy timid bevels.

"Ah, what torture that man endured!" the prisoner exclaims with rising pity. And he continues narrating between ongoing silences, during which he undoubtedly tries to ensnare terrible memories:

"His was an indestructible obsession to keep from falling, consolidated by God knows who. Many people said, 'Palomino is mad.' Mad! Is it possible for someone to be mad who, under normal circumstances, is concerned for his endangered existence? And is it possible for someone to be mad who, suffering the claws of hate, even with the very complicity of the justice system, takes steps to avoid that danger and to try to put an end to it with all his exacerbated might of a man who deems everything possible, based on his own painful experience? Mad? No! Too sane perhaps! With that formidable persuasion over such unquestionably possible consequences, who gave him such an idea? Although Palomino had often exposed the hidden grim wires that, according to him, could inwardly vibrate to the very threat of his existence, it was hard for me to clearly see that danger. 'Because you don't know those wicked men," Palomino grumbled undaunted. After arguing with him all I could, I fell silent. 'They write to me at my house,' he said to me another day, 'and they make me see it all over again; while my release could come soon, they'd pay any sum to keep me from getting out. Yes. Today more than ever, danger is at my side, my friend . . .' And his final words choked me with thrashing sobs. The truth is that, facing Palomino's constant despair, I ended up suffering, at times, and especially as of late, sudden and profound crises of concern for his life, admitting the possibility of some form of even the darkest treachery, and I even verified for myself, arguing with the rest of the inmates, thereby testing, with who knows what kind of unexpected grounds of decisive weight, the sensibility with which Palomino was reasoning. But that's not all. Occasions also arose when it wasn't doubt I was feeling, but an indisputable certainty of the danger, and I myself left him and went to the meeting with new suspicions and vehement warnings of my own, about the horror of what could transpire, and this is exactly what he did when he was calmly standing in some visionary oblivion. I loved him very much, it's true; his situation was of great interest to me, always scared stiff from head to toe; and I tacitly helped him search for the carabids[59] of his nightmare. In the end, I actually investigated the concealed pockets and minor actions of countless inmates and officers at the establishment, in search of the hidden hair of his imminent tragedy . . . all this is true. However, given what I've said, you'll also see that by taking so much interest in Palomino, I slowly became his torturer, one of his own executioners. 'You be careful!' I'd say to him with foreboding anguish. Palomino would jump in place and, trembling, turn in every direction, wanting to escape and not knowing where to go. And then we both felt terrible despair, fenced in by the invulnerable, implacable, absolute, eternal stone walls. Of course, Palomino barely ate. How could he be expected to? He barely drank too. He might not have breathed. In each morsel he saw latent deadly poison. In each drop of water, each atom of the atmosphere, his tenacious scrupulousness nuanced to the brink of hyperesthesia made the most trivial movements of other people seem related to nutrition. One morning, someone at his side was eating a roll. Palomino saw him lifting the piece of stale bread to his lips, and in an energetic expression of repulsion, he spat in his face repeatedly. 'You better always be careful!' I'd repeat more often each day. Two, three, four times a day this alarm would sound between us. I'd let it out, knowing that this way Palomino would take better care of himself and thereby stay further away from the danger. It seemed to me that when I hadn't recently reminded him of the fateful disquiet, he just might forget it and then—woe betide him! . . . Where was Palomino? . . . Thrust forward by my vigilante fraternity, in a snap I made my way to him and whispered in his ear these garbled words, 'You better be careful!' Thus I felt more at ease, since I could be sure that for the next few hours nothing would happen to my friend. One day I repeated this more times than I ever had before. Palomino heard me, and after the ensuing commotion, he surely was thanking me in his mind and heart. But, I must remind you once more: on this road I crossed the limits of love and goodness for Palomino and I turned into his principle torturer—his personal henchman. I started realizing the double meaning of my behavior. 'But,' I said to myself in my conscience, 'be that as it may, an irrevocable command of my soul has invested in me the power to be his guardian, caretaker of his security, and I shall never turn back for anything.' My alarming voice would forever beat alongside his, on his angst-filled nights, as an alarm clock, as a shield, as a defense. Yes. I wouldn't turn back, not for anything. Once, late into the night, I awoke in a sweat, as a result of having felt a mysterious vibrant shock in the middle of a dream. Perhaps an open valve of strife was throwing a bucket of cold water on my chest. I woke up, possessed by immense joy, a winged joy, as though an exhausting weight had suddenly been lifted, or as if a gallows had jumped out of my neck, all busted up. It was a diaphanous, pure, blind joy, I don't know why, and in the darkness it stretched out and fluttered in my heart. I fully woke up, regained consciousness, and my joy reached its end: I'd dreamed that Palomino had been poisoned. By the following day, that dream had overwhelmed me, with increasing palpitations at the crossroads: Death—Life. In reality I felt utterly seized by him. Harsh winds of unnerving fever charged my wrists, temples, and chest. I must've looked sick, no doubt, since my temples and head were heavier than ever and my soul mourned its grave sorrows. In the evening, it fell to Palomino and me to work together at the press. As they do now, the black steel bits were clanging, smacking into one another as if in an argument, scraping against one another. Hell-bent on saving themselves, they were spinning madly and faster than ever. Throughout the entire morning and into the afternoon, that stubborn irreducible dream stayed with me. And, yet, for some reason, I didn't shy away from him. I felt him at my side, laughing and crying in turn, showing me, impulsively, one of his hands, the left one black, the other one white, extremely white, and both always coming together with strange isochronism, at an impeccable terrifying crossroads: Death—Life! Life—Death! Throughout the day (and here I also forget why) not once did the vigilant alert from before reach my lips. Not once. My prior dream seemed to seal my mouth shut to keep from spilling such a word, with its right whitening luminous hand of fleeting, limitless, blue luminosity. Suddenly, Palomino whispered in my ears with a contained explosion of pity and impotence: 'I'm thirsty.' Immediately, driven by my constant obliging fraternity with him, I filled a reddish clay pitcher and brought it for him to drink. He thanked me fondly, clutching the handle of the mug, and he quenched his thirst until he could drink no more . . . And at twilight, when this life of prickly carefulness became more unbearable, when Palomino had drilled holes in his head, on the brink of a breakdown, when a febrile yellowness of an old bone aged yellow placated his astronomically restless face, when even the doctor had declared that our martyr had nothing more than fatigue brought on by an upset stomach, when that excessively peccary uniform was torn to shreds in corrosive agony, even when Palomino had formed his tall ephemeral smile—oh harmony of the Heavens!—with the wrinkles on his forehead, which didn't manage to jump down to his cheeks or to the human sadness of his shoulders; and when, like today, it was raining and foggy in the unreachable open spaces, and a causeless, labored, surly omen worsened down here, at twilight, he approached me and said, with bloody splinters of voice, 'Solís . . . Solís! Now . . . Now they've killed me! . . . Solís . . .' When I saw his two hands holding his stomach, writhing in pain, I felt the blow strike me at the bottom of my heart, the feeling of a roaring fire devouring my innermost recesses. His complaints, barely articulated, as if they didn't want to be perceived by anyone else but me, were floating toward my inside, like flared-up tongues of a flame long contained between the two of us, in the shape of invisible tablets. So surely and with such lively certainty had we mutually awaited that outcome! Yet after feeling as if the asp had filtered through the veins of my own body, a sudden, mysterious satisfaction came over me. A mysterious satisfaction! Yes, indeed!"

At that moment, Solís made a face of enigmatic obfuscation mixed with such deaf intoxication in his gaze that it sent me wobbling in my chair, as during a furious stoning.

"And Palomino didn't wake up the following day," he mysteriously added afterward, hoarse, without provocation, bearing many tons. "So had he been poisoned? And perhaps with the water I gave him to drink? Or had that only been a nervous breakdown? I don't know. They only say that the next day, while I felt obliged to stay in bed during the early hours, due to the overbearing distress from the night before, one of his sons came to inform his father that his pardon had been handed down, but he was nowhere to be found. The administration had replied to him, 'Indeed. The pardon of your father, handed down, he's been released this morning.'"

The narrator had in this a poorly contained expression of torment that drove me to say to him, with thoughtful consternation, "No . . . No . . . Don't start crying!" And, making a subtle parenthesis, Solís again asked me with tenderness as deep as before, "Are you cold?"

"And then?" I interrupt him.

"And then . . . nothing."

After that, Solís falls dead silent. Then, as an afterthought, full of love and bitterness at once, he adds, "But Palomino has always been a good man and my best friend, the most loyal, the kindest. I've loved him so much, taken such great interest in his situation, helped to examine his endangered future. I even ended up investigating the contents of the pockets and deeds of other people. Palomino hasn't come back here, doesn't even remember me. That ungrateful bastard! Can you imagine?"

Again come the sounds of the penitentiary band playing the Peruvian national anthem. Now they are no longer sight-singing. The chorus of the song is played by the entire band in symphony. The notes of that anthem echo, and the prisoner still silent, sunken in deep deliberation, suddenly flicks his eyelids in a lively flutter and cries out with a stunned expression,

"It's the anthem that they're playing! Do you hear it! It's the anthem. But of course! It seems to be making out a phrase: Weee-aaare-frrreee . . ."

And as he hums these notes, he smiles and finally laughs with gleeful absurdity.

Then to the nearby fence he turns his astonished eyes that glow with burning tears. He jumps from his chair and, stretching out his arms, exclaims with jubilation that sends a shiver down to my spine:

"Hi Palomino! . . ."

Someone approaches us through the silent, unmoving, locked gate.

[JM]

WAX

That night we couldn't smoke. All the bodegas in Lima were closed. My friend, who led me through the taciturn mazes of the renowned yellow mansion on Calle Hoyos, where numerous smokers converge, said goodbye to me and, with soul and pituitaries porcelained,[60] he jumped the first streetcar he saw and fled through midnight.

I still felt somewhat woozy from our last drinks. Oh, my bohemia of yore, bronzemongery[61] ever cornered by uneven scales, withdrawn into the shell of dry palates, the circle of my costly human freedom on two sidewalks of reality that lead to three temples of impossible! But you must excuse this venting that still emits a bellicose odor of buckshot smelted into wrinkles.

As I was saying, once I was all alone I still felt drunk, aimlessly traipsing through Chinatown. So much was clearing up in my spirit. Then I realized what was happening to me. Unrest emerged in my left nipple. A carpenter's brace made of a strand of black shiny hair from the head of my long-lost girlfriend. The unrest itched, smarted, shot inside and through me in all directions. So I couldn't sleep. No way around it. I suffered the pain of my stunted joy, its glimmers now engraved on irremediable ironclad sadness were latent in my soul's deepest brackets, as if to tell me ironically, that tomorrow, sure, you got it, another time, swell.

So I craved a smoke. I needed relief from my nervous breakdown. I walked toward Chale's bodega, which happened to be nearby.

With the caution warranted by such a situation, I reached the door, put my ear up to it, nothing. After waiting a moment, I got ready to leave, when I heard someone jump out of bed, scampering barefoot inside. I tried to catch a glimpse, to see if anyone was there. Through the keyhole I managed to discern Chale lighting the room, sitting noticeably disturbed in front of the oil lamp, its pathogenic greenness in a mossy halftone welded to El Chino's layer of face, harangued by visible ire. No one else was there.

Chale's impenetrable appearance made him seem to have just woken up, perhaps from a terrifying nightmare, and I considered my presence importune, deciding to leave, when the Asian man opened one of the desk drawers, captained by some inexorable voice of authority. With a decisive hand he removed a laconic coffer of polished cedar, opened it, and fondled a couple of white objects with his disgusting fingernails. He put them on the edge of the desk. They were two pieces of marble.

Curiosity got the better of me. Two pieces—were they really marble? They were. I don't know why those pieces, at the outset and without my having touched them or clearly seen them up close, traveled though the space and barraged my fingertips, instilling in me the most certain sensation of marble.

El Chino picked them up again, angling egregious, flitting observations so that they wouldn't unscrew certain presumptions about the motive of his watchfulness. He handled and examined them at length in the light. Two pieces of marble.

Then, with his elbows on the table and the pieces still in hand, between his teeth he let out one hell of a monosyllable that barely entered his beady eyes, where El Chino's soul welled up in tears with a mixture of ambition and impotence. Again he opened the box perhaps out of an old determination that he now relived for the hundredth time, taking out several steel pieces, and with these he began to work on his cabalist marble pieces.

Certain presumptions, I was saying, jumped out in front of me. Indeed. I had met Chale two years prior. The Mongol was a gambler. And as a gambler he was famous in Lima; a loser of millions when he was at the table, a winner of treasures when he speaking with peers. So what was the meaning of that tormenting all-nighter, that furious episode of nocturnal artifice? And those two stone fragments? Why two and not one, three or more? Eureka! Two dice! Two dice in the making.

El Chino was working, working from the very vertex of night. His face, in the meantime, also was working out an infinite succession of lines. There were moments when Chale went into a frenzy and tried to break those little objects that were to be rolled on a felt-covered table chasing each other, in search of a random or lucky win, with the sound of one person's two closed fists pounding hard against each other until they emitted sparks.

As for me, I had taken considerable interest in that scene, which I could hardly think of leaving. It seemed to be an old endeavor of patient heroic production. I sharpened my wits, wondering what this ill-destined man was after. To engrave a set of dice. Could that be it?

This much is affirmed about digital maneuvers and secret deviations or willed amendments in the game's shaker. Something similar, I said to myself, comes through this man for sure. And this, because of what he rolled in the end. But what intrigued me most, as one will understand, was the art of the medium and its preparation, which had seemed to demand Chale's complete commitment. This is the correlation that must be preestablished, between the kind of dice and the dynamic possibilities of the hands. Since, if this bilateral type of element was not entirely necessary, then why would El Chino fashion his own dice? Any material kicking around would've worked. But no.

There's no doubt that the dice are made of a specific material, under this weight, with that edgility,[62] hexagonned[63] on this or that untouchable cliff to be bidden farewell by fingertips and then to be shined with that other dimple or almost immaterial coarseness between each frame of the points or between a polyhedral angle and the white exergue on one of the four corresponding faces. Therefore, it's necessary to bear the flair of the random material so that—in this always improvised (and therefore triumphant) point—it is always obedient and docile to human vibrations of the hand that thinks and calculates even in the darkest and blindest of such avatars.

And if not, one simply had to observe the Asian man in his creative, tempestuous task, chisel in hand, picking away, scraping, removing, crumbling, opening up the conditions of harmony and jaggedness between unborn proportions of the die and the unknown powers of his fickle will. At times, he'd momentarily stop working to contemplate the marble, and his depraved face would smile syrup in the glowing light of the lamp. Later, with an easy deep breath, he'd tap it, swapping one tool for another, and give the monstrous dice a practice roll, tenaciously inspect the sides, and patiently ponder.

A few weeks after that night, there were people amid scruffy crowds and others with similar opinions, who spread stupefying unbelievable rumors about amazing events that had recently transpired in the great casinos of Lima. From one morning to the next, the fabulous legends would grow. One evening last winter, at the door to the Palais Concert, an exotic personage whose goatee seemed to be dripping[64] was speaking to a group of gents, who lent him all their ears:

"Chale had something up his sleeve, when he gambled those 10,000 soles. I don't know what, but El Chino possesses a mysterious unverifiable ability to summon when he's at the table. This can't be denied. Remember," that man stressed with sinister gravity, "that the dice El Chino plays with never appear in anyone else's hands. I'm talking about unmistakable facts drawn from my own observations. Those dice have something to them. What it is, I don't know."

One night I was driven by my distress into the hole in the wall where Chale used to gamble. It was an affair for the most ostentatious of duelers at the table, and many people were standing around the table. The crowd's attention, haltered by the ganglionic cloth covered with piles of money, told me that a low pressure system had set in that night. A few acquaintances led me through and encouraged me to place a bet.

There was Chale, at the head of the table, presiding over the session in his impassive, torturous, almighty appearance, two vertical straps around his neck, from the stumpy parietal bones of a bare hide to the livid bars of his clavicles, his mouth deceitfully forged in two taut pieces of greed that would never open in laughter out of fear of being stripped bare naked, his heroic shirt rolled up to his elbows. The pulse of life beat in him over and over, searching for the doors of the hands to escape from such a miserable body. Nauseating lividness on his predatory cheekbones.

He seemed to have lost the faculty of speech. Signs. Barely articulated adverbs. Arrested interjections. Oh, how the bronchial wheezing of the walking and living dead sometimes burns in each of us!

I decided to observe El Chino's minutest psychological and mechanical ripples as discreetly and meticulously as I could.

The clock struck one in the morning.

Someone placed a bet of 1,000 soles in the hands of fate. The air popped like hot water pierced by the first bubble of the ebullition. And now if I wanted to describe the appearance of the surrounding faces in those seconds of scanning, I'd say that they all oozed out of themselves, scrubbed and squeezed along with Chale's set of dice, lighting on fire and standing there in a line, until they needed and wanted to extract a miraculous ninth face on each die, as if it were the weary grin of Fate herself. Chale violently rolled the dice, like a pair of sparking embers, and he groaned a terrific hyenic obscenity that made its way across the room like dead flesh.

I touched my body as though I'd been looking for myself, and I realized that I was there, shaking in awe. What had El Chino felt? Why did he roll the dice like that, as if they had been burning or cutting his hands? Had the spirit of all those gamblers—naturally always against him—managed to do him harm, before a bet as lofty as this?

While the dice were released upon the emerald cloth, through my mind flashed the two pieces of marble I saw Chale engraving on that now distant night. These dice I saw before me certainly came from the nascent gems of yore, for I noticed they were of a whitened and translucent marble on the edges and of a firm almost metallic glow in the center. Beautiful cubes of God!

After a brief hesitation, El Chino picked up the dice again and continued to play, not without a certain convalescing spasm in his temples, which may have been perceived only by me. He threw them again, shuffled, threw them a second time, a third, fourth, fifth, sixth, seventh, eighth time . . . The ninth landed: a five and a six.

Everyone seemed to dangle from a pillory and come back to life. Everyone became human again. Someone asked for a cigarette. Other people coughed. Chale paid 2,500 soles. I let out a sigh, swallowed my spit; the heat was stifling.

New bets were being made, and the tragic dispute of luck verses luck carried on.

I noticed the loss Chale just suffered didn't completely disturb him, a circumstance that cast an even greater shadow of mystery on the motive behind his previous unusual rapture of anger that, in view of the foregoing, couldn't be attributed to any bright nervous flash, since it was groundless and undermined my spirit's growing deliberations over El Chino's possible knowledge with currents or powers beyond concrete facts and perceivable reality. Just how far, in effect, could Chale get fate to side with him by using some infallible wise technique when he was rolling the dice?

In the first game that followed that other one with the 2,500 sol bet, the stakes were the same. Many other people joined in with bets lower than 500. And the combative ambiance around the banker waxed utterly hostile.

The dice jumped out of El Chino's right hand, together, at once, donned with the same thrust forward. With a measuring instrument that could register the most infinitesimal rigorous human equations of action in unnamable numerals, the absolute mathematic simultaneity with which both marbles were released could've been affirmed. And I'd swear that, while sounding the headlong relation that arose between those two dice at the start of their flight, that which is most permanent, most alive, the strongest, most unchanging and eternal in my being converged—all the powers of the physical dimensions fused—and this I could feel in the truth of my spirit during the material departure of those two flights, at the same time, unanimously.

Chale had thrown the dice while squeezing his entire sculpture into an anatomical deviation so rare and singular that it clouded my already-influenced sensibility. One might say at that very moment, the gambler had sterilized his animal nature, subordinating it to a single thought and desire while taking his turn.

In effect, how can one describe such a movement of his boney sides, grinding against each other, over the blare of a silence standing in suspense between the two pebbles of the march, such a rhythm of the shoulder blades being transfigured, brooding under truncated wings that suddenly sprout out, before the blindness of all the gamblers who perceived none of this and who left me at such a spectacle that punished me square in the heart! . . . And that unmoving confluence of El Chino's right shoulder was waiting for his forehead to finish gaining the rest of its arc, which the intuition and mental calculation of forces, distances, obstacles, accelerants, and even the maximum intervention of a second human authority were unfolding, shaking, adjusting from the highest point of man's soothsaying will to the bordering hills of divine omnipotence . . . And that pallid, wiry, neurotic wrist, as if casting a spell, was almost diaphanized by the light that seemed to carry and transmit the dice in vertigo, which were waiting for it in the basin of his hand, jumping around, hydrogenic, palpitating, warmed, soft, submissive, perhaps even transubstantiated in two pieces of wax that came to a halt only on the farthest point of the table, as was secretly required, smashing down on the two sides that pleased the gambler . . . Chale's whole presence and the entire atmosphere of extraordinary, unavoidable sovereignty that arose in the room right then and there had sucked me in too, like an atom in the middle of a solar fire at noon.

The dice were flying or, rather, running and stumbling over each other, skating, isochronally leaping at times, with the stabbing buzz of the snares that, in a stone drumroll, played a march of the irreversible, despite even

God himself, before the poor faces of that salon, more solemn and congregated than at church when the consecrated host is raised . . .

Along a trembling grayish line each die hobbled as it rolled. One of these lines began to thicken, started to unfold in stains some whiter than others; it then painted 2 black dots, then 6, 4, 3, 3, and finally stopped on the 5. The other marble—oh, the sides and the back, the man and the front of the gambler!—the other marble—oh, the simultaneous departure of the dice!—the other marble advanced three finger-lengths more than the first and, in a similar process of evolution toward the unsuspected goal, also showed 5 carbon dots on the table. A winner!

With the serenity of someone who reads an enigma that long ago was familiar, El Chino placed the 5,000 soles from the bet in his bag.

"This is madness!" someone shouted. "The highest stakes always go to Chale. He's unbeatable."

El Chino, I repeated for myself, undoubtedly dominates the dice that he himself manufactured, and in addition to this, since he's the owner and master of the most indecipherable designs of fate, they obey him.

The most powerful gamblers seemed to grow angry and grumble at Chale in the wake of the last game. The entire room rippled in a spasm of spite, and the muzzled protest of that crowd, whipped by fate's invincible shadow incarnated in the fascinating figure of Chale, was on the brink of becoming a bloodbath. One single great misfortune can do more than millions of various minor triumphs, and it allures and binds them in its hurricaned guts, until finally anointing them with its incandescent funereal oil. All those men must've felt hurt by El Chino's most recent win, and, had it come to it, they might've stripped the winner of his life. Right about then, even I—nettled by remorse as I recall—even I furiously hated him.

He followed it up with a bet of 10,000 soles. We all trembled in anticipation, out of fear and infinite compassion, as if we were about to witness some heroic feat. The tingling tragedy spread through everyone's skin. Eyes whinnied nearly pouring out grief. Faces straightened violet with uncertainty. Chale tossed his dice. And with this single crack of the whip, two sixes stared up at him. A winner!

I felt someone brush by me and push me aside to get to the edge of the table, nearly breaking my neck with brutal depravity, as if an irresistible deadly force were driving the intruder to such behavior. Those who were next me partook in the same gaping as I.

And instead of grabbing the money he had won, El Chino made it into an unwonted oblivion so that, moving like a spring, he could immediately turn his face back to the new contender. Chale's expression changed. Both men's eyes seemed to collide, like two beaks that feel each other out hovering in the air.

The newcomer was a tall man with proportionate and even harmonious breadth, a lofty air, a large cranium on the sturdy horseshoe of a lower jawbone that reposed in a collected manner constructed with excessive teeth for chewing whole heads and torsos, and the slant of his cheekbones widening downward. Minimal eyes, very sunken, as if they withdrew only to later attack colorless girls in unexpected onslaughts, taking on the appearance of two empty sockets. A toasted complexion, coarse hair, curved and untamable nose, tempestuous forehead. The kind of guy who takes to fighting, to adventure, who's unpredictable, full of suggestions as bewitching as boas. A disturbing mortifying man, despite his goodish well-centered looks. His race? One couldn't tell. That fleeting human presence just may have lacked any ethnicity at all.

He had undeniable traces of worldliness and even appeared to be an irreproachable club member, with his appropriate and distinguished suit and the curious ease of his expressions.

No sooner had this personage assumed a position alongside the table, than all the gas poisoned with booze and greed we breathed in the casino—even that of the last game of 10,000 soles, the largest all night—thinned out and suddenly vanished. What hidden oxygen did that man bring? Had we been able to see the air, it would've looked blue, serene, and peacefully azure. I suddenly snapped back to normality and the light of my awareness, between a cool breath with renewed blood and relief. I felt freed of something. There was a peaceful expression on all the faces. The dominion of Chale and all his spellbinding postures met their end.

However, something over there was being born, something that at first took the shape of curiosity, followed by surprise, and then tingling unrest. And that unrest came forth, without a doubt, from the presentation of the new patron. Yes. For he—I would've affirmed so much with my neck— brought an extraordinary proposal, a mysterious plan.

El Chino was disturbed. Once he noticed the stranger, he didn't look at him face-to-face again. Nothing could get him to. I'm sure that he was frightened by the stranger and that, in him more than in anyone else present, the repulsive deplorable effect that man awakened was far too great to keep hidden. Chale hated him, feared him. That's the word: he feared him. What's more, no one had ever seen this gentleman in the casino. Even Chale didn't know him. This was also the reason why his presence was explosive.

The club member's breathing suddenly grew labored, as if he was hyperventilating. He huffed hard, glared at El Chino, whose downcast expression seemed crushed by that gaze, mutilated, reduced to pitiful ashes, his entire moral character, all his self-confidence from before, all his belligerence triumphing over fate now next to nothing. Chale, woeful as a child caught in the act, shook the dice in his right hand's trembling cupped fingers, wanting to demolish them out of impotence.

The crowd slowly turned its eyes to the outsider, who had yet to utter a word. Silence befell the room.

"How much are your winnings?" the newcomer finally addressed El Chino.

El Chino blinked, making an apocalyptical and ridiculous face of neglect, as if he were about to receive a deadly shot to the face. And turning in to himself, he babbled, without knowing what he was saying.

"That's everything."

The winnings were nearly 50,000 soles.

Mr. X named that sum, removed from his billfold the same amount of money and masterfully placed his bet on the table, to the astonishment of the onlookers. El Chino bit his lips and, still dodging the gaze of his new adversary, began to shake the marble cubes, his cubes. No one else joined in such a monstrously daring bet.

The solitary gambler, absolutely unknown to anyone except for El Chino, removed a revolver from his pocket, stealthily held it against Chale's head, with his finger on the trigger and the barrel aimed at its target. No one, I repeat, no one perceived this Sword of Damocles that remained suspended over El Chino's life. Quite the contrary, everyone saw it dangling over the stranger's fortune, since his loss had been taken for granted. I remembered what, just minutes before, had been whispered through the room:

"The highest stakes always fall to Chale. He's unbeatable."

Was it his good luck? Was it his wisdom? I don't know. But I was the first to foresee El Chino's victory.

He tossed the dice. Oh, the gambler's sides and back, his shoulders and his chest! With optimal eloquence, before my eyes the extraordinary spectacle repeated, the anatomical curvature, the polarization of all the will that tames and subdues, enters and performs the most inextricable plans of fatality. Again, before the creative force of the dice thrower, I was overtaken by a mysterious cataclysm that ruptured all harmony and reason for being of the events, laws, and enigmas in my stupefied brain. Again, that simultaneous release of the dice before the same fortuitous terms of the bet. Again, I opened my eyes, gorging them to verify the luck that was going to grace the great banker.

The dice tumbled and tumbled and tumbled.

The barrel and the trigger and the finger all waited. The stranger didn't look at the dice, he only stared terribly, implacably, at the head of El Chino.

Facing the unnoticed defiance of that revolver against that pair of dice about to paint the number that would submit to the invincible shadow of Fate, incarnated in the figure of Chale, anyone would've said I was there. But no. I wasn't there.

The dice came to a halt. Death and Fate had everyone at wit's end.

Snake eyes!

El Chino began to cry like a child.   [JM]

1

Balta Espinar got out of bed and, rubbing his drowsy eyes, carelessly walked toward the door and headed down the hallway. He approached the column, unhooked the small mirror from the nail, looked at himself, and experienced a sudden shudder. The mirror shattered on the stone floor and a sharp, quiet sound of crystal and tin echoed through the peaceful air of the house.

Balta stood there pallid and trembling. Overwhelmed, he quickly turned around, then in all directions, as through the shudder had been occasioned by his surprise at sensing someone lurking behind him. He found no one. For a long time he stared at the trunk of the camphor tree in the courtyard, and faint strands of blood, clotted by the recent repose, bulged in his exorbitant sclera and, in a sort of mysterious warning, ran down both sides of his frightened eyes. Then Balta looked at the broken mirror near his feet, hesitated for a moment, and picked it up. Again he tried to see his face in it, but the only remnants of glass still fixed to the frame were a few tiny fragments. Over those shiny shards, similar to thorns and the sharpest of swords, Balta passed it over his face repeatedly, splitting into bits and pieces, his nose elongated, his forehead bent sideways, his lips slivers, his ears shooting out in unprecedented flight . . . He gathered a few more pieces. In vain. The entire mirror had been turned to subtle, minute ingots and hyaloid dust, and it would be impossible to put it back together.

When Adelaida, Balta's young wife, returned home, he said to her with the voice of a child who has seen an evil shadow, "You know what? I broke the mirror."

Adelaida looked upset.

"How did you break it? What a shame!"

"I really don't know how it happened . . ."

And Balta turned flush with presentiment.

Evening came. He sat at the dinner table. From his seat, with manly Andean kindness, Balta was looking at the sky, a pink and placid sky of July that canopied the sown fields of the far-reaching countryside with profound variants. On the slope of the orchard appeared the spirited chestnut head of Rayo, Balta's favorite colt that he had made his pet. It looked at him, and the steed rested its equine eyes for a moment on its master, until a hen in the coop disturbed the evening's serious silence by mournfully crowing in fright.

"Balta! Did you hear it?" Adelaida cried out from the kitchen.

"Yeah, I heard it. What a stupid hen. Seems like it was the *'pulucha.'*"[66]

"Jesus! God help me! What will become of us . . ."

And Adelaida burst through the kitchen door, avidly staring toward the side of the chicken coop.

Then Rayo fearfully whinnied and perked up its ear.

"We've got to eat her," Balta said, rising to his feet. "When a hen crows, it's very, very bad luck . . . Before my mother died, one morning, many days before the misfortune, an old fava bean–colored hen we had started crowing."

"And the mirror, Balta? Oh, Lord! What will become of us . . . ?" Adelaida sat down on the other bench, placed both hands on her face, and began to weep. She cried in silence. Her husband was thinking quietly for several minutes.

Happily married until then. Still a young man, he tenderly adored his wife. Pale, angular, with a gaze that was healthy, agrarian, one might say, vegetal, and a lapidary expression in his lively countenance, tall, strong, and always happy, Balta spent his honeymoon full of delicacies, with high expectations and his trust placed in the future of his home. He was a farmer. He was a good country boy, more than 50 percent dark villager from the sticks. Adelaida was a sweet, smiley, teary-eyed *chola*,[67] happy with her recent wifely curve, and pure and loving toward her dear man.

Adelaida, moreover, was a real homemaker. At the rooster's crow she was getting up, almost always without stirring her husband; with the utmost caution, she'd quietly cross herself, offer her morning prayers under her breath, and in the moist light of dawn stabbing through the bars on the windows, she'd walk on tiptoe with her flat-heeled shoes across the bedroom and leave. By the time Balta got out of bed, Adelaida had already gone to fetch water from the stream on the corner with her two large jugs, the tarnished one and the glass one, which would barely fit in the water at the same time. Adelaida had those jugs for so many years! She'd received them as a gift from her maternal grandmother, Magdelena, when Adelaida was a little girl, as thanks for the warmth and impassioned assistance with which she used to keep her company day and night during her ailing and solitary old age. For her part, the elderly donor had received them as a gift from her uncle Samuel, who had purchased them the day that Magdalena, who then was still a young lady, was honored to be admitted into the local faction of the Society of the Sacred Heart, a congregation of high esteem, formed by people of stature in the village.

The jug that Adelaida called the tarnished one, actually, was not very stained; the moniker corresponded to years of use and her penchant for nicknames. The glass jug, on the other hand, possessed a most original and fantastic merit. One day, when these vessels still belonged to the grandmother, Adelaida, who was barely six years old, went to the well with the glass jug to get some water. It was very clear in her memory. She couldn't carry the two jugs at once, on account of her small size, and she'd fallen over with them. Her silky white lapdog, Picaflor, had followed her. Suddenly, while she had dunked the jug deep into the water behind the sluice-gate, a pack of dogs in heat walked by. Picaflor got tangled up with them and ran off until she disappeared around the next corner, in spite of Adelaida's appeals and admonitions. When she returned, the inflamed animal was panting and growling. When the dog approached the little girl, she seemed to grow even more irritated, began to furiously scrape the ground with her hind paws, and showed her sharp fangs and red gums, growling through the corners and contractions of her rancorous mask. She barked, growing ever angrier. Adelaida called to her, "Picaflor! Down . . . Down . . . Picaflor!" And that ingrate of a dog kept panting and seething, standing on a stone, about to bite; she kept sniffing the ground, searching, missing something, with loving earnest. Then she turned her threatening snout to Adelaida, and there were even moments in which she'd jump up and sink her teeth into the dress of the girl, who started to cry, clinging to large rocky crags and innocently kicking the rabid beast.

The stream continued to echo in the dark cavern.

Without warning Picaflor flared her nostrils rhythmically, with a mysterious grimace of cordiality in her moist little eyes, the color of dead bile. She suddenly stopped barking, went up to the edge of the sluicegate, stuck her entire head into the murky depths, licked the vague glass figure, and began to wag her tail with maddened delight. She leaped toward Adelaida and, rising on her hind legs, bent her slavish paws, as though she were begging for forgiveness, and licked the little girl's uncovered, toasted arms, with the blind, jubilant affection of an animal that recognizes its master . . .

2

By the time Balta was waking up, Adelaida had already watered the plants and, with the broom that she herself had made with green fragrant *yerba santas*[68] brought that morning from the countryside, had swept, gleaming silver, the two hallways, the front- and backyard as far as the first landing of the terraced garden, and the small room upstairs, as well as the gutter and street in front of the house. She had washed up and when she was about to serve her placid husband a steaming bowl of soup, with delicious dried potatoes, scalloped with slices of perfumed golden rocoto, a couple of womanly drops of water fell from her long black braids.

Adelaida was a true housewife. All day long she'd do her chores, ever busy, incited, matrix, flush, going and coming and even doing the work of men. One day Balta was on the farm, far away. The woman, whose tasks were finished, as is proper to female incumbency, went to the pen and took out Rayo. The horse was happy to come at the rearguard of Adelaida, who tied him to the camphor tree in the yard and quickly brought the sheers. She began shaving him, singing one yaraví after another.

She had a sweet and flowing voice: that contentious and long-suffering voice that, to the oxen, is a guide through wild bulrush and an incentive or admonishment through expansive sown fields; that voice that nigh the torrents and under the arching wooden bridges made of the densest marble edges, lulls to sleep bloody dentate saurians on their slow expeditions into alvine backwaters, and the black and yellow botflies during their roving from petiole to petiole; a voice that grows hoarse and turns into lancing tin in the throat, when that lucuma-colored billy goat, still just a kid, out of a bristling heron panic and with the prickly shape of an incubus, heads out to damage the neighbor's barley field, and you've got to call him with the sharpest of fifes from a good sling's throw[69] away, rubbing up against the one with the green and gold wool sewn as a gift by loving hands, which is why it hurts so much to ruin and end her, a voice that in the basaltic indigo crag across the way has an enchanted sister, eternally traveling and eternally captive . . . That's what Adelaida's voice was like.

Rayo wasn't putting up a fight.

"Tomorrow, Mister, you're gonna behave yourself. Your owner wants to throw the book at you. You should know by now. Lay off, lay off. You'd better look beautiful tomorrow."

The colt stretched out, listening to the insistent woman's sweet voice, exposing the folds of its shiny, strapping, handsome neck.

Adelaida finished the trimming.

"What are you doing?"

Balta arrived, his wife started laughing and, under a blazing halo of virtuous bashfulness, said to him, "Nothing. All through. I've just finished."

"And the only reason I came was to shave that animal, putting off so much other work over there . . . Oh, this woman of mine!"

She laughed even sweeter still, and her husband hugged her, moved, filled with passion.

3

The day the hen crowed, Adelaida was groaning until bedtime. It was a sad day at home. Balta couldn't sleep. He tossed and turned in bed, sunken in dismal thoughts. Since they got married, it was the first disturbance to cloud their happiness. From time to time Adelaida's griping became unbearable.

A strange thing had occurred to Balta when he looked into the mirror: he had seen an unknown face pass before his eyes. Stupor struck his nerves, making him knock over the mirror. After a few seconds, he believed he saw someone in the glass appear behind him, and after looking in every direction, he thought that his sleep-filled eyes must have been playing tricks on him, since he had just gotten up, and so he calmed down. However, now, in the middle of the night, listening to his wife lie awake weeping, the scene of the mirror surged through his mind and mysteriously tormented him. Still, he felt that he should console Adelaida.

"Quit playing, Adelaida," he said. "Crying because the hen crowed! . . . Come on . . . Don't act like a little girl!"

He said this mustering up the courage, since a very sharp needle was prickling the length of his tense veins and stitching one bend to another, one firm quivering taste bud to the next, with a tough black thorn that he had never seen sprout from broad prickly pear paddles in season . . . That thorn was tough and it stung, and that needle vertiginously roamed through his irritated blood. Balta wanted to grab it, but it slipped through his fingers. The truth is, he was suffering. He didn't want to give any importance to the incident of the mirror, and yet this seemed to follow him and gnaw with blind obstinacy.

The following day, Balta immediately headed for the street to buy a mirror. He'd had that fantastic obsession since the previous day. He didn't grow tired of looking into the glass hanging from the column. Pointless. The projection of his face was now normal and no longer cast even the slightest strange shadow. Without saying anything to Adelaida, he went to sit on one of the enormous camphor trunks, cut for rafters, which he had bound in the yard and leaned against a wall, and there he remained for hours on end in front of the mirror. The morning was gorgeous, a cloudless sky.

Adelaida's mother, old lady Antuca, surprised him when she showed up at the house to ask for a candle. What an incorrigible mother-in-law she was, half-blind from cataracts she contracted many years prior when she stayed up past midnight, alone, walked passed a house where they were holding a wake, and the *air* did her harm.

"Haven't you been to the farm, Balta? Don José says the wheat in the pampa is ready for harvest. Says he saw it on Saturday, when he was coming back from the Salinas's . . ."

Balta threw a stone.

"Shu! . . . Shuu! Adelaida! That hen!"

The hens were pecking at the wheat that had been washed for flour and that, laid out on large blankets across the yard, was drying in the morning sunlight.

When the old lady left, she forgot to close the gate and a black dog from the neighborhood ran in. It went up to Balta, who was still sitting on the orange-colored beams, and it began to sniff around and wag its long bushy tail, making a riot with poorly disguised acrobatic priggishness. Entertaining himself by directing the glimmering sunlight with the mirror every which way, Balta angled it in front of the dog. The wandering mutt silently stared at the bottomless blue surface, sniffing it, and then barked at its image with a harmful yelp that agonized in elastic torsion, sharp as a whip.

Harvest time came.

Balta never remembered anything else that happened in the house that afternoon when the hen decided to crow, until one September day, when Adelaida, at the stockpile of wheat, said to him without warning, "Lift up this saddlebag. I can't hold it any longer."

"Are you sick?"

Adelaida lowered her sweet womanly eyes, with an ineffable air of emotion.

"When did this start?" he replied, in a low, paternal voice, lacerated by tenderness and tears.

Adelaida cried, and then father embraced mother.

"As I recall," she muttered timidly, shyly, "since July."

When Balta heard these serious words and had thought about them for a moment, a dark cloud arose in branded flight to his forehead. "Since July," he said to himself. And then he remembered, after a while, the ungodly vision that, as if in a dream, he had in the mirror, that remote afternoon in July, when it broke from the stupor the vision had caused him. "A strange coincidence," he said, "very strange indeed." A mysterious atrocious omen breathed a long-lasting shudder into his veins.

Harvest time passed.

Summer came and went and autumn arrived with its hard windy days, the time for planting. One day after another a hard rain would fall, and high stormy clouds filled the atmosphere.

Balta and Adelaida moved out to the farm.

4

Out on the farm, when Balta was headed home from work one evening, he went to let his oxen have a drink in the stream across from the cabin. He, in turn, likewise thirsty and beset with fatigue, went to the clean water source that flowed between the scrub brush, kneeling down to drink from it directly. He heard gulping for several seconds, while his lips were submerged. Suddenly Balta jumped, took three or four steps back, staggering and stomping and bending the tender branch of a camphor tree, the foliage of which deafeningly and lugubriously tickled the trees of the meadow. He looked from side to side to figure out who was behind him, but he couldn't find anyone; he scoured the brush—no one. Some alarmed pigeons took flight in multiple directions. A buzzard, hovering slow as dripping oil, passed from one tree to another, where it hopped on several branches until it finally vanished along with a faint trickling rustle of dried leaves.

After a few months, something happened to Balta that was very similar to what occurred that July afternoon in front of the mirror. Amid the ripple of waves his lips produced as they sucked up the water, his eyes had perceived a strange image, its ephemeral traces thumping and bumping against the fast moving shadows of the weeds that cover the spout of the natural spring. The noisy slurping of water trickling from his lips as he drank dreadfully rippled the specular vision. Who would follow him like that? Who was toying with him, behind his back, only to scuttle away with such trickery and swiftness? What was it that he had seen? Anxiety sunk into all his membranes. It was extraordinary. He thought for a moment and felt he was being ridiculed, mocked. He turned his head from side to side. It was strange. Maybe his wife was playing him for the fool? No. She respected him too much for that. No!

Balta may not have been an intelligent man, but he possessed great common sense and was very even-keeled. He had studied, for better or worse, his five years of primary education. His bloodline could be traced back to uproarious tribes, whose flesh was and forever would be of the fields,[70] rustic souls at the level of the patriarchal serf. So he grew up like a good rational animal whose mind could identify boundaries, hopes, and fears in the sole light of an instant driven with greater or lesser efficiency by ancestral scions of race and custom. He was a barbarian, but wasn't distrustful.

After that, when the strange image appeared for the second time, now in the water before his perplexed eyes, Balta started acquiring an air of concern. He was given to thinking at length on the hallucinatory episode. What could all that have been? He wanted to mention it to Adelaida, but he decided to keep the incident to himself, afraid he'd look ridiculous in front of his wife.

The following Sunday he went to town. In the plaza he ran into an old friend who had gone to the same school as him. He couldn't resist the temptation to tell him his worries. He told the story laughing, doubting at moments, and other times his spirit became crowded with a thousand suspicions, wounded with childish indignation, or grimly intrigued. The other man started to laugh at Balta's first words, and then he replied with a serious tone of conviction, "It's not strange. Every once in a while something similar happens to me. Occasionally, and this occurs when I least expect it, a light and a world of things and people I want to trap with my thought strike like a bolt of lightning in my mind, but they strike and fall apart, barely discernible. When I was in Trujillo, the man I said this to told me that these were signs of madness and that I had better watch out."

Balta couldn't understand any of this. His friend's story was too profound and complicated for him.

Meanwhile, the weeks of planting passed.

One morning Balta went to the pasturelands, near a clearing in the woods, at the edge of an irrigation ditch. He went alone. Suddenly, without realizing it, his eyes lowered to the stream, and he had to step to the side in terror. Again someone appeared in the mirror reflection on the water. A fleeting murmur blew through the willow trees that stood at the edge of the stream. He turned his face in that direction and, among the dense branches of vines and hollyhocks, saw the leaves resume their natural position, after having been disrupted by a volatile and crushing escape, like that of a startled, astute, untamed beast or a crafty, agile person.

"Who's there?" Balta shouted in alarm. "Watch out, you scoundrel!"

And he followed his prey with great determination, but it was all in vain. He wandered around the entire vicinity, scrutinized the treetops, the backside of rocks, under the footbridge, to no avail.

It was the third time that a strange, perfidious presence had surprised him. Nor did he tell this bit of news to his wife, although an instant later his wandering mind—with that blasted freedom of thought—started to suspect horrible and offensive things for her; or perhaps, for that same reason, he said nothing about it and, with rigorous discretion, kept to the road of all that could overcome his suspicions . . .

As days went by, Balta appeared more taciturn and gloomy. From time to time he'd wind up in long bouts of seclusion, in which he'd become absorbed like a sleepwalker, or he'd wander away from the house by himself, without letting anyone know where he was going or why he had left. That *cholo* considerably changed his way of being. He began to behave very differently around his wife, having unusual fits of exalted and painful passion for her.

"Hey, come here. Sit down," he said to her one day.

The two of them sat down on the bench at the door that opened to the fence on the street. He gave her a terrified kiss, and with ungrounded anguish he sighed and said, "If one day you stop loving me, Adelaida . . ."

She kept silent, leaning in. Never had he been untrusting; never had the finest needle of infidelity pierced her heart! Fraternal tenderness, blind religious faith, a pure and candid bosom has always united them. She walked into the yard, and he stayed in the same place, alone, sunken in meditation.

Balta had acquired a vague aversion to mirrors. He remembered them with dark, shapeless displeasure. One night he dreamed of an exceedingly strange location, flat and colored monotonous blue; he was there alone, and possessed by a tremendous ringing as he faced his solitude, he tried to escape, but couldn't. No matter which way he turned, a surface was already there. It was like an incommensurable mirror, infinite, like an unmoving ocean, limitless. In the spellbinding clarity of the midday sun, his castaway eyes barely managed to find his shadow on their own, a murky intermittent shadow that, moving to the rhythm of his body, now appeared enormous, wide, long; then shrunk down and thinned out until it was nothing but an impalpable thread; or then slipped away completely only to follow him every once in a while, like a black bolt of lightning, playing this sort of game of merciless ridicule that increased his dread to the point of desperation . . . When he awoke to the calls of his wife, tears were laying waste to his eyes.

"What were you dreaming about," Adelaida asked, solicitous and unnerved. "You've been complaining so much! . . ."

"It was a nightmare," he muttered.

And they both fell quiet.

The strange thing was that Balta didn't involve his wife at all in these incidents. With regard to her, he maintained the most hermetic silence. And in this way, like an immense tapeworm hidden away, a nervous root began to grow in his spirit, the sap of which had risen from the sterile lymph of a fateful crystal . . . Why hadn't he informed his companion of all this at the outset? Why, on the contrary, along with that torturous worm that was to skewer God knows what, would he set ablaze a mysterious garnet between the arms of his love? Why would he lower that charged tempestuous kiss? What had given birth to that exalted and painful passion? Thus, the tragedy began to rot, out of sight, layer by layer, from the core outward, that hard thousand-year-old camphor trunk that served as the central beam suspended from one end of the roof of their home to the other, like a vertebral column . . .

For no good reason Balta started to feel jealous of his wife — a dark jealousy of which he wasn't aware. She didn't realize it either, although she did notice that her husband was changing the way he interacted with her in a very palpable way.

"Let's go to town," Adelaida said one day, as the triptolemic[71] chores had come to an end.

"But there's still so much to do," Balta replied mysteriously.

Since the Sunday when he spoke with his friend in the plaza, he hadn't returned to town. Whenever the need arose for him to go and resolve some domestic affair, he'd deny it, invoking an array of inconveniences or using any trifle as an excuse. He seemed to be avoiding the ruckus and seeking out solitude, undoubtedly keen to comprehend such a timid pursuer who apparently was trying to do something to him, and something certainly not entirely good, since this was how the pursuer was bothering him, by watching him, following his footsteps, to confirm it was him, Balta that is, or to deal him a mysterious blow . . . But he was also afraid of the solitude of the house in town, then abandoned and deserted, with its hallways in which the hens and rabbits must have defecated and filled with trash. Thinking about this inevitably evoked the column where the widowed empty nail would still be sticking, on which the mirror once hung. Then a grim discomfort possessed him. The excuse to go to the village became rotund and unavoidable.

A sad and sinister expression started taking over his countenance. During the days of January, filled with downpours or terrible hailstorms, when the dark fallow fields resembling thick burial shrouds were wrung out, folded in large random pleats, or apathetically swaying in the wind, the storm clouds of his anxiety grew high and menacing.

The squalls, which sometimes lasted for hours, made numerous puddles in the cracked patio outside the dwelling. If he hadn't gone to the plowed fields or if, due to the rain, he was obliged to suspend his work and clean up, Balta would remain seated on one of the benches in the hallway, his arms crossed, absorbed as he listened to the buzzing of the storm and wind on the thatch rooftop, which was threatening to collapse. He'd stay there until some circumstance requiring his attention could no longer be held at bay, such as shooing away the pigs that, due to the electric flow of the air, were nervously rooting around the gate of the sty, snorting and making a deafening racket. He'd beat them with a stick and, with new posts, fix and secure the entrance to the pen; but the animals wouldn't stop and they kept grunting and furiously, savagely pushing the stones of the postern. "What's wrong with these damned animals! . . ." Balta exclaimed, possessed by anger and the subtle restlessness of an omen.

The noise of the storm grew louder, and as if dishing out lashings with a long whip to the entire body of the old hut, it triggered intermittent shudders of fear, in response to the easy squeaking of a lose eyebolt, the uncertain fall of a tile pulled up by the moisture, that vertexilar[72] sprout that—following the sublime interplay of fresh and stale air, the density of the rain from which the amazed ozone fled, and the invisible slants of ailing light—ejected, accentuated its curve all the more astonishingly, and suddenly competed for another exit among the whirling hay on the rooftop. It was the familiar pounding blows of the mortar and pestle, where Adelaida would do her grinding, all this detonation in his nerves, and a vague sensation of foreboding creeping through his soul.

A piglet, with a reddish coat and large dorsal bristles, which had recently stopped suckling on account of having lost its mother who knows where in the *jalcas*,[73] started to squeal like crazy, running here and there, among the rest of them. Balta threw a stone at it, and the poor little thing slowly but surely lowered its voice and complained all afternoon along. Oh the frightful voice of animals, when grave misfortunes befall us!

Without knowing why, Balta was afraid to go outside and went into the kitchen. As he crossed the puddle-filled yard, he briefly saw a blurry silhouette ripple in the water that danced beneath the storm. When he entered the kitchen, he did so running as if he was being chased . . . Adelaida was grinding with the pestle and mortar. They began to speak enthusiastically. He apparently wanted to be shocked, and he spoke to his wife closely about the increasingly colder winter and other trifles. Again Adelaida told him that the time had come to return to town.

"There's still so much to do!" he repeated. "We'll go in February."

José, the old sharecropper,[74] and his two sons, arrived completely drenched. Along with them, sobbing and hunched in pain, was Santiago, Adelaida's younger brother. From one of his mud-covered feet, blood was flowing bright like the innocent, unbidden crimson of warm pomegranate temperas.

[JM]

Letters

TO *LA REFORMA*

Huamachuco, August 12, 1920
To the Editors of *La Reforma*, Trujillo.
Dear Gentlemen,
Today I address the following words to *La Industria* of this city: Huama-chuco, August 12, 1920. Dear gentlemen of *La Industria*, Trujillo. My dear gentlemen, in your prestigious newspaper's volume 7 of this month I have just read the charges being pressed and wired in by Carlos Santa María, of Santiago de Chuco, concerning the supposed fault of numerous gentle-men and my own fault for the fire and plundering that, according to the claimant, occurred in his commercial store in that city.

I am surprised by and amazed at slander as brutal as this, with which the aforesaid Santa María intends to bring me down. I energetically protest this and hereby invoke my rights in the face of such infamy before the jus-tice system. I had no other choice. Let this Santa María beware of the legal repercussions for the despicable slander that today I denounce.

I respectfully request that you, gentlemen, publish the present letter.

Much obliged for your consideration, sincerely and without further re-quests at this time.

Yours truly,
César Vallejo   [JM]

TO ÓSCAR IMAÑA

Trujillo, October 26, 1920
Dear Óscar,
I've read the last letter you wrote to Antenor. As I see from it, you're ruined by boredom and by Pacasmayo. It's the pits. Here you've got me as eaten away by monotony as you. What are we going to do, Óscar? Endure it, endure it.

I bet by now you've already received news that I'm being civilly prose-cuted and criminally charged in Santiago de Chuco and also that I was sought after by the law at the doors of the Panopticon. There you have what I must endure to live. Now you see. So for two months now I've been in hiding, and for one month, living in Mansiche with Antenor and Julio.

When are you coming by here, so we can laugh together until it hurts. God I wish you'd drop in for a bit. I think it's rather simple, just a matter of fifteen soles at most. Come on, get over here; don't be a lug.

Maybe in a few days the case will be solved, and will be solved in my favor. I find it hard to believe. But, maybe. I'll let you know what happens.

Probably within two months or so we'll set off on a trip outside of Peru with Antenor. Let's at least plan on it. As for me, I think it's a sure thing.

And you? When?

Before leaving, we'll plan to edit a book, a work by all of us in collaboration. It will be the crystallization of our fraternal life for so many years of our best childhood times. Send us your writings and let us know what suits you best, poems or prose. You'll choose. The book will be two hundred pages. It doesn't seem too bad now, does it?

I've just gone to sleep after lunch and have woken up with a bit of a cold.

Don't keep silent. Write to me always, by way of Antenor. I'm sorry that this isn't longer; I feel somewhat ill.

Highest regards.

César   [JM]

TO GASTÓN ROGER[75]

[Trujillo, December 1920]

My Dear Friend,

For the past month, I have been imprisoned in this city's jail, calamitously judged for a series of despicable crimes that I did not commit. It is this provincial environment. The misguided distrust of local slander: I am from the heartland. I am now a victim of one out of so many gratuitous or brutally cajoled infamies that abound, reeking of bats, in every heap of district affairs. For I am from the same land as those who accuse me, and I passed through Santiago de Chuco, months ago, when there were killings and fires in that province. It is this provincial environment. That is all.

And what is more, I have been prosecuted with utter impunity and utter impudence. And, as now I am in grave danger of being found guilty by the criminal court, one of these days, I hope that you, who valued something in my artistic work, may want to show, along with the rest of our friends in Lima, some gesture of sympathy and of interest in my favor, on the occasion of this outrage and this mortal wound, by which they want victimize me, indifferent to my innocence and the law. I would imagine that this thoughtfulness, on your part, would lead to the acquittal to which I have a right in the case at hand.

The days are numbered until the hearing, and I am almost sure of the compassion with which this fraternal petition will be received by the resilient intelligentsia of Lima.

Affectionately yours,

César Vallejo [JM]

TO ÓSCAR IMAÑA

Trujillo, February 12, 1921

Óscar,

Today I put down these lines for you from prison still. How about that. Oh how I would've liked to write you with news of my release, but these attorneys!

I know that by now you're in Pascamayo. And yet I know that you've got to let yourself out of the moment-to-moment to come by here. I hope that you do, and they let me go to Salaverry to wrap my arms around you.

Two public prosecutors have argued for my release, and the court even today has yet to hand down a ruling on my case. Not even because Morales sits on the bench. Clericalism is more than wretched.

You can imagine how I'm faring. At times I lose my patience and everything grows dark; very rarely am I well. I've got four months in prison under my belt, and now they must weaken my hardest fortresses.

We received the memorial from the ladies of Chiclayo. Today I'm writing a telegram to Cornejo's wife, expressing my thanks for such a considerate gesture.

In my cell I read every once in a while, and in brief I brood and gnaw my elbows out of rage, not exactly because of that *honor* thing but because of the material privation, completely material and my animal freedom. Óscar, this is awful.

I also write from time to time, and if any sweet breath fills my soul, it's the light of memory . . . Oh the memory in prison! How it gets here and falls upon the heart, which it oils with melancholy already so decomposed . . .

In short, I don't know what these people will do. We soon shall see.

Your brother,

César [JM]

TO ÓSCAR IMAÑA

Lima, June 1, 1922
Óscar,

I received news from you yesterday. Tello, our old schoolmate, told me you were in Chiclayo. I had received your last letter a while ago, but without a return address, so I didn't know where to address my reply. Only today have I finally learned where you are. And I write to you with all the affection that has always bound us like brothers.

I heard that you've become a lawyer, and this pleased me immensely. As you know, all that's necessary to make it in life. Unfortunately, I cut my career short and don't know what my future holds in store. God be with me.

I received the beautiful writings you attached to your note. In the next few days I'll see that they get published in a fashion you deem most suitable. You'll have to excuse me for not doing so sooner, but, as you may suspect, I live quite a ways away from the literary bustle of the capital and hardly ever find myself in the company of literati. That's why I let you down. But in the next few days I'll do it, my dear Óscar.

I repeat. Antenor, who was here in March, has seen just how far I live from other writers. Completely. Only by brute force was one of my stories picked up by *Variedades*. It was strictly a question of friendship and nothing else. So that's how I'm living. And so I'm happy and content. Doesn't that seem good to you? It does.

My second book is at the printers. I'll send it to you shortly. It will have a prologue by Antenor. Say hello to Dr. Puga and your whole family, and receive for yourself affectionate regards from your brother who never forgets you.

César

[JM]

TO ANTENOR ORREGO

[1922]

The magnificent words of your prologue have been the only comprehensive, penetrating, generous words to cradle *Trilce*. On their quality alone, they suffice and exceed. The vital groans and urges of the creature at its time of birth have bounced off the vegetable coast, off the shriveled tinder bark of Lima's literary sensibility. They've understood nothing. For most readers, it's merely the delirium of a poetic schizophrenic or literary lunatic who seeks only the shrillness of the street. The book is disputed, rejected, ridiculed, and hammered in the watering holes, among groups on the street, everywhere by the most diverse of people. Only a handful of young still-unknown writers and several college kids have shuddered at its message.

As for everyone else, the book has fallen into the greatest abyss. I feel that I'm teeming with ridiculousness, plummeted to the bottom of that burlesque cackle of stupidity on the surroundings, like a boy who clumsily sticks a spoon on his nose. I'm responsible for it. I assume all responsibility for its aesthetic. Today, and perhaps more than ever, I feel hovering over me a thus far unknown, most sacred human and artistic obligation: to be free! If I'm not to be free today, I never will be. I feel the arc of my forehead gain its most imperative heroic strength. I submit to the freest form I can, and this has been my greatest artistic harvest. God knows unto where my freedom is certain and true! God knows how much I've suffered so that the rhythm would not overstep that freedom and fall into licentiousness! God knows at which hair-raising borders I've peered, fear-stricken, afraid that deep down everything would die for my poor living soul; and how many times I've been ambushed by heinous ridicule, sealed in with my jaw dropped, with the sort of air of a boy who sticks a spoon on his nose! At this moment I nearly relive the entire rumble that brought *Trilce* and *The Black Heralds* to life.

César Vallejo   [JM]

_____

TO MANUEL NATIVIDAD VALLEJO

Lima, June 16, 1923
My Dear Little Brother Manuel,
God be with you, Juanita, and all your children.

I'm writing these lines to let you know that tomorrow I'm leaving for Paris. I'm going for a few months, certainly only until January or February. I'm going for literary matters, and I'm hoping it turns out well.

I wish I could've visited you before leaving, even for just a few days. It wasn't in the cards, so what are we going to do? Today I'm sending you my affection and farewell and offer you my quick return. Please console Dad. I'm guessing this letter sounds rather sad and won't comfort you much.

It's three in the morning, as I write. For a trip so far away, I've exhausted myself over the past couple of days. At this very instant I'm just about dying of nervous fatigue. Today I'm going to write to Godoy and Echeverría about the lawsuit. Let me know what happens, and don't lose yourself to silence, as it will drive me to despair.

Write to me at the following address:

Monsieur

CÉSAR VALLEJO

Legation du Pérou   Paris

(France)

I'll write to you as soon as I get there. Don't worry.

With my warmest affection for you and my regards for Juanita and my Panchito, I'll miss you and now must say good-bye.

Your brother,

César   [JM]

TO CARLOS C. GODOY, ESQ.[76]

Lima, June 16, 1923

To Carlos C. Godoy, Esq.

Trujillo

Dear Sir,

Tomorrow I set off for Paris. There I hope to receive good news from you with my greatest desire that they also inform me of your good health as well as that of your good family. I would've liked to stop in Salaverry when I passed through, but, unfortunately, the *Oroya* doesn't stop at that port so I'm left with my hand waving in the air, without being able to embrace the few friends like you for whom I reserve a place in my heart. What are we to do? I'll stop by on my way back.

Would you be so kind as to take a quick look at the file on the case from August, if it's not too much of a bother, which, I am to understand, has been swept under the rug[77] of the Trujillo Court? I urge you to do so, sir, in my stead and for the peace of my dear ones, over whose fate I bitterly distress.

They soon will write to you personally, from Santiago, and, in any case, my brothers will meet with you at an appropriate time.

My respectful best wishes to your wife, siblings, and children, all of whom I remember with fervent gratitude, and you, sir, receive warm wishes from your friend.

César Vallejo   [JM]

TO VÍCTOR CLEMENTE VALLEJO

Paris, July 14, 1923

My Dear Little Brother Víctor,

May the Almighty let these words reach you, Dad, and the rest of the family, filled with well-being. The Almighty let me arrive without any setbacks to this great capital, which according to common consensus, is the most beautiful that God created on Earth. So here I am, and it all seems like a dream to me. A dream! A dream! I want to cry now, seeing myself here, so far from you all . . . ooph, so far! I want to bawl my eyes out because my suffering and sadness emerge in my eyes and don't allow me to write . . .

Paris! Paris! Oh, what grandeur! What a marvel! I have fulfilled the greatest desire that all educated men feel when they look upon the globe. Oh, marvel of marvels!

I arrived yesterday, the thirteenth, at seven in the morning, on the express from La Rochelle. My health is fine. I haven't seen too much. Only the Eiffel Tower, L'Hôtel National des Invalides, the Seine, the Arc de Triomphe, the Palace, and Lake of Versailles. That's nothing. Paris has no beginning or end. It's designed to be endless.

Today, the fourteenth, is Bastille Day in France. Just now I have returned from the legation of Peru, where I was the guest of honor for a lunch with the minister plenipotentiary Mariano H. Cornejo. What a luxurious lunch! Butlers in coattails served us. Cornejo toasted to the joy of having Vallejo the poet with him. Such were his words, verbatim. I've savored the authentic champagne of France. Soon you'll have to see the newspapers, where all this is reported.

From Spain, I wrote a card to Dad, which I imagine he has already received.

My little brother, as a boy I never dreamed that one day I'd be in Paris, mingling with great personalities. It all seems like I'm dreaming, and I look at myself and don't recognize me. We've been so humble, so poor!

Now then, God shall look after me. I trust him and in him place my hope. Here I continue to work on a novella to be submitted to the Contest of Paris this year, with a prize of 10,000 francs. Hopefully I'll win the prize, and with it I'll have attained the definitive laurel and worldwide recognition. I'll let you know soon.

This is the hotel[78] where I'm staying, a photo of which I'm enclosing in this envelope. I have a room on the fifth floor, which you'll see is highlighted; that's where I am as I write this to you, at five in the evening. From the boulevard there comes the rumble of musicians, laughter, voices, the rattling of underground cars, etc., etc. I dedicate this moment to the sacred memory of my father and to all of you who are in Santiago right now, at home, perhaps together talking, laughing, or even crying. I think of you and start choking on melancholy, and I can take no more. I'll return to America soon, God willing, very soon. We shall see.

Paris is in the middle of summer. There's a terrible heat wave.

Little by little I'll speak French correctly.

Write to me always. Don't forget about me. I'll write to Dad tomorrow.

Tell me what's happening with the lawsuit from August. I've been worried about that.

I'm going to write to Nestítor right now.

My address:

"Monsieur César Vallejo—
Legation du Perou
14 Rue Chateaubriand (8º)
Paris."

All my love and affection,
César

[JM]

TO CARLOS RAYGADA

Paris, September 15, 1923

Dear Raygada,

It's going on three weeks since I've been in Paris. On a daily basis I live in utter brotherhood with Silva, who's the only man of greatness I've found in Europe. The rest undoubtedly hide behind curtains I've yet to whip open.

Alfonso wants to go to Peru. It seems to me that he should go right away. Here he has nothing to do now. My impression is that a longer stay in Paris might even do him harm. It would be good if you and our other friends could facilitate his trip, without wasting any time. Otherwise, life here is going to inflict a harmful gash, terribly harmful. Europe is like this: sometimes it can give and other times it crumbles your soul from which it repossesses something that it gave and something it did not. Alfonso no longer has anything to take away from here. He must return. Get him out of here, as he says; get him out of here right away.

Strong best,
Vallejo

[JM]

Articles and Chronicles

THE BLUE BIRD

Paris, 1923

The theater of Cora Laparcerie has just staged this famous *féerie* of Maurice Maeterlinck: one hundred artists, forty children, in marvelous decoration and costumes, created by the master, Granier, and designed in the fine drawings of Georges Lapape. The economic audacity for the staging of this comedy, its Paris premiere, amounts to much more than what the great vanished artist Réjane had displayed. Naturally, this time, the triumph of the author and of Mme Laparcerie has lived up to expectations. Twenty thousand francs at the box office for the debut alone! The record for ticket sales of all the grand theaters and music halls of Paris!

In unanimous tone the Parisian press has celebrated Cora Laparcerie's success and on all the posters this autumn forecasts her abundant harvest of applause and francs.

As for the author, yesterday the critics said, and I paraphrase, that the beautiful adventure of the children, Tyltyl and Mytyl, is immortal, the best of all Maeterlinck's work, made of obscurities, lofty metaphysics, and certain imbalances. The critics have exposed the theme of *The Blue Bird*, vertebra by vertebra, all the way up to the neck, and even higher. The critics, full of sufficiency, have sketched out the comedy, allegorizing it more and more, interpreting it, situating it, and failing from as close as they can get. Good critics, and better Frenchmen still, know that what they say is true.

But I want to say something for myself regarding *The Blue Bird* and its production by Cora Laparcerie. Of course, before such a fantastic mise-en-scène, before such an outpour of epidermal sensuality, emotions piling up on the floorboards, my nerves start bucking, get out of control, and the sensation of unusual asperity attacks them, grinding them with giant molars. Why does it harm us so, burying heat in our skin all the way down to the word-knobs? Why the inferno, transformed into sevens like swords in the retina's seven Satans? Why does the sensibility pound us so? Why does it berate and stone our soul? Could it be that we're deaf or dull? Could that by chance be a session of vile pyromania? Light, in shining ornamentation, of gemstones and pearls like hysterics; Time, in a white silver suit, gray eternalfather[79] yataghan sideburns made of 181 degrees of the quadrant; an oak tree, in unredeemable green . . . Why does the sensibility pound us so, scorching us with color? Yes. The Light. No doubt. But the fact that it's Light doesn't suffice. It must be dressed in Light. And each of its veils must clarinate[80] all ears: Light! It moves the scandalous woman to return and respond, in a pithy act, with an order to the lackey, so as to remove her from us thereafter.

This speaks of an undeniable decadence in the sensibility, a consistent decadence, no longer the Byzantine hyperesthesia, but rather an alarming anesthesia. Has Paris grown dull? Is it blinded beneath twenty years of senile sleep in its eyes? Is it seeking, in every corner, the spasm, the ichor of form and feeling, though it may be at the worst of times and obliquely? Could it be that it lies in ruins and isn't sufficed by the natural, just, and harmonious measure of things? Does it wish to double its length and width? Does it want to turn around and head back? It's lost.

The production of *The Blue Bird* has cast a spell on all of Lutetia. The critics, in particular, reveal their own satisfaction; these critics, French and all, prognosticate the eternity of Maeterlinck's comedy even though it just may happen that the bland run-of-the-mill allegory of Time could wield its no less academic Catholic yataghan and eviscerate Tyltyl and Mytyl, the witch or fairy Berylune, the Allegories, and the blathering bird too. Personifying Time armed with patriarchality and, at once, such a sizable sickle, runs certain risks for the duration of worldly things. Rear time and it will run away with your life. M. Maurice Maeterlinck, if you, sir, with some new fresh graceful feature, had symbolized Time, not with an eternalfatherly beard and damoclean scythe, but rather as a grinning ephebe, crowned with doves and Arcadian blackbirds! . . . you would've flopped at the splendid theater of Cora Laparcerie.

But, the 20,000 francs per day!

[*El Norte* (Trujillo), February 1, 1924]   [JM]

LA ROTONDE

Paris, 1924

Behold this ambiguous hypogeum, its iridescent paneling, a boisterous alveolus of cosmopolitan mange. Behold the loud café, armed with artists, with slackers, with snobs and wavering skirts, between Mimí and Margarita, between *grisette* and *garçonne*.

La Rotonde! Boulevard Montparnasse, under the autumnal night, with sad rain, and its brows streaked with suspended cables that come from off-lying bays to wrap around the chestnut trees, the pedestrian silhouettes, and the ringlet of the exile's pallid ear. La Rotonde! Strange hearth, its flames in suspension, on the olive hill of the night.

La Rotonde! Here are the endlessly long, warm chaise longue chairs; the frenzied canvases of the latest NOVIESPACIAL exhibit; the maître d'hotel, with the correct jacket and hummingbird moustache. A polyglot crowd fills the dance salons, the *amourette* rooms and the terraces. We see Aichia, the Senegalese who laughs beneath his herbaceous green turban while he poses for the Montparnasse Academy; that sad gaunt Swiss man, donning a white turban draped in the style of Hyderabad . . . Near that corner, where two innocent maroon Englishmen gobble apricots, the rounded figure of Japanese painter Foujita appears, wearing his tortoiseshell glasses, through which his expressive jubilant eyes look upward. Then Mme Lourioty of the Theater Pitoëff will show up; as the night goes on Hilda de Nys will appear, the most beautiful singer who not long ago performed a magnificent recital of Wagner, and then nearly at dawn, Emilienne d'Alençon, with her violin d'Ingres.

La Rotonde! The café where conversations are often held by Maurice Maeterlinck, his already-whitened hair in view, with the no less aged Enrique Gómez Carrillo, from whom he is inseparable; where Claudio Farrère spends a pluvious twilight, the continent calm and contemplative, with his famous pallor; and where Tristan Tzara, Max Jacob, Pierre Reverdy, and the entire dadaist squad drink and wave at the galleries from behind their masks of absurd satraps of chance.

An exceedingly fascinating physiognomy has its roaring place and nervous mixture and saturnal prestige; here there seems to burn a wick woven from many tormented hides of the artist; of the eccentric millionaire, who out of curiosity comes to see the immortal effigies; of the modern woman *parisién*; of the pilgrim and the sybarite. An ambiguous hypogeum, I say, a boisterous alveolus of cosmopolitan mange, where hidden fingernails scratch an unspeakable scar on our skin.

Here the heart settles into its place on the left; it rattles like a matchbox to see if inside itself there are any sticks, and all night long it burns burns burns its little yellow twigs. The rain has continued to fall, and at one point big fat drops of sweetened grease doused a stick.

Yet here's the great Spanish painter, my ultraist friend, Francisco Miguel. He walks in, quite late at this point:

"You hear the latest? Julio Herrera Reissig is Vicente Huidobro's father! See for yourself!"

Before me he opens the latest volume of the magazine of the newest Spanish art, *Alfar*, where I read a critique by Guillermo de Torre—

"Forerunner of Creationism: Julio Herrera Reissig"—and one more restless discussion unravels at La Rotonde.

[*El Norte* (Trujillo), February 22, 1924]   [JM]

COOPERATION

On the tenth of this month, a significant gathering of *Peruvianness* has taken place in the Theater Caméléon of Paris, which is directed by French writer Alexandre Mercereau, where on Mondays foreigners have the objective of presenting their cultures in an endeavor of quite praiseworthy spiritual solidarity or cooperation. The soirée dedicated to Peru consisted of a talk by Lima intellectual Francisco Elguera about the Inca civilization and its influences in the Peruvian regions; a reading of poems representative of the culture, by José Santos Chocano, Leonides Yerovi, and César Vallejo, given by the poet Pablo Abril de Vivero, adjunct at the legation in Rome; a concert of national arias and melodies that, over the folkloric documentation of Alomía Robles, the celebrated Parisian singer and actress Valentine Stern performed, accompanied on the piano by Alfonso de Silva, the Peruvian composer who has just triumphed in the conservatories of Madrid and Berlin; and a discourse by Mariano H. Cornejo, minister plenipotentiary in France. People are saying that the soirée was attended by all the Peruvian families residing in Paris, a large colony of the rest of the countries from America, along with the French public. People are also saying that the party had suggestive influence, due to its unforeseen exotic nightlong procession through and for Europe.

There's a lot (though none of it good for Europe) to say when the skin of solidarity touches us Latin Americans. Solidarity with Europe? One does not comprehend the extent to which there may be that parity of hearts—between Europe and South America—necessary for such a *human* objective and not for mere diplomacy. Solidarity? Comprehension? None of this exists in Europe with respect to Latin America. We stand up to Europe and offer our open heart to all the nodules of love, and Europe answers us with silence and premeditated clumsy deafness, if not with an insulting sense of exploitation. With premeditated deafness does Europe observe our life and childish agitations. I've already said this elsewhere. But we must insist as many times as possible, touching the inaccessible murals until our fingers break, or until we see emerge thereon the callus that makes stones spark and bramble patches scratch, like that other historical callus, beneath whose blow the grass never grew again. For some reason we're pre-judged as barbarians.

As many times as it's necessary, one must grab Europa by her grand-motherly chin and shove this buckshot through her nose: do you smell that? It's the great virile vapor of a new continent . . . This is how one must shout it day and night until she knows to hear us and value our leading role in intercontinental cooperation. She must at least declare that she knows us, doesn't understand us, and doesn't respect us. Why the deafness and silence? Europe can disdain or ignore the Africans, the Australians. But us? To respect and admire India—which she announces stupendously—a Tagore has sufficed; to respect and fear Japan—which has already left its mark on the world—a Yamagata has sufficed; to respect and fear the United States—which already has in its hands, like a diabolical evil, the stomach of the world—a Grant sufficed. To respect us, the Latin Ameri-cans—we who've just announced ourselves and are going to make our mark—does not a Simón Bolívar suffice? A Rubén Darío? Hypocrites! We know the trick. Europe pretends to ignore us, laboring with ridiculous simpleton insistence to demonstrate that she ignores and disdains us. It's not that she strives to get to know us. She knows us all right. It would be useless for her to pretend to ignore us. The deceit is plain and pitiful. It's the vulgar investigation of someone who intends to take down his adver-sary and, unable to attack him, resorts to feigned disdain, not even giving a visible warning—for such is his insignificance—when in reality, this per-son is surreptitiously observing his adversary's most minor movements, afraid and stricken by nightmares.

For half a year I've been in Paris, and I can say that, except for daily in-formation coming out of New York—*Le Figaro* dedicates one full spread per week to the United States—never in any paper have I seen the slightest news from America. What does this boycott mean?

Solidarity? Cooperation? The cooperation of chancellors, the protocol of conveniences frequent and always to the advantage of Europe. Coopera-tion? Soon enough we shall demand it of them by way of the fist. In the meantime, let's breed a *ferpery*, a brood of Firpo,[81] and Carpentier, soon you shall see.

Down with the Empire. Here we are, the barbarians!

[*El Norte* (Trujillo), February 26, 1924]   [JM]

BOOK THREE 1924–1928

Articles and Chronicles

PARIS CHRONICLE

There's liberalism and then there's liberalism – The new philosophy – One sol per fifteen hours of work in Shanghai – Communist uprising at the Legation of China in Paris – Plausible apostrophes of Léon Daudet – Scheherazade in the Grand Palais – Sandals are in fashion – The eyes said to Death: Enough! – Mysterious threats to the police of the Seine – One thousand francs for a seat at the theater and two thousand artists on one stairway – The Eiffel Tower gets rented out to Citroën – Pascal's metaphysical consolation – The "Cadum" soap among the chimeras of Nôtre Dame – Verifying paternity – Introducing the Socratic method to the chronicle – Amundsen's journey to the North Pole.

Paris, July 1925

Liberalism, I mentioned in my previous chronicle. Since when has this philosphy existed? Since the encyclopedia? Since Luther? Since Pico della Mirandola? Since Jesus Christ? Surely, it can't be since Eastern philosphies, wise as they were and inspired by synthetic unity, because Eastern philosphies, rather, from Confucius to Zoroaster, overflowed with wisdom on the contrary, that is, on the basis of their intolerance, their despotic dogmatism, their sacred sectarianizing passion, their wonderful xenophobia toward other men and other sentiments.

Reading Saint Augustine's *Soliloquies*, one can grasp the thread of religious liberalism that seems to stem from that terrible punch that Jesus yearned to receive with his other cheek. But the truth is that the roots run far deeper, all that way to Buddha. It's just that in the Lord of Meekness as in the Master of Clarity, liberalism cries out for strong applause, strong spirits; they demand and receive the opposing argument or spear thrust with the sonorous virtue of the firmament: by returning it. Liberals, therefore, are the strong-hearted; liberals, in the pure and constructive sense of the word, are those who keep close to Serenity.

But as soon as that religious liberalism became political and marched from the Bastille to Versailles and jumped from tribune to tribune in the *états généraux*, it became plebian, meager, rhetorical, and what had been a concrete path, in substance and morality, became a cowardly dossier of vacuous weakness. In all democracies, from 1789 to this day, so-called liberal political parties are the dentures of the ill who smile. This pseudo-

129

liberalism as of late, this sickly, effeminate intolerance, devoid of any vital affirmation, which had the governments of almost all European countries in its hands around 1914, sponsored and precipitated the war.

Two new writers of the world are right, and at this very minute they're marching against political liberalism, the trunk of all twisted horizons. This reaction is backed by a protoplasmic principle of historical continuation. Down with the liberals! More selective passion, more intolerance, greater centrifugal force. It's not enough to say: my idea is good. An intolerable role. The true liberalism—high, religious, vital—doesn't entail a moral defensive or one of cold eclecticism but rather a pungent offensive temperament, which manages, in its inner forge, to convert the contrary and adverse into an element of self-amplification.

* * *

The intellectual youth of China, who study at the Sorbonne by the thousands, have united with the Chinese workers and risen up against the legation of its country in France, to grab documents that will be of service to the strikers of Shanghai. The trembling, wavering government of Painlevé is overwhelmed. Moscow! Moscow! Investigations are carried out; guilty parties are arrested, and statements are demanded of their leader, Yen Choum Siem,[1] director of such communist propaganda organs as the *Ciel Rouge* and *Rayon Rouge*. The center and fringe republicans grow flustered and cast inquisitive stares at M. Léon Daudet:

"What say you, M. Daudet!" the French Left and Right ask, waiting for the recalcitrant realist to give them a burning fuse with those beautiful apostrophes of his, so beautiful they resemble nothing, or resemble the most refined flattery.

"Fire on the Chinese in France! Thugs! Traitors! Cowards! Thieves!"

M. Daudet is quite short-tempered.

However, on the other hand, in Shanghai there are English and French yarn factories, where Chinese men, women, and children work day and night under the flags of France and England for salaries of two shillings, eight pennies, per twelve hours of work. That's right, ladies and gentlemen. And without a law governing accidents on the job, without insurance, without anything . . .

* * *

While poor Chinese students gather in some secret flat on rue de l'Ecole de Médecine, in the Latin Quarter, to hatch their vindictive attack, in the houses of the Duke of Rouen, Count Greffulhe, Marquis de Malayessie,

Prince of Murat, Baron de la Motte, the heir of Sweden, the Maharaja of Kapurthala, and Lord Rothschild, elegant pretty women discuss surprises and the new revelations that the Paris dressmakers will launch at the Nuit du Grand Palais celebration. Next to the bronze *L'homme au nez cassé* by Rodin, one princess, a tad advanced in her years, while petting an irate Briard dog that wouldn't let her speak, was saying, "Gellé makes footwear out of Brazilian gold, crocodile or buck skin, in a perfectly crafted braid, with two or three morning glories, in the style of the Greek sandal."

"I'll wait to see the drawings of Les Sieyeux at the beginning of summer," the daughter of a banker adduced. "They've offered to send me them by the sixteenth . . ."

"But the party falls right on the sixteenth."

"It doesn't matter. As slaves to fashion, we don't dress ourselves, it's the tailors . . ."

"And the mannequins . . ."

"And the beaus!"

Then came the grand celebration. And while the Chinese workers, spying on the police, gathered for the last time, in a hotel on the outskirts of Luxemburg, to seal their pacts of rebellion, fine women, very worldly men, cheerful artists, fortunate writers, wealthy foreigners, and nobility were entering the Grand Palais. . . . Once in the glamorous gilded salon, some people evoked Scheherazade, others Dinarzade, and some even evoked the melancholic sultan of the final night. Then the magnificent heralds began to file in, announcing the wonders about to appear. And the retinue of fashion paraded in, standing upright, on the ramp, spasmodically, to the sounds of Korsakov's "Scheherazade," the retinue of decor and precious stones, with a giant bushy-browed diamond tilted in the center, worthy of a crippled finger. With gestures and expressions of famous artists, the procession paraded in suits likening the theater of Molière; the retinue of the Dance of Dances, the stunning Rainbow, comprising outlines and drawings of the most important designers of Paris; and then, the procession of theater types of D'Annunzio, to the sounds of Debussy's *Sirens* . . . Mistinguett, Ida Rubinstein, etc. The eyes, possessed by light and line, said to Death: Enough! . . .

Yet halfway through that glitzy spectacle, someone came and hastily whispered a few words into the ear of M. Morán, prefect of Paris . . . A few days back, there had been anonymous pamphlets, mysterious threats on the celebration at the Grand Palais. Official orders were given. Signs of unrest were revealed. Divisions of officers and squads of firemen began to mobilize immediately. The mysterious shudder reached as far as the stairway, the splendid stage of the affair. At that moment, the *Entrance of the*

Clowns was taking place to the picturesque sounds of Berlioz's *Carnival*. Laughter then was bound between the funny faces of the Frattelinis, who started to quiver with well-deserved anxiety.

The following day, there was no shortage of frightening rumors: "The Bolsheviki were going to throw a bomb, protesting against the insulting orgy of wealth and luxury" or "They were going to set fire to the entire palace like they did last time, at the Bazar de la Charité" or "The grand stairway was about to collapse under the weight of so many artists," and so on.

In the end: 600,000 francs in ticket sales—barely anything!—despite the thousands of francs each theater seat cost and the two thousand artists who took part in the parade. "A celebration of commercial advertisements for the fashion leaders," the photophobes grumble.

But, with regard to the ads, there are none from the United States. However much M. Citroën would like to compete with the Yanks, he won't be able to do so. Ford's grand rival has just signed a contract with the Municipality of Paris to light the Eiffel Tower with his name, that is, Citroën.

The journalists, the poets (who aren't Montherlant or Géo-Charles), the spiritualist philosophers, who actually persist in France, have aimed their shouts at the sky: "That does it! The name of Citroën on the flagstaff of the highest building in the world! Where the name of God should be! Petulance," yelled Maurice de Waleffe, foaming at the mouth. "It's going to be the new Babel. God will unleash his punishment; the borders of nations will blur more than they already have, since languages are already quite mixed up. Not even Ford, that heathen, has dared to put his name in the lights on Niagara Falls . . ."

"But it's only for the length of the exhibit of Decorative Arts," M. Citroën insists, "and to give a better view of the city at night."

"No, sir! Not even for one night. Time doesn't matter in certain cases. Profanation desires but once, as in adulteries and the egg of Columbus . . . Therefore, the contract is null."

Yet, despite the protests, everything makes us think that the name of Citroën will glow atop the flagstaff of the magnificent tower, for the metaphysical consolation of Pascal, the pale aficionado of heights, and for the sales of mass-produced automobiles.

And what's worst of all is that the example will spread among the competitors. There will be no reason to prevent Cadum from placing its famous ads for soap among the chimeras of Nôtre Dame. Pink brand pills will stake their flag into the terrace of the Arc de Triomphe. Cook will illuminate the obelisk de la Concorde. Etcetera.

* * *

To each his own. The industrialists with their ads and the physiologists with their fingers.

An infallible procedure to investigate paternity has just been discovered. Legislators and judges must be congratulating one another, civil law, guaranteed, and women no longer will have to argue so much to resolve that problem, which really isn't a problem at all, but often gets inextricably and salaciously entangled. The procedure is simple: a comparison of fingerprints between the children and the plausible father.

* * *

Do you want a sample of the modern, Parisian, off-the-cuff, insinuating, cinematic chronicle? Here's one, taken from *Paris-Midi*:

From *Noon to Noon*
Who will win First Prize, Belfonds or Chubasco? Will M. Léon Daudet be elected senator of Maine-et-Loire, or his opponent, M. Villeneau? Will the girls who go to Magic City find a boyfriend at the amusement park, or will they return old maids? Are bond holders content with their financial loans backed in gold, or are they dissatisfied? Will Marshal Joffre recover his light blue ID card or is it lost forever?

On its way back from Morocco, will the Parliamentary Commission have a good trip or will it have an accident? Will the corpse discovered at the Sénart glade be identified, or will it remain anonymous? After such a cram-packed week, will M. Painlevé really give two speeches in Versailles and in Sens, or will he give the same speech twice?

Will the salvos that the Beauvais women and girls fire in honor of Juana Hachette crackle or will it be a slow burn? Will the franc go up or down in value? Must we carry a cane or an umbrella?

So many mysteries in just one day!
Pierre Audiat

Does this really mean the introduction of the Socratic method into the journalistic chronicle? In spite of this sample's execution, it's speaking rather in the tone of a popular oracle.

* * *

On the other hand, our epoch is eminently interrogative. Everything is problematic; everything is a mystery. We live among countless, distressing problems, insoluble many of them. This is the resonance of the war.

A few days ago, the great Norwegian explorer Roald Amundsen gave us another reason for inquiry. One fine morning he boarded a plane and, following one of the directions on his magnetic needle, got lost in the polar fogs of the north. Days and days went by and the silence became absolute behind the fierce propellers. Then a thousand questions emerged: "Could he have died from the cold? . . . Could he have suffered a fall, and the hero's remains now be mourned by melancholic seals? Could he have been devoured by the monsters that, like ugly virgins, have two hearts, likening those that Conan Doyle spoke of? . . . Could another one of Poe's maelstroms have swallowed him? . . . Could he have reached the end of the earth and there been crowned emperor of the meridians and parallels? Could he have turned up down under, that is, at the South Pole? Could he have discovered another America, like Columbus? . . ."

They searched everywhere to rescue him. And one gray afternoon the explorer returned by sea. Nothing had happened to him. Or rather, he had suffered the tragedy of having nothing happen to him.

[*Mundial* (Lima), no. 270, August 14, 1925]   [JM]

SPAIN IN THE INTERNATIONAL EXHIBIT OF PARIS

I speak with sculptor José de Creeft – In the manner of Marcel Proust – The interpretative and the creative in art – Aesthetic conflict of the portrait.

Paris, September 1925

It seems to me that the only people who could appreciate the excellence of portraits are the same people who posed for them.

"Here I look quite good."

"Here, quite bad."

But does the portrait really exist in photography, in painting, in sculpture? I'm afraid you may say it does. I'm afraid you may say it doesn't, that the portrait is already an extinct artistic genre, an aesthetic species that, like the milodon in zoology or like the bone *pfeilstrecker* in Barbarian sculpture, now belongs to archaeology. Yet I'm more afraid that one may not know whether to tell me that the portrait does or doesn't exist in art. Critics have managed to complicate things so much for us that nothing can be affirmed or denied anymore; nor in this case is there any more chance for skepticism, that convenient cowardly easel of uneven legs, which, not being a tripod, the surrealists so righteously abhor.

By all means, the only people authorized to pass judgment on portraits are the ones who posed for them. Thus, Jean Cocteau speaks of his, made by Picasso, which is like saying, made by Father Eternity; Pierre Reverdy speaks of his, also made by Picasso; Maurice Raynal likewise speaks of his, made by Alexander Archipenko, which is like saying, made by the spring solstice; Vicente Huidobro speaks of his, made by Lipchitz, which is like saying, made by Lenin. And, so that everyone is at the table, Anatole France speaks of his, made by Bourdelle, which is like saying, made by the Tarpeian Rock, etc., etc.

Now, César Vallejo speaks of his portrait, of the work that José de Creeft has just shown at the International Exhibit in Paris, but he speaks without the tone of a critic, like M. Choquet on the portrait that Paul Cézanne made of him.

I decisively declare that I do not feel portrayed in what De Creeft has made of me. This is something very different from what I am. If I must judge it, I shall say that the portrait doesn't exist in sculpture, and I don't know whether or not it has ceased to exist or will soon exist, since I've never felt portrayed—not by photographers, sculptors, painters, or writers.

Much like Ventura García Calderón was exclaiming to Toño Salazar and me one afternoon, while viewing a caricature of himself, "I look like a priest!" Facing the work of De Creeft I may likewise exclaim, "I look like a horse!"

Has De Creeft, by chance, made a caricature? Has the portrait, by chance, evolved into a freer and deeper, higher and more harmonious interpretation, connecting its spirit with that which we have thus far called "caricature"? Or could it be that the portrait never did and never will exist? Is the caricature or any other artistic genre thus far unknown or in progress? And carrying this still further, could it be that, with regard to portraits, as has transpired in all other fields of art, the *interpretative* aesthetic has died, ceding its place to the *creative* aesthetic? . . . I mean, is the artist no longer bound strictly to the data of the origin, but only makes use of it as a mere springboard to create something absolutely new and different? . . .

In this regard, questions such as these, as one will see, are proper to the profane or, better yet, to the simple mortal. As for what in the sculpture of De Creeft would concern me as a critic or initiate, there's much that I could say, were I a critic or initiate. I'd say, for example, "José de Creeft is a great sculptor. Spanish by blood and upbringing, his aesthetic is a genuinely Spanish aesthetic, for it carries on the sovereign tradition of Goya, Veláz-quez, Ribera . . ." Or I might say, "The sculptures of this brilliant worker suggest a positive, enthusiastic temperament, filled with resources. Few others at his age have gathered together a group of objects as beautiful as they are numerous. He knows the material in which his hands work breadthwise and possesses delicate sensibility to make the most out of the diorite, as much as out of smooth Sicilian wood. If he continues working, De Creeft will arrive. We're sure."

On the other hand, if I were a critic, I'd say, "In these times of disorientation and chaos, when everything rattles in psychical and social anarchy, the effort of José de Creeft must be enjoyed and encouraged by all. To get to where he has gotten, let us note that De Creeft has had to endure a terrible struggle in Paris; to put bread on the table during the wartime years, he donned the large blue tear of fat-broached painters and makers of liturgical icons of the Rive Gauche."

Then, I'd write, "In De Creeft's direct cuttings one notices an authentic breath of a creator, an architectonic distinction and simplification that bespeak his models and leave a scent of blood in the museums. De Creeft isn't a stonemason, as was said of Mateo Hernández by the wretched Corpus Barga, in whom, let us add but briefly, the Barga outweighs the Corpus.[2] De Creeft is a sculptor of undeniable nobility, whose cuts and scrapes are Michelangelic[3] and not monolithic. Perhaps he lacks a touch of courage in his technique and another touch of pensive repose, for one thing and another, courage and repose fuse and tend to flourish in first-rate works."

Perhaps I'd adduce something else: "Like in the death of Wagner's Isolde, the women depicted by this sculptor possess a strangely extra-organic dejected aspiration in their fine Faustian gullets, fashioned for ineffable cocktails. And what would Dante Gabriel say of the maternities sculpted by De Creeft? Pre-Raphaelites? From the fourth century? I stay put with my opinion in private, far from the patrons and critics of the school. I stay put with my plain, elusive impression, with my critical illiteracy, sitting down, absorbed before the marvels of this artist, as did Bósforo's amiable half nudes, before the lapidary wonders of the great primitive sculptors whose confusing imprecise names half transmit to us Pausanias, Maximus of Tyre, among the ancients, and Winckelmann, for example, among the moderns."

Yet since I'm not a critic or a literary professional, I shall say nothing. Nor should I be taken as a new Marcel Proust, who loved pastiches, no longer about the famous Lemoine affair, the diamond manufacturer and imitator of Renan, akin to a Saint-Simon or Théophile Gautier, but rather about José de Creeft, by emulating five or more writers whose names I leave in the shadows. Nothing at all like this am I nor do I wish to be as I smudge the present article. I only wish to thank José de Creeft for his effort to portray me, which likewise has managed to produce, not a portrait, but an absolutely new creation independent of the *original*. Much obliged and much applause.

* * *

One time someone was disputing portraiture with me.

"The likeness of a portrait is of least importance," he argued. "It's the character that's essential."

Likeness. Character. What kind of a tangle is this?

A portrait must contain a spirit in its essence. The essence of a certain spirit means a certain individual lot, a certain physiognomy that stands out and differs from the rest: a personality. This personality doesn't correspond only to a given instant but to the infinite personality, the figure past, present, and future of a life, in other words, its essential role. Therefore, the sculptor must delve into the mystery of that life, discover a permanent sense of beauty and make it sensible in lines and colors, planes and movements. More than a captured moment, a portrait is the revelation of a life, from the beginning to the end of its trajectory. A portrait is oracular data, the code of divination, an explanation of the mystery. All this is character.

But the creation of a portrait, like all creations, does have its heroics. These heroics stem from a struggle between the infinity of a being (the character), which is discovered and revealed by the artist, and the location of this being in circumstantial space and time. This location is the likeness. The artist will administer the points of conflict in accordance with his emotion. Yet the circumstances of space and time, within which the infinity of the spirit is discovered, mustn't waver or fall in defeat, until it's possible to recognize the persona against the stone or bronze. The greatness of the creation depends on a certain mysterious balance, between the visible and invisible of a portrait, between the circumstantial and the permanent, in other words, between the likeness and character.

Character. Likeness. They are conflicting values in portraiture, and as a result, they harmonize and integrate. Each has its role of emotion and fullness.

This is what José de Creeft has done.

[*Mundial* (Lima), no. 280, October 23, 1925]   [JM]

MODERN MAN

They say that our time is characterized by the horsepower that hauls the carriages, the color guard, the horns of life as a whole. Speed is the sign of modern man. No one can call himself modern except by being fast. This is how philosophers portray it in statues. The English orators have reduced the delivery of their orations to mere outlines, and there are liberal representatives, like Mr. Jiwons, who have won their elections with a single speech, in a country where every great enterprise entails a thousand anginas caused by inflamed vocal chords. In the United States the mayor of New York has just been elected without having given a single speech. It could be argued that silence doesn't mean quickness. That's another story. It's possible that the time the mayor would've spent delivering a political speech could've been spent on something else. The rhythm of velocity doesn't consist only in doing something quickly but also and especially in correctly choosing the opportune use of time. Let's imagine two people who want to walk down the avenue de l'Ópera; whoever *seizes the moment* to cross the street will be faster, and so the saying goes: waking up earlier won't make the sun rise sooner . . . Naturally, in our example, what must be chosen is the moment, that is, the time and not the kind of work, as in the case of the mayor of New York. At any rate, in both cases, speed stems from knowing how to choose the use of time. Aside from that, one mustn't forget that speed is a phenomenon of time and not of space; there are things that move rather quickly without changing place. This has to do with physical and psychic movement in general. In a line from *Trilce* I said that I once sat down to wander.

But we've gotten off track. Speed is the sign of our time. I'm not the one who says so; I only interpret the general concept.

"In what way is one fast?" some people wonder. "What must be done for us to accelerate? Is it a discipline that can be learned at will?"

These are the people who believe that speed is taking us down a good path. We already know that these believers tell everyone else to suck a yucca,[4] and not even a saint could change their minds, except if they turn their backs to the machine.

Whether inherited or learned, the discipline of speed exists. It consists of the possession of a faculty of *maximum insight* for the perception or, rather, to translate into consciousness the phenomena of Nature and of the subconscious in the least amount of time possible; to become excited with the greatest brevity and instantly realize the true, universal meaning of events and objects. There are men astonished by the activity of others. There are European writers, for example, who in the course of a single day have read a beautiful book, savored a grand musical performance, fought and reconciled thrice with their wives, spent an hour arguing with an adversary,[5] written two chapters in a book, changed their suit four times for different occasions, attended a play, taken a nap, cried, directed a firm gaze at God and at the mystery . . .

One must not confuse speed for swiftness, this word taken in the sense of banality. This is very important.

Two people stare at a great canvas; whoever is first to be moved is more modern.

[*El Norte* (Trujillo), December 13, 1925]   [JM]

BETWEEN FRANCE AND SPAIN

The new literature of America – Racial emotion of a visit to Spain – As in Pérez de Ayala: Reconquest of the countryside – The city and the mountains – Dizziness in a smoking jacket – Oscar Wilde and César Vallejo – Noisy polemic about pure poetry – Spain and Russia, the purest countries of Europe.

Biarritz, November 1925

Some months ago, I amused myself in Paris by reading an article by Astrana Marín in the *Imparcial* of Madrid, regarding my literary work.[6] The celebrated Spanish critic, whom, it should be said, I don't even have the honor of knowing in person, began his article with this salutation: "Things are renewed. Light shines on us from America. The poets of the other world prepare to indoctrinate the Castilian generations in their rhythm . . ." An entrance to Jerusalem it would seem, amid psalms and hosannas. Several years ago, Astrana Marín welcomed the presence of Vicente Huidobro in Madrid with a similar tone.[7] It's just that—and this was the reason for my hilarity—contrary to what Marín believes, I've never stepped foot inside Spain's precincts. As of yet I've barely gotten to know green Horatian Santander.

Only now am I going to Madrid for the first time, Mr. Marín. From the Cantabrian coast, where I write these words, I can make out the Spanish horizon, possessed by a deep, strange, and unprecedented emotion. I'm going to my land, without doubt. I return from my Hispanic America, reincarnated by the love of the word that salvages distances, on Castilian soil, seven times pierced by the nails of all columbeid adventures.[8]

"What are you going to do in Madrid?" argued my friends in Paris like examiners.

"Learn about its glories, the glories of Spain, about El Greco's irreproachable, disastrous anatomies; the authentic golden stirrups gifted by popes to despotic kings; the small corner of the ruined Bishop's Chapel in La Puerta del Moro; the sweet circles of veiled, anachronistic, sensual women; the high clear sky; the first manuscript in the language written on parchment in which Don Rodrigo Diaz de Vivar and his wife, Jimena, leave their estate in testation . . . etc. For that you've got to go to Madrid."

"All right. For that you do, but only for a few days. Afterward, *il n'y a rien a fáire*,"[9] add my friends, with a terminal case of Parisitis.

Therefore, I am on a trip to Madrid, a tour that is not literary—God spare me!—but simply of good will for life. That's all, Mr. Marín. I'm not going to "come, see, and conquer," as you believe. If there's anywhere in this world to conquer, Madrid certainly wouldn't be the most suitable place.

I have lingered here, in Biarritz, to graze my labors on the harmonious vegetation of the Pyrenees. On this escape from Paris, I can recover the bloody force of existence, my feeling for harsh, pathless nature, which I notice a bit crouching among civilian afflictions. How pleasant it is to slip or struggle in the dense virgin forest, in an atmosphere and land without roads. How pleasant it is to lose oneself for lack of roads. Now I'm itching to get lost permanently, no longer in the world nor in morality, but in life and by dint of nature. I hate the streets and paths. How much time have I spent in Paris, without the least danger of losing myself. The city is like this. The loss, though not the perdition of a spirit, is impossible. One is far too surrounded by routes, arrows, and signs to get lost. Contrary to what happened to Wilde, on the morning he was to die in Paris, I always awake in the city surrounded by everything, by the brush, by the bar of soap, by everything. I awake in the world and with the world, in myself and with myself. I call and inevitably they answer, and my call is heard. I go out onto the street, and there is a street. I starting thinking, and there always is thought. But now there is not. Now, between the buttresses of the Pyrenees and the beautiful sea of Gascony, on autumn days when the summer season has come and gone, and everyone has retired to Paris, London, Rome, Madrid, or a faraway America, I'm finally free of streets, rails, corners, telegraph offices, towers, theaters, newspapers, writers, hotels, brushes, soap, and everything else that in one way or another is a road; I am free even of thoughts. Ah yes, my dear Vicente Huidobro, I shall never concede to the excessive importance you place on intelligence in life. My votes always go to sensibility. Bergsonism? *Pas de tout!* M. Paul Souday, whose rationalism has just pulverized the brave abbé Bremond in his polemic on "Pure Poetry," confuses the French philosopher's theory of intuition with sensibility as a function that's more physiological than psychical, of which I've sometimes spoken to you, my dear Vicente.

Here, covered by sea and mountain, without roads—which are values exclusively of memory, since the idea is a mere history of the fact of life, and roads in the world, mere history of the progress already made—here, I repeat, without roads, saturated in earth and sea foam, the taste of the bread of pain and the water of grief disappears from my mouth, on which we survive in cities, in prisons, in convents . . . Here, before my grateful eyes, I behold the mobile leaf of the international poplar, the black and excessive wind that neither comes nor goes over the hills. Beyond, the placid Río Bidasoa on the border, the atmosphere, cracked but not split by the bone of the city. Here is Biarritz, its rocky places of the Virgin, bathed by ever-boisterous waves; the lighthouse, more ornamental than useful to castaways; the Chambre d'Amour; the desolate mount of the Rhume; the steamboats of fishermen; the white villas with red roofs; the old melancholic port . . . A delightful panorama! And below, the marshy Hendaya, where now the good Miguel de Unamuno whiles away his days of exile; on the other side of the Bidasoa, San Sebastián, traversed by tributaries. In a round horizon, who knows whether to the north or east, being a far cry from here, the chryselephantine region where Pierre Loti once lived must be far away, far, very far . . .

But finally this Basque coast, this mountain chain—what are they but city divisions, civil colonies overlapping one another, pieces of Paris, rags of London, metropolitan posts! Nothing. The fields of Europe, the seas of the old continent, these fields are salons; these seas are tuxedoed, urban, civilized, policed. The clearings between the oak trees are nothing but rough drafts or skeletons of small plazas; an islet between waves is but a monument on a stand. Small and distant from one another as things may be, none ever lacks an automobile in the driveway, a spare tire on the door: that one dominating the environment with its ruckus; this one returning to normal the entrance and exit of love on the far side of the wall. The tower itself of a hamlet chapel is tamed by some clock, as though life in time did not have much to do with faith in the eternity of life. There are no longer any fields or seas in Europe; there are no temples or homes—a misconstrued and poorly digested form of progress has crushed them.

But tonight, as I continue my trip to Madrid, I feel a deep, strange, and unprecedented emotion: they say that only Spain and Russia, among all the European countries, preserve their primitive purity, the purity of feats of America.

[*Mundial* (Lima), no. 290, February 1, 1926]   [MLR]

Paris, 1926

Gentleman,

It is my pleasure to hereby proclaim that death, more than a punishment, sentence, or limitation imposed on man, is a need—the most imperious and irrevocable of all human needs. Our need to die surpasses the need to be born and to live. We could forgo birth, but we could not forgo death. Thus far, nobody has said, "I need to be born," and yet it's indeed common to say, "I need to die." On the other hand, to be born is, or would seem, rather easy, as nobody has said that it has been especially difficult and especially challenging to come into this world; while dying is more difficult than one believes. This proves that the need to die is enormous and irresistible, for it is well known that the harder it is to satisfy a need, the greater the need becomes. One yearns the most for that which is least accessible.

If a man were to receive letters always saying that his mother remained in good health, he would finally end up feeling a mysterious discomfort, not exactly suspecting that he was being deceived and that his mother must have died but rather bearing the burden of the subtle, tacit need for his mother to die. That person would make his respective reckoning and think to himself, "This cannot be. It's impossible that my mother has not yet died." In the end, he will feel an anguished need to know that his mother has died. Otherwise, he will end up taking it as a given.

An ancient Islamic legend tells of a son who managed to live for three hundred years, in the midst of a race where life reached its end after fifty years at most. In the course of his exile, the son, at two hundred years of age, asked about his father and was told, "He is well." But, fifty years later, when he returned to his village only to learn that the author of his days had been dead for two hundred years, he remained very calm, whispering, "I've known it for many years." Naturally. The need for his father's death, in its time, had been irrevocable and fatal in him and had, in its time, been fatally fulfilled in reality.

Rubén Darío has said that the gods are sentenced not to reach death. As for humans, if they, by dint of their awareness, were sure that they would reach death, they would be blessed forever. But, unfortunately, humans are unsure about dying: they feel an obscure desire and craving to die, but forever doubt that they will. The sentence of humans, we shall say, is to be forever unsure of death.

[*El Norte* (Trujillo), March 22, 1926]   [MLR]

THE HISTORY OF AMERICA[10]

Paris, April 1926

I'm told that the Peruvian millionaire, Víctor Larco Herrera, has recently tasked Ventura García Calderón with arranging in Paris an exhibit of the Incas, the cost of which will be covered by the disconcerted sugar producer. It will be a complete collection of samples from the Quechua civilization and a compilation of Peruvian history so vibrant that we will be able to place our surest hopes for ripe fruit in it.

We belong to those who believe in resurrection of the messianic order, or at least in a second medical-legal disinterment. The past of America, or rather, the Atlantean feat, disappeared or was buried without an autopsy—this omission being of serious import for natives and foreigners alike. The brand new European *competitors*, as is natural, remain indecisive about going to America to sow fields about which they lack sufficient information; and with regard to the aboriginal heirs, they don't know if they should cultivate those people's estate, hand it over as a gift, sell it, or rent it out, and how much they could charge. Tremendous difficulties really, due solely to the fact that so far they've neither taken the inventory of pre-Columbian artifacts nor performed a rigorous autopsy on America's past. If the United States possessed a history like ours, along with such ancient traditions, by now they would already have taken inventory twenty times and liquidated all the ancestral work. But we, from the South, are very different Americans, very romantic in our own way, very distant from science in historical regulations as in notarial codes. (I'm talking about autopsy because there once was life; about inventory because there once were cultural goods.)

Yet from yesterday to today we are changing. We have begun to realize the need for historical examination, now that we have a history. Lord Carnavon and the Carnegie Institute have shown us the wheezing tombs and fine mummies of history. We now realize that if we want great towers in the future, we must look at the strata from which all this concern for life emerges, driving us to persevere. He who has no knowledge or wisdom of his forebears won't foresee or know anything about his children. By heading into the past one reaches the future.

America isn't a new continent, as fashionable sociologists say; it's an unexplored continent, which doesn't mean the same thing. New for Europeans; simultaneously new and old for the aborigines. A new continent? New in what sense? New as a synonym of primitive? New as a race? New as a geologic event? America will be discovered soon enough. As for what's existed for many centuries prior to the arrival of Columbus—as a solid fact, as a race, and as a culture—it's not new. If you want to open your heart to this, go listen to the Aymara[11] rhapsody exhaled by the mouths of the finest *huacos*[12] at the Nazca ruins in Peru.

The historical examination of America is just beginning. It has started by way of art, because art, among social activities, is the first to produce, the first to transcend space and time, the first to reveal and convince. In the exhibit of Larco Herrera and García Calderón, preference will undoubtedly be given to the artistic treasures of the Incas—their textiles, visual art, music, decoration, ceramics, and architecture. If only that exhibit were continental and not exclusively Peruvian, that is, displaying the entire Indo-American civilization: Aztecs and Tarascas, Toltecs and Mayas, Shiris[13] and Chimús, Quechuas and Amayaras. To our knowledge, such a reevaluation of history has yet to be made.

Thus, to come full circle, our historical exploration must continue to intensify, and in the interim it must be based on surveys of artistic folklore. Fortunately, this is beginning to materialize. Numerous research projects of this character are now being carried out all over the continent with the goal of achieving a better understanding of our history, within America herself. La Misión Peruana de Arte Incaico, directed by the eminent Luis Valcárcel, traveled last year to Bolivia, Argentina, and Uruguay; a theater company Los Guachos Argentinos, directed by the great Porteño actor, José Franco, has recently visited Chile, Brazil, and Uruguay; another similar theater group, Los Charros Mejicanos, is currently traveling through South American countries introducing the art of the North; and, finally, a scientific mission will shortly leave Guatemala on its way to the South to carry out explorations and studies of the architectural and social order with exclusively indigenous personnel. On the other hand, we must not forget two facts of great historical value: the musical work of Alomía Robles[14] in New York's Metropolitan and the English edition in progress of *Los hijos del sol*, a book of Incan legends by the great polymath, Abraham Valdelomar. Let us also point to the musical work that is being developed in Paris by the Brazilian composer Villa-Lobos[15] and that which is being carried out in the United States by the Mexican Julián Carrillo, inventor of the thirteenth sound theory.

These two great artists don't count as simple reconstructors of historical art but as creators of a totally human and universal aesthetic—which is more substantive and precisely historic—straying from the path and obtaining that higher air of the very spiritual disciplines of the race and tradition. This is what Stravinsky has done, based on the Russian steppe, and the Frenchman, Erik Satie, based on the Druid stones. Similar to such Indo-American efforts, of late there's been space in Paris for an Exhibit of Argentine Art, in the Musée du Jau de Paume; a recital of Peruvian music, in the Paris-Amérique Latine Association, performed by young artists of Cuzco—César Enríquez, Edgardo Rosas, César Valdivieso, and L. Enríquez—under the direction of Peruvian composer López Mindreau. The Argentine exhibit has been a hit, and the critics are welcoming the remarkable painters of the future who have come to unveil unexpected secrets of the great American wilderness. As for Incan music, this has constituted an unprecedented revelation for Paris, as Francis de Miomandre has said. The Andean *quena*[16] has conquered Paris, and there is no doubt that in a not so distant future, it will become the love and admiration of Europe, as the *chalumeau*[17] of the Volga has performed with its heroic squeals and the refined, lethal *drumba* of Caucasia.

[*Perú, Organo del Consolato Generale del Perú in Genova: Rivista Mensile Illustrata di Vita, Cultura ed Intercambio Commerciales fra l'Italia ed il Perú* (Genoa) 2, no. 12, May 1926]   [JM]

THE ASSASSIN OF BARRÈS

M. Pierre Laval, the new minister of justice in France, has just prohibited the public from attending judicial hearings. Before that, slackers without money to pay for the theater or a dance hall could while away their boredom in the courtrooms, without it costing them much. A few minutes of waiting in the elaborate patios, some stamping of feet, some entreaties to the guards, and—in you go! A spectacle of great interest, these hearings, in which edifying nuances of the urban environment played out. There was the spectacle of criminals, judges, witnesses, prosecutors, and lawyers, on the one hand; the spectacle of the public, on the other; and, on a separate string, the spectacle of the public and the machinery of justice together. What more could one ask for? People came out completely satisfied. It didn't cost them money. From a theater people usually come out dissatisfied because the spectator almost always believes, there in the aesthetic-economical accordions of his heart, that those hours at the theater weren't worth what he paid: it was too hot or the protagonist was bad or the decor insipid or the guy in the next seat was a spy or the usher was rude . . . By contrast, judicial hearings in Paris filled people with a perfect, unobjectionable, selfless emotion. One needn't add the artistic range and intensity of each hearing: the tragedy, the drama properly called; sometimes, the comedy, the vaudeville, the comic sketch, and even the *guignol* farce, the burlesque, opera, even dance. Occasionally, for certain medicolegal dem-onstrations, movies were offered and the occult arts lent important ser-vices, inasmuch as the astrological world of fortunes was involved.

But suddenly here now M. Laval, who belongs to a revolutionary youth group in the French Parliament, like Herriot, like Jouvenel, like Lamour-eux and others, comes to take away from us such an abundant spectacle, just out of fear that the law courts could turn into, for example, a school for delinquency. A majority of Parisians is left without entertainments. Life has gotten more expensive, since now many will have to pay for their fun. The theater and the cinema feel obliged to spill or to pretend to spill—which in this case is the same—more blood on the stage and the screen, in compensation for the blood that's no longer seen in the courtrooms. Well, M. Laval may not know what he's messing with.

Aside from these collective inconveniences in the prohibitive decree, each person suffers some particular resonance in turn. Among the old clients of the hearings I know a representative of a sleeper-car agency in whom that decree has not managed to destroy what we might call the judi-cial or, if you like, police habit. This brave initiate in the affairs of penal justice has begun to make intricate steps toward acquiring a collection of famous weapons, the kind that served great criminals. His belief is that the venture is feasible and that the collection could then basically serve the State, Science, Humanity.

In Paris everything is possible. All of a sudden, one thing happens and that's that. A good proof of that is the conduct of this other type, strangely judicial or judiciable, whom you're going to meet at once. A strangely judi-cial type, because he's not, like the representative for sleeper cars, a type classifiable in one or another judicial pigeonhole, rather he is inside of jus-tice, without ceasing to be outside of it.

M. Ferand Scatel is a jurist at the Sorbonne who—how original!—takes a great interest in the life of America. I was with him yesterday, at the fa-mous café Le Boeuf sur le Toit in Montmartre drinking an aperitif. A youth entered the room and stopped by to shake hands with M. Scatel. M. Delfau, as the lad is named, must be around thirty-four: he is elegant, though lean and very nervous. It seemed to me I'd seen him before. It seemed to me I'd seen him precisely at a judicial hearing, since Delfau has a rather judicial air. If I haven't seen him in a courtroom, as a spectator, I must have seen him on the stand, in a seat for the defense, in a police cordon, in a row of witnesses, or on a bench for the accused. This friendship between Delfau, a judicial type, and Scatel, a lawyer, seemed perfect to me for they both had an air of hearings. There are friendships that go very well.

But, as I learned after, M. Delfau has never been a lawyer, a judge, a witness, nor a policeman, and not even a bailiff. M. Delfau has not been a criminal. Nor a spectator at hearings. His strange judicial atmosphere comes from a role that he's played and that I can qualify only as rigorously judicial. M. Scatel, jurist at the Sorbonne, likewise can qualify that role only as judicial and not even as criminal. M. Delfau assassinated Maurice Barrès. But I think I've said a lot. M. Delfau himself is content to tell us, M. Scatel and me, while he sips his glass of *amourette*:

"I was supposed to have assassinated Barrès, the day he died of pleurisy. That is, I wasn't going to assassinate him but punish him, as a judge punishes a criminal or as an executioner guillotines a condemned man."

Readers will imagine our surprise at those words. But, as I said, in Paris everything is possible. M. Delfau talks to us at length: "My action, unfortunately, only came down to letting him die on his own, like a doctor who lets a sick man die or like a witness who lets an assassin be condemned or a prosecutor who ardently demands capital punishment or a guard who, because he fell asleep, allows a serious stabbing . . . I'm not speaking as a lawyer who lets an accused man be condemned, nor as an accused man who does not defend himself because you (Delfau lowers his voice, looking at Scatel) are a lawyer and because maybe I am accusing myself before you."

M. Delfau crosses his legs and adds in a dramatic tone, "Barrès, though on his own, died at any rate; he was a bad writer, that is, a great criminal. The dadaists judged him at a literary hearing. But that wasn't the main thing. Cocteau said of him that he made one think of the corpses swollen with honey by the Greek embalmers. But that wasn't the thing either. Bad writers should be assassinated, as rulers are assassinated. We should assassinate bad poets, bad painters, bad sculptors, bad musicians, with greater reason than politicians. Already in Munich the famous actor Schlosser was murdered right when he was doing a disastrous job playing a role at the theater. In Tokyo, the same thing happened to Koyague the painter, in the middle of painting a portrait: Count Masakoru, who was posing, exasperated, for a canvas in which he was being mistreated, shot his revolver at the artist. I thought of assassinating Barrès for being a bad writer. I know they would have lynched me afterward as a national response. I would have even turned myself in. Some want to assassinate Clemenceau in Paris and Mussolini in Rome. Why not, in Paris, assassinate Barrès and, in Rome, D'Annunzio? . . . Bad literature is a great offense, not only for the State but for Humanity.

"For this great crime of being a bad writer, I thought of assassinating Barrès, that is, to punish him as a *sanction of man to man*! I thought to punish him the same day that he died of pleurisy. But I am consoled, at least, by having let him die on his own. In effect, Barrès was growing old, and I let him grow old. Barrès suffered, throughout his legislator's heart, the mockery of the free young voters, and I let him suffer that. Barrès happened to cough frequently, and I also let him cough. Hours he had of treacherous winds, leaning out his windows over the Bois de Boulogne, and I let those winds lash him. Barrès happened to need *death*, while *voluptuousness* overflowed and his *blood* held council in democratic silences, and I left him with his blood, his voluptuousness, and his death. Because one must know that Barrès died from suffering a great shortage of death. It's very important to know this. Barrès died from a lack of death.

"Contrary to what happens with most people who die from a lack of life, for Barrès it was the lack of death that killed him, which should not lead us to confuse him with the great men who also die from lack of death. Know that for great men, death from lack of death puts an end to that rarefied death, while for lesser men, who are even lower than most people, death from lack of death puts an end to an exuberant life, as with Barrès, for example. Christ and Judas are a good example of these two classes of death from lack of death. They are the great man and the lesser subject. Between the two are all the rest—you, me, and people in general who die from lack of life. These subtleties are very important. Paul Valéry thinks he is worth what he is lacking, since he possesses the clear and profound science of what he is lacking. So a great spring of wisdom lies in the knowledge of what we are lacking: life or death, money or beauty, hate or love . . ."

At the end of his explanations, M. Delfau adopted the terrible expression of a saint. He is the assassin of Barrès, the one who should have assassinated him. That's what I thought from the first moment I met him: this lad is a strangely judicial fellow.

It's written that in Paris everything is possible. All of a sudden, one thing happens and that's that.

[*Variedades* (Lima), no. 958, July 10, 1926]   [JW]

THE POET AND THE POLITICIAN
The Victor Hugo Case

San Sebastián, July 1926
Day by day Victor Hugo's literary work is falling out of favor. Why? The reason according to the people who are in the know, is that Victor Hugo owes his glory not to the intrinsic literary value of his work but to its politi-

cal value. If Hugo had not called Napoleon III a green candle,[18] *Orientalia* would awaken less emotion. If Hugo had not joined the ranks to defend the nation in 1870, *The Legend of Centuries* would move people even less than *Orientalia*. Victor Hugo the poet owes a lot, everything in fact, to Victor Hugo the elected deputy. His fame and spiritual influence come from his democratic stance, his libertarian speeches in the Comédie Française, his patriotic oratory in Parliament, in sum, from the fact of being a political apostle. If Hugo had shut himself in his room like Mallarmé, he would never have achieved his universal trajectory, in spite of all the volumes of his literary work.

Now that people's political sensibility has evolved and the ideal of democracy, with all its romanticism, has been replaced by more recent social ideas, not to say more profound and essential ones, two things must happen, inevitably and logically. In the first place, there will be a fatal depreciation of Hugo's political values and then, consequently, a depreciation of his literary standing. His contemporaries molded Hugo's literary fame with the same hands that were inflamed by applause for the politician. It's not that they admired his writing directly, but simply because it came from an apostle of freedom, from the tousled lion's head that spectacularly and every day uttered apocalyptic speeches amid tongues of fire: in international conflicts, in elections, in Parliament, in the town council, on the people's barricades. Hugo knew how to be seen and applauded. The public naturally became mad with enthusiasm when they read the works of this man who they'd so often seen with the thirty towers of Nôtre Dame over his head, in the light of the sun.

At the same time, Hugo's work is essentially that of a political ideologue and not a poet. Hugo uses literature solely to spread the doctrine of the Third Republic. His literature is didactic. A moral can be extracted from every line of his poetry. He conceived a political idea or theme and then dressed it in literature. Sometimes it's "give to the poor man what's his" or else "redeem the delinquent" or "free the prisoner" that he's proposing. In all his poems, novels, and plays, there's some obvious social, economic, or religious doctrine. And this, unfortunately, can be everything bar art.

It was an easy and cheap way of becoming a "great poet." That's the way it was. Everyone has their role in the world. But what's not tolerable is mystification. We must distinguish the poet from the politician. The poet is a person who works in the sphere of the highest synthesis. He also has a political nature, but this is so in the highest degree and not in the mode of a spokesperson or sectarian. The poet's political doctrines are clouds, suns, moons, undefined and universal movements, insoluble conjunctures, first causes, and final ends. And it's the others, the politicians, who have to serve as exponents and interpreters for the multitude of this universal, chaotic language, full of the most contradictory trajectories. That's the difference between the poet and the politician.

Tagore, Romain Rolland, Barbusse are politicians rather than poets. Their fame will end when the political sensibility of the epoch changes, as has happened with Hugo. But what never finishes are the clouds, suns, first causes, and final ends, everything that preaches nothing in particular; in other words, the poet's work.

[*El Norte* (Trujillo), August 15, 1926]   [WR]

THE STATE OF SPANISH LITERATURE

The literary youth in Spain and America is currently hard up for teachers. Not even Unamuno, the strongest among the elder writers, manages to inspire direction in youngsters. No young man loves him enough to make him a mentor. Where has even a word of Unamuno been invoked as a generational model? Where are Unamuno's two apostles? Where is that Great Nation that sees him as a guide? When he speaks they applaud him; when he shouts or blasphemes or goes to jail, they sing his praise and shower him with flowers—but he doesn't stir the man or men who, under the contagion of his enlightenment, shoulder the whole weight, the whole responsibility of the future. The same admiration and enthusiasm that Unamuno awakes in the general public is proof of his mediocrity. As for Ortega y Gasset, I don't believe I'm wrong to deny him even the lowest of teaching positions. Ortega y Gasset, whose poorly germanized mentality constantly creeps over merely literary ground, is just a white elephant in creative teaching. In Hispanic America the shortage of teachers is greater.

Certain puppet-show acts of late between Chocano, Lugones, and Vasconcelos plainly show that our elders claim to be inspired—at a time like this!—by remote defunct cultural resorts. Some of them, moved by neopuritanism, with signs of undoubted tartufism, and others, stirred by a bastardized Nietzscheism in the raw, and nonprimitive (which is another matter)—all these agents of idealism, each on a path of its own, strive for an upstart methodology and are played out and sterile anyway. Besides, over there no one knows what they want, or where they're going, or how to get there. Magnificent arrivistes, most of them. Others haven't a clue. On each of these masks the egotist is painted, a yellow of greed, of mummification, of deranged fanaticism.

The rest of the writers from Spain and America keep to the naturalist novel, in purebred style, in rubendarionian verse and realist theater. Curious to note that even within these clichéd orientations, not one of these writers seduces the youth or points in any direction except the strictly literary.

Amid this dearth of spiritual command, new writers in the Castilian language don't show their outrage over an empty past, toward which in vain they turn for direction. Such outrage appears only in the most gifted, who are almost never the most spectacular. They disown their elders, when they don't renounce them from the start.

From the generation that comes before us, we can expect nothing. It is a failure for us and forevermore. If our generation manages to break its own trail, its work will crush the previous. Then, the history of Spanish Literature will leap over the past thirty years, as over an abyss. Ruben Darío will raise his great, immortal voice from the other shore, and from this one the youth will know how it must respond.

We pronounce vacant all directorial ranks from Spain and America. Without teachers the youth is on its own to face the present in ruins and a rather uncertain future. For that reason our coarse will be as hard and heroic as they come.

Manifest from one hour to the next by the strongest and purist of vanguards, may the outrage of the youth be the first creative shock wave already.

[*Favorables París Poemas* (Paris), no. 1, July 1926]   [MLR]

DA VINCI'S *BAPTIST*

Paris, August 1926

One time I read in *Treinta años de mi vida* by Enrique Gómez Carrillo an anecdote about the days when Oscar Wilde was around in Paris dreaming up *Salomé*. Those were days when "the king of life" used to talk about the Jewish princess in Nimrod's stormy plot of land in the forests of art, after the sweet Herodian piece. Remy de Gourmont, in particular, enjoyed talking with Wilde and seems to have helped the great Englishman[19] a lot concerning historical and Hertzian elucidations about the strange daughter of Antipas.

As a result of finding myself the other day with Leonardo da Vinci's *Baptist*, in the galleries of the Louvre, I remembered Gómez Carrillo's evocative pages, and I've gone to look for him at his apartment on the rue de

Castellane, eager to hear from his own lips, written in pure air, the afore-mentioned anecdote. But on the way I recalled that Gómez Carrillo spoke to me the other day of his upcoming vacation to Nice. In effect. His concierge answers me, "He left for the Alpes Maritimes."

That's a pity. Because this John by Leonardo da Vinci tells me, in his voice of a virgin Florentine faun, how he was carried away to Oscar Wilde's sublime tragedy, just as he appears in his secular painting at the palace of the Tuileries. Wilde's *Baptist* undoubtedly comes from da Vinci's. One refers to the other and they both complete each other and harmonize into a single aesthetic fullness.

As far as I know, no one before the Italian painter gave a more earthy spirit, a more human life to the historic figure of the Precursor. No one showed him grammatical gender in more expressive heroic lines. Within his Galilean racial mysticism, John stands out in da Vinci's canvas with a grace, a force, and a purpose of such chaste and natural sensuality that contemplating him produces a slight tingling on the skin. Contemplating him immediately inspires in us the feeling of an impossible tragic erotic nature. Beardless, barely adolescent, his long hair preened by the desert wind, he seems to throw his wild cascade of curls to bite the head of the crowd. That undulating hair, traced over his temples like famished teeth, will go straight to casting upon the ardent Salomé's breast the great shadowy mane of desire. One day Salomé will see those leonine curls and will no longer be able to live without caging them in the bars of her fingers. Oh, that hair biting the temples, even before the slingshots of light come crashing down upon the brow, a mere draft for the brow of The One at whose feet the Magdalene would come sobbing! Oh, that taciturn hair, suitable for the naked face that bends there, even with all its light, terrified!

The erotic suggestion of John begins in that carnivorous fleece. That fleece acts as a threshold to the wheat festival, to the sacred apple orchard of the thorax and the arms. And see that right arm, entirely naked. It starts at the armpit, then makes a turn that's almost absurd it's so smooth: bent upward at the elbow, instead of making the vertex of strange protection.

A chilling and sulfurous fingertip thus raised? To brandish the index finger on high, in a sharp ferocious jab, that we think we feel in who knows what strange pore, the lowest of the flesh. A chilling and sulfurous fingertip! A germinal stamen! (Something of this gesture transmigrates to the arm of the *Baptist* in Rodin's bronze.)

But look at the left arm. How it hides behind the other and how it insists on fading into the thorax, so subtly and wingedly, to the point that it is not missed. In the impression given off by the whole body, that arm near the heart is as if it weren't there. Before that embarrassed arm, which conceals and negates itself and defends its vivid nakedness, "Victor Hugo would be amazed." While the right arm, owner of the entire body, challenges desire face-to-face, here the left arm escapes, shields itself, resists, repels the supreme contact. The mere play of the arms is showing the tenor of the Baptist's nature: an innocent, irreducible ferment of sexual passion. The layout of the terms is clear. The conflict of the arms synthesizes and presents the tragedy.

The conflict then spreads and reaches a climax. And if not, pay attention to the play of edges and tips throughout the whole figure. In the eyebrows, the nose, the closed smiling lips, the rim of the eye sockets, in the shoulders, and oh, in the savage index finger! A whole vivid cresting of axes. The whole tragedy in a nutshell.

The gust of earthiness in da Vinci's John is such that it suggests direct similarities with *Bacchus*, by the great Florentine painter. Except that his *Bacchus* is a serene, pagan earthiness, without conflict, without tragedy, while in his *Baptist* the opposition of arrows is at its boiling point.

No other artist has offered a more natural and human version of the one before whom lions trembled. None has presented him in such a healthy and vital manner. Solario[20] is missing the Jewish ethnic form. Luini[21] lacks a tragic pulse, despite the haughty touch of the executioner's hand, on holding the Baptist's bloody head by the hair. Guerchin[22] is the one who most rises to the level of da Vinci, with the disturbing Herod in his canvas. Da Vinci, without spilling a single drop of blood in his picture, without even showing Salomé, and the drunken stepfatherly crown, nor Herod, suggests to us better than any other painter the dance of love and death.

Only Oscar Wilde produced in literature something about John the Baptist as great as what the genius from Florence depicted in his canvas. Both versions recall each other and fit together in a marvel of predestination. Except that Wilde, no doubt, was inspired by da Vinci.

Does Gómez Carrillo know anything else about Wilde's *Salomé*? I'll wait till he comes back from the Alps.

[*Variedades* (Lima), no. 968, September 18, 1926] [JW]

Paris, October 1926

I can't concur that the *Pastoral Symphony*[23] is any more valuable than my little five-year-old nephew named Helí. I can't accept that *The Brothers Karamazov* is more valuable than the gruff, poor old porter at my building. I can't agree that Picasso's harlequins are any more valuable than the pinky of the world's evilest criminal. Life before Art. This must be repeated today more than ever, while writers, musicians, and painters manage to avoid life at all cost. I know more than one modern poet who likes to lock himself in his study and furnish disconcerting verses of ingenuity, the most agile of rhythms, phrases where fantasy reaches daunting outbursts. His life? The life of this poet is reduced to sleeping until two in the afternoon, waking up without the least concern or, at most, to yawning out of tranquility and boredom, while he sits down to have lunch with fine cigars until four o'clock. Then he reads the newspapers and goes back to his room to fashion his ultramodern verses, until he grows hungry again when eight rolls around. By ten at night he's at some hip café, rejoicing as he remarks on the words and deeds of his friends and colleagues, and at one in the morning he returns to his room to forge shocking verses, until six in the morning when he falls back asleep. An existence like this, as I have said, produces work full of imagination, brimming with technique, dazzling metaphors and images. But from that same sort of existence nothing else is produced—only a great technique in verse and a supreme, subtle skill in composition. With regard to the vital content, nothing.

In these bourgeois poets who live on a government salary or a family allowance, the flaw of the sensual slacker from the worst courtesan times is still alive today. Not even an inkling of human unrest, beyond their court-jester concerns. Not even an atom of sincere astonishment, of fear for the eternal dilemmas of things, for hunger, or even for personal misfortune. With sufficient funds to subsist in mediocrity, they lack even circumstantial cravings, like eating and drinking better. These artists wander in medias res, as Giraudoux would say. They don't venture down the right side of the street because they're so lazy they don't want to seek the counterweight—ideal instinct—to the left side of the street. And vice versa. Tranquil, complete, balanced, prudent, cowardly, happy spirits are these. They neither break an arm on the train, nor ever have too much for lunch, neither lend nor borrow, neither sweat nor cry—they don't even get drunk or suffer from insomnia. Organically indifferent, they constitute the purest image of death.

Instead, their artistic vocation is slavery and servitude. One day some-one said the following to one of these artists: "During a fire a dilemma arises: You can either cut off the hand of the fireman to save an El Greco canvas, or leave that hand intact and lose that painting to the flames. Which do you save: the man's hand or the man's work?"

"Cut off the fireman's hand already and save that canvas!" responded deafly the imaginative artist, the marvelous maker of images, the perfect technician.

These artists are trying to scam life. They won't succeed.

[*El Norte* (Trujillo), November 21, 1926]   [JM]

A GREAT SCIENTIFIC DISCOVERY

Cause of excessive modern fatigue – New offensive against revolutions,
earthquakes, and child prodigies – The economic meaning of Nature – How the
maelstrom of history ends – Picasso versus cubism – Latest Russian literature –
Warning to American literary youth – The 1926 Nobel Prizes.

Paris, November 1926

Those who believe that life detests revolution are back on the offensive. Enough with the earthquakes and riots. The process of perfection runs the length of an extremely delicate wire, which doesn't resist convulsive urgency or excessive velocity. Life repels improvisation and assault. The old maxim *natura non facit saltus* trumps all objections. When we witness an earthquake or the massacre of a family of despots, we face absurd acts— abortive, momentary failures in life's lineal process. Life does not desire these failures but seeks to transpire economically, without wasting itself in unexpected adventures and precocious illuminations. Precociousness is another form of revolution in nature, another form of abortion in life. Pre-cocious children have done nothing great, in spite of those people who, out of vanity, are shocked by the six-year-old Mozart, for example. Radiguet[24] used to say that whiz kids always turned out mediocre and end up with failed lives. So life desires to transpire lineally, flowing straight, without constraint, along the length of its heroically and temporally subtle wire. Time gives the wire its length. One can't speed up or slow down events. *Natura non facit saltus*. It doesn't jump ahead or back. From this point of view, reactionary politicians are just as harmful as revolutionaries.

History shows us that bloody movements have ended by staggering backward, reforming and restraining their emergencies and excesses.

Articles and Chronicles   155

Their goals were always too great. The speed of movement was always so excessive, that it illuminated the opposite of what it desired. The standard-bearer of human rights, Napoleon, ends up becoming emperor, perhaps even without realizing it. At other times, these bloody movements are reconciled with previous situations, which makes them natural and just in a more deliberate way. This is the case with "The Soviet." Russian communists are rectifying and moderating what's excessive in their intentions, especially in the organization of the economy and industry.

Still unknown is what will become of art through this worldwide dusting and shaking, year upon year, school after school, since the days of war. What will become of cubism, constructivism, dadaism, and surrealism? And as for science, we don't know what will happen to film, aviation, radio broadcasting,[25] and the sum of these new endeavors of life, to which we now give overwhelming, limitless importance. For people are quick to say that Picasso and Stravinsky have already become classics, and Léon Daudet, a sincere intelligent soul, thinks that film is an immensely inferior art to the one it's believed to be. As for contemporary horsepower, it's entirely possible that the *surmenage*[26] of the great capitals may come exclusively from a discrepancy between the modern possibility of speed and our nerves at present. On a telephone set with a slight delay, Parisians erupt in a fit of rage. Too much is asked of science. We wish that planes would never fall. For the sake of the radio, atmospheric interference should be totally avoidable and avoided. What good are cabs, cry many people foaming at the mouth, if we wait for hours on street corners trying to hail one that's empty? These people forget that nature does not leap. One shouldn't ask too much of things. Inventions aren't as formidable as they're thought to be. For planes to fly us from Paris to Buenos Aires in twenty minutes flat without ever crashing, hundreds or thousands of years must pass. Meanwhile, let us listen to those who preach against leaps and earthquakes, in scientific matters and in everything else. We're wrong to grow angry over a delay on the phone. Our sensibility has taken a false journey toward excess, has made a sudden leap into the future, leading us to situate ourselves at a point where telephony has yet to arrive. It's time for us to rectify and work out the excesses of our propelling temperament. Let us reconcile ourselves with the modest natural evolution of things. There's no need to run away. The wheel of a car is scarcely distant from the very blue dawn of the ox's hoof. For everything else many more years must pass.

In literature the movement toward modernization and toward balance is still further off. There are still poets who fashion dark verses, and Apollinaire's calligrams continue to serve as a standard of concern. In Russia a new fictional genre is just sprouting, without any staggering humpback clowns or Chaplin rip-offs. The novel *The Naked Year* by Boris Pilnyak, recently translated into French,[27] is likely the herald of a new measure, a new balance, a new spirit. This intense, triangulated tale of pain concerning the 1917 Revolution could be an alert for America's young writers who stubbornly seem to proliferate—even in 1926—a thousand European literary schools that are false, spectacular, and (what's most painful) superficial, effeminate, and outmoded. The youth of America mustn't forget that the eighth anniversary of the armistice has not just elapsed in vain.

Yesterday, the wise austere Frenchman, M. Georges Claude, announced to the Academy of Science in Paris his invention to convert the sea into a giant endless fountain of mechanical energy. Based on Carnot's theory of the steam engine, Claude proposes to transform into mechanical energy the heat differential between the sea's twenty-five-degree surface temperature and that of the five-degree temperature of the water underneath. Claude's experience, carried out at the Academy of Science, has been conclusive. But let's not forget that industrialists are wrong to demand huge magical returns of Claude's invention. Laying pipe and turbines under the sea entails significant costs, and they'll have to content themselves with the fact that the benefit arising from this new mechanical energy will increase but slowly, always very slowly.

What will never be excessive is the glory creators deserve, in science as in art. A Nobel Prize proves to be ridiculous for men as worthy as Bernard Shaw and Jean Perrin.

[*Mundial* (Lima), no. 343, January 7, 1927]   [MLR]

LATEST SCIENTIFIC DISCOVERIES

Deafness cured by means of noise – Aesthetic divagations and scientific exactitudes – Human microcosms and macrocosms in progress – The best city street of Paris – The construction of Blvd. Haussmann took seventy years – Winter in the mountains, on the lakes and streets – The fate of war widows.

Paris, January 1927

A great English physician has just discovered an ingenious device to cure deafness. Traveling in an automobile with a deaf friend, he realized that the more noise the car was making, the better his friend could hear his words. After long experiments in the laboratory, the professor has built a "vibrator" designed to emit vibrations of great intensity, which surpass the limit of normal auditory perception. A deaf man, subjected to hearing this excessive noise on a regular and everyday basis, has managed to communicate such sensation to his ears in unprecedented, perceptual power. The hope is for this trial to culminate in the definitive and infallible cure of deafness.

From this invention one may deduce delightful and perfect paradoxes. I once wrote, with reference to the changeability of aesthetic symbols, that the color black is not the negation of all colors, but a positive optical sensation just like white, which is the sum of all colors. I also said that, regarding optics, black and white possess the same revelatory value in the visible world, since white and black are the two poles of equilibrium of this world and no one knows, at least as of yet, which is positive and which negative. To figure this out, it would be necessary first to know which of these colors gives the greatest impression of infinity. Is infinity black or white? Infinity probably lacks color, or rather, it's neither white nor black. Color limits.

And following this discourse, I said that it is not necessary to attribute to things a halfway belligerent value, but that each thing may contain virtuality to assume every role, all oppositions, consequently giving rise to the possibility that the color black may sometimes symbolize pain or pleasure, death or epiphany, according to the hemispheres and the epochs. And taking this discourse still further, I said that along auditory lines a great noise can either jolt us awake or put us to sleep. It just may happen that a person, according to his nervous system, can reconcile sleep and silence only through the action of an awful racket. Anyways, I also stated that one can become deaf as a result of listening to excessive silence, which can even go so far as to cause death. Pythagoras held that, in an ordinary and natural way, men listen to a formidable, terrible noise in the air: the fatal passing of the universe. We don't perceive or realize it because we've been born with it and, over the course of centuries, our ears bring it close and surround us with it. If, when a man is born, he were suddenly abandoned by the noise of the world, he'd drop dead on the spot. The English physician, in curing deafness, has done nothing but apply these principles. He has not discovered death with a great silence, nor has he deafened anyone, but, rather, he has returned the hearing by means of a great noise. Tomorrow that same physician could commit murder just by unleashing a great shriek in someone's ear or by curing deafness with excessive silence. The law is the same across the board; only its consequences and applications vary.

All this proves that each thing possesses a great multiplicity of vital values and that, for example, a certain kind of coldness can become so strong as to produce combustion. Each thing contains all energies and directions of the universe in the making. The human being is not the only microcosm. Each thing, phenomenon of nature, is also a microcosm in progress.

It's just that this progress can't be made on a boulevard, because that would be a crime, due to traffic's flow into bottlenecks and the fact that new city lanes open up slowly, say, every seventy years. The construction of Blvd. Haussmann in Paris began in 1857, under Napoleon III, and only yesterday, Sunday, January 15, was it completed and opened to public traffic. This vast new road, responsible for a thousand demolitions and expropriations, has cost 1.2 billion francs. The land alone on which the new arterial has been laid cost 62 million, since it measures 2,500 meters in length, from what was formerly Blvd. Haussmann to the Place de la Bastille. This boulevard will very shortly be the widest and longest of the city, where one is sure to feel, as in no other place, the subtle and high-handed pulse of Parisian life. Upon that recently paved gigantic carriageway, one can see elegant women coming and going, bundled on their winter errands, in the snow, in the wind.

On the frozen ponds of Paris and in the snow of the Pyrenees and Alps, women ice-skate, and swans and white bears die. But on the boulevards of the city, the winds reap vengeance on the poor animals, blowing toward the women, as in fabulous religions.

With regard to women, there are never any evil winds. Not even the winds of death. European women were widowed in 1914 by millions and, as this statistic claims, 40 percent of them keep remarrying every year. In England 4,500 widows of the war marry per year. And, wont for a second spouse, the Charleston is a very good cure for the heart's evil winds.

[*Mundial* (Lima), no. 352, March 11, 1927]   [JM]

THE IDOLS OF CONTEMPORARY LIFE

Toward a just discipline – End of the revolutionary spirit – Need for an examination of individual conscience – Movement in favor of good sense – Pneumatic laughs and precise tears – Fear of the skilled and faith in life – Balance, not regression.

The hour of balance draws nigh. Revolutions still tend to apply their maximum demands, but from the red flag's handle a green shoot of another flag begins sprouting on the right: the handle of fertile control. And little by much, the banner's dye and that of the shoot, in the new grace of their connective hardware, will come to ripen hope and kindle the blood's fire. Little by much, control will come to muzzle foaming mouths. The balance is already here. The same revolutionary spirit already senses the need for the opposing disciplines of consideration and justness. Enough with the foot stamping and excruciating barroquism. In politics, art, and economics, attempts are already culminating and foretell the advent of complete formulas, creative formulas. Only the complete creates. Only when a machine's springs and gears have reached organic rhythm—an infallible cardiac rhythm of repetition, a rhythm of constructive pursuit—is it qualified to work and work with vitality.

This era of excess we witness will live the least excessively. Excess is good only on the condition of its being an excess of life, never an excess of head or feet. And so it seems to us that this era of extremes will not produce in the future the extreme Left, the extreme Right, or even the extreme Center. It will produce only the just in the future, the exact of historical exactitude.

The popular trend revolutionaries are falling into is the best sign of the postwar revolutions' agony. It's already hard to meet someone who's not a revolutionary or who, at the very least, doesn't subscribe to contemporary notions of revolution. All of them—and not by snobbery, but sincerely—step into the frontline of politics with hardline communists, of economics with Marxists, of literature with surrealists, of music with jazz, of visual arts the Negroes, of pure science with Einstein, of applied science with film, of gymnastics with tennis. People relish all this so much they burst into spasms. As can be seen, nowadays there is no struggle between the hierophants of these new life forms and the vast blockheaded clientele. These revolutions have secured absolute victory. Therefore, with regard to revolutionary spirit, their historical journey has reached its completion.

What more do you want? We don't see the cause of the spectacle those revolutionaries offer when they leap out in the middle of great boulevards to shout, with the voice of Daniel in the lions' den, "In truth I say unto thee that the avant-garde will save humanity. In truth I say unto thee that the avant-gardes are gifts from God. To hell with those who don't believe in Charlot, in Josephine Baker, in Lenin, in Einstein, in Susanne Lenglen, in the radio, in poems written sideways, in the Eiffel Tower, in Tunney, etc. . . ."

We don't see the reasons behind these imprecations, or why they're directed against whom they are, as our daily experience tells us, since we're all in agreement with such brand new glorious godsends. Who'll deny the divinity of Baker, Einstein, Douglas Fairbanks, or Dempsey? No one. Millions upon millions prostrate themselves at the feet of these authentic idols. The janitors, cooks, ministers, kings, have-nots, haves, the meridians and the poles of this poor earth unanimously adore them. As for the Soviet avant-garde, one must not speak to them, who, like the Russian ambassador to England, at his death left a fortune of several million pounds of gold coin . . . So, we don't know what lack of appreciation the apostles of the revolution are bickering about.

But we're already on the cusp of another movement's birth, one that is to go against trickery, ingenuity, mechanical ability, antivitality, in sum, against all postwar fanaticism. This movement won't be one of reaction—say it ain't so Pero Grullo!—but of dynamic equilibrium, of evolutionary justness and that good sense which Keyserling preaches, so dear to creators, compasses, and the cosmic concert. This movement will come to put key and measure to our epoch. And this movement will sift through current values, separating the chaff from the grain. No one knows what will arise from this act of justice and rigor. I fear for the savvy, the magicians, the technicians, the theorists, the jongleurs of last straws, the subtle heroes of trickery, pneumatic laughter, precise tears.

And I'll answer to whatever is vital in that fanaticism, which probably won't be much.

[*Mundial* (Lima), no. 358, April 22, 1927]   [MLR]

AVANT-GARDE RELIGIONS

Polemic on film and Charles Chaplin – Conflict between the cinema, the circus, the music hall, and the theater – Worldwide consequences of the divorce of the Tramp[28] – An artist's opinion and a man's opinion – Rift between filmmakers – Douglas Fairbanks and Rio Jim, characters of an Italian comedy – Spirit and men in modern minorities.

Paris, March 1927

In these disputes over film, only the profane are authorized to opine. In film-related matters, as in all the arts, initiates and professionals are called on the least to speak their views, especially when the task is to situate the freely human and extratechnical scope of art. Thus, as the search is on today to determine whether or not film assumes a supreme artistic role and, therefore, possesses its own peculiar means of expression, independent from the other arts—the opinions of critics, authors, actors, and metteurs en scène have no authority. Neither Jean Epstein nor Louis Delluc, neither Jannings nor Chaplin himself would say what must be said. Technicians speak as technicians and very rarely as men. It's very difficult to be a man, my dear North Americans! It's very difficult to be this and that, artist and man, at once. A man, who's an artist, can no longer do or say anything related to art, except as an artist. A poet will judge a poem not as a mere mortal, but as a poet, and the same occurs with filmmakers. Abel Gance, metteur en scène of *Mater Dolorosa*; Douglas Fairbanks, protagonist of *The Black Pirate*; Charles Chapin, author, metteur en scène, and actor of *The Gold Rush*; Leon Moussinac, historian and film critic, will not succeed in expressing a fair criterion regarding the fate of film for humankind. And we already know to what extent technicians get tangled up offstage in the fly ropes, falling through the weak side of the system, from indoctrinating prejudice or from professional interest, consciously or subconsciously, and in this way fracturing the complete sensibility of man.

In the debates on film, at most, free writers who have nothing to do with the inner workings of the profession can offer an opinion. This is why I'm pleased in this polemic that an idea of Paul Valéry, of André Saurés, of Blaise Cendrars, or of Dr. Allendy may or may not be to my liking. But, in general, all that's worthwhile in this matter is the appearance of a rigorously profane man who, naturally, isn't a complete boob.

Readers will know soon enough that a red-hot polemical commotion has arisen in the world from the lawsuit Chaplin's ex-wife (Lita Grey) is bringing against him, concerning the artistic personality of the Tramp and, therefore, in respect to the aesthetic value of film. In Paris, a group of writers, headed by—what a surprise!—the Catholic poet Max Jacob, has made the defense of and apology for Chaplin and for the *ècran*.[29] On the other side, a second group of writers, whose figurehead, André Saurés, charges against trampism. On this occasion a great Parisian newspaper publishes a poll about the value of film, of the circus, of the music hall, and of the modern theater, in which the opinions of very significant writers and artists of Paris appear. No one yet knows what will become of this conflict. Who knows if theater, the music hall, or the circus, or all three may end up waxing silent art? So far no one knows.

At the heart of the poll is, namely, whether or not film exists as a new art independent of the other arts, and if it does, what the state of its development is and what its possibilities are in the future. The debate over Chaplin, in essence, tends to resolve an identical postulate. No one, I repeat, foresees the definitive terms of the solution. In the short term, from the debate one can already deduce that "the filmic or trampistic religion," as André Saurés sarcastically calls it, captured 90 percent of the population worldwide. Eight percent is made up of die-hard, irreconcilable enemies of film. The remaining 2 percent is made up of free and changing people, who manage to give sincere, human intonation to their attacks and praises, without systematizing them or letting themselves be carried away by trends or troglodytic skepticism, by following the fluctuations of their own taste and the peripeteia of the development of film.

Does film exist? Fire! Fire! At this stage of the game, the question is already burning and few dare respond in the negative. Ninety percent, as we have said, are ready to vote for the existence of film. Eight percent, with all their hands, are voting against it. Neither one gang nor the other is honest though, because both have become fanatic. According to the remaining 2 percent of the people, only the freely and humanly variable opinion is of interest. When these people deny the existence of film, they deny it honestly. When they affirm it, they also do so honestly. To the first group "everyone" belongs, to the second group "another everyone," and to the third, "the best of all."

Among worshipers of the *ècran*, there are those—without counting the bulk of the public and operating among units—who ground their filmic faith in very symptomatic motives. Madame Rachilde prefers the cinema because it's cheaper. Bib prefers the movies because "there's nothing in the circus, in the theater, or in the music hall comparable to Chaplin's genius." Gabriel Trarieux believes and has faith in the *ècran*, because it's a global art. "Besides in music," he says, "very few art works radiate so far."

Dominique Braga believes and has faith in film because it's the art of the fifth dimension. "The metteur en scène," he says, "will manage to penetrate, from the angle of the *prise de vue*, the inside of his character, so as to interpret his life cinematically, in a way that's visual and, at once, intellectual" and so on and so forth.

From time to time one hears a dissonant voice, a snorting at the machine, an irreverent yawn. It's Léon Daudet, or Georges Kaiser, or Henri de Naussanne, or André Saurés himself, or one disillusioned morose moviegoer or another who, like Galtier Boissiére, will confess the departure obliquely. "In reality," he states, "film is nothing but an art of interpreters and Douglas, Rio Jim, and others have very rightly been compared to characters of the Italian comedy."

The polemic continues and, therein, the bets in favor of film grow with each birth and even with each death.

[*Mundial* (Lima), no. 359, April 29, 1927]   [JM]

AGAINST PROFESSIONAL SECRETS
On Pablo Abril de Vivero

The current generation of America is no less lost than the ones that came before it. The current generation of America is just as rhetorical and devoid of spiritual honesty as the preceding generations that it rejects. I raise my voice and accuse my generation of being unable to create or manifest a spirit of its own, made of truth, life, and healthy, authentic, human inspiration. Today I sense a disastrous outcome of my generation, fifteen to twenty years in the making.

I'm sure these young men of today do nothing but change the labels and names of the same lies and conventions of the men who came before them. The rhetoric of Chocano, for example, reappears and persists, perhaps more inflated and hateful, in the poets that have come after him. As during the romantic era, America currently borrows and wears the European dress shirt of the so-called new spirit, driven by incurable historical ingratitude.

Today, like yesterday, writers from America produce a borrowed literature that's working out tragically awful for them. Now more than ever, the aesthetic—if that grotesque, simian nightmare of American writers deserves such a name—lacks a physiognomy of its own. A line from Neruda, Borges, or Maples Arce is no different than one from Tzara, Ribemont, or Reverdy. At least in Chocano there was some cheap Americanism in the themes and names. In today's writers, not even that.

Let me make this concrete. The current generation of America has its foundation on the following principles:

1. New orthography: Deletion of punctuation marks and capital letters (European postulate from futurism twenty years ago to the dadaism of 1920);
2. New calligraphy of a poem: The ability to write vertically like Tibetans, or in circles or diagonally like kindergartners; essentially the ability to write in any direction, according to the objective or emotion one wishes to suggest graphically (European postulate, from San Juan de la Cruz and the Benedictines of the fifteenth century to Apollinaire and Beaudouin);
3. New topics: The radiotelegraph overtakes the moonlight (European postulate, in Marinetti as in three-dimensional synopticism);
4. New devices for image making: Substitution of comparative and ecstatic alchemy for calculating and dynamic pharmacy in the so-

called *rapport* of poetry *d'après guerre* (European postulate, from Mallarmé twenty years ago to the surrealism of 1924);

5. New images: Advent of the unstable, caustic polarity of metaphoric terms, according to laws in systematic opposition to the aesthetic terms of Nature (European postulate, from the precursor Lautréamont fifty years ago to the cubism of 1914);

6. New cosmological consciousness of life: Accent on the spirit of human and cosmic unity. The horizon and distance acquire an unprecedented meaning, due to communication and motion facilitated by scientific and industrial progress. (European postulate, from Laforgue's stellar trains and Hugo's universal fraternity to Romain Rolland and Blaise Cendrars); and

7. New political and economic sense: The spirit of the democratic, middle-class man is replaced by the hardline communist (European postulate, from Tolstoy fifty years ago to the surrealist revolution of our day).

The raw materials and intangible, subtle tones that can't be found in perspectives on or theories of the creative spirit simply don't exist in America. In the aesthetic disciplines I've just enumerated, European poets continue to flourish on both sides of the pond. Yet in America those very disciplines don't help writers reveal and realize themselves precisely because they've been imported and practiced by mimicry, because they don't respond to the peculiar needs of our psychology and environment, and because they haven't been conceived by the genuine terrestrial drive of those who now cultivate them. With regard to this kind of spiritual movement, endosmosis, far from nourishing, is poisonous.

Therefore, I accuse my generation of propagating the same methods of plagiarism and rhetoric from preceding generations as those which they themselves reject. What we have here is not a warning in support of a nation, continent, or race. I've always thought those labels have nothing to do with art and that, when writers are judged in terms of them, one becomes increasingly confused and one's uncertainties, all the more uncertain. For example, take Jorge Luis Borges, who practices that Porteño fervor as false and superficial as is the Latin Americanism of Gabriela Mistral and the cosmopolitanism fashionable among all young Americans of late.

As I write these lines, I invoke a different attitude. There's human tone, a vital and sincere heartbeat the artist must foster, although it doesn't matter in which creative disciplines, theories, or processes. Find that dry, natural, pure, powerful, eternal emotion and the needs for style, manner, and procedure are no longer of any importance. In the current generation of America, no one manages to feel that emotion. And I single out those writers of gross plagiarism, because I think that their plagiarism prevents them from expressing and realizing themselves humanly and highly. I single them out for their lack of spiritual honesty, because while they imitate foreign aesthetics, they're aware of their plagiarism and they nonetheless plagiarize, boasting with insolent rhetoric that they create out of autochthonous inspiration, out of the free and sincere drive of life. Autochthony does not consist in saying that one is autochthonous but precisely in being so, even when not saying so.

While reading the latest book by Pablo Abril de Vivero, *Ausencia*, I have reconsidered American culture. Books like this represent a very significant moment in continental literature. The nobility of these verses can be seen from afar — noble, because, in the middle of 1927, they don't intend to discover the cure for tuberculosis or even another school of poetry. This is a book of human beauty, plain speech, and the rare virtue of arousing excitement in the reader. That's why this is one of the noble books of America. Abril could've tangled up the syntax and logic to join those masses of quacks who, with this or that avant-garde label, completely infest the environment. (I say masses because today, as opposed to what could or should occur, most writers are revolutionaries.) The spiritual aristocracy stands there being conservative, and the defensive status quo stands there proclaiming itself avant-garde. Abril could've been more deceiving and written with his eyes closed, and this might have impressed the dazzling and highest of circles. Had Abril even written not with capital letters, but skyscrapers instead — this, a quite avant-garde paradox — he surely would've made it big in the salons.

But the book by Abril, like other sincere books from America, was swept away by the genuine, creative emotion and finds a way to stay outside of any school, showing the signs of a free and invigorated personality. *Ausencia* is the work of a profound and simple poet, human and transparent. This is how true creators are characterized: by devoting themselves without anointing themselves and without besmirching anyone else. Artists like Abril, who have something in their heart to give, do so soundly and naturally. And that's also far from the avant-garde. It's out of cowardice or destitution that almost all artists take to the avant-garde. One fears that the melody may not come adequately or that it won't come at all and, as a last resort, takes refuge in the avant-garde. This much is certain. In pseudo new poetry there is plenty of room for every lie but no room at all for oversight. These are the "professional secrets" that Jean Cocteau defends; it's "the kingdom that is not of this world," according to abbé Brémond. The soundness of Paul Souday, his good taste and sacred need for authentic human emotion—that's not welcome there.

Fortunately, every so often in America books like Abril's come out and, between the vanguard Charleston, achieve a well-balanced step, a voice of sanity, a refreshing glow without pretensions. Thanks to these books, every once in a while one is allowed to perceive in America unquestionable silhouettes of great lyrical emotion. The section from *Ausencia* titled "Nocturnos" reaches that high poetic tone.

[*Variedades* (Lima), no. 1001, May 7, 1927]   [JM]

THE NEW DISCIPLINES

Paris, July 1927

The war has given rise to a new structure for life in Europe. This cannot be denied. Whoever lives here a few years and absorbs the intimate European social atmosphere has to confirm the existence of cultural forms and disciplines that are absolutely distinct from those before the war. Everything differs from the previous era: the economy, thought, sensibilities, fashion, and even worries and vices.

The young intellectuals of the new continent, to whom I address these lines especially, don't know or know poorly the existence, quality, and reach of European culture *d'après guerre* (culture, yes, though it might be only an attempt or simply feeling around in the dark). Few are the men of America who really notice the new vital state of Europe. And that's because such a phenomenon of renovation can be known only, in all its authenticity, by living long years in close contact with European life. Not many South Americans come to Europe to live in this way. Some are here as if they were not. Their daily life goes by as a continuation in Europe of South American life: their social dealings are solely with South Americans and Spaniards; they speak only Spanish; they read (when they read) newspapers and books only in Spanish; their conversations and topics turn around America or American things; their smallest acts are directed, in intention and motives, toward America; and even in the matter of shows, they seek and attend only Spanish theater, Indoamerican concerts, Andalusian dance, conferences about the homeland, and native oratory. Clearly, such people can be many years in Europe, and it's as if they were not. As for the rest, they pass through, traveling all over the old hemisphere in six or eight months and barely seeing anything, like at the movies or in Paul Morand, in order to bring back, on their return, only a rushed album of blurry images that haven't passed through the retina and so, as a consequence, get erased before they disembark in Buenos Aires or Valparaíso. I know both classes of South Americans, and, at any moment, I can point out intuitively a thousand examples of each of them. In the best cases, there are South Americans who live isolated in a single European social field, in the bourgeoisie or the aristocracy, that is, in the areas least likely to reveal the new European spirit. Anyway, some people from America spend twenty or thirty years in Paris, walled up with books and newspapers, far from the living palpitating life of every day and with no connection to the warm circumstantial trance of individual psychology, these particulars truthful and infallible documents for penetrating the life of a society.

The new European structure for life is not what the young writers of America generally imagine. It is not Mistinguette, or Paul Morand, or the Black Bottom dance, or Margueritte, or fashionable literary schools, or Chevalier, or the Tour Eiffel. These things are just simple motifs for show, as cheap as they are gaudy, which the press and the boulevard artists exploit right and left, often from native and irremediable unawareness of those artists, and almost always taking full economic advantage to cheat the good impressionable visitors. Apart from the fact that all those clichés date from before the war. Chevalier and Mistinguette have been singing for forty years in Montmartre; Morand has been writing about bathrooms and bicycles for twenty years; the Tour Eiffel uses identical measures and the same distribution of forces as in 1899; butch women have existed since the years of Musset and George Sand; surrealism has existed, as André Breton himself declares, since Poe and his contemporaries; and, as for dance that aims for the *grand-écart* or die trying, the cakewalk was already a common dance back in the time of Debussy. So none of this constitutes the new European life. America should know that Europe is getting worked up these days, in a way that's more serious and deeper than what you'd imagine, to be reborn toward a life that is likewise purer and happier than before. The restlessness and yearning to be reborn are expressed and demonstrated in Europe by means of other phenomena that are not the banal and decadent numbers that I've just indicated. There are other manifestations of the new kind of European life. Others that my contemporaries in America know poorly or barely suspect.

One of the disciplines characteristic of the new European life is the feeling for order and method. Young people here have understood that life, to be successful individually and socially, must obey a rigorous discipline of order and method. Order and method in work, in leisure, in joys, in sorrows, in public, in private. Order and method in the tasks of the body and in the functions of the spirit. Order and method for sowing and for reaping, for dying and for living. Order and method for wrecking and for building. The romantic generation of Hugo and the ascetic one of France both lacked the feeling for order, the first because of an excess of faith in nature's wisdom and in the natural destinies of life, and the other because of not having that faith. In every aspect, life *d'avant guerre* was messy, *bataclanesque*, to use a term current at the time. The irregular and anarchic habits of the bohemian were typical and representative. It was a sign of strength and spiritual aristocracy to shake off, as much as possible, every law, every rule. One had to break free of the yokes and even of oneself. People flaunted the disorder and the anarchy, like lovely personal qualities. Artists threw themselves into their work, blindly, taking it all the way. The myth of improvisation and the phobia of the scientific dominated in art as in other fields of life.

But the best among Europeans *d'après guerre* have reacted against this discipline. Like no other animal, man is a being of order par excellence. A schedule and a plan are now indispensable for every enterprise, material or spiritual, subjective or collective. The watch, once staunch enemy of the artist, is not missing now on the wrist of the poet and the aviator. An authentic geometric inclination leads people to act and to manage—dancing in the *Fantasio* or crying before a tomb—by means of sketches and in view of maps and guides. Even sleep is adjusted now—on the right, to the hands of the watch, and on the left, to the needle of the compass. We understand now that order and method, far from slowing down and opposing freedom and the natural proportions of life, favor and encourage them. Beauty, says Paul Valéry, comes from difficulty. There is no construction possible without rules or a system, that is, without science. Because in man nothing should be blind.

One of the signs of the new European life, then, is the advent of the man of order and method and the disappearance of the bohemian and anarchic sort from the previous era. Raymond Radiguet's work, its fullness of beauty, its constructive and organic finished spine, calls our attention for that reason. In this sense, Radiguet has been a new spirit, an authentic avant-gardist.

[*Variedades* (Lima), no. 1017, August 27, 1927]   [JW]

LIFE AS A MATCH

Paris, August 1927

Who flies farther? Who throws better punches? Come on, who? Who breaks the record in tennis, in football, in duration, in altitude, in weight, in resistance, in intensity? Who earns more money? Who's the fastest dancer? The record for fasting, smoking, philately; the record for music, laughter, piety, matrimony, divorce, murder, revolution! . . .

The feeling or perhaps just the pruritus of the record spreads through all spheres of life. No one does anything anymore without an eye on his rival and his gaze on the goal that must surpass all goals thus far achieved. The aviator flies, no longer out of the natural and free vocation of flight, but to do what no other aviator has done before. The dancer dances, no longer out of the free and natural urge to rhythmically move, but to do what no other dancer has done before. The murderer kills, no longer in a fit of violence, passion, or morbid instinct, but to do what no other murderer has done before. The same occurs everywhere. Man moves in comparison with man. It's a joust, no longer of forces that oppose one another directly, which would be more noble and human, but of forces that compare and rival one another, which is stupid and artificial. Today man can't live and step forth on his own, while looking straight ahead, as the parallel order of things has it, but instead he lives and bears in mind the advance of everyone else, that is, while looking sideways at the horizon.

The prevailing criterion is quantitative in this society of records and heights. Quantity, be it large or small, is sought for all units of measurement. The quality of actions thus remains completely external to life, or if it's brought inside for something, it's to be measured to the decimal. In boxing one jab is better than another, insofar as it tipped the scale of the fight one driblet in the crusher's favor. Following the criterion of the record, even humor (when there is any) is assigned a quantitative value.

As a criterion of life, the record comes to us from sports. The philosophical soul of this criterion, Quantity, arrives from the United States—that country of the standard—where even tears are appraised and coveted because they're not and can't be mass-produced. In New York, someone who cries profusely and accumulates endless tears becomes a great industrial resource, a lively hotspot of human activity.

The world, like this sports trend, keeps adopting the feeling of the record in all activities. Life is now a stupendous, plural, multifaceted match, in the way a terrible, bloody battle used to be waged. (Some people prefer the latter character of life.) The manifestations of this matchism are countless, joyous, comic, dramatic, banal, tragic, metaphysical, mystical, material-ist, scientific. Its forms and variations are no less diverse. The forms of the match, pure and typical, ambiguous and disguised. In Cannes they're pre-paring for a strange competition, a midday game for women, on a gigantic quadrilateral mowed into a meadow where an army of country girls will dress as white pawns, and some odd adolescents, black pawns. Two great champions will play this match, and during the classic feasts at the Swiss vineyards of Vevey it will have nothing to envy, in fertile grace or the move-ment of eternity.

Sports uphold these arduous values of life. Due to the sports trend, the most minor act of man has become a duel — be it express or tacit — with the likeness of one's neighbor. Are you pleased with this? Of course you're not.

To say it with Antenor Orrego, life as a match is the devitalization of life. The moral pulp of the match is slavery and effemination. I don't live by comparing myself to anyone or defeating anyone or even pushing others down. I live by supporting and, in sum, concentrically relating to every-one else, but not by rivaling them. I don't want to break any records. I seek in myself the free and universal triumph of life. I don't want to break the record of one man over another, but instead the centripetal and centrifu-gal record breaking of life. The record of life is one thing, and the triumph of life is another. Life is not war or farce of war. It is but stimulus and noble emulation. But the match necessarily rests on stimulus and emu-lation that are far too extreme and narrow. This man trains more because he knows his contender is, in turn, better trained. Dempsey prepares and works more to fight Tunney than he does to fight Wills.[30] In life one lives and advances, not because other people live and transform, but because of the lone, free feeling of living. If there was not more than one man in the world, that man would live alone, without contenders, without emulators, and even without cohabitants.

Therefore, the match entails the neighbor and the mirror. It's played out of self-love, patriotism, greed, or for one of the countless other stupid and egotistical reasons in which the malice of man mixes together with the good sweat of the beast.

[*Variedades* (Lima), no. 1021, September 24, 1927]   [JM]

ARTISTS FACING POLITICS

Warning to true artists – A mistake by Diego Rivera – The difference between political propaganda and political creation – From Mayakovsky to Dostoevsky, from Déroulède to Marcel Proust – The extent to which an artist is a political being – Take caution with phonographic records – Ideas in the air and clouds in the heart – Let emotion be given and theories discarded.

Paris, November 1927

The artist is an unavoidably political being. His neutrality, his lack of political sensibility, would prove spiritually shallow, humanly mediocre, aesthetically inferior. But in what sphere should the artist act politically? His field of political action is multiple: he can vote, join a protest, like any other citizen; lead a group of civil volunteers, like any other statesman on the block; head a doctrinaire movement on the national, continental, racial, or global scale, like Rolland. In all these ways, the artist without a doubt can be politically active, but none of them responds to the powers of political creation, peculiar to his proper nature and personality. The political sensibility of the artist arises, preferably and in its maximum authenticity, by creating political concerns and clouds, vaster than any catechism or collection of ideas (that are express and, therefore, limited), from whichever political moment you please, and purer than any newspaper's polls or political ideology, be they nationalist or universalist. The artist must not reduce himself to turning the tides of an electoral vote of the masses or to reinforcing an economic revolution, but, before all else, he must give rise to a new political sensibility in humankind, a new political raw material in human nature. His action isn't didactic, transmitting or teaching emotions and civic ideas that already infest the air. Essentially, it means stirring, in an obscure, subconscious and almost spiritual way, the political anatomy of man, waking in him the aptitude to engender and summon new civic concerns and emotions. The artist isn't circumscribed to cultivating new vegetation in the field of politics or to geologically modifying that field, but chemically and naturally he must transform it. This is what artists did prior to the French Revolution and as the creation thereof; this is what artists have done prior to the Russian Revolution and as the creation thereof. The harvest of such political creation, brought about by true artists, is visible and palpable only after centuries, and not the next day, as occurs with the superficial action of pseudo-artists.

Diego Rivera believes that Latin American painters must take men and the social strife of Latin America as artistic motifs and themes, as a political medium to combat the aesthetic and economic imperialism of Wall Street. In this way, Diego Rivera debases and prostitutes the political role of the artist, by converting it into the instrument of political ideology, a cheap didactical medium of economic propaganda. "It is an incontrovertible truth," he says, "that power, in the first place, is an aesthetic factor economically shifting the reference of consumer goods and, in the second place, a psychological factor capable of channeling the mind and will of the proletariat down the shortest path toward the achievement of what befits its class interests." Diego Rivera forgets that the artist is the freest of beings and works far above political programs without escaping the realm of politics. He forgets that art isn't a medium of political propaganda. I'm talking about true art. Any versifier, like Mayakovsky, can defend the excellence of Soviet sea fauna in good futurist poems, but only a Dostoevsky, without pigeonholing his spirit in any political, concrete, and, therefore, already-annihilated creed, can give rise to great cosmic urgencies of human justice. Any versifier, like Déroulède, can stand up straight in front of the crowd and shout whatever democratic banter he fancies, but only a Proust, without registering his spirit with any political party, be it his own or his neighbor's, can give rise to, not new political tones in life, but new chords on which those tones ring.

Diego Rivera manufactures a record and intends to give it to the artists of America so that they make it spin. All political catechism, even the best of the best, is a record, a cliché, a dead object, when compared to the creative sensibility of the artist. This political action is fine in the second-rate hands of a look-alike or knock-off artist, but not in the hands of a creator. It would be good, even in Rivera's theory, to locate the moxie, but history offers no examples of an artist who has successfully created a great work based on polls or political parties that he supports or opposes. In general, theories hamper and hinder creation.

Before shouting on the streets or getting locked in jail, in a tacit and silent heroic act the artist must create the great deep political aqueducts of humankind that become visible and flourish only over centuries, precisely, in those ideologies and social phenomena that later echo in the mouths of the men of action, apostles, and opinion leaders we mentioned earlier.

If the artist refuses to create what we might call political clouds in the human wilderness, reducing his work to the secondary role of propaganda or the barricade itself, to whom might that great spiritual thaumaturgy fall?

[*Mundial* (Lima), no. 394, December 31, 1927]   [JM]

CONTRIBUTION TO FILM STUDIES

A serious metaphysical problem – Universal sound and silence – Rhetoric in theater – "Chantecler" drags on – Are we headed for silence or sound? – Greetings to Einstein – An essential element of silent art – Synchronism in film – Eternal adultery in French theater.

Paris, November 1927

In Paris rhetoric stills receives applause. For *Chantecler*, Edmond Rostand still gets a twenty-year-old ovation, and the crowing of the rooster in his story still moistens the eyes of fiancées with the usual tears. When Victor Francen, of Theater Saint-Martin, with his luxurious dark orange plumage and his valiant cardboard crest, climbs atop the hedges and crows, "Cock-a-doodle-doo! Cock-a-doodle-doo!" the balconies still creak, and the audience responds with grand syncopated applause.

The actors know this: a well-recited monologue is enough to keep a play onstage for a year. Rhetoric determines the cost of theater, by means of the prosody of the phrasing or feeling. If Francen makes it big by busting his tongue, Ivonne Printemps makes it big by hyperbolizing the thunderous emotion of adultery for the thousandth time. The former is the rhetoric of the word; the latter, of the nervous system.

However, no one can deny that the year is 1927 and that the internal or external acoustic conditions of life differ from those a quarter century ago, when *Chantecler* was first produced. Could noise have increased since 1905? Could it have decreased? Over the past twenty years has there been more or less noise in the universe? But, here I seem to have asked too much. I've practically boxed dear Mr. Einstein's ears with questions so sizable that, unbeknown to me, have become real stumpers as soon as they left my mouth! No. All I wished to know is if life, over time, becomes noisier or quieter. Materialists will reply that life is headed for silence; spiritualists, for the apotheosis of the immortal Word; and centrists will hold that the amount of sound existing in the universe remains constant and that what changes is the proportion in which it mixes or alternates with silence, in accordance with time and space.

"Be that as it may," M. Jean Renouard says, "the truth is that, in a time when noise despotically rules the world and our nerves are subjected to the mortal battle cries of all these engines, chased by modern progress, silence has sought refuge in the dark rooms of the cinema. As a (perhaps unconscious) reaction, the crowd rushes to these tranquil oases where our nerves are eased and dreams momentarily allowed to fly . . ."

The thesis of universal sound as a constant is thus supported and confirmed almost completely. If modern life has invented so many deafening machines, with all their resonating consequences, in return it has given us the cinema where silence still reigns. Sound has grown on the street but has decreased in the rooms of the cinema. More categorically, the same amount of noise exists now as it did twenty plus years ago.

And when M. Jean Renouard and I were going to enjoy a viewing of *Chantecler*, watching it in the silence of a room at the cinema, the film *Ben-Hur*—kablooey!—unleashed a wretched racket of trumpets, rattles, applause, and chariot crashes . . . It's the orchestra. We see on the *écran* a lofty imperial parade of ancient Rome, and the orchestra accompanies the spectacle with a sonorous expression. It's the synchronism of image and sound . . . M. Jean Renouard and I left the cinema.

"Where shall we go tonight in search of silence?"

"To planet Venus! Since all the noise in the universe these days appears to have invaded Earth. Even film, called 'the silence art' with such good intention, becomes the focus of insufferable racket."

We forget that music should be radically excluded from film and that one of the essential elements of the seventh art is absolute silence.

[*Mundial* (Lima), no. 391, December 9, 1927]   [JM]

MADNESS IN ART

A few abstract theodolites – The Mad Salon – A chronicle of favorite pastimes –
Art among the mad or the mad in art – The opinions of two great French
psychiatrists – Thoughts written in the margin of insane pictures – The fatal
breakdown of vocation – The restless creativity of an Indo-American – Madness,
the secret of human destiny.

Paris, December 1927

The Countess de Noailles's favorite pastime is painting. Max Jacob's and Francis Picabia's is painting too. Charlie Chaplin's is musical composition. Lindbergh's is singing. The French senators' favorite pastime is the Basque Ball, and the deputies' is drawing. Mariette de Rauwera's favorite pastime is classical dance. The favorite pastime of the deaf is sculpture, and of the mad, painting. The favorite pastime is a current phenomenon, because a human never devotes both arms to a single vocation, but always reserves the left for what, even for an instant, could've been.

The principal vocation of the mad is madness. Such is their art, its fundamental motive in life. But the mad also make concessions for the remainders of a problem. They seek to bite off the whole right arm, but meanwhile with their left eye wield a critique of pure reason or discover a new dimension in the visual arts so that they don't get bored. Similarly dividing their concern, the mad go halfsies, which is to say, they're almost equally enthused by both activities. This is one of the most important differences that distinguish the sane from the mad. The sane man's right foot differs enormously from the left, and this marks out the irreproachable citizen who's never strayed or a serious child who never plays. By contrast, the mad man's right foot is hardly distinguishable from the left. If you ask a mad man of great prestige what the difference is between day and night or between the past and future, he'll respond with wonderful and distinguished stupidity. Contrary to what one might think, the mad don't completely devote themselves to madness, but rather divide their sensibility almost equally between their predominant life vocation and some other sphere of life. The mad don't put too much east in this, or too much west in that. We're almost tempted to attribute a meridian position to them—the terrible metaphysical golden mean.

When the mad, apart from being mad, get into painting, they aren't left-handed because, following what's been said, they nearly paint with both hands, or at least in the act of painting they don't know their left from their right, or light from shadow, or a simple point from a line, and, as a result, their pictures are magnificent, disastrous.

In an intrepid gallery on rue Vavin, a few madmen from various countries offer a copious exposition of drawings, paintings, and sculpture for communal sanity. While rational decorative architects prepare us for Christmas with harmonious illuminations in storefronts and on the Tour Eiffel, the favorite pastime of the mad strangely vibrates, but the purity and clarity of their sad melodies, in a creative surge, surpass even the music of the celebrated Theremin. Without a doubt, the mad are admirable people.

Some critics dare to believe that this exposition could actually support a fundamentally creative aesthetic. "Picasso already wants," ventures a critic in *L'Art Vivant*, "to possess the amazing resources of the mad Juni, one of those exponents who's written slogans and thoughts like this in the corner of their drawings: 'And the bells of Meudon go ding dang dong!' and 'These same walls, sir, have eagle eyes.'"

"The art of the alienated," says another critic of *Crapuillot*, "has a guiding significance as great as that held by black art twenty years ago." Called on to rule in this matter, celebrated psychiatrists Maré and Vinchon agree in affirming that "modern art seems to connect at a certain point with insane art, because both take their inspiration from the domain of the unconscious and express it in a more or less direct way. It should likewise be noted," explain said geniuses, "that when artists suffer a mental disturbance, their spirit generally returns to primitive notions of art, and a similar tendency can be seen to manifest itself in our modern schools, just as it manifested itself in the past in the case of Renaissance artists, such as El Greco, for example."

What would older people back home say to all this? Recently, no less, on the occasion of an exposition of the work of Peruvian artist Juan Devéscovi in Paris, people from overseas stood in front of that direct expression, as described by Maré and Vinchon, which characterizes the painting of this brave Indo-American artist, and they don't want to be convinced that what humankind lacks in order to be completely happy is precisely a few more Spanish flies of madness.

[*Mundial* (Lima), no. 401, February 17, 1928]   [MLR]

THE PASSION OF CHARLES CHAPLIN

More on artists facing politics – Lessons of objects with examples – Secret laws and trajectories in art and artists – The political spirit of Chaplin's work – A great frieze of the modern economic tragedy – What the United States does not know – A new Philistine incarnation: Lita Grey – The chronicler can admire but not be enslaved – Chaplin's dog facing the Tramp.

Paris, January 1928

The Ninth Symphony was humanly born key by key from the law of Mariotee, which the Estachian tube couldn't disprove to Beethoven's auditory nerve. In turn, the five luxury automobiles of Charles Chaplin, multimillionaire and gentleman, lead the most dispossessed and absurd of men into the future, wearing fifteen bowler hats, five other people's suites, six pairs of *godillots*,[31] and twirling four magical canes . . . Thus, Chaplin engenders the Tramp, in the splendid film *The Gold Rush*. Beautiful are the lost letters, and secretly humble are the facades of the giant skyscrapers.

Here, in this film, is Charles Chaplin, gentleman and multimillionaire, scratching the crotch of the Tramp, that beggar eaten away by giant honorable lice. For the length of the film, Chaplin, high poet of human misery, turns his back to his dollars. An avatar of art has made him poor in them, great in them. The actor here, as in no other film of his, is completely absorbed by the character. Good night, Mr. Pirandello . . . There you have Bill, Chaplin's white dog, howling outside the gate of the dressing room waiting for his owner. The Tramp has just come out with a bag over his shoulder, and he heads off to the gold rush in Alaska. Bill, who hasn't recognized the Tramp as Chaplin, will wait for him at the gate for an entire year, whereupon the pilgrim returns to the dressing room, puts on the millionaire's clothes, and leaves reincarnated as the mastiff's owner. Bill licks his substitute gloves, joyfully recognizing him . . . That is the storyline of *The Gold Rush*, Chaplin's aesthetically broadest work. Good morning, Mr. Unamuno!

This film formulates the best interrogation of social justice of which all art *d'après-guerre* has been capable. *The Gold Rush* is a sublime explosion of political unrest, a great economic complaint of life, a heartrending argument against social injustice. The fin de siècle Europeans, who could find no salvation in literary skepticism and scientific materialism, sit through this film fomenting a torturous frieze of misery, avarice, desperation. They're the heralds of the Russian Revolution. The economic desolation of one of them, the most pain-stricken of all and the least adapted to the conventional fickle logic of humans, lets out hair-raising roars.

In this work Chaplin is depicted as a red or hardline communist. But there's more to it. He proves to be a pure and supreme creator of new and more human, political, and social instincts. If he has not yet been understood as such, history will tell. "In Russia," Chaplin himself has stated, "one walks out of these showings, eyes glistening with tears, because over there I'm considered an interpreter of real life. In Germany, I'm seen from an intellectual point of view. In England, from the point of view of a clown. In France, as a comedian. I don't think I'm any of this. I am, rather, a tragic man."[32] A tragic man in our day and age must necessarily address economic and social pain.

For its part, the United States hasn't perceived, even at a distance, the profound and tacitly revolutionary spirit of *The Gold Rush*. I'm lying. In a subconscious way, perhaps, the gringos have teamed up with Lita Grey to stone Chaplin, just like the other Philistines stoned Our Lord, equally unconscious of the historical meaning of their hatred.

So it is, without a cheap protest against subprefects or ministers; without even uttering the words "bourgeois" or "exploitation"; without political adages or maxims; without childish messianics, Charles Chaplin, millionaire and gentleman, has created a marvelous work of revolution. This is the role of the creator.

Over time, unsuspected political platforms and economic doctrines will be yanked out of *The Gold Rush*. That will be the work of second-rate artists and imitators, propagandists, university professors, and candidates for the government of the people.

[*Mundial* (Lima), no. 404, March 9, 1928]   [JM]

INVITATION TO CLARITY

Theory of theories and all theory – The exaggerated importance of education about nativeness – Deficient words of an academic – It is as difficult to be clear as it is to be obscure – Simplicity in art – The moral merit and the aesthetic merit of an artistic work – Journalism, school of clarity.

Paris, January 1928

In the lecture that M. Gabriel Hanotaux gave at the French Academy, held in the reception of M. Paul Valéry, the eminent historiographer said to the great poet, "You, sir, should be clearer and the world will more readily receive your poems." Valéry glared indulgently at Hanotaux. Had the protocol permitted the new academic to rebut the discourse of his fellow, Valéry could've returned the advice of the venerable Hanotaux by saying, "You, sir, should be more obscure and the world will more readily accept your historical work." For the time being, let's leave aside these herbalist bifurcations and get to the words of Hanotaux.

A fine liqueur wouldn't elicit such an invitation to clarity from the mouth of a free critic like Paul Souday or a juvenile critic like Frédéric Lefèbvre. But this wheezes from a legitimate lung in the academic spirit that still believes, or so it would seem, in the *desired* technique or the volition and not in the native or extravolitive technique. In a dynamic aerated spirit, as is Valéry's, the word of Hanotaux must've resonated with a chord worth getting to know. Will the advice manage to jostle Valéry's creative playbook? Although I don't much admire his poetry, I respect his undeniably great strength as an essayist and, for this reason, doubt that the words of his illustrious colleague may especially resonate in Valéry. The authentic greatness of his spirit repudiates the desired disciplines, the exercises deliberately proposed by him or gathered, from night to morn, on the public street. Let the philosopher of *Eupalinos* say what he might; great work is the native origin and never a result of the will. This is the jurisdiction of the same psychological law that Ferdinand Vandérem applies to simplicity in art. "There exists," says Vandérem, "the simplicity achieved by conscious forces of the will. The history of art often confuses them, but they're as distinct as the poles of an electric battery."

Nonetheless, Hanotaux's words awoke in Paris many other opinions regarding Valéry's work. "You should work in journalism and you'll attain your style with clarity," some people told him. Others spread the rumor that Valéry had set out to write a novel as a way of "clarifying himself." And still others, hitting the nail on the head, finally said that Valéry was not a poet at all, but a philosopher who, as such, had a certain obligation to be obscure. When a philosophical idea obtains a stranglehold on the spirit until locking its grip all the way, the obscurity is complete. Only great thoughts are obscure.

Hanotaux, whose work is very clear and comprehensible, appeared pitifully mediocre in the light of this last thesis. And if Valéry had said to him, "You should be more obscure," no one knows if Hanotaux, out of the blue, could've been more obscure. It must not be very easy to suddenly become profound and brilliant. Perhaps the difficulty of being obscure in historiography is as insurmountable as the difficulty of being clear in poetry.

Thus, the debate has led nowhere. It has barely become an opportunity to remind passersby that, until proven otherwise, the intrinsically aesthetic merit and style of a work of art don't depend on the will. Application doesn't create a genius or give him a tone. A great literary worker, like Balzac, has a moral merit at most. As for obscurity and clarity in art, this is also a question of temperament and not volition. And so the application or will to clarify or obscure oneself is meaningless.

[*Mundial* (Lima), no. 405, March 16, 1928]   [JM]

PROLETARIAN LITERATURE

Establishment of the VAPP in Russia – The political position and the ethical position – The progressive attitude of Trotsky and Pilnyak – The opinions of Lenin and Gorky – The historical role of the State and of politicians – Criterion of the politician, moralist, and artist – Intersection of bourgeois literature and proletarian literature – The debate lingers on without a solution.

Paris, August 1928

A Soviet State communiqué of the first of July 1925 announced that proletarian literature now officially existed. "The class struggle," as one of the clauses of this decree states, "must continue in literature as in all other spheres of society. In class society, a neutral art does not and cannot exist."

The VAPP (All-Russian Association of Proletarian Writers),[33] endorsing the spirit of the official ruling, describes the character of proletarian literature in the following terms: "Literature," it declares, "is an incomparable weapon. If, as Marx observed, it's undeniable that the ruling ideas of an epoch are always those of a ruling class, the Dictatorship of the Proletariat is incompatible with the notion of a nonproletarian literature. Thus under current conditions, literature is one of the fields in which the bourgeoisie conducts its supreme offensive against the proletariat."

Such a definition of the necessarily proletarian nature of literature in Russia is clearly a response, based on a political conception of art, to a scientific and technical necessity at the level of the State. History shows that all States have always seen art through a political lens. Such is their right and obligation. The State and its personnel must see, or have the capacity to see, in all social phenomena the means to realize their political doctrine. Such has been the understanding of governments and political leaders—whether reactionary or revolutionary—of yesterday and today. They have required writers, willingly or not, to operate within spiritual horizons that match their social and political conceptions of life. Any government or representative of the State not adopting this attitude would be betraying himself by depriving his political ideal of an important means of fulfillment. Lenin would not be acting truly if he did not extend the modus operandi of the Dictatorship of the Proletariat to the works of the spirit. The same would apply to Mussolini if he did not act likewise with regard to the dictatorship of the bourgeoisie. Both sides are obliged, if we adhere to a vital and creative conception of politics, to spare no means, including art, of realizing the political experiences that they might in other ways achieve totally or partially. The architect should not be held back by respect for the beauty of trees, if he wishes to obtain from them the wood required by the design of the monument.

However, artists' concept of art is distinct and should be so. When Haya de la Torre emphasizes the need for artists to contribute with their work to revolutionary propaganda in Latin America, I reply that, generically, as a human being I find his demand highly cogent politically and that I sincerely sympathize with it, but that as an artist I accept no injunction or prescription, whether from myself or others, that, however well-intentioned, might subordinate my aesthetic freedom to the service of any type of political propaganda. My political conduct as an artist is particular to itself even though both aspects in the end go in the same direction, however little that may at first sight appear to be the case. As a human being, I can sympathize and work for the revolution, but as an artist it's not in my hands or anyone else's to control the political outcomes that may be implicit in my poems. Have Russian writers rejected the spiritual framework that the Soviet regime has imposed? We don't know.

Apart from this debate about the right of the State to impose a given aesthetic stance upon writers, the question of proletarian literature has produced heated discussion on the nature of proletarian art.

Lenin's criterion, by which art should be an instrument of the State so as to implement a political doctrine, has given way to Trotsky's: from a wider examination of the problem, Trotsky extends the proletarian notion of art to wider and deeper territories of the spirit and declares that no Russian poet of the revolution, starting with Blok and Gorky, has succeeded in establishing the essential coordinates of proletarian art. This position, which is less political and more human than that of the Soviet State, is shared by Boris Pilnyak, one of the most interesting young writers in Russia. But proletarian literature, in Trotsky's and Pilnyak's version, is still confined within the spiritual catechism of the communist State. Compared with the political stance of VAPP, their view is only relatively broader. Both stances see art from a political point of view that depends on the State, and not from a free, aesthetic point of view.

There's a third way of characterizing proletarian art. On the occasion of the official apotheosis of Gorky in Russia, some critics such as Plekhanov[34] and Gorler believed, in line with Trotsky and Pilnyak's thesis, that Gorky has nothing in common with the working class. Others, like Lunacharsky and Bukharin,[35] took the opposite view, taking their cue from Lenin, who said that the author of "Malva" and other stories is a great proletarian artist. Finally, the Pokrowsky literary circle asked Gorky himself to express his opinion on what proletarian literature is or should be. Gorky said, "The typical mark of the proletarian writer is the active hatred for everything that from inside or outside oppresses the human race, stopping it from realizing its free development and the full extension of its faculties. The proletarian writer tends to intensify his readers' participation in life and to give them a greater confidence in their own strength and in the means to overcome all inner enemies, helping them at the same time to find the larger meaning of life and the immense joy of work. In brief that's my idea of a writer who belongs to the world of the workers."

Gorky's opinion disillusioned the Soviet critics and experts, and disagreement about the issue continues and grows more complex. The stance of the author of *The Mother* is tied up, in reality, with the spirit of bourgeois literature, which tries to achieve the same aims that Gorky attributes, in a highly vague and general way, to proletarian literature. Gorky fails to describe a strictly proletarian art. What he says about it has been said about bourgeois art by bourgeois critics and by aesthetes of all times. At the same time, Gorky's idea belongs to a moral conception of art and not an aesthetic one, in the vital and creative sense of that word.

In Russia the nature of proletarian literature hasn't yet been clarified. As long as a type of judgment that's foreign to the substantive laws of art, as is the case with political and moral criteria, attempts to dominate the debate, the question will become ever more obscure and confused.

[*Mundial* (Lima), no. 432, September 21, 1928]   [WR]

COLONIAL SOCIETIES

Words and deeds of tourism – Illusions and disillusions of American tourists –
Belphegor on our continent – The meaning of measurement in the French spirit –
A Paris of fairytales and monsters – The farces of boulevard literature – Psychology
of the European villager – A triangle of study: Oslo, Paris, Rio de Janeiro – French
influence in America.

Paris, March 1928

Some South Americans who've come to Paris for the first time were complaining about it, as follows: "How disappointing! I thought Paris was something else, nicer, more interesting. But we see that it's a city approximately the same as all the big cities. In Paris there's nothing extraordinary. It's a real letdown to arrive at the 'capital of the world' and find nothing otherworldly about it."

"The Bois de Boulogne," says an Argentine donning argyles, "is smaller, if you will, than the Palermo of Buenos Aires. The avenue de l'Ópera of Paris measures 1.5 meters less than the Ópera of Buenos Aires."

"There's no doubt," says one Colombian, "that the Place de la Concorde, the avenue des Champs-Élysées, Nôtre Dame, Les Invalides are beautiful . . . But they offer nothing extraordinary, I mean, nothing that truly captivates my attention."

As one can see, South Americans have come a long way and no longer let themselves be conned by this Paris that literary culprits have made famous with magical legends. Gómez Carrillo now proves to be either a knucklehead or a wise guy. Paris wasn't what was painted by this chronicler who died in a café on some great boulevard; Paris wasn't a marvelous city, with literary taverns, romantic and disinterested women, absinth and tubercular artists; in reality, Paris is just the opposite: a city common and identical to all cities, like Buenos Aires, Havana, Montevideo, and Mexico City.

"I find only one difference," adds a South American. "Paris is quite a bit prettier than other cities. That's it. Yet there's quite a difference between this and supposing that Paris is Glory herself and has wonders that one can't find in other cities."

This South American, like Belphegor (the symbol of our epoch), exercises his sacred right to experience this feeling. He demands of Paris more of something that other cities can give him to a lesser extent or degree. Once the South American has familiarized himself with Paris, he feels swindled by the naturalness and measure with which life in the Ville-Lumière transpires. Paris does not offer him anything extraordinary, anything that exceeds the current proportions of all cities. Everything in Paris is within the mark of what's foreseeable by logic and reason or within the mark of what has already been seen in other cities. Nothing in Paris strays from the norm. Pedestrians walk on two feet, as they do everywhere; the rain falls, as it does everywhere, from the sky; the trees on the avenues, as they do everywhere, sprout, grow, and die . . . etc. The traveler's fantasy and curiosity undergo an effect of disappointment. Only a few weeks after arriving in Paris, the South American ends up sitting on a bench in the hotel lobby, stretching his arms, and yawning.

The South American, upon embarking in Valparaiso or Veracruz, was promised he would see marvelous, phenomenal, authentic typically Parisian things: a man with three backs, a stone that speaks, an epicene ballerina, a square circle, endless movement . . . His thirst for sensations, as he sees what Paris is, gets tripped up over the unexpected restraint of Parisian existence, with this sense of restraint in the French spirit, as tight-fitting, premeditated, and human as few are.

European country folk and provincials, on the other hand, are not hard to please. Their thirst for sensations seems more modest. When a Hungarian, Norman, Russian, or Scandinavian villager visits Paris for the first time, his admiration for the great city is manifest and exuberant.

One might say that, in the eyes of the European villager, the life of Paris is a patent revelation of unforeseen principles of human cohabitation; meanwhile, in the eyes of an American villager (the best cities of America are nothing less than villages), Paris is but a repetition of city life in America.

And so it probably is. From this point of view, there is less difference between the city standards of Oslo and Paris than there are between the former, the latter, and those of Rio de Janeiro. Moreover, the civic habits in Oruro, Bolivia, are more akin to those of a Parisian's than to a provincial's in France itself. In this aspect, South Americans bear a closer resemblance to Parisians than French provincials do.

To this extent Latin America is culturally and socially colonized by Paris.

[*Mundial* (Lima), no. 410, April 20, 1928]   [JM]

THE PSYCHOLOGY OF DIAMOND SPECIALISTS

Introduction to the surrealist method – In the diamond quarter of Paris – An amorphous awareness, changeable and multiple – The beings of surprise – The diamond's influence on wood, or vice versa – A burial in the manner of a Stevenson story.

Paris, March 1928

Since Paul Éluard and Benjamin Perret demonstrate to men of reality the surrealist importance of crime in order to get ahead, we see diamond dealers on rue Lafayette at their secretive trade, in the doorways of their jewelry shops, and headed to their serious commitments.

On rue Lafayette, near its junction with rue Châteaudun, there's a café with a counter almost carbonized by the human frequency of diamond specialists. Billfold underarm, they sip their coffee there, collating rings, earrings, broaches, watches, bracelets, necklaces. What better forces for great legal phenomena! . . . Awareness—this historical relation between the boat and the water—attained between the unsuspecting jewelry and the countless forms. No mold escapes the awareness of those diamond specialists. As a result of his craft, a diamond specialist acquires a polymorphic diaphragm and eager flesh that lends itself to metamorphosis. Unstable, changeable, accommodating, and casuistic—according to the multiple and, at times, simultaneous stock-exchange fortunes of jewelry— the diamond specialist becomes a man whose nature and way of being are such that, in mysterious contrast with the diamond's geometric laws, he escapes all regularity of behavior. An extraordinary novelistic essence lubricates his nerves and endows him with a disconcerting agility to launch himself into unexpected psychological adventures. His capacity for evil can be improvised just as easily as his capacity for good. In sum, the diamond specialist can evince great powers of transformation and surprise. He is the kind of being that's capable of anything. His contact with the diamond's terrible hardness—due to a revenge of Nature's physical laws—makes him soft as wax, which is to say, prepared for any hand that life deals him.

Has a diamond specialist painted a picture superior to all the paintings of Picasso? It was to be expected. Has a diamond specialist passed by on the arm of God himself at the corner of my house? It was to be expected. Has a diamond specialist made many more millions laugh than Chaplin has? It was to be expected. Does a diamond specialist get bored? It was to be expected. Does a diamond specialist have a wife? It was to be expected. Has a diamond specialist discovered the secret of Lenin's political force? It was to be expected. Does a diamond specialist sell foreign jewelry to a French movie star? It was to be expected that this star is Mlle Falconetti.

A circle of diamond specialists! What better eggs for beautiful lurking crocodiles? A diamond specialist, M. Charles Mestorino, has personally attended the burial of a man he killed. Why did he kill him? Because Mestorino is a diamond specialist and his victim, a dealer in diamonds too. What greater motive could you want?

On the day of the burial, the police watched the procession in which the murderer very seriously stepped forth, side by side with his wife, both old friends of the dearly departed. "What a conscience," all of Paris exclaimed, "to be present at the burial of his own victim! This calls for the guillotine, ipso facto!"

These are the onlookers in this valley of tears and, especially, on rue Saint-Agustin of Paris. They still don't know that in Russia there are no longer prisons for common law offenses like robbery, murder, and so on. Prisons and the death penalty remain only for political crimes.

So in Russia very interesting surrealist maxims are practiced in public affairs.

[*Mundial* (Lima), no. 412, May 4, 1928]   [MLR]

LITERATURE BEHIND CLOSED DOORS

Several young rebels of French criticism every so often touch upon heated and lively topics with the tact of an amateur fisherman's coldcock in the effluent or eddy of some salon. It's Ribemont-Dessaignes facing the mess of universal suffrage, or André Coeuroy facing the problem with European music, or Breton, spraying his hose of vitriol all over the postwar nationalist boils. Other essayists, like André Maurois in *Voyage au pays des Articoles*, take pleasure in blowing their noses at the trickery of those topics, and the rest of them, like Jean Cocteau in *Le secret professionnel*, give themselves a pedicure, or, like Lt. Conceito de Eça de Queiroz, bathe their skulls in holy water and egg yolks.

One of these heated and lively topics is literature behind closed doors, the heated topic of the day par excellence, from which almost all modern hacks flee, like chilly lizards, escaping between the cubist furniture of their study, knocking over the inkwell, and tearing the inseam of their *robe de chambre*.[36]

"Stop! Don't be startled!" said the elemental man to the terrified scribe, as he was walking into the office. "Sit back down."

The hack sits down, since the state of his spirit is seated, so to speak, it's at rest. His work doesn't stand on four feet, as would occur with the profane work of an illiterate savage, but rather on one foot, like a mass-produced piece of furniture, or it hangs by a string on the wall, like a perfect family portrait.

The writer behind closed doors knows nothing about life. Politics, love, economic strife, the heart-rending disaster of hope, the direct clash of man and men, the frequent immediate drama of opposing forces and directions of reality—none of this personally ruffles the writer behind closed doors. A typical product of bourgeois society, his existence is a historical outcrop of successive and inherited interests and injustices toward a sterile neutral museum-like cell. He's a mummy with weight but no rigidity. To be more precise, this infected hack is the direct descendant of bourgeoisdom's economic gaffes. Proprietor, landlord, with stipends or sinecures from government or family, food and shelter guaranteed, so he can skirt the economic struggle, which is compatible with individual isolation. More often than not, that's the economic situation of the private study writer. The scribe may also feed his belly with a tacit economic meaning, inherited from the collective sociology that bears him, which makes him come up short on rent, like any old parasite on society, but gives him the temperament he needs to produce expensive literature. He unwittingly possesses and is driven by a series of production instincts that are typically as bourgeois in nature as his conservative feelings and ideas. The ankylosis of his art and cloister covertly corresponds to the ankylosis of his readers. In a society of belching bores and complacent exploiters, the most agreeable literature smells like a moth in a pettifogger's office. When the French bourgeoisie was happier and more satisfied with its empire, the literature of greatest elegance slouched behind closed doors. On the eve of the war, king of the plume, Anatole France. Even today, in countries where the bourgeois reaction is more recalcitrant than in France, Italy, or Spain—so as not to reference only Latin countries—the writers of most immediate influence are Valéry, Pirandello, and Gómez de la Serna, whose works essentially contain an exclusive and evident sensibility of the private study. That mental refinement and game of talent epitomize the man who softly delights behind closed doors.

As the stuffy air of a windowless flat rises but only to disperse, facing this literature in pajamas the free immensity of life rapidly gathers before the natural lungs of man. And while Lord de Régnier in his silk upholstered armchair struggles to eke out a new poetic symbol from his exacerbated talent, under the clear sky, sweating and muscular, the French rugby team defeats the British at Colombes.

Life must get even somehow.

[*Variedades* (Lima), no. 1056, May 26, 1928]   [JM]

VANGUARD AND REARGUARD

It's the fashion at film showings in Paris for each event to be made up of three distinct parts: an old or rearguard movie, a futuristic or vanguard movie, and a contemporary movie, according to the era in which they were made. The same program will have a film shot in 1906, for example, another shot in 1928, and another that's also current but in which bold innovations are ventured.

The fashion appeared for the first time in the revolutionary theater of the Vieux Colombier, then repeated in the Cinema des Ursulines, in Studio 28, and finally in theaters on the grand boulevards and even in the suburbs. The original purpose was of a strictly technical order, seeking in the chronological confrontation of styles the springs of perfection or failure in the material. But it seems that this interest in a simple laboratory grew into a vast experimental attempt on the very eyes of the clientele. Now it seeks out the secrets of technique and, moreover, initiates the public to swing sharply, in a single soirée, between bad taste and good, between the perfect and the imperfect. The cinema thus achieves two correlative and concentric results: it perfects technique and it refines and crystallizes cinematic taste in the public.

A man who is not a film artist, nor a "director" or even a cameraman, and who watches from his seat the old, the futurist, and the contemporary films, can nonetheless relinquish his own role as customer or initiate and escape in this way to be the subject of the cinematic experience that we have been discussing. This man can counteract the cinematic bacillus and, without ceasing to be a spectator—which is not the same as a customer or an initiate—become simplified into a mere human being, without pro or con from the screen, without good taste or bad, and solely possessed by the central sentiment of the gaze upon things. How does it work in this free man, the confrontation between periods of cinema's development and the life it expresses? . . .

This man, contrary to what happens to the customer or the initiate and to the very creator of the screen, doesn't laugh too much at the old film, nor is he too amazed by the futuristic film, nor does he take much delight from the film of our current time. He finds that between the old, present, and future techniques, there is a calm ebb and flow, like the passage from one second to another on a clock face and not an abrupt syncope, like the brutality of Hindemith's music or the sudden trance of twilight. He finds, as well, that between the life expressed by the old film, that expressed by the modern film, and that heralded by the futuristic film, barely a death or a life passes, but not an eternity.

It is often said that progress advances from shade to shade and not from color to color. The hours of every creation are counted by thousandths of thousandths of a second and not by centuries. The leap, which the old Latin wisdom so feared, is incompatible with the almost absolute continuity of the terrain. The rhythm of fashion itself, so quick and epileptic, abides by this same continuative law of movement. Between the enormous hat of the woman *d'avant-guerre* and the shortest toque worn today, the distance is only a female head, that is, practically nothing. Finding a greater difference between both hats would be to reduce the criterion of proportion to the volume or physical size of things.

The return to the ancient arts is proof that there was a leap in the process of technique and that the spirit withdraws and tries to rejoin the natural, continuing rhythm of creation. In the vanguard experiences of the current cinema, we see that the magic lantern, for example, again tries out its possibilities that were scorned and abandoned many years ago and from them it may be feasible, in effect, to extract great cinematic effects. Fernand Divoire believes, for now, that the magic lantern is perhaps, by its daring synthesis of movement, and by the schematic simplicity of its expression, the true style of the future screen.

[*Variedades* (Lima), no. 1059, June 16, 1928]   [JW]

ANNIVERSARY OF BAUDELAIRE

The most beautiful sepulchral stone of Paris – Baudelaire's lay diabolicalness –
Rebellion and innocence – Baudelaire and Voltaire – A poetry reading in the
cemetery of Montparnasse – The cat, the bat, and "Les Fleurs du Mal."

Paris, May 1928

In the cemetery of Montparnasse the anniversary of the death of Charles
Baudelaire was commemorated. The scene was an aesthetic kidney stew
with a simplicity that was almost vegetable.

The ceremony took place in front of the monument to the poet, one of
the most beautiful sepulchral stones in Paris. Its meaning is literal and
direct, yet, at the same time, it is quite original. The sculptor has taken an
enormous block of stone, split it in half, and given it the form of a compass. This is the skeleton of the monument. A compass. An airplane, one
whose wings drags at great length on the ground. Like the symbolic alba-
tross. The other half of the stone rises perpendicularly behind to present,
near the top, a great bat with extended wings. Above the living, floating
creature rests a gargoyle whose hands hold a chin that is pensive, vigilant,
almost aggressive.

Another sculptor would have chiseled, instead of a bat, the heraldic cat
of the bards. But this sculptor chipped deeper into the stone and chose
the bat, that zoological binomial, between mammal and bird, that ethic
image—between Lucifer and angel—that incarnates so perfectly the spirit
of Baudelaire. For the author of *Les fleurs du Mal* was not diabolical in the
Catholic sense of the word but was rather the raised sum of those two large
and inseparable figures: rebellion and innocence. Rebellion is not possible
without innocence. Only children and angels rebel. Evil never rebels. Show
me an old man who rebels. It would be impossible. An old man can only
grow resentful and bitter; he can't rebel. Like Voltaire. Rebellion is the fruit
of an innocent spirit. And the cat carries evil between his paws.

In contrast, the bat—the flying mouse of the crypts, that hybrid piece of
the soffits—has the instinct for height and, at the same time, for darkness.
Its realm is the dark kingdom, yet it inhabits the copulas. From its double
nature—flight and darkness—one could say that it possesses the wisdom
of the shadows, and one could say that it falls upward . . .

It was there, then, in front of this authentic cathedral stone and this
reverent crowd, that Gustave Kahn spoke of the cult of the great artists of
the world, among whom, he said, Baudelaire occupies an eminent posi-

tion. M. Valmi Baysee then talked about the growing influence of Baude-laire on foreign literature.

Some women from the general public and actresses from the Comédie Française and the Odeon recited the poet's verse, intoning a scene of in-effable, human, and living color, communicating a simplicity of free and natural trance, stripped of the airs of societies and chapels.

The contralto voice of an actress spoke "L'éstranger." Another recited, with a fluidity that was truly moving, "L'invitation au voyage," and M. Alex-andre gave a supreme declamation of "Danse macabre," and M. Lambert another, no less captivating, of "La mort des amants."

The group to the rear broke up by the side of the statue "Souvenir." On the leafless avenues, the wind remained behind, singing, in two silences, its silence.

[*Mundial* (Lima), no. 421, July 6, 1928]   [EW]

THE MASTERS OF CUBISM
The Pythagoras of Painting

The greatest contemporary painter is a Spaniard from Málaga: Picasso. Next to Picasso and embracing a no less powerful artistic personality is another Spaniard from Madrid: Juan Gris. In Paris, the fame of both, at least among the elites of the vanguard, has helped in large part to impose the new painting, which under the name of cubism offers now figures so towering as Braque, Derain, Matisse, Marcoussis, whose works are being celebrated far and wide, that they can almost be considered classics al-ready. I've just now finished reading an article by Sabord where he tells of his surprise on seeing how the cubist revolutionaries are starting to enjoy a popular and absolute consecration, as if they weren't such revolutionaries. Every show of decorative models from Parisian shops is currently domi-nated by the motifs and drawings of Braque, Matisse, Gris, and, naturally, Picasso himself. Generally, starting with the International Exposition of Decorative Arts in 1925, cubism has invaded the world of commerce to a resounding degree. Cubism has spread to furniture design, luxury goods, architecture, posters, the theater, etc. The famous and dazzling concert hall the Salle Pleyel has the most old-school polygons. The ads for the Cook Agency on locomotives haul along entire squads of geometry from *les fauves*. People get all caught up trying to locate the characters from *Doctor Caligari* among the truncated pyramids and the loony bin's lack of perspective, etc., etc. The year 1923 marks the apex of Muscovite influence on decorative art in Paris. Upon this Russian prevalence of taste and heights followed the cubist prevalence of taste and depth, which has now reached its greatest scope. Okay, fine. To this irradiation of a new art, profoundly human and, above all, of its time, Picasso and Gris have contributed with ideas and works of the highest order. An overly patriotic Spaniard might claim that the current cubist prevalence in the Paris fashion industry is in the end a Spanish triumph, since cubism has Picasso and Gris for leaders.

But that's not why one could think that cubism, on getting around and put within reach of commercial taste, is on the threshold of passing into the domain of the vulgar, that is, by that road it's on the point of going up in smoke and disappearing, due to the superficiality and coarseness of its trajectory. The spread of cubism proves only that there breathes a broadly human content, a universal vitality. This spread is, at the same time, natural and logical. The great aesthetic currents of history have had equal luck and the same consecration. The works of Picasso and his friends, like the marvels of the Renaissance, will pass into the category of celebrities, not for having descended to the majority of people but rather for having educated those people to the point of making them ascend toward the works and for enclosing there a cosmic rhythm. We must not forget that there is celebrity and celebrity. One thing is Paul de Kock and another is Victor Hugo.

Among the first creators of cubism, Gris has toiled away heroically. Hero against the recalcitrant public and hero against many sectarians of the school itself. Since his first paintings, Gris has shown a rigorous, mathematical sense of art, against the reigning celestinesque metaphysics. Gris paints in numbers. His canvases are real top-grade creations, brilliantly resolved. Beside other cubists more or less wavering from capitulation or disbelief, Gris preaches and carries out, from the dawn of the new aesthetic, around 1908, an intransigent, red, vertical belief. Nothing of Bergsonism nor of empirical rationalism. Gris preaches and carries out a conscientious and scientific knowledge of painting. He wants the painter to know conscientiously what he is painting and to avail himself of a wise technique and vigilant practice, by which he may properly make use of his natural gifts. His work, in this way, is made of precision, of pure certainty, of Goethean infallibility. Without sinking in any narrow scholasticism. Gris always adjusts himself, like the sainted hermit Popes, to the severe and apostolic numbers. Because of that, the critics have called him the Pythagoras of painting and proclaimed him the initiator of what could be called "pure painting," like the "pure poetry" of abbé Brémond. Such appreciations spring up of their own from the serene contemplation of his work, where he strictly practiced the doctrine upheld, shortly before his death, in his conference at the Sorbonne.

Gris has been perhaps the most rebellious painter in Paris. He was not the sort of artist who compromises out of hunger, or love of fame, or out of "lousy doubts," as Apollinaire would say. Gris is always Gris, against aces and queens, even against time and against himself. And through this rigorous spirit of artistic austerity and through the scientific possession of his creative forces, without unconfessable fog or elaborate and complicit mysteries, Juan Gris will remain the most representative painter of our time.

[*Variedades* (Lima), no. 1069, August 25, 1928]   [JW]

TOLSTOY AND THE NEW RUSSIA

Debate over the type of culture of modern man – One apparent confusion and another, artificial – The three current positions of the debate – Between a French criterion and a Saxon criterion – Still afoot, amid all, the Russian ideal.

Paris, September 1928

Now that we're in the presence of a great recasting of history, in which some ways of life end and other, different ways, proceed from the former, in America we must insist on the concept of *culture*. We must determine, once again, when a man is cultured and when he's not. With such surfeit and cruelty has the word *culture* been reserved for philosophy and the word *cultured* for psychology that few people can discover their vital content anymore. We're not referring to the inevitable—albeit apparent—confusion that emanates from the different interpretation these words deserve, as the racial stance, climate, and history of the people. This confusion refers to external, short-lived qualities of a man and in no way to the fundamental values common to mankind. Therefore, this confusion is apparent or, at most, superficial. Beneath it prevails a universal criterion to show the content of the word *culture* and to determine when a man is *cultured* and when he's not.

This most voluminous confusion—no matter how artificial and consequently avoidable it may be—proceeds from the lexicon and speech of the philosophers. Within a certain mentality (Western, for example), it's still difficult to find two writers whose concept of culture is identical. That person calls cultured the man who enjoys the music of Stravinsky, while this person calls cultured the honorable gent who demonstrates absolute deafness toward the *Apollo Musagetes*. Another person calls cultured the man who masters Latin and Hebrew at the French Academy, meanwhile a fourth person calls cultured the fellow who scrupulously comes through on his daily promises, even though he's a full-fledged boob.

English writer Stacy Aumonier recently classified countries according to their degree of culture, in the following manner: (1) cultured countries, by order of their merits: Sweden, Scotland, Denmark, Holland, England, Norway, Hungary, Switzerland, and Germany; (2) semicultured countries: France, Belgium, Austria, and Czechoslovakia; (3) Barbarian countries: Italy, Ireland, Portugal, Spain, Greece, Turkey, and the Balkans. Contrary to this, French writer M. Rosny, of the Goncourt Academy, believes that Aumonier is mistaken and that a country like France—which has renewed philosophy and mathematics with Pascal, created electromagnetism with Ampère, revolutionized medicine with Pasteur, made painting illustrious with Watteau, and in literature has produced Montaigne, Rabelais, Molière, and Balzac—has the right to figure into the first group of cultured countries. But surely Aumonier calls cultured the man whom Rosny believes is barbarous, and vice versa. Rosny probably thinks that a chemist is a cultured man, for the sole fact that he's created a great scientific formula; meanwhile, Aumonier understands cultured only as the man healthy in body and spirit, chaste to sensuality, honest inside and out, happy with life and sad with life—a man who, in a word, naturally and humanly *comprehends* life despite the fact that he's not a chemist and doesn't revolutionize medicine. As it turns out, this confusion is typical and flagrant.

After the war of 1914, the debate over what type of culture corresponds to the new man who's come out of the war has emboldened the chaos surrounding the concept of *culture* itself. The centennial celebration of Tolstoy comes to kindle this debate, forking it into three positions: the way back toward the quality of sagacity in primitive or patriarchal man who detests the whirlwinds of progress and the disheartened race of modern industrialism (Tolstoyan ideal); the way of growing, epileptic progress, which eliminates the leisure and contemplative simplicity of the old sage (ideal of the United States and the West *d'après-guerre*); and, finally, the way that wants the truly cultured man to fuse the natural qualities of simplicity and of human *sagesse*, with the dynamic qualities obtained by the infinite action of progress (the Soviet position).

On the occasion of Tolstoy's centennial, the Russian press has been careful to clarify and concretely specify the communist notion of the cultured man. It has, in the first place, defined the opposition that exists between the new Russian spirit and Tolstoy's maimed, absurd conception.

It has then demarcated the opposition between socialist culture and the civilization of the West and North America *d'après-guerre*. Trotsky's study on the author of *War and Peace* is a particularly magnificent synthesis of the profound abyss between the type of cultured man of Moscow, Paris, and New York. Here Trotsky keeps his distance from the retrograde bourgeoisdom of Europe as well as the advanced bourgeoisdom of America, which, together, represent one decrepit period of history.

The Russian ideal undoubtedly owns humanity's future.

[*Mundial* (Lima), no. 437, October 26, 1928]   [JM]

From *Art and Revolution*

THE REVOLUTIONARY FUNCTION OF THOUGHT

Confusion is a phenomenon with a permanent, organic character in bourgeois society. Confusion grows ever thicker when it is addressed as already confusing problems by the very historical terms of its utterance. The latter occurs with the brand new and, at once, very old problem of the intellectual's obligations with regard to revolution. As posed by historical materialists, this problem is already a tangle. When formulated or simply outlined by bourgeois intellectuals, it acquires the aspect of insoluble chaos.

* * *

"The philosophers," Marx says, "have only *interpreted* the world in various ways. The point is to *change* it."[37] The same can be said of intellectuals and artists in general. The finalistic function of thought has allowed them only to interpret the interests and other valid forms of life—leaving them intact—when it should have enabled their transformation. The finalism of thought has been conservative, rather than revolutionary.

The point of departure in this transformational or revolutionary doctrine of thought stems from the fundamental difference between the idealist dialectic of Hegel and the materialist dialect of Marx. "In its mystified form," says Marx, "dialectic became the fashion in Germany, because it seemed to transfigure and to glorify the state of existing things. In its rational form it is a scandal and abomination to bourgeoisdom and its doctrinaire professors because it includes in its comprehension and affirmative recognition of the existing state of things, at the same time also, the recognition of the negation of that state, of its inevitable breaking up; because it regards every historically developed social form as in fluid movement and therefore takes into account its transient nature not less than its momentary existence; because it lets nothing impose upon it, and is in its essence critical and revolutionary."[38]

* * *

The object or matter of transformational thought resides in things and events of immediate presence in tangible reality. The revolutionary intellectual always operates near life in flesh and bone, facing beings and phenomena in his surroundings. His works are vitalistic. His sensibility and

196

method are this-sided[39] (materialist in Marxist language), that is, of this world and not of any other, extraterrestrial or cerebral. No astrology or cosmogony. No abstract masturbation of some hotshot lawyer. The revolutionary intellectual sets aside the messianic formula that says, "my kingdom is not of this world."[40]

* * *

By the transformational nature of his thought about and action on immediate reality, the revolutionary intellectual incarnates a danger for all the forms of life around him, which he tries to abolish and substitute with other, new, fairer forms that are closer to perfection. He becomes endangered by the prevailing laws, customs, and social norms. Thus, he turns into the target par excellence of the prosecutors and reprisals of conservatives. "It is Anaxagoras, banished," says Eastman, "Protagoras, prosecuted; Socrates, executed; Jesus, crucified."[41] And, let's add, it's Marx, vilified and driven out; Lenin, shot. Therefore, the revolutionary intellectual's spirit of heroism and personal sacrifice is an essential characteristic of his destiny.[42]

[JM]

THE WORK OF ART AND THE SOCIAL SPHERE

Is there even a narrow correlation between the life and work of the artist? Is there absolute synchronism between the work and life of the author? Yes. Synchronism exists in artists great and small, in conservatives and revolutionaries alike. Synchronism has been produced in the past, is currently produced, and will be produced forever. Even in the case of artists whose work seems to lack the peculiar tone of their life at first sight, the profound and sometimes underlying concordance is evident. To reach that tone, suffice an auscultation in good faith, with a bit of sensibility.

Let's look at a few examples. Nietzsche was a physically weak, sickly man. Is one to deduce from this that *The Birth of Tragedy* is the wincing of a wasted loser? Tolstoy never had financial burdens. He didn't know what it means to put bread on the table by working. He lived the life of a petite bourgeois man or, rather, a feudal lord. Is one to deduce from this that *Resurrection* is a feudalizing work? Mallarmé lived in perpetual political abstention, neural to the ebb and flow of parliaments, absent at elections, assemblies, and political party gatherings. Is one to deduce from this that *The Afternoon of the Faun* is devoid of political spirit and social meaning? Of course not. Such conclusions are reached only by run-of-the-mill, empirical critics. Akin to a poor photographer who seeks in photography the formal reproduction and external imitation of the original, the poor critic scours the work of art to find the literal reproduction and reflection of repetition in the artist's life. When he does not find that reflection—which, let us add, occurs precisely with the great artists—he concludes by saying that there is no synchronism in the life of the author and his work. This is how people proceed who believe that concordance exists in some but not all artistic objects.

To find truly profound aesthetic synchronism, one must bear in mind that the phenomenon of artistic production, as Millet says, is an authentic operation of alchemy, in the scientific sense of the word—a transmutation.[43] The artist absorbs and concatenates the social unrest of the environment as well as his own individual unrest, not to return it exactly as he absorbed it (which is what the poor critic would want and what occurs with inferior artists), but rather to transform it within his spirit into other essences, distinct in form and identical at the core, into the raw materials as absorbed. At first sight, as we said, one might not recognize the vital raw material as absorbed in the structure and emotional movement of the work, just as at a glance one might not recognize in a tree the nutritional chemical bodies extracted from the soil. However, if one analyzes the work in depth, one will necessarily discover—in its innermost viscera and through the personal peripeteia of the artist's life—not only the circulating currents of socioeconomic character, but the mental and religious currents of its epoch. An alchemical analysis of a vegetal substance would likewise establish a similar biological phenomenon in the tree.

The correlation between the individual and social life of the artist and his work is therefore constant. It operates consciously or subconsciously, whether the artist wants it to or not, no matter if he accepts or denies it, and even if he tries to escape it. The challenge for the critic—we repeat—is knowing how to discover it.   [JM]

GRAMMATICAL RULE

Grammar, as a collective norm in poetry, lacks a raison d'être. Every poet forges his personal and nontransferable grammar, his syntax, spelling, analogy, prosody, his meanings. He is sufficed by not leaving language's jurisdiction. The poet can even change, in a certain way, the lexical and phonetic structure of a word itself, depending on the case. And this, rather than restraining the socialist and universal scope of poetry, as one might suspect, expands it unto infinity. For it's well known that the more personal (again, I don't say individual) an artist's sensibility, the more universal and collective his work.   [JM]

POETRY AND IMPOSTURE

Makers of symbols, appear in public nude and only then will I accept your pants.

Makers of images, return your words to men.

Makers of metaphors, forget not that distances announce themselves from three to three.

Makers of borders, see how the water flows, on its own, without a need for floodgates; the water, which is water made to come, yet not to make us comely.

Makers of heights, one can see from afar that never in your life have you died.   [JM]

TELL ME HOW YOU WRITE AND
I'LL TELL YOU WHAT YOU WRITE

Technique doesn't lend itself much, as a simple view might suggest, to falsification or simulation. Technique, in politics and art alike, reveals the true sensibility of a man better than all programs and manifestos. There's no document more convincing or data more authentic of our sensibility than our own technique. The original schism of Russian social-democracy between the Bolsheviki and Mensheviki arose from nothing less than a discrepancy of revolutionary technique. "But we agree on everything except the technique," the Mensheviki argued to Lenin in 1903, to whom he replied, "Yes, but precisely, technique is everything."

There are artists who call themselves surrealists and would like to practice the aesthetic of Breton, but his sculpture, his drawing, or his literature reveals, by means of its technique—a complex display of profound personal and social factors—a sensibility that is, let's say, impressionist or cubist or simply *pompier*.[44]

Many believe that technique is the refuge for the trick or the simulation of a personality. It seems to me, on the contrary, that it always undresses what in reality we are and where we're going, albeit by contradicting the false pretenses and external parvenu cerebrations with which we'd like to dress up and be seen. [JM]

UNIVERSALITY OF VERSE FOR THE UNITY OF LANGUAGES

A poem is a vital entity much more organic than an organic being in nature. The limb of an animal gets amputated, and the animal continues to live. A branch gets cut from a plant, and the plant continues to live. But if from a poem one amputates a verse, a word, a letter, a punctuation mark, it dies. Since the poem, when translated, cannot preserve its absolute vital integrity, it should be read in its original language, and naturally this limits, for now, the universality of its emotion. But one must not forget that this universality will be possible the day all languages unify and fuse, through socialism, into one single universal language. [JM]

AESTHETIC AND MACHINISM

The heavenliness of the moonlight in poetry has been superseded by the heavenliness of the cinema, the airplane, the radio, or whichever other quasi-"futurist" smack you please.

Bourgeois professors, philosophers, and artists have a concept sui generis of the role of the machine in social and artistic life and attribute a sort of divine character to it. The idealism and inclination toward mysticism, located in the foundation of these people's criterion, made them see the machine, at the onset of Fulton's invention,[45] as an idol or new divinity as mysterious as all divinities, before which one had to kneel in simultaneous adoration and fear. And even now they take up this attitude. Bourgeois artists and writers, particularly, have used the machine to symbolize Beauty with a capital *B*, while philosophers use it to symbolize Omnipotence with a capital *O*. Among the former is the fascist, Marinetti, inventor of futurism, and among the latter, the patriarch, Tagore, whose shouts and cries for help against the Jupiterian empire of the machine haven't managed to jostle the accursed Fordic mindset of capitalist "culture."

But the revolutionary artist has a different concept of and feeling toward the machine. For him, a motor and a plane aren't more than objects, like a table or a toothbrush, with one difference: the former are more beautiful and useful, in sum, they possess greater creative efficiency. Only that. Following this hierarchical evaluation of objects in social reality, the revolutionary artist can do more when placing them in the work of art. The machine isn't an aesthetic, moral, or even economic myth. Just as no worker with class consciousness sees a deity in the machine or falls to his knees before it like a resentful slave, so too does the revolutionary artist refrain from using it to symbolize Beauty par excellence, the new aesthetic prototype of the universe, or the unseen and revealed muse[46] of artistic inspiration. Nor has the Marxist sociologist assigned the tractor a totemic value in the proletarian family and socialist society.

In the wake of the October Revolution, the futurist wave that rolled through Russian art and, specifically, through poetry was quite explainable and fortunately has been ephemeral. It was an undercover, old-fashioned surge of the recently crushed capitalist era. Mayakovsky, its major representative at the time, ended up recognizing it as such very quickly and, together with Pasternak, Esenin, and others, boycotted all machinist residuals in literature.

When Gladkov exclaims, "the nostalgia for machines is stronger than the nostalgia for love,"[47] he says it only as one could say, "the nostalgia for machines is stronger than the nostalgia for my room" or anything else. It's not that the machine is elevated, but that love is terrifying. And in this case the sentiment that Walt Whitman possesses is excluded, for he, unaware of its social and aesthetic value, set it in motion and applied it with impressive justness.

So mistakenly wander today's poets who make the machine a goddess, like those who before them made a goddess out of the moon, sun, or sea. Neither deification nor heavenliness of machines. This is but an instrument of economic production and, as such, only an element of artistic creation, like any other, similar to a window, a cloud, a mirror, or a path, etc. Everything else amounts only to a newly coined animism that is arbitrary, morbid, decadent.   [JM]

AUTOPSY OF SURREALISM

Among other symptoms of its agony, the capitalist intelligentsia offers the vice of the cenacle. It's curious to observe how the most recent devastating crises of economic imperialism—war, industrial rationalization, misery of the masses, financial and stock market crashes, development of the workers' revolution, colonial insurrections, etc.—synchronously correspond to the furious manipulation of literary schools, as improvised as they are short-lived. Around 1914, expressionism was born (Dvorack, Fretzer). Around 1915, cubism was born (Apollinaire, Reverdy). In 1917, dadaism was born (Tzara, Picabia). In 1924, surrealism (Breton, Ribemont-Dessaignes). Not to mention the preexisting schools: symbolism, futurism, neosymbolism, unanimism, etc. Finally, since the advent of surrealism, a new literary school bursts forth on a nearly monthly basis. Never before has social thought been sectioned off into so many and such fleeting formulas. Never before did it experience such a frenetic pleasure and such a need to be stereotyped into prescriptions and clichés, as though it were afraid of its freedom or unable to emerge in all its organic unity. Such anarchy and disintegration hadn't been seen except among the decadent philosophers and poets at the dawn of Greco-Latin civilization. Those of today, in turn, reveal a new decadence of the spirit: the dawn of capitalist civilization.

The last school of the main cartel, surrealism, has just officially died.

The truth is that surrealism, as a literary school, didn't represent any constructive contribution. Instead, it was a prescription for making poems about restraint, as are and will be all literary schools of any period. And yet. It wasn't even an original prescription at that. The entire pompous theory and abracadabrant[48] method of surrealism was condemned by and, in a few thoughts on the topic, sketched out at the hand of Apollinaire. Based on these ideas of the author of *Calligrams*, the surrealist manifestos limit themselves to creating intelligent parlor games of automatic writing, morality, religion, and politics.

Parlor games, I say, and intelligent ones at that—cerebral games, rather. When surrealism arrived through the ineluctable dialectic of things to confront the living problems of reality, which don't exactly depend on the abstract metaphysical lucubrations of any literary school, it seemed to be in a hurry. To stay consistent with what the surrealists themselves used to call the "critical and revolutionary spirit" of this movement, it had to jump into the middle of the street and take charge of, among other things, the political and economic problems of our time. Surrealism then turned to anarchism, this being the most abstract, mystical, and cerebral form of politics that best reconciled the ontological and even occultist character of the cenacle par excellence. As anarchists, the surrealists were able to keep gaining recognition, given that, as such, they managed to cohabit and even cosubstantiate with the organic nihilism of the school.

But over the course of time, the surrealists came to see that, outside the surrealist catechism, there was another revolutionary method as "interesting" as what they were proposing: I'm referring to Marxism. They read, thought about it, and, out of a very bourgeois miracle of eclecticism or out of an inextricable "combination," Breton proposed to his friends the alignment and synthesis of both methods. The surrealists immediately became communists.

It's only in this moment—not before or after—that surrealism acquires certain social importance. From the simple fabric of poems in series, it transforms into a militant political movement and into live, revolutionary, intellectual pragmatism. Surrealism then deserved to be acknowledged and qualified as one of the most vibrant constructive literary trends of the age.

However, this concept wasn't devoid of inventive benefit. One had to follow the ulterior surrealist methods and disciplines in order to know the extent to which certain contents and actions were truly and sincerely revolutionary. Even when it was known that aligning the surrealist method with Marxism was nothing more than juvenile nonsense or provisional mystification, there remained the hope that they'd gradually continue to radicalize the brand new, unforeseen, militant Bolsheviki.

Unfortunately, while agitating and refuting in shrieking claims of Marxist faith, Breton and his friends subconsciously and unavoidably kept being incurable intellectual anarchists. The pessimism and desperation from surrealism's first moments, which were able to effectively set the conscience of the cenacle in motion, became a permanent static system—an academic lesson plan. Those moral and intellectual crises, which surrealism claimed to promote but (yet another lack of originality in the school) shied away from, had debuted most expressively in dadaism, ankylosed in psychopathic legalese and literary cliché, despite the dialectical injections from Marx and the restless youngsters' formal and unofficial dedication to communism. Pessimism and desperation must always be stages, not goals. To stir and ignite the spirit, they must develop until transforming into consecutive affirmations. Otherwise, they don't amount to more than pathological germs, condemned to devouring themselves. While mocking the law of vital transformation, the surrealists became academics, I repeat, for their own sake and intellectual crises and didn't have the strength to go above or beyond them with truly revolutionary destructive-constructive forms. Each surrealist did as he pleased. They broke off with numerous members of the party and its publishing organizations and took up everything, in constant divorce with the great Marxist directives. From a literary viewpoint, their productions continued to be characterized by evident bourgeois refinement. The commitment to communism wasn't at all a reflection of the essential meaning and forms of their works. For all these reasons, surrealism declared itself incapable of comprehending and practicing the true, unique, revolutionary spirit of our age: Marxism. Surrealism rapidly lost the social prestige that had been its only raison d'être and began its irremediable agony.

At present, surrealism—as a Marxist movement—is a corpse. (As a merely literary cenacle—I repeat—it always was, like all schools, the imposture of life, a regular scarecrow.) The certification of its bereavement has recently transformed into two documents of interest: *The Second Manifesto of Surrealism* by Breton and another, with the title of *A Corpse*, which numerous surrealists, headed by Ribemont-Dessaignes, have signed against Breton. Along with the death and ideological decomposition of surrealism, both manifestos establish its dissolution as a physical group or aggregate. It's a split or complete collapse of the chapel. Now the most serious and last of the series emerges from the rubble.

In his *Second Manifesto* Breton revises surrealist doctrine, showing that he's satisfied with its performance and result. Breton continues to be, until his final moments, a professional intellectual, a scholastic ideologue, a rebellious lawyer, a recalcitrant *dominus*, a Maurrasian[49] polemicist, and, finally, just another anarchist on the block. Once again he declares that surrealism has triumphed, because it has obtained what it proposed: "to provoke a crisis of conscience, from the intellectual and moral point of view." Breton is wrong: If he really has read and subscribed to Marxism, this doesn't explain how he forgets that the role of the writer in that doctrine isn't to provoke moral and intellectual crises, serious or general as they may be, that is, by creating the revolution "up above," but rather on the contrary, by creating it "down below." Breton forgets that there's only one revolution—the proletarian—and that this revolution will be created by workers in action and not by intellectuals in their "crises of conscience." The only crisis is the economic crisis, and for centuries now this has been put forth as fact and not simply as a concept or as "dilettantism." As for the rest of the *Second Manifesto*, Breton wields attacks with the vitriol and personal insults of a literary cop aimed at his old brotherhood—insults and vitriol that evince the bourgeois character of his "crisis of conscience" as bourgeois to the bone.

The other manifesto, *A Corpse*, offers lapidary and necrological passages about Breton. "For an instant," says Ribemont-Dessaignes, "we were smitten by surrealism: youthful loves, the loves, if you will, of manservants. Youngsters are authorized to love even a guard's woman (this woman is incarnated in the aesthetic of Breton). A false companion, a false communist, a false revolutionary, but a true and authentic farce, Breton must beware of the guillotine. What am I saying!? One does not behead a corpse."[50]

"Breton scribbled," Roger Vitrac says. "He scribbled in revolutionary and holier-than-thou style about subversive ideas and obtained a curious result, which continued to astonish the petite bourgeoisie, the petite merchants and industrialists, the minions of the seminary and the cardias of the first schools."

"Breton," says Jacques Prevert, "was a deaf-mute who confused everything: desperation and liver pain, the *Bible* and *Les Chants de Maldoror*, God and God, the ink and the table, the barricades and the divan of Madame Sabatier, the Marques de Sade and Jean Lorrain, the Russian Revolution and the surrealist revolution . . . This lyrical foreman handed out diplomas to lovers who wrote poems and, in the days of indulgence, to newcomers, out of desperation."

"The corpse of Breton," Michel Leiris says, "disgusts me because, among other reasons, he is a man who always lived among corpses."

"Naturally," says Jacques Rigaud, "Breton spoke quite well about love, but in life he was one of Courteline's characters."[51]

Etc., etc., etc.

These evaluations about Breton can be applied without exception to all surrealists and to the defunct school itself. It will be said that this is their circumstantial prankster side and not the historical foundation of the movement. Quite right. Assuming that this historical foundation really exists, which in this case is not so. The historical foundation of surrealism is almost null, from whichever perspective it's examined.

But this is how literary schools come to pass. Such is the fate of all unrest that, instead of becoming an austere creative laboratory, merely amounts to a formula. Useless then are the booming complaints, the calls for the vulgate, the color advertisements, in the end, the sleights of hand and professional tricks. Alongside the aborted tree, dead leaves asphyxiate.   [JM]

NEW POETRY

New poetry has been used to classify verses whose lexicon is made up of the words "cinema," "jazz-band," "motor," "radio," and in general all terms of science and contemporary industry. It doesn't matter whether or not the lexicon corresponds to an authentically new sensibility. It's the words that matter.

But this isn't new poetry, or old poetry, or anything else. The artistic materials offered by modern life must be assimilated by the artist and transformed into sensibility. The radio, for example, is destined to awaken a newly nerve-stricken mentality, a more profound sentimental perspicacity, proof, and understanding that amplify an ever-denser love, rather than just making us say "radio." So it is that anxiety builds and one takes the breath of life. This is the true culture that makes progress. That is its only aesthetic purpose: not to fill our mouths with newly coined words. There's often a lack of new words. A poem may not say "airplane" and still possess the emotion of aviation in an obscure and tacit, yet effective and human way. This is the real new poetry.

Otherwise, there's barely enough to combine such and such artistic materials, and, accordingly, a more or less beautiful perfect image is produced. In this case, it's no longer a matter of "new" poetry based on new words, but on new metaphors. Yet this too falls into error. There may be a lack of new images in truly new poetry—its function being one of ingenuity and not genius—but in a poem the creator relishes and suffers a life in which new relations and rhythms of things and men have become blood, cell, something anyway that's been incorporated vitally and organically into sensibility.

"New" poetry by means of new words or new metaphors is distinguished by its novel pedantry, its complications, and its baroqueness. New poetry by means of new sensibility, on the contrary, is simple and human and, at a first glance, could be taken as ancient or doesn't call into question whether it's modern or not.   [JM]

THE IMAGE AND ITS SYRTES

In an image by Guyau, life is represented as a mad virgin, the delusional bride of a groom who doesn't exist and for whom she joyfully waits each dawn and weeps each dusk because he hasn't arrived. In this image, life—life itself—disappears and what we have before us is a mad bride. By trying to communicate a greater visible pulse to the presence of life, Guyau, on the contrary, makes life disappear and shows us, in its place, another presence, something else: a woman. For no one will deny that life is one thing and a woman, another.

Such is the fate of all images by way of substitution. Ambiguous, hybrid, inorganic, false, these images lack poetic virtuality. They aren't aesthetic creations, but rather painful, artificial articulations of two natural creations. One mustn't forget that grafting isn't a phenomenon of artistic biology. Nor is reproduction. In art, each form is an infinity that begins and ends with itself.

Cubism hasn't managed to avoid this genre of images. Nor has dadaism. Nor surrealism. Much less, naturally, populism.   [JM]

THE MAYAKOVSKY CASE

At a gathering of Bolshevik writers in Leningrad, Kolbasiev said to me, "Contrary to what's presumed abroad, Mayakovsky isn't the greatest Soviet poet or anything of the sort. Mayakovsky is nothing more than a thespian hyperbolist. Before him are Pasternak, Biedny, Sayanov, and many others . . ."

I knew Mayakovsky's work, and my opinion was in absolute agreement with Kolbasiev's. And, a few days later, when I spoke in Moscow with the author of *150,000,000*, our conversation confirmed Kolbasiev's judgment for all of eternity. In reality, Mayakovsky isn't the greatest Soviet poet. He's merely the most published. If one read more of Pasternak, Kaziin, Gastev, Sayanov, Viesimiensky, the name Mayakovsky would vanish from many radio waves.

But, why did my conversation with Mayakovsky have to be the definitive key to his work? To what degree can a conversation define the spirit and, even more, the aesthetic value of an artist? In this case, the answer depends on the method of critical thought. If we start with a surrealist, Freudian, Bergsonian, or any other reactionary method, we cannot ground ourselves in a simple dialogue with an artist to locate the tendency of his work. According to these different spiritualist methods, the artist is an instinct or, to express ourselves with a more orthodox lexicon, an intuition. His work flows from him naturally, unconsciously, subconsciously. If one asks his opinion on art or his art, he will surely respond with banalities and many of them; the exact opposite of what he does and practices. Accordingly, a genius denies, contradicts, or almost always loses in his debates. Therefore, to abide by one of these, as critical grounds, results in falseness, absurdity. Yet this doesn't happen if we start with the method of historical materialism, so dear to Mayakovsky and his communist friends. Marx conceives of life solely as a vast scientific experiment in which nothing is unconscious or blind, but rather is reflective, conscious, and technical. According to him, the artist must proceed with a rigorously scientific method and complete understanding of his means so that his work may dialectically reverberate through history. That's why there's no better exegete of a poet's work than the poet himself. What he thinks and says about his work is or should be more accurate than anyone else's opinion. In the statements he made to me, Mayakovsky thus described, better than any critic, the true meaning and sum of his work.

Mayakovsky spoke to me with a visibly pained and bitter accent. Contrary to what all his critics say of him, deep down he was suffering an acute moral crisis. The revolution had arrived in the midst of his youth, when the forms of his spirit were already settled and even consolidated. The effort it took to suddenly turn around and face that new life with a boxing glove broke his spine and made him lose his center of gravity, converting him into a *désaxée*,[52] as occurred with Essenin and Sobol. Such has been the fate of this generation. It has suffered in a completely individual aorta the psychical consequences of the social revolution. Situated between the pre- and postrevolutionary generations, this generation of Mayakovsky, Essenin, and Sobol has been crucified. Within this generation, the cavalry has been greater for those whom the revolution took by surprise, dispossessed of all tradition or revolutionary initiation. The tragedy of personal, psychological transmutation has therefore been brutal, and only the indifferent have managed to escape from it by wearing a revolutionary mask—the numb posing as Bolsheviki. The more sensitively and warmheartedly the individual were to penetrate social events, the deeper the disturbances must have been in his persona, derived from political convulsion, and the more exacerbated the pathos of his inner and individual revision of history. The final judgment has therefore been terrible, and suicide (material and moral) was fatal and inevitable, the only solution to the tragedy. On the contrary, for the others—for the insensitive and indifferent "Bolsheviki"— it has been easy and not at all risky to pipe out "revolutionary" cries, since for them the revolution stayed outside, as a phenomenon or spectacle of the State, and didn't end up becoming an inner, psychological, personal revolution. Thus there was neither difficulty nor danger in associating with the trend started by others. This is what most writers have done and do in Russia and elsewhere. What? Are these other writers going to go so far as to be put to death for the "sacred cause"? Well, are they? . . . That proves nothing. History shows that many have been put to death for much less.

In the case of Mayakovsky, two aspects must be distinguished: his life and his work. After his suicide, the former has reached completion as one of the greatest and purest individual expressions of collective action. Without a doubt the suicide has been nothing more than the millionth stage of the long moral via crucis of the writer, a *déraciné*[53] of history, and a powerful will to fully understand and live in powerful social relationships. This inner struggle between the past, which resists, despite its complete lack of leverage, and the present, which demands authentic thunderous transformation, in Mayakovksy was drawn out fiercely, terribly. At the bottom, the tenacious, irreducible, petite bourgeois sensibility would survive with the set of all its fundamental social values of life, and only on the outside would the voluntary thirst, virile from suffocating the profound being of the old history, slave away to replace it with the equally profound being of the new history. The grafting of the latter on the former was impossible. On the day after the revolution, in vain he exchanged his futurist vest for the Bolshevik poet's button-down shirt. In vain he walked around thereafter reciting his Soviet poems in the streets and plazas, factories, fields, *izbas*,[54] unions, in the barracks of the Red Army . . . In vain he sought in the masses the suggestion necessary to sovietize his intimately *désaxée* spirit. With a gigantic strong body, with a robust steely megaphonic voice, he would recite, "Oh my country! You are a beautiful child. Oh my young Republic! You pull up and buck like a youthful filly. Our momentum is aimed at the future. And to you, old countries, we shall leave you one hundred kilometers back. Fare thee well, oh my country, you the youth of the world . . ." In vain, all of it . . . In vain . . . Shackled to counterfeit formulas of an external and inorganic Leninism, on the inside the poet truly continued to suffer in silence, feeling the complete opposite of what his poems were saying. While Mayakovsky continued to get mixed up in literature with that entourage of "revolutionary" artists, who appear to be so with the same ease that they would appear to be brave, senior citizens, or creatures of the night, the inner life of the poet, in open disagreement with an art that did not translate it, continued to struggle under the surface, debating itself in agony. It was the tragic, piercing breakdown of all synchronicity between the work and life of the author. And neither a revolutionary nor reactionary poet became of him. His inner struggle completely neutralized his sensibility and artistic expression. Mayakovsky was a mere intellectual, a simple wordsmith, a hollow rhetorician.

"War on metaphysics," he said to me in Moscow. "War on the subconscious and the theory according to which the poet sings as sings the bird . . . War on apolitical poetry, on grammar, on metaphor . . . Art must be controlled by reason . . . It must always serve as political propaganda, and even work with preconceived, clear ideas, and it even must be developed with a thesis, like an algebraic theory. The expression must be direct, point blank . . ."

Did his poetry respond to these claims? Evidently, it did. However, the theory of Mayakovsky served to turn him into a manufacturer of cold, dead poems *sur commande*.[55]

The claims of Mayakovsky express the truth about his work in the sense that they confirm the fact that it responds to an art based on formulas and not on affective personal sincerity.

By binding himself to an artistic platform, taken from historical materialism, Mayakovsky merely made unprecedented poems deprived of inner warmth and meaning, produced by external, mechanical traction, that is, by an artificial heater.

Mayakovsky was a soul exemplary of his environment and his time, but he wasn't a poet. His life was likewise great due to its tragedy, but his art was declamatory and null since it betrayed the authentic and truly critical moments of his life.

[JM]

REGARDING ARTISTIC FREEDOM

"I protest," a poet said to me, *au dessus de la mêlée*,[56] "that the artist and writer should submit to the yoke of any government or social class, whether it's the Soviet government and the proletarian class or not. The artist and writer have nothing to do with political parties and classes and must work on their art with absolute freedom and independence."

"Do you think," I argued, "that in all of history there have ever been artists and writers who were free and independent in this regard?"

"Naturally. Even today, we have Bernard Shaw, Stravinsky, Picasso, Chaplin."

"Is that right? Free of what? Independent of what?"

"Of the politics of Chamberlain, Stalin, Chautemps, Roosevelt."

"Hold it right there. Let's understand each other. Suppose one day Picasso paints a cubist Laval, making the French weavers scrounge off the police, because they demand a raise in their wages. What would happen? This is what: neither Mr. Rosember—*marchand* of Picasso—nor any other *marchand de tableaux*[57] of Paris would want to show that painting to the public in their galleries; second, the public of rue la Boétie—a crowd indeed *chic, le tout Paris cultivé et riche*, capable of buying Picasso's most expensive paintings—would be indignant and find the theme and even the artistic execution of the canvas *drôles*,[58] in poor taste, crafty, and, finally, annoying, if not *pas intéressants*[59] (and we already know why!); third, the critics of *Le Temps, Le Figaro, Paris Midi* . . . etc. would cry out to Heaven;

and, fourth, the secret police of famous Mr. Chiappe would visit Picasso one afternoon and serve him a surely not so desirable summons. In the end, the painter would lose his prestige, and his career (aside from earning him premeditated surveillance) could consequently end up sending the artist to Irun. What happened to the painter's freedom? And let it be known that the theme of the painting wouldn't be Picasso's invention, but would be taken from the reality of what happened in July 1930, when Laval was minister of labor.[60] And let it be known, finally, that the tragedies—and all the more if they're social—contain premium artistic suggestions."

"But, exactly," the poet said to me somewhat defeated, *au dessus de la mêlée*, "the artist is not to mess with political themes." Picasso will never paint such a canvas and, thus, what you say never will happen . . ."

"But of course. Surely not. Picasso and the other 'free' artists don't mess with political themes for this reason: so that nothing happens to them. They're ignorant to Zola's phrase: 'My duty is to speak; I don't want to be an accomplice.'[61] It's very pleasing to watch the bulls from a safe distance. What does it matter if those themes are extraordinarily great on their own account? As soon as you mess with them, say good-bye to 'freedom.'"

"But, Picasso, like other great artists, is far from doing this out of cowardice or egotism."

"Okay, okay. It's an unconscious egotism and a dependence on class and the bourgeois government, which is equally unconscious."[62]   [JM]

MY SELF-PORTRAIT IN THE LIGHT
OF HISTORICAL MATERIALISM

A portrait must contain the essence of a life, that is to say, the infinite personality, the past, present, and future figure, in brief, the entire role of a life. The artist will poke around the mystery of that life, discover its permanent and changing sense of beauty and will make it felt in lines, colors, surfaces, movement, mass, directions. A portrait is, then, the revelation of a life, from the beginning to the end of its trajectory. A portrait is data from an oracle, the cipher of a prophecy, an explanation of the mystery, the excavation of a fable. All this is the character of a portrait.

But the creation of the portrait, like all creations, has its heroic side. This heroism is rooted in a battle between the infinity of a being, or rather his character, which is revealed by the artist, and the situation or circumstance of that being in space and time. This situation, this finiteness is his appearance, what he looks like. The artist will dole out aspects of the conflict according to his emotions. The circumstances of space and time within which we unexpectedly encounter the infinity of his life must not be subordinated to the point that we cannot recognize the person in the portrait. Upon a certain mysterious balance between what is visible and invisible in a portrait, between circumstance and permanence, or, what amounts to the same thing, between appearance and character is what the greatness of a creation depends.

Character and appearance are embattled values in the portrait, which is why they harmonize and integrate with each other. The feeling of plenitude in the portrait, as in a compass, resides in both. They constitute the thesis and antithesis of dialectical movement in this art. [SJL]

From *Against Professional Secrets* [63]

FROM FEUERBACH TO MARX

When an organ carries out its function fully, there's no possible malice in the body. At the moment a tennis player masterfully tosses the ball, he's possessed by animal innocence.

The same occurs with the brain. At the moment the philosopher discovers a new truth, he's a complete beast. Anatole France said that religious sentiment is the function of a special organ of the human body, yet to be discovered. One could also affirm that, at the precise moment that this organ of faith functions at its peak, the believer is also a being so devoid of malice that he could be called utterly animal.   [JM]

EXPLANATION OF HISTORY

There are people who are interested in Rome, Athens, Florence, Toledo, and other ancient cities, not because of their past—static and immobile—but because of their present—lively and dynamic. For these people, the world of El Greco, the green and yellow robes of his apostles, his house, his kitchen, his crockery, are not very interesting. What do they care about the cathedral of Toledo, with its five doors, its seven centuries, its refreshing cloisters, its silver choir, and its enchanting Mozarab chapel? What do they care about the Inn of Blood, where Cervantes was to write *The Illustrious Kitchen Maid* . . . ? What do they care about the Palace of Carlos V, all of its stone and its distinguished coffered ceiling? The celebrated Castle of San Servando on the other side of the ravine might as well disappear in broad daylight. The tombs of the heroes and cardinals of the cathedral might as well disappear. The Munitions Factory in Toledo—what do they care!? The Tránsito Mosque, constructed in the fourteenth century by the Jew Samuel Levi—what do they care!? These passersby are utterly indifferent to history in a text, in a legend, in a painting, in architecture, in tradition.

While the guide explains the date and political circumstances of its construction on the Bridge of Alcántara, I note that one of the tourists becomes a disengaged schoolboy and stares at an old Toledan, who is just arriving home on the back of his donkey. The old man laboriously gets down, in the middle of his receiving room. "Ah . . . !" the old man snorts and begins to loudly call to the watchmen on the corner so that they help him remove the donkey's saddle. This happens on the street that bears the name *Sponge Cake Oven Way* or on that slightly rougher one called *Don Pedro's Path to the Chicken Coop.*

These are the scenes that interest certain people: the historical present of Toledo, not its past. They want to submerge in the fleeting present, which in the end recasts and crystallizes the essentials of past history. That old man, seated atop a donkey, summarizes in his snort El Greco, the cathedral, the palace, the mosque, the munitions factory. It's a living and transitory scene of the moment, synthesizing, like a flower, Toledo's uproar and defunct deeds.

The same can be said of all the ancient cities, historical ruins, and treasures of the world. One does not narrate history, or see it or hear it or touch it. One lives history and feels it live.   [JM]

––––––––––

An animal is led or is pushed. Man is accompanied in parallel.

––––––––––

There exist questions without answers, which fill the spirit of science and common sense with uneasiness. There exist answers without questions, which are the spirit of art and the dialectical consciousness of things.

––––––––––

THE HEAD AND FEET OF DIALECTICS

Facing the stones of Darwinian risk that compose the Tuileries Palace, Potstam, Peterhof, Quirinal, the White House, and Buckingham, I suffer the pain of a megatherium, who meditated standing upright, the hind legs on the head of Hegel and the front legs on the head of Marx.

––––––––––

THE DEATH OF DEATH

In reality, the sky isn't far from or near the land. In reality, death isn't far from or close to life. We are always before the river of Heraclitus.   [JM]

Parallels exist neither in the spirit nor in the reality of the universe. It's but an abstract supposition of geometry. There's no room for a parallelism within the single and linear continuity of life. History and Nature unfold linearly and, in this single, solitary line, human events and natural phenomena occur, one after another, successively and never simultaneously.

The parallelism of a railroad does not have a greater living reality than that of two lines drawn on a chalkboard. Two trees or two children born at the same instant do not constitute an effective parallelism either. In all these cases, the geometric illusion doesn't sustain objective events but participates in the nature of so many other fictions of the senses or abstractions of intelligence, like when we see, from a train in motion, that the houses are on parade or when a burning stick is moving in a circle (see Pascal), we believe that we see and affirm an arc of fire, etc.

Life is a succession and not simultaneity. The apparent parallels of a railroad don't develop at once, but one after another. Men don't live together, but they occur one after another. Towns don't live together either, but occur. Plurality is a phenomenon of time and not of space. The number 1 is solitary of place. The number 2 and the subsequent single or compound numbers don't exist as objective reality, but as abstract suppositions of thought.

Life doesn't play out in various forms at once. But in various successive forms. One planet doesn't have a destiny different from that of other planets, but the same and unique end that all the others have managed to carry out. A stone meets a destiny identical to that of a mollusk, and it goes before or after a man, but not at the same time as he. If one could depict the evolution of life, it would be represented by a line of beings and things, with one at the end. In abstract terrain, beings and things unfold with an apparent myriad character. But this isn't substantive reality. Beneath the illusory simultaneity of things and beings, reality, at the end, is solely a succession in the motion of the universe. The masses are more a parade than a crowd. The asyndeton surging from history is more a line than a point.   [JM]

INDIVIDUAL AND SOCIETY

When the interrogation began, the murderer gave his first answer, staring at the members of the tribunal. One of these, Milad the substitute, gave off an astonishing likeness to the defendant. The same age, the same muti-lated right eye, the cut and color of the mustache, the line and thickness of his chest, the shape of his head, the haircut. An absolutely identical double. The murderer saw his double, and something must have happened in his conscience. He made his left dead eye turn in a strange way, took out a handkerchief, and wiped the sweat from his hard cheeks. The first background question, formulated by the president of the panel, was this:

"You, sir, took a liking to women and, aside from Malou, you had your maid, your sister-in-law, and two other lovers . . ."

The defendant comprehended the procedural scope of this question. Poker-faced,[64] he fixed his only good eye on Milad the substitute, his double, and he said, "I took a liking to women, as all men take a liking to them . . ."

The murderer seemed to feel a knot in his throat. The presence of his double began to cause in him a visible yet mysterious discomfort, a great fear perhaps . . . Every time a serious and terrible question was formulated, he stared with his only eye at his double and responded each time more defeated. The presence of Milad caused him greater and greater pain, dis-astrously influencing the course of his spirit and of the judgment. At the end of the first hearing, he took out his handkerchief and burst into tears.

On the afternoon of the second hearing, he looked even more dejected. Yesterday, the day of the sentence, the murderer facing his ruling, was a wreck of a man, a devastated, hopelessly lost culprit. He barely even spoke anymore. As the verdict of death was being read, he was slouching in his chair, his head resting on his hands, numb, cold, like a stone. When the bailiffs took him away, amid the clamor and murmuring of the dismayed crowd, he only fixed his gaze on the face of Milad, his double, the substi-tute.

To that extent the individual conscience is social and collective.   [JM]

NEGATIONS OF NEGATIONS

André Bretón says that Philippe Soupault left his house one morning and began running all over Paris, asking from door to door, "Does Mr. Philippe Soupault live here?"

After going through various streets, at an unknown house they an-swered the door and said, "Yes, sir, Mr. Philippe Soupault lives here."

A detective who appears in a Chesterton novel, bent on finding the place where the criminal was hiding, discovered him, guided and attracted by certain odd details in the architecture of the house where the criminal was hiding.

One day when I was coming out of the Louvre, I ran into a friend at the door to the museum who asked me where I was going. I said, "To the Louvre Museum."

It would be good to remember that Columbus, as biographer André de Loffechi tells us, experienced his first feeling of the earth's roundness as he was entering his bedroom in Genoa. "If instead of entering his bedroom," Loffechi observes, "let's say, Columbus goes out to the garden, then he would not necessarily have discovered America."

Marquis de Vasselot unwittingly used a somersault in his bed to discover the scientific principle by which certain Chinese bronze pieces from the Tsing dynasty period maintain a bluish coloring when in contact with the air.

Lord Carnavon, who in February 1923 discovered the third underground funeral tomb of Tut-Ankh-Amon, suffered from a mysterious nervous illness, according to what has been learned after his death. His companion in archaeological adventure, Mr. Howard Carter, tells us that the unfortunate Lord, while still in London before his pharaonic finding, without knowing why, would become ill and would be struck by melancholic thoughts each time the scent of resin reached his nose. He then would enter his library and open up his volumes. After finding the object of Carnavon's search, the gold sarcophagus of the Tut-Ankh-Amon's mummy, Mr. Carter has stated that said mummy was found covered with a thick layer of sacred resin.

The Eiffel Tower's three hundred womanly states are frozen. The tower's Hertzian mane of culture, its fuzzy sights, its living steelwork, stapled to Descartes's moral system, is frozen.

From *Against Professional Secrets*   217

Le Bois de Boulogne, green from a private clause, is frozen.

The Chamber of Deputies, where Briand exclaims, "I hereby appeal to the peoples of the land" while the doorkeeper unconsciously caresses his capsule of human uneasiness, his simple pump of Man, according to Pascal's principle, it is frozen.

The Champs-Élysées, gray from a public clause, is frozen.

The statues that circuit[65] the Place de la Concorde upon whose Phrygian caps time is heard studying the infinite, they are frozen.

The dice of the Catholic cavalries of Paris are even frozen on the face of the threes.

The civil cocks, suspended in the gothic needles of Nôtre Dame and of Sacré Cœur, are frozen.

The maiden of the Parisian countryside, whose thumb measures the horizon with her eyes only once, is frozen.

The two textured andante in Stravinsky's *The Firebird* is frozen.

Einstein's scribbles on the chalkboard of the Richelieu amphitheater at the Sorbonne are frozen.

The airline tickets for the trip from Paris to Buenos Aires, in two hours, twenty-three minutes, eight seconds, are frozen.

The sun is frozen.

The fire at the earth's core is frozen.

The father, meridian, and the son, parallel, are frozen.

History's two deviations are frozen.

My minor act of man is frozen.

My sexual oscillation is frozen.

-:-:-:-:-

I want to get lost from a lack of roads. I'm itching to get lost permanently, no longer in the world nor in morality, but in life and by dint of life. I hate the streets and paths that don't allow one to get lost. The city and country are like this. In them, the loss, though not the perdition of a spirit, is impossible. In the country and in the city, one is far too surrounded by routes, arrows, and signs to get lost. One is without fail limited there, to the north, to the south, to the east, to the west. One is inevitably situated there. Contrary to what happened to Wilde, on the morning he was to die in Paris, I always awake in the city surrounded by everything, by the brush, by the bar of soap, by everything. I awake in the world and with the world, in myself and with myself. I call and inevitably they answer, and my call is heard. I go out onto the street, and there is a street. I starting thinking, and there always is thought. This is exasperating.

-:-:-:-:-

Technicians speak and live as technicians and rarely as men. It is quite difficult to be a technician and a man at the same time. A poet judges a poem, not as a simple mortal, but as a poet. And we already know to what extent technicians get tangled up offstage in the fly ropes, falling through the weak side of the system, from indoctrinating prejudice or from professional interest, conscious or subconscious, and in this way fracturing the complete sensibility of man.

-:-:-:-:-

Everything wears its hat. All animals wear their hats. The plants wear theirs as well. There is not in this world anything or anyone that doesn't cover their heads. Even though men may remove their hats, the head always stays covered by something we could call the innate, natural, and tacit hat of each person.

From man's point of view, hats are classified as natural hats and artificial hats. We call a natural hat one that is born with each person and is inseparable from him even in death. In the skeleton, the presence of the natural and tacit hat is palpable. We call an artificial hat one that is acquired in hat shops and from which we can separate ourselves momentarily or eternally. In the skeleton, the lack of this artificial hat is, likewise, evident.

-:-:-:-:-

Those who take to the shoulder and not to the road itself will be rejected. Woe betide he who spawns a monster! Woe betide he who radiates a straight arc! Woe betide he who manages to crystallize some utter nonsense! This is how the differences of distichous leaves march on the Pantheon of the big deals, crucified in useless straitjackets.

-:-:-:-:-

I know a man who used to sleep with his arms. One day they amputated them and he stayed awake forever.

-:-:-:-:-

Water invites meditation. Land, action. Meditation is hydrographic, action, geographic. Meditation comes. Action goes. That one is a centripetal; this one, centrifugal.

–:–:–:–:–

Dance, when repeated, gets stereotyped and becomes cliché. Each dance should be improvised and die shortly thereafter. This is how the Negroes do it.

–:–:–:–:–

If one doesn't want theater, as a performance, to disappear, it would be good, at least, for each component—text, scene, movement—to be improved by the actors themselves, who, in effect, should also be authors and regisseurs of the works that they act out. This is what Chaplin does on the silver screen.

–:–:–:–:–

A doctor affirms that to furrow the brow, one must flex sixty-four muscles, while to laugh thirteen muscles suffice. Pain, therefore, is more athletic than joy.

–:–:–:–:–

People and things that cross each other in opposite directions don't go to different places. They all go to the same place; it's just that they go one after the other.

–:–:–:–:–

Those who travel on the bow carry the port side; those who travel on the stern, the center. The starboard side, the skipper's got that.

–:–:–:–:–

The idea is the history of the act and, naturally, posterior to it. First one lives an act and, then, this act is minted into an idea, its correlate. Paul Valéry will have to excuse this small landing, this conjugation of the infinitive of *Soul and Dance*.

–:–:–:–:–

The knife is always being taken by the blade instead of being taken by the handle. There are men destined to engender geniuses and there are others destined to create works of genius. The coitus in which Dostoevsky's father engendered the great novelist is worth as much as *The Idiot*. Between one thing and another there lies a chained clock.

The day has the night locked inside. The night has the day locked outside.

I saw him pass by so quickly that I didn't see him.

Who will win a race between a bicycle and a frog? Averchenko would say, the frog.

I was far from my father for two hundred years and they wrote to me saying that he was still living. But a profound feeling from life gave me the deep and creative need to believe that he was dead.

Renan said of Joseph de Maistre, "Every time that there is an effect of style in his work, it is due to a lack of French." The same can be said of all great writers in every language.

One can speak of the horse's bit only when dealing with cerebral activity, founded on reason. Feeling is never in excess. It has its measure in itself and proportion in its own nature. Feeling is always the right size. It's never deficient or excessive. It needs neither a bridle nor spurs.

The noise of a car, when it goes slowly, is ugly and unpleasant. When it goes quickly, it becomes melodious.   [JM]

REPUTATION THEORY

I have been in the famous Sztaron tavern on Seipel Street, in Budapest, a tavern, they say, of a secret Bolshevik company whose manager, Ossag Muchay, has been quite courteous to his clientele. Muchay has been with me for quite a while, talking at length and sipping Viennese absinthe, that religious and potent liqueur, the color of an inchworm that he extracts from a strange wild grass called *sleeping spirit*. This evening, the tavern was visited by a great number of customers, who entered, stretching out their limbs, drinking maliciously at the bar and then leaving with utter perfection. In the corner on the first floor, two young girls were playing a game of leapfrog[66] with tiny caped turtles bedecked in ribbons. In the doorway of the same room, good Muchay and I were talking. We spoke about the superstitions of Asia Minor, about the salubrious sciences of apprehension, about witchcraft.

I said good-bye to Muchay and left the tavern. I headed toward the corner and took Prague Street, which appeared to be invaded with people. The crowd was looking over the brick walls at the police maneuvers. I realized, through timely waning swells in vignette, that they were chasing the criminal of a high crime, one which no one could identify. A group of officers left one of the towers of the Ravulk church, leading a man in handcuffs. As they led the prisoner down the steps of the entrance hall, I could see him through the crowd, wearing a coat with lozenges, enormous eyes, a large well-bred dog, who had just bitten a queen.

I followed the throng of people to the station. The commissioner himself interrogated the prisoner in a tone of legal indignation:

"Who are you? What is your name?"

"I don't have a name, sir," said the prisoner.

His name has been sought in Loeben, the village where the shackled man was residing, but to no avail. There is no official record of his family. Nor was any paper at all discovered in his pockets. All that is proven is that he lives in Loeben, because everyone has seen him there on a daily basis, walking through the streets, sitting in the cafés, reading newspapers, talking with passersby. Yet no one knows his name. How long has he lived in Loeben? This remains unknown, as does whether he is Hungarian or a foreigner.

I returned to Ossag Muchay's tavern and explained the case to him in great detail and even gave him the minute description of the prisoner. Muchay told me, "That individual, in all truth, lacks a name. I am the only one who holds his name. Do you want to find out what it is?"

He took me by the arm, we went up to the second floor, and he led me to a desk. There, he took a scrap of paper out of a tiny case, where appeared, in thick and loose lines, but so crumbled that it was impossible to decipher them, a signature penned in frog green ink, like the kind Hungarian country folk use. I argued with Muchay, "Can one really take a person's name and hide it in a case, like a simple ring or bill . . . ?"

"Nothing more or less," the tavern owner replied.

"And what is the explanation of all this? So then, what is that name?"

"Neither you nor anyone can know it, since this name is now in my sole possession. You, sir, can find out what it is, but you cannot know it . . ."

"Mr. Muchay, are you mocking me?"

"Not in the least. That man lost his name and he himself, although he would like to, cannot know it now. It is absolutely impossible for him, as long as he does not have in his possession the signature that you see before you."

"But if he signed it, it will be easy for him to sign it again and again."

"No. The name is but one alone. Signatures, there are many of these, no doubt, but the name is only one out of all the signatures."

His unexpected billiard subtleties began to make my mind swim. Muchay, on the other hand, spoke without faltering. He lit his pipe with two flicks on his Croatian flint. He closed the steel case and led me down.

"The life of a man," he said, walking down the stairs, "is completely revealed in only one of his acts. The name of a man is revealed in only one of his signatures. To know that representative act is to know his true life. To know that representative signature is to know his true name."

"And on what grounds do you believe that the signature you possess is the representative signature of that man? What's more, what does knowing a person's true name matter? Doesn't one know everyone's true name?"

"Listen, sir," argued Muchay, placing a prudent inflection on his words, "the true name of many people remains unknown. This is why the worker from Loeben, and not the owner of the factory where he worked, was imprisoned."

"But do you know the crime he is accused of?"

"An assault on Regent Horthy."

I lowered my eyes, blowing air into my medium-sized organs and remained Vallejo facing Muchay.   [JM]

NOISE OF A GREAT CRIMINAL'S FOOTSTEPS

When they put out the light, I felt like laughing. Things in the dark resumed their labors, at the point where they had paused. In one face, the eyes looked down at the nostrils: there they took an inventory of certain mislaid optical values and immediately put them back in place. The scales of a fish hollered at the shell of a ship; three drops of rain paused at the parallel height of a threshold, to await another drop that had been delayed for some unknown reason; the policeman on the corner blew his nose noisily, insisting upon blowing only the left nostril, singularly; the highest and lowest step of a spiral staircase turned to make suggestive signs at the last passerby who climbed them. Things, in the gloom, resumed their labors, freely animated with joy and behaving as if they were upper-class diners at a banquet in which the lights suddenly went out and everything was in the dark.

When they put out the light, frames and markings in the world were distributed in a much better way. Each rhythm went with its music; each weight on the scale moved the least that any destiny can move by itself, exactly, until almost acquiring absolute presence. In general, a precious balance of liberation and justice among things was produced. Seeing this I was content, since in myself as well the grace of the numeral shadows arched and bucked.

I don't know who created light again. The world was again crouching in its bedraggled skins: the yellow skin of Sunday, the ashen skin of Monday, the damp skin of Tuesday, the prudent skin of Wednesday, the sharkskin of Thursday, the sad skin of Friday, the ragged skin of Saturday. The world thus went back to appearing still asleep, or pretending to be asleep. A horrifying spider, with three broken legs, crept out of Saturday's sleeve. [SJL]

CONFLICT BETWEEN THE EYES AND THE GAZE

I've often seen things that others have seen as well. This fills me with subtle and tiptoeing vexation, in whose intimate presence my supportive sides flow with blood.

"The sun has broken through," I say to a man.

"Yes," he replies. "A sweet and tawny sun."

I've felt that the sun is, truly, tawny and sweet. So I get the urge to ask another man what he knows about this sun. He has confirmed my impression, and this confirmation causes me pain, a dull pain that aggravates my ribs. Is it not, then, true that as the sun broke through, I was facing it? And, like this, that man has come, as if from a rearview mirror, close up to murmur at my side, "Yes. A sweet and scrawny[67'] sun." An adjective is cut out from each of my temples. No. I shall ask another man about this sun. The first has made a mistake or is joking, trying to undermine me.

"The sun has broken through," I say to another man.

"Yes, quite cloudy," he responds.

"The sun has broken through," I said to another, still further away.

"A half-baked sun,"[68] this one contended.

"Where might I go to avoid a rearview mirror, whose surface comes to smack me in the face, no matter how far I push on sidelong and gaze straight ahead?"

Alongside Man, beautiful absurdities come and go, a plodding cavalry on the move, in need of a leading ox, number, and rider. Yet men love to hit the brakes out of love for the rider and not out of love for the animal. I must hit the brakes, out of love only for the animal. And no one will feel what I feel. And now no one will be able to undermine me.   [JM]

LANGUIDLY HIS LIQUEUR

We must have been at a compassionate age when my father ordered our entrance to school. A priestess of love, one rainy afternoon in February, Mom was serving a prayer-time snack in the kitchen. In the downstairs hallway, my father and older brothers were sitting at the table. And my mom was about to sit down next to the household hearth itself. Someone knocked on the door.

"Someone's knocking on the door!" my mother.

"Someone's knocking on the door!" my own mother.

"Someone's knocking on the door!" my whole mother said, plucking her entrails on infinite frets, over the whole height of who's here.

Nativa, the daughter, goes to see who's there. Without waiting for maternal consent, Miguel outside, the son, who left to see who had thus arrived, opposing us breadthwise.

A time of thoroughfare contained my family. Mom went out inversely moving forward and as if she had said, the parts. A patio was made outside. Nativa was crying over such a guest, over such a patio, and over my mother's hand. Then and when, pain and palate roofed our foreheads.

"Because I didn't let him go out the door," Nativa, the daughter, "Miguel has kicked me out of the cocoon. Out of his cocoon."[69]

What a right hand of the subprefect, the right hand of my father, revealing the man, the filial phalanxes of the boy! He could grant the fortune that the man would later desire. However, "and tomorrow, to school," the father masterfully expounded, before the weekly audience of his kids.

"And thus, the law, the order to show cause. And thus also life."

Mom must have cried, the mother barely groaning. No one wanted to eat anymore. A thin spoon that I know fit in the lips of the father, only to come out broken. The son's absorbed bitterness got stuck in the fraternal mouths.

But later, unexpectedly, a hen, not a distant or an egg-laying hen, but a brutal and black one, came out of a rain gutter and from that same patio of the guest, it clucked in my throat. It was an old hen, maternally widowed by some chicks that didn't manage to incubate. Origin forgotten in that instant, the hen was a widow of her children. All the eggs were found empty. The broody one later had the last word.

No one startled her. And startling her, no one stopped cooing for her great maternal chills.

"Where are the old hen's children?"

"Where are the old hen's chicks?"

"Poor little things! Where could they be!" [JM]

VOCATION OF DEATH

The son of Mary leaned in and asked, "What are you reading?"

The doctor raised his eyes and shot a surprised look at the speaker. Other scribes returned to the son of Mary and the wise rabbi.

Attendance at the temple that day was spare. A Greek man was judged for his debt. The creditor, a young Syrian from the land of Hermon, was seated at the base of a column in the portico and, due to all the allegations before the judges, he wept in silence.

"I'm reading Lenin," the doctor replied, opening a pamphlet written in foreign characters in front of the son of Mary.

The son of Mary read to himself from the book and both exchanged gazes, later separating and disappearing into the crowd. Upon return to Nazareth, the son of Mary ran into his brother-in-law, Armani, who was arguing out of jealousy with his wife, Zabade, the younger sister of the son of Mary. Both spouses grew more irritated when they saw him, out of their deep hatred for him.

"What do you want?"

The son of Mary was lost in thought and he shuddered. Coming to, he took to the street without uttering a word. He was hungry and remembered his cousins, the good children of Cleophas.

"Jacob, I'm hungry!"

"There's a phone call for me. I'll be right back," Jacob replied to him in that sweet and winged Hebrew of ancient Galilee.

Evening came and it had been three days since the son of Mary had eaten anything. He went to watch the workers pass through the intersections of Nazareth, some toward the west, through the gentle skirts of Mount Carmel, whose final abrupt peak seems to submerge into the sea; others toward the mountains of Samaria, beyond which sad Judea rests, dry and arid. He went up to a wall and leaned against it. He was exhausted—his heart more than ever felt void of hatred and love, and his thought, more than ever uncertain.

The son of Mary turned thirty years old that day. Throughout his life, he had traveled, read, and meditated a great deal. His family hated him, due to his strange demeanor, in which he rejected every profession and concern with reality. A rebel against the practices of townsfolk, he eventually abandoned his job as a carpenter and no longer had any vocation or concrete direction. In his house, they called him an *idiot*, because in all reality he seemed brainless. He almost died from hunger and from exposure several times. His mother loved him more than her other children because he was *poor in spirit*. He often disappeared without anyone knowing his whereabouts. He returned with a wild hyena in his arms, his clothes torn to shreds, staring into space and sometimes weeping. He also used to bring home the branch of a fig tree from one of the holy places of the patriarchal age, the flowers of which refined spiritual therapists of devout life had rubbed against their habits.

The son of Mary managed to see a great stone, not far from him, and he went to sit on it. Night was falling.

Then, from Nazareth a group of people with a strange vagrant air left on the deserted and stony path. The boatman, Cephas of Capernaum, came over there and his mother-in-law, Juana; Susana, the wife of Kousa, the governor of Antipas; and Hillel, the one who always had an austere aphorism, who was the mentor of the son of Mary. In front of everyone, a young man with striking beauty and mild manners stepped forth. Worried, Hillel said, "Rest in God, behold the fundamental idea of Philon of Alexandria. What's more, for him, like for Isaiah and even for Enoch himself, the course of things is the result of God's free will.

As she noticed the son of Mary, seated on a stone, Susana went up and spoke to him. But the son of Mary did not reply: at that very moment he died.

Hillel, always prone to pondering, experienced a sudden visionary exaltation and, turning to the young man of striking beauty who was with them, he said, in a Syrian dialect, these unexpected words:

"You, Lord, are now the Son of man! In this moment, Lord, you begin to be the Son of man! In this moment, Lord, you begin to be the Messiah, proclaimed by Daniel and awaited by humanity for centuries."

"I am the Son of man sent by my Father," replied the young man of striking beauty and mild manners, as if he had just had a revelation thirty years in the making.

Around his Jewish head, a bluish glow began to appear.   [JM]

From *Toward the Reign of the Sciris*

1. THE OTHER IMPERIALISM

That rumble came from the army led by the prince and heir to the throne, as it reached the city limits, on its way home from a deadly tour in Quito. From the terraces at Sajsahuamán,[70] the receiving line formed near the entrance to the Intipampa[71] at the end of the wide highland road.

With the build still of a boy (as this was his first military campaign), at the head stood Hauyna Cápac, who had grown bronze from exposure, scorchers, and the deep freezes of the north. Decimated by ice in the heroic land of the Chachapoyas, the army now forded the first rivers of Cuzco, at a slow march, paced by the war drums' beat. The weapons of the empire followed up behind, and just a sling's throw away, the *rumancha*[72] masters. Then the rainbow flag was unfurled, embroidered onto a banner of wool and feathers, with holes left by a *suntupáucar*[73] spike through which a golden egret beam of light was shining. Angular heroes pushed on, triangulated by wrinkles, on their shoulders the dense mass of *queschuar*,[74] gaptoothed and gouged during counterattacks; gaunt and gangrene slingers; skeletal hunchback archers with flimsy bows; a third of the metal poison-tipped arrows in bundles, reed bows resting on their shoulders; lancers with enormous dangling arms wearing *guayacán*[75] headpieces with tassels; ax men falling out of formation, painfully limping . . . In the middle was an old *apusquepay*,[76] with a protruding chin and serene eyes, wearing his yellow turban, tied by a piece of stretched bow string and feathers.

Downcast and damaged, the army entered the city. Only a few generals, officers of nobility, and veterans smiled as they walked through the streets. Instead, the soldiers and even the heir apparent were possessed by great sorrow as they pushed on.

As the last soldiers disappeared from sight at the heart of the city, the workers of the fortress saw them and were overcome by a strange indifference. There was no applause or enthusiastic shouting. The women and children, who appeared at the doors, watched the warriors coldly. Some women crossed the road and gave a returning relative some *chicha*[77] or a few handfuls of fried hominy and sweet *ocas*.[78] The heralds kept quiet. Mouths filled with a turbid silence instead of the usual victory *hailli*.[79] When the army crossed in front of the Monastery of the Chosen Women in Hanai-Cuzco,[80] an old woman burst into tears.

War horns sounded in the distance as the army entered Cusipata.[81]

Muted were the murmurs of those bugles made from the skulls of dogs that had been hunted in enemy camps. Strings of sonorous monkey teeth from the north were fastened to the mouth so that, when the barbarous instrument was filled with air, a spine-tingling chatter came out, and as those sounds rung clear, the city swathed itself in pity and silence.

When he learned that Huayna Cápac was approaching, Túpac Yupanqui waited for him in the palace's patio of copper, surrounded by the court. His face was shriveled with rage. The prince arrived at the foot of the imperial throne, uncovered his head, and bowed. He expressed his fealty and obedience before recounting the story of the expedition in a submissive, prostrated tone.

"Father," he said, "the conquest of the Huacrachucos has been consolidated. Five hundred *mitimaes*[82] come with me, and I've left fifty Children of the Sun on the shores of the River Marañón. The Quechuas' bravery was heroic when they forced that province to surrender, whose young men fought ferociously, and had it not been for the advice from their elders, whom I won over with generous incentives, the surrender of the Huacrachucos would never have come to pass . . ."

The Inca remained indifferent. The eyes of the others turned to him, eager to see the effect that would be elicited by the word of the prince, whose arrival at Cuzco was early and unexpected. He had been unprepared for the current disposition of the Inca, in view of the largely unsuccessful results of the tour. The hearths in the mountains, the *chasquis*,[83] nothing had announced such a sudden return.

"After many journeys through the jungles," Huayna Cápac continued, "I attacked the Chachapoyas at their own walls and forts. Their resistance was even greater than the Huacrachucos' had been. Over the course of three moons I laid siege to the city. There I lost the brunt of the army. My ax men died trying to cut back the jungle, while the natives used it as a line of impenetrable defense. It was there that many veterans of Maule[84] and Atacama fell. I remounted the attack. Looking for a weaker flank, we backtracked at nightfall and climbed into the punas of Chirma-Cassa . . ."

When he reached this point, Huayna Cápac uttered his words in a tragic tone. The court stood at attention to listen. Only Túpac Yupanqui maintained his unaffected expression, as though he knew ahead of time everything the heir apparent would have to say.

"In that deadly region," added the prince, "all strategies failed, except at the price of a great abnegation. In faraway lands beset by hostility, I chose to take the most direct roads, and this was our greatest risk and sacrifice. So it was. I lost three hundred Warriors of the Sun, frozen in the cold on the eve of our final and fatal encounter with the enemy. Battle in those conditions was impossible. We withdrew and, since the army had been almost completely cut down, I consulted my advisers and decided to return to Cuzco . . ."

Thus spoke Huayna Cápac as he knelt before his father. The Inca's expression suddenly changed and, in a fit of rage, he raised his voice, loudly addressing the terrified court, and said, "The Children of the Sun have been defeated first in the mountains of Beni, whence returned to Mojos only one thousand soldiers of the ten thousand who embarked on boats that had been built over the course of two years; then, as the conquest of the Chirihuanas began, they were afraid of the savage cannibals, tried to cross the Maule again, but gave in to the fierce Promoncaes. And today, my son, prince and heir to the throne, on your first military campaign, you make an embarrassing withdrawal and thereby disrupt the conquest of the Sciris . . . Very well: the Conquest is over. Let us tend to the work of peace!"

Túpac Yupanqui rose from his golden seat and entered his chambers, followed by Raucaschuqui. The others were not sure how they should behave in the wake of the Inca's fit of rage. The heir apparent covered his jaguar head, and, with an expression of anger and pain, he flung his cape over his shoulder, headed toward the portico, and disappeared, followed by two young *huaracas*,[85] his campaign advisers.

2. THE SEER

According to the calculations of the *llacta-camayocs*,[86] the day the hunt was supposed to end, necessary preparations were made for the Emperor to attend the final phase of the *chacu*,[87] at his express wish.

Sixty thousand Quechuas had been sent out through the territory for the hunt. There were five thousand participants in the region of Cuzco, who had sojourned into the mountains and ravines three weeks earlier, carrying hundreds of ropes, a variety of weapons, hunting *alcos*,[88] and plentiful provisions. The stockade was already waiting on the Vilcamayo plains, south of the Colcapata Palace. It was an immense semicircle that opened toward the mountains, in a clearing that measured half a sling's throw deep. That morning, several women were tying fantastically painted tassels to the ropes, which were supposed to help corral the animals. At dawn several escaped guanacos reached the city slums, jumping over walls and fences.

The city dressed up for the celebration. Smoke rose from homes where preparations of food, *chicha*, and coca were being made for the town. Strong and stout women, with uncovered arms, water dripping from their braids, barefoot or with flimsy pita *llanques*,[89] were coming in and going out of the houses, carrying casks of fermented *chicha* on their shoulders or with both hands. Others were carrying enormous pots, brimming with hot Patasca;[90] wide-mouthed cups that had no handle, overflowing with hominy for the children; rosy wicker baskets from Puno, packed with *masato*;[91] towers of calabash *mates* and *potos*,[92] from largest to smallest tattooed with white hot burins; tobacco; *molle*;[93] saffron; ripe lucuma; oranges from the north; and clay from Nazca. Hundreds of llamas had been slaughtered for the celebration, and ropes of *charqui*[94] were hanging in the courtyards and corridors, salted and infused with pepper and chili. Rocoto of the temples was ground with pestle and mortar and mashed with *quinoa* and *olluco*.[95] Behind the houses, hearths were crackling white hot baking potatoes, sweet potato pies, and stuffed rolls, whose dense, porous scent impregnated the air with maddening subtlety.

From the moment he decided to lay down the arms of conquest and exchange them for plow and loom, Túpac Yupanqui had an especially kindhearted air of simplicity about him. Now he'd go out to see the farmwork; now he'd visit the shrieking forges of goldsmiths and smelters, where metal sheets and ingots whined when attacked by the sharp line of a sacred effigy or the angle of a splendid pick; now, as he'd walk through the outskirts of the capital, he'd gaze upon a hut, and take a strand from a skein for rugs and runners, whose threads were resting against the dried-out *pircas*,[96] dripping bright dyes from bloodwood, *molle*, bitter *quinoa*, and oilbirds; now he'd call to an *amauta*[97] and formulate elaborate questions about feats of the Incas of yore, the movements of time, the next new moon, about boundaries, distances, winds, birthrates, life, and death . . . Túpac Yupanqui found himself completely delivered to a profound life as a serene and constructive guardian, which tinted him with a sort of peaceful and smiling healthiness.

Noblemen joined the Inca in his enthusiasm for peace and work; however, deep down they lamented the Emperor's new policy, in the name of the race's warrior spirit and, especially, because of what it meant for their class, since expeditions of the conquest, in the long term, for them held the promise of promotions in the court and greater wealth in their coffers.

That morning there was talk in the corridors of the palace, in small boisterous crowds. "This is all very well," muttered a young grief-stricken *antun-apu*[98] to a few *curacas*,[99] "but I find no opposition between the *chacu* and the battle. You all know that the Children of the Sun have a divine mission on earth: to endlessly expand the region of the Inti[100] and its favorable fruits. The Inca is wrong. A great catastrophe is brewing . . ."

The *curacas* settled down. Making sure he wasn't overheard, one of them replied, "A great catastrophe is brewing. I've dreamed that a gigantic black *alco*, with fiery eyes and hairless skin, devoured the whole harvest of a *quinoa* field in an immense stockpile of the Raymi.[101] I dreamed that the mysterious *alco* was scared away by thousands of Quechuas who were letting out painful groans when they saw him eating the grain."

A few young princesses approached. The soldier and *curacas*, called by a servant, went off to join the others.

On the step of a small doorway, there were two granular friezes, riveted to the fire that they depicted (in one, the sacrifice of a boy; and in the other, the birth of Maita Cápac), and here two *ñustas*[102] appeared, one of them glowing with beauty and the other with lamentable homeliness.

Arm in arm they walked up slowly, leaning on each other. The princesses vanished out the side door of these premises that would eventually be the prince's, at the precise moment that an unforeseeable event occurred, leaving everyone paralyzed. A seer, unknown to all, entered the palace through the portico that faced Cusipata, letting out shrieks and shaking a sharp-tipped staff.

With long mangy hair, features distorted by terror, a tattered purple robe wrapped around him, and eyes sunken by anguish and hopelessness, he was running and jumping around, as if he had stepped on millions of red hot nails, looking for mysterious, terrible, and unheard-of things in the walls and gold-plated monoliths, on the rafters, statues, and pilasters— even in the air itself. He raised his staff and thrust it at the rosettes and arris on the wall. As if he were chasing insects or spiders, he bent over and then squatted to search the pavement and the patchwork of pelts and tapestries with the tip of his staff or his finger. He moaned and wept with infinite desolation.

The court stood witness to this scene in bewilderment. They let him run around in a circle, where his madness seemed to gravitate. He screamed, grunted, and groaned unintelligible words. He fell to the ground and removed his rags. Then it seized him by force, threatened him, but soon after they had left him alone, as though his body was burning, he started to speak.

"I'm the Seer!" he shouted. "The spider's legs grow inward! Catastrophe! Catastrophe!"

They took him to the Inca who noticed the prophetic air about the Quechua.

"Let him speak," he ordered in a tone of vague consternation. "Go ahead."

Between trembling pauses, the terrified Quechua, in whom the strange flame was burning the endless wick of the stars, spoke in sublime agony.

"I see *quipus*[103] tying themselves in knots like frightened serpents!" he said. "One of the chords keeps growing and knotting the tabernacles of the Coricancha;[104] it's red like an aqueduct filled with blood. The *malaquis*[105] and mummies of the emperors knot up too . . . I see a foreigner, with a white bearded face, sacking the sacred relics of Rimac and Titikaka . . . I see the *yllapa*[106] crossing a new sky and disintegrating into three different things, linked by the identical pace of their paths . . . Now they're gone! I can't see them anymore. What terrible blindness has gripped me! I see an innumerable army made of warriors and a chief who are all the same size, such that all appear to be chiefs or ordinary soldiers . . . Other armies come and wage war against one another, without shedding blood or tears. More than combat, it resembles a friendly and innocent game . . . Some pestilent clouds seep from the cracks in the earth and smother or stifle the fighters, disrupting the rhythm of their fight and replacing its order and harmony with sweat, fatigue, and unrest. Ah, the catastrophe! I hear the way the roads grow, coiling into dens, dolmens, and nests! . . ."

The Seer was removed. He had an enormous skull, the upper part flattened into a perfectly horizontal plane, from the height of the hairline on his brow to the occiput of his head. If it was not for the scalp that covered his skull, one would think that he had been scalped with a machete. The width of his face reached an excessive diameter, similar to the image that convex mirrors produce.

Once in Cusipata, the monster showed symptoms of calmness. He slowly recovered the normal state of his consciousness and returned to his prodigious world, alluding and referring to things and circumstances in reality. To the questions directed at him, he gave increasingly reasonable answers. Finally, when he reached the sick house, his words and actions became coherent and meaningful.

"What is your name?" they asked him.

"Ticu."

"What *ayllo*[107] are you from?"

"The Collahuatas."[108]

"You're obviously a Chuco.[109] Where do you live?"

"In the ghettos of Hurin-Cuzco,[110] near the palace at Yucay . . ."

"Who do you give predictions for?"

The Chuco was in a cold sweat that beaded on his forehead, and mortal lividness covered his large face. In the patio of the sick house, amid high and wide-reaching walls, they made him sit on a crumbling bench.

He then was surrounded by guards and the oldest nurse of the infirmary, a sweet old Aymara, dressed in a black *lliclla*.[111] Ticu showed signs of deep depression. His voice became hollow and weak, until he lost it altogether. Although the whole demonstration of cerebral disorder has ceased, his molded cranium, his irregular face and phenomenal, unnatural expression instilled tremendous fear. His eyes were frightening on their own—those sunken, simple, dismembered eyes, beneath his uncovered eaveless forehead—and they suddenly lost their air of rationale. Everyone looked at him from a distance, scrunching their noses, as though they were in the presence of a corpse that was starting to rot. Again they asked, "Who do you give predictions for?"

He continued to shake his head, revealing one and the other temple. The Chuco stretched out his arms and legs, like a sick man on his bed, and did not reply.

"Who do you give predictions for? Or do you smear yourself with live bugs just for the fun of it?"

"Leave him alone!" shouted the elderly woman, whose heart was aching with mercy. "Let him be. Don't torment him. He can't take too much more."

Ticu looked at her from head to toe and turned his eyes to the pond, surrounded by blossoming *molles*, which tinted the patio blue in the clear morning. He remained still for a moment—a silhouette against the stuccoed white wall. In the corners of his foreboding mouth, some foam had formed, which his fever dried out. And there, among the rest of his teeth, one could just discern two yellow and twisted incisors jammed into his jaw.

"You're a sycophant!" they said.

Human sanity suddenly peered through the monster's eyes. His face reorganized itself, cleared up, and brightened. His nose appeared to curl at the tip, his lips quivered, and even his ears seemed to try to get a better look at the rest of his mask. The Chuco looked at the guards and old woman, one after another, staring at their faces, clothes, feet, and the ground they stood on.

"Leave me alone," he said with a smile in a serene tone. "I'm not a seer. Go tell the Emperor I'm just another Quechua. Ask him to let me go to my hut. I've done nothing wrong. You're mistaken to think I was out of line. My head has nothing to do with this. Aren't there droves of Collahuatas roaming the Inti's realm? The splints simply gave me a flat and obedient forehead. I'm just a Quechua who fills the water troughs and pools at Yucay. Oh, father Viracocha,[112] Lord of the Incas, Light of the Empire! May they let me return to my shovel that waits for me to dig irrigation ditches between sacred trees!"

From *Toward the Reign of the Sciris* 235

The old woman stared at the ground in sorrow. Ticu felt compelled to convince them that his mental state was actually normal. The guards shouted in unison, "You're a sycophant! You've slandered the nobility. Wretch of the Sun! Pestilent worm! Leech of the Sacred Oracle!"

A sad little poor boy came running. It was Ticu's son. He jumped onto his lap and wrapped his arms around his neck, kissing him. Ticu looked at him strangely, and sliding out the bone that had been sheathed in the mantle wrapped around his shoulders, he tested the tip in the palm of his hand, as if it were a knife, and then he took the boy by his chin and plunged the bone into one of his eyes until it disappeared . . .

The child let out a chilling scream.

3. THE PEACE OF TÚPAC YUPANQUI

Countless military troops were dissolved, and those veterans moved on to the labor of farming, finishing the roads from the capital to the heated Tumbes-Coquimbo border, as well as fortifying and beautifying Cuzco, Chanchán, Cajamarca, and Huánuco. From *tambos*[113] scattered throughout the territory entire regiments of soldiers started to arrive, disarm, and head to the quarries at Anta and Collao, or to Aclla-Huasi,[114] near the capital to rebuild the temple that had suffered serious damage during a recent earthquake.

The disarmament freed up thousands of hands for all activities in the reign. The arts of metal, ceramic, stone, and textiles were given a new thrust forward. From forge and burin emerged multiple types of fountains; large baskets for worship; statues of animals, plants, and herders beautifully engraved; brooches; and pitchers with serpents and birds etched in, which emitted surprising whistles when they were poured. They brought to the Inca's palace beautiful wooden cups and carafes made from palm trees and carved *guayacán* filigree, with drawings in indelible colors recounting episodes of battles between the armies of the Tahuantinsuyo[115] and the occidental tribes, as well as some scenes that depicted the celebration of Túpac Yupanqui's coronation. In the Monastery of the Chosen Women, a precious alpaca sash was woven in just a few days for the Almighty. On the sash, embroidered in gold and a vibrant, vegetable dye were all the animals of the empire, each species in its own climate and habitat. The subtlety of the textiles and their composition, in terms of their colors and hues, was so shocking that the skill and precision with which the anatomical shadows and lights fell upon the fur coats and plumage disconcerted many an observer. Eyes would strangely turn away from the sight of the marvelous sash, wanting to organize the parts, specify the shapes of the animals, or locate a panoramic image of the fauna. When the sash was wrapped around the Inca's waist and gazed upon from afar, it didn't look extraordinary at all, save for the sumptuous glow of its dyes, but viewed up close, it left one with an astonishing, nearly distressing sensation. Some people weren't able to accurately recognize its artistic value, and others, observing the work in excessive sunlight, were still unable to identify even one animal. Whether the object was moved far away or brought near, without leaving the line of sight, the observer seemed to be blinded and couldn't see a thing.

"I can't see any animals," many people said. "Not even the sky or land—nothing."

An *auqui*[116] from the imperial court, to whom the Almighty had just given a beautiful infant wife (daughter of the Inca from the Yunga[117]), gazed at the sash in an attempt to record its details and nuances, marveled, and then went blind. In response to this, the court attributed to the gleaming object an accursed and sentimental meaning. They whispered that a vestal virgin in love with the prince found out about his engagement to the infant and, to avenge her love, produced the sash, which would be the end of her.

The refurbishment began at the Palace of Chanchán in the great corridor that led from a chamber of colorful arabesques toward the back of the building, where fifty secret rooms were tucked away, which no one but the *rumay-pachaca*[118] would enter only once per year to distribute plots of land. These secret hidden rooms had possessed an aura of mystery and enchantment since the time of the Chimús. Their walls abutted the city cemetery, rising barely above the sea, and the tides would sometimes even lap against the gravestones. It was over one of the walls of that corridor—a vast passageway toward such sad estates—that an artist had started to fashion a chilling bas-relief like no other. Not a soul dared ask him about the motive or meaning of that frieze.

The relief depicted a skeleton playing a *quena*, made from a necklace of shrunken human skulls. It portrayed dancers of both sexes and all ages. Although the macabre musical instrument was already finished, it still looked like a sketch, since in a way it resembled a perpetual draft, an eternal gestation of lines. At the rear of this first part of the frieze, sculptors were chiseling the second section of the bas-relief, which depicted a choir of mourners. One of the artists chiseled the shawl of a weeper; another worked on a bare foot, raised backward, about to take a step; the former dissolved into overwhelming shock on a woman's lips, the latter delineated a tear, falling at the height of a young sallow neck, which had been fighting to attenuate the pensive flutter of eyelashes for the last couple of days. The stone cutters worked arduously.

"Gold!" one of them exclaimed, surprised in the midst of his work. "Where in this stone is the gold coming from?"

With the blow of the chisel, a golden spark appeared in the palm of an engraved hand in the relief. The artist meditated for a moment, deciding not to file down the thorn of sacred metal. From various points of view he contemplated the hand and touched it several times with utter caution, putting his soul in his fingertips. Again he meditated at length and an ineffable smile illuminated his face: The hand was perfect. Neither one more line nor one less atom!

In his desire for peace and labor, Túpac Yupanqui also paid attention to horticulture, hunting, and fishing. New herds were amassed. Mobs of hunters invaded the forests, *jalcas*, lakes, rivers, and seas, in pursuit of the delicate plume, the song that had never been heard, the painted flesh, the shiny claws, the sharp horns, the diamond scales, the polished fangs, the silent pearls, and the grunts in heat. The Almighty ordered the preparation of a great *chacu* for the celebration of the Raymi, an operation that hadn't been carried out for six years. The regional *chacu* of Cuzco was to be attended by the Inca himself and would be held on the plains that lay at the foot of Colcapata Palace, in the Vilcamayo valley.

A few moons following the retreat of Huayna Cápac, the Tahuantinsuyo transformed into a gigantic beehive. Aside from a few regiments stationed on the borders and in one or another rebellious province, all the subjects of the reign—natives or *mitimaes*—gave themselves solely to the work of increasing the empire's wealth. Incan politicians suddenly stripped themselves of their proselytizing and bellicose character. The people worked without reprieve, completing projects that already were under way, extending the scope of other endeavors, and laying out plans for new ones.

It's not that Túpac Yupanqui rejected the life of arms and conquests. In fact, throughout his reign he'd done nothing but fight in wars. His father, Pachacútec, left him a great deal to do. All the territories in the north, from Chancas[119] to Tumbes, whose ruler still remained a hostage in Cuzco, ended up submitting to Túpac Yupanqui. Long years of blood and ambition: heroic expeditions, unprecedented in the dynasty, first over the powerful Nazcas, as skillful at craftsmanship as they were in the defense of their freedom, and then into the domain of the Chimús, the proud rivals of the Incas. This final offensive lasted eight long years, twists and turns of all sorts, with bloody battles of incalculable losses. The siege and assault alone of the impenetrable fortress at Paramonga that began the invasion cost five thousand Quechua lives. Túpac Yupanqui himself had ordered the strategy and was wounded by an arrow in the arm. Then there was the toppling of the densely populated, brilliant, almighty Chanchán, capital of the Chimús. No forebears of theirs had ever achieved such feats and victories. There was the history; the eloquent truthful *quipus*; the chronicles and testimonies of their generals, soldiers, and people; the odes of the *aravicus*;[120] the triumphant hymns; the war dances; the trophies; the reliefs; and monuments that dwell in the *tambos* and theaters of grand events . . . Therefore, Túpac Yupanqui was a warrior emperor. Yet now he yearned for a haven from the rugged journeys, though he didn't know how long it would take to build. He yearned for peace and labor. That the mind might work on its subtle peaceful stamen and the soil produce the stalk that gives shade and freshness, the seed that it feeds and grows, the flower that blossoms for the tabernacles, cribs, and tombs. He yearned for peace and labor. That happiness might exhale hardy comforting laughter, the sky unfurrow the brows of farmhands and herders, the husband kiss his wife, and that the burning twilight of the reign might douse priests with docile light, those stormy figures of ovular heads and long beards . . . The Inca now yearned for love, meditation, the seed, leisure, great ideas, eternal images.

4. AN ACCIDENT ON THE JOB

Túpac Yupanqui spent one afternoon with Mama Ocllo, surrounded by his entourage, amid the sacred city's columns, visiting the work sites at the Sajsahuamán fortress, which was being rebuilt. Twenty thousand Quechuas had left for work that day. At that time they were just about to finish the second tower. The Inca went forth to where they were and, observing the bustling crowd at work, turned toward one of the laborers.

"Where is the stone of this doorway from?" he asked.

"Father," he said kneeling down, "it's from Pisuc."

The imperial entourage shuddered at the sound of the eastern quarry.

A muted and convulsive murmur of voices and shouts came from the other side. At the base of the third and final tower of the fortress, the crowd was swarming around a gigantic stone that was about to be raised. For six years that stone had traveled from the shores of the Urubamba. Many years had passed since it grew tired in the middle of the road and no longer wanted to go any farther. They'd gotten it to rock by beating it. They berated it at the top of their lungs and pushed it from all sides. The stone stayed right where it was, deaf to all calls and provocations. Days, moons, and years went by. Many men fell on its behalf. Rainwater washed away some of the soil beneath it, but the stone stayed put, fixed in place. As herders from afar would look for their flocks in the evening, they'd often gaze at it with fearful piety, as though they were staring at graves. Vultures and owls perched on it at night, and their caws and hoots would coo it to sleep. But men returned there one day and managed to stir it. They were bringing it up, about to lift it onto the terrace of Sajsahuamán.

"It's the tired stone," the Inca said pensively, "it's also from Pisuc."

The rock field of Pisuc lay on the other side of the Urubamba, far beyond the shores of the river. According to tradition, it was from there that scores of the fortress's rocks were brought, though many were used for the foundation. Entire, beautiful blocks—mountains in one single piece—of basalt with grains fitting for the great cogs and subtle agglutinations of simple rapprochement. The architects preferred the blocks of Pisuc over any others and, if all the walls, towers, and tunnels were not constructed of that material, it was because their transportation through copious rivers proved impossible. One singular circumstance surrounded the grim appearance of the Pisuc stones: from the time they leaped from the quarry until they were embedded in their destined place, they left in their wake the extermination of many lives, the misfortune of others—always a gash of blood and tears. The Inca was contemplating this lugubrious aura of Pisuc when an *auqui* came up to him.

"Father! Did you want to see how the doorway of the second tower has turned out? They've just finished it."

Notified that the sovereigns were coming back, the crowd knelt in silence. The master stonemasons were giving heated orders, which the drudges endeavored to follow with haste and skill. A series of pikes ran through some of the holes in the higher end of the wall and disappeared upward and downward, only to reappear as thick cables in the hands of the workers. From every direction came a distressing roar of stones rumbling, pikes creaking, footsteps rushing, and chests panting. When the monolithic door began to rise, the crowd fell into a deep silence, deaf to all but the noise of the ropes, threaded through the holes in the wall, and one energetic snort after another. Túpac Yupanqui and Mama Ocllo took a few steps back to get a better view. They were awestruck by the way the stone was being lifted. In the device, the stone's weight and size (proportionate to its height) took on so much more shape and acquired so much more importance that it roused the vague sensation of terror. An unexpected interruption suddenly paralyzed the mechanism of arms and rigging, and a few people from the imperial delegation went up to inspect it. One of them stretched out his hand and, barely reaching the suspended block with his fingertips, dug his nails into it and turned toward everyone else.

"The basalt stones of Pisuc are the most beautiful in the reign!"

Unexpectedly, a ghastly event occurred. In the callused hands and on different points of the cyclopean object, the cables began to crack. Terrifying cries of alarm echoed round. Stones fell from that refined door's threshold, and the gigantic rocky body crashed down like a clap of thunder. The entire wall shook. Deep silence followed the fall of the stone, as though it would stay there dead forever . . .

In his arms the Inca held Mama Ocllo, who'd fainted in horror. Some of the *sipacoyas*[121] and ladies of the court were wailing for help. Muffled screams escaped the tower.

"He's over here. And my brother?"

Some questions went unanswered.

"No, I haven't seen him. No, I haven't seen him . . ."

"Blood! Blood!"

A giant, long, unending, collective shriek filled the space and proceeded to echo through the city and off the slopes of Mount Huanacaure.

5. BYZANTIUM, WEST LONGITUDE

Runto Caska was a relative of the Inca. A young man with remarkable masculine beauty and a knack for music and weaponry, he enjoyed extraordinary influence on the Emperor. Túpac Yupanqui rarely made decisions on the affairs of the realm without first speaking with his relative, oftentimes replacing the Council of Elders with his noble relative in matters of consultation. But the influence of Runto Caska wasn't based on his capacity as relative to the Inca, but rather on his capacity as artist.

The *antara* of Runto Caska was a series of polished gold tubes, with drawings on the metal itself, enclosed at one end and set side by side, in order of length and width, from the greatest to the smallest, no more than an inch in length by a barely measurable diameter. They were aligned and tied in knots by a double net of tendons that had belonged to over-sized Collas, who'd died a bloody death in a battle Runto Caska had fought during the first tour of the conquest, shortly after his sixteenth birthday. Through the two small nets, a series of green and red wool and alpaca strings ran toward the center, and where these reached the tubes on the ends of each side they formed knots and ended in four large tassels. When this sonorous triangle was being played, it would hang from the artist's neck by a braid of silver filigree, and when it was not in use, it would be kept in a frog-skin pouch, lined inside with valerian, red angel's trumpet, and other *vilca*[122] herbs that terrible diviners would use in their practices.

On his way back from the Intipampa, Runto Caska reached his ranch with a feeling of pensive melancholy. The artist crossed a small gallery of bare rock, rough-hewn by chisel, coldly and randomly left there, then headed inside to a room, where a tortoise-shell cauldron was burning in the middle, radiating welcome heat and the voluptuous aroma of coca and banana peel. The musician sat down on a copper stool, upholstered with jaguar hides. There he stayed, lost in thought, with his gaze fixed on the soffit. The artist was suffering. Kusikayar hadn't attended the *huaraco*[123] celebration, and her absence was filling him with anxiety. He was in love with her. Ever since the day she came of age and her womanhood was celebrated in accordance with Quechua custom—in the humble shack of the then obscure, poor village girl—Runto Caska, who'd been present at the *quipuchica*,[124] loved her with all the strength of his youth. In response to the musician's insinuations, the Inca had made her a *ñusta*, on the merit of her gift for performing sacred dances.

Strange was the beauty of Kusikayar. No one knew for sure the origin of her line, which had been lost in the shadows of the reign's lower class. Some used to say that her forebears hailed from an eastern country, beyond Pacarectambu, the dwelling where dawn cracks, the place of the four dimensions. Others used to explain that the young girl's cradle had been in the dry salt fields of the south, whose farthest limit, sharp and craggy as it was, rested in the shape of a *pata*, that is, a hoof, which is why her people were often called *patagones*. This was the most common rendition, inviting some to attribute the symbol of Kusikayar's miraculous feet to that origin. But there were also other people, priests in particular, who used to claim that her family had come from a remote reign during very ancient times, located near the border where light makes its mysterious bed.

"That's where her line came from," the young *villac*,[125] Ananquizque, said. "That caste wasn't brought here by force. On their own accord, they arrived one evening at the city and, so say the elders who read it in banana leaves, this occurred precisely when the *coyllur*[126] was seen in the daytime sky, early enough in the summer that the columns still lacked shadow in the sunlight."

The figure of Kusikayar came to acquire great renown in religious rituals. Her dance became a special liturgy in the Festival of the Sun. During the celebration of the Situa,[127] as the rains were beginning to fall and illness was running rampant, Kusikayar danced at the Coricancha doors to the beat of inscrutable musicians. Amid the gyrations of her body, taciturn priests gazed at the uncertain future and the mortality of the year. People adored and feared her, as if she were an *aclla*[128] among virgins of the Sun.

And it was during the final celebration of the Situa that a subtle, vague event befell Runto Caska and appeared between him and Kusikayar like a mysterious ghost.

Contrary to the astronomical calculations registered in the Kalasa-saya,[129] on the morning of that day of the Situa the air suddenly grew strange and darkness engulfed everything, as if night had fallen. The *yllapa* crossed the space and was pursued by a god-awful rumble coming from the ground. Some walls and roofs fell down. An old man dropped dead in the middle of the street. Mothers wept and, in their arms, babies moaned and scratched at their breasts. Many a pregnant wife violently delivered an eternally sleeping creature. In Hurin-Cuzco a young lady went mad and threw herself into the River Huatanay. The Quechuas' terror had no limits. Everyone ran out of their abodes into the plazas, howling in fear and shouting at the *yllapa* to quell his anger. The city bustled about in an immense spasm of dread. Men and women, children and seniors, the entire community gathered in Cusipata, in front of the Coricancha's door. The priests, their faces sharpened with terror, and the *amautas*, filled with majesty, predicted peace. A *villac* touched by visions spoke up.

"The *yllapa* is angry," he said. "It's because the conquest of the Tucumanes hasn't been carried out. So says the oracle. Leave your homes to dispel the evil of the sown fields and then come back to hear the prophesy at the Dance of the Situa."

The crowd left for the fields. Among them some frightened *alcos* went, sniffing around the rocks and grassy trails, scratching the ground and plaintively howling. Every *piruc*[130] went at the head of their people, and the entire crowd was praying and moaning. Some of them, to placate the anger of the *yllapa*, left pouches of coca and maize in the hills and higher up in altitude. Others were having a drink from the streams or were pouring a few drops of *chicha* or flicking it into the air. They arrived at the granaries, knocked on them, and belted out warnings to apostrophize the evil and make it go away.

They were met by peace when they returned to the sacred city. Crowded in front of the Coricancha doors, they waited to hear predictions come out of the seers' mouths based on the feet of Kusikayar.

Donning a fine transparent tunic, the *aclla* came out, surrounded by priests. Her short hair was let down, and she wore no bracelets, hair ties, or any other accessory, save for the long sash of a princess.

The Inca was there, on his golden litter, accompanied by his court. A deep silence befell them. The people in the crowd bowed their heads. Then sacred music slowly arose in great phrases and overwhelmed the *aclla* with exaltation. They sang the liturgical *ytu*,[131] then the priests addressed the crowd.

"The *yllapa* shall calm his anger," they said. "Conquest must be waged on the Tucumanes. The first tour shall depart tomorrow and shall consist of five hundred slingers. The death count this year shall be low. Go back to your abodes and pray that the sacrifices bear fruit . . ."

When the words of the oracle had been heard, the crowd dispersed. Some groups went on their way to temples and *huacas*[132] to make Viracocha an offering of silver and bronze objects, painted pebbles, handfuls of soil, guinea pig bones, and *chuño*.[133] Others carried perfumes and coca leaves, which they lit on fire at the base of the sacred pilasters.

Runto Caska remembered all this, as he returned from the celebration of the *huaraca*. He also remembered that, ever since that Dance of the Situa, the ñusta would acquire a strange fear of him and experience mysterious reservations, even during their most tender and passionate moments. The artist asked about it, but her reply was incomprehensible. Runto Caska was suffering.

[1923–24]   [JM]

From *Moscow vs. Moscow*

THE FINAL JUDGMENT

In the house of ATOVOV, *the pawnbroker. Winter morning, Moscow, a few years after the revolution. A miserable room, harsh light, loneliness and decadence. On a cot, the pawnbroker, about to die, confesses to* FATHER RULAK.

RULAK (*paternally*): Speak slowly, my son (*placing a hand on his forehead*).

ATOVOV (*panting*): I was never afraid of death. But, all night, my moral strength has failed me . . .

RULAK: The cause of fear is death, my poor son. It's not the mystery of the afterlife, but the sinful existence that one has lived in this world. Children and saints die without shuddering in the least.

ATOVOV: I'm afraid it's too late . . . My sin is more serious. Help me, Father, help me confess it to you . . .

RULAK: The Almighty will know, even if you don't have time to tell me.

ATOVOV (*with a raspy voice*): Water, please . . .

RULAK (*giving him a glass of water*): Don't forget that life is but a valley of sorrow and that death, even for the most unworthy, is the supreme liberation and a step toward a better world.

ATOVOV (*in a painful memory, to himself*): It was . . .

RULAK (*attentively*): What are you afraid of? Place your trust in God.

ATOVOV (*decisively*): Father, I've committed murder! . . .

RULAK: Murder?

ATOVOV: Yeah, during the revolution. I killed Rada Pobadich, the jeweler; I killed him so I could take his money.

RULAK (*filled with mercy*): My poor son! You have killed . . . and so that you could steal!

ATOVOV: I killed him and I robbed him.

RULAK: Under what circumstances did you kill that man?

ATOVOV (*enraged*): Wretch! Scoundrel!

RULAK: Lord, open the door of thy infinite mercy!

ATOVOV: Father, I haven't told you everything . . .

RULAK: I know, but patience. Pull yourself together.

ATOVOV: It was at night, in Red Square, a few days before the Bolshevik uprising . . . Rada Pobadich was there. I was following him . . . (*he coughs*).

RULAK: Breathe now, my son, don't work yourself up . . .

ATOVOV: Lenin was rallying the crowd . . . Rada Pobadich, I don't know how, had managed to position himself behind him, very close, almost touching him . . . Suddenly, a shot rang out. Like in a flash of lightning I saw Pobadich aiming a revolver at Lenin, and I . . . I thought that the overthrow would fail so I shot Pobadich . . .

RALUK (*paralyzed by these last words*): He was aiming at Lenin? . . .

ATOVOV: Yeah, he wanted to kill him . . .

RULAK: But . . . But, my son . . . But, then you have prevented the death of Lenin?

ATOVOV (*continuing his confession*): And I . . . took advantage of the confusion in the crowd to search his pockets . . . And the key . . . The key was there . . .

RULAK (*growing eager*): But, let's see, my son. Rada Pobadich was truly going to kill Lenin? You're sure that he would've killed him?

ATOVOV: Absolutely sure.

RULAK: I mean, that he would've taken out the head of the revolution and therefore stopped the Bolsheviki from coming to power . . . (*stupefied*) So it's your fault the red catastrophe has become a reality? . . .

ATOVOV: Ah! Father Rulak! . . .

RULAK: So you saved the life of a man who brought misfortune to Russia and atheism to its souls? . . . (*in an exclamation of holy anger*) You wretch! You heinous man! The true culprit of the Russian disaster! . . .

ATOVOV (*profoundly*): Let the wicked be forgiven! . . .

RULAK: Be forgiven!? . . . (*horrified*) An infinite sin! . . . A sin that surpasses all theological categories of sinfulness! . . .

ATOVOV (*weakly outstretching his arms*): Have mercy on me, Father Rulak! . . .

RULAK (*raising his eyes to the sky*): Adesto nobis, Domine Deus Noster, et quos tuis mysteris recreasti, perpetuis defende subsidis, Per domine! . . . Join us, Lord our God, and defend, with the constant help of thy grace, those whom thou have created to participate in thy divine mysteries! . . . Illuminate, Lord, my judgment with thy divine light! . . . (*withdraws in reflection, abruptly sits up to listen and, full of anguish, exclaims*) I hear the screams of the outraged Church! . . . I hear the screams of the souls led astray by the Bolshevik devil! . . . The screams of my priestly conscience begging for punishment! . . . (*leaning over the*

moribund man) You wretch! . . . Listen to your confessor! . . . Receive
your verdict! . . . Do you hear me? . . . (*waits, a deadly silence*).

ATOVOV (*in a weak, barely perceptible voice*): He had an affair with your
woman . . .

RULAK (*shuddering*): An affair . . . Who? . . . Who had an affair with my
woman? . . .

ATOVOV: Rada Pobadich! (RULAK *is petrified*).

RULAK (*suddenly enraptured by a chaotic fit*): You're lying! . . . You're mad!
. . . You're mad or lying right at the moment when you're about to die!
. . . Rada Pobadich didn't know Svodna Ilivocha! . . . Who was he, this
Rada Pobadich? . . . At least tell me how you knew him . . . Who told
you? . . . Speak! . . . Tell me how! . . . (*suddenly falls silent, anxiously
leans over the man on his deathbed, fixing his crazed eyes on him*) You're
not dead yet, right? . . . (*calls to him*) Atovov! Atovov! My son! . . . (*the
pawnbroker has died*; RULAK *collapses, stunned*) Good heavens! He's
dead!

RULAK *lies there, pauses, and then, painfully pulls himself together. He
gets up from the corpse and walks in darkness, like a blind man, like
someone sleepwalking. He covers his face with both hands, falls to his
knees, and humbly holds the crucifix against his chest, bowing his head
ever lower. Then, calmly, sweetly, he whispers with infinite mercy.*

RULAK: Lord God, with the same mercy reap every soul, large or small,
that has fallen into sin . . .

[1930]   [JM]

DEATH
A One-Act Tragedy

*Moscow. A cubbyhole that is part of a monastery-cum-hospice. The only
furnishings are a few stools, a lectern, a cot. In the back wall, a door
opens on darkness. A court or corridor, parallel to the ramp, runs in the
foreground, in front of the cubbyhole, disappearing stage left and stage
right.*

*When the curtain rises, there's no one on set. A bell rings, slowly and
calmly, on a winter afternoon.*

Two priests, SOVARCH *and* SAKROV, *enter from the corridor, stage
left.*

SAKROV: Faced with this situation, what, I ask myself, is the duty of the Church?

SOVARCH: The duty of the Church? Toward who?

SAKROV: But toward the whole of the family. Toward all the Polianovs. No matter what their political tendencies may be.

SOVARCH: You are asking me? I don't have the slightest idea.

SAKROV: The children fight for and against the Soviet. The mother, faced with the perspective of seeing the younger ones becoming fully involved with Bolshevism, is losing her head. The case of the father just gets worse. You know his hidden and mysterious hatred for his son Volni.

SOVARCH: But he denies that. He says that's just one of your own totally unjustified ideas. As for me, I can't explain that hatred. What could be its cause? When he abandoned his family, that child was only five or six years old . . .

SAKROV: Father Sovarch, I do not know the cause of that hatred either, but believe me: it exists.

SOVARCH: I tend to believe rather that he hates everybody, that's all.

SAKROV: No doubt. And yet in regard to his son, especially, he is hiding feelings that we need to keep an eye on, because what makes this aversion a serious problem is the fact that he hides it, although there are times when his gaze betrays him when he speaks of him.

SOVARCH: All I can say is that, from time to time, he has gestures that scare me.

SAKROV: And let's not even mention Varona Jurakevna's determination to join and follow her husband, even as far as the . . .

SOVARCH: Father Sakrov, there is but one path to reach God, and you know it.

SAKROV: That's not my understanding . . .

SOVARCH: In other words, there is but one death, and that's the death of the soul. The Church's only duty is to save people from this death.

SAKROV: Father Sakrov, there is the death of life and then there is the death of death.

ROLANSKI (*entering stage right*): Gentlemen! Before all there is misfortune! Osip Dvoschine Polianov has just eaten his shirt!

SOVARCH: You mean he drank it.

ROLANSKI: Father Superior is scolding him right now. It seems that the NEPman on the other side, Rulkof, may have given him a few drops of vodka for doing it. A shirt that was nearly new! Now he's in his undershirt.

SAKROV: What is he answering Father Superior?

ROLANSKI: He is weeping like a child. He claims that he's fed up with the monastery and that one of these mornings he'll scram. Can you hear the Superior's voice?

SOVARCH: The Superior is wrong . . . (*voices from the back of the house*: "Father Rolanski! Hurry up! Where is the antiphonary? . . .")

ROLANSKI (*leaving on tiptoes stage left*): Excuse me. The antiphonary! . . . (SAKROV *also leaves, stage right.* SOVARCH *sits down at the lectern and with a needle he pulls from his cassock starts to darn one of his pockets.*)

ZURGUES (*entering with* POLENKO, *stage left*): Well! A monastery is not a shelter! He may be the metropolitans' nephew, but this is too much.

SOVARCH (*without raising his eyes*): Now then, has the Superior finally calmed down?

POLENKO: Your cassock, Father Sovarch, is the shabbiest one in the monastery. What do you do with your personal alms?

SOVARCH: There is no such thing as personal alms, my friend.

POLENKO: You beg at the best spot in the city, on Pushkin Boulevard.

ZURGUES: If his pocket is constantly ripped, it's for a good reason.

SOVARCH: I take with my left hand, and give with my right hand.

ZURGUES: Still, you are clearly obsessed with your pocket and that is suspect. Smells of cupidity. You should see your face when you darn: a usurer's.

POLENKO: The idea of a pocket is contrary to the idea of a heaven. Our Lord's tunic had no pockets.

SOVARCH (*still mending*): Chatterboxes. Peace . . . (*again the sound of bells*).

ZURGUES: Father Polenko, the call to service. (ZURGUES *leaves, followed by* POLENKO.)

SOVARCH: Pharisees! Just look at Father Superior's cassock: it is studded with pockets! (ZURGUES *and* POLENKO *have disappeared. Pause.*)

SAKROV (*returns*): Everybody rushes to the service . . .

SOVARCH: And the prince? Did they take him too?

SAKROV: Of course, they took him. He reeks of alcohol from afar and in that state he prays to God. He dragged himself there sobbing all the way, hanging on the Superior's arm. It doesn't make any sense. We have tried to turn the prince into a good man for years now. And what have we achieved? Is success even possible?

SOVARCH: To the contrary, he's getting worse and worse. At least from the point of view of reason.

SAKROV: Just last night he nearly kidnapped the NEPman's woman.

SOVARCH: I know. And it is you who kept him from doing so.

SAKROV: I kept him from doing it, indeed, and by the same token, saved him from a major whooping the husband was ready to dole out.

SOVARCH: Oh, the guy would have earned it.

SAKROV: Erotic madness. A well-known . . .

SOVARCH: His madness is short-lived. Can you imagine, my friend, that yesterday morning, at the exact moment of the Angelus prayer, he had a sudden fit of laughter that put everyone very ill at ease.

SAKROV: But, Father Sovarch, the only conclusion one can come to is that the Church's action is fruitless and, let's admit as much, in fact, harmful.

SOVARCH: That may be an exaggeration.

SAKROV: No! Our advice, our reasoning, our preaching is fatal for him. These mental exercises simply exhaust a brain already strongly shaken by alcohol and all the rest.

SOVARCH: My friend, here in the monastery I have on several occasions made known my belief that we need to insert a few hours of physical labor into his regimen, which would give a bit of a rest to his introspective life.

SAKROV: You're on the right track, Father Sovarch.

SOVARCH: I think so. This man is subjected to an effort of abstraction incompatible with his nervous condition. I have observed him closely: when he prays, his demeanor darkens visibly and his gaze fixes the ground strangely . . .

SAKROV: Father Sovarch, do you know how I got the idea of trying to take the prince to a kolkhoz?

SOVARCH: While praying?

SAKROV: You'll see . . . Mornings he takes walks with me along the Moskva. We chat, we watch the waters flow beneath the bridges, the faraway roofs of the houses, the domes of the Byzantine temples, the sky, the trees, the passersby . . .

SOVARCH: A bad thing, those walks, as far as I am concerned. Contemplative life and day dreaming in general . . . bad, bad!

SAKROV: I don't disagree. However, these walks produced very strange symptoms in him. On the left bank of the Moskva, opposite the Kremlin, construction of collective housing has been going on for some weeks now. Laborers are working there at all times. The construction sites make up one vast and massive throng. Now, Father Sovarch, do you know what Osip Polianov does as soon as we reach the building sites? He quickly and spontaneously approaches the laborers and starts to help them in their work . . .

SOVARCH: That does not surprise me at all.

SAKROV: And not just once! It is reassuring, let me tell you, to see such enthusiasm in a man like him, a being plagued by all sorts of vices. And the result: an enormous and immediate moral well-being.

SOVARCH: This is very normal. I always knew.

SAKROV: One hour of such exercise is enough for him. When we return you are looking at a totally different person: less unstable, less clownish, less cynical, more serious, more reasonable, and quieter . . .

SOVARCH: So what is your conclusion . . .

SAKROV: Elementary. Basic: the only thing that may heal him from his moral and intellectual decline is work, physical labor.

SOVARCH: That's quite possible. I'm not saying no. But carry on.

SAKROV: Don't forget, Father Sovarch, that work is a peak experience, a springboard. Starting from there, everything is possible . . .

SOVARCH: Even a fall!

SAKROV: Even the most desperate of flights, and salvation. The prince may well emerge from a solid period of organized work much more supple, more human, understanding, and tolerant, not to mention that he'll have stopped drinking and skirt chasing. He could thus start playing a more conciliatory and appeasing role for his children.

SOVARCH: So all that needs to be done is to send him to a kulak's or any other peasant's farm—but not to the Bolsheviki. Are you aware that the whole monastery is awash with talk that your stubborn wish to hand the prince over to the Bolsheviki is nothing more or less than a deviation from your ministry . . .

SAKROV: Blindness! What blindness! I am totally convinced that acting as I do, I am working rigorously inside the frame of the Church.

SOVARCH: Beware! I have heard this: "This ploy of throwing people into the kolkhozy is deep down just indirect soviet propaganda."

SAKROV: Charity, this cardinal principle of Jesus's doctrine, has to be done any which way and by any means available . . .

SOVARCH: There is only one way to come to God, Father Sakrov! I'm telling you again!

SAKROV (*firmly*): The prince has to be saved! His wife and children have to be saved! If this situation goes on for just one more day we can expect the worst. I can see, I can feel disaster approaching . . .

SOVARCH: I'm telling you, take him to a peasant.

SAKROV: His horror of the muzhik is unsurmountable. He hates primitive rural life. His inclination for modern mechanical work is, however, undeniable. He is animated by clear and obvious pleasure when he is among machines, scaffoldings, and teams of workers. (*Here, in silence, like a shadow,* OSIP POLIANOV *enters stage left. His expression is painful, absent, that of a somnambulist. He seems to be looking for someone.* SAKROV *asks him, affectionately*) Are you looking for something, prince? (OSIP *doesn't answer. He collapses on a seat.* SAKROV *and* SOVARCH *observe him.* SAKROV, *again, same tone*) Are you coming from the office? . . . (OSIP *stays silent*) Is it over already? . . . What's the matter? Are you not feeling well? . . .

OSIP (*gaze lost in the distance*): This night I dreamed of an enchanted grave, a strange, extraordinary grave. But did I only dream it? . . . Or did I actually come to know it while awake? No matter . . . And this grave, while being Lenin's, was my grave . . .

SOVARCH: That's weird.

SAKROV: And then? Tell us the rest.

OSIP: But the style of my grave was rather gothic. Are you familiar with Christian medieval sarcophagi? Now, just translate their sculptural style into architecture, and there you have it. (*Becoming animated*) A golden sickle and hammer, crossed, crowned the facade of the entry . . . But then, when I leaned to look down into my casket, what did I see? . . . My two arms, alone, separated, absent from the rest of my body, lay there, rigid, dead . . .

SOVARCH: A strange symbol.

ROLANSKI (*reentering*): My brothers, the latest news: they want to rip the hearts out of men . . .

SOVARCH: Who wants to rip the hearts out of men?

ROLANSKI: The Bolsheviki, of course! There's proof of it, absolute proof!

OSIP: The good people!

ROLANSKI: The French Revolution already tried to put a similar reasoning machine into the hands of the bourgeoisie!

OSIP: Well, Father Rolanski, I keep coming back to my question: at certain periods of history does reason hold the monopoly of light? Why have recourse to it each time the world stumbles and staggers about in darkness? And the heart? For when, the heart?

ROLANSKI: Then, during the Restoration, an unfettered romanticism arose, maybe the most sentimental one humanity has ever known.

SAKROV: History, my brothers, never repeats itself.

ROLANSKI: But it spirals up, dear friend. Here's the proof: we, here, in Soviet Russia, are already witnessing a similar revenge of human sentiment against Marxist rationalism . . .

OSIP (*with a sudden start*): Wait . . . A second . . . This is weird . . . A shadow, or rather a strange breath, just descended from the roof to the floor. It went out near my feet, among the stools . . .

ROLANSKI (*inspecting the floor near the stools*): Oh, you're joking. A breath? A shadow?

OSIP: No. It was not a breath. I was wrong. It is indeed as I said: a shadow, clearly.

ROLANSKI: Didn't it fall into your pocket? Or, even, didn't you crush it with your clogs?

OSIP: For some time now, during my nights of doubt and fear, of emptiness and anxiety, I like to come sit here, at this lectern. I stay here for hours on end. And here my eyes see, as they fall from Heaven, shadows . . . shadows . . . shadows . . .

ROLANSKI: "Theologal" rain, no doubt!

SAKROV (*to* OSIP): Prince, you are sick, you have to get your health back.

OSIP (*hallucinating*): Black is made of white; night is made of day. Chaos, that's skepticism in reverse, the confusion of the fingers, vertigo . . . (*He stumbles as if blind.*) Hold me, my friends . . . (*They hold him and sit him down. He whispers, painfully*) Here I am . . . I'm not thinking about anything. My head sounds hollow. No thought without sensations.

ROLANSKI (*correcting*): Come on, Polianov, there's no sensation without thought.

OSIP: It's the same. What comes first? The egg? The chicken? Or the hatchery?

ROLANSKI: May I say something? Are you listening to me?

OSIP: Hum! . . . No. My ears are closed for fear of nothingness.

ROLANSKI: And yet you think that you can listen to me?

OSIP: By God, no! I hear myself thinking. (*Abruptly*) Are you here? All three of you? Well, illustrious Church fathers, I am truly sorry to have to confess this, but you are not here. No. You are not here. (ROLANSKI *and* SOVARCH *look at each other.*)

ROLANSKI: What?

SOVARCH: That we are not here! But . . . Prince, contrary to what you say, I dare maintain—and I do hope that my dear colleagues will say the same—that all three of us are here, in front of you, in flesh and cassock. Look at us, please.

OSIP (*scandalized*): You, here, you say? In front of me? You?

ROLANSKI: Indeed. Here, in front of you. The three of us.

OSIP (*still scandalized*): Oh what blindness! What shortsightedness! That's the summon of the arbitrary!

SAKROV: Enough of these Byzantine polemics! Listen, Prince, seriously now—I have to speak to you about a most urgent matter . . .

OSIP (*interrupts, moving toward* ROLANSKI, *offering him his arm*): Father Rolanski, take my arm, I beg you. Hold me tight. Do it, I grant you permission. (ROLANSKI *obeys mechanically.*)

ROLANSKI: Like this? . . . Tighter? . . .

OSIP: Tighter! Tighter!

ROLANSKI: There! Good heavens!

OSIP (*surprised*): I don't feel anything, I swear!

ROLANSKI: How can it be that you don't feel anything?

OSIP: Nothing at all. I've lost all sensitivity. I'm swimming in nothingness. (SAKROV *signals* ROLANSKI *to release* OSIP's *arm. The latter jumps at that.*) Oh! . . . It isn't true . . . God be thanked. I now feel your hand. Now I do, yes . . .

ROLANSKI: Osip Polianov, whatever you want, my friend, but permit me to point out that at the present moment you are completely permeated by dialectical materialism.

OSIP: And yet, Father Rolanski, I walk neither on the left nor on the right side: neither with you, who wants to overthrow the Soviet government, nor with Sakrov, who wants us to go to a kolkhoz. I remain firmly rooted in the exact metaphysical middle ground. Leave me be. I am in need of solitude . . .

ZURGUES (*entering stage left*): Gentlemen, it's a quarter to five. Aren't you going out?

ROLANSKI: Out? What for?

ZURGUES: It is time to go begging. Everybody's rushing into the streets.

ROLANSKI: Did the Superior also go out?

ZURGUES: Of course! Hurry up. Are you coming?

ROLANSKI (*ready to leave*): Sovarch, Sakrov, come on! Dear Prince, let us go outside for a bit. (SOVARCH *leaves in silence.*)

SAKROV (*while* OSIP, *somber, remains seated in silence*): Not me. Thank you. As you know this is not my trade.

ROLANSKI (*leaves with* ZURGUES): And yet it was that of the twelve apostles and of the Lord himself. (*They have disappeared.* OSIP *and* SAKROV *stay for a moment, in a pensive mood. In the distance, the noise of doors closing. Followed by complete silence.*)

SAKROV (*with authority, but gently and fraternally*): Now, Osip, let's quickly focus on where we stand. We have agreed that you no longer love Varona Jurakevna . . . (OSIP *keeps silent, seems absent.* SAKROV *moves toward the left side of the corridor.*) Wait, let me check . . . (*He goes out and* OSIP *walks about nervously.* SAKROV *comes back right away.*) Indeed, everybody has left . . .

OSIP (*agitated*): She's a saint! I'm a bastard! Goodness inhabits her; evil resides in me. Wretch! Sinister billy goat! You reek of the devil! . . . (*He smacks his own face with great force and tears out his hair, sobbing*) Vara! Little Vara! Despise me but forgive me! . . .

SAKROV (*stiff*): I know, in the end you will go back to your wife . . . I was charged by Father Superior to help you get back on your feet and turn you away from your aberrations and follies—yet you have done nothing but deceive me. (OSIP *weeps, his head buried in his hands.*) You had promised me that you would not return to your wife and yet you underhandedly continue to love her and search for her. You are pursuing her, don't deny it . . .

OSIP (*stops weeping and with his face still hidden grumbles like an angered child*): Old rabbit! . . . It's the first time I sin, calling a priest a rabbit, forgive me.

SAKROV (*like a doctor putting up with his patient's exasperation*): Osip, be careful, little brother!

OSIP (*same tone*): What do you want me to be careful about?

SAKROV: As far as I can judge, you are playing us to some degree, and that is very serious.

OSIP (*same tone*): Okay. So what!

SAKROV: You do not venerate the so-called holiness of Varona Jurakevna. You don't even love her: you desire her, that's all.

OSIP (*same tone*): You make your pendulum run widdershins . . .

SAKROV: Recidivist! Does she know your address? Who knows if you don't even besiege her at her home, without your children's knowledge?

OSIP (*same tone*): That's not true.

SAKROV: More deceitfulness. You lie.

OSIP (*in a doleful and passionate invocation*): One and only spouse! Singular woman! United heart! Believe me, I loved only once in my life! I loved only you! And you, my great one, I loved you only once! One single summit! (SAKROV *looks at him, exasperated.*) Oh! . . . how much I've wept at the feet of this, the summit of our love! . . . Once only one loved! Neither before, nor after! . . .

SAKROV: You have loved after. You have loved many times.

OSIP (*still in his invocation*): Never, since the day after this unmatched zenith, have I been able to find again in you that lost love! . . .

SAKROV: You found it with other women.

OSIP (*same tone*): No matter how often I erred from woman to woman, my companion was always only the sadness of the exiled one.

SAKROV (*indulgent*): Lower your voice . . .

OSIP: Such is the poverty of the human heart!

SAKROV: We could be overheard! Father Superior could return . . .

OSIP: I am drunk with sadness! And wealth is gay but all my wines are sad! As the romantic poet put it. (*In a light, relaxed manner*) Well, little brother, to put an end to this, rest assured, Varona Jurakevna disgusts me, for me, she is lethal . . . (*He has moved very close to* SAKROV.)

SAKROV (*exhales violently*): Again! You have been drinking the archbishop's wine again!

OSIP: Clearly and positively, Sakrov, God appears to me to be my only reason for living . . .

SAKROV: That is accurate. That is very accurate, my friend. Except that there remains the problem of how to draw close to Him.

OSIP: I had to surrender to the obvious, not so very long ago, on a day when the idea of suicide presented itself to me, after a conscientious examination of my heart and of my fate. At the bottom of it all, of everything, is emptiness. But suddenly, beneath this bottom, at the deepest level of emptiness, I saw that Being of Beings arise and call me back to life, with a mighty, magnetic voice . . .

SAKROV (*who is completely focused on* OSIP's *reactions*): Ad majorem dei gloriam! That's it!

OSIP: And then this idea comes to me: I have too much muzhik blood in my veins to be skeptical or to be just a bastard. At most I may be a nihilist, but not a skeptic, which is not the same thing at all.

SAKROV (*forcefully*): Come now, Prince, let's be precise. I have told you: it is given to man to rise up to God only if he leans on the shoulders of other men. We have to be in communion with them. Which means, let us go toward them, let us join their efforts, their struggles, their pains, their joys, their lives. The isolation of the hermits of the Middle Ages is no longer of our times. A single man no longer has strength enough for the supreme ascension. And it is a given: God can be discovered only in the midst of the great human gatherings, amid the crowds. This is the religious statement of our times!

OSIP: Father, here you come again, hammer and sickle in hand; I am stopping you. No! Wrong floor, once more! (*He walks about, sits down, stands up nervously.*)

SAKROV: And yet, far from me the intention to throw you into the arms of the Bolsheviki!

OSIP: It sure looks like it to me.

SAKROV: All I want is to restore you through work.

OSIP: I appreciate it.

SAKROV: Drop the irony! You are becoming more and more unbearable. (OSIP *remains standing, head lowered.*) You show a very strong interest in the labors of the masses, and you even experience pleasure taking part in such work.

OSIP: Indeed. Working with many others, physical labor, the process of the big machines pleases and captivates me.

SAKROV: So? . . . Isn't labor more beautiful than love or even than prayer? Admit it!

OSIP: I admit it. I admit it readily. And as to pleasure, let's not mention it: it horrifies me.

SAKROV: Excellent. What about Varona Jurakevna? . . .

OSIP: Poor Vara! There's nothing left between us. And yet, to be totally frank, there is something in her that attracts me and pulls me back to her when I least expect it. It overpowers me, Father Sakrov. Is it the love of our children? Is it the past? Is it she herself, without me being conscious of it?

SAKROV: And yet you know it. Confess to it.

OSIP: And it is strange but I have to own up it: I never feel attracted to her, except when I have a few glasses of vodka in my blood. It is bitter to admit as much.

SAKROV (*taking him by the shoulders*): Come on, Osip, listen to me: why do you feel it necessary to turn away from Varona? Answer!

OSIP (*in a low voice, mechanically like a child repeating a lesson*): because I am not worthy.

SAKROV: And why is that?

OSIP (*same tone*): Because she is not worthy of it either.

SAKROV: Why are you both unworthy of making a new life together for yourselves?

OSIP (*same tone*): We think only of ourselves, of loving ourselves, and we don't care about our children.

SAKROV: Be more specific. If you managed to live . . .

OSIP (*same tone*): If we managed someday to live together, I would continue to dirty my home with my misbehavior.

From *Moscow vs. Moscow* 257

SAKROV: And Varona Polianov, what about her?

OSIP (*same tone*): Her . . . she would not care if I besmeared the heart of my children, as long as I slept with . . .

SAKROV (*finishes the sentence with severity*): Because she too, no doubt, is interested by vodka as a stimulant for your ardors. (*And as* OSIP *wants to object something*) What? What do you want to answer?

OSIP (*in a low voice*): Nothing, nothing at all, Father Sakrov.

SAKROV (*assertively*): Come on! Say it!

OSIP (*simply*): Just that I'll never go for your escape from the monastery plot . . .

SAKROV (*with a start*): I heard a door opening! I think . . .

He listens. Steps can be heard. He runs out through the door at the back of the stage. OSIP *listens too. Time passes.* VARONA JURAKEVNA *appears timidly from stage left. Catching sight of her, the prince shudders. He hesitates. He wants to run away. Finally he signals her to stop and keep silent. He goes toward the backstage door, wants to follow or stop* SAKROV, *but returns. He is possessed by a great agitation. Finally, he makes up his mind and moves toward his wife.*

OSIP (*calmly*): God be with you, Varona Jurakevna! . . . (*He shakes her hand.*) Come in, please.

VARONA (*anxiously in a low voice*): Good day, Prince. Are you alone? Am I disturbing you?

OSIP (*during this scene he will constantly watch the door through which* SAKROV *left*): Not at all, dear friend.

VARONA: I entered without knocking. I had first made certain that you'd be alone . . .

OSIP: Alone, that is to say . . . Father Sakrov is close by. But then, of course, entrance to the monastery is open for everyone. It is God's house.

VARONA: I should not have entered.

OSIP: But why not, dear lady? What is happening? Sit down, please. Speak confidently.

VARONA (*in an even lower voice*): First, I beg you to forgive me for not having let you in last time you came . . .

OSIP: Not to have let me in? Last time? . . .

VARONA: I was out of my mind, forgive me, after a terrible discussion with Zuray. I didn't understand exactly what he was telling me . . .

OSIP: But what is it you want to say, madame? (*He watches the backstage door.*)

VARONA: And the children were about to return . . .

OSIP: I do not remember ever knocking on your door. (*He keeps watching the door.*)

VARONA (*brusquely*): A great misfortune has befallen our house, Osip. Volni and Zuray have left us. They finally became members of the Communist Youth organization.

OSIP (*indifferent*): They've become komsomolki? When did that happen?

VARONA: A month ago. I haven't seen them since . . .

OSIP (*as if just a spectator*): That's annoying! And you, of course, are in despair?

VARONA (*breaks into tears*): Zuray was able to console me of you, of your cruelty, your absence . . .

OSIP (*eyes fixed on the back door*): Oh, don't start with that again, I beg you.

VARONA: My life without you was made bearable only by her presence, she who among all our children most reminded me of our defunct happiness, our broken fate . . .

OSIP: Here we go again . . .

VARONA: Recently, her voice had the inflections of yours.

OSIP (*eyes still fixed on the back door*): Come on! And the forehead! Where's the resemblance?

VARONA: The forehead. Well, that one rather deviated from the paternal lineaments.

OSIP: A shame, what a shame. Finish!

VARONA: But since she is not there anymore, I can live no longer . . .

OSIP (*with a facetious or hallucinatory start*): Shut up! (*eyes still fixed on the back door*)

VARONA (*worried*): What's the matter?

OSIP: Come closer. (*as he moves closer to the door*) Come look at it, in this dark room, if you want to, come . . .

VARONA (*anxiously tiptoeing toward the door*): See what? Eh?

OSIP: My corpse. Look at it, please.

VARONA (*thunderstruck*): . . . ?

OSIP: Come. Here. Look. Do you see it?

VARONA (*looking, dismayed, upset*): Prince . . .

OSIP (*solemnly*): It is he himself who laid himself down there. In other words, I fell by the weight of my own gravity.

VARONA: I'm scared. You are not well.

OSIP (*interrupting her, eyes fixed on the door*): The cold in my life has dropped so far down on the scale of my thermometer that in the midst of my soul's and my body's distress, I don't even suffer, I don't even despair any more. I am less than a corpse. I am the corpse of a corpse.

VARONA: Your eyes are far away, my dear. I was wrong to come . . .

OSIP (*very close to her, sternly*): I do not think I am mistaken: you have tortured them with your hatred of the Bolsheviki. You have pursued them and chased them from the house. Confess! I want you to tell me everything.

VARONA (*plaintively*): Ah, so much remorse! It is not their absence that torments me the most, it is the remorse.

OSIP: Come on now. Explain. What did you do to my children?

VARONA (*in tears*): In the evening Zuray would usually sit on the edge of her bed to read her brochures. I'll always see her thus. Last winter, on a day the two of us were alone in our room, she was leafing through a fat volume on the history of the Bolshevik coup d'état, I think. As she suddenly turned kind of dreamy while giving me a deep and grave look, I approached her tenderly. For to see her prey to revolutionary ideas made me suffer untold . . .

OSIP: Varona, I beg you, my remorse sleeps calmly, don't wake it up.

VARONA: That day she was prettier than ever. But of a sad and clouded prettiness that, I don't know why, pleased my heart while at the same time distressing it. (OSIP *tenses up, takes a few steps.*) Why did she speak to me like this? I'll never know. Suddenly she asked me, "Tell me, Mother, what if Daddy was not dead?" That's how the conversation began, and we talked all afternoon long. Then, as Volni was coming up the stairs, she hastily laid a convulsive and absent-minded kiss on my forehead. (VARONA *sobs.*) I never found out why she kissed me like that. Why did she speak of you to me in that way . . . I know only that kiss; I cannot forget it, now that she is far away, now that the reds have stolen her from me, maybe forever . . .

OSIP (*sullen, torn*): My daughter, I will never speak to her! I who have never come close to her, who have never talked to her, never heard her . . .

VARONA: She is not wicked at all! No! She is a Bolshevik; that's her flaw, her error, her sole mistake. I can no longer live without her. I have tried, I cannot. I thirst for her! I hunger after her! Osip! Open yourself to my distress! I am coming to you, to seek refuge.

OSIP (*deep, penetrated*): No! The revolution is not the fall of the tzar, nor the power takeover by the workers. What is happening right now in the heart of the families and of the people, that is the revolution.

VARONA: It breaks my heart to think what politics can lead us to! It is stronger than anything! It separates the most united beings, creating hatred there where there had been only love. I remember Volni and Zuray when they were little. It makes me want to weep and pray to God . . . (*She sobs.*) . . . To tear oneself away from one's own children! . . . Why? . . . Why? . . .

OSIP (*takes her in his arms*): Get ahold of yourself, dear! We are not the only ones in this situation. There isn't a day goes by without hearing of children of the bourgeoisie or even the nobility who have broken with their parents to become revolutionaries.

VARONA (*eyes in his, in one deep breath*): Osip! My big one!

OSIP (*looks at the door and lets go of* VARONA): The youngest son of the Wolfs did the same thing.

VARONA (*follows him and suddenly beseeches*): Listen! Come home!

OSIP (*surprised*): What's that? (*He moves away.*)

VARONA: Yes, Come home!

OSIP (*looks at the door and raising his voice*): Madame, you are going astray. Come home, me! To our children?

VARONA: I need you. I feel so alone. Ever since our Zuray left, a horrible solitude has been overtaking me; it goes through my bones and tears at my entrails . . .

OSIP (*same look and tone of voice*): But, madame, you are forgetting my dirt, my infamies.

VARONA: No matter! My solitude, my abandonment, you, you alone can console it. Osip! My companion! Spouse of my life! Come back to us.

OSIP (*same look and tone of voice*): Madame, my regrets. While I bow most respectfully before your maternal distress, permit me to disappear one more time. My filthy carcass . . .

VARONA: You are absolved. I forgive you . . .

OSIP: My consciousness overflows with darkness . . .

VARONA: Come back.

OSIP (*watches the door*): I would at least need to consult Father Superior, obtain his permission . . .

VARONA (*rearing up, with dark purpose*): Would you prefer me to go among the reds and force them to return?

OSIP: There we are! That's an idea! Go bring them back.

From *Moscow vs. Moscow*   261

VARONA: I can't promise. Do I have your permission?

OSIP: By the way, you can also go into a church and ask God for refuge . . .

VARONA (*her mind made up*): Very good. I will go fetch them from among the Bolsheviki, even if they don't agree and refuse to see me. (*She moves toward the exit.*)

OSIP (*imperturbable*): That's it, go fetch them. And let me know as soon as they'll have returned to you. That will please me. (*He dismisses her.* VARONA *rushes out, in the grip of a tempestuous agitation.* OSIP *makes a gesture of mortal exhaustion and staggers, leaning on a corner of the lectern just as* SAKROV *returns onstage through the back door.*)

SAKROV: She has left . . . (*Catching sight of* OSIP, *about to faint*) But what is the matter with you my friend? She wouldn't have beaten you? (*He holds* OSIP *up.*)

OSIP (*weakly*): It's the effort I had to make. Oh, what a battle! What temptation!

SAKROV: I know. Temptation. But the All-Powerful is with you!

OSIP (*raises himself with difficulty*): And then, this accident . . .

SAKROV: What accident?

OSIP: This moral accident. Sentimental, rather. In an excess of sincerity, my heart stopped momentarily.

SAKROV: Don't move. Don't move. (*Holding him up*) Are you in pain. Is it true?

OSIP (*resting*): No. Done. Momentary stop. Sincerity, you see, has some use, especially under a socialist system: the bore has left me in peace.

SAKROV: And she will not see you again. That's what matters. (*Suddenly, in a low, pressing voice*) Prince, make a decision, once and for all.

OSIP (*his mind elsewhere*): But deep down, she no longer wants me, no matter what she says.

SAKROV: Let's leave for the kolkhoz.

OSIP (*same tone*): The children! The Bolsheviki! What do I care?

SAKROV: Let us leave for work, if at all possible, early tomorrow morning!

OSIP (*with painful lassitude*): It is rather the priests that are my nightmare. Oh! . . . What a mess! . . . They don't stop lecturing me: God! Soul! Eternity! And whatever else! . . . (*He sits down and leans against the lectern, his head fallen between his hands.*) And that's what they call refuge and consolation!

SAKROV (*grabs him passionately by the wrists*): Osip Dvoschine Polianov, let's leave! Let's leave right away! This minute! Let's go! Work in the fields is awaiting us! (OSIP *doesn't answer; his head still lowered*) The great machines! The tractors! The formidable noise of the engines! The breathless flurry of workers! The green and blue horizon, the embrasures, in spring time! The abundant sun! The strong and healthy air! The end of all thought! An end to this stultifying life in the monastery! . . . (OSIP *raises his brow and looks at* SAKROV, *absentmindedly.*) Come! Yes! Let's hurry up! My hands are already impatient to move, to get ahold of a muscular task! An unknown potential is biding its time in each one of my cells! . . . (OSIP *walks, hesitatingly, toward center stage.* SAKROV *grows more and more exalted.*) Oh, what a surge of active forces life is! It comes at you from every point in the universe! It grabs you and lifts you up and carries you away! (*While speaking thus, he grabs* OSIP *by the elbow and moves toward the left side of the corridor.*) Cheerful and moving and harmonious—that's the world of matter! But before all, moving! . . . Let's hurry up! Come one! That's it!

OSIP (*suddenly turning away*): Sakrov! To the end of the centuries man will always be the Son of man! I'm sitting down! (*He sits down.*) I am sitting. I am thinking. You are standing . . .

SAKROV: Off to the kolkhoz, Polianov!

OSIP: You are trying to save me, and that is a very bad thing for you to do, my poor friend.

SAKROV: You are annoying me. Let's go!

OSIP: Leave? Never! I am already unhappy enough as is! If on top of it all you save me, what a mess! No, no, my friend! That: never.

CURTAIN

[NP/PJ]

From *The River Flows between Two Shores*

ACT 1
Scene 1

> *Moscow. Midnight at a square submerged in penumbra and silence. In the background, far away, the cupolas of the Kremlin. It's snowing.*
>
> *Rising from a short base, in the center of the square a statue of Lenin appears. Standing up, with his left thumb stuck under his right arm, outstretched, pointing straight ahead into the distance with his index finger, Lenin appears in the familiar posture of riling up the crowd.*
>
> *In a visible state of drunkenness,* MUKININ *enters the square. The finger of the statue points at him, and when the* NEP*man notices, he vibrantly shudders. He stops, takes a few steps back, looks around himself, tries to get on his way. In vain. His discomfort grows in the presence of Lenin, who points at him and fills him with terror.* MUKININ, *in his drunkenness, no longer knows for sure if in reality it's just a statue in front of him or if it's Lenin in the flesh. For a moment he bravely approaches the statue, but, again, he steps back. He wants to run away and again stops. At that moment, the statue comes to life and, continuing to point at him implacably, staggers toward* MUKININ, *who takes off in a sprint, petrified, disappearing stage left, with Lenin chasing him.* OSIP PETROVITCH POLIANOV *briefly crosses the square in the same direction as the* NEP*man. Stumbling as he goes, the prince is drunk too.*

CURTAIN

Scene 2

> *Inside a store. Doors to backstage and to the right. Complete darkness and silence. We hear a door being opened cautiously. They flip on the light switch. Light.* MUKININ *and* OSIP PETROVITCH *appear at the door downstage, in the same state of drunkenness from the previous scene.*

OSIP: Come on! Out with it! You're mad! Mad I say!

MUKININ (*removing a granite hand from under his fur coat, frightened and in a low voice*): Mad? But it has suddenly come to life and chased after me, as though it were a person in flesh and bone. (*Places the hand on the counter.*)

OSIP (*looking it over and laughing*): Strange, strange! Epic! (*Laughs again.*) The hand of Lenin! Piece number one of the heavy artillery!

MUKININ: I may be drunk but . . . it was you, when I threw the stone . . .

OSIP (*absorbed in contemplation of the hand*): Shh! Quiet! . . . Fifteen years ago, I remember it as if it was yesterday, I saw that hand alive, the forefinger pressing against a fountain pen, run across a wrinkled sheet of faded paper. They were the celebrated April Theses of Petrograd.

MUKININ (*locking the upstage door*): My life is hanging by a thread! I'm dreaming! A statue that walks and chases me! Saint Andrew!

OSIP: Plebeian soul! "Human, all too human!" Desperately in need of a fabulous meaning! Don't you know that there are stones and even rocks that move by themselves, that step forward and even gallop? Haven't you even seen in your dreams those geologic cuirassiers that the great Apocalypse speaks of?

MUKININ: Please, don't turn me in. Don't tell anyone what I've seen!

OSIP: And the evidence? Why have you brought it to your store?

MUKININ: The hand . . . I don't know. I didn't realize. Without knowing what I was doing, I picked it up off the ground and hid it . . . to cover the tracks . . .

OSIP (*severely*): In any case, sir, throwing stones at great men . . .

MUKININ: But it's just a statue.

OSIP: Even more so, at their statues.

MUKININ (*anxiously*): Why? Is that what you think?

OSIP: Let's suppose that you, for example, were rich before the revolution. And let's suppose, for example, that the "reds" had dispossessed you of your property . . .

MUKININ (*suddenly scrutinizing* OSIP): Who are you?

OSIP: That would not be a sufficient cause . . . Take great caution, my friend, with the hand of a statue!

MUKININ: But I haven't . . .

OSIP: The hand of a statue is evil or, so they say, very evil. Kindly do me the favor of raising it up (*referring to the hand of the statue*) with both hands. Come on! (*insisting*) Come on! (MUKININ *obeys but suddenly drops it on the counter out of terror, gasping and turning away.* OSIP, *sarcastically*) Ah, you fool! Fool! What have you gone and done to Lubianka, just a moment ago?

MUKININ: To Lubianka? Me?

OSIP: Yes, you. It's useless to deny it. I've got you in my mitts. Just one word from my lips and you, sir, are a goner.

MUKININ: I was returning . . . returning from the union meeting.

OSIP: Yes. And look at this coincidence. You suddenly grew thirsty . . . But . . . are you crying? What's wrong with you?

MUKININ: Crying, me? Why would I be crying?

OSIP (*drawing near*): You're not crying? Honestly?

MUKININ: No. Honestly.

OSIP: And, nonetheless, you rogue, you cunning man, your whimpering is physical, undeniable.

MUKININ: By the Virgin of Kazan, crying, me?

OSIP: It's your muscles that are crying bitterly. Your fibers, your cells, your chemical entities. Perhaps unbeknown to you . . .

MUKININ: My muscles? What muscles? I don't feel anything.

OSIP: You don't? And that friendly man?

MUKININ (*turning his ear to the street*): My brother-in-law . . .

OSIP: When he sees her with a stranger, who's going to watch their backs?

MUKININ: Whose backs?

OSIP: Who keeps watch on the night of the mystery? Who becomes our guardian angel?

MUKININ (*again turning his ear to the street*): The police!

OSIP (*furiously*): Stupid, ignorant fool! The electron!

MUKININ (*lowering his voice*): The police! I'm telling you. (*without removing his ear from the upstage door*) Yes! The police! . . .

OSIP (*raising his voice*): You illiterate fool, come here!

MUKININ (*obeying*): I'm coming! I'm coming! . . .

OSIP: Where's your electron?

MUKININ: Excuse me, but I believe . . . (*suddenly, again trying to identify him*) Take off your glasses! I know your voice!

OSIP (*sidestepping*): Moderation . . . Respect . . .

MUKININ (*doubting*): It's a mask! Alexandrovitch? Livekerov? Who? . . .

OSIP: Okay, okay. Let me explain myself, listen up. In a system that's bourgeois, capitalist, or whatever you want to call it, 51 percent of people are wretched, but in a system that's proletarian, socialist, or whatever else you want to call it, the wretchedness is negative 101 percent. This is how the middle ground between Hegel and Marx is reached, and it accounts for less than does . . . You say it . . . than does? . . .

MUKININ: Than does . . . Than does . . . (*lowering his voice and peeking out the upstage door*) Whatever you know it does.

OSIP: Wrong! For the second time! Than does madness! And let me say, you old fox, I have met Lenin in person . . .

MEKNIN (*on his own*): The things that come from your mouth! You're a nut job!

OSIP: So be it, and I will add, this adventure (*alluding to the hand of the statue*) will entail no consequence for you. Absolutely none.

MUKININ: Thank you so much. But . . .

OSIP (*interrupting, with his hand*): As for me, I couldn't care less. I've seen nothing. What statue? Neither when I was walking nor standing still! You pretend to have thrown a stone and broken off the hand of the statue . . .

MUKININ: I did it in legitimate defense, sir.

OSIP: Right! That's your alibi . . .

MUKININ: The statue was attacking me and I defended myself.

OSIP: Therefore, the granite, especially the granite of a statue, occasionally has brittle, vulnerable parts—the wrist especially. However, that would surprise me in the case of Bolshevik granite . . .

MUKININ: There's no such thing as Bolshevik granite or bourgeois granite. That's for the birds!

OSIP: In my judgment, this hand must be from some saint or idol, fractured in frantic transportation . . .

MUKININ: Sir, I am sure. It's from the statue.

OSIP: Well, no matter where it's from, in my desire to shield you from a deplorable outcome . . .

MUKININ: Are you going to get rid of it?

OSIP: I'll take care of it . . .

MUKININ (*kissing* OSIP's *hand*): Baron!

OSIP: Under one condition.

MUKININ: Which is?

OSIP: That I leave here in absolute darkness. Turn off the light.

MUKININ: Did you say? I don't understand . . .

OSIP: Are you denying me? I'm sorry. (*takes a few steps toward the door*). Good night.

MUKININ (*immediately begging him*): One moment, by God! Save me! Take it with you! . . . (*in a shudder, his eyes on the door to the street*). They've knocked!

OSIP (*quietly*): It seems they have . . .

MUKININ: I hear footsteps . . .

OSIP: Their footsteps . . . Yes . . .

MUKININ (*anxiously*): Whose footsteps, Baron?

OSIP: The police! (MUKININ *falls into a chair, as if thunderstruck, plunging his head in his hands; immediately thereafter,* OSIP *refers to himself authoritatively in a raised voice*) Stalin!

MUKININ (*frightfully raising his face without understanding anything*): Stalin? Where?

OSIP (*glowering, upright in front of* MUKININ): Me! Stalin! Right in front of you!

MUKININ (*in a flash of lucidness*): You? The comrade? . . .

OSIP (*in an irate shout*): Stalin! (MUKININ *stumbles backward.*) A seat!

MUKININ (*with haste, trembling*): But of course, Comrade Stalin, excuse me, I beg you! (*brings him a seat*).

OSIP (*sitting down magisterially*): Where is your wife at this hour?

MUKININ (*now trying hard to hide his drunkenness*): Comrade Stalin, she's at work in the factory . . .

OSIP: What are you thinking, you cuckold!

MUKININ: Comrade Stalin, who can know . . .

OSIP: Doesn't your forehead itch?

MUKININ: Communism extols . . .

OSIP: You drunken two-bit communist! (*with subtle indulgence*). Come here and sit down next to me, or in front of me. (MUKININ *obeys.*) So now you see . . . (MUKININ, *disoriented, observes* OSIP *through his drunkenness.*) I am Stalin, it's a great pleasure, absolutely charmed. Yes, for sure . . . (*A shadow of incredulity passes over* MUKININ, *who wants to speak.*) What are you alleging? What do you have to say?

MUKININ (*wavering*): Me, nothing, Comrade Stalin, excuse me. (*The upstage door bursts open and* SPEKRY *enters, with an accordion under his arm; he too is drunk;* MUKININ, *overwhelmed*) Who are you? What do you want?

OSIP (*immutably*): My secretary. (*to* SPEKRY) Come in, come in, Comrade. (*turning back to* MUKININ) So I was saying . . . indeed, I am Stalin. Now you see.

SPEKRY (*to* MUKININ): But, are you blind, man? (*pointing at* OSIP) Comrade Stalin, right here, and you doubt. (MUKININ *doesn't know if he's dreaming or awake.*)

OSIP: I'm the general secretary of the Communist Party. What's the general secretary of the Communist Party? Nothing. A man like any other.

SPEKRY: Except that Nature has endowed him with greater talent and heart than all men combined.

MUKININ (*leaning close*): Comrade Stalin, my utmost admiration.

SPEKRY (*to* MUKININ): Now you see, in proletarian democracy, the most intelligent and honorable men are the ones at the head of society.

OSIP (*to* MUKININ): Give us something! Aren't you going to offer? What do you suggest?

SPEKRY: How impolite. Look at this miser!

MUKININ (*running to serve some drinks*): Oh, Comrade! It would be my pleasure and honor.

OSIP (*to* SPEKRY): And you, play that contraption of yours. Something deep. My soul is deathly sad.

SPEKRY (*starts playing his accordion with the damper on*): What will it be? Tears? Sighs? Shrieks of passion?

OSIP: Play . . . a lament . . . a complaint that's strange and at once familiar. Some music about a great man . . . let's say . . . a great man who has not had dinner and whose wife nonetheless has adorable lips, exquisite as strawberries . . .

MUKININ (*serving the liquor*): Comrade Stalin, a NEPman drinks on proletarian orders. May I?

OSIP (*all three have their glasses*): I'm drunk, NEPman. It's evident.

SPEKRY: Comrades, to the Soviet order!

OSIP: But I'm still Stalin. Let Troy burn!

MUKININ: You're still him all right, the spitting image. Come on, ching-ching. (*They clink their glasses together and drink.*)

SPEKRY (*playing a sad tune*): "Each night . . . Each night my soul keeps scouring the darkness . . ."

MUKININ: What an unexpected honor, Comrade Stalin! I'm astonished by your frankness, your simplicity, your manner . . .

OSIP: What do you expect! This can occur only in a socialist order. If Hitler goes out for a stroll, on any given night, like I do . . . they'd kill him.

SPEKRY (*playing*): "Your reproach that's jailed the wind . . ."

OSIP: The folklore of the steppe. A black horse that whinnies!

SPEKRY (*stops playing*): Comrade NEPman, it appears there's something you haven't noticed.

MUKININ (*filling the glasses again*): But I have, I have noticed.

SPEKRY: You haven't noticed that I am mute. Have you noticed this?

OSIP: Completely mute. Mute, without ifs, ands, or buts.

MUKININ: Would you look at that! What a quality!

SPEKRY: And what am I saying to you right now? At this very instant.

MUKININ: At this very instant . . . Nothing. Nothing specific.

SPEKRY: My true language is my accordion.

MUKININ: Ah, right! Now, I understand.

SPEKRY (*plays a chord and asks* MUKININ): What did I say to you there?

OSIP: The smile of a nubile virgin.

SPEKRY (*to* MUKININ): What did I say? Did you hear me?

MUKININ (*trying to understand*): What did you say here? What did you say? I'm going to tell you. Something . . . like . . .

SPEKRY (*plays other chords, forming a melody and then asks* MUKININ *again*): And here? What did I say here?

MUKININ (*who has understood*): That you're tired. Isn't that it?

OSIP (*breaks into laughter*): The thorniest thorn of the patch[134] is indisputably a NEPMAN.

SPEKRY (*to* OSIP): No, sir! I didn't say that! (*to* MUKININ) You listen now. (*plays a whining tune and adds*) Someone is crying at the front door!

MUKININ (*hurries to open the door to the backstage area*): It's my wife! My wife! (*He opens the door and* OLGA *enters.*)

OLGA: Good evening.

MUKININ: What's the matter, my dear? Has something happened?

OSIP/SPEKRY (*bowing*): Madame . . .

OLGA: Nothing. Why?

MUKININ (*introducing her*): Here, Comrade Stalin, our chief . . .

OLGA (*astonished*): The comrade . . . Stalin! Who? This guy?

MUKININ (*grabbing* OSIP *by the arm*): In the flesh. Comrade Stalin, disguised. He's charming. Not proud at all. A good guy.

SPEKRY: A simple man. Natural. During a night out or in.

MUKININ: Without makeup or making a fuss.

OLGA (*with timid incredulity*): The comrade . . . At this hour? Like this? In that? . . .

SPEKRY: Exactly, madame. It's his normal state: simplicity. Not despotic at all; just the opposite . . .

MUKININ: As you understand, Comrade Stalin has his grief, his anguish, his inner human struggles, like every man.

OSIP: To serve you, my lady: my personal torment and pain.

OLGA (*scrutinizing* OSIP *from head to toe*): That's quite natural. In any case, Comrade Stalin, please make yourself at home.

MUKININ: Comrade Stalin, another drink? Please. (*fills the glasses*) And what about you, accordionist: "Your reproach the wind . . . a prison, the winds and reproaches" (SPEKRY *plays*) Olgashka! Come here, my darling!

OSIP (*gallantly, to* OLGA): So, look, madame: we great men, like all men, medium and small alike, have a heart that suffers humanly . . .

MUKININ (*exhausted, suddenly collapsing in a chair*): Shit, I'm shot!

OSIP (*to* OLGA, *while* SPEKRY *plays his accordion muted*): Because they surely haven't hidden from you that there's been electricity for more than two, three, or four years of the Five-Year Plan.

OLGA (*believes, for moments, that it is Stalin speaking*): Comrade, that seems correct.

OSIP (*nuzzling up closer to* OLGA): The proletariat, the machine, the global revolution are an indubitable reality. But no less real and existent are the mysteries of God, love, and death. (*turning to* MUKININ). Right, NEPman?

MUKININ (*half asleep, in a groan*): Fuck off!

OLGA: Oh, Comrade Stalin, excuse him, please . . .

OSIP: What? It's nothing, madame. I shall tell you that I'm especially fond of this language. I am sick and tired of bureaucratic words. When I go out at night like this, incognito, I warn you that I do so only every once in a while, what I try to find in my strolls are people from the belly of the populace, from the base of the masses, who speak and act on their toes, without hypocrisy or duplicity. (SPEKRY *slowly stops playing, starts falling asleep.*)

OLGA: You are a kindhearted man, Comrade. I had heard so much.

OSIP (*almost in her ear, quietly*): Here, between us, right now, I beg you, don't see me as the head of the workers of the Soviet Union but rather as just a regular friend.

OLGA: You are very modest as well, Comrade Stalin.

OSIP (*suddenly taking* OLGA's *hand and raising it to his chest*): Touch my heart. (OLGA *allows him, confused, surprised.*) Terrible is the thirst that devours me. I am Stalin, yes. A fighter, a man entirely dedicated to humanity . . . (*holding* OLGA's *hand between his hands*) But, Comrade, no one knows, I swear, that this fighter is a sensitive man, burning with passion and, nonetheless, lonely, Comrade, very lonely! (*face-to-face, with fire*) What a look! And that mouth!

OLGA (*pulling her hand back*): Oh, Comrade!

OSIP (*quieter, impassioned*): I've known you for a long time! I've seen you on many occasions, without your noticing . . . (*kisses her hands*)

OLGA: Comrade . . . my husband . . .

OSIP: It's only for you that I've come here tonight.

From *The River Flows between Two Shores*　271

OLGA: Please, be quiet!

OSIP: Come with me to the Kremlin. Come. Right now.

OLGA: Comrade . . .

OSIP: To be frank, it's the first time, the only time really, that I've gone out in disguise. I've done it only to speak with you. To make your acquaintance, I've had to get drunk (*nodding toward* MUKININ).

OLGA (*convinced that it's Stalin speaking to her*): Shh! . . . Slow down! I beg you!

OSIP: He's already sleeping. My Olgashka! Come now. Let's go! (*Stands up.*) In silence . . . We shall speak in the Kremlin . . .

OLGA: But . . . (*with great anxiety*) Are you really Comrade Stalin?

OSIP: What naivety! I am Stalin! Now you're going to see!

OLGA (*standing up*): But . . . you're not well . . . I'm afraid of you . . .

OSIP (*leading her by the hand, tiptoeing toward the upstage door*): Shh! . . . Silence! . . . I'll show you soon enough . . . I am Stalin, I swear.

OLGA: By the Virgin of Kazan! And tomorrow, Comrade?

OSIP: Tomorrow? I'll still be Stalin. Don't worry (*quietly opens the door*).

OLGA: And my coat? . . . Hold on. My hat . . .

OSIP (*without letting go of her*): Superfluous! Superfluous! I have many in the Kremlin.

OLGA (*indecisively*): And what am I going to do in the Kremlin?

OSIP: Work! We shall prepare the Five-Year Plan together! Come on! (*opens the door to leave; at the moment they're about to close it behind them,* VARONA *enters, astonished.*)

VARONA (*to* OSIP): Prince! My husband! Good God, come home!

OLGA (*turning to* OSIP *and falling from the clouds*): Prince? You?

OSIP (*with rigid dignity, to* VARONA): Madame . . . Me, come home?

VARONA: Yes, Osip! I can't take it anymore! Come home this instant!

OLGA: Go back to his home? (*to* MUKININ, *in a loud voice*) Hey, you! Get me away from these bold-faced liars!

OSIP (*to* VARONA): Madame, look past my defects, my coarseness . . .

VARONA: No, Osip. It doesn't matter. I forgive you. Come back! Come back, Osip!

MUKININ (*waking up*): There's only one path God leads us down.

SPEKRY (*waking up, in turn*): Comrade NEPman!

MUKININ (*standing up, staring at the circumstances*): Or, in other words, there's only one kind of death: the death of the soul. (*approaching* OSIP) Comrade Stalin!

OLGA: Stalin? Stalin, my foot! You shysters! Time to close up! Out! (*VARONA has taken* OSIP *by the arm and leads him.*)

SPEKRY: Comrade NEPman, there are two kinds of death: the death of life and the other, the saddest, most implacable, the death of death. Saint Augustine of Hippo, *The City of God*, chapter 3, page 67.

VARONA: Osip Petrovitch! Would you please!

MUKININ (*moved by a sudden, exuberant joy, opens his arms up to everyone*): Tovarishchi![135]

OLGA: To bed I said! Hot shots!

MUKININ (*embracing* OSIP): Stalin or not, you like me because of the wine, because of the stat—and because of the . . . of the sta—You know what I mean?

VARONA: Osip, let's get out of here, I'm begging you . . .

OSIP (*embracing* MUKININ *back*): My brother in defeat, my brother in God . . .

SPEKRY (*behind a stormy, echoing tune, to his accordion*): What now? Tears? Kisses? Sighs? Scoffs?

OLGA: Aspaso Ivanovitch! It's already two in the morning! (SPEKRY *strikes up a loud, fast Cossack's song*; OSIP *and* MUKININ *dance.*) Enough, please! Everyone, out!

VARONA: Careful, Osip! Get up!

OSIP (*upon finishing the dance, suddenly, mysteriously, wobbling*): Silence! Silence! . . .

VARONA: Osip Petrovitch, you're going to fall . . .

OLGA (*to* MUKININ): Aspaso Ivanovitch, I have to get up early.

SPEKRY: Kotoryi chas!?[136]

OSIP (*in a sudden startle*): How strange! A joke . . . A breath perhaps . . . has just fallen from the ceiling and scattered at my feet, between the stools . . .

SPEKRY (*looking around on the floor and in between the stools*): What did you say? A breath? . . . A shadow? . . . Or are you joking?

OSIP: No. I'm confused. It wasn't a breath. It's exactly what I told you to begin with: a shadow, purely a shadow.

SPEKRY: Couldn't it have fallen from your pocket? Or, maybe you crushed it under your shoes out of carelessness . . .

OSIP: For the short time I've been here, on my nights of fear and anxiety, doubt and emptiness, I've enjoyed sitting down to wander for hours without beginning or end, amid the silence, solitude, and darkness. I've felt the shadows falling from the sky . . . shadows . . . shadows . . .

MUKININ: Bolshevik manna.

VARONA (*impatiently begging*): Prince, let's go!

OSIP: And I have seen my fingers blur together: what a terrible thing!

From *The River Flows between Two Shores*   273

The chills, the vertigo, the sinister zeroes! (*steps backward*) Hold me up! (VARONA *holds him up and makes him take a seat.* OSIP, *like a sleepwalker, mutters*) It's written on the walls: without thought, there is no feeling.

VARONA: What's come over you, Prince? Do you feel sick?

SPEKRY (*vehemently*): Quite the contrary, Osip Petrovitch! Without feeling, there is no thought!

OSIP: It's all the same, Mr. Accordionist. What came first? The chicken or the egg?

MUKININ (*patting him on the shoulder*): Whether you're a prince or not, can I or can't I say one word to you?

OSIP (*wavering*): That is ... uh ... no. I've plugged my ears out of the fear of nothingness. (VARONA *slips by and leaves through the upstage door, without uttering a word. Once she is gone,* OSIP *stands up and exclaims*) A saint! She's a saint! And I am scum! There's Good in her, and Evil in me. (*pulls his hair with force, moaning in a low voice*) Vara! Vara! Despise me but forgive me!

SPEKRY: Osip Petrovitch, you just relax, please.

MUKININ: Yes! Damn it! You've got to suffer! You've got to live! You've got to drink!

OSIP (*philosophically, very seriously*): I tell you, Comrades, indisputably, God is the only reason for my existence.

SPEKRY: Nothing more natural. (OLGA *is dozing off, sitting by herself.*)

OSIP: I've arrived at this certainty not long ago, on a day when the idea of suicide came to me, after a painstaking assessment of my life and fate. At the bottom of everything, of everything, the void. And then, deeper down, at the terrible bottom of the void, I saw the Being of beings take shape and come to life, calling me to life with its strange magnetic voice ...

OLGA (*half asleep*): Aspaso Ivanovitch ... they should leave ...

OSIP: What's more, I have too much muzhik blood in my veins to be a skeptic or mere degenerate. At most, I could be a nihilist, but never a skeptic, which isn't the same ...

SPEKRY: Prince, we've already told you: the isolation of the medieval hermits has lost meaning and power in our day and age. To rise up to God, one must communicate with one's neighbor.

MUKININ: Exactly! You've got to live! You've got to suffer! You've got to drink! (*Drinks.*)

SPEKRY: A man on his own lacks the strength necessary to ascend to

God. We wouldn't know how to discover it, except in the great human collectives . . .

OSIP: I see you, Spekry; come closer again, hammer and sickle in hand . . .

SPEKRY: Labor is more beautiful than love and . . . even more beautiful than prayer . . .

OSIP (*to* SPEKRY): Play, play your accordion! "Each night . . . each night my soul . . ." (SPEKRY *plays an infinitely sad song from the steppe, muted.*)

MUKININ: Olgashka!

OLGA (*nodding off*): Ah! I'm falling asleep . . .

MUKININ: I'll speak quietly so that I don't wake you. (OSIP, *sitting next to* SPEKRY, *hears the melody, sticking his ear to the instrument.*) Look, Olgashka. We have to become proletarians.

OSIP (*ecstatic*): Until the centuries' end, man will also be the Son of man!

MUKININ (*to* OLGA, *who continues to nod off*): What do you expect? The taxes go up, I drink all the vodka in the store. There's no other choice than to close it and become laborers. You'll take the sickle, and I, the hammer.

OLGA: Fine . . . okay . . .

OSIP (*standing up, with rage and repugnance*): The woman? Ah! . . . (*spits*). The hammer? (*spits*) The sickle? . . . The sickle? (*approaching* OLGA). My lady, do you know the sickle?

MUKININ: Slowly, Comrade. Speak to her quietly so that you don't wake her . . .

OSIP (*frowning and pensive*): Varona Gurakevna is immortal to me . . .

MUKININ: Olgashka, I'll grab the hammer, and you, the sickle. Down with the NEP! (OSIP *has stuck his ear against the accordion again and is captivated by his chords.*)

OSIP (*while* SPEKRY *continues to play*): Play . . . Play . . . Play . . .

CURTAIN

Scene 3

The apartment of VARONA GURAKEVNA *and her children,* NIURA *and* ZURAY. *Aged furniture. On the walls, photographs of characters from the time of the tzars and religious prints. Doors on the right and left, leading to the rest of the house, which is large and has several floors. The door on the left is functional and leads to the room of* VLADIMIR *and* ILITCH; *the door on the right, which leads to a flat occupied by other tenants, is condemned. Upstage, a large door over the corridor. For several seconds the scene remains empty. At moments, footsteps and voices outside can be heard. Then the upstage door opens.* VARONA *and her uncle,* BORIS KOLOVITCH, *come in from the street.*

VARONA: Come in, Uncle. They haven't arrived yet. (*opening the door on the left*) However, given the time, they could be here shortly.

BORIS (*tired*): Ah! . . . There's no doubt, evidently, one way or another, we're witnessing the universal breakdown of the family. In Russia, the United States, France, Germany . . . everywhere.

VARONA: Please have a seat, Boris.

BORIS (*sitting down*): A legacy of the war. Ah, my legs are stiff.

VARONA: The little one no longer comes home until very late at night. And him! I often don't see him for two or three days straight. Even today, it would be nothing out of the ordinary if they didn't come home for supper (*starts setting the table*).

BORIS: But we have to be fair: they are still just kids. In my time, it was more serious. We used to go out onto the steppe in gangs of ten or fifteen, for one or even two weeks at a time. Our parents, meanwhile, would run to the police. However, that back then was the simple mischief of pipsqueaks, whereas this that's going on today . . .

VARONA: And he's the one who drags my little girl to those Bolshevik rallies. Here, at the house, in my room, red clouds form at any hour.

BORIS: Tell me . . . Have you tried—I'm afraid to ask—to show them that these habits of theirs upset you?

VARONA: It's just that I can't stand them, Uncle Boris . . .

BORIS: Awful! Awful! Awful!

VARONA: It's the voice of the family, all together, that lifts you up after such a loss.

BORIS: Varona Gurakevna, I must insist: your intolerance is counterproductive.

VARONA: Boris Kolovitch, I can't share your opinion . . .

BORIS: To be frank, aside from the fact that I fear the rigor you use to judge your younger children—rigor that should be inspired by healthy reason and unquestionably righteous feeling—is nothing more than a disguised form of your hatred for the revolution . . .

VARONA: I don't think so, uncle. You're mistaken.

BORIS: And that your children are filled with hatred whose remote cause came long before their Bolshevik ideas.

VARONA: I'm listening to you, Boris Kolovitch.

BORIS: I don't know if I'm making myself clear. What I'm proposing is to take measures against an error that could turn Ilitch and Zuray into two innocent victims of events they've had nothing to do with . . .

VARONA: It's easy to see what you're getting at. But go ahead . . .

BORIS: Varona, it's nothing more than a warning, a word of precaution . . .

VARONA: I understand, Uncle. However, let me tell you: you aren't entirely right . . .

BORIS: I hope I'm not, I hope I'm not! That's my greatest wish.

VARONA: Ilitch and Zuray, without a doubt, are far removed from the events that gave rise to my downfall. But I assure you, Boris Kolovitch, I know nothing more atrocious for a mother than to see her children—her very own children—in the face of her misfortune, express that indifference, that coldness, that lack of . . .

BORIS: Excuse me, but that generally doesn't turn my head. Those are the inevitable effects of the Bolshevik education they've received from their most tender age.

VARONA: What else can I do? Resign myself? Appeal to violence? To a lashing that might stir deep in their guts the filial feeling of solidarity that my disastrous life deserves?

BORIS: That's the question, the key to the problem.

VARONA: Don't I have the right to be outraged that their political feelings overshadow my wretchedness and go in the direction opposite to mine, both of them snuffing out all mercy for me?

BORIS: You're getting at the knot, the nerve of the matter.

VARONA: I know, Uncle, a mother cannot and should not attack the political freedom of her children . . .

BORIS: See! Even you say so . . .

VARONA: I know that law, morality, and even good sense prohibit it . . .

BORIS: It's prohibited to do so knowingly, under penalty of falling into an injustice that could entail serious consequences.

VARONA: It's just that this, Uncle, is nothing but pure theory and, between theory and action, the heart rises up.

BORIS: Sometimes it does . . . Who can deny it?

VARONA (*with energy*): And mine, Boris Kolovitch, doesn't accept that, doesn't want my children to become Bolsheviki. Never! This house, on a daily basis, is a wasp's nest. There's not one conversation that doesn't end in a political dispute. For all we know, one day it might degenerate into a horrendous drama before us . . . But not even that can be foreseen! . . .

BORIS: That's what I think too . . .

VARONA: . . . and when the moment arrives, no one would be able to avoid it. I'm well aware of all that. There's no remedy. Ilitch and Zuray are my children, and, as such, (*harshly*) I shall keep them at my side, even by force, if it comes to that.

BORIS: It's your right and, to a certain extent, your duty . . . At least as long as they're minors . . .

VARONA: I'll beat their rebelliousness. No matter what happens. (*aggressively*) No matter what it takes . . .

BORIS: My daughter, I am your uncle and I am in your home, at your side, to help you, to give you as much advice as I can, and to give you strength in your misfortune. Look at my resignation, Vara; yours truly could be an example for you. God has come to my pleas for help. Taking refuge in the house of some charitable friends, I face my fate like a good, humble, peaceful Christian, and I can say so without bitterness or grudges. Do it for yourself, Varona Gurakevna. Let us suffer, my daughter . . . Suffer and hope!

VARONA: It's just that, Uncle, you're a good man . . .

BORIS: What I am, poor Vara, is reasonable.

VARONA: Your fatherly words do me good.

BORIS: One must bow before the will of God the Almighty. It's your duty as a mother and a Christian. You recognize in your conscience that you don't have the right. Therefore, tolerance and patience, Vara. Serenity and more tolerance: this must be your role in your home at every instant.

VARONA: How will I do it, Lord? Tolerate their ideas? By not speaking to them anymore about my torments? And shall I let them think and do as they please?

BORIS: You must close your eyes, Vara.

VARONA: What can I do so that none of my kids abandons me? (*indistinct voices stage right*)

BORIS (*getting ready to leave*): Don't oppose their way of thinking, Varona. Don't prosecute them for their ideas. I say this to you for everyone's sake. (*quietly*) And your husband? Have you heard anything?

VARONA: Oh, the same as always . . . And your wife?

BORIS: Nothing . . . Rumors . . .

VARONA: Of course, there are plenty of people who come telling me they saw him at night in the slums, staggering around drunk as a skunk . . .

BORIS: Pay them no attention. (*more quietly*) Be careful with the younger ones!

VARONA: I do everything I can to keep them in the dark as to his whereabouts. I don't think they suspect a thing . . . Although sometimes in their eyes, it's as if they intuited that they're not supposed to recognize anything relating to their father . . .

BORIS: Hmm . . . it's possible. (*ready to leave*) Well, Varona Gurakevna, have courage. I must be on my way to the station now. (*kisses her on the forehead*) Good-bye, Vara. See you soon.

VARONA: When are you going to come back, Boris Kolovitch?

BORIS: I don't know exactly. Perhaps at the beginning of the month. Give your kids a kiss for me.

VARONA: Good-bye, Uncle. See you soon and thank you very much. (BORIS *leaves through the back.* VARONA *remains pensive. A sudden impatience possesses her. She continues setting the table, arranging some objects, takes out a book to read and, after a few seconds, throws it and puts her ear to hallway door just before sitting back down.* ILITCH *and* NIURA *enter upstage.* VARONA *gets up anxiously*) And Zuray?

NIURA *and* ILITCH (*dressed as komsomolki*): Good evening, Mother. How was your day, Mom? (*They kiss her.*)

VARONA: Where's Zuray? I said.

NIURA: You already know, Mom. It's too early for her to leave work. (*Behind them, enter* VLADIMIR.)

VLADIMIR: Mother, good evening. How is my Mom? (*kisses* VARONA)

ILITCH (*suddenly, reading a newspaper*): "Serious interruptions in the General Electric of Dnieprostroi." (*indignant*) Again! Sabotage yet again! (VLADIMIR *looks closer at the newspaper*; ILITCH *keeps reading.*) "A severe investigation is under way in the technical administration of the station. There are indications that suggest it is another act of sabotage . . ."

VLADIMIR (*who has taken the newspaper*): For sure it was the Germans.

VARONA: I just love the Russian internationalists who don't want to recognize that, today, among nations and races there isn't anything but prejudice, revengeful instincts, and deaf rivalries. (ILITCH *paces angrily.*) What's proved by these sabotages of foreign engineers?

NIURA: What else are they going to prove except that the universal love communists predict is couched in utopia? Period.

VARONA: Utopia the country has been paying for with its blood since the Soviet took power.

VLADIMIR (*who has finished reading the news*): Yes, sir. To my understanding, the only one responsible for all that is the government. Why isn't the decision made to throw out those German technicians? Don't they know that in every German—bourgeois or proletarian—an enemy of Russia surreptitiously sleeps?

ILITCH: Not in the worker, Vladimir. No. That's already been said and proven: an immense abyss, in Germany as everywhere else, separates the soul of the worker from the soul of the bourgeois, large or small . . . (*shrieking voice in the hallway*)

FIRST VOICE: And let's suppose that's so!

VARONA (*moving her hand to her ear*): These guys again!

SECOND VOICE: What do you know, son of a kulak? The resurrection of the dead is a reactionary fact and has nothing to do with the Marxist explanation of history. It deeply upsets the people who come back to life. They're a bunch of wanderers.

FIRST VOICE: Who are you to talk? Read the ABC of communism! . . .

SECOND VOICE: But suppressing fatigue, a vital problem, is a physical, animal fact!

FIRST VOICE: And all facts are physical . . . (*The voices withdraw.*)

SECOND VOICE: Have you read Dostoevsky? Yes or no? Dostoevsky says clearly . . .

VLADIMIR: Suppressing fatigue! What a problem!

VARONA: Exactly! Marotitch would be better off sewing buttons back onto his britches.

NIURA: Which he always leaves open! (*starts darning her socks*)

VARONA: And what's worse is that these clowns don't do anything, except get drunk.

ILITCH: They'd get a good lashing, if I was on the inspection team looking into their radio station.

VARONA: What's more, we live in the middle of a wholesale food market . . .

NIURA: A good lashing, says Ilitch. Only those screams would justify it . . .

ILITCH: Yet we shouldn't exaggerate our rigor either. One must not forget that these defects are nothing more than a manifestation of the natural upheavals proper to the development of a new society . . .

VLADIMIR: Aha! So then you forgive them?

ILITCH: I just mean that they're only partially responsible for it.

VLADIMIR: Partially? We could suppose. But for that portion of responsibility, would you ask them for their books? To whom do they surrender them? They live and work as they please. And if this is how it is, it's precisely because of this tolerance, indulgence, or indifference that the Soviet observes with them, as though the loss of various generations is indirectly preferred.

NIURA: Various? We're entering the third.

ILITCH: Excluding this youth sector that surrounds us, which is nothing more than the remnants of the old "intelligentsia," the survival of the old bourgeois notion of what intellectuals should be: bohemians, slackers, alcoholics, madmen . . .

VLADIMIR: Which doesn't take away from the fact that, whether you like it or not, this is the prevailing sort of intellectual in the Soviet.

ILITCH: It's not in the hands of the Soviet, or in anyone else's, to abolish from night to day the intellectual generations of many centuries by decree.

NIURA: However, it has abolished—and by decree—other older institutions and laws, even circumstantial with human nature, like private property, for example . . .

VLADIMIR: And universal suffrage . . .

VARONA: And freedom of religion . . .

ILITCH: And the right to be lazy and the right to exploit your neighbor . . . No one hears about that!

NIURA: And the VAPP? Hasn't it been created by decree? Doesn't it exercise the most hateful literary tyranny? Isn't it the VAPP and its unquestioned, arbitrary directives that penetrate and strangle the minds of today's youth—and not the bourgeois tradition as you believe?

ILITCH: Don't waste your breath. In the first place, you ignore that what characterizes the intelligentsia is—

VLADIMIR: Of course I ignore it, since in the Soviet this "intelligentsia" has never existed and never will exist.

ILITCH: The new intellectuals aren't those (*points to the room on the right*) that we've got there. The new intellectuals are elsewhere and you know it: they're in the factories, in the mines, in the fields, in the laboratories . . . (VLADIMIR *and* NIURA *start laughing.*) Laugh all you want! What's important is that we correct an error: the new thinkers and artists are being fostered by the proletariat right this very minute. The rest, I repeat, are nothing more than the recalcitrant fodder of the past.

NIURA: Stop, please! Take the official statistics: last year, 75 percent of the largest college stipends were given to students from a bourgeois background.

VLADIMIR: Pow! Knockout!

ILITCH: And who, may I ask, has provided instruction to this 75 percent? Is it not the Soviet? Answer me that.

VARONA: Polemics once again!

ILITCH: Aren't they the workers who from the start have laid the foundation of this new university?

VARONA: Enough already, Ilitch!

ILITCH: You can crunch the numbers—

VARONA: Didn't you hear me?

ILITICH: After all, you're right, Mother: silence is a better option (*returns to his newspapers*).

VLADIMIR: Anyway, you can't say that the Totchas and the Marotitchs have grown up in the debacle of the civil war and that they do nothing but reflect the defects and imbalances of the times?

ILITCH: But they're barely twenty years old!

VARONA: Silence!

NIURA: Leave it alone, Vladimir. To each his own criteria . . .

ILITCH: To each his social class, you mean to say, and we agree (*pauses*).

VARONA: Meanwhile, it's going on nine o'clock and here we are, with the table set, waiting for Zuray (*ironically*), who's still at work . . .

NIURA: Until she becomes a komsomolka like this one here (*pointing to* ILITCH), and she signs up on a day as early as next week.

VARONA: That's it! . . . as long as I'm alive, we shall see about that . . .

VLADIMIR (*yawning loudly*): Ahhhhhhhhh! Anyways, Mother, are we going to eat?

VARONA: Let's wait a while longer . . .

VLADIMIR: I'm just so hungry . . .

VARONA: Ten minutes more and if she doesn't arrive . . . we'll have to eat supper without her (*goes to the hall and listens*).

VLADIMIR: What to do for ten minutes? Write poems? Fall seriously ill and die of boredom? . . .

ILITCH: Your club isn't far from here: go see your comrades . . .

VLADIMIR: The comrades of my club? What for?

ILITCH: To change your mind . . . to invest that extra energy and time of yours in something worthwhile.

VLADIMIR: Ah! Do workers have ideas?

ILITCH: Try to answer that question for yourself . . . The collective, you know, despite all its problems, cures neurasthenia without causing pain . . .

VLADIMIR (*scoffing*): The collective! (*scoffs again*) The col-lec-tive.

ILITCH: Unlike you, workers don't have time to burn, reading, drawing, and everything else . . .

VLADIMIR: Forced laborers don't have time to burn either. So what?

ILITCH (*sharply*): With one difference: the forced laborers of the Soviet laugh, sing, and amuse themselves. And what do you mean by "forced laborers" anyway? Am I a forced laborer? Are you? And everyone else, forced laborers? Aren't you yourself repeating every chance you get that the only gainful people in the Soviet are the workers? What do you say to that? Come on.

VARONA (*returning*): If you guys don't stop arguing this instant, I'm leaving.

NIURA: And I am too, Mom. I'm going to go darn my socks in Red Square.

VARONA: Listening to you two, one would think you're not siblings but enemies about to face off . . .

ILITCH: Unfortunately, Mother, we're not far from that . . .

VARONA (*violently*): What! Please!

VLADIMIR (*thumbing through a magazine, reflecting, ironic*): Hmm . . . It is undoubtedly the determinism of life . . . It is a fact . . . The determinist law rules over everything. Isn't that it, brother Ilitch?

ILITCH (*his blood boiling*): Are you going to allow this, Mother, that they gang up on me?

VARONA (*flighty*): But read, write whatever you want instead of getting upset.

NIURA: Shoot! We can't even talk about what we want to anymore . . .

ILITCH: But what do you get out of speaking deviously about Marxism every day and precisely at the moment when I'm here? To what end? To get me to leave like so many other times?

NIURA: As you please.

ILITCH: Well, not this time! Now, I'm going to read Marx aloud! As loud as I can! (*leaves stage left*) At the top of my lungs!

NIURA: Is he being serious? (*All three wait with visible anxiety.*)

ILITCH (*returning with a book*): Here I have my Marxist reader. Let the dialogue commence. I'm at your disposal (*sits down and gets ready to read aloud*).

VLADIMIR: Hey, enough jokes already! I advise you not to turn on your faucet of recycled water . . . (*goes and grabs one of* VARONA's *religious books from the shelf*).

ILITCH (*with strong inflection*): With moral oxygen! With ideological oxygen! With this I shall penetrate your ears!

NIURA: Listen to the proletarian metaphor. Moral oxygen! Ideological oxygen! How original!

VLADIMIR (*with his book open as well, sits down facing* ILITCH): Ready! Let's go! But I warn you, if you start up one more time, I'll top you fourfold.

ILITCH: Enough, enough! The question is not knowing who should start, but knowing how it will end . . .

VARONA: Get out of here!

VLADIMIR: Come on, Mother. The duel is ready to go off!

ILITCH (*waiting to read*): Ready?

VLADIMIR: On your mark, get set, go! (*Both burst out reading simultaneously, overlapping one another, as loud as they can.*)

NIURA (*exaggerating a scoff*): A camera! A recorder! (ILITCH *abruptly stops reading.*)

VLADIMIR: What's the matter?

ILITCH: If you guys don't stop busting my chops, I'll start reading again.

VLADIMIR (*throwing his book triumphantly and making a trumpet with his hands*): Tu-tu-tu-tu-tu-tu! (NIURA *splits her sides in laughter.* VLADIMIR *very loudly*) Listeners: for the umpteenth time, the Red is on the ground!

ILITCH (*enigmatically*): Look at yourself in the mirror! (*triumphantly resumes his reading in silence;* VLADIMIR *looks at him, taking large victory strides*).

NIURA (*pretending to look for something in the dresser*): Yes . . . However, (*bitterly*) it's no small feat to recognize it . . . In the end, who always makes sure he gets his own? Ilitch! This guy!

ILITCH: Princess Osipovna Polianov sometimes forgets that she lives under the Dictatorship of the Proletariat . . .

VARONA (*exasperated*): Scorpion! (ILITCH *remains imperturbable, pauses.*)

NIURA: Vladimir, have you read the Khlebnikov I lent you last week?

VLADIMIR: Of course! Really impressive! (VARONA *enters the hallway to wait for* ZURAY.)

NIURA: Isn't it though? It left me with an obsessive emotion. It reaches the most unforeseen frontiers of human intelligence.

VLADIMIR: To be precise, I don't remember having read a subtler, more disconcerting work. (*looking at* ILITCH) Therefore, that book isn't for everyone.

ILITCH: Admire Khlebnikov! He's a fool! A decadent! A clown in argyles who thinks he's the president of the world!

VLADIMIR: In this domain, my dear little Soviet, you don't have the floor. We forbid you from judging works that are over your head, over the tip of your hat.

ILITCH (*powerfully scoffing*): What you haven't even managed to suspect, my dear little bowler-capped anti-Soviets, is that you've fallen right into one of his traps, since Khlebnikov sought nothing more than to make bourgeois jaws drop in fear of his genius! (*doubles over in laughter*).

NIURA: You Marxist puppet! What can some squalid materialists know about pure creations of the spirit, if they have only oven fumes for a soul?

VLADIMIR: For example, do you by chance comprehend the akeists?[137]

NIURA: And the hardliners?

VLADIMIR: And the Adamists?

NIURA: And the Friends of the Hammer?

VLADIMIR: And the Shock Battalions of Memory?

NIURA: And the painters with eyeglasses?

VLADIMIR: And the bygoners,[138] do you comprehend them?

ILITCH (*slowly*): And the honorary tzarists, do you guys comprehend them? (VLADIMIR *and* NIURA *grow quiet*)

VARONA (*returning, frowning*): Supper time! Right now! (*with supreme impatience*) For me, a cup of tea. (*to* NIURA) But later on, naturally. Only when you guys have finished.

NIURA: No, Mom, no. First you'll have supper with us.

VARONA: No. I don't have an appetite.

VLADIMIR: You have to eat something solid, Mom.

VARONA (*very concentrated, absent*): Eat supper, I beg you . . .

NIURA: That daughter of yours! What a punishment!

ILITCH: Mom, eat something with the three of us . . . (*Seated at the table, all look at* VARONA *indecisively, who endeavors to disguise her extreme anxiety.*)

NIURA: You don't eat . . . You don't sleep . . . It's suicide! (*Leaning over,* VARONA *crumbles up a napkin with her fist.*)

ILITCH: Zuray is late for supper, it's true, but that's no reason to work yourself up, Mom . . .

From *The River Flows between Two Shores* 285

VLADIMIR (*with bitterness to* ILITCH): Oh, for you, it's not such a serious reason, of course.

NIURA: You've got to be reasonable, Mom. (*hugging her*) Besides, the three of us are with you. (VARONA *is weeping in silence;* VLADIMIR *and* ILITCH *violently throw their napkins on the table and one by one turn their backs toward one another, taciturn;* NIURA *to* VARONA) I'm going to look for her! Okay, Mom? (ILITCH *stands up, grabs his hat and sullenly goes out onto the street without uttering a word.*)

VARONA (*more hurt upon seeing him leave*): You get out of here too! Leave me alone!

NIURA: Us too, Mom? Don't kick us out!

VARONA (*moving from pain to violence*): I want to be alone! Alone! Do you understand? (NIURA *and* VLADIMIR *look for their hats.*) Get out of here! What are you waiting for?

Slowly, VLADIMIR *and* NIURA *leave. Alone,* VARONA *paces back and forth, agitated, then slumps down into a chair. She perks her ear to the hallway. The upstage door softly creaks open and* SPEKRY *sticks in his head.* VARONA *has now stood up.*

SPEKRY (*quietly, confidentially*): Excuse me, madame . . . Good evening . . .

VARONA (*confused*): How can I help you?

SPEKRY (*closes the door, looks around, and approaches* VARONA): I've been sent by the prince, your husband . . .

VARONA: What? (*overcome by a profound disturbance*).

SPEKRY (*maliciously insinuating*): Yes, madame. He's staying here, close by, very close, in the little square. He's a bit tipsy, to be honest, but he's come sincerely to see you . . .

VARONA (*reacting*): Get out of here! Get out!

SPEKRY: He has explained everything to me, and it's obvious that he's not stopped adoring you, and that—

VARONA: Get out, I said!

SPEKRY: . . . he adores you and loves you . . .

VARONA (*showing him the upstage door with irrepressible disgust*): You wretched man! Leave this house at once! . . .

SPEKRY (*prying*): Might not something be weighing on you? There's something in those eyes . . . in that mouth! . . .

VARONA: Get out! I'm going to scream! (*cupping her ears*) And call for help!

SPEKRY: You are lonely. They are still young . . . Enjoy them.

VARONA (*in a scream*): Help!

Mumbling a sardonic laugh, SPEKRY *disappears. Alone again,* VARONA, *a prisoner of her own angst, approaches the upstage door, listens, comes back, hesitates, turns to put her ear against the hallway wall, reflects, pauses. Someone knocks on the door. With her back to the door,* VARONA *quietly covers her face with her hands, standing still, pale, shaking. They knock again on the door, which creaks open and* FATHER VAKAR *cautiously sticks his head in and, casting a gaze around the room, moves forward, step-by-step, very prudently, toward* VARONA. *Her face still covered, she mutters with a quivering voice.*

VARONA: Go away! Go away! You'd better get out of here!

VAKAR (*severely, though paternally*): Don't speak. You would've just taken him in again. (VARONA, *recognizing the voice as* VAKAR's, *gasps, frozen in place.*) Maybe he saw me and was deterred from entering.

VARONA (*imploring*): Father Vakar!

VAKAR: Varona Gurakevna, maybe the love you have for your children, and especially for Zuray, who resembles him so much, is actually for none other than your husband . . .

VARONA: Oh, Father! Not that!

VAKAR: Then what wall confines you to a depraved man who abandons his family to live a life of scandal and vice?

VARONA: Perhaps because he's the father of my children . . .

VAKAR: Now, maybe you've forgotten that, out of the two disasters of your life—his alcoholism and the revolution—he's the one who's most at fault?

VARONA: How can I forget, Father?

VAKAR: Indeed, back in 1917, if instead of crawling through those old red-light dives, he had set out to save your fortune from the Soviet paws, your existence and that of your children would be quite different.

VARONA: He has dragged us through all disgrace . . . through all dishonor . . .

VAKAR: Tell me, Varona, with complete sincerity: how do you currently feel about him? Tell me the truth once and for all. Are you still set on working things out with him?

VARONA: No, Father, never . . .

VAKAR: Never? And, yet . . .

VARONA: Working things out with him, Father? No.

VAKAR: . . . if only you could've heard yourself but a moment ago . . . Oh, the way you were talking about him! . . .

VARONA: Father!

VAKAR: Your flesh dreams of his, aspires to it, perhaps even to your regret. Don't deny it, my child: abysses attract.

VARONA: But, Father, I suffer from something else . . . a more tyrannical, atrocious obsession.

VAKAR: I know your character, you won't confess. You'll secretly brood over the tormenting pulse of your blood, even though you know that revealing our conscience to the Creator lifts from us much of the weight of our guilt. Wretched woman, do you relish the greedy torture of sin? (VARONA *cries;* VAKAR *goes up to her, fed up.*) Varona Gurakevna, look me in the eyes! Face-to-face! Do you intend to besmirch your children by making them think that their father will return? Do you intend to tell them he's in Moscow? I refuse to think that the idea of getting Osip back has entered your head, which would go against all my advice and once again put you at fault in the eyes of morality and religion. You have been forewarned: A home with a pervert of his kind as head would be an insult, derision of the sacrament and the matrimonial union . . .

VARONA: Woe betide me, Father! (*She collapses into a chair, weeping.*)

VAKAR: Have courage, Varona! In all sincerity, what do you think about your husband?

VARONA: Father . . . you already know: I've wanted to kill the final remnants of my love with the cilice . . . I've lashed myself brutally, furiously, desperately . . . and then . . . about two months ago, when my flesh and soul, my heart and conscience, started to feel released from his image . . . (*hesitates*).

VAKAR: Don't hold back—the Savior is listening!

VARONA: . . . suddenly, Father, I experienced the blow of the cilice, bloodying my skin upon contact . . . a strange sensation that seeped through my whole body in a sort of intoxication . . . a mysterious and at once painful and disturbing feeling . . . a kind of mystical pleasure of suffering and bleeding for him . . . (*hides her face in her hands*).

VAKAR: Unfortunate woman! That's why the inflection on your words of rejection, a moment ago, revealed a plea of your weakness! . . .

VARONA (*with her face still hidden in her hands*): Oh, the regret, Father! How shameful!

VAKAR: That's what I was saying. When you talk about Zuray, a subtle, imperceptible, though sharp and tenacious tone of passion for her rings through your words, your gaze, your silence . . .

VARONA: Protect me, Father.

VAKAR: You obsess over her and, by wrapping your arms around Zuray, you try to escape your conjugal complex.

VARONA: Oh, Father, that's not why I love her! . . .

VAKAR: Yes it is, Varona, that's why you prefer her over your other three children.

VARONA: I love her because she's come into the world during the hardest and saddest of circumstances in life . . .

VAKAR: Foolish woman! Just like before, you continue to deceive me!

VARONA (*absorbed in thought about* ZURAY): And I shall never be able to resign myself to losing her. She is my entire existence! Out of all my children, she's the one who's still innocent, tender, and loyal. (VAKAR, *concerned, paces slowly*.) Ilitch, now completely converted to Bolshevism, has become a komsomol member. Niura and Vladimir— why pretend?—they've placed their hearts outside the house . . .

VAKAR: Those are the laws of Nature.

VARONA: If the Reds now take Zuray away from me, what will I be left with? . . . This morning, she started reading in silence, leaning on her elbows at the table. I stood here watching her for quite a while. The expression on her face, Father, is so noble, so sensitive . . . Just seeing her is compensation for my horrible misfortune. She wraps me up in peace, eases my pain, restores my zest for life. Her inspiration, her presence at my side makes me, to put it this way, fortunate . . .

VAKAR: Nothing could be more natural . . . more understandable.

VARONA: If I just have my daughter—ah, Father—how much easier life would be for me! What fate has become of me! This nosedive of my life! This sinister man, Osip! This hellish society! This constant hair-raising fear that one day Zuray could become a komsomolka too and leave the house to join the Reds. It's torture, Father Vakar!

VAKAR: Varona Gurakevna, listen to me. You're threatened by one precipice alone, and it's that you continue to be tied to your husband. Everything inside you gravitates around you. It's stronger than your will, than your reason, perhaps even stronger than your own heart . . .

VARONA (*timidly hesitating*): Sometimes . . . I think that maybe his presence, his return to our home . . .

VAKAR (*shocked*): What do you mean to say?

From *The River Flows between Two Shores* 289

VARONA: Maybe it would fix everything . . .

VAKAR: You relapse! You relapse again like so many other times! You hellish creature!

VARONA (*with a distracted expression*): Without him, I feel defenseless. Without him, it's the disorder of the family, the chaos . . . I'm going to lose my mind . . .

VAKAR: Fear Heaven, Varona Gurakevna! (VARONA *weeps in silence.* VAKAR *removes a crucifix from his soutane and raising it up with both hands*) Come, Varona.

VARONA (*approaching him*): Father . . . (*bows her head in front of the crucifix*).

VAKAR (*with the crucifix on high*): Stay right where you are, collect yourself, and place your whole soul in your ear to listen to the Sacred Heart of Our Lord beating all around you.

VARONA: Yes, Father . . . (*silence and short pause*).

VAKAR (*gravely, very concentrated*): In the name of the Father, Son, and the Holy Spirit, I forbid you from thinking about your husband under any pretext whatsoever, from being with him, looking for him, and even calling him by name. He's a soul irreversibly condemned by Heaven. Jesus sees you, Varona Gurakevna! Heed his order, his holy word! I thee warn! Obey him! Amen . . . (*short silence, then* VAKAR, *with great unction, blesses* VARONA. *He puts the crucifix back and, gravely, paternally*) As for the situation with your children, don't get in the way of the course of things. Have faith: everything will work itself out. This relationship between your stubbornness for Osip and your fear of losing Zuray is real, I repeat, but the day you forget about Osip forever you'll become someone else, more tolerant of your children, more tolerant of their ideas, and, let me add, they may even be indifferent to you.

VARONA: I don't believe it, Father.

VAKAR: Yes, Varona. At the bottom of your problem with your children is a question of the second order, just sociopolitical issues. What's essential is the morality of our life, the salvation of our souls in the Lord.

VARONA: But they spend less and less time at home! They spend all their time in the factory and their clubs! And, I can sense it, Zuray is breaking away.

VAKAR: Faith, Varona, I repeat! Let divine mercy illuminate you!

VARONA: Just the idea of seeing her succumb to that Bolshevik gangrene makes me go crazy, sends me off the deep end . . .

VAKAR: Beg the Almighty to give you the humility to overcome! (*suddenly, footsteps are heard,* VAKAR *lowering his voice*) Humility, my daughter! I shall return next week. See you very soon. Varona. Humility and more humility.

VARONA (*also lowering her voice*): I'll see you very soon and thank you, Father. Thank you. (VAKAR *leaves upstage, followed by* VARONA, *pause.*)

VOICE OF VARONA (*in the hallway, addressing a third person, with surprise*): What are you doing here? Are you eavesdropping?

VOICE OF GIRL (*embarrassed*): I'm not eavesdropping, madame.

VOICE OF VARONA: Then what were you doing hiding over there?

VOICE OF GIRL: I was looking for my mom.

VOICE OF VARONA: Does she live in this building?

VOICE OF GIRL: No, but a lady walked down the street and came in here, and I thought she was my mom. She went up the stairs, and, suddenly, I couldn't see her anymore. I live in an orphanage. My name is Saloja Dajchin.

VOICE OF VARONA: You say you live in the orphanage? Come in for a moment.

VOICE OF GIRL: Oh, no, madame, it's very late!

VOICE OF VARONA (*insisting*): Just for a moment and then you'll leave.

VARONA *returns from backstage, followed by the* GIRL, *whose face—that of an impressively pure peasant—reflects the immense desolation of the orphan. She's wearing bright, new clothes.*

VARONA: Sit down! (*offers her a seat and looks her over*) What did you say your name is?

GIRL: Saloja Dajchin, madame (*keeps looking at the room*).

VARONA: And you live in the orphanage.

GIRL: Yes. My mother came to see me this afternoon. She came from Rovorroe. Do you know Rovorroe?

VARONA: Rovorroe, yes I do. (*sitting close to the* GIRL, *facing her*) That's pretty far.

GIRL: She came to tell the director that I should be educated for the Soviet and I should become a komsomolka, but I don't want to. I wanted to leave with my mom.

VARONA: What? I don't understand; why then did you run away from your mom's house?

GIRL: My mom told me to become a komsomolka and, since I didn't want to, I escaped. They caught me here.

VARONA (*touched*): Poor little girl! And your dad, what did he say?

GIRL: My dad died, madame. A kulak killed him. Mom detests the kulaki and the bourgeoisie.

VARONA: Ah . . . And you? Do you hate them too?

GIRL: Yes, I do too, madame. They threw my dad into an oil pit, over in Rovorroe . . .

VARONA (*terrified*): How awful! And why did they do that?

GIRL: Because he was Bolshevik.

VARONA: Is that what your mom said?

GIRL: Yeah, and everyone else says so too. (VARONA *thinks about the* GIRL, *moved by diverse sentiments, and the* GIRL *continues*) I was hanging from my mom this afternoon so that she wouldn't leave me, but she has taken off without me. So I escaped from the orphanage to look for her . . . My mom will be leaving for Rovorroe soon . . .

VARONA: How old are you?

GIRL: Ten, madame.

VARONA: And do you know how to read?

GIRL: Yes. I'm just two years shy of getting my diploma.

VARONA: Hey, that's good. So you're more or less educated. And do you have any siblings?

GIRL: No, madame. My mom and I lived alone.

VARONA: Poor little girl . . . (*staring at her*) You unfortunate, poor little thing! I can see in your face and the way you speak that you're very affectionate, very sensitive . . . (*takes her by the hands, and the* GIRL *lowers her eyes*) Don't become a komsomolka, my little girl. Your mom will eventually call you and keep you at her side . . . (*and as the* GIRL *shakes her head no*) She won't? How do you know?

GIRL: My mom hates my dad's murderers. She suffers so much the death of my dad and, seeing her cry so much makes me cry a lot too. Maybe she's right in wanting me to become a komsomolka . . .

VARONA (*placing her hands on the* GIRL's *hands*): But, my dear, what is becoming a komsomolka going to achieve? Your dad died and becoming a komsomolka isn't going to bring him back . . .

GIRL: Young people today are also against the kulaki. And when you see what they do sometimes, it makes you want to kill them! (*A flash passes through her eyes.*)

VARONA: Why would you want to kill them? Do they go around killing everyone's dad?

GIRL: The kulaki steal, beat, and kill! But . . . I don't want to be a komsomolka. The komsomolki don't spend any time at home; they barely live with their parents; they're always outside, working, and I never ever want to leave my mom!

VARONA (*stroking her hair*): Why . . . (*hesitates*) don't I have a daughter like you? . . .

GIRL: You don't have a daughter, madame?

VARONA: I do . . . Two daughters . . . Two . . . But, my daughters are very different . . .

GIRL: Two? (*staring at her*) Are you suffering too?

VARONA: Yes . . . a great deal . . . (*The* GIRL *abruptly stands up and kisses* VARONA *on the forehead.*)

GIRL: Now it's very late, madame. I'm afraid I must go . . .

VARONA (*holding her back*): Where are you off to if you have nowhere to go?

GIRL (*nervously*): I'm going back to the orphanage to write to my mom and tell her that I'll never bring her misfortune again and that I'm going to become a komsomolka just as she pleases. Good-bye, madame. I'll come back . . . (*leaves running upstage.* VARONA, *sitting down, as if awakening from a siren's song, puts her tired head between her hands, deeply lost in thought.*)

CURTAIN

[JM]

Letters

Paris, May 14, 1924
Dear Pablo,

I'm so sorry I didn't give you a hug before you left. The news of your trip came to me as a surprise, and I was told by none other than the great Rey y Lama, in a vague, skittish way. But I then had the pleasure of receiving your letters addressed from Madrid, and they've done me so much good, first due to the intense affection I hold for you, and second, because here I've remained nostalgic for you, your generational encouragement, and brotherly support.

I'm confident you'll enjoy a warm reception among people of intelligence and social worth in Madrid. You're going to play a beautiful role with outstanding South American spirit that will lead you to experience enviable and praiseworthy moments. You, my dear Pablo, know this very well. I shall attain true inner fruition only as long as you rejoice, sing, be praised, and fully integrate. May you succeed, Pablo. Work be thy name. Steer clear of the dandies and spiritual posers. Work, Pablo, and be nourished by your unrest, your talent, and your immense heart. So much I wish and hope for.

Don't forget about me. Let's see if, with Sassone and that friendly talented Angélica Palma, you can get me something in the magazines of Madrid, for some of the things I've been working on here. Don't forget about me.

Tomorrow I'm going to see Moreira. Thanks very much for your attentive recommendation. Maybe one of these days he'll return from Meudon, where so many Parisians love to go, because next summer it's apparently going to be terrible. Meanwhile, I live over there, and only three or four days do I come to Montparnasse. Today I write to you from La Rotonde. You'll suppose so much by the stationary I'm writing on: pardon its meticulous lines.

Don't forget about me. Get me something, kindest, magnanimous Pablo, as a correspondent or chronicler of Paris. Once you're settled in and rested up, don't forget about me.

Strong, fraternal, grateful regards,
César Vallejo

I forgot. I picked up the suitcase at the Legation. I appreciate that. Its contents have done me very well. Thank you very much. Jiménez, Ibáñez, and Gálvez send their regards. [JM]

TO PABLO ABRIL DE VIVERO

Paris, May 26, 1924
Dear Pablo,
I wrote to you at the beginning of this month. I suspect you must already be at the Palace of the Borbones, in the company of the minister to present your credentials. Now I imagine the days of revelation and understanding you'll be savoring in Madrid. I hope that, when you have a cordial disposition, peace, and time to write to me, I'll learn from your lines humorous details about Madrid, taken at random and in broad brushstrokes, as is your style. Good, joy-filled moments await me, isn't that true, my dear, unforgettable Pablo?

I've broken off from an unpublished novella (you know well that wretched word) a chapter you'll allow me to share with you. I don't think you'll care for it, as I'm not satisfied with it either. It's custom-made *for the most demanding taste* of the public. Therefore, Pablo, don't you think you might be able to see that it gets published? As always, in exchange for a few pesetas for your work. What can I do? I need to figure out how to get by. I don't really have a career or profession in anything. However, I long to work and live my life with dignity, Pablo! I'm no bohemian: the misery hurts me terribly, and it's no party for me as it is for others. You've seen my situation in Paris. Is it that I don't want to work? I've gone to the factories scores of times. Could I have been born completely unarmed for this fight in the world? Perhaps I was. But this daily fright clouts me right in the will, strangles it, and seems to have taken it as its favorite prisoner. In the midst of my most horrible hours, it's my will that trembles, and the breadth of its movement goes from one deadly ledge where a man must let death come to another ledge where he's tempted to conquer the world with blood and fire! But my will is sterile, crippled.

I went looking for Moreira, but couldn't find him. Tomorrow I'll look again.

Some francs from America finally reached me. They're a terrible lot. They've only sent me a portion of what they owe, promising to wire the remainder shortly. With this bit of scratch I'm getting by, and I want to take advantage of this relative peace it's afforded me, to find a job for when it runs out, which *irremediably* will be soon enough. (I don't know why in my mind I see one of your most spiritual attitudes, through this memory, as I comment on the irremediable way that money runs out. If we were together, talking about this, you'd give my woe such an agile, noble, and juvenile tint that all my momentary bitterness and ungratefulness would've dissolved in chuckling and lyrical solace.)

I keep your encouraging words in the front of my mind, the ones in your letter from Madrid. They energize me so often. I'll look forward to hearing news from you soon, and I send you my warm regards.

César

[JM]

TO ALCIDES SPELUCÍN

[Paris, July 1924]

Dear Alcides,

I've just gotten out of a horrible crisis of body, soul, and hope. Sick and poor, wearing a funeral suit even at the bottom of my heart, I've felt the whirlwind of fate's brutal strength. But everything has passed. Come on. Even now I have to restrain my pain. What can I do!

Julio sent you a cable. The day before yesterday we received 1,500 francs. I await news from you to find out where these funds come from that you have just sent me, with such brotherly affection and kindness. My soul is fraternally grateful too and sends you affection from overseas.

I'm going to ask you a favor. As soon that you receive these lines I beg you to write to Néstor, to Juli, Department of Puno, by way of Mollendo, telling him my situation is bad, and that the ten libras he has to send me he should send to you instead. Do this as soon as possible. After receiving the ten libras from Néstor, I ask you to wire them to me immediately, although we'll have to discount the cost of the cable, which won't be cheap. It doesn't matter if only a small portion of that money makes it to me; it would be something anyway, and something would be better than nothing.

Alejandro Sux is offering me a position with a news outlet in Paris that in September is going to launch a magazine in Spanish and French, called *Nuestra América*. I'll be waiting. We soon shall see. Oh, this fight, tenacious, patient, desperate! Will I never be rewarded? No matter what, one must face up to it, right down to the end.

Write to me, all of you. And to you, Antenor, and all our unforgettable brothers, I send my adoration and aching soul.

César

Julio and I will stay in Paris for a few more months. We'll let you know if we leave. Spain is frightful. They tell me that we're more likely to die of misery there than anywhere else in the world.   [JM]

TO PABLO ABRIL DE VIVERO

Paris, October 19, 1924

Dear Pablo,

It seems that back luck is determined to do me in. I write you this letter from the Hospital Charité, Boyer Room, bed 22, where I've just been operated on for an intestinal hemorrhage. My dear friend, I've suffered twenty horrible days of physical pains and incredible spiritual battles. In life, Pablo, there are hours of darkness shut off from all consolation. There are hours more, perhaps much more sinister and terrible than the tomb itself. I didn't know what they were until this hospital showed me, and now I'll never forget them. In the process of recovery, I often cry for any reason at all. An infantile facility for tears keeps me saturated in an immense mercy for things. I often remember my house, my parents, and lost loves. One day I'll be able to die, in the course of this hazardous life that has befallen me to live, and so I shall see myself, then just as now, an orphan of all family encouragement and even of love. But my luck has already landed. It's written. I'm a fatalist. I think everything has been written.

The doctor thinks I'll leave the hospital in six to eight days more. Life, no doubt, is waiting for me on the street, to beat me whenever it pleases. Bring it on. There are things that must follow their natural course, and they can't be stopped.

I've read the kindhearted reply from Leguía regarding the grant. I hope they don't snatch it out of my hands.

As soon as I'm better I'll write to him with my thanks. No matter what, Pablo, I beg you to be mindful of securing the grant.

From my bed of misfortune, brotherly regards and all my thanks.

César   [JM]

TO PABLO ABRIL DE VIVERO

Paris, November 5, 1924
Dear Pablo,

My sickness has dragged on and on. Yesterday marked a month that I've been in bed. Since the operation, I've had another hemorrhage, and it's nearly taking me away. The night of Sunday the twenty-seventh could have been fatal. Horrible! But today I am better again. Since Tuesday, I have been in my room, still bedridden. The doctor told me to stay in bed and take care of myself.

Pablo! There are hard, cruel people in the world. There are frightening pains, and death is an evident, dreadful fact. There are people hard in heart, and one can die of misery. Fine. But what can one do? I again believe in the Lord Jesus Christ. I've become religious again, but taking religion as the supreme consolation in life. Yes. Yes. There must be another world of refuge for the many on earth who suffer. Otherwise, existence is inconceivable, Pablo.

In looking at my desperate situation, Cornejo has finally requested a ticket for my return to Peru. Postmarked October thirtieth, the process began. I've already asked him to say that, yes, I will return to Peru. But I beg you, dear Pablo, please tell them in Lima to give me the ticket as soon as possible and then tell them in London to give me the value of the ticket in cash. With that money I'll be able to live until I receive the grant from Spain, which we're expecting to come in January. In any case, see if there's any incompatibility between the ticket and the grant. If there is, I'd naturally prefer the grant, every time. If the ticket would cause problems for the grant, I'll forego the ticket. Doesn't that seem right, Pablo? However, I'd imagine both issues could be resolved in Lima, since the ticket can be acquired in a day, whereas the grant, not until January. So, they don't seem incompatible to me. Anyways, you'll see what's best and your great heart will do for me what it has always done: Good.

If the ticket comes through, hopefully it will be soon, as you already can imagine my distressing economic situation.

Good-bye, my unforgettable Pablo. May God protect you and may you enjoy well-being.

Kind regards from your friend,
César

I'll reply to Leguía in the next couple days. Please let him know about my illness.

TO JUAN LARREA

Madrid, March 12, 1926

Juan,

I arrived at eleven o'clock last night. I'm going to have to stay here until Monday, because they haven't paid me yet. What I got today was a back payment, which I thought I had lost. I hope to pick up the other payment on Monday afternoon and that night I'll take the 9:30 train to arrive in Paris on Wednesday the seventeenth, at eight in the morning. So I'll write to Lasala right away.

Tomorrow I'll take the 7:45 train to Toledo. I need to take advantage of these days to get to know Spain some more. The day after tomorrow, Sunday, I'll go to El Escorial.

I'm writing to you from Café Anís Benavente in Plaza del Sol. I have had a beautiful day for a thousand different reasons: pay, the promise of future pay, diaphanous air, and pretty Spanish women in the streets.

Herrero left yesterday for Sigüenza. So I sent the package by land, as you had requested. I'm attaching the receipt. I managed to get it through customs without any funny business, that is, without paying any tariffs, thanks to the admirable air of my traveling mate, the toothy woman.

This afternoon I met Guillermo de Torre, introduced to me by a Chilean friend. They've invited me to his house tonight at seven, but I got out of it, saying I'd be returning to Paris tonight.

While I write to you, the orchestra of the café plays sad, sad Spanish tunes. I remember the Regence, the English girls from *The Thousand Harlequins*.[139] I think about Paris and the fact that, all in all, life is beautiful and kind. Be strong, Juan. Better, more interesting and dynamic days are still to come.

Do me a favor and drop by my hotel to tell them I've written you from Havre, saying I'll arrive in Paris on Wednesday and that I'll leave the hotel later and will stay there for another fifteen days. Go as soon as this letter reaches you, because it's not beyond them to throw out my things, since the rent is up on Tuesday and I won't arrive until Wednesday.

You can expect me on Wednesday. I'll phone you as soon as I get in so that we can have lunch together that day.

Strongest regards from your friend,

César

Vallecito sends his best.   [MLR]

TO RICARDO VEGAS GARCÍA

Paris, May 15, 1926
Dear Friend,

I have decided to send you a chronicle to be placed in *Variedades*, the magazine in which you generate so much enthusiasm with your generosity and brilliance. For this chronicle, I wish to be paid the amount that you deem suitable. Those of us without material goods in life have to do something to stay above water, each within his means. Good friends, like you, are able to help me out immensely. So stretch out your hand, if you would. Life is Paris is terribly hard, as you know.

If you find it suitable, I would ask that you let me know if I can send you chronicles regularly for *Variedades*, for which I would be paid a price that you would need to set. Naturally, the chronicles would go with photos. Furthermore, you would suggest the type of chronicles, the way they should be handled, and the payment method.

The good friendship that unites us and your notorious generosity and camaraderie inspire in me the blind hope for welcoming news from you. Meanwhile, you can count as you please on your colleague and friend, with my best regards, and thanks for your kindness in advance.

César Vallejo   [JM]

TO JUAN LARREA

Paris, July 26, 1926
Dear Juan,

I appreciate your kindness in sending me the money I borrowed from you, due to my distressing situation brought on by those sons of bitches at *Mundial* who've yet to pay me what they still owe me. What do you say? I'm bursting with indignation. I wouldn't have bothered you again, if I had received those payments from America as I was expecting to. I thank your blessed soul for your brotherly courtesy and interest in my life.

I've finished sending off *Favorables* to the four cardinal points of the world. North America, South America, Europe, and Istanbul. Two hundred copies have been sent. I've also placed some for sale in Spanish bookshops on rue Richelieu and rue Bonaparte. Every day I buy eight to ten Parisian magazines to see if they give us any play. So far, nothing. We'll see soon enough. One must wait. We've got to wait. I'll let you know when there's news.

I'm waiting for you to send me a photo of you and one of Diego for my article in *Mundial* of Lima and for *Alfar* of A Coruña. I've written to Picabia, Ribemont, Éluard, and Reverdy, sending them the magazine and requesting their contributions for August. I await their replies from one day to the next. Gris has written me and asked for your address in Madrid. I've already sent it to him: Hotel de la Estación-Vallecas-Madrid.

In general, Hispanic American circles are *étonnés*[140] by *Favorables*. They don't know whether they should laugh or cry. We, naturally, neither laugh nor cry, nor do we stop laughing or crying altogether. Meanwhile, we must wait. We've got to wait.

The old *montparnos* dogs send their regards. Faura left yesterday for London and didn't go to Nice. Pepe is in Deauville. Vallecito asked me to send his regards. He's going to write an article for *Variedades* of Lima, about *Favorables*, saying how much he liked it.

I hope that you'll come no later than the tenth, as you say in your letters. In any case, let me know the day and time of your arrival at Paris so that I can be there at the station.

I owe you 300 pesetas. If you get here before my grant money arrives, I'll have Pablo pick it up, and I'll pay you here. Anyway, I'm sending you my card so you can present it on the first to the paymaster. Life is becoming terribly expensive. You'll see when you get here. If it's within your means, would you lend me another 100 pesetas, as soon as possible, since I'm afraid to say that *Mundial* continues to keep its silence, and I'm on the verge of hitting rock bottom again. If you can, send me the 100 pesetas at your earliest convenience. As soon as I receive the money from *Mundial* I'll pay you back. You can count on it.

I've given *congé*[141] again at my hotel, so I can leave around the tenth, the date you return to Paris. I'll take it upon myself to find a hotel for us in the best conditions possible. In my next letter, I'll let you know what I came up with concretely.

I imagine it must be very hot over there and that you're screwing in superlative doses. Ah, you old dog! In the meantime, over here, Marie Louise keeps asking me about you, wanting, no doubt, to dance the Charleston with you in the hall and in the bed. I'll look forward to your reply soon.

All best regards from your brother,

César   [JM]

TO ALCIDES SPELUCÍN

Paris, September 14, 1926
Dear Alcides,

El libro de la nave dorada has filled my heart with memories and hopes, not only because of what it contains circumstantially with regard to our childhood, but also because of the greatness of the eternal song that breathes through its pages. Brother, you've managed to create a well-rounded, even-handed, definitive work, brimming with infinity. Víctor Raúl and I have read it with love for all our fraternity, and it has filled our eyes with tears.

Your book is a masterpiece, which will serve as a spiritual guide for the youth of America. I don't think there is a precedent in the continent of an original work of so much technical control and of such finished verbal mastery. Your book is a classic work in the sense of perfection of the word.

For that I send you an embrace from your brother,
César   [JM]

TO JOSÉ CARLOS MARIÁTEGUI

Paris, December 10, 1926
Dear Comrade,

I am expressing my thanks with regard to the kind review that you send me published in *Mundial*, concerning my literary work. Several passages of your affectionate essay are driven by such a will to comprehend me and they successfully interpret me with such penetrative agility, that while reading them I felt as though I were discovered for the first time and were revealed conclusively. Your essay is especially full of good will and talent. I am grateful, my dear comrade, for both of those things.

I have received *Amauta*. With fraternal, fervent sympathy, I am following the hardships and cultural endeavors of our generation, at whose head I see you standing alongside other sincere souls. In the next few days I'll gladly send you some work for *Amauta*, whose success and renovating action in America I celebrate wholeheartedly, since it is, as you say, "our message." I believe that this resonance must grow, thereby contributing to ever condensing the healthy Peruvian inspiration of our action across the continent and the world.

I will write to you shortly about the book that you request of me for Editorial Minerva. There's a chance that it will be ready soon.

Kind regards for all the good friends of *Amauta* and for you, all my best from your devoted comrade.

César Vallejo   [JM]

TO EMILIO ARMAZA

Paris, December 10, 1926
Dear Comrade,

What a pleasant surprise it has been for me to receive your book *Falo*. For some time now I've been thinking of writing you to ask for your new address and inquire about our friends. Your book has filled me with pleasure, and your affectionate card reminded me of those days in Lima, when we had drinks at the Paredes' on jirón de la Unión. I suppose you haven't forgotten.

Your book especially struck me with its disciplines of balance and measure. In these kinds of epilepsy, a work like this (eurhythmy and justness) does good and reconciles us with "the severe and apostolic numbers" that things eternally enjoy. Neither one mass more, nor one volume less. Your book *Falo* responds to this fundamental demand of life and art. Beyond this merit, truly exceptional in these times, your poems breathe Peruvianness, that is, humanity, with broad, salubrious, *titikaka* lungs. The straw of the *jalca* reverberates through *Falo*, against the snowdrift and for the fortune of domestic hominy and limestone. What beautiful stanzas pop white, white! I've really enjoyed it. A magnificent book, dear comrade. A strong embrace for that.

Write to me always and let me know about your new publications. I'll do the same. Give me news about our friends.

You can count as you please on your old friend and comrade from way back.

César Vallejo   [JM]

TO PABLO ABRIL DE VIVERO

Paris, July 24, 1927
Dear Pablo,

Xavier arrived yesterday and already seems better in health. He tells me that his arrival alone has filled him out *sur-le-champs*.[142] So much better. His stay here will surely do him good so he can confront his life vitally, de-literaturizing[143] himself as far as possible.

Only yesterday, I learned through Xavier of the minister's arrival and went to see him. He was in bed, sick. But I believe he's already feeling better today. I still haven't told him anything about my novel, as I await your opinion to decide how it should be handled.

It would mean requesting government funding for a French translation of my novel about American folklore, *Toward the Reign of the Shiris*, which I've finished and typed. As credentials, I point to the modest yet effective work I've done for some time now in the press to support Peru, and I say that the object of this French version of my novel is to promote and publicize in Europe Indo-American and particularly *Peruvian* culture. What I request in return for this book, which will be illustrated with wooden engravings of Incan motifs, is the sum of 500 Peruvian libras. Naturally the edition would become government property, and I'd merely take only one hundred of the total two thousand printed copies. Would this work? What are your personal thoughts about this? I don't know if the minister will agree and actually sponsor it. Won't Salomón's presence in the government hinder my application? Anyway, I ask you, dear Pablo, to answer me as soon as possible, giving your advice, which will sway me one way or the other. I certainly hope it will come before the minister leaves Paris, which I believe will be within eight days.

As for the grant, I frankly don't know what to do. Xavier must have mentioned the difficulties placed on us day by day. I'm rather for deciding against it, whatever the outcome. For a young man in his early twenties, it's good enough, but for me it's already very outdated to keep gnawing on so tiny a crumb. On the other hand, if nothing comes of my novel, I may liquidate my life with a single stroke and go to New York. I'm tired of this. It's terrible. Anyway, Pablo, you know how unsustainable it is.

The news of his new post in the embassy will come out tomorrow, as today is Sunday. I'll send you the newspapers. It's rudeness, alone, that you should return to unpaid work. When will the day of *redress* arrive?

You know how much I'm endeared to you, Pablo. I will assist Xavier with equal care here. Don't worry. Awaiting your next line, as a brother does, receive warmest regards from your grateful, unwavering friend.

César

[MLR]

TO LUIS ALBERTO SÁNCHEZ

Paris, August 18, 1927
Dear Colleague,

I am so grateful to you. You've always been so good to me. Your understanding spirit is great, which is why my brotherly embrace reaches you wholeheartedly.

I'm enclosing some newly harvested poems. You know, my dear Sánchez, that I'm a tightfisted miser when it comes to my unpublished things, and, if I open myself up to you, I do so in a pleasant impulse of intellectual sympathy. For friends as great as you, everything. That's why these poems have come to you. They're the first ones to see the public light since my departure from America. Even though they've continually asked me for poems, my vote of aesthetic conscience has been unshaken until now—a decision not to publish anything that doesn't fulfill a dear need of mine, so dear it's extraliterary. Now, my dear colleague, if you like you can publish the poems I've sent you. And I certainly hope you like them, as that would give me sincere joy. In this way, your reading them would pay in part for the generous stimulus I've always found in you.

Could you please let me know about your new works and intellectual concerns? You know there exists between us a good, sincere, and spiritual understanding and an enthusiastic admiration on my part for all you write.

Write to me and don't give me up as forgotten. Strong best from your unwavering friend and companion,

César Vallejo   [MLR]

TO PABLO ABRIL DE VIVERO

Paris, September 12, 1927
Dear Pablo,

I've just received your letter of the eighth, which suffered the delay of *La Razón*'s change of address. This office is on 26, avenue de l'Ópera, Ex-printer.

Your letter has made me reflect deeply and seriously. Your indications about the grant and my novel are very optimistic, owing to the affection and brotherly criteria with which you customarily treat anything that involves me. I'm grateful to you, dear Pablo, with all my soul. But, unfortunately, at present I'm going through an acute crisis of distrust in the success of all my affairs. Motives exist for this distrust: the strongest being the long years of useless, perhaps even harmful optimism with which I've lived in Europe, always clinging to the eternal eve of a better day that has never arrived. I say "harmful optimism," because, as you know, Pablo, nothing is more awful and more suicidal than a prolonged wait. Within this wait we can do nothing, given that we believe, from one instant to another, that things are going to change and that we'll be able to bring life into some other mirage. Till now I live immersed in a provisional parenthesis, always at the gates of another mode of existence that, I repeat, never arrives. This is how I take everything: with a provisional character. And so five years in Paris have gone by. Five years of waiting, without being able to take on anything seriously, nothing settled, nothing definitive, and menaced by a continuous economic shock that prevents me from undertaking or handling anything thoroughly. Is there anything more horrible? And it's no longer possible to postpone this deceitful situation any longer. I'm beginning to prefer definitive misery over the rickety insecurity of the future. I'm beginning to resign myself. I'm beginning to recognize that my true and only existential path is misery. It seems I'm mistaken in looking for economic security or, at least, bread at its hour or water at its hour. I was born for solemn poverty, and all that I do to avoid it will be useless, just as it has been so far. Apparently this isn't literature, since I depart from reality and head toward reality.

I thank you with all my heart for what you always do to help me get out of this situation, dear Pablo. I'm tired of waiting and don't want to tire you anymore with my requests and your running around.

You know what Madrid is. Our affairs drag on at an interminable pace. The Spanish and their environments are invulnerable. We know them well enough, and you know them better than I, because you've felt more closely that soporific Biscayan attitude. My misery outside of Madrid may not be as bad as it is within. The university demands a "certificate of attendance." The last time I went to collect it, that's what they said. This isn't a hypothesis of what might happen but what they've already demanded of me. I had to appeal to Jiménez de Asúa, whom I never thought I'd fall to, so that I could collect it. Any other way, I'd remain, even being in Madrid, without means to stay above water on a monthly basis.

I've reflected much about all of those things. I've compared everything. You know I've already suffered enough, to be precipitate. Here, in Paris, I'll confine myself for now to *La Razón* and to the sporadic payments of *Mundial* and *Variedades*. And after, we'll see what I do, when I get the ticket money to Peru: either I'll go to New York or stay in Paris.

It looks like corresponding holiday payments go through September. I ask you, in any case, to find out for sure about all this. Córdoba has offered, at the beginning, to collect in my name for August, and, not wanting to bother you again, I've given him the power to make the collection. A thousand thanks, Pablo, for your kind offer. As for Xavier, I've already indicated to him the content of your letter, and he tells me he'll write to you today. Xavier lives far from my hotel, near the Porte de Champerret. There it's calmer, somewhat in the countryside of Paris. He's better from his illness and tells me that what he lacks is only money to continue in his healing. We see each other with certain frequency, but not always, given the distance. I've observed that he's ready to go back to Madrid at the end of this month. I say "observed" because, as he wavers so much in his decisions, we should not rely much on what he says "by means of words." It would be suitable for him to do this, that's to say return to Madrid, as soon as possible. There are many reasons for that: for your peace of mind, for his own, and even from an economic standpoint.

I'm sorry you can't come to Paris, as I would've liked. It would've done much good for your health and spiritual well-being, and we would've talked at length about all our questions. Unfortunately, life here becomes more expensive by the day. The franc has certainly stabilized, but the price of everything continues to rise. Anyway, it would be magnificent were you to find a way of making your trip to Paris, even with sacrifices. I await further news.

Write and tell me what you'd like me to do for Paco's school. I'm always waiting for your instructions. My foot's already better.

I looked for Vuillermoz again and it seems he's on holiday. I've already told you, that this man is beginning to prove unreliable. I'm going to bear down on him every day. I haven't *La Gaceta* nor *El Sol*. Thanks for the Puno bulletin, which I'll return with my next letter. *El Repertorio* has also just published my article about you. Have you seen it yet? If you haven't, I could send you the issue, taking it from *Les Journaux*. Write to me always at 11, avenue de l'Ópera. It's very safe.

Affectionate greetings to Vallecito and for you, strongest regards from your grateful brother,

César   [MLR]

TO PABLO ABRIL DE VIVERO

Paris, October 19, 1927

Dear Pablo,

I've just received your telegram, which I'm answering immediately. We don't know if our presence alone is enough to receive the payment or if, once we're there, they'll ask us for something else, such as September's exam certificate, for example. I imagine the paymaster doesn't know that we've given up the scholarship and, therefore, requires our presence in Madrid, given that school is already in session. But I don't know if, to avoid the journey, it's advisable to tell them we're no longer students and that, as a consequence, we're under no obligation to be in Madrid. I fear our journey will be useless and force us to spend 700 francs we don't have. Pablo, I truly don't know what to do about this. Your telegram leaves me with insoluble doubt, because what they want could be an exam certificate. If this is the case, September's payment is lost and showing up leads to nothing.

It seems that, if we say we're no longer students, we may not need the exam certificate. But if they already know we've given up and we're still required to take the exam, we're lost, and there's nothing left to do. Anyway, I ask you to answer just how certain it is that they'll pay us for September based on our presence alone and without other requirements that are impossible to meet. I await your answer, ready to take the train the same day your telegram arrives, unless you tell me otherwise, to the extent that my presence won't be enough for payment. As for Xavier, he tells me he doesn't have the means to go to Madrid, nor does he see where he can get money for the journey. This is terrible. I don't have a cent either, but I'm going to see about a 500-franc loan. Xavier is completely broke and we're absolutely thrown by your news, which has fallen on us unexpectedly.

You'll receive this letter the day after tomorrow (on Friday), and I ask you to send me a telegram as soon as possible, so we know what course to take. I ask you, Pablo, so as to save time, to make a prompt decision. And for this favor, I offer a thousand apologies.

Anxiously awaiting news from you, I send the strongest embrace from your fraternal, grateful friend,

César

P.S.

If the September payment is lost, don't bother to telegram. Your silence will tell us there's no remedy. [MLR]

TO RAFAEL MÉNDEZ DORICH

Paris, February 17, 1928
Dear Rafael,
I've read your poems, and I know that in you there's a poet hunter of time and health. Insist, persist, and you'll see the words arrive when you call them very early. I hope you still go to *La Estación* and drink that nectar from Ica. Tomorrow I'll try to find the book you asked me for. Sadly there's not a bookstore that sells books recently published in Spain; they're late to arrive but arrive they do, and I promise I'll take care of it.
César Vallejo   [JM]

TO PABLO ABRIL DE VIVERO

Paris, March 17, 1928
Dear Pablo,
I've run all your errands, but haven't been able to see Vuillermoz yet. As soon as I see him, I'll hand over your letter, or, in the opposite case, I'll send it by mail. Then with Zevallos I'll see what needs to be done to adjust your account, according to your instructions.

Would you be so kind as to write to Solar in London, asking him to send me the necessary cash for my trip, which should be arriving today or tomorrow in London. Don't forget this errand, which you promised to do with such good will. According to your promise I still haven't asked this same favor of Zevallos, who would've recommended me to Mackehenie. If you can't make this recommendation, I'd be grateful if you could tell me, so as to look for the recommendation of Zevallos or someone else. In any case, let me know if you've written to Solar, for my government. Today I'll write to this gentleman alluding to your letter.

The truth is I don't deserve the least bit of help, in the Peruvian concept. The most unfortunate and obscure of Peruvian vagabonds get tickets and tickets in money. Recommendations cross in the air and rain down tickets, lodging, salaries, prizes, gifts, etc., etc. Only this poor native remains on the margin of the feast. It's really something. And it seems that even randomness feeds my misfortune: a technical error in the ministry still deprives me of something so modest and insignificant that others obtain in the blink of an eye. If we ascribe to the Marxist thesis (on which Eastman extrapolates), then the class struggle in Peru must reach these heights, which are full of reward for people like me, who live under the table at a bourgeois banquet. I'm not entirely sure if revolutions actually proceed from the pariah's rage, but if they do, in my life those "apostles" of America will find more than my fair share. Anyway, it's better to keep silent for now.

Strong best from your brother,

César

[MLR]

TO PABLO ABRIL DE VIVERO

Paris, April 26, 1928

Dear Pablo,

I've received the letter from Minister Leguía. Hopefully the claim is made to Lima as soon as possible. For my part, ten days ago I sent a letter by means of the diplomatic mailbag to Dr. Dulanto for Rada. If nothing comes of all this, then we'll see what's to be done. The truth is that it has to be settled in some way. Don't you think so?

Leguía's letter couldn't be harder or more hostile. My situation doesn't allow me to give it the response that it deserves. Everything in due time.

Meanwhile, since I was counting on this money that never arrives, I'm dying of misery. One sees that all are thieves in Peru: some denying what one rightfully requests and others holding onto what belongs to someone else. My agent, who invoices the newspapers for my chronicles, remains silent and only every six months sends whatever he feels like. I don't know who's robbing me: him or the magazines. The fact of the matter is that my chronicles are published in almost every issue of *Mundial* and *Variedades*, which should bring me in about 1,200 francs per month, but this money never arrives. And here I am, enduring dark hours, without any bread. My back is against the wall.

Strong regards from your brother.

César

[MLR]

TO PABLO ABRIL DE VIVERO

Paris, October 19, 1928

Dear Pablo,

I'm leaving for Moscow today. As I get ready, my thoughts are with you, and I jot down these lines to send you my fraternal regards.

I have spoken to you at length about this trip for quite some time. Today

I take it, after having rested for nearly three months in the countryside. I feel like a new man, ready to face life and all its setbacks once again.

In the midst of my recovery, I feel (perhaps more than ever) tormented by the problem of my future, and it's precisely with the drive to resolve this problem that I'm setting off on this journey. I realize what my role in life is not. I haven't found my path yet, but I want to find it, and perhaps in Russia I will, since on this other side of the world where I live, things move on springs similar to the rusty wing nuts of America. I'll never do anything in Paris. Perhaps in Moscow I'll find better shelter from the future.

I'll write to you constantly from Russia. I don't know if I'll be able to stay there definitively, which would be ideal. And if I do return, I know not when that would be. All I'm afraid of is the terrible Russian cold. I'll write to you as soon as I reach Moscow.

Unfortunately, the ticket I got was only for second class, which is to say, it cost fifty libras. Had it not, my ride to Moscow would've posed fewer risks. Nonetheless, I must do this, come what may.

I don't know if you were able to do anything with my recommendation concerning Bustamante; don't trouble yourself with it anymore. It appears that he's already resolved the matter. I'd appreciate it if you'd return the paperwork in an envelope to him, Consulate of Peru in Paris. Thanks so much, Pablo.

Write to me about your promotion. What news do you have about it? I hope you get it as soon as possible. You already know how dear you are to me and that I feel as if your affairs were my own. I know that the day you're in a position to help me out, you will as you have so many times with such generosity.

Until I write to you from Moscow, receive fond regards from your unwavering friend.

César   [JM]

TO PABLO ABRIL DE VIVERO

Paris, December 27, 1928
Dear Pablo,

I'm affectionately replying to your letter from the eleventh. In truth, I'm the one to blame for not receiving your news as soon as possible, but ever since my arrival in Paris, I've been so engrossed by a series of "minor concerns" that I've not been able to write you the long letter I wanted to send you about my trip.

I share your indignation with the minister of foreign relations, who seems to back that conspiracy to prevent your promotion. You already know that whatever is done to you I feel as if it were done to me and, if I can contribute in any way to oppose this swinish official, who combats "with malice, treachery, and viciousness," avail yourself of my brotherly offer as you see fit. But, what can be done against people whose values in life stray so far from our own?

Perhaps this New Year will finally bring your ascent, once your enemies fall into the trap of fate's immanent justice. I certainly hope this happens, dear Pablo. I desire it, with all my heart.

As for my trip to Moscow, I've at least managed to secure collaboration with some Russian magazines that will pay me regularly. I've already started sending my articles on America, and I hope things go just as I've arranged there.

Beyond this and my experience in the wonderful Soviet system, I couldn't take any more away from the trip. The language and material difficulties of a method poor in fundamental resources forced me to turn tail immediately. The problem of rooming, on its own, is insoluble, even for Stalin himself—except if one earns a fantastic salary, which is about what a hotel costs. But salaries there aren't so great that people are able to pay the five francs daily for a room.

So I've returned to my pastries. The payment from *Mundial* has been regulated, owing to the interest put in by a good friend from Lima. In consequence, I've started to send columns for every issue of that magazine. I've also started to collaborate in *El Comercio* of Lima, with two monthly articles. This is all that will come to me from Peru, as something fixed. In Bogotá I've obtained the collaboration for *Cromos*, which is the Colombian *Mundial*. This is just a monthly article. In Chile I'll also have a monthly article. In short, if these payments are made on time, I'll be able to live in relative peace. We'll see if they do.

Once more I'm in the small hotel I had on rue Molière, where you once stayed. I'm prepared to work as much as I can, in the service of economic justice that's currently absent and making us suffer: you, me, and the majority of men, to the benefit of a few thieving pigs. Everyone who suffers from this capitalist fraud must unite to cast down the current state of things. I'm feeling revolutionary—more from experiences I've lived than ideas I've learned.

Write to me always, Pablo. I'll do the same. And receive all the brotherly affection of your unwavering grateful friend,

César

[MLR]

Notebooks

My friend Alfonso Reyes, Mr. Minister Plenipotentiary: it is my pleasure to affirm to you sir that, today and always, all working theses, in art as in life, mortify me.

* * *

The object that reaches the masses is an inferior object. If it reaches only the elite, it's considered superior. If it reaches the masses and the elite it's considered genius, unbeatable.

If Beethoven stays put in the spiritual aristocracies and remains inaccessible to the masses, too bad for him.

* * *

Latin America.

There you have two words that have been exploited in Europe by every conceivable social ambition. Latin America. Here we have a name that's carried away and brought back from one boulevard of Paris to the next, from one museum to the next, from one magazine to the next, merely as literary as it is intermittent.

In the name of Latin America they manage to get rich, become well known and prestigious. Latin America knows about the lectures, verses, tales, film debuts with music, pasta, beverages, and humor on Sunday. In the name of Latin America someone prowls though the European offices that extract the easily infatuated humility of America in an attempt to publish a folklore and archaeology that get yanked by their manes for the use of memorized apothegms on cheap sociology. In the name of Latin America they play the dangerous diplomatic role of the orator who, at banquettes and anniversaries, is easily sweet-talked into favoring the flaming conventional chimeras of European politics.

For all this these two words suffice. People who can't do anything by themselves benefit greatly from them, without clutching their country of birth, background, and family records. Even Maurice Barrès, the same Barrès from the "cult of the self," has reaped benefits from Latin America.

* * *

I don't want to refer, describe, turn, or persist. I want to clutch birds to the second degree of their temperatures and men by the doublewide tongue of their names.   [JM]

BOOK FOUR 1929-1935

From *Human Poems*

GOOD SENSE

—There is, mother, a place in the world called Paris. A very big place and far off and once again big.

My mother turns up the collar of my overcoat, not because it is beginning to snow, but so it can begin to snow.

My father's wife is in love with me, coming and advancing backward toward my birth and chestward toward my death. For I am hers twice: by the farewell and by the return. I close her, on coming back. That is why her eyes would have given so much to me, brimming with me, caught red-handed with me, manifesting herself through finished tasks, through consummated pacts.

My mother is confessed by me, named by me. Why doesn't she give as much to my other brothers? To Víctor, for example, the eldest, who is so old now that people say: He looks like his mother's younger brother! Perhaps because I have traveled so much! Perhaps because I have lived more!

My mother grants a charter of colorful beginnings to my stories of return. Before my life of returnings, remembering that I traveled during two hearts through her womb, she blushes and remains mortally livid when I say, in the treatise of the soul: That night I was happy. But the more she becomes sad; the more she would become sad.

—My son, you look so old!

And files along the yellow color to cry, for she finds me aged, in the sword blade, in the outlet of my face. She cries over me, saddens over me. What need will there be for my youth, if I am always to be her son? Why do mothers ache finding their sons old, if the age of the sons never reaches that of their mothers? And why, if the children, the more they are used up, come nearer to their parents? My mother cries because I am old from my time and because never will I grow old from hers!

My farewell set off from a point in her being more external than the point in her being to which I return. I am, because of the excessive time in my return, more the man before my mother than the child before my mother. There resides the candor which today makes us glow with three flames. I say to her then until I hush:

—There is, mother, in the world, a place called Paris. A very big place and very far off and once again big.

My father's wife, on hearing me, eats her lunch and her mortal eyes descend softly down my arms.

[CE]

I AM GOING TO SPEAK OF HOPE

I do not suffer this pain as César Vallejo. I do not ache now as an artist, as a man or even as a simple living being. I do not suffer this pain as a Catholic, as a Mohammedan or as an atheist. Today I simply suffer. If my name were not César Vallejo, I would still suffer this very same pain. If I were not an artist, I would still suffer it. If I were not a man or even a living being, I would still suffer it. If I were not a Catholic, atheist or Mohammedan, I would still suffer it. Today I suffer from further below. Today I simply suffer.

I ache now without any explanation. My pain is so deep, that it never had a cause nor does it lack a cause now. What could have been its cause? Where is that thing so important, that it might stop being its cause? Its cause is nothing; nothing could have stopped being its cause. For what has this pain been born, for itself? My pain is from the north wind and from the south wind, like those neuter eggs certain rare birds lay in the wind. If my bride were dead, my pain would be the same. If they slashed my throat all the way through, my pain would be the same. If life were, in short, different, my pain would be the same. Today I suffer from further above. Today I simply suffer.

I look at the hungry man's pain and see that his hunger is so far away from my suffering, that were I to fast unto death, at least a blade of grass would always sprout from my tomb. The same with the lover. How engendered his blood is, in contrast to mine without source or consumption!

I believed until now that all things of the universe were, inevitably, parents or offsprings. But behold that my pain today is neither parent nor offspring. It lacks a back to darken, as well as having too much chest to dawn and if they put it in a dark room, it would not give light and if they put it in a brightly lit room, it would cast no shadow. Today I suffer come what may. Today I simply suffer.

[CE]

—No one lives in the house anymore—you tell me—; all have gone. The living room, the bedroom, the patio, are deserted. No one remains any longer, since everyone has departed.

And I say to you: When someone leaves, someone remains. The point through which a man passed, is no longer empty. The only place that is empty, with human solitude, is that through which no man has passed. New houses are deader than old ones, for their walls are of stone or steel, but not of men. A house comes into the world, not when people finish building it, but when they begin to inhabit it. A house lives only off men, like a tomb. That is why there is an irresistible resemblance between a house and a tomb. Except that the house is nourished by the life of man, while the tomb is nourished by the death of man. That is why the first is standing, while the second is laid out.

Everyone has departed from the house, in reality, but all have remained in truth. And it is not their memory that remains, but they themselves. Nor is it that they remain in the house, but that they continue about the house. Functions and acts leave the house by train or by plane or on horseback, walking or crawling. What continues in the house is the organ, the agent in gerund and in circle. The steps have left, the kisses, the pardons, the crimes. What continues in the house are the foot, the lips, the eyes, the heart. Negations and affirmations, good and evil, have dispersed. What continues in the house, is the subject of the act.

[CE]

HEIGHT AND HAIR

Who doesn't own a blue suit?
who doesn't each lunch and board the streetcar
with his hired cigarette and his pocket-edition pain?
I who was only born!
I who was only born!

Who doesn't write a letter?
Who doesn't talk about something very important,
dying from habit and weeping from hearing?
I who was solely born!
I who was solely born!

Who isn't called Carlos or some other thing?
Who to the kitty doesn't say kitty kitty?
Ay! I who only was solely born!
Ay! I who only was solely born!
    1927   [CE]

HAT, OVERCOAT, GLOVES

In front of the Comédie Française, is the Café
de la Régence; in it is a room
set apart, with an armchair and a table.
when I enter, the unmoving dust has already risen.

Between my lips made of rubber, the ember
of a cigarette smokes, and in the smoke can be seen
two intense fumes, the thorax of the Café,
and in the thorax, a profound oxide of sadness.

It is important that autumn graft itself to autumns,
important that autumn integrate itself with sprouts,
the cloud, with semesters; with cheekbones, the wrinkle.

It is important to smell like a madman postulating
how warm the snow is, how fleeting the turtle,
how simple the how, how fulminating the when!

                                                          [CE]

BLACK STONE ON A WHITE STONE

I will die in Paris in a downpour,
a day which I can already remember.
I will die in Paris—and I don't budge—
maybe a Thursday, like today, in autumn.

Thursday it will be, because today, Thursday,
as I prose these lines, I have forced on
my humeri and, never like today, have I turned,
with all my journey, to see myself alone.

César Vallejo has died, they beat him,
all of them, without him doing anything to them;
they gave it to him hard with a stick and hard

likewise with a rope; witnesses are
the Thursdays and the humerus bones,
the loneliness, the rain, the roads . . .

[CE]

And don't say another word to me,
since one can kill perfectly,
now that, sweating ink,
one does what one can, don't say another . . .

We will, gentlemen, see each other again with apples;
late the creature will pass,
the expression of Aristotle armed
with great hearts of wood,
that of Heraclitus grafted on that of Marx,
that of the gentle sounding coarsely . . .
This is what was well narrated by my throat:
one can kill perfectly.

Gentlemen,
sirs, we will see each other again without packages;
until then I demand, I shall demand of my frailty
the accent of the day, that,
as I see it, was already awaiting me in my bed.
And I demand of my hat the accursed analogy of memory,
since, at times, I assume successfully my wept immensity,
since, at times, I drown in my neighbor's voice
and endure
counting on kernels the years,

brushing my clothes to the tune of a corpse
or sitting up drunk in my coffin . . .
    [1931/1932]   [CE]

———————

   It was Sunday in the clear ears of my jackass,
of my Peruvian jackass in Peru (Pardon my sadness)
But today is already eleven o'clock in my personal experience,
experience of a single eye, nailed right in the chest,
of a single asininity, nailed right in the chest,
of a single hecatomb, nailed right in the chest.

   So do I see the portrayed hills of my country,
rich in jackasses, sons of jackasses, parents today in sight,
that now return painted with beliefs,
the horizontal hills of my sorrows.

   In his statue, with a sword,
Voltaire pulls his cape to and looks at the square,
but the sun penetrates me and frightens from my incisors
an increased number of inorganic bodies.

   And then I dream on a verdant
stone, seventeen,
numeral boulder that I've forgotten,
sound of years in the needle rumor of my arm,
rain and sun in Europe, and, how I cough! how I live!
how my hair aches me upon descrying the weekly centuries!
and how, with a twist, my microbial cycle,
I mean my tremulous, patriotically combed hair.
    [1931/1932]   [CE]

———————

   Today I like life much less,
but I always like to live: I've often said it.
I almost touched the part of my whole and restrained myself
with a shot in the tongue behind my word.

   Today I touch my chin in retreat
and in these momentary trousers I tell myself:

So much life and never!
So many years and always my weeks! . . .
My parents buried with their stone
and their sad stiffening that has not ended;
full-length brothers, my brothers,
and, finally, my being standing and in a vest.

   I like life enormously,
but, of course,
with my beloved death and my café
and looking at the leafy chestnut trees of Paris
and saying:
this is an eye, that one too, this a forehead, that one too . . . And
   repeating:
So much life and never does the tune fail me!
So many years and always, always, always!

   I said vest, said
whole, part, yearning, said almost, to avoid crying.
For it is true that I suffered in that hospital close by
and it is good and it is bad to have watched
from below up my organism.

   I would like to live always, even flat on my belly,
because, as I was saying and I say it again,
so much life and never! And so many years,
and always, much always, always always!
   [1931/1932]   [CE]

EPISTLE TO THE PASSERSBY

   I resume my day of a rabbit,
my night of an elephant in repose.

   And, within myself, I say:
this is my immensity in the raw, in jugfuls,
this is my grateful weight, that sought me below as a pecker;
this is my arm
that on its own refused to be a wing,
these are my sacred writings,
these my alarmed cullions.

A lugubrious island will illuminate me continental,
while the capitol leans on my innermost collapse
and the lance-filled assembly brings to a close my parade.

But when I die
of life and not of time,
when my two suitcases come to two,
this will be my stomach in which my lamp fit in pieces,
this that head that atoned for the circular torment in my steps,
these those worms that my heart counted one by one,
this will be my solidary body
over which the individual soul keeps watch; this will be
my navehall[1] in which I killed my innate lice,
this my thing thing, my dreadful thing.

Meanwhile, convulsively, harshly,
my restraint convalesces,
suffering like I suffer the direct language of the lion;
and, because I have existed between two brick powers,
I myself convalesce, smiling at my lips.
　　[1932]　　　　　　　　　　　　　　　　　　　　　　　　[CE]

THE HUNGRY MAN'S RACK

From between my own teeth I come out smoking,
shouting, pushing,
pulling down my pants . . .
My stomach empties, my jejunum empties,
misery pulls me out between my own teeth,
caught in my shirt cuff by a little stick.

Will a stone to sit down on
now be denied me?
Even that stone on which trips the woman who has given birth,
the mother of the lamb, the cause, the root,
that one will now be denied me?
At least that other one
which has gone cowering through my soul!
At least
the calcarid[2] or the evil one (humble ocean)

or the one no longer even worth throwing at man,
that one give it to me now!

   At least the one they will have found lying alone across an insult,
that one give it to me now!
At least the twisted and crowned, on which resounds
only once the walk of moral rectitude,
or, at least, the other one, that flung in dignified curve,
will fall by itself,
avowing true entrails,
that one give it to me now!

   A piece of bread, that too denied me?
Now I no longer have to be what I always have to be,
but give me
a stone to sit down on,
but give me,
please, a piece of bread to sit down on,
but give me
in Spanish
something, finally, to drink, to eat, to live off, to rest on,
and then I'll go away . . .
I find a strange shape, my shirt is
filthy and in shreds
and now I have nothing, this is hideous.

                                                                    [CE]

——————————

   Considering coldly, impartially,
that man is sad, coughs and, nevertheless,
takes pleasure in his reddened chest;
that the only thing he does is to be made up
of days;
that he is a gloomy mammal and combs his hair . . .

   Considering
that man proceeds softly from work
and reverberates boss, sounds employee;
that the diagram of time
is a constant diorama on his medals

and, half-open, his eyes have studied,
since distant times,
his famished mass formula . . .

   Understanding without effort
that man pauses, occasionally, thinking,
as if wanting to cry,
and, subject to lying down like an object,
becomes a good carpenter, sweats, kills
and then sings, eats lunch, buttons himself up . . .

   Considering too
that man is truly an animal
and, nevertheless, upon turning, hits my head with his sadness . . .

   Examining, finally,
his discordant parts, his toilet,
his desperation, upon finishing his atrocious day, erasing it . . .

   Understanding
that he knows I love him,
that I hate him with affection and, in short, am indifferent to him . . .

   Considering his general documents
and scrutinizing with a magnifying glass that certificate
that proves he was born very tiny . . .

   I make a gesture to him,
he approaches,
I hug him, and it moves me.
What's the difference! It moves me . . . moves me . . .
   [1934/1935]   [CE]

————————————

   Idle on a stone,
unemployed,
scroungy, horrifying,
at the bank of the Seine, he comes and goes.
Conscience then sprouts from the river,
with the petiole and outlines of the greedy tree;
from the river rises and falls the city, made of embraced wolves.

The idle one sees it coming and going,
monumental, carrying his fastings on his concave head,
on his chest his purest lice
and below
his little sound, that of his pelvis,
silent between two big decisions,
and below,
further below,
a paperscrap, a nail, a match . . .

This is, workers, that man
who in his work sweated from inside out,
who today sweats from outside in his secretion of rejected blood!
Cannon caster, who knows how many claws are steel,
weaver who knows the positive threads of his veins,
mason of the pyramids,
builder of descents through serene
columns, through triumphant failures,
idle individual among thirty million idle,
wandering multitudes,
what a leap is portrayed in his heel
and what smoke from his fasting mouth, and how
his waist incised, edge to edge, his brutal tool, idle,
and what an idea of a painful valve in his cheekbone!

Likewise idle the iron before the furnace,
idle the seeds with their submissive synthesis in the air,
idle the linked petroleums,
idle in its authentic apostrophes the light,
idle without growth the laurels,
idle on one foot the mobile waters
and even the earth itself, idle from stupor before this lockout,
what a leap is portrayed in his tendons!
What a transmission his hundred steps start up!
how the motor in his ankle screeches!
how the clock grumbles, wandering impatiently in his back!
how he hears the owners knock back
the shot that he lacks, comrades,
and the bread getting into the wrong saliva,
and, hearing it, feeling it, in plural, humanly,
how lightning nails

its headless force into his head!
and what they do, below, then, aie!
further below, comrades,
the dirtypaperscrap, the nail, the match,
the little sound, the stallion louse![3]

    [1934/1935]   [CE]

PARIS, OCTOBER 1936

    From all this I am the only one who parts.
From this bench I go away, from my pants,
from my great situation, from my actions,
from my number split part to part,
from all this I am the only one who parts.

    From the Champs-Elysées or as the strange
backstreet of the Moon curves around,
my death goes away, my cradle parts,
and, surrounded by people, alone, estranged,
my human resemblance turns around,
dispatching its shadows one by one.

    And I move away from all, since all
remain to provide my alibi:
my shoe, its eyelet, as well as its mud
and even the elbow bend
of my own shirt buttoned up.

                                           [CE]

    And if after so many words,
the word itself does not survive!
If after the wings of the birds,
the standing bird doesn't survive!
It would be much better, really,
for them to blow it all and be done with it!

    To have been born to live off our death!
To raise ourselves from the sky toward the earth
through our own disasters

and to spy the moment to extinguish our darkness with our shadow!
It would be much better, frankly,
for them to blow it all, what's the difference! . . .

And if after so much history, we die,
no longer of eternity
but of those simple things, like being
at home or starting to ponder!
And if then we discover,
all of a sudden, that we are living,
to judge by the height of heavenly bodies,
off the comb and the stains of the handkerchief!
It would be much better, really,
for them to blow it all, yes of course!

It will be said that we have
in one eye much sorrow
and also in the other, much sorrow
and in both, when they look, much sorrow . . .
Then! . . . Of course! . . . Then . . . not a word!
  [1936]   [CE]

TELLURIC AND MAGNETIC

Sincere and utterly Peruvian mechanics
that of the reddened hill!
Soil theoretical and practical!
Intelligent furrows: example; the monolith and its retinue!
Potato fields, barley fields, alfalfa fields, good things!
Cultivations which integrate an astonishing hierarchy of tools
and which integrate with wind the lowings,
the waters with their deaf antiquity!

Quaternary maize, with opposed birthdays,
I hear through my feet how they move away,
I smell them return when the earth
clashes with the sky's technique!
Abruptly molecule! Terse atom!

Oh human fields!
Solar and nutritious absence of the sea,

and oceanic feeling for everything!
Oh climates found within gold, ready!
Oh intellectual field of cordilleras,
with religion, with fields, with ducklings!
Pachyderms in prose when passing
and in poetry when stopping!
Rodents who peer with judicial feeling all around!
Oh my life's patriotic asses!
Vicuña, national
and graceful descendant of my ape!
Oh light hardly a mirror from shadow,
which is life with the period and, with the line, dust
and that is why I revere, climbing through the idea to my skeleton!

Harvest in the epoch of the spread pepper tree,
of the lantern hung from a human temple
and of the one unhung from the magnificent barret!
Poultry-yard angels,
birds by the slipup of the cockscomb!
Cavess or cavy to be eaten fried
with the hot bird pepper from the templed valleys!
(Condors? Screw the condors!)
Christian logs by the grace of
a happy trunk and a competent stalk!
Family of lichens,
species in basalt formation that I
respect
from this most modest paper!
Four operations, I subtract you
to save the oak and sink it in sterling!
Slopes caught in the act!
Tearful Auchenia, my own souls!
Sierra of my Peru, Peru of the world,
and Peru at the foot of the globe: I adhere!
Morning stars if I aromatize you
burning coca leaves in this skull,
and zenithal ones, if I uncover,
with one hat doff, my ten temples!
Arm sowing, get down and on foot!
Rain based on noon,

under the tile roof where indefatigable
altitude gnaws
and the turtle dove cuts her trill in three!
Rotation of modern afternoons
and delicate archaeological daybreaks.
Indian after man and before him!
I understand all of it on two flutes
and I make myself understood on a quena!
As for the others, they can jerk me off! . . .[4]

    [1931/1932, 1936, 1937]   [CE]

    The miners came out of the mine
climbing over their future ruins,
they girdled their health with blasts
and, elaborating their mental function,
closed with their voices
the shaft, in the shape of a profound symptom.

    Just to have seen their corrosive dust!
Just to have heard their oxides of the heights!
Mouth wedges, mouth anvils, mouth apparatus (It is tremendous!)

    The order of their tumuli,
their plastic inductions, their choral responses,
crowded at the foot of fiery misfortunes
and aerent[5] yellowing known by the saddish and the sad ones,
imbued
with the metal that peters out, the pallid and humble metalloid.

    Craniated with labor
and shod with viscacha hide
shod with infinite paths,
and eyes of physical weeping,
creators of the profundity,
they know, from the ladder's intermittent sky,
how to climb down looking up,
how to climb up looking down.

    Praise for the ancient game of their nature,
for their sleepless organs, for their rustic saliva!

Temper, edge and point, for their eyelashes!
May grass, lichen and frogs grow in their adverbs!
Iron plush for their nuptial sheets!
Women to the depths, their women!
Much happiness for their people!
They're something prodigious, those miners
climbing over their future ruins,
elaborating their mental function
and opening with their voices
the shaft, in the shape of a profound symptom!
Praise for their yellowish nature,
for their magic lantern,
for their cubes and rhombs, for their plastic misfortunes,
for their huge eyes with six optical nerves
and for their children who play in the church
and for their tacit infantile parents!
Hail, oh creators of the profundity! . . . (It is tremendous)

    [1931/1932, 1937]   [CE]

From *Reflections at the Foot of the Kremlin*

8. LITERATURE
A Meeting of Bolshevik Writers

It took me a long time and a lot of work to find Kolbasiev's house. After London, Leningrad is the most expansive city in Europe. Add to this the current lack of public transportation, the newcomer's unfamiliarity with the city, and, what's worse, the Russian language, and you can imagine the hardship a foreigner feels when he tries to go anywhere on his own. Plus, the numbering of Leningrad houses follows an order and progression so esoteric and intricate that only initiates know how to use it. By luck, I met Vigodsky on time, a critic who was also going to the meeting of Bolshevik writers. And, in the same way, Vigodsky led me through another labyrinth: once in Kolbasiev's building we had to decipher room numbers and apartment numbers, which are much more complex and meticulous than those on the street. Leningrad doesn't suffer from the shortage of lodgings prevailing in Moscow, but it doesn't suffer a surplus of houses either. The population just barely fits inside the city's current perimeter and, to prevent conflicts and disorder occasioned by the increasing proximity of city and countryside (proximity triggered by the socialization of Soviet politics), its housing system has been rigorously organized down to the T. Every house has become a hive by right of its meticulous order and the regularity of its divisions.

The apartment we enter is spacious, comfortable. Leningrad is generally a laid-back city, clean, clear, and even joyful. Tzarism turned it into a Western and almost Parisian city with regard to its overall layout, its architectural style, its municipal aspect, its embellishment. A residence for nobility and gentry, it was equipped with a thoroughly Western sense of comfort, at least in its central districts. There are scores of apartments that have their Parisian counterparts on the Rive Gauche. Kolbasiev's building is one of these, except that, within Soviet life at present, many families inhabit each apartment, occupying four rooms, three, two, and even a sole studio, according to the number of family members and the kind of work they do.

Kolbasiev is a young man, about thirty-five years old, with certain personal distinction. He used to be a diplomat. Somewhat banal and courtly, his manner and ease reveal the protocol of a traveler, a worldly man. When the other Bolshevik writers arrive, his ceremony is even greater. However, Kolbasiev is also a great revolutionary storyteller. Against a mediocre first impression, I come to see him as an orthodox and profoundly Bolshevik man. From the bourgeois salon he has gleaned only the desire to please, grace of gesture, and has found the rest of capitalist society a cause for sincere repugnance. There are many revolutionaries like Kolbasiev, who have graduated from "high" society, such as Chicherin, Lunacharsky, Mayakovsky, Pilnyak, Volin, and others.

Sayanov arrives. Lipatov and Ehrlich follow. Later Verzint, Chitzanov, Sadofiev. All young, under the age of forty—poets, novelists, critics, essayists—they make a merry and picturesque uproar. Healthy joy, fruitful exuberance, generous force, collective life instinct, creative praxis. They dress without proletarian pretension, without a Bolshevik mise en scène, no revolutionary uniform, or yellow blouses, or black shirts, even the long pants of the sansculottes from the convention. No, this is the involuntary negligence of a threadbare jacket, an absent necktie, and worn-out shoes. This poverty is proper to men of justice and in no way is the professional abandon of scruffy bohemians. These are largely white Russians from the north; blue eyes of polar desolation, bruised faces, their breath a maelstrom, frown of rounded closure. Some have come to literature, directly and consciously, from the working class, others from the *itzba* and the tide of civil war; others have come from the petite bourgeoisie, sent by a Leninist lashing, and more than a few from the lumpen proletariat, repaid and victorious in a life of work and order. They don't act toward me with that mild protective curiosity that eminently bourgeois men of the plume tend to demonstrate in the presence of an unknown foreign writer. They address and treat me with fraternal simplicity.

Sadofiev is the most relaxed and the most respected of all. They consult him continually, listening to him with affection and devotion.

"Sadofiev is our great proletarian poet," Kolbasiev tells me.

"Greater than Pasternak and Mayakovsky?" I argue, surprised.

"The greatest of all," Kolbasiev repeats firmly, and his opinion proved to be common among and confirmed by everyone there. Kolbasiev adds, "Mayakovsky is just a histrionic hyperbolist. As for Pasternak . . ."

Nonetheless, I'm more interested in collective modalities than that individualistic way of considering and judging literary matters, which allow me to incite my Russian friends in conversation. I take note of the following statements formulated by the Bolshevik writers as signs of their aesthetic:

There is no apolitical literature; it's never existed in the world, nor will it ever. Russian literature defends and exalts Soviet politics.

War on metaphysics and psychology. Only sociological disciplines determine the reach and essential forms of art. The issues and problems dealt with by Russian literature correspond strictly with Marx's dialectical thought.

Intelligence works and must always work under the control of reason. Nothing like surrealism, a decadent system openly opposed to the Soviet intellectual vanguard. Nothing like Freudianism or Bergsonism. No more *complex*, *libido*, *intuition*, or *dreams*. The method of artistic creation is and must be conscious, realist, experimental, scientific.

Literary themes are production, work, reorganization of family and society, the vicissitudes and unspeakable struggles to create the new spirit of man, with his collective feelings of creative emulation and universal justice. Russian literature has two ways of focusing on social realities: the destructive way of belligerence and world propaganda against the spirit and the bourgeois/reactionary interests on one side and, on the other, the constructive way of a new order and new sensibility. The last is distinguished by two concentric movements: proletarianization of society in toto and the socialization of the proletarian State.

The age of schools and literary cliques is a thing of the past in Russia. No more akmeism, or presentism, or futurism, or constructivism. There is nothing other than the United Front of Revolutionary Writers, whose spirit and technical experiments can be summarized in the doctrine of *heroic realism*.

Current Russian poets' teachers and precursors are Pushkin and Khlebnikov. Block contributes nothing profound or enduring. Foreign influence is reduced to ballads in English (Kipling, Coleridge) and German (Heine, Rilke).

Russian writers form a professional syndicate, as in other branches of Soviet life. They publish and catalog works in conjunction with a special section of the Administrative Office of Public Instruction, and these, in order to operate, must meet State criteria.

The exercise of literature is free and isn't organized by any school or official preparatory academy; it isn't subject to programs or coercive Soviet questionnaires either.

The revolutionary writer leads a life of action and constant dynamism. He travels and is in direct contact with rural and working life. He lives outdoors, feeling in an immediate way the living social and economic reality, the customs, political battles, collective joys and pains, the work and soul of the masses. His life is an austere laboratory where he scientifically studies his social role and the means of fulfilling it. The revolutionary writer is aware that he, more than any other individual, belongs to the community and cannot confine himself to any ivory tower or to egoism. The writer in his study, in his frock coat, is dead in Russia, the bookish monocled prince who sits at the foot of a mountain of books and papers day and night, ignoring the flesh and blood life of the street. The bohemian dreamer, ignorant slacker, this writer is also deceased.

Soviet literature, in certain measure, betokens ancient realism and ancient naturalism, but its historical foundation and creative sequences surpass them. It's not a school, but a living and moving trance of daily life. Hence, its substantial difference with all other literatures in history.

[MLR]

9. THE DAY OF A STONEMASON
Love, Sports, Alcohol, and Democracy

For an entire day, I've followed a stonemason's every step. At seven this morning, I began at his home on Pushkin Boulevard, a small studio in house number 8. With two floors and three courtyards, this larger house is an old dilapidated structure from millennial Moscow. I've entered with the pretext of looking for an imaginary person. While making this inquiry, I've leisurely observed the worker, who has just jumped out of bed. He's with his companion, a young copyeditor who works at *Pravda*. They don't have children, aren't married, and have been together for a year. Do they love each other? Love! What a different meaning this word has in Russia! For us, love exists only rarely. By love we refer to a mere sympathy born directly from an interest, be it economic or any other, which has nothing to do with the affective world.

A woman conceives of this sympathy, always based on the quality of the man, blind to the values that determine the sentiment. The same occurs in the man with respect to the woman. That quality may be wealth, worldly position, or the possibility of obtaining one thing or another, sooner or later. In these bourgeois relationships, only rarely does that sympathy emerge from beyond these perspectives. One person who loves another, the first lacking economic means or social status, resembles an extravagant fool. To love a tramp—someone who barely earns enough to keep from starving or who has no name and social stature and will never successfully obtain these or a better income—constitutes madness or impudence. The well-to-do or aristocratic man always goes for a well-to-do or aristocratic woman, and he who's neither of these strives or is tempted to love the woman who resembles him. Most often, the subjects of this "love" don't completely recognize the true foundation of their relationship. In these cases, one discovers in his or her beloved a collection of charms, seemingly unique and endearing personal attractions to an inner spiritual makeup. "I don't love her for her social or economic position," he says sincerely, "but for her moral fibers. If she ends up a penniless no-name, I'd keep loving her," and she says the same of him. These "lovers" are convinced of this, but they don't know that such fibers of the beloved come directly of his or her economic or social position—and they don't know this, because the relation of cause and effect between this position and those fibers is contributing and hidden, but nonetheless direct and indisputable.

Other times the subjects of this "love" are perfectly cognizant of the social or economic and extra-affective character of their relationships. This transpires in the highest worldly spheres of the bourgeoisie or nobility, while the case presented here occurs in the mid- or lower-level bourgeoisie.

Why is love disfigured and denaturalized like this in the capitalist world? It could be that it's in step with the insatiable individualism that has engendered countless appetites and egotistical preoccupations: the desire to distinguish oneself from others, by taking advantage of them at all cost, not to mention vanity, concupiscence, sybaritism, and laziness with its vice and cowardice. In response to these concerns, love—if that's what we call such an appetite—is classist, which is to say, that a man and woman of one social class unite only with a woman and man from the same class; no one wishes to lower his or her position. Only from time to time, I repeat, does one jump to another class, but in this case it's not the person of the higher class who falls; it's the person from the lower class who ascends. As we said, this doesn't mean that the upper class won't regard them as a fool or a strange bird. Generally, these leaps between classes appear so anomalous to everyone's eyes that people interested in taking them prefer to keep such relationships covert, like a crime or something shameful, unspeakable.

Love has stopped being classist in Russia, ever since the moment that social classes disappeared. Socially and economically, everyone is equal. Individualism and its derived appetites are kept in check by a new collective balance and within a new moral and legal order. Work is obligatory. There's no time for leisure or pleasure in refinement. Vanity has been overtaken by pride, in the collective sense of the word. Therefore, men and women have been freed from all preoccupation or socioeconomic concerns upon choosing their companion. The initial thrust and inspiration of love resides entirely elsewhere: in the affective world, where the freedom of sentimental choice is absolute and inalienable. When a man is united with a woman, he's united in love, since there's no other interest that could join them. Proof of this exclusively sentimental foundation is the countless couples made up of some great writer and a streetcar conductor, a union director and a hotel porter, or a journalist and a stonecutter—and these aren't hidden or shameful, but forthcoming, and many of them official. In this way, love also contributes to erasing once and for all the differences or moral barriers that arise between different types of work. With regard to love, all jobs, careers, and professions are equal and decent in Russia.

The stonemason who inhabits this narrow flat with the copyeditor from *Pravda* surely must love her and be loved by her, or else it would be hard to understand how they could live together and share a bed on a daily basis. What other link could there be between them? A simple physiological sympathy? Perhaps, but for it to last a year, that physiological sympathy must be undoubtedly strong, healthy, profound. On the other hand, one senses in their words and mannerisms a great shared fraternity. She speaks to him and behaves spontaneously. He appears a touch paternal. They're cheerful, agile, and childish. They laugh and play while they wash up and get dressed to go to work.

My interpreter and I have sat down to watch them. The Soviet Russian is more cordial than the Russian of yore. He opens up to strangers immediately and without reservations. Some foreign journalists allude to a secretive atmosphere, inhibited, cordoned off, in which he lives under the Dictatorship of the Proletariat. As for me, I haven't found this atmosphere on any of my trips to Russia. Quite the contrary, people, including officials, toast the newcomer with a forthcoming and cheerful candidness.

The stonemason's room doesn't have much furniture. It's modest, but also pleasant, located on the ground floor of the second courtyard. On the left and right, it's connected to the rest of the house, where other families and couples reside. The bed is a very low, rustic divan. There's a small table against the wall, with books and magazines in Russian and German. Across the way, a rickety wooden chair and a box that resembles a trunk or a bench. Photographs of Lenin, Stalin, Voroshilov,[6] and Rykov[7] in postcards and magazine cutouts hang on the whitewashed walls. The stonemason and his companion have gone into the courtyard to wash up, and they return, drying themselves off and singing.

"Don't you have a bathroom?" I ask.

"No, not in the house. This place is very old and completely uncomfortable—an inheritance from the era of the tzar. But we shower where we work, at four in the afternoon, just before lunch."

"And breakfast?"

"In the co-op on the corner."

She grabs a book from the table, *Theoretical and Practical Leninism*, by Stalin,[8] and she gets ready to leave. Her clothes are light. She puts almost all of them on in front of us. Her skirt is as short as that of any *midinette*[9] on rue Saint-Honoré. Lively colors juxtaposed. White cotton socks. Black shoes, with a sporty English heel. Short hair, under a blue beret with narrow seams. A square neckline, down to where her cleavage begins. Then, a thin gray jacket, without any fur. No makeup. Medium-sized, well-built, vivacious, pink complexion, rotund, and deeply feminine expressions, her head thrown back with rustic grace, the stonemason's companion is ready to leave. She doesn't stop talking and laughing, but thumbs through the book and sternly, enthusiastically, says to the interpreter, "Did you read Stalin's article in *Isveztia* yesterday?"

"No," the non-Bolshevik Russian replies.

"It's remarkable! There he talks about the Marxist theoreticians and their scholastic shortcomings."

A heated dialogue ensues.

The stonemason is also ready. His outfit is even more schematic than his companion's. Pants, an astrakhan-lined coat and coarse yellow shirt. He wears no hat. This is certainly not the proletarian uniform of buildings in Chicago, with their standard button-downs, their standard pockets, their standard hats. Nor are these the clothes that U.S. shoe, shirt, and hat factories give construction companies for their workers, on the condition that these garments bear the initials or advertising logos in the colors of those factories. The stonemason's outfit is just an object made by the unions of the Soviet, but it's not a uniform, since it lacks the decorative element, which is the repetitive feature that characterizes a uniform.

We leave. Here I observe a difference from our world of salons. In Russia, there's no social etiquette. People give and take, deny and consent, without formalities. Even in the terrain of friendship, solely justice prevails. One gives a seat to the person who's tired, and the owner of the house takes it, if he needs it more than the visitor. And this goes for everything else too. The stonemason and his companion leave without excusing themselves, because they need to leave, because leaving isn't bad for anyone. "We're leaving" is all they say. In a house on Unter den Linden or Champs-Élysées, people would say, "How rude!" Only on Fifth Avenue do things, at least among business people, occur in a similar way to what we see in Soviet Russia. It's not in vain that the Yanks' technique of production is so similar to the socialists'.

Now on the street, I likewise notice that neither his nor her behavior changes. Among us, people are different on the street than they are in their homes. A man takes more manly breaths, is more solemn, more upright, distinguished, or important. A woman becomes more graceful, more of a coquette, more elegant, respectable, and even demanding. The spirit of the street permeates us and turns us into foolhardy hypocrites. We falsify ourselves on the largest scale, and all this for the eternal concern of distinguishing ourselves and outdoing everyone else. Our falseness and individualism grow insofar as there are ever more people around us, watching us, and listening to us. The solitary man is the most sincere. As can be seen, these two positions are paradoxical and even absurd, without any rational or creative character. One is sincerity without witnesses—which socially doesn't interest or concern anyone—and the other, an equally subjective and abstract collectivism that doesn't concern anyone either.

The spirit of the street especially predominates the bourgeoisie and is more demonstrative the older and more orthodox this bourgeoisie is. The capitalist proletariat, with its bureaucratic capes, is also saturated with the spirit of the street.

The stonemason and his companion indistinctly walk in the road or on the curb, because neither one nor the other has a real need to use the sidewalk.

Foreigners are deeply curious to understand with certainty the new relations introduced by the revolution between a man and woman. With regard to these, one has only the most fantastic and salacious of ideas, yet the reality is less unbelievable than most people believe. New relationships in the Soviet begin with a simple and universal principle: the man is not stronger or weaker than the woman. That question of the stronger or weaker sex is nothing but a false formulation, which everyday experience squashes. This is the true formulation: in some areas the man is stronger than the woman, and, in others, the woman is stronger than the man. The secret of this harmony resides in the balance of these signs—negative and positive—according to the role and possibilities of each sex. The woman, in the Soviet system, isn't higher or lower than the man in a permanent way. Sometimes the scope of her actions exceeds his, and other times his exceeds hers. Otherwise, they're equal every step of the way. Thus, the legal, economic, political, and moral statutes of the sexes—on these new foundations—have been established in the Soviet. The rights and obligations of the woman in the family and civically, with regard to everyone else, are equal to those of the man. Regarding children, the same occurs. The man is just as responsible as the woman. Politically, she can elect and be elected for the same positions as he can. Finally, meekness, modesty, and dignity aren't any more severe or less required for the man than they are for a woman.

"What are the differences between the man and the woman," people aboard inquire.

These differences reside in the very nature of the sexes, which vary according to their strengths and weaknesses. If these conditions inherent in the male and the female were to be simplified and classified in two large fields, we could say that physically the male, for the time being, has fewer rights and more obligations than the female, while spiritually the equality is rigorous. This criterion, with provisional and inevitable exceptions, seems to determine the position of both sexes in Soviet society.

"But, in my opinion," our female interpreter says, "this is all wrong. Spiritually, men are superior to women."

The stonemason's companion asks us what we're talking about, and when she finds out she responds. "No," she says, "because if men are more permanent in their passions, women are more ardent and sharp. If men are more apt for synthesis, women are apt for analysis. Men are more rational; women, more intuitive. Men are more patient and tenacious on the creative front; women are the same during crises and hardships . . ."

Seven forty-five. We go out to have breakfast at the neighborhood co-op, and they say good-bye on the way to their respective jobs. A firm handshake as between two friends.

"See you later."

"See you later."

At four in the afternoon I go looking for the stonemason where his job lets out. It's on the far shore of the Moskva River, in the vast buildings that the Construction Cooperatives are erecting for workers' housing. When I cross the bridge, I see two sets of workers on the stairs and scaffolding of the buildings. Some are about to stop their work and get down; others who start, climb up. As I reach the outer walls, a wave of workers lets out and floods the street. No uniforms, I repeat. Many wear caps, though more than a few heads go uncovered. Very few have beards, and those that do are the oldest, over fifty years old. Almost all of them are shaven, American-style. They form a great pandemonium, spilling onto the corner, some on foot, others taking streetcars.

Here's the stonemason from this morning. He comes with three others, in a heated discussion. Introductions. They ask about my profession and my political affiliation.

"He's a nonpartisan writer," they say to one another, and we continue together toward the river's other shore. We head to the restaurant of the co-op that's close to the stonemason's house.

"How do you like Russia?" the four of them ask me at once.

"Very well. It's admirable."

"What have you liked the most?"

"The working masses."

"And then?"

"The hope and faith that drive them."

"And what are they saying abroad about the Russian Revolution?"

"They don't know much about it. They have only confused and false notions."

"What difference do you find between the workers of the Soviet and the workers of capitalist countries?"

"Here, you're free, while the others are slaves."

"Why do you think we're free? What about the dictatorship of the Soviet?"

"Your freedom is a freedom from class. Your individual freedom, on the other hand, is relative and very limited, but this is what's demanded by the needs of the first freedom. Marx has said that freedom is nothing more than the rational understanding of need. Individual freedom has never been complete in history. Its application can be somewhat limited and conditioned by collective interests. While the former continues to allow it, individual freedom in Russia will keep expanding and consolidating."

I see that my words rouse interest and acceptance in them.

"That's right," they say. "That's the truth. We're glad you understand the meaning of the Dictatorship of the Proletariat. Well done."

One of them speaks to the others at length, and from one or another Latin particle or ending, I realize they're talking about workers' politics and imperialist politics. The speaker is a former secretary of the Workers' Committee of Construction, where the four of them are employed. He must be around twenty-eight years old. His voice is gruff and somewhat monotonous, but full of warmth and intelligence.

"Are you communists?" I ask them.

"No, we don't belong to a party."

"But you trust the system?"

"We place our full trust in it."

"Then why not join the party that governs you and that you accept with such confidence?"

"Because to be a communist you need to have free time and strength for all the work entailed by being a party member. As simple workers, we already have enough and even too much responsibility."

"What kind of responsibilities?"

"Aside from our work in construction . . ."

"Are you technical workers or manual laborers?"

"One of us is a carpenter. The rest of us are regular workers. Aside from construction, which pays us a salary, we have other duties that go uncompensated but are inseparable from our role as day laborers, such as forming the workers' cells of the industry we belong to, the workers' committees and assemblies; helping monitor this industry; exercising socialist emulation whenever the needs of production demand it; forming policy and new trade techniques for education; and so on . . ."

"What's the role of the workers' cells, committees and assemblies?"

"To discuss and make decisions on administrative, technical, economic, and cultural issues of the profession and the industry."

"And socialist emulation?"

"That's what capitalists would call a system of record. For example, when the Soviet urgently requires living quarters due to the influx and growth of the city's population, the workers of a building decide to increase labor, doubling or even tripling it, to finish much sooner than the project's original deadline. Among the workers, there's a sense of civic emulation at the service of the collective interest. That's how most of the Gosplan (Five-Year Plan) is being completed in four, three, and two and a half years."

"What reward does the worker receive for his effort in favor of the common good?"

"No personal reward. It arises solely from a high sense of real, practical communism."

"And what about the campaigns for progress?"

"They're just a form of socialist emulation. They're groups of workers that form with the goal of spreading ideas and constructive enthusiasm about the Soviet in the still reluctant or ignorant sectors of the rural masses and in the factories, to help them understand . . ."

We get off the streetcar. They all live in the same neighborhood and eat at the same co-op. When we enter the restaurant, the stonemason and the carpenter—who's the one that was speaking to the others in Russian about the proletariat and imperialism—look for someone in particular among

the crowd of numerous diners seated around the long tables. They're looking for their companions. There they are. We walk up to them, but there's
no room, so we end up sitting far away on the opposite end of the immense
hall.

Later on, the two of them meet up. The carpenter's companion is older,
a beautiful woman. They sit down and smoke. The conversation turns boisterous and fills with laughter. When we leave the co-op, I notice that each
of the women pays her own tab.

I also learn that the carpenter and his companion have been married for
five years. But this couple doesn't have any children either. Why? Because
he has tuberculosis and the law prohibits him from becoming a father
until he's been cured. The doctor has prescribed a special diet for this reason, which he follows, under penalty of a severe legal sanction in the event
that he breaks it.

My attention is drawn to the utter equality of the two couples from the
viewpoint of social morality. Even though the stonemason and his companion are in a free union, they receive the same social respect, consideration, and esteem as the carpenter and his companion, who are married.
In the Soviet system, free love has the same moral and social dignity as
marriage.

Two of the workers say good-bye.

"Where are you going now?" I ask.

"To Union Hall. At five o'clock there's a session of the Construction
Union Section."

One of the two who leaves is the carpenter. His wife stays with us. The
couple says good-bye as the stonemason and his companion did in the
morning:

"See you later."

"See you later."

Like two simple friends. No kisses, like the workers of Saint-Denis, or
the mawkish sickly sweetness of the tacky Argentine Porteños. The Soviet
husband and his wife, before all else, are good friends. Conjugal love in
Russia is more friendship than passion, more fraternity than sexual attraction.

Ten minutes to five. We walk through the Great Square.[10] The ladies stay
here. They're going to take the streetcar. They're in a hurry, running late.
They have a childcare lesson at a special section of the Central Committee for Breastfeeding,[11] designed for married women who've yet to become
mothers.

"We're going to the Workers' Club," the stonemason and his workmate say to me, "to prepare a report on construction lumber from the pine re-gion of Lapland. We need to have it ready by Thursday. We're going to read something at the club's library."

"What time will I see you again?"

"At eight, when the club lets out."

What a different life this is from that of the capitalist worker! No cof-fee, or alcohol, or card games, or yawns of boredom. No one drinks cof-fee, even at breakfast. Russians prefer tea, which prior to the revolution was consumed heavily, nearly as a drug. The Soviet has rationed it out, though not with traumatic measures, but rather incremental elimination backed by propaganda and education. The same has been done and is being done with alcohol. At first, the Soviet radically prohibited alcoholic beverages in one fell swoop. Like in the United States, the Dry Law met tre-mendous resistance, discontent, and violence, especially in provinces and the countryside. If the Soviet was saturated with Saxon rigidness—so dear and worthy of imitating as certain Latin countries do—the Dry Law would still be upheld in Russia today, and this country would still be, as in the United States, a theater of the most absurd scandals among the wet and dry. But Leninism possesses shocking ductility. In view of the difficulties presented by the Dry Law, the Soviet immediately changed its tactic and resolved to combat alcoholism incrementally by attacking the vice from below. Police enforcement was then replaced by propaganda among the masses and education in schools. Countless action groups were formed. Antialcoholic prophylaxis quickly gained member support in the fields and factories. The government assigned this policy a preferential place in its annual plans. Currently, the situation is very promising. Every day in vari-ous villages the sale of alcohol is suspended at the request of the residents themselves. In general, these are the people who in public elections de-mand the elimination of alcoholic beverages. But, there's more. A friend of alcohol is considered an enemy of socialism. The phobia of alcohol is par-ticularly stronger in the younger generations. Every year the consumption of alcoholic beverages decreases by 10 to 12 percent.

However, the Soviet is well aware that neither propaganda nor educa-tion would be sufficient weapons against alcoholism, if a second factor were lacking, the most important and decisive of all: the improvement of the worker's living conditions. Propaganda and education are tools often used today by capitalist governments. This is the priestly and even rhe-torical side of the enterprise. The practical and determining aspect of the campaign's success is constituted by the means created to channel the worker's daily pleasures and inclinations toward another plane of concerns and satisfactions. Do capitalist governments do this? No. There, in-finite concerted efforts attempt to stop this sort of policy in favor of the working class. And the beverage manufacturers? And the wineries? And the distributors? And the landholders of the vineyards? And the owners of other industries whose interest resides in recharging the spent workers' energy by means of alcoholic stimulants, since the infinitesimal salaries don't allow them to do so by means of better nutrition and a better life-style? And the consumption taxes? In the Soviet system none of these interests exists. Thus, it has been and continues to be easy for the Soviet to stir up the diverse factors of everyday existence of the masses, with the goal of directing them through new channels away from the fascination with alcohol.

Among these new channels is the real, practical, and daily participation of the worker in the direction and administration of collective affairs. The worker lives inebriated with the pleasure and effort he exerts at all hours during his social endeavors. His enthusiasm and civic inebriation stem from his conviction that he, as an individual, is alive and important to the collective, since every day his eyes see for themselves that what little he does or says directly weighs into the business of all. This is also the founda-tion of his feeling of responsibility—a sentiment that absorbs him and at once fills him with pride and political fervor. It's a fact of historical experi-ence that people and epochs of the broadest and most effective democracy correspond to a greater purity of customs among the masses.

On the contrary, despotic nations and minority governments yield a re-laxation of customs among the people. There's no sport that could distract people from their vices more than the exercise of sovereignty, with all its democratic rights and functions. Without a doubt, a worker would much rather write an official letter that, according to him, is going to determine to this or that degree the kind of houses that many people will inhabit, instead of playing a card game or a football match. On the other hand, a worker from the capitalist countries prefers to go to the tavern over going to vote, because he knows that his vote won't weigh into the fate of so-ciety. The bourgeois State apparatus co-opts suffrage and covers it up as it pleases. It's a sleight-of-hand game, an abuse capable of all tricks, vio-lence, and falsification.

At eight o'clock in the evening the stonemason leaves the Workers' Club. Now he's alone.

"Are you tired?" I ask.

"Quite the contrary," he smiles. "Study and reflection on rather unusual things is good for my manual laborer soul—it's comforting. When I got off work, at four o' clock, I was starting to feel physically tired. But now, after reading and thinking, I have the urge to do something, go running or move something heavy with my arms."

"Do you play sports?"

"Yes, I belong to a cross-country team. The doctor thinks that construction workers need this kind of exercise to counterbalance our line of work."

"How do you Russians choose your sports? According to your individual tastes, or is it the government that imposes the one it deems most suitable?"

"Government doctors examine us every so often, ask about our vocation, and then decide."

"So, you're not free to choose the sport you want to play?"

"Our individual freedom ends where the interests of society begin. If the former were unlimited and absolute, we'd often take to a sport contrary to what our health and working condition require. Taste for a sport is one thing, and the rational benefit of this or that sport is another. In order words, reason trumps taste."

"And when do you practice?"

"The hours and days vary quite a bit. In general, we do it three times a week, so, almost every day. (Remember that the new Russian workweek has four days.) But that always depends on a series of conditions and relative needs for work; on our proletarian deeds outside of work, the ones we've already spoken about; on the sporting boards of the tactical plan that corresponds to them, and so forth."

We reach a co-op where they serve tea. There are a lot of people, teams of workers whose schedules are similar to the stonemason's. They keep a similar diet, at the same time, and as often as he: breakfast, a cup of tea, and a small roll at seven in the morning; lunch, a sort of bean soup with a piece of beef (borscht) and a pie filled with ground meat and potatoes and black bread at four in the afternoon; and, finally, another cup of tea with a sort of biscuit at eight or nine at night. Around eleven in the morning the workers have a snack at work, consisting of tea with a bite of cheese or a very seasoned vegetable stew. For drinks, water and on occasion a white, rather strong Russian beer. But lots of tobacco. Russia is probably the place in Europe where people smoke the most.

There are many vegetarians, especially in Moscow. I've been informed that prior to the revolution there were even more. The moral ideas of Tolstoy, along with his ascetic practices, rapidly decline in Russia. Vegetarians are currently looked at in mockery as a retrograde sect, given the revolutionary elements.

From *Reflections at the Foot of the Kremlin*   347

"Do you want to come tonight," the stonemason asks me, "to the Theater of the Professional Union?"

This is a new theater, created after the New Economic Policy (NEP) had been established. Its scenic spirit, aesthetic, funding, and staff are of proletarian origin. Tonight they're putting on *The Rails Are Humming*,[12] a piece by Kirshon, metallurgic worker and author of the play *Red Rust*,[13] which has just been performed with resounding success in theaters of Berlin, Paris, and London.

As we reach the box office, the stonemason shows me his ticket, and when I ask him where he got it and how much he paid, he replies, "Our union gives us these tickets for next to nothing."

"How much did it cost?"

"Twenty-five kopeks."

And I purchase mine for the same type of seat as his, and it costs me one rouble, twenty kopeks. Oh, the Dictatorship of the Proletariat!

Soviet theater is a mirror image of Russian social life. Applyling Jules Romain's unanimist theory to the case at hand, it's not difficult to feel, in a lively and visual way, the entire socioeconomic structure of the Soviet incarnated in the audience of the theater.

At first sight one immediately notices the division of the crowd in two classes of spectators: on one hand, the proletariat, and on the other, the NEPmen, diplomats, and concessionairs of foreign enterprises. It's not just a matter of suits, but the heads and their expressions. The dividing line is more ostensible than I've ever seen before in any European theater. The NEPmen are distinguished from the petite bourgeois of capitalist countries by their dress and behavior on the whole as the nouveau riche that they are. They lack neither theater glasses nor a gold chain. Along with the diplomats and consessionairs of foreign industrial countries, they shrivel their faces in a pejorative, disgusted expression. The latter, because they're already suffering from the revolution; the former, because of the risk their respective countries run of suffering from it some day in the not-too-distant future.

"That lady," he says to me, referring to an elegant and overbearing woman, "is the wife of the German ambassador."

"Why does she look angry?"

"Whenever she's in public she looks like that. She hates the Soviet with a passion. Everyone knows it."

"And you guys? . . ."

"What are we going to do! She's only defending her class."

Bolshevik and Soviet workers don't feel the slightest personal resentment toward bourgeois foreigners. Outside of Russia people believe that the Soviet masses hate and harass bourgeois foreigners as much as they can. They don't. This is only imaginable in the empirical and romantic rabble of the old rebellions. Now, the Russian proletariat operates on a collective plane and a plane of class verses class. Revolution isn't created by stoning bystanders; it arises from crowd to crowd. With regard to the NEPman, the tactic changes, because he doesn't belong to any social class in Russia but rather tries to remake it through different individual efforts. Hence, it's necessary to combat him individually.

With the exception of this minute sector of spectators, the entire audience is made up of workers, Soviets. Their domain, in breadth and depth, is complete in the theater. The mass reigns freely and without obstacles. Their movements, their shouts and words, approving or rejecting, decide the tone and collective temperament of the show. Here, as in all other activities of the country, workers are the owners and masters of the social atmosphere. The NEPmen, diplomats, and foreign industrialists appear to be oppressed, cowering from the crowd, and they do nothing except adapt and follow the social directives of the proletariat, albeit reluctantly. This too is the Dictatorship of the Proletariat, as opposed to what occurs in capitalist countries, where workers are the ones who suffer, even in theaters, the dictatorship of the owners.

The working mass is distributed throughout the sections of the venue, not according to the price that each person pays for a ticket, as occurs in bourgeois society, but according to a rare and special turn beyond all economic consideration, since all the tickets cost the same price. This turn or rotation is established and monitored by the unions or co-ops that the spectators belong to. In this way, for example, today I see spectators in the box seats, front row, and other places of preference who will occupy less comfortable and elegant places and seats next time, because the theater venues of the tzarist period, naturally, maintain their hierarchical seating arrangement. Soon enough strictly Soviet venues will be built, and the architectonic layout will reflect Russia's new social structure.

The social aspect of Muscovite theaters bespeaks the intimately democratic spirit or, to be more precise, the proletarian spirit of the viewers. In this compressed scene of Soviet society, the old and well-worn ideals of equality and fraternity are made palpable. But note that such fraternity and equality are made manifest here in proletarian scale. In the bourgeois system, equality and fraternity have been and will be impossible, since the out-of-control individualism entailed by capitalist society is the gateway to all competition and war, not to social solidarity and harmony. The proletarian world, on the contrary, is based on the collective instinct, the motor and driving force of social equilibrium. A great homogeneity prevails in the expressions and movements of the mass. Nobody or nothing stands apart from the crowd. No one makes a difference. No one is higher or lower than anyone else. *Pas de vedettes*.[14] Everyone balances out to the same social status.

In these Russian theaters, we're far from luxury, presumption, concupiscence, envy, and the courtesan gossip of the bourgeois soirée. Everything here is sober, essential, truthful, modest, forthcoming, fraternal. It's not the pomp of a few and the misery of the many, but the summary cleanliness and decency of everyone equally. The outfit and expression, the gaze and word transcend confidence, proper of the proletarian soul. Neither the sideways glance of resentment, nor the insulting brow of vanity; neither gallantry nor betrayal; neither muted murmurs nor shameful adulation—and no starchy etiquette. Here, there's no place to shout, "How well that woman knows how to turn her head!" or "What a terrible laugh that lady has!" or "What dignity she places in a greeting!" Here, people act naturally, though always adhering to a new and profound sense of harmony and social modesty.

From his revisionist position Henri de Man haggles with the proletariat over the appropriation of most or almost all the social norms, uses, customs, rules, pleasures, and inclinations of the bourgeoisie. Henri de Man formulates this allegation with the goal of proving that class division doesn't offer the depth the original Marxist doctrine claims it has and that, instead, the capitalist and worker are linked by a series of social practices and habits that are common to both. This is how the author of *Beyond Marxism* tries to whisk away the revolutionary notion—which entails class struggle—by substituting it with the evolutionary notion, that is, an understanding between workers and employers, since both social levels are supported by an identical mindset and identical lifestyle.[15]

But the illustrious Belgian ex-Marxist jumps to generalizing and confusing conclusions. He's not wrong in stating that many sumptuary pleasures and social benefits of employers have been transferred and continue to be transferred over to the worker, but let's be clear. This transfer occurs in three stages. First, the worker acquires from his employer what the latter does for the common good, no matter the social class. This occurs with the taste for comfort, such as an automobile, telephone, etc. Second, the worker takes from the employer the latter's malpractices, in the same way that a healthy person contracts an illness from someone that he or she is obligated to visit frequently. This happens with the inclination toward jewelry, self-marketing, womanizing, etc. Third, the worker takes from the employer what the latter does in passing that doesn't belong to any particular social class. This can be said of all snobbery and trends, like certain sporting games and many public shows.

In the first case, what's unique and characteristic of the bourgeois man stays in him and doesn't transfer over to the worker. The part of these practices that stays in him is the excessive, refined, and depraved: a belch, a callus, a Byzantine sting. In the second case, the contagion is more or less avoidable and, for the most part, curable. The third case is unimportant. Therefore, the Russian proletariat has taken and will keep the habits and social inclinations that the bourgeoisie practices, which count as patrimony from all social classes on account of their justness and usefulness. Among these habits, we find decency in dress and manners.

The masses, with all their elemental strengths and weaknesses, fill the theater's spiritual hull to the seams. A new and more natural civility controls the caliber of their actions from the inside out. This is the same working mass of all countries, but with some differences: here it's freer and less libertine, more level-headedness and less privation, more equality and spiritually balanced and less monotonous; it lacks superiors; it has no need for police supervision or moral oversight from anyone; and it contains justness and control of all its movements. This is what elicits the impression that whatever they do is good, which is just the opposite of what occurs with the working capitalist masses, whose every action seems prone to error and failure, frequently requiring external control and coercion.

Many Russian theaters have completely eliminated the curtain. The first to set the example was the Meyerhold Theater. It responded to an imperative of greater scenic verism. Thus, the performance loses its sense of illusion but gains its realism. The curtain is childish and conducive to daydreams, to fantasy. The curtain is the top of a jack-in-the-box. It contains an element of puerile and supreme convention. It suggests ideas of shirking, trickery, and ruse. It's reminiscent of those children's games in which one child has to turn around in order not to see what's around him or how the other child prepares the mystery or surprise. The spectator, who's no longer a child—no matter how much effort bourgeois aesthetes put into making art a simple children's game—has rejected the fairytale implied by the curtain and asks to see everything with his own material eyes. This preference is made manifest particularly in countries where the social drama of history has been or is more gory and intimate.

Despite what idealist artists and critics would like to argue, the economic tragedy of today certainly has nothing of an illusion to it—no dream or children's game. This debate and dramatic conflict of our epoch are of a raw realism exempt of fiction. Or rather, the social tragedy of today is determined by consummated and irrepressible factors and events of history, which no convention or volition can now degrade or destroy. In the same way, art that addresses this tragedy also must treat it and recreate it by subjecting itself as much as possible to the same realism and to the same determinism of the conflict. Therefore, the conventional element of the theater—since this art form, more than any other, resides in fiction—must be possible at least and the least conventional as possible. The Soviet notion of art doesn't accept the theory of certain bourgeois literary chapels, according to which the laws of art are completely different from the laws of life. This formula, aside from being arbitrary, is deliquescent and casuistic, and it expresses the morbid cerebralist fixation of capitalist aesthetics.

Nonetheless, the theater of the professional union still has a curtain. As it is raised, a booming noise of the boiler works erupts. The action of the piece occurs in a car maintenance center, and the decoration is extraordinarily original and powerful. While the rest of the theaters of the world limit themselves to the usual decorations based on bourgeois residences, the castles of counts, or, at most, pastoral farmhouses, here the Russian regisseurs—for the first time in history—are staging scenes of the factories and electromechanical plants, that is, the most tedious and yet most fertile atmosphere of modern labor. Here it is, in its authentic and marvelous reality, with its entire aesthetic and creative dynamo. It's the mise-en-scène of industrial labor. The apparatus of production.

The emotion that the decoration awakes is of an exultant grandeur. From the pulleys and transmissions, from the motors, anvils, pistons, and winches bursts forth the spark, the violet flash, the dazzling zigzag, the isochronic crack, the implacable ticktock, and the burning, pneumatic wheezing, similar to that of an invisible angry beast. We're not looking at a simulated boiler works, fashioned out of cardboard and synchronized with sounds of allure. This is a real workshop, machinery in flesh and bone, verist-realist scenery, a throbbing piece of life. The workers bustle about, in great angular movements, as in an etching. The dialogue is erratic and geometric, hence, a bundle of electrical wires. The circuits of the proletarian word and those of the workshop's mechanical energy take shape and break away, superimposing and crisscrossing each other like the rings of an invisible *jongleur*. I, who don't know Russian at all, limit myself to and am pleased with only the phonetics of the words. However—perhaps precisely because of that—this symphony of unintelligible voices mixed with the shrieking machines strangely fascinates and fills me with enthusiasm. I could keep listening to it indefinitely, while I watch the workshop's movement.

The decoration alone is worthy of an entire theatrical study. I'm sufficed to realize the revolutionary scope of the Soviet scene. A theater capable of such a mise-en-scène, so audacious and radically new, undoubtedly fosters the equally new revolutionary spirit and contents on the world stage. Yes. Here one feels a new world beat. Until today, theaters have been reduced to addressing matters related to the squandering of production, its reaping by social parasites, the lords. Until today we could see only in stage lights the dramas of the bourgeoisie's distribution among itself of the wealth created by the workers. The characters were professors, priests, artists, deputies, nobles, landowners, merchants, financiers, and, at most, artisans. Never did we see onstage the other face of the social coin: the infrastructure, the foundation of the economy, the root and birth of the collective order, the elemental forces and human agents of economic production. Never did we see as theatrical characters the crowd and the worker, the machine and the raw material.

The plot of *The Rails Are Humming* develops around the revolutionary consciousness of the Bolshevik worker, around his political and economic duties within the Soviet, his efforts, pains, struggles, classist satisfactions, the dangers and enemies from within and without the proletariat. The scenes and acts occur in the workers' meetings, in front of a half-assembled locomotive, in the manager's office of a factory, in the laborers' quarters, at the workers' clubs.

The dramatic focus of the action, the social myth of the piece, cause and end of all interests, ideas, and feelings in play, resides in the revolutionary predicament of history. In the wake of the gods of Greek tragedy, the hagiography of medieval drama, the mythical Nibelung of Wagnerian theater,[16] the symbology of the bourgeois stage, here we have the materialist fable of the Dictatorship of the Proletariat.

The Bolshevik worker, the scenic personification of the social destinies of history, consciously shoulders the weight and responsibility of the dialectical mission of his class. As in sacred theater, his soul is mortally sad. He also has his vultures, like old Prometheus. They are foreign capitalism, the kulaki and the NEPmen, the ignorance of the muzhik, the recalcitrant clergy, Geneva, the engineers and technicians, the Soviet bureaucracy, the deviations of the party's Left and Right, the soft reaction.

In this piece there's a culminating scene that, on account of its tragic and universal grandeur, recalls the best passages of the Passion and Aeschylean drama. The worker, shift manager of the Factory Counsel, returns to his room at night. He is exhausted. His struggle with a thousand hardships, derived from the behavior of other people and, what's worse, from his own human nature, has been a bloody battle. Oh man, is he bad. The worker's awareness of his duties on one hand, and on the other his moral conviction of terrible, passionate, interested resistances in which his daily revolutionary efforts ceaselessly tumble and crash, do battle in his soul like two wild beasts. His duties are as overbearing and unyielding as the obstacles are enormous and invincible. His moral drama is pathetic, heart-rending.

When he enters his room, he finds his son, about twelve years old, asleep on a bench. His companion isn't home, still at work. It's nine o'clock at night. There's great desolation in the family nest. As always. Such is the life of the revolutionary worker. For now, the home has ceded all spiritual importance to the factory. The home exists only for a few seconds each day. Today the factory is the true home of the Soviet worker. A question of quantities and qualities. The classist family is nothing more than the Roman family, enlarged and liberated.

The worker doesn't want to go to bed. He wouldn't be able to sleep. He's pensive and suffers. He thinks about his great efforts; perhaps they're vain and useless. Here's the son, the poor thing, alone, abandoned. Seeing him asleep, like a little fragile thing, his heart is torn. His personal sacrifice, in favor of the collective good, is only a concern to him; but the sacrifice of his family . . . because man, in the end, no matter his social class, is a being with the instincts of father and husband. Socialism usually doesn't suppress or shackle these instincts except to make them rational and just. But we're not in the socialist system yet. The Soviet social order is revolutionary, and the revolution has its provisional, still-terrible demands, among which are the momentary breakdown of the family and the concentration of sentimental energies and interests of the worker on his revolutionary workshop.

The dramatic vigil of the worker culminates in a bout of desperation. He takes a jar and is going to down its contents. (Do you remember Sobol, Yesenin, Mayakovsky? Suicide in Soviet society is one of the many intermittent and reluctant residuals of the revolutionary psyche. It subtly reappears by the dozens.) But the worker hesitates. He's still fighting. It's time to sweat blood and "take this cup from me." As he lifts up the jar, a small hand suddenly stops him. It's the hand of his son, who wasn't sleeping. The boy's action is of far-reaching historical significance.

A shudder runs through the crowd, and they exclaim, "Long live the social revolution!"

[*Nosotros* (Buenos Aires), no. 266, July 1931]   [JM]

14. FILM
Russia Inaugurates a New Era on the Silver Screen

Vladimir Mayakovsky has taken me to the *générale* of *The General Line* by Eisenstein. After a contradicted or, rather, debated explanation by the film operator, Sneiderov, the onscreen inauguration is received by the audience—of critics, artists, and writers—with endless ovation. Classist ovation for the film's propagandistic character? Ovation in admiration of Eisenstein? To a very small degree, ovation for the great artist and, almost entirely, ovation for the propaganda. It's understood that the dominant plane in Russia today is constructed by the political economic revolutionary. This doesn't mean—as jealous professors and bourgeois aesthetes suppose—that the Soviet believes that economics and politics are superior, and art, inferior. The Marxist organization of social phenomena in infrastructures and superstructures—economy, politics, law, morality, religion, philosophy, art—doesn't entail any hierarchy at all. When Marx states that the foundation of human society is the economy, he doesn't pretend that it's superior to politics, law, or art. All he does is state a fact, a reality. It's like when one states that there are feet at the base of the body: by this one doesn't mean that the feet are superior or inferior to the head, torso, or arms.

Could it be that other countries don't enjoy the same social distinction in economics and politics as Russia does? Indeed it could. The economics and politics of all countries have an identical social distinction to that which Russia has, and so it has been throughout history. The difference is that, in Russia, economic and political activities are the domain of everyone and at the service of everyone, while in capitalist or feudal countries, the economy and politics are managed and directed by a select few and at the service of a select few. Here we have the mass that produces the wealth with which all social phenomena are supported and develop, yet only a few—the employers or lords—take it upon themselves to gear those phenomena toward the benefit and well-being of said few. So then, apparently, for the majority and in its eyes, economics and politics lack social distinction from the moment they no longer depend on the positioning and maneuvering of a tiny chapel of vedettes.

Who in France takes it upon himself as a personal challenge to study, channel, and perfect the methods of transportation? Just any bystander, man or woman? Of course not. The only one who takes it upon himself is the manufacturer of engines, wheels, or tires, or the entrepreneur of streetcars, or the steelmaker, or the railroad concessionaire. The bystander believes that it doesn't concern him. (In effect, it concerns him only when the time comes to pay his train fare or luggage fees or when he must uselessly wait for the broken-down locomotive.) And in England, who takes it upon himself to improve and humanize the penal system? Just any bystander? No. The only one who takes it upon himself is the parliament member, minister, lord, magistrate, or professor at Cambridge or Oxford. This is of no concern to the bystander until the time comes to go to prison for having said some truth to the equivocal prince of Wales or for having publicly condemned the war of bourgeois countries. And down this road, all the bystanders of the capitalist world—who are a mass—have reached the conclusion that economics and politics aren't more than occupations of remote, hazy initiates that the collective can eschew without too much difficulty. In sum, bourgeois political and economic phenomena consent to and demand the intervention of the people only to make them suffer their consequences and to place on the shoulders of the masses the apparatus of production, the base of those phenomena, but in no way to have a bearing to direct these men. Consciously or unconsciously, professors and bourgeois aesthetes defend this reality.

In Russia, politics and economics are carried out in the public light, in the open air. They depend on everyone's direct and effective management. They've democratized. Those problems belong to and are resolved by everyone, given that their solutions and transformations are to the detriment or for the benefit of the collective. The Soviet management of the res publica—with its broad electoral base, its right to revolution, and the union in the hands of the masses or legislative and executive branches—contains the most direct and genuinely democratic core that any government has had and exercised throughout history. The Greek republics almost resemble them, although only in formal and external regards, but not because of their content of truly democratic and creative masses. In this way, economics and politics in Russia may have a visibly menacing bearing on the people.

* * *

As in *The Battleship Potemkin*, Eisenstein executes a revolution of media, technique, and objectives of film in *The General Line*. What Eisenstein brings is an aesthetic of labor (not an economic aesthetic, which is a non-sensical, absurd notion). Labor is elevated as the primary substance, genesis, and sentimental fate of art. The thematic elements, the scale of the images, the découpage, and the caesura of the composition in all of Eisenstein's work is based on and concurs with the emotion of labor in which everything hinges on the brand new myth of production: the mass, social class, proletarian consciousness, class struggle, revolution, injustice, hunger, Nature with its raw materials, History with its implacable materialist dialectic. What do we see and feel at the bottom of these forms of the social process? Labor, the great re-creator of the world, the drive of drives, the act of acts. What's most important is not the mass but the motion of the mass, the act of the mass, just as the matrix of life is not matter but rather the motion of matter (from Heraclitus to Marx). Eisenstein, who is currently taking the theory of historical materialism to the screen, has stuck to the leitmotif of labor in *The General Line* and in *The Battleship Potemkin*, setting the entire social apparatus in motion for the performance: the government—reactionary and revolutionary—army, clergy, bureaucracy, navy, bourgeoisie, nobility, proletariat, factory, farm, city, tractor, airplane, wealth, and misery. These diverse social factors aren't more than the creation of labor. Without it, human society is impossible. Labor is the father of life, the center of art. The rest of the forms of social activity are merely specific, diversified expressions of the primary act of economic production: labor.

Eisenstein addressed this central leitmotif on various filmic registers. The first of these is the social mechanism of labor, its mode of human realization: the way work is and should be done by the members of a collective. Does labor correspond to a single man, to many, or to all men? It is this coarse and, at once, sleek statement that Eisenstein dialectically poses and resolves in his films. Labor was individual in the presocialist era, but it started to become social with the rise of the human collective, yet this was born the day two men first joined forces to work. Labor is the father of human society. In humans labor is an essentially collective phenomenon, an act of the many. Everyone must work. But, what are, in effect, the social modalities of current-day economic production? This leads Eisenstein to the social drama of labor, originated by the wickedness of a few select men for whom the effort of production must be exerted solely by certain social levels, while other levels have a sort of right to do nothing, and for whom, on the other hand, the wealth created by labor must follow a distribution method inverse to that of its production: those who produce it take barely 5 percent of it, while those who produce nothing, 95 percent. The struggle between the former and the latter is the class struggle in all daily areas of cohabitation: in the home, on the street, at the temple, on the farm, in the workshop, on the ship, in the barracks, at the office, in the bank. It's the exploitation of man by man. The most violent forms of this social drama of labor are the famine of the workers, the luxury of the parasites, the protest of the masses, the massacre of the latter by their exploiters, the insurrection and occupation by the producers and the consequential reaction of their exploiters.

In the end, the integral and fair socialization of work—in the production and distribution of wealth—constitutes Eisenstein's second filmic aspect. This is the socialist edification by the proletariat, the infinite collectivization of the workers' life. Socialism. Here Eisenstein arrives at the glorification of labor, no longer as a myth based on the origin of human society—a springboard in the development of Eisensteinian art as a whole—but rather as a myth based on the future. This is the celebration of hope, faith, effort, good will, fair practice, and universal love.

As one can see, the two filmic moments in Eisenstein are not more than forms and modes of dialectically determining the leitmotif that is labor, the base of every artwork, just as it is the base of the social apparatus of history. This leitmotif embraces and tacitly fills—by omniscience—the entire development of Eisenstein's oeuvre.

The images of labor! This artist has almost always been accurate in the selection, composition, and *découpage* of the images. The filmic creation is newer in the history of the silver screen than in the contextualization of the leitmotif. For the first time in film, the elemental powers and tools of economic production, the State apparatus, the imponderables of industrial technique, the forms of social wealth, the avatars of raw materials, the dialectical materialism of history, the movement and resting of life, are discovered, composed, and *découpe* with an astonishing cinedialectical effect—to use an epithet by Eisenstein himself. In *The Battleship Potemkin* and in *The General Line* there are prodigies in this point, for example: a frieze of tractors, seen from an airplane, coiling like a serpent on a plot of land in the kolkhoz; a carpenter's saw, cutting like the bow of a violin a Nordic pine trunk or slicing through the middle of a joist with the isochronal flux of a shuttle; the steel spiderwebs in a section of a *kombinat*,[17] where a group of workers are spread out like gigantic nightmarish ganglia; a parade of turbines running eight deep, in focus up close and elevated in the gigantic electrical installations of the Dnieper; a series of pistons firing point-blank in the lower machinery of a ship; the hand that orders and the machine that orders, the latter based on the former with a Marxist leap from history; the bull in rut, at the moment it shoots like an arrow toward the distant cow that awaits it; a firing squad taking aim at the masses; bank notes falling successively from the hands of the poor onto the table of the kulak; the transformative process of milk into cheese, butter, and other derived products; the dizziness of a wheat field, swaying in the breeze (negative frame) and gilded—all the chromium from the gold—by the sun and the clouds (positive frame).

Here, the human forces of work reach unprecedented expressions and images. This is a psychological risk unknown to capitalist subjectivism in film. Here, we're in the presence of a new psychology. The psyche that Eisenstein reveals to us isn't an individualist, introspective psyche, but one that's socialist, sane, and objective. It is in function with the collective tribulations of life, for example, the visual of a scream of contempt in the mouth of a marine; the expression of pain on the face of a worker wounded by the machine gun of capitalism; ten thousand pairs of proletarian hands applauding an agitator; swarming masses retreating in horror at their employer's howitzers; the curve of a revolutionary's chest acquiring its greatest convexity in the face of the squad about to fire at him; the bloated greasy eyelids of the employer who sleeps like a log; a crowd at a protest rally; a fat black fly grazing on the sweat of the adipose cheeks of a NEPman brutalized and immobilized by exuberant digestion; a procession of icons with ad hoc decor; the bone dry expression of a ship's captain when he gives the order to shoot the starving sailors; the luminous and euphoric smile of the muzhik, civilized and liberated by the Bolsheveki . . .

One brief distinction is to be made between *The Battleship Potemkin* and *The General Line*: the first film contains the deconstructionist[18] moment in the process of production; the second contains, most of all, the constructionist moment of that process. The first is more psychological; the second is more sociological. The former is more painful and episodic; the latter is more painless and permanent. That one exposes the events of history as they are; this one exposes them as they should be. Therefore, they complete each other in the filmic explanation of the social process, as two sides of the same coin.

How far we are here from Hollywood and all its schmaltzy, decadent dressing rooms! [JM]

From *Russia Facing the Second Five-Year Plan*

WHAT IS THE WORKERS' CLUB?

The Workers' Club in an institution that was created after the October Revolution in Russia, and there's no other club like it in the world. It's an extension of union life, a branch of class solidarity and proletarian cohabitation that has the following distinguishing characteristics: its scope of action surpasses the interests of the union and is intimately focused on the interests of the collective; its activities are beyond the technique of career, profession, or its components, and they encompass all forms of creation—artistic, political, literary, moral, judicial, and economic; it's usually a cultural center where problems of national and international interest are debated and elucidated; it's a home, conducive to the spiritual peace of each worker and to the exchange of ideas and initiatives among laborers, one on one; and, finally, there's room for all workers without distinction of profession or union to pursue creative endeavors, particularly in public sessions and performances at the club. The structure, mechanism, and scope of the Workers' Club remarkably differ from those of the union. To this regard, it's an institution possible only during an advanced stage of the proletariat and during a relative peace in class struggle, an organ of socialist construction, whereas the union, naturally, is an organ of class warfare—an economic barricade. They cohabit and complete each other in the Soviet, since these two genuinely belong to the Dictatorship of the Proletariat.   [JM]

WORKERS DISCUSS LITERATURE

The group discussion of Soviet literature offers many suggestions and teachings. The workers of the club—mostly manual laborers, the "servants"—argued that night over a study by Lunacharsky that appeared a few days earlier in *Isvestia*,[19] about the new French literary school, populism, along with its similarities and differences in relation to contemporary Russian literature. Abroad one must exclaim with a bit of skepticism and a good bit of mockery: "The servants, discussing and publicly criticizing the aesthetic theories of an ex–minister of public education and fine arts?"

The response was obtained ahead of time, as talk about "servants" had already been heard in Moscow.

"This populism thing," one of them said, "is nothing but a trend. Since bourgeois writers have already exhausted all 'inventions,' today they come turning to us with the same facility as they might have turned, or still may turn, at a later day, to criminals, for example, to the mad, or to athletes. It's going nowhere, because it's mere eccentricity."

"Besides," another man added, "novels have been written about the 'servants' for centuries now. The Russians and the French have already done just that."

"What they want," said a female worker, "is to court the laborers, to plate them with gold, with literary dreams, the bitter pill of life."

"I don't know anything about those things," Yerko interjected. "I won't have bourgeois writers coming to make me read anything. What little I have read is nothing more than corruption, adultery, murder, luxury."

"He's right," an officer from the Red Army said. "Populist writers always address the same things in their books: adultery and corruption. The difference is that they see these things from the other side, as though they weren't complicit. And yet those populists write in the great newspapers of Paris, disguised and defending the bourgeoisie and its culture. Therefore, by describing the existence of the popular classes, what the populists do, as Lunacharsky says, is elicit mercy for them. Mercy, my friends, is not what we the workers desire. We don't want them to pity us. Nothing is gained from that, aside from an affront and insult. A worker begs for nothing and demands only social justice for all. The revolution is the struggle for justice and must not be confused for panhandling. It's not gratuity we're owed, but justice, justice, justice. And this justice is won only by force, with weapon in hand, because capitalists don't want to return, out of the good of their heart, what they've taken from us and keep taking every day—from us, the workers and true owners of the world. Comrades, down with the bourgeois, populist, surrealist writers and the rest of them! Long live the revolutionary writers!"

I notice that the words and ideas expressed by the different speakers are clearly comprehended by the whole crowd. Frequent are the interruptions, designed to specify and clarify the terms of the discussion. Questions from the least initiated and educated rain down and get answered with patient detail. There are moments when the intellectual tone falls back into nearly childish simplicity. Even so, the examination is always held tight to the simple and human essence of each problem. This is how one learns to comprehend what is simple in the most arduous social problems — how far we are from the ideological shells and the philosophical complications of bourgeois judgment! In group discussion, the argument is sincere; the word, fair; the conviction, bare; the idea, clean; the intention, diaphanous; the framework, dialectical, schematic; the process, swift. The results of this confluence of factors lead to fertile conclusions that are practical and operational. Group discussions and, more generally, ideological activities of the Workers' Clubs constitute one of the most potent and illuminating strengths of revolutionary doctrine in Russia. If instead of expecting the League of Nations to solve the world's problems, humankind were to expect it from the Workers' Club, one could be sure that war would be as impossible then as peace is now.   [JM]

THE MECHANICAL LANDSCAPE

Russia is sad. The sadness of strength. I get a strange feeling from the immense kolkhozy spread along the infinite steppes and from the cyclopean factories that rise from the nerve centers of its geographic economy — a feeling I've had facing the titanic masonry of the Panama Canal, the London docks, the factories in Dresden, the mines at Ruhr, the workshops and laboratories in Grenoble, and the grasslands on the outskirts of the Danube. It's the sadness of the heroic struggle of human beings or nature for higher forms of life.

Dnieprostroi! From the railway platform, my eyes feast on a panorama of the industrial city under construction. The morning is terribly cold. The air, a squall. The land, a tundra. It has rained all night. It rains here ten months out of the year, nonstop. So, due to its level and flow, the Dnieper lends itself to a Marxist *leap*, a five-year plan, a bold industrial undertaking in any case. Thus the Soviet has here laid out the foundations for an enormous electric power plant, designed to produce a propelling force for the intensive modernization and industrialization of that region. Once all the work is complete, according to the project laid out in the Gosplan, in Dnieprostroi Russia will own an electric power plant with a capacity of five million horsepower — the largest in the world.

We descend the gentle slope on a switchback toward the city, literally up to our knees in mud, and a glacial wind envelopes us, blowing across the river from the far bank. A vast perspective through and through. A constant feeling of distance prevails everywhere in this immense country, this Russia. It's just the opposite of what happens in France, England, or Italy, where everything seems to be jammed in our ribs. Could this be due to nature? Or because human beings, in a social activity, stamp their weights and measures onto objects?

The urban conglomeration that we see from afar—the industrial city—comprises a myriad of concentric hamlets, coiling one after another. The oldest of these dates back to the ancient times of the tzars. Nowadays, the sector of laboratories, studies, and offices (recently installed to direct and drive engineering and mechanical projects to fruition) rises from the heart of everything. The panoramic aspect of the city is completed by and takes all its character from the gigantic constructions erected alongside the river, occupying the southern tier of the region.   [JM]

ART AND REVOLUTION

A second outstanding moment in the session of the Workers' Club occurred during the domestic dances, whose themes come from the *servants'* everyday chores. It's a strictly proletarian affair for that reason, because the artists—men and women—are most likely workers. The expression, style, and lexicon are proletarian too, as is the mentality with which they've designed the costumes and decoration, the choreographic composition, and finally the song: solos, duos, and choruses. In this way, the emotion turns out to be rational and profoundly revolutionary, since the idea of the proletariat entails the idea of revolution. Everything in these dances effectively comes together with the feeling of class struggle, social justice, and, in a word, the socialist sentiment. This mixes—tacitly or expressly—with the lyrics of the songs and the hymns, the figures, the musical development, the literal allusions, and simple suggestions.

Here propaganda undoubtedly constitutes the tip of the performance's prow; however (and this is what's extraordinary about Soviet art), propaganda and political agitation aside, in such artworks there can and in many cases there really does remain for years to come a respectable balance favorable to the aesthetic of all places and times. The proof is in the influence that current Soviet theater, music, and film exerts on the most advanced of art circles worldwide, from a strictly aesthetic perspective.

The musical numbers reveal to me another no less illuminating and unexpected form of the revolutionary spirit in Russia.

On the piano and balalaika: Tchaikovsky's *Sad Song* and then *Rhapsody No. 2* by Liszt. I must confess that the announcement of the music by the Hungarian romantic struck me as somewhat anomalous, here, in the

Soviet workers' center. But I was even more surprised when it was played. Behind the applause apportioned to Tchaikovsky, whose herbaceous and idyllic sweetness had plunged the crowd into tenderness, the rhyming sounds of the rhapsody quickly and irresistibly pierced their proletarian hearts. For the duration of this music, I saw and felt the crowd tremble, gripped by a vast spiritual shudder. This revolutionary mass, the mass of historical materialism, which has made the greatest economic revolution in history with its own blood and hears nothing but the hammer of the factories and the motor of the tractors, this socialist, dynamic, and technical mass was showing me, a contemplative and arbitrary, indolent and egotistical, petite bourgeois man, what is and what is to be the course, the sign, the dialectical formula of the new society that it's fighting for. Tomorrow, when the fight ends—supposing it will end, supposing that such is the law of history—the way to love will be the definitive embrace of humankind. And it will then hold in store for all the combatants of today, forgers of that future, everything that in one way or another expresses the existence of history's raw material, which is, at once, the raison d'être of all rebellion and social struggle: love. On this day, during times of relative peace, the workers can already perceive (and every so often they do) through the everyday struggle, outside of combat, those direct expressions of love for humankind. This is what the crowd tells me and tries to get me to understand, while the balalaika of the steppe lets the last notes of the Hungarian rhapsody ring through its strings. I grasp the teaching, submissively, rationally.

An extended ovation follows the music. In the eyes of the workers—men and women—I notice that there's a different, unusual, almost extraordinary light.

"What did you think of that?" I ask Yerko. "Did you enjoy Liszt?"

"Yes," the *servant* of Europe replies with conviction.

And I know, from personal experience, just how much monosyllables are worth when they come from a Bolshevik's mouth. [JM]

DIALECTICS AND MANUAL LABOR

The female workers set off toward the embankments. Some of them wear boots and others, thick, wide shoes, like those of a man, and we see them stick their feet into the swamp, their faces lit up, their waists hefty, their gait quick. We follow. After a short walk, we turn on a hillock and arrive at the stonework encampment number 8. Many laborers come from different directions to the workplace, an immense area, situated on the left bank of the Dnieper, where gravel is dug and extracted for the production of bitumen.

As the day goes on, the wind builds up and blows harder and colder with each bluster, but almost everyone comes dressed in short, lean, tight-fitting garments, from skirt to smock. If this skirt was divided in half vertically, the whole exterior would suddenly become masculine. With this outfit, in its most simple expression, I have before me the economic border between the sexes. With this outfit, anyone will feel completely geared up for work on the banks.

The labor commences. After the instruments and tools are handed out and all the female workers are reviewed, they disperse in teams, undoubtedly following an outline previously set by off-site technicians. A few minutes in and around us we see a crowd of bodies engaged in different activities, with distinct rhythms and different timing. The workers labor in direct contact with the land. All that separates them from it is this: the tool. This is the position of manual labor within production: closer to nature than to thought. Consequently, its action is strictly subjected to telluric rigors, which thought—that supreme inventor and dispenser of commodities— has not as of yet managed to overcome, save in a negligible part.

"Poor people!" The socialist says to me. "Manual labor is undoubtedly hard work, and even harder when a woman has to do it. You sure have got to be strong, and even stronger outside in this weather."

Indeed. No matter how accustomed these women are to the weather and material labor, I clearly see reflecting in their eyes and expressions the toilsome, difficult endeavor and the reluctant trance of production. Custom doesn't alter the character or objective nature of the act to which one grows accustomed. The toilsome act is still toilsome. What one has done is grown accustomed to toil, which continues to be toil. Here custom is figured by the callus, but this is a natural excrescence, an organic expression of health, if not an abnormal sort of endurance, a sickly sign, the externalization of pain. The bourgeoisie often reiterates that the hard jobs of the workers are reserved for those who aren't accustomed to them, but not for the workers who habitually do them. If only that custom had the divine virtue of making the toil of the endeavor joyful or at least pain-less! But it doesn't. Custom sanctifies nothing. One step further: custom in itself contradicts the law of incessant motion and transformation of history. Everything else is merely a classist position of conservative sociology.

Working right now in the great construction sites of the Dnieper, these women patently suffer as they do their jobs, and in pain they step up and see them through to the end. Their effort is splintering. At the bottom of this, however, there is collective enthusiasm and abnegation—a tragic, tenacious, inherent principle to the labor. While they do their job, the workers aren't happy. Work here is wretched. The Austrian socialist is right. Manual labor is hard and even harder when women have to do it in a stormy climate and out in the open. Behold, the abbreviated tragic formula of these feats. In the equation, there's barely room, with a second subtraction sign, for the revolutionary fervor of the worker. The endeavor always ends up being dramatic, with all the proportions and characters of struggle and heroism.

Within production, as long as humans do what the machine could and should do, their endeavor will always be toilsome. By replacing the human arm at all the jobs that it's capable of executing, the machine will deliver man back. Manual labor awaits total redemption. Among other objectives of social welfare, the technician contemplates and seeks the definitive onset of joyful work, which must replace and is replacing painful work. So demands the dialectic of production. This transpires, in part, within the capitalist system and not as a practical effect of any employer's altruism, but rather as the ineluctable result organically entailed in the objective historical process of the economy.   [JM]

Articles and Chronicles

THE LESSONS OF MARXISM

There are men who formulate a theory or borrow it from their neighbor so that, with pitchfork or fist, they can try to stick or stuff life into that theory. As such, life ends up being at the service of doctrine, instead of the latter at the service of the former. Hardline Marxists, fanatical Marxists, grammatical Marxists, who pursue the realization of Marxism to the letter, forcing social reality to literally and loyally prove the theory of historical materialism—even while they denaturalize facts and distort the meaning of events—belong to this lot of men. By dint of seeing in this doctrine certainty par excellence, definitive, irrefutable, and sacred truth, they have converted it into a horseshoe, striving to make the evolution of life—so fluid, as luck would have it, and so pregnant with surprises—wedge that shoe on, even though it's bruising the toes and weakening the ankles. These are the doctors of the school, the scribes of Marxism, the ones who oversee and, with the jealousy of amanuenses, guard the form and letter of the new spirit, just like all the scribes of all the gospels throughout the course of history. Their adoption of and compliance with Marxism is so excessive and their vassalage so complete that they don't stop at defending and propagating it in its essence—which is what only free men do—but rather they go so far as to interpret it literally, that is, strictly. Thus, they end up becoming the first traitors and enemies of the very thing of which, in their trifling sectarian consciousness, they believe they're the purest guardians and most loyal depositories. It was no doubt with this tribe of slaves in mind that the master himself, the first one, resisted becoming Marxist.

What a pitiful orgy of parroting eunuchs the traitors of Marxism get in on. Based on the conviction that Marx is the only philosopher of the past, present, and future, who has scientifically explained social motion and who, as a consequence, has once and for all hit the nail on the head of the laws governing the human spirit, their first vital disgrace consists of amputating their own creative possibilities at the root, relegating them to the condition of panegyrist parrots and parrots of *Das Kapital*. According to these fanatics, Marx will be the last revolutionary of all time, and after him no man in the future will be able to create anything ever again. The revolutionary spirit ends with him, and his explanation of history contains

367

the final incontrovertible truth against which no objection or repeal is or ever shall be possible—not today, not ever. Nothing in life can or could be conceived or produced that won't fall within the Marxist formula. All universal reality is nothing more than a perennial and quotidian verification of the doctrine of historical materialism.

From astral phenomena to the secretory functions of the sex of euphorbia, everything is a reflection of man's economic life. To decide if they should laugh or cry at the passerby who slips and falls on the street, they must first pull out their pocket edition of *Das Kapital* and consult it. When they're asked if the sky is clear or cloudy, they open their Marx reader, and whatever they find there, that's the answer. They live and work at the expense of Marx. There's no strength demanded of them anymore when they face life and its vast changing problems. It's enough for them that the master once appeared before their eyes and has spared them the virile chore and noble responsibility of thinking for themselves and making direct contact with things.

Freud would easily explain the case of these men, whose behavior responds to instincts that precisely oppose the revolutionary philosophy of Marx. No matter how much a sincerely renovating intention inspires them, their effective subconscious action betrays them and turns them into tools of class warfare, old and occult, underlying and *refoulé*[20] in their innermost recesses. Formal Marxists and slaves of the Marxist letter are almost always of aristocratic or bourgeois roots or social stock. Education and culture haven't managed to expurgate these blights. Such is, for example, the case of Plekhanov, Bukharin, and other fanatical exegetes of Marx, descendants of bourgeois or aristocratic lines, converts.

Lenin, on the other hand, had separated himself and, on many an occasion, spoken out against the Marxist text. If he had adhered and restricted himself, down to the letter, to the ideas of Marx and Engels, regarding the incapacity and lack of capitalist maturity in Russian society, only to go ahead with the revolution and the implementation of socialism, the first proletarian government wouldn't currently exist.

Trotsky offered us many lessons of liberty too. His own opposition to Stalin is proof that he doesn't follow the flock when it disagrees with his spirit. In the midst of the colorless spiritual communion that the communist world observes before Soviet methods, the Trotsky insurrection constitutes a movement of great historical significance—the birth of a new revolutionary spirit from inside the revolutionary State, a new left inside the other left that, by natural political evolution, has turned out to be on the right after all. From this viewpoint, Trotskyism is redder than the red flag of the revolution and, consequently, the purest and most orthodox of the new faith.

[*Variedades* (Lima), no. 1090, January 19, 1929] [JM]

THE YOUTH OF AMERICA IN EUROPE

Paris, December 1928

Let us specify, once more, that America lacks a cultural home of its own. Does a Latin American spirit exist? Let us specify again that this does not exist nor will it exist for a long time yet. The first condition for bringing it about and creating it must come out of our sincere conviction that it does not exist, nor is it even glimpsed. The first step toward an original culture—that is, a vital culture—consists of creating the awareness that we still do not possess it. Let's try, then, to create in America the austere and rigorous awareness that we lack our own spirit and culture. Let's take charge of the need for this awareness, which is not a confession of more or less empirical vulgar humility but rather the first scientific and, if you like, technical act in an effective creative evolution. Let us conceive of that awareness, which in Cartesian terms could be called methodical or provisional awareness; let's try to engender it and make it count as the only point of departure for our reason for being. To achieve that, let's put into play all the destructive means against all the illegitimate traces and simulations of culture that sustain our continental pedantry. The surrealist movement—at its purest and most creative—can help us in this cleansing of our spirit, with the healthy and tonic contagion of its pessimism and desperation. Our state of spirit demands an active pessimism and a terrible creative desperation. Pessimism and desperation. Such are, for the present and to begin with, our first acts toward life. We haven't created anything. We have not even begun. We lack hope as much as bitterness, horizons as much as darkness. Our trouble lies not in a specific crisis of politics, economics, religion, or art. Our trouble resides in the fact that we haven't created anything, not truths nor errors; nor have we tried anything. Our case lies in chilling vital desolation.

In America the question is not understood in this way. The best intellects—most of them—start from another notion and another sentiment. A vulgar and exaggerated optimism, a facile and pedantic smugness, constitute the common base of every effort, whether sincere or simply for show, toward a Latin American culture. Whenever we're faced with the spirit of foreign societies, we are inclined in advance to find a constant balance of values—in facts or immediate perspectives—in our favor. A comfortable and foolish parti pris disposes us to always come out winning in these assessments. That is the humorous case of the Catherine Wheel in *The Remarkable Rocket* by Oscar Wilde. It's about one of the most disastrous forms of mistaken faith with its sudden slope toward indolence and inaction.

Other times, such optimism does not derive from a confrontation between foreign ways and our own. Most often, optimism arises from the individual and zoologically egotistical pretension of those who play the role of intellectual leaders of America. A frequent and well-known phenomenon can serve us as proof of this prodigiously foolish and alarming pedantry. When young intellectuals from America come to Europe, they don't come to honestly study foreign life and culture but rather to "triumph." They bring in their suitcases some books or canvases made in America and, barely do they arrive in Paris, no other wish stirs them but to triumph. Let the newspapers deal with them so they can return as soon as possible to their native land, tell their friends and fellows that they triumphed in Europe. They embark on the voyage from America to foreign lands, drawn not by life's concerns and by the healthy yearning for knowledge and perfection, but thinking about the return by steamship, carrying in their suitcase a few books with prologues by more or less questionable literary eminences, or an album of press clippings. They don't come to learn and to live but rather to get flustered and to return. They come with their feet, but they stay put with their skull and thorax.

Not long ago, a sculptor came and, eight days after his arrival in Paris, had a show of his work.

"You can't imagine," he told me in a heroic tone, "what this show cost me. The thirty pieces on exhibit I did in the few days that I've been in Paris. It's a tremendous effort. I haven't even had time to see the Eiffel Tower . . ."

"And who obliged you to do this show, so suddenly like that and right after arriving in Paris?" I asked him rather intrigued.

"No one. But I promised myself. You have to work, work, work . . ."

And you have to triumph, the sculptor meant to tell me.

They return, in effect, triumphant and celebrated. In their person and in the case of every one of them, what returns to America strengthened and consolidated is the sick continental optimism.

[*Mundial* (Lima), no. 450, February 1, 1929]   [JW]

Spengler has inadvertently perverted the youth of America. *The Decline of the West* has bruised the necks and ankles of more than one Latin American schoolboy. Diagonally, blame falls not on the philosopher for the fact that there are people who don't know how to read and, much less, deduce scientific outcomes from what they read, on account of their impartiality. (Science does not exclude passion.)

What teaching does America deduce from Spengler's work? The teaching that Western culture is in agony, calling for help to the constructive powers of other societies. And what are the powers that can substitute the Western spirit? The students of America think that in between the lines of *The Decline of the West* there subtly slithers the allusion to Latin America as the society, chosen by the dark unfathomable power of history to succeed the West in the cultural direction of the world. In virtue of what specific rhythm of history must Latin America be the focus of the next civilization? Latin American students don't know with certainty, and their explanations that endeavor to promote such a candidacy for the next cultural hegemony are drawn from imperialism and with complacency inborn in the soul of the creole.

This Latin American attitude, as improvised as it is desirous, is undoubtedly well known throughout the rest of the world. Even when no one truly believes in that mission of America, they're condescending—not without malicious, sarcastic winks behind our backs that we innocently keep straight with ambition that so many people leech off as the price of the tolerance they require to behold it—toward this or that form of economic imperialism (as in the United States) or this or that economic movement of social justice (as in the Soviet Union), only so they can oppose it head on or ambush it from behind.

But the Latin American thesis in itself—to say the least—is ridiculous, since it's not in keeping with our historical experience, our current cultural structure, or the objective reality of other societies.

No matter what have been the historical conditions in which we've lived thus far, we can't deny that our development has been awfully mediocre. Other people, as in the United States, have achieved in the same period a form of existence all their own. For an entire century of political freedom, we've done nothing. What has contributed to our disastrous historical inheritance and, especially, the lie of our independence? This very notion can be argued against a candidacy in the cultural direction of the world. A new culture is not pulled out of a pocket, from night to morning, and even less so, out of a pocket with a hole in it. The awakening of Russia proceeds not from an unexpected spark, as surmise certain mystics or romantics (enemies of all scientific concept of life), but rather from a slow, subterranean stirring of Muscovite society. The leaps of history addressed by Marx don't signify the suppression of procedural, successive phases of society but only the transformation—not unexpected but rather anticipated—of one phenomenon or system of phenomena into another. That after 11 comes 12 doesn't mean that one whisks away the unity that must be added to the eleven digits so that they "become" a dozen. In other words, the leap is rooted in the change from one "quality" to another, but not in the suppression or abbreviation of the "quantities," which are necessary precisely to produce a quality of social phenomena.

Western culture, on the other hand, is not the domestic, exclusive home of Europe. It's an organism whose nuclei and arms throb beyond that geographic parcel and vertebralize[21] the spirit of many other contemporaneous societies, among which we find Latina America. As for the case that said culture may truly be reaching its dawn—a phenomenon that Spengler locates in a very elastic period—it would likewise have to die in the societies whose cultural foundation bears its seal, and this includes Latin America. A rigorously European shoot, deprived of all autochthonous character, our social spirit now more than ever must follow the historical peripeteia of the parental home from which it proceeds and on which it feeds. It's a fact of everyday observation that the parasite (and especially the apterous parasite, the symbolic genera of the tortoise, or any rudimentary species that can't escape, due to its inability to move on its own) which has contracted the fatal contagion of the organism that nourishes it, rots along with the being it feeds on.

Another difficulty for a forthcoming Latin American hegemony arises from our confrontation with other societies whose development places them as possible successors of the Western spirit, compared to whom we end up irremediably inferior. Russia and the United States—where all unrest and power is currently polarizing—would undoubtedly be prescribed to insufflate new life into men. They're called to that role by their great natural resources, their own cultural disciplines, their enormous population, their homogeneity; as for Latin America?

In the abstract terrain of these hypotheses, to the claim that we don't know what people are capable of, we'll respond that perspectives on the future unfortunately are made of pliable resources that are more or less real and malleable. When these resources emerge from vagueness, improbability, or randomness and slip between our fingers, we can say nothing about the future.

With regard to sociology, Marx has once and for all decreed the bankruptcy of sentimentalism, utopia, and patriotism, lesser or greater as they may be.

[*El Comercio* (Lima), February 3, 1929]   [JM]

THE ECONOMIC MEANING OF TRAFFIC

On rue de Rohan, which connects rue de Rivoli to the Place du Théâtre Français, all the vehicles are currently stopped. It's one of the countless bottlenecks in the downtown arterials of Paris and, since it's so cold, a writhing scandal ensues. The chauffeurs, pedestrians, and traffic police all shout, protest, and furiously argue. Frozen gales blow in off the Seine, and one cannot just stand there without dying from exposure. The cars try to move on; they screech, and one tire after another goes flat. Many fumes, of a blue that comes from the paschal Baltic to the June-time Mediterranean, are emitted from the vehicles. Shortly thereafter, the jam clears up and, once again, wheeled are the wheels that wheel[22] with the feel of a Greek hexameter.

Yet two minutes later the bottleneck forms again in the same street. In one hour the traffic has jammed thirty-fold. The pedestrians grow absolutely livid. In Paris, one cannot walk, yet one can't simply go for a ride either, given that not everyone can afford a fare. Some pedestrians miss their train, others their date, others lose their lives. One recent statistic shows that the number of traffic victims increases proportionately with the number of new cars on the road. In cities with the most automobiles, the number of victims is the greatest across the board. Regarding the quantity of cars and the number of victims, the descending scale is this: New York, London, Paris, Berlin, Vienna. And we must note, moreover, that the depiction of victims does not follow the depiction of the progress of the industrial machine's safety features implemented to prevent accidents. U.S. and British car manufacturing certainly offer greater solidity and assurance than the French and Germans do, and yet it's precisely in New York and London that more people perish in traffic accidents. Might we attribute this to the poor system of traffic flow? Let's suppose we can. Even still, it can't be denied that the most advanced, if not perfected, traffic systems are those of London and New York.

There's one very significant detail in bottlenecks and traffic jams worth pointing out. Along with the protests of pedestrians, the protests of chauf-feurs explode. This is quite interesting. The pedestrian protests, because he believes that he's a victim of the automobile and, logically, of its driver, at whom he blatantly growls, without realizing that it's not always the chauffeur's fault. On the other hand, the chauffeur directs his insults at the pedestrian, who's clearly the one that's immediately blocking traffic, without realizing either that the pedestrian isn't always to blame for these conflicts. And in the midst of both protests, as slanderous as he is irascible, the policeman emerges and usually gives the right of way to the higher-up, that is, to the one in the automobile . . . The order is thus reestablished, tip-ping the scale upward against "the underdogs," as Azuela[23] would put it. In bottlenecks, collisions, and other traffic accidents, as one can see, there's an underlying socioeconomic conflict. These are sharp and lively dramati-zations of class struggle. They're the picturesque and, at once, tragic peri-peteia of the political scene of history. Except that the chauffeur—one of the underdogs—unknowingly defends the higher-ups, the car owners or passengers able to pay cab fare, and the pedestrian attacks the chauffeur, when he should seek solidarity with him. These two errors are the blun-ders and irony inherent in the drama, and they make it all the more bloody and painful.

The social phenomenon is supported by multiple, innumerable, histori-cal tactics. Sometimes it's a man who shoots at his own head and doesn't kill himself, or it's that other man, who aims at four in order to get three. Or else it's Andreyev's governor,[24] who gives himself to dreams of justice for his constituency. Or it's the traitor from *The End of St. Petersburg*.[25] When Great Britain and the United States intensify their fight for naval domination of the world, what they're really doing is increasing the un-employment rate in both countries and exacerbating proletarian distrust.

With the dialectic of Marx no one is placed in danger.

[*Mundial* (Lima), no. 459, April 5, 1929]   [JM]

NEW POETRY FROM THE UNITED STATES

Paris, June 1929

We all know that poetry is untranslatable. Poetry is tone, the verbal ora-tion of life. It is a work constructed with words. Translated to other words, synonymous but never identical, it's no longer the same. A translation is a new poem that hardly resembles the original. When Vicente Huidobro claims that his poems perfectly lend themselves to loyal translation into all languages, he's mistaken. Into the same error fall those who, like Huidobro, work with ideas instead of working with words and search in the version of a poem the letter or text of life instead of searching for the cardiac tone or rhythm of life. Gris was telling me, quite intelligently, that also riddled by this error are many modern painters who work with objects instead of working with colors. One forgets that the strength of a poem or painting comes from the way that the simplest and most elemental materials are placed. After all, the most elemental and simplest material of the poem is the word, and of the painting, color. Therefore, the poem must be worked with simple, loose words, moved and arranged according to the poet's creative taste.

The same occurs in architecture, music, and film. A building is constructed with stone, steel, and wood, not with objects. It would be absurd to build a palace out of tables, animals, drums, thrones, boats, with their peculiar movements and roles. Along the same lines, music is the arrangement of simple, loose sounds, not sonorous phrases. It would be absurd to compose a rhapsody out of the mooing of cows, laughter, footsteps, vegetable murmurs, or meteorological rumbles. In the *Consecration of Spring* one can detect—as if in a vivisection—the free birth of sounds, independent of all sonorous organization or any harmonic and melodic combination. Embryonic film worked with scenes and entire episodes, that is, with masses of images. Today, it begins to work with simpler elements: instantaneous scenes at a millisecond, combined and *découpées* according to the filmic sense of the "maker." Example: *The Three Mirrors*, running at the avant-garde cinema of the Ursulines and, to a wider and more essential degree, all Russian film.

Pierre Reverdy also votes for the impossibility of translating a poem. After I asked him if he'd like to see what I came up with for *Favorables* in Spanish translation, he told me that he preferred his poems be read in French. Naturally. What's important in a poem, as in life, is the tone with which something is said and, secondarily, what's said. The latter, in effect, is susceptible to passing into another language, but the tone used to say it is not. The tone remains, immovable, in the words of the original language. Consequently, the best poets are least conducive to translation. What gets translated of Whitman or Goethe is philosophical qualities and accents, and very little of their strictly poetic qualities. In foreign languages, one knows only their great ideas and mammalian movements but can't perceive the great numbers of the soul, the nebulous shades of life that reside in a turn, a *tournure*, as it were, of the word's imponderables.

In all likelihood, new poetry of the United States is something altogether different from what French and Spanish translators would lead us to believe. However, and ever remaining on the other side of the idiomatic barrier, one can establish, if one is attuned to what little gets over the wall, some of its characters and points of contact with other aesthetics.

One fact has been unanimously registered by European critics: the decisive influence of postwar European art in the new poetry of the United States. Here, we're not dealing with the European influence on the Yankees' so-called literary "renaissance" of 1912, whose dominant traces—imagism and free verse—evidently seem to emerge from Parisian and symbolist suggestions. European criticism now refers to cubist, expressionist, dadaist, and surrealist influences. "The Americans," Bernard Fay says, "are far too slow to invent synthetic rhythms and channels. While European poets, with cold mediocre inspiration, excel at inventing new forms, the Americans, though animated by a vast poetic delirium, are timid and crude at form as demanded by expression. This explains how American poets have avidly set out to learn new techniques: French, German, and English."[26] But the phenomenon appears to be different. It is, rather, the new European poets who are beginning to Americanize, by universalizing themselves without claiming to do so. The new spirit of the world demands an undaunted vitalist drive, a profound sanguine sense of life, a supreme realism, a uniformly accelerated dialectic. Though presenting its deepest human urgency and its vastest scientific horizons in Russia, this vitalism nonetheless sets a more spectacular, ostentatious precedent in the United States, which (along with the cultural vicinity between the United States and Western Europe) brings about the slow and tacit Americanization of the European youth.

Moreover, in this case there's one fact that bears tremendous force: the vitalist imperative of our epoch is recognizably of the North American tradition. Walt Whitman is indisputably the most authentic precursor of new poetry worldwide. The European youth, the best of them, lean with both hands on *Leaves of Grass*. Beyond Walt Whitman, the new European schools remain on the peripheries of life with their formulaic poetry. They're stuck in the poem of the private study—masturbation. The most interesting European youth Whitmanize, taking from Walt Whitman what universal and human aspects there are in the spirit of the United States: his vitalist feeling, in the individual and collective, which even now acquires an unforeseen historical preponderance worldwide.

New poetry from the United States offers an identical orientation. It comes from the Whitmanian tradition and carries it on, rectifying it. Alongside this fraternal, synchronistic tendency of Europe's better caliber, a second direction in the United States has been discovered: European importation, which follows the formulas and *poncifs*[27] mentioned by Fay—formulas and *poncifs*, we repeat, that are equally bookish and decadent.

To the first strain belong the writers of proletarian origin or, at least, those of the people, Negroes many of them. This is a sensibility that, without having managed to purge the capitalist sin, still translates the most noble strengths and concerns of that people. Let us cite, as examples, Hart Crane, Michael Gold, Gwendolyn Haste, Langston Hughes, Ell Slegel, and Vachel Lindsay. To the second tendency belong the recalcitrant imagists, with Ezra Pound and Hilda Doolittle at the head, and the equally recalcitrant dadaists, whose chief is Gertrude Stein.

In neither of these two tendencies does the "hoped for" accent appear, the transformative accent that, without breaking off with the profound and sane historical nexus, breaks with the artificial conventions and social errors. The result echoes a timid, liberal anger, and its scope even now doesn't surpass those Whitmanian *Vistas*. However, out of the young writers of the first tendency, undeniably revolutionary shudders surge, at times, and express a state of collective spirit, which, on certain underlying levels, is equally saturated with the social unrest at hand.

[*El Comercio* (Lima), July 30, 1929]   [JM]

BURIED ALIVE

Paris, June 1929

A recent statistic claims that four million people in Europe have been buried alive since the beginning of the Christian era to our time. Currently, the ratio of those buried alive is one out of every thirty thousand interments. In France they calculate six hundred burials of the living each year. In the United States the proportion is five out of every thousand. No matter how much Dr. Farez doesn't believe these figures, discarding them as arbitrary, one can't deny that premature interment is an evident fact that recurs with greater or lesser frequency. Let's suppose that these figures are embellished. This doesn't destroy the essential gravity of the phenomenon that resides in its constant possibility. The statistic shows that it transpires in the current state of science with the same frequency as it did two thousand years ago, when medicine was still in its infancy. Scientific progress has thus far been unable to bring the number down. Will the future hold similar findings in store for us? Might there not be a way, if not to radically avoid this phenomenon, then at least to reduce its frequency?

We're not reading some tale by Poe or playing an unofficial, spiritualist, merely athletic game. We don't wish to jostle our ontological fibers out of disinterested metaphysical pleasure. Here we face a serious problem of reality that concerns life and the most basic rights thereto before it concerns death and the mysterious death rattle. Can we be erased from life by mistake or due to the professional negligence of the people in charge of verifying the bereavement? Does science truly feel incapable of certifying that an individual, at a given moment, is dead or alive? These are the main points of the problem, as posed in an advanced society like France or the United States. In underdeveloped countries, it can occur because there's no physician to make the call or because of the interested parties' ignorance or superstition.

In many respects to the question, let's agree with Dr. Farez that the aforementioned figures are embellished and capricious, that in this embellishment one notices the interests of certain traffickers who try to exploit the credulity of one's neighbors to the benefit of some lurid insurance company, and that other propagandists of this danger are the obsessed, phobic, organic cravens who've given their pathologies the character and value of objective realities. Let's agree, most of all, that the majority of the cases of people buried alive is nothing more than legends, stories, or tall tales—melodramatic inventions through and through. These false cases are found by the thousands in daily newspapers, and the public believes them as words of the gospel since they're in print. Sometimes, it's a novelistic story that comes from beyond the sea. Readers here don't perceive a merely imaginative work but a case of unimpeachable, loyally transcribed reality. Other times, it's a *fait divers* invented by the local media, relating to an event that is presented as though it really occurred somewhere, on such a day at such a time. Most often it's the transcription made by the press of truly abracadabrant and fantastic hubbub, without proof of any kind.

Point in case: Marie Logstel, a civil servant in a major central European city, is on the cusp of getting married. Certain difficulties arise at the last minute. Marie writes to her relatives so that they come to pressure her fiancé. Said relatives, a gaggle of greedy peasants who don't want to waste their time, play deaf and refuse. One day they receive the following telegraph: "Your daughter, Marie, has died." This time they come to see her, with the fear of regret that their denial could've determined Marie's suicide. And when they get off the train, their surprise has no limits: Marie, the daughter, in flesh and bone, is there to welcome them. As for the telegram about her death? A simple subterfuge to oblige them to come. But in the newspaper the date of her death has already been registered and, when they tried to correct the information, it didn't say what had actually occurred, but this instead: "Marie Logstel, whose death we reported to our readers, has come back to life . . . etc." And the newspapers worldwide throw the news of this sensational case into the wind. They adorn it with details, dramatize it, describe the horrifying situation of the poor girl in the coffin and, nonetheless, it remains registered as authentic.

Let's agree with Dr. Farez on all this, but also move on to true cases of premature interment and ask the illustrious wise man and his eminent colleagues, is there an infallible sign that indicates when a person has died? "Yes," we are told. That sign is the green stain on the abdomen, the unmistakable signal of putrefaction. This is the classic sign of death, its irremovable seal. "However," Dr. Farez adds, "the green stain often appears quite late and the habitual conditions of existence require the interment to occur without too much delay. The prognosis of death must therefore be pronounced prior. To do so physiologists have come up with numerous experimental methods." These methods demand exceptional professional implementation and scientific education rarely found among doctors. So the same distress lives on as always—no one can avoid the risk of being buried prematurely due to scientific deficiency or professional negligence, because if the doctor that treats us is inept or deliberately disdains his professional duties, we're goners.

One mustn't forget that the verification of death, by means of the methods proposed by Farez's physiologists, poses serious scientific problems that are most likely to be resolved by the particular sensibility of each doctor than by general formulas and rules. Dr. Farez himself recognizes these difficulties when he says, "It's a mistake to believe that death is sudden and definitive—that it immediately replaces life. Life goes away, but death hasn't come yet." Therefore, there is neither life nor death. All mortals pass through this intermediate state. Ah, if the arrival of death could be postponed and stopped from insensibly reaping the whole organism! . . . Ah, if that life in limbo could be revived, as occurs with the hanged! . . . Utopia? Literature? Give me a break. Full perspective of practical possibilities. Everything depends on the scientific capacity of doctors and their professional dedication.

In sum, at times like this, science provides infallible resources to verify whether a subject, at any given moment, is still alive or dead. If cases of people buried alive occur, they're due to the ineptitude or immorality of the doctor who verifies the bereavement.

[*Mundial* (Lima), no. 480, August 30, 1929]   [JM]

At eight in the morning, the train pulls away from the platforms at Warsaw, heading toward the Russian border. The travelers return to their compartments or stand in the corridor to watch the landscape march by. I've stayed in my own compartment. Two young Polish students, who had been with me since Berlin, just got off. I go through various cars in search of French speakers going to Moscow, as I need to obtain reports to guide my first steps at the border.

Seated in the corner of a budget-class compartment, I see a young woman, slim and pale, donning a beret in the quaint style of the Parisian *midinette*. My footsteps make her to turn around. Her blue eyes look at me with that universal unspoken sympathy that a foreigner feels for another foreigner in a foreign country. The Bolshevik tendency in Paris, Berlin, London, Warsaw—a warmhearted spirit of solidarity toward foreigners— seems to stem from a socialist will, consciously or subconsciously, to unite all travelers of the world to counteract the troglodytic xenophobia that prevails these days. This young woman is certainly Bolshevik. Her foreign expression, her economic desolation in third class, and, especially, the universal cordiality of her socialist gaze, attract me out of the blue. A shiver runs over her, so I ask if I should close the small window of the compartment. She thanks me in bad French with a raspy cough.

"Are you going to Moscow?" I inquire.

"Yes," she responds with another cough. "Are you going to Moscow too?"

"I am. Are you Russian?"

"Yes. Russian," she says with a faint smile.

An interesting friendship, I think. And since I saw the coat and hat of a man in her compartment, I ask her if she's traveling with a companion.

"No," she says. "I'm traveling alone. My husband stayed in Paris. A gentleman is sitting here. I don't know him; he just got on in Warsaw. I think he's Russian too."

I've spent all morning conversing with these two travelers, whom a precious coincidence brought together here to reveal to me, in a lively and dramatic way, the current double feature of Russian society: moribund bourgeoisdom and nascent socialism. While our friend is a hardline communist (the fanatical type of woman from the Russian Revolution), our companion is a bourgeois doctor, a white Russian man from whose mouth I've seen spew edifying apostrophes against the proletarian State.

The doctor sat down across from the young woman and speaks to her tenderly, as to a sick patient he's treating, "Do you feel okay? . . . Has anything changed? . . . Do you have enough air? . . . Do you want me to open the window? . . ."

Traveling in fine clothes, he's a polished professional bourgeois type — ginger blonde, his nose curved down as if from a wallop, his eyes roll around in an unpleasant movement that pronounces his evident well-being. He hums and looks at the landscape or reviews his briefcase, and I observe that he, a man of great stature, surreptitiously and disdainfully glances as me, an inferior stranger.

Since the doctor came in, the woman has sunken into complete silence. She coughs less often and focuses on the landscape, as though she didn't wish to get in the way of our words. I venture to interpret this attitude as directed against the doctor, whose courtesy and requests don't seem to have provoked in her any greater echo than a few dry formulas of gratitude.

What an eloquent and dramatic silence this is, between two people who incarnate the two historical fronts of the Russian Revolution! The noise of the train, running over the Slavic land, strangely and profoundly reaches consonance with the silence of the compartment. The noise of the machine over Nature; the silence of one social class facing an opposing social class; the rattling noise of the machine, which must be understood and cooperate with the land, for the sake of economic production; and the militant silence of the revolutionary, hounding and cornering the bourgeois exploiter — the henchman of the workers. In the presence of the sound of the train and the silence of my compartment, I'm attacked by a host of images from the revolution and a boisterous, processional panorama of history.

[*Mundial* (Lima), no. 484, September 27, 1929]   [JM]

MUNDIAL IN RUSSIA

Leningrad, October 1929

Two cornerstones allow anti-Soviet foreign media to declare the failure of the current Russian system: the so-called economic crisis and political crisis.

What is the actual economic system at present? Is it the system of the NEP? Has it slanted to the right, favoring the development of the elite bourgeoisie? Has it slanted to the left, returning to wartime communism? Are we in outright socialism? Are we in outright capitalism? Among other organizations of the reformist press, *Le Populaire*[28] was recently claiming that the Soviet has decreed the suppression of the NEP since the end of last July. Is it true that the NEP has been suppressed and that, as they add, the Soviet has returned to wartime communism? Is it true that this suppression has suddenly been decreed as an extreme and distressing measure that would foretell a real catastrophe and failure for the NEP? Neither one nor the other is true. The NEP hasn't been suppressed, and this measure hasn't been taken in the *ex abrupto* fashion that the newspaper claims. The NEP continues to frame Russian economic life just as Lenin thought it would. What *Le Populaire* deems "suppression of the NEP" is nothing but the increasing swiftness with which this economic form elicits the action its founder had designed it to execute: the progressive elimination of the elite bourgeoisie. The NEP gave rise to the NEPman, to later suppress him by the spontaneous function of the economic phenomenon of the Soviet. With the NEPman dead, the NEP disappears. That's what's happening. *Le Populaire* spins the facts and lies, because it wants to discredit the Dictatorship of the Proletariat, which has unmasked the newspaper before the eyes of French workers, stripping it of any political influence over them and of any possibility of exploiting them.

Yet this leads to the second argument against the Soviet: the political crisis. "How do we explain," says *Le Populaire*, "while socialism progresses in Russia," as the Soviet sustains, that "the old Bolsheviki, the heads of the revolution, capitulate to capitalism by sliding toward reformation or turning into government opposition?" Here, *Le Populaire* wants to swindle the public with ambiguous, sybaritic questions. Who are those old Bolsheviki that capitulate by opting for reformation? Are they alluding to Rykov? *Le Populaire* knows very well that, since the beginning of the revolution, Rykov was a moderate in the Bolshevik party. Rykov has been and is, by his temperament, an opinion of counterweight—a skeleton key in the government. With regard to international politics, the voice of Rykov singlehandedly reaches for peaceful methods with a technique of calm. It has heavily influenced the recent attitude of Russia in the eyes of the aggressors, the Chinese government.

As for the supporters of the revolution, who join the opposition, the allusion to Trotsky is palpable in the words of *Le Populaire*, but in this case we're also dealing with someone who comes from very far away. The action and thought of Trotsky, even before the revolution, has notoriously been extremist in essence. His extremism is nowhere to be found today. Most of Trotsky's disagreements with Lenin are explained by the former's temperamental, incurable leftism. During the days of the revolution, long after he formally became part of the Bolshevik party, Trotsky kept addressing the problems of the civil war and the organization of the proletarian government with exacerbating intransigence. Only the profound, ideological, and political devotion he felt for Lenin contained the excesses of his extremist tactic and permanent rebellion. Therefore, Trotsky is a revolutionary and a hardline combatant. During Lenin's life, what for Trotsky was simple spiritual propensity or a controlled, muzzled action turned into the disappearance of the powerful, respected chief—an unleashed and uncontrollable action. Once Lenin died, no one was left in the party with the ideological authority and personal influence capable of harnessing that "moral monster," as Lenin used to call Trotsky.

While judging the current politics of the members of the Soviet government, if one forgets or consciously ignores the historical and biographical analysis, the most pitiful pitfalls are unavoidable. *Le Populaire* wants to present the current action of different communist leaders as events without history, produced from night to morning by unforeseen, insurmountable difficulties of the system. But this method is neither healthy nor scientific. In the study of facts and social problems one can't eschew situations originated by the individual and psychological factors of each actor, since they strongly influence the course of history and, as Marx says, the social superstructures.

Naturally, when one's opinion is incomplete and oversimplified, as occurs in the case of *Le Populaire*, self-deception is a snap.

[*Mundial* (Lima), no. 495, December 13, 1929]   [JM]

MUNDIAL IN EASTERN EUROPE

Vienna, October 1929

Since the war, at the height of U.S. global power, German influence has survived to this day *au relenti*[29] in almost all countries of Central and Eastern Europe. On a trip with lengthy strides through Austria, Czechoslovakia, Hungary, and Yugoslavia, I discover this subsistence of the German spirit most notably in the technique of production. Marx teaches that to know the character, trajectory, and future of a country, one must be guided by the state and physiognomy of its technique of production. For a momentary evaluation the traveler must leave aside whatever art, literature, religion, and philosophy he's trying to understand. First and foremost, he must focus on the forces, environments, and instruments of economic production, if he wants to dive straight into his survey and observations.

With clarity greater today than ever before, one sees that on the eve of the war Germany was indisputably lord and master of all countries to its west. Yet while Great Britain was dominating Scandinavia and even many of the Latin counties of Europe, Germany went so far as to try to rape those markets by injecting its machinery and industrial methods into Norway and Sweden, into Italy, Romania, Spain, and, covertly, into France. As for influences on Russia circa 1914, we must distinguish two: German and French. How could these two contrasted, secular enemies coexist in Russia, despite tzarism's Francophile politics and French surveillance? There's nothing strange about it. The phenomenon of coexistence and even the provisional agreement between two forms of imperialism has occurred and often does occur within a single nation. There's one precondition: the tacit *but delimited* distribution of the zone of influence. In Latin America today, from one side French thought prevails over the mentality and customs, and from the other, Wall Street rules the economy.

Similarly, France used to dominate in the intellectual worldly concerns of Russia, that is, what Marx calls ideology and social superstructures. The spirit of study, literature, art, philosophy, prevailing morality, public opinion—they all were French. Germans had the engines, dynamos, giant kilns, metallurgical formulas, industrial plates, and agronomic recipes. Attracted by the tzarist government, French capitals used to dominate strictly high-end fashion trade, unable to venture too far into the terrain of technical production, due to the peculiar limitations proper to the French industrial spirit. The more I get to know Russia, the more I realize how deep German influence has reached there. This claim may well seem false, if one considers the permanent offensive unleashed by the entente against all German politics and imperialist intentions, but the reality has been just that. Even now, factories preserve their German markings. Soviet industry maintains this machinery, a little old already, yet lacks the money necessary to increase and radically renew its technique of production.

In the countries I'm passing through, the methods of exploitation are almost completely primitive. The factories rumble. The tractor is still a strange animal in the fields, and in the capitals—Vienna, Prague, Budapest—the traffic of cars and automobiles is incipient. As I've said, all that machinery bears the German seal. Most of the metallurgical centers I've visited are based on Teutonic mechanics. Czechoslovakia, however, is starting to turn its back on Germany and focus its national curiosity on the United States. Czechoslovakia is rapidly Americanizing.

The same can't be said of Austria and Hungary. The German spirit here appears more recalcitrant. The ancient empire of Franz Joseph hasn't lost a drop of its Germanity, with the fall of the kaisers, the separation of Hungary, or with the republicanization of both countries. These events haven't been overly important from the viewpoint of their political transformation. They're three lead roles—external and conventional—of a single political outlook that remains identical. The government is still in the same hands as it was yesterday, and, at bottom, it maintains the same structure. Only the government agency has changed. And German imperialism continues its proliferation, perhaps with greater diligence than before, its action, and propaganda to realize the *anchluss* or definitive formal annexation, first of Austria and then of Hungary. In reality, this annexation has been a long enforced fact. The absorption has been performed through the economy, the deepest and most lapidary—so deep it's even had time to transform into an organic design and flourish in a culture identical to these countries.

But the nationalist bustle of German imperialism in Austria and Hungary (as in Germany itself) will be toppled by the proletariat. The workers and peasants of Eastern Europe are conscious of their class—a clear fate laid out into the future. The Hungarians already had their Dictatorship of the Proletariat, even if it lasted only for a few weeks. The Austrians had theirs in 1927. The Germans, theirs, in 1919. No matter what the appetites of the international bourgeoisie may be, the social process of these countries, like that of the rest of the world, depends on the role and the strength of the proletarian class.

[*Mundial* (Lima), no. 497, December 27, 1929]   [JM]

THREE CITIES IN ONE

A burg between Mongol and Tartar, Buddhist and schismatic Greek, Moscow is one giant medieval village that from its crushed barbarian gut still exhales the iron oxidation of the gallows, the rust on Byzantine kupolas, the vodka distilled from barley, the blood of the serfs, the grains of the tithes and first fruits, the wine of the feasts at the Kremlin, and the sweat of primitive, bestial entourages. Every corner of the city bears witness in form: its irregular and abrupt plane, its yellow and white walls, the cobblestone carriageways, the red rooftops spotted with moss, the elemental Asiatic decor.

Yet, aside from the ruins of the past, prior to 1917, one notices the ruins and devastation produced by the October Revolution and by the civil wars that followed it. The bombardments, plundering, and destruction remain imprinted on the unhinged doors, in the broken windows, on the blasted roofs, cracked walls, mutilated monuments and buildings. The churches, palaces, and statutes underwent an especially implacable historical revision. At first one thinks that all this is the effect of time, but when one patiently penetrates the city, it becomes apparent that, alongside Ivan the Terrible's crumbling citadel crumbles the citadel of the revolution—the vestiges of a tremendous political hurricane.

But, in addition to being a collection of prerevolutionary ruins and the revolution's collected rubble, Moscow is the capital of the proletarian State. The urbanization of the worker accelerates with surprising rhythm and encompasses two activities: the construction of new homes and the transformation of old ones into collective housing for workers. One-third of the city is already new. On the left fringe of Moscow, almost all the houses have recently been constructed. Their style? Rigorously Soviet: conceptually sober, simple lines, right angles, solid material, engineering unconcerned with the engrossing, monumental, decorative myth of the Western worker's architecture. Nothing further from the architectonic misery of the capitalist "workers' houses"—four walls and a roof—as though the intention was to lock inside not even human beings but droves of beasts of burden or livestock soon to be slaughtered. The proletarian houses of the Soviet are spacious, comfortable, and especially hygienic. Each building is a miniature city: with yards, a library, bathrooms, a club, and even a theater. No bright-colored murals, nothing banal or superfluous, nothing baroque or Churrigueresque. Attempts have been made to assimilate these constructions into the New York cubist skyscraper and new German architecture, but neither one nor the other pulls it off like the Soviet—the comfort, modesty, elegance and simplicity, the solidness and beauty.

A particular social sector corresponds to each of these three urban aspects of Moscow. The feudal or prerevolutionary population stands out and blatantly differs from the Bolshevik element of 1917 and the postrevolutionary working masses. These three social levels, with different (and sometime opposing) mentalities, customs, and interests, nonetheless coexist in the current city. An impartial observer can't deny it. To attribute only one character to Moscow—as many foreign writers have done—is false. This kind of mixture is not so diffuse as to be missed at first sight. To a certain extent Luc Durtain has stated this, but he classifies population by generations (individualist criterion) instead of classifying it by the cycles of social progress (collective criterion), thus following a geologic procedure to study the civilian phenomenon and making vertical cuts instead of following a biological procedure and sectioning it off horizontally. Doctor or not, Durtain forgets Darwin's method. We'd like to see how he studies the stem by slicing it fiber by fiber, instead of cutting against the grain.

[*Bolívar* (Madrid), no. 5, April 1, 1930, from a longer series of articles, "A Report in Russia"] [JM]

LATEST THEATER NEWS FROM PARIS

Paris, 1930

Edison has said that every man must tempt all fates and activities. Old as we are, we must leave one career to pursue another to see if we might be better off thus and realize ourselves more completely. Edison wanted one and the same individual to pass from tailor to poet, electrician to diplomat, painter to soldier. That's how the Yankees do it. The United States is a multanimous[30] laboratory where everyone is constantly testing all of life's formulas in the most varied of careers. Rare is the man who settles in one career or job forever. Edison himself has been a farmer, cabinetmaker, scribe, nurse, mechanic, teacher, etc. The biography of the great U.S. creator is a true mosaic of trials and tests, a multicolor embroidery of trajectories, in any case, an impressive puzzle of activities. Thus, the foreigner who goes to the United States in search of a better life will have no prior knowledge of what he'll be or may become. If he's a journalist, he isn't free to become a stocktrader. If he's a musician, he isn't free to become an accountant. If he's a stonemason, he isn't free to become a movie star. If he's a cook, he isn't free to become a poet. The foreigner can't subtract himself from the social laws of such an experimental whirlwind. Once economic necessity has hitched him to the pinions of Wall Street, there's nothing left to do but keep up with the rhythm of the environment.

In this sense, the Yankees are, or would seem to be, taking a good look at socialism—the kind with a doctrine on the socialization of labor. According to Marx, in the society of the future, each man must be polytechnic. In socialist production, each worker knows and works at all positions, performs all functions, and bears all economic responsibilities. The Yankee concept of life, as a vast laboratory under constant experimental surveillance, looks strikingly similar to the socialist concept. The socialization of technique isn't possible without an uninterrupted process of simplification and perfection of the methods of work, which must be made ever more elemental so that learning them becomes easy and accessible to all intellects and doesn't require much time. If this were not so, a man with an average intelligence would be impotent and all his life he'd fall short in learning the total technique of the job.

Placed in front of this information, people who ignore or refuse to accept socialism for this or that personal or classist reason won't be able to deny the example and capitalist doctrine from Edison and his compatriots. On various roads one reaches the same point insofar as it's ineluctable and determined by scientific premises.

Jean Giraudoux seems to follow Edison's advice, without even proposing to, strictly out of subjective unrest. Giraudoux is forty-five years old and has been a druggist, diplomat, poet, novelist, and stage actor. His only two works of theater—*Le Limousin* and *Amphitryon 38*—one adapted from a novel of his and the other written directly for the stage, have earned him heaps of praise from licensed critics.[31] But they go so far as to claim that Giraudoux is the author we've needed for a decade to save French theater from its imminent doom. If one judges that Giraudoux is "dehumanizing art," one evidently can't deny that his work renews—if not revives—the French stage. His intellectual salon games, his cerebral juggling act, his aesthetic of phrases, his elegant spiritual acrobatics are new and novel *ad absurdum*. French theater—if one honorable exception after another can be made—is irremediably halted with Sacha Guitry and his store window characters, with Tristan Bernard and his kindergarten *boutades*,[32] with Paul Géraldy and his boudoir sentimentality, with the French comedy and its everlasting classic repertory, not to mention the asphyxiating street production that infests almost all the stages of Paris.

But if one judges that Giraudoux is not dehumanizing art, there is the danger of recognizing that Giraudoux isn't following Edison's advice in its authentic and sane terms. Edison wants life to be tried out, but not mocked or kept hidden. He wants one to go through all activities, not as a dilettante in silk pajamas but as a blacksmith in a smock for high temperature kilns. The theatrical work of Giraudoux lacks passion, humanity, vital inspiration. It betrays life as much as Guitry's, Bernard's, or Géraldy's. The difference is only in the means. Géraldy betrays it from above, which is more serious and treacherous. Guitry does not pass through but rather beneath life; Giraudoux doesn't pass through life either, but rather above it, which is insulting. Tristan Bernard addresses it with his feet. Giraudoux addresses it with his head, which is more idiotic. All of them, in substance, ignore it, substituting shoes for feet, hat for head.

But life does not let itself be cheated by impunity. While in the Comédie des Champs-Élysées *Amphitryon 38* is being staged, I notice that Theater of Art[33] is putting on *The Criminals* by Bruckner—a work that doesn't exactly achieve greatness but does contain problems and conflicts of un-deniable human interest. *The Criminals* is a naturalist, Zolaesque piece from the orthodox period of naturalism. Bruckner accuses too. His play is a pamphlet against courts and attorneys, against the customs and vices of today, against the entire social apparatus, and he reaches the overly natu-ralistic conclusion that deep down we're all criminals. Pamphlet, dema-gogy, anarchism, nihilism, and there is even declamation in *The Criminals*. An abundance of conventional cheap tricks, academic pedantry, and ideo-logical disorientation, however, *The Criminals* draws on certain features of great theater even without the metaphysical loftiness of Pirandello, the social profundity of Shaw, the psychoanalytic clouds of Strindberg, or the sociological sanity of Selvinsky. Let him be praised, however, and let his meticulous collective documentation suffice, his naked shuddering social veracity, his destructive scope of our times.

The resonance of *The Criminals* in the audience is proved by the legal de-bate the play has elicited in Paris to elucidate some of its passages that re-late to the sentencing of certain delinquents in the work. Eminent French criminologists, like Henri Robert, Moro de Gaffieri, and Paul Boncour, are now discussing the theories and criminal situations of this play. It's the first time in Europe that such a debate has been provoked by the agitating force of the stage.

[*El Comercio* (Lima), June 15, 1930]   [JM]

AN INCAN CHRONICLE

One day in the Intipampa, during the celebration of the *huaraco*, they were performing a final ceremony to make men out of eight hundred boys of the empire, whose military preparation had reached its end. Around the Inca hundreds of noblemen were bustling—the magistrate in whose peaceful expression throbbed the sign of justice; the severe and pensive amauta, a broad green tunic hanging over his shoulder; the general who only gazed forward, with his seven-colored crest and silver sandals that knew the crags of auroral regions; the sad *arabicus* of blue garments, with dazzling insects from the north embroidered in aloe threads; the taciturn hermit, who came from the distant *paccarinas*;[34] the *rymay-pachaccas*, his face still toasted from a recent trip to the turbulent Pongoa or Lake Titi-caca, on whose shores the Inti's maize grows in miraculous grains . . . To his right the Inca has the High Villac, dressed in white wool sheared from alpacas of Hatun.

The *calli-sapas*,[35] who were to take part in the epic contests of the Inti-pampa, appeared adorned in the luxury exterior that corresponded to their stock, and they carried beauteous carafes of glazed clay filled with liturgical *chicha*. They emerged on one side of the city, escorted by a sentry of infantrymen, whose pikes and bows sparkled under the sun.

The crowd howled with joy and took a long time to quiet down. An elderly woman wept, holding in her arms a bundle of fresh live forevers.

"Last night," between sobs a young girl said, "when the guards were sleeping at the base of the Saccsahuamán walls, an evil serpent bit him."

She pulled from her bosom a jaguar claw filed and shined in the shape of a half-moon, put it in her hand, and, with great unction, raised it to her lips and disrobed.

The line of paladins drew near in their race. When their yellow suits could be seen from afar, the *calli-sapas* sang in unison an ancient aria, in whose melody love and glory sweetly trilled. They sang for the shadows of the ancient heroes, the unmovable dolmens of Accora, the mummies that, in the crouching flexion of nocturnal birds, contemplate the sacred niches and porphyry ashlars of the silent *chulpas*.[36] They sang for the victorious battles and bones buried on endless roads of the conquest. Some princesses raised their voices; others yelled to the rhythm of the song with their shoulders erect, their throats wide open, heart-shaped wombs enclosed and new, where the great curtain that opens up to eternity was being raised; and there were still others who momentarily stopped singing and their tongues were then at ease, while the mouths of their allegorical cups widened in a rictus of unspoken revelation.

When the song ended and its echo lingered in the hollow carafes, the young men and women of the town bowed their heads. The Inca honored the victors to the triumphant sounds of the *hailli*, chanted by the people. The heroes put on their woolen sandals, synching the *huara*[37] in a sign of virility, and the mothers crowned their temples with green live forevers.

[*La Voz* (Madrid), May 22, 1931]   [JM]

THE INCAS, REVIVED

Paris, January 1935

The primordial periods of American prehistory remain obscure for many reasons; one of these resides in the type of research that has been carried out on this theater of feats: rudimentary studies that lack any method or systematization, any long-term encompassing plan that, worst of all, is smitten by the lesser interests of museums, when it's not shamelessly chasing profit. Or else, the exploration has been led by lazy, literary snobs, utterly profane in the matter, and when Indo-American nationals have intervened, they've almost always tried to draw conclusions — damaging the objective scientific course of the studies — about some vainglorious, foolhardy nationalism.

Another reason resides in the fact that for a long time — centuries in some cases — many archaeological centers have been abandoned as though they were worthless. The attention American prehistory deserves in the eyes of men of science dates back approximately one century from this juncture. Before, it was believed that the new continent was in fact *new* and that its inhabitants appeared on it during a relatively recent period. The result has been the destruction, dispersal, or disappearance of the most valuable treasures, due to mindless hands or simply the action of time and the natural elements.

In this regard, it was in no small part responsible.[38] Without a doubt, there were many intelligent Spaniards — distinguished men and government officials — who realized the extraordinary value of aboriginal cultures at the outset of the discovery of America, but the same didn't occur inside provincial administrations, which, on the contrary, focused on wiping out the natives to establish the imported institutions with all the greater ease — a common practice in colonial systems of all epochs and metropoli. For these reasons and others, when America is considered as an organic whole, one could nearly claim that its prehistoric process thus far hasn't been grasped, except for some fragmentary and provisional scientific terms.

Until further notice, American archaeology remains in question. Even the most insignificant problem can't find two like-minded authors. Each uses his own logarithmic table, until joining the wise men who belong to a single school or scientific tradition. This contradiction is evinced in the form of the most piebald confusion, in scriptural terrain — a discrepancy and confusion all the more grave since the orthographic knowledge of the Quechua and Aymara languages is of decisive importance, as a philological exponent of Incan civilization, the crowning historical key of, if not all, then at least the most representative of past cultures.

On the other hand, it seems that research hasn't especially followed the thread of economic production in those societies. From the corresponding literature, what stands out is the fact that almost all methods of exploration, from geologic to religious, have been pursued. A stone, fossil, race, custom, architectonic style, word, textile, moral axiom, hieroglyph of war, or myth blows hot air into twenty historical lungs and gives rise to many hypotheses and superstitions. Yet very rarely has a tilling or fishing tool been used, much less a hunting or rearing procedure, to build on the technical meaning or economic scope of the entire plausible social system they belong to. However, it's readily accepted that, circumscribing the examination of the southern part of the continent, it was in modern-day Peru and part of Bolivia that the ancient American humans achieved the most advanced, wealthiest, most complex social organizations.

According to what we know, Andean cultures synthesized their slow, grueling endeavors with a higher calling, of the different (successive and simultaneous) populations from both slopes—eastern (Atlantic) and western (Pacific)—of the great cordillera, comprising therein the migratory reactions in the Amazon and the north, although this hasn't been proven yet.

How many centuries did those people need to form the Inca Empire, the culmination of South American prehistory? "Twenty thousand years," some people say. "One thousand," argue others.

The social feat of this hemisphere is such an impressive spectacle!

Despite the poorly coordinated and scant archaeological material discovered so far, in the winding, chaotic, and labyrinthine disputes of wise men and professors, one certainly can't deny that we're facing a millennial and most remote sociological process. Certain paleontological studies lead some bigwigs to hold that societies of advanced organization already lived on the current South American soil, under other telluric conditions, long before the geologic transformations that gave rise to it. Many of these social seeds have been rescued from such geologic disruptions—megalithic constructions more than anything—whose materials and forms represent some of the many other native landmarks of subsequent cultures. The social genesis of America, in the judgment of these professors, would date back to the Tertiary period.

What territories and what races contributed to the crystallization of the Tahuantinsuyo? Through the vicissitudes of life, did these races know one another? Did they make contact and organize into a high collective order? What laws and interests, what instincts or ideals, moved them—in war and peace—to manifest a destiny whose historical essence and meaning seem to contain extraordinary kernels of wisdom and organization?

Some authors have fallen into the error of wanting to clear up these mysteries through direct study and observation of nature and the indigenous of our day. Such a method, as was to be expected, has failed, at least concerning the human factor.

Again, two main considerations are made: first, the psychology and even physiology of the autochthonous race or races have been profoundly modified by the social atmosphere over four centuries; and, second, the way in which this atmosphere has prevailed over them and continues to do so today.

The first colony and, to a lesser extent—though it may seem rash—the republic, have treated the indigenous like foreigners in their own land. And as such, the indigenous roam, hyperbole aside, completely on the margin of the social life that surrounds them. They're unaware. In reality, they don't know who organizes and directs them to wherever it is they go. What does such an existence signify, except suffering and incurable suffering? Regarding the present and future, it's as if the indigenous have been turned to stone by the jerking halt of the process deep in their being—a suspension of their social and human senses.

It's evident that, just as a paralysis of indigenous evolution has come to rise, so too will an atrophy of the race transpire in the long run. Like a moving train that's suddenly brought to a screeching halt, the individual and social framework of the indigenous has been broken and dismantled. As for its evolutionary force (in the sense of its objective social constructions), there's nothing left but rubble, which can do nothing but affect this or that surviving form of the long-deceased creative entity.

How can one try to identify or explain a historical process of such immense value as that of South America's past by using the shadow or corpse of the powerful races that created it? Such an effort turns so absurd that, as a form of dissuasion, one need only cite what a German pedagogue exclaimed when he compared the indigenous of today to the creatures of their history: "No!" he said. "Such a great civilization hasn't been able to slip the grip of those pariahs."

However, the human document is there, in flesh and bone, waiting to give us not the key to feats of the past, but an explanation of what can be done in the future. Thus, the importance and profit of all historical study: clear the horizon of the future with the knowledge and comprehension of the past.

In this terrain, one would have to create a new research method that, by applying the scientific study of historical matter—man, landscape, and ruins—would be apt to devise a social formulation in stride with this matter's possibilities and potential characteristics. All else is the masturbation of sterile slackers—the morbid pleasure of the museum and for the museum.

Man, landscape, and ruins!

Ruins undoubtedly are wonders; the landscape is a miracle of the world;

only man is small. What could such interplay of unequal forces bring about tomorrow?

The "Indian problem," as the natives' current situation tends to be called in Peru, has given and continues to give rise to a great deal of messianic rhetoric and little, if any, reflection of austere scientific rigor. The mystical passion of the Indigenists and the blank skepticism of the enemies of the races of color (which there are in Peru as well!)—the former deifying the descendants of the Incas, whom the latter despise and condemn for their rapid breakdown—are equally shaky in their most elemental sociological foundation.

Indeed, the indigenous of today are not going through the crisis of psychophysiological breakdown, which some people suggest, nor do they rejoice in the creatrice racial euphoria,[39] as other people claim. It's just as inadmissible to think that "the indigenous will be the creator of the future of humanity, the world's only hope," since they previously built an extraordinary civilization, as it is to think that "the indigenous are beasts, without any chance of the smallest ascent in humanity," because today they find themselves sunken into a coma of senses and soul, brought on by their despicable state of slavery.

The "Indian problem" appears intimately hindered by the current global problem. Its solution, for the natives, will be favorable or unfavorable insofar as the solution to the global problem is fair or corrupt. In other words, everything in this question is possible, as long as all social factors—by sovereign, decisive, international arbitration—are subject to the most radical revisions, unexpected reinforcements, and crushing liquidations too.

The same can be said of nature. As a telluric matrix, America is sublime, but, as a source of material progress, the matter either is or isn't important, since in her womb she either has or hasn't great wealth, according to the economic perspective—of space and time—through which it's brought into focus. Also to this regard, a worldwide displacement in the distribution and industrialization of raw materials would in a single shot transform continental stockpiles on an international scale.

Until these perspectives become reality, the indigenous, abandoned (or, rather, exiled by society), lie immobilized, dangling, facing a wilderness of arid gorges (in the *puna* and highland steppe, principle centers of the indigenous population), devoid of produce (the food most consumed by the indigenous is barley and their beverage, ice), a harsh climate that can annihilate even the youngest, most robust, and resistant of races. That highland steppe and *puna* have been handed down to them as punishment for the crime of losing an unfair fight.

It's flagrant foolishness to believe that the indigenous and the Andean highland steppe "are in admirable harmony." No! That would be like saying that the prisoner, annihilated and brutalized by twenty years in prison, is in admirable harmony with his dreary, narrow dungeon.

Naked, starving, his bones and marrow hollowed by exposure to temperatures of fifty degrees below zero, his brain and heart benumbed by the permanent vertigo from the immense cordillera's horizontal silence and the vertical desolation of his own tragic fate, repeated with the atrocious monotony of penitents pacing in circles, indigenous man—a human after all—must surely get the feeling (perhaps he's seen it in a dream) that other people are living not far from his place of exile, and over their souls and bodies the progress and victory of society have allowed an infinitely perfectible state of well-being to hover.

What a different spectacle of archaeological data, whose revelatory scope, like a performance report of prior factors, truly spills admiration and astonishment onto the world!

Tiahuanaco! Nazca! Chimú! Machu Picchu! Cuzco! The Colla and Aymara and the Quechua Cuzco!

The seal of the Quechua was left engraved in the ruins of all pre-Columbian civilizations. The vestiges of the Tahuantinsuyo preserve convergent footsteps. The panoramic examination of some here and there suggests a play of reciprocal forces whose last axis was in Cuzco, the holy city, the stone polis, the capital (*Cozko*, naval), summit and summary of those societies' historical movement.

Situated on the shores of the Watanay, with forty thousand inhabitants, 820 kilometers from the Pacific Ocean and at an altitude of 3,335 meters above sea level, in the heart of Vilcanota, formed by the western and eastern cordilleras of the Andes, Cuzco is undoubtedly the oldest city in America.

What first catches the attention in the ancient Incan capital is the stone unit of its construction: the megalith. Some of these measure up to twenty cubic meters. Disconcerting is the montage of these immense masses at enormous altitudes, their setting and agglutination (they say a pin won't fit between one block and the next), the cut and shine of each piece, and, finally, the diversity and wealth of the architectonic styles that go from the cyclopean style of the barbarian age to the cellular pavement of the decadent period, passing through the polygonal, ashlar, rectangular cellular, and others.

The fortresses of Ollantaytampu and Sajsahuamán (the Cuzco acropolis); the Coricancha, or Temple of the Sun; the Ayllawasi, or Monastery of the Chosen Women; the palace of Kolkapata; the Yachaywasi, or House of Knowledge (University of the Incas); the Sunturwasi, or Quechua capitol; the *intihuatanas*, or clocks of the solar year; and other constructions of recreation and culture in the outskirts of Cuzco, of which now merely foundations and megalithic walls remain—these give an approximate idea of the Tahuantinsuyo's architectonic evolution. The citadel of Sajsahuamán alone, in which not long ago the foundational vertebrae were unearthed (bastions, towers, terraces, and embankments), just may form a schematic summary of pre-Columbian architecture.

Advances in engineering stunning for that time (hydraulic systems through channels at great heights—the Incas knew the principle of communicating vessels—subterranean galleries, techniques of fortification, etc.) bear witness to the existence of a constructive organizational mentality that rivals, at times triumphantly, ancient Rome, Babylon, and Egypt. Garcilaso's enthusiasm leads him to deem Sajsahuamán "the most celebrated work of antiquity." Squier and Nadaillac[40] don't hesitate to compare it to the pyramids, Stonehenge, and the Coliseum.

It's impressive to take in the panorama of Cuzco today, a triple city—triple? Better yet, a tower of cities, a cyclical stairway of the capital of one hundred successive nations, integrated by pre-Columbian foundations, Spanish buildings elevated on top, and, finally, the developments of the republic. Hills and valleys, mountains and rivers, skies and distances, Upper Cuzco (Janan Kozko) and Lower Cuzco (Urin Kozco) rest—and this one sees at first sight—directly on formidable autochthonous foundations, which gives those colonial cathedrals and republican palaces the appearance of visitors, since one can't tell whether they're staying or going. The aspect of the architectonic ruins is even more impressive in the Tampu region.

At 2,850 meters above sea level, "the mysterious city," capital of this region, in the so-called Song of the Urubamba, a river that farther down feeds the Ucayali and the Amazon, Machu Picchu indisputably offers the most original, audacious, grandiose lapidary constructions of the pre-Columbian period across the Americas.

The circumstance of the discovery of this city, suspended between vertical ravines of seven hundred to a thousand meters in depth, in the valley that forms the Urubamba below, combines its megalithic complex with a stunning orographic value overwhelming in a mixture of astonishment and nightmare. There, land and sky seem to have joined forces through human effort to sculpt to scale a real City of God upon the immensity of the heights. Boroughs, staircases, posterns, towers—a great part of Machu

Picchu has been carved directly into the crags of the Andes. The rest has been fastened and constructed, stone by stone, with choice porphyry transported from far away, down below, and even from the other side of the voluminous river. Engineering of today, using modern techniques, would be hard-pressed to move and lift whole rocks like those. The Incas, unaware of man-powered vehicles and even the wheel, probably executed both jobs on the shoulders of men.

There are no signs remaining of the transitory life that the Tampus led in the "mysterious city," but this energy and pleasure for the feat of such urban planning reveal a very advanced society. In Machu Picchu they've found remains of bunkers, lookouts, solar calendars, temples, palaces, plazas, burial grounds, and staircases from 10 to 150 steps.

Tiahuanaco is something else altogether. Its constructions are highlighted by the ornamental care and refined detail of its most important architectonic periods, from the white sandstone in cyclopean style, to the andesite of the so-called Wiracochas style. The mass and volume, the weight and height are of secondary importance in the constructions of Lake Titicaca or the high planes, after the tactical-military concerns for urban defense, the symbolic sculptures, and elegance of the walls. The Temple of the Sun in Tiahuanaco is celebrated as central to the mythical and cosmogonic ideas of a great many Andean cultures, sculpted in their monoliths.

The other pole of attraction of the worldwide curiosity in these civilizations was surely established by the lesser arts: ceramics and pottery, as well as gold and silver smithing, in their double value as a document: archaeological and artistic.

Vases (keros[41] and huacos), pitchers, aríbalos,[42] crockery, household items, figurines for decoration and worship, and idols, carved in metal (gold, silver, and copper), in precious stones (many of them unknown to the science of today), alabaster, bone, clay, and wood (palm tree, guayacán, quechuar[43]). Incised, colored, flat, and in relief, the styles of these arts vary in accordance to the regions and cultures from which they come, by the continuity of the colors, revealing the engraving's expressive clarity, the solidity of the material, the grace of its forms, the boldness of its composition and its great thematic freedom.

Here we don't mention other aspects of Incan life: social organization, political structure, economic system, scientific development, music and literature, morality and religion. That would give these lines a scope and extension that I have not proposed.

[*Aula Vallejo* (Córdoba), nos. 11–13, 1972–74]   [JM]

From *Tungsten*

Owner, at last, of the Quivilca tungsten mines in the department of Cuzco, the New York management of U.S. Mining Incorporated green-lit the immediate exaction of the mineral.

An avalanche of laborers and workers came out of Colca and places along the way to the mines, and it was followed by another and another, all hired for the settlement and mining project. The shortage of manual labor on the outskirts and regions neighboring the deposits, for a fifteen-mile radius, forced the company to take a vast throng of Indians from far-away villages and rural populations and send them to work in the mines.

Money began to flow at an alarming velocity and in abundance unprecedented in Colca, the capital of the province and home to the mines. Business transactions reached unheard-of heights; people were everywhere, at general stores and markets, on the streets and in public squares, finalizing purchases and financial holdings. A host of rural and urban estates changed hands, and a constant bustle was boiling over in the offices of notaries public and judges. The money from U.S. Mining Incorporated brought uncommon commotion to provincial life, which had been so peaceful until then.

Everyone radiated the air of a traveler—even the way they walked, previously slow and lethargic, became brisk and impatient. Men came through dressed in khakis, gaiters, and riding pants, talking with a voice that also had changed in tone, about dollars, documents, checks, legal seals, meeting minutes, payments, tons, tools. Boys from the poor quarters would come out to watch them go by, and a sweet uneasiness would make them shudder and think about the distant minerals whose exotic charm possessed an irresistible attraction.

"Are you going to Quivilca?" they asked, smiling and blushing.

"Yeah. First thing in the morning."

"How about those go-getters! Going to get rich in the mines!"

So came the idylls and loves that later would dwell in those fabulous mine veins' dismal domes.

During the first push of laborers and miners, the company's managers, directors, and middle managers also headed to Quivilca. First of all, there was Mr. Taik and Mr. Weiss, manager and assistant manager of U.S. Mining Incorporated; the company's bookkeeper, Javier Machuca; the Peruvian engineer Baldomero Rubio; the merchant José Marino, who held exclusive rights to the general store and to contracting manual labor for U.S. Mining Incorporated; the commissioner of the mining organization, Baldazari; and the land surveyor, Leónides Benites, Rubio's right-hand man. He'd brought along his wife and two young kids. Marino didn't bring any other relatives than a ten-year-old nephew he liked to beat at least once a day. The rest ended up going without any family.

They settled an unpopulated mountainside on the eastern slope of the Andes, overlooking the woodland region. There the only sign of human life they found was a little shack of natives: the Soras. This circumstance, which permitted them to utilize the Indians as guides through that remote region, plus the fact that (according to the map) this was supposed to be the company's center of operations, forced the mining population to sprawl around the Soras' shacks.

Massive, hazardous efforts were made to settle down once and for all to a normal life in those *punas* and a job in the mines. The lack of lines of communication from the civilized towns, reached from that settlement only by a trail steep even for llamas, constituted an almost invincible hardship at first. Countless times work was suspended for want of tools and due to the hunger and exposure of these people, harshly subjected to an implacable glacial climate.

With their innocent, cheerful docility, the Soras were infinitely helpful to the miners and played such an important role there that, on more than one occasion, the company would've folded had it not been for their timely intervention. When the provisions ran out and no others arrived from Colca, the Soras handed over their grain, cattle, cookery, and dining ware, without a fee or a spare, and without receiving any compensation either. They were contented to live in harmony and disinterested friendship with the miners, whom the Soras with certain childish curiosity would watch grow agitated night and day in the systematic wrangle of their fantastic, mysterious machines. As for U.S. Mining, from the outset it had no need for what manual labor the Soras could offer to the operations, since it had brought from Colca and places along the way a numerous and sufficient throng of laborers. In this regard, the company didn't disturb the Soras' peace, until the day the mines started requiring greater power and more men. Would that day arrive? For the moment, the Soras continued to live exempt from labor in the mines.

"Why do you always do that?" a Sora asked a worker, whose job it was to oil the cranes.

"It's to scrape out the debris."

"And why do you scrape out the debris?"

"To clean the vein and free up the metal."

"And what are you gonna do with the metal?"

"Don't you like to have money? You stupid Indian!"

The Sora saw the worker smile and he too smiled, mechanically, for no reason. He looked on that whole day and many others, trying to see what that job of oiling cranes was all about.

"Do you have money yet? What is money?" he asked that same worker, whose temples were dripping with sweat.

"This is money," the worker responded paternally, jingling the pockets of his shirt. "Check it out. This is money. You hear that?"

The worker said this and took out several nickel coins to show him. The Sora looked at them, like an animal who has just failed to understand something.

"And what do you do with money?"

"You buy whatever you want. Man, you're stupid!"

The worker laughed again, and the Sora went on his way, skipping and whistling.

On a separate occasion, as if under a spell, another Sora was staring at a worker hammering on the anvil of the forge, and he broke clear into tears of joy.

"What're you laughing about, half-breed?" the blacksmith said. "Want to work with me?"

"Yeah. I wanna do just like that."

"No. You've got no idea, man. This is really hard."

But the Sora was determined to work in the forge, until he finally gave in, and he worked for a period of four days, managing to offer effective assistance to the mechanics. On the fifth day, at noon, the Sora paused next to the ingots and suddenly left.

"Hey," they said, "why are you leaving? Keep working!"

"No," said the Sora, "I don't like it anymore."

"They're gonna pay you. They're gonna pay you for your work. Just keep workin'."

"No. I don't want to anymore."

Shortly thereafter they saw the same Sora throwing calabash buckets of water onto a tray where a girl was washing wheat. Then he offered to carry the tip of the rope into the shafts. Later on, when they'd started to transport the mineral from the pithead to the appraisal warehouse, he was pushing a wheelbarrow. One day Marino, merchant and labor contractor, went up to him.

"So I see you've been working too," he said. "That's good, half-breed, real good. You want me to save your life? How much do you want?"

The Sora didn't understand this language of *saving his life* or *how much do you want.* He wanted only to get some exercise, do some work, and amuse himself. The Soras never could sit still: they'd buzz around, jolly, breathing hard, their veins tense and muscles tight while they pastured, planted, mulched, hunted vicuñas and wild guanacos, or climbed up rocks and cliffs in an endless or even disinterested endeavor. They had no sense of utility whatsoever, demonstrating such confidence in other people that it was sometimes downright pitiful, and they lived life as if it was a generous, expansive game, without calculating or worrying about the economic outcome of their actions. Nor did they know what a purchase was, much less a sale, which is why those operations appeared to them as entirely entertaining.

"Sell me a llama for *charqui*."

The animal would be handed over, without anyone quoting its value or requesting that quote. A few times for the llama one or two coins were exchanged, which the Soras would accept only to give them away to the first person who walked by or asked for them.

* * *

No sooner had settlers arrived in the region than employees and laborers realized they'd need to surround themselves with the basic necessities of life that this place might offer—on top of what came from elsewhere— such as beasts of burden, llamas for slaughter, grain for feed, and more. Yet this required the patient work of exploring and clearing untilled terrain to convert it into arable fertile plots.

The first to work the land—with his sights set not only on obtaining products for his own subsistence but on increasing his wealth through animal rearing and farming—was José Marino, store owner and exclusive labor contractor of Quivilca. He formed a secret corporation with Rubio, the engineer, and Benites, the land surveyor, assuming the administration, since he could manage the company from the general store with certain ease and special advantages. Moreover, Marino possessed an extraordinary economic sense. Short and stout, with a snide and stingy demeanor, the merchant knew how to guide clients, like a fox herds hens. Rubio, on the contrary, was a meek fellow, despite his remarkable height and the slant of his shoulders, which endowed him with the stunning resemblance of a condor preying on a goat. As for Leónides Benites, he was nothing more than a skittish student of the Engineering School in Lima, straight-laced and feeble, both useless and even counterproductive qualities when it came to business matters.

Right from the start, José Marino had his eye on the Soras' recently planted fields, and he decided one day to make them his. Even though this meant entering a cheek-by-jowl race with Machuca, Baldazari, and others, who began to strip the Soras of other things, Marino ended up winning the battle with these two weapons: the general store and his eminent shamelessness.

The Soras began to be seduced by certain objects, strange for their savage minds, which they happened to see in the general store: color flannel shirts, picturesque bottles, multicolored packets, matches, hard candy, shiny buckets, transparent glasses, etc. The Soras felt drawn into the store, like certain insects toward the light—and those who didn't feel drawn were forced to come in by Marino's loan-shark guile.

"Sell me the *oca* field next to your shack," he said to them one day in his store, capitalizing on the fascination that had befallen them in front of the merchandise.

"What's that you say, *taita*?"[44]

"Give me your *oca* field, and I'll give you whatever you want from the store.

"That's fine, *taita*."

The sale, or rather, the exchange was sealed, and as payment for the *oca* field, José Marino gave one of the Soras a small blue carafe with red flowers.

"Careful you don't break it!" Marino said to him paternally.

Then he showed the Sora how he should carry the carafe, ever so carefully, in order not to break it. The Indian, surrounded by two others, slowly transported the vase to his shack, like a sacred guardian. They covered the distance—about a half mile—in two and a half hours. When people came outside to see, they burst into laughter.

The Sora hadn't realized whether or not exchanging his good field for a carafe was a fair transaction. In substance, he knew that Marino wanted his crop, and so he gave it to him, supposing that the other part of the deal—the reception of the carafe—was separate from and independent of the first. He was fond of that object and thought Marino had given it to him strictly because of that fondness. And so the merchant continued to acquire the Soras' fields, which they in turn continued to hand over in exchange for small picturesque objects from the general store with the greatest imaginable innocence, like children who know not what they do.

While the Soras were losing their property and livestock to Marino, Baldazari and other U.S. Mining employees hadn't stopped struggling against the vast virgin wilderness, attacking the *punas* and lowlands, the vegetation on the cliffs, new oases to plow and new animals to tame and rear. The dispossession of their personal effects didn't seem to inflict them with even the slightest prejudice. On the contrary, it gave them the chance to be more expansive and dynamic, since their unbegotten mobility thus found a more jubilant, effective application. The Soras' economic awareness was simple: as long as they could work, had a way and place to do so, to acquire life's basic necessities, nothing else mattered to them. Only on the day when they were wont for a place and way to work just to stay afloat would they then open their eyes and oppose their exploiters with unmistakably fierce resistance. Their fight with the miners would be a matter of life or death. Would that day come? In the short term, the Soras lived in a sort of permanent withdrawal, facing the astute, unbearable invasion of Marino and company.

For their part, the workers, with pity and mercy, criticized these robberies.

"How bold-faced!" the workers exclaimed, looking out the corner of their eyes. "To take their fields and even their huts! And to steal from them what's theirs. What a dirty trick!"

"But, fault falls only on the Soras," one worker observed. "They're a bunch of fools. If they pay the price, they're fine with it; if they don't, they still don't care. If they're asked for their shacks, they laugh like it's a joke and they hand it over on the spot. They're a bunch of animals. Those idiots! Gettin' just what they deserve! . . . Screw 'em!"

The workers would look at the Soras as if they were mad or unreal. An old woman, the mother of a coal merchant, took one by the jacket.

"Hey, you animal," she angrily grumbled. "Why do you give away your things? Don't you work for them? Are you going to laugh now? . . . You see? Now you're going to laugh . . ."

The lady turned red with rage, and she all but pulled him by the ears. The Sora, in every response, left to bring her back a pile of *ullucos*, which the old women rejected.

"But I'm not saying this so you give me something," she replied. "Keep your *ullucos*."

Then she was stricken by sudden regret, imagining that if she'd accepted those *ullucos*, the Sora would've interpreted her act as an expression of tenderness and mercy.

On another occasion, a stonemason's wife shed tears when she saw how generous, naive, and guileless they were. She had purchased from them a crop of harvested pumpkins, and, rather than paying the price the crop was worth, at the last minute, while putting some coins in the Sora's hand, she said, "Take four reales. I don't have any more. Do you want them?"

"Sure thing," the Sora said.

Yet since the woman was in need of money to purchase remedies for her husband, whose hand had been shredded by a dynamite explosion in the mines, and since she saw that she might still be able to skim a little more off those four reales, she started pleading.

"Actually," she went on, "just take three reales. I need the other one."

"Sure thing."

The poor woman went on to realize that she could skim off yet another real. She opened the Sora's hand and removed another coin.

"Actually, take two," she said with fearful hesitation. "I'll give you the rest another day."

"Sure thing," the Sora meekly replied once again.

It was then that that woman lowered her eyes, touched by the Sora's gesture of innocent goodness. In her hand she felt the two reales that would be used for her husband's remedy, and a strange feeling came over her and caused her to weep all afternoon.

* * *

In José Marino's general store, Mr. Taik and Mr. Weiss, Rubio the engineer, Machuca the bookkeeper, Baldazari the commissioner, and Zavala the newly appointed schoolmaster used to gather after work to talk and drink cognac, all dressed smartly in thickly lined clothes and leather to combat the cold. Sometimes Leónides Benites would also show up, but he hardly drank and generally would leave on the early side. There they'd also play bank craps and, on Sundays, go on benders, firing off gunshots in beastly inebriation.

At the beginning of the gathering, there was talk of matters in Colca and Lima, then, of the war in Europe, and later they passed on to topics pertaining to the company and the exportation of tungsten, whose value was rising by the day. Finally, they conversed about the gossip in the mines, the domestic rumors linked to private life. When they reached the topic of the Soras, Leónides Benites felt inclined to speak.

"Poor Soras!" he said with a philosophical air and pained redemptive tone. "They're a bunch of cowards and idiots. They do everything because they don't have the courage to defend their interests. They can't say no. What a feeble, menial, humble race—incredible. They make me so sad and yet so angry!"

"Don't be so sure," said Marino, already two sheets to the wind. "The

Indians know damn well what they're doing. And that's life: a continuous dispute and struggle between men. The law of selection. One man loses, so that another man wins. My friend, you, of all people . . ."

These last words were spoken with noticeable sarcasm. And due to his obsession with mocking and silencing everyone else, this was a dominant feature of Marino's personality. Benites understood the allusion and grew visibly disturbed, unable to counter such a cocky man, because, aside from other reasons, he was drunk. But the other conversationalists were surprised by the detail, shouting in unison and jest, "Ah! Of course! Naturally! Naturally!"

Rubio scratched the zinc on the countertop with his fingernail, as was his custom.

"No," he argued with his distant stammering voice. "It seems to me that these Indians are fond of an active life, of work, of digging holes in untouched lands, of trailing wild animals. This is their custom and lifestyle. They get rid of their things only to throw themselves back into a search for new cattle and shacks. They're pleased and happy to live like this. They're ignorant to the law of propriety and think that anyone can take anything without distinction. Do you guys remember the incident with the door?"

"The door to the office?" asked the Bookkeeper, coughing.

"Exactly. One day, out of the blue, this Sora grabbed the door, put it on his shoulder, and stuck it in his chicken coop, with the same confidence as he would have, had it been his own."

A cackle echoed through the general store.

"That's funny. So what did they do to him?"

"When they asked him where he was taking the door, he said, 'to my hut,' with a smile of comical childish candor. Naturally, they repossessed it. He thought that the door was there for the taking, if one had a need for it. They're really funny."

"They play the fool," Marino said, winking and sticking out his paunch, "but man, are they shrewd!"

"I disagree," Benites said, opposing this notion and making a face of disgust and mercy. "They're weaklings. They let others take their possessions purely out of weakness."

"Do you call them weak," Rubio contested, losing his temper, "because, to make a life for themselves, they face the forests and *jalcas*, amid fierce animals and all kinds of dangers? Why don't you, or anyone else here for that matter, do that sort of thing?"

"That's not bravery, my friend. Bravery is fighting man to man; he who ends up on top is the brave. The rest is a different story."

"So you believe the strength of a man, his valor, has been created to be invested in pushing another man down? . . . Brilliant! It seemed to me that an individual's courage must help him work toward collective wealth and not be used as a weapon against other people. That theory of yours is really something! . . ."

"But that's just it. I couldn't hurt anyone. Everyone knows me. Yet I think I'm obliged to defend my life and interests, if I'm attacked and robbed of them."

"I'm not saying another word," Marino interjected. "A closed mouth attracts no flies . . . What are we drinking? Who's pouring? Come on! Enough with the nonsense!"

The land surveyor paid him no attention.

"Here, for example, I've come to work," he said, "not to let them take from me what I earn, but to save the money that I needed. Aside from this, I take nothing from anyone, nor do I want to bury the son of any of my neighbors."

Marino grew tired of asking who wanted a drink, and since Benites, his partner in their livestock farms, had ignored him, spellbound by the argument, the merchant said, with a chuckle of cutting irony to shut him up, "I'm not saying a word. Benites! Benites! Benites! . . . Remember: A closed mouth attracts no flies . . ."

Machuca let out a long cough, after which, by the power of the congested rolls of his neck, he said, "I, on the other hand—" He coughed again. "I, on the other hand, say that—" He couldn't continue. He coughed for a while and finally cleared his throat. "The Soras are thick-headed Indians, insensitive to the suffering of others, blind to the world around them. Just the other day I saw one of them hang a rope that was tied around a boy's waist at the other end. The Sora, with all the weight of his body, tightened the rope and adjusted it in such a way that he was going to cut that boy in two, who had no way to get out and was kicking in pain, sticking his tongue out and his face, turning purple. The Sora saw him and, nonetheless, continued his stunt, laughing like an idiot. They're a bunch of cruel, heartless bastards. They need to become Christians and practice the virtues of the Church."

"Bravo!" said Marino. "Were you asking for the glasses?"

"Hold on, I'm speaking."

"But were you asking—"

"God damn it! Just help yourself!"

Leónides Benites did nothing more than express in words what he truly practiced in his everyday conduct. He was the economy personified, and he saved his last cent with dignified jealousy. Better days would come, when he'd gather his little reserves and get out of that situation, but for the time being, he had to work and save, without any other perspective than the future. Benites wasn't blind to the fact that in this world people with money are happier and that the best virtues, therefore, are work and saving, since they procure a peaceful, fair existence, without attacks from anyone else or the reprehensible fostering of greed, spite, and other base inclinations that corrupt people and crumble societies.

"You should teach the children only two things," Benites would say to Julio Zavala, the schoolmaster. "To work and save. You should summarize the Christian doctrine in those two supreme teachings, which, in my mind, synthesize the morality of all times. Without working and saving, there's no chance for peace of mind, charity, justice, or anything else. That's what history shows us. Everything else is a load of crap!" After saying something to this effect, he'd grow excited, inflect his words with a tone of sincerity, and add, "I was raised by a woman, and I'm grateful to her for having brought me up as she did. That's why I can live the life that everyone knows me to lead: working day and night and forging a better economic position for myself, humble as it is, but nonetheless free and honorable." His chronic expression of anguish vanished, as if he had remembered something, and he said, "I don't believe you . . . It's one thing to save and another to covet. For example, that's the difference between Marino and me: greed versus saving. You understand . . ."

The schoolmaster nodded, and then he seemed to reflect deeply on Benites's ideas.

In general, the land surveyor held a firm conviction that he was a good, young, hard-working man, organized and honorable, with a bright future ahead of him. He had always alluded to himself as a paradigm of life that everyone should follow, and although he didn't express so much explicitly, his words exuded it, pronounced with apostolic dignity, on occasions when problems of morality or fate arose among his friends, whereupon he'd take intransigent stances on issues of good and evil, truth and lies, sincerity and hypocrisy, and other important matters.

* * *

Due to the orderly life that Leónides Benites led, he had never been under the weather.

"The day that you fall ill," Marino would yell, since in Quivilca medicine was an empirical trade, "you'll never get up again!"

Facing these dismal words, Benites would take even greater precautions for his self-preservation. His personal hygiene and the cleanliness of his room were painstakingly immaculate—and this he ensured at all cost. He'd go on endless searches for physical well-being, by establishing a routine that no one but he, with the patient meticulousness of a distrustful curmudgeon, would be able to execute. In the morning, before he left for work, he'd try on multiple pairs of underwear to see which was suitable for the current weather and state of his health, and just as often he'd return from halfway down the road to change his shirt or undergarment, because it was too cold out or because the ones he was wearing were too warm. The same would occur with his use of socks, shoes, hats, sweaters, and even with gloves and his briefcase. If it was snowing, he wouldn't pack only as many papers, rulers, and ropes as possible, but rather, to put his skills to better use, he'd also take his levels, tripods, and theodolites, even though they'd serve no purpose. Other times he'd grow agitated, jumping up and down and running around like a loon, until he had nothing left in him, or he'd refuse to leave his room for anything, and if someone came by, he'd slowly and stealthily open the door so that a bluster of wind wouldn't suddenly sneak in. But if the sun was shining, he'd swing all the doors and windows wide open and refuse to close them. Thus, one day while Benites was at the bookkeeper's office, the boy he'd charged with minding his door got distracted and someone broke in and stole the sugar along with his portable stove.

But that wasn't all. As preventative measures against the contagion of evils, Benites's pulchritude was greater. He wouldn't accept a drop or morsel from just anyone, but only from someone he had previously exorcized, after blessing that drop or morsel five, count them, five times. The bookkeeper came to see him one Sunday morning when the cook had just brought a gift of piping hot *humitas*,[45] and he entered just as Benites was blessing them for the third time, but he lost count of how many blessings he'd given, and this was why he no longer dared taste the gift and just gave them to the dog. Shaking his hand was utterly futile. When he had no other choice, he'd ever so slightly touch the other hand with his fingertips and start worrying, making a face of disgust, and it wasn't beyond him to go wash his hands with two kinds of stockpiled disinfectant soap. Everything in his room was always where it belonged, and even he, Benites, was always where he belonged, working, pondering, sleeping, eating, or reading *Self-Help* by Smiles,[46] which he considered the greatest work of modernity. During the religious holidays of the Church, he'd thumb through the Gospel according to Matthew—a pocket edition gilded in gold that his mother had taught him to love and in it comprehend all that true Christians deem worthy of comprehension.

Over the course of time, his voice had grown considerably hoarse, as a consequence of the snowfall in the cordillera. This circumstance appeared as one of the worst possible flaws in the eyes of José Marino, his partner, with whom he'd often dispute this issue.

"Quit your fussing!" Marino would say, entreating him in the presence of the general store's clientele. "Speak up, like a man! Enough with your humbleness and excessive piety! You're too old to play stupid. Drink up, fill your belly, fall in love, and you'll see how your voice clears up . . ."

Leónides Benites said something that couldn't be heard over the laughter brought on by Marino's prickly phrases, and his partners started to mock him, "What was that? Huh? What did he say? Which one now? But, I can't hear a thing!" The laughter redoubled and Benites, hurt by the ridicule, blushed, stood up, and left.

Benites generally wasn't liked in Quivilca. Why? Because of his lifestyle? Because of his moralist mania? Because of his physical weakness? Because of his withdrawal from and distrust of other people? The only person who participated in close proximity (and with any affection) in the land surveyor's life was a lady, a lathe operator's mother, a half-deaf woman already up there in her years, who was famously beatified and, therefore, friendly, possessing all the good customs and leading an exemplary life of austerity. Benites was never satisfied by being anywhere, except the ranch of that devotee, whom he'd join for long gatherings, playing cards, commenting on Quivilca life, and often discussing serious moral dilemmas.

One afternoon they came to tell the woman that Benites was sick in bed, whereupon she went to see him and discovered that, in effect, he was stricken with a fever so high it made him delirious and seized him with anguish. She prepared him a strong eucalyptus infusion with two fingers of alcohol and saw to it that he take a mustard bath, which would make him perspire profusely, the sure sign of the body's ridding itself of the malady, which seemed to consist only of a bad cold. Yet, as the two remedies were administered and the sick man started to sweat, the fever persisted and, at moments, even worsened.

Night had fallen when it began to snow. The front door and window of Benites's room had been sealed airtight. The woman stuffed rags in the cracks to keep out gusts of wind. A candle was burning and projected sad yellow tones onto objects of the room and the patient's bed. According to him, were he to move or shift his position, driven by the fever, the shadows would flicker—now short, now long, cut off, or full-sized—on the planes of his unibrowed face and between his pillows and bedsheets.

Benites tossed and turned and let out confusing nightmarish phrases. Beside herself over his increasing gravity, the woman began to pray, kneeling in front of a painting of the Sacred Heart of Jesus that hung above the headboard. He turned his pale inexpressive head, like the death mask of a corpse, and she collected herself again to pray. Then, she stood up, revived, and stood alongside the bed.

"Benites?"

His breathing now sounded quieter and more irregular. The woman stepped closer on tiptoe, leaning over the bed and staring at him for a good while. After thinking for a moment, she called him again, feigning her calmness.

"Benites?"

The sick man let out a dark groan potent with orphanhood, which struck the woman in her womanly womb.

"How do you feel? Shall I prepare you another remedy?"

The man made an awkward, abrupt motion, formed two fists in the air, as if he were crushing invisible bugs, and opened his bloodshot eyes. His gaze was ambiguous and, nonetheless, threatening. He smacked his black-and-blue chapped lips, whispering nonsense.

"Nothing! That curve is greater! Leave me alone! I know what I'm doing! Leave me alone!" he said and, in a single jerk, turned to face the wall, bending his knees and sticking his arms under the covers.

Quivilca had no doctor. They'd complained to the company about this to no avail. Each person combated illness according to his or her own understanding, except for pneumonia, because José Marino, the empirical store owner, had become a specialist in that treatment. The woman tending to Benites didn't know if she should go to the merchant in case that's what it was, or if she should focus on procuring some other prescription on her own and waste no time. She kept pacing across the room in desperation, and, from time to time, she'd observe the patient or put her ear to the door, listening to the falling snow. Maybe her son or someone else would decide to come by and help her search for advice or aid.

Although the sick man at times would fall into absolute silence, which the woman didn't perceive on account of her deafness, the night generally dragged on, filled with painful screams and delirious words. Adjoining the entire area, there had been an extensive deposit of the mineral. The rest of the ranches were far away, right on the skirt of the mountain, and she would've needed to shout for someone to hear her.

The woman decided to prepare him another remedy. Among the useful items that Benites kept on his table as a precautionary measure, she found a bit of glycerin—a substance that immediately gave her an idea for the new prescription. She lit the burner again, and tiptoeing over to the bed, she examined the patient, who'd been calm for quite a while, and she realized that he was asleep. She decided then to let him rest, postponing the remedy for later in case the fever kept up. She knelt before the sacred painting and, with painful vehemence, mumbled countless long prayers mixed with sighs and tears. Then she stood up and returned to the bed, drying her eyes with the cuff of her percale blouse. Benites remained calm.

"God is great!" the woman exclaimed, touched, and with an almost imperceptible voice, she added, "Oh, Sacred Heart of Jesus!" raising her eyes to the effigy and bringing her hands together, swollen with ineffable frenzy: "Almighty God! Watch over Your creature! Aid him and abandon him not! With Your sacred flame! Father, protect us in this valley of sorrow!"

She couldn't contain her emotion and started to weep, took a few steps, and sat down on the stool. There she began to doze.

Suddenly she awoke.

The candle was about to go out and had dripped, creating a narrow deep crevasse through which it had melted, continuing to heap up and cool on one prong of the candlestick, in the shape of a closed fist whose forefinger was raised, as if pointing at the flame. She adjusted the candle, and as she noticed that Benites hadn't switched positions and was still asleep, she leaned over to look him in the face. "Sleep," she said, and decided not to stir him.

In the midst of his febrile visions, Leónides Benites had often seen the painting of the Sacred Heart of Jesus that hung over the headboard. The holy image mixed together with the images of his delirium, embroiled in the light glow of the flakes coming off the whitewashed wall. The hallucinations were related to what worried Benites the most in the tangible world, such as his work performance at the mines, his business in the corporation with Marino and Rubio, and his desire for sufficient funds to go to Lima to finish his engineering studies as soon as possible, so he could start up a business on his own in his profession. In the delirium he saw Marino complaining about his money and threatening to hit him, backed by all the settlers of Quivilca. Benites energetically protested, but had to withdraw in defeat, due to the immense number of attackers. He was slipping on precipitous rocks, and when he suddenly came around the bend in that craggy terrain, he ran into another group of his enemies. The scare made him jump. The Heart of Jesus immediately entered the conflict and frightened the aggressors and thieves with its mere presence, only to later disappear without warning, abandoning him precisely at the moment when an angry Mr. Taik said to him, "Get out of here! U.S. Mining is canceling the appointment because of your disgraceful conduct! Get out of here, you wiseass!"

Benites kept begging him, plaintively pressing his hands together, but Taik ordered he be removed from the office, and two Soras came in smiling, as if mocking his disgrace. They took him by the arms, dragged him out, and, without being asked to, threw him to the ground. At this juncture, the Sacred Heart of Jesus left, as everything had been resolved, and the Lord disappeared in a flash of lightning.

Shortly thereafter Benites caught a Sora stealing a bundle of bills from his register. He lunged at the thief, chased him, compelled not so much by the amount he was taking, but the barefaced smile the Indian wore to taunt him, while he saddled the back of an alligator in the middle of a wide river. Benites reached the riverbank, and just as he was about to step foot in the current, he suddenly felt stupefied, deprived of all voluntary movement. This time Jesus appeared before Benites with a blazing halo around his head. The river suddenly surged, covering all visible space, even the most remote confines. A massive crowd was surrounding the Lord, attentive to his plans, and the feeling of a terrible crux lay on the horizon. Dread suddenly possessed the land surveyor, when he realized that, in an obscure though certain way, the hour of the final judgment had arrived.

Benites tried to examine his conscience, which might afford a glimpse into the place that would be his eternal destiny. He tried to remember his good and evil deeds on earth, and naturally he recalled his good deeds first. He avidly gathered them and into the most suitable, visible part of his mind in order of importance: beneath them, those deeds relating to past actions of the more or less disputable or insignificant type of goodness and above them, at an arm's reach, those deeds relating to the great features of virtue, whose merits were reported from far away, leaving no room for doubt about their authenticity and importance. He then asked his memory for the bitter remembrances, and his memory gave him none—not even one rat-scented recollection.[47] At times, it would timidly insinuate a fuzzy deed that, examined closely in the light of reason, ended up vanishing into the neutral corners of the classification of values or, studied even more closely, managed to lose any tint of guilt, replacing this with not just any other indefinable hue, but with the exact opposite: this recollection essentially became a meritorious deed that Benites recognized with true paternal fruition. Fortunately, he was intelligent and had very carefully cultivated his discursive critical faculty, with which he knew how to elaborate on things and give them their true, accurate meaning.

Very rarely was Benites unprepared (or so he felt) to be introduced to the Savior. As he reasoned it out, a great fear made a cocoon for him out of his own thought. Then, an Accoya alfalfa farmer he hadn't seen for years who used to sell his mother grass for her guinea pigs was berating him with curses for his covetousness and greed. Through a rapid association of ideas, Benites recalled that he sometimes loved money—perhaps excessively. He remembered that one night in Colca, at a huge abandoned estate where he was sleeping alone, he'd heard the noise of lost souls. In the darkness they began to push open the door, and Benites was scared silent. He remembered that, the following day, he'd told his neighbors about what happened, not forgetting to guarantee to them and everyone else that souls would often linger there, due to the burial of gold left by a colonial Spanish *encomendero*.[48] As the nocturnal sounds kept repeating, the thirst for gold finally tempted Benites, and in the late hours of one of those nights, the land surveyor invoked the lost souls.

"Who's there?" he asked, propping himself up in bed, his teeth chattering out of fear. When they didn't answer, but kept pushing the doors, Benites asked again, panting in a cold sweat, "Who's there? If you're a lost soul, then tell me what you want."

"I'm a lost soul," a nasally seemingly otherworldly voice replied in a pitiful tone.

Benites knew it was bad to run from lost souls, which is why he argued without delay, "What's wrong? Why are you lost?" and nearly weeping, the soul replied, "In the corner of the kitchen I buried five cents, and that's what's keeping me here. Chip in ninety-five cents more and pay the priest for a Mass in my name, for my salvation . . ."

Indignant over the unexpected, onerous detour that the adventure was taking, he started to club that lost soul and yelled, "I've seen shameless dead men before, but never one like this!" The following day, Benites left that estate.

Now, remembering all this, already far from worldly life, he judged his conduct sinful and deserving of punishment. However, over the course of long reflections, he decided that his words, harmful to the lost soul, were communicated during an abnormal state of his spirit without any malevolent intention at all. With regard to morality, he did not forget that the physiognomy of actions is given by intention and intention alone. As for his refusal to pay for the Mass requested by the lost soul, guilt didn't fall on him, but on the parish priest, whom a strong dyspepsia impeded from giving Mass. It wasn't hidden from Benites, let it be said in passing, that the priest's illness wasn't so severe as to take him completely away from the fulfillment of his sacred duties, and this motivated a more judicious and serious analysis: perhaps in reality it wasn't a lost soul at all, but a nasty prank played on him by one of his friends, who had learned of his ailments. In this context, had the Mass been held, the prank would've had a repercussion of mockery and impiety, entangling Benites as one of the culprits. There was no doubt that he had, as it were, done well in proceeding as he did, subconsciously defending the Church's charters of seriousness, and his conduct therefore just might garner enough merit to be rewarded by the Lord. Benites placed this memory in the middle, exactly in the middle of all his memories, moved by a singular, inextricable dialectic.

A feeling never before registered in his senses, born at the very bottom of his being, suddenly announced that he was in the presence of Jesus. The light that filled his thought was so bright it possessed his vision of all that was, is, and shall be—the entire consciousness of time and space, the plenary image and one of the objects, the eternal, essential meaning of the limits. A flash of wisdom enveloped him, serving him up in a single shot the sensitive and sentimental, abstract and material, nocturnal and solar, even and odd, fractional and synthetic concept of his permanent role in God's designs. Then he could do nothing, think nothing, want nothing, feel nothing for himself or in himself alone. Like the *ego* of egotism, his personality could not be subtracted from the invigorating and caring court at his sides. In his being an orchestral note of the infinite had lingered from the footsteps of Jesus and his holy standard hanging from the heart's tallest mast. He turned inward, and when he felt separated from the Lord, condemned to wander through fate like a scattered number, dislocated from universal harmony, in some gray vague expanse, without dawn or dusk, an indescribable pain he'd never experienced filled his soul to the top and choked him, as if he was chewing on coins in the dark and couldn't manage to swallow them. His inner torment, the fateful misfortune of his spirit, was not due to the paradise lost but to the expression of infinite sadness he saw or felt ripple across the Nazarene's divine face, when he bowed at his feet. Oh, what mortal sadness is Yours! And, oh, how I could not contain even the Enigma's two-mouthed glass! That great sadness made Benites suffer an incurable, unlimited pain.

"Lord," whispered Benites, pleading, "At least, let your sadness wane! At least let a bit of it pass into my heart! At least let a few pebbles roll down to help me reflect Your great sadness!"

Silence ruled the transcendental extension.

"Lord! Blow out the lantern of Your sadness, for my heart is not ready to reflect it! What have I done to my blood? Where is my blood? Oh, Lord! You gave it to me, and I've accidentally left it coagulated in the pits of life— poor in blood and coveting it!"

Benites cried to death.

"Lord! I was Your sinner and poor sheep who strayed! When in my hands I had the chance to be a timeless Adam, without afternoon, evening, night, or the day after! When in my hands I had the chance to bridle and harness the Edenic murmurs for all of eternity and overcome the Absolute and the Changing! When in my hands I had the chance to stake out my frontiers homogeneously, as in simple bodies, claw by claw, beak by beak, pebble by pebble, apple by apple! When in my hands I had the chance to slice up the path lengthwise and sideways, through diameters and altitudes, to see if I might thus leave for the meeting with the Truth! . . ."

Silence began to grow quiet on the side of nothingness.

"Lord! I was Your criminal and ingrate, Your unforgivable vermin. If only I hadn't been born! If only, at the very least, I had immortalized myself in the cocoons and vespers! Happy are the cocoons, for they are jewels born of paradise, even though they sleep in their sealed womb, in their coarse stamens! Happy are the vespers, for they didn't and won't have to arrive at the time of definable days! I might only have been the egg, cloud, the latent and immanent rhythm: God! . . ."

Benites erupted in a scream of infinite desolation that, after screeching to a halt, left silence silent forever.

* * *

Benites awoke abruptly. Morning light poured through his bedroom window. Next to the bed sat José Marino.

"What a good life, partner!" Marino exclaimed, crossing his arms. "Eleven in the morning and still in bed! Come on, let's go! Get up! I'm going to Colca this afternoon."

"You, to Colca?" Benites gasped. "You're going to Colca today?"

"Yeah, man! Get up!" Marino said, anxiously pacing the length of the room. "We need to go take care of some accounts! Rubio is already waiting for us at the store . . ."

"Okay," Benites shuddered, sitting up in bed. "I'll get up in a second. I'm still running a slight fever, but it doesn't matter."

"A fever, you? Quit pulling my chain, man! Get up! I'll wait for you at the store."

From *Tungsten* 415

Marino left and Benites began to get dressed, taking his customary precautions: socks underwear, shirt, everything had to be appropriate and suitable for that particular moment on account of his recent subpar health. Neither overdressed nor under.

At one in the afternoon, the horse Marino was going to mount stood waiting in its saddle near the door of the general store. The merchant's nephew was leading it by a rope. Inside, loud voices were arguing between cackles. Once the deals between Marino, Rubio, and Benites had been sealed, Machuca, Zavala, Baldazari, Taik, and Weiss said good-bye to the merchant. Tumblers abounded, and Machuca, already half in the bag, chided Marino and asked, "So who are you going to leave the Rosada girl with?"

The Rosada girl was one of Marino's girlfriends. An eighteen-year-old, beautiful sort of highland girl, with large black eyes and innocent purple cheeks, she'd been brought to Colca by a prompter from the mines, and her sisters, Teresa and Albina, came along lured by the mystery of that life that wafted a strange irresistible seduction over the astonished, naive villagers. The three of them came to Quivilca, after running away from home. Their parents—a couple of miserable old peasants—bemoaned their disappearance for hours on end. In Quivilca, the girls set out to work, making and selling *chicha*, in an enterprise that often obliged them to drink and get drunk with their clientele. The prompter was upset that Graciela had this type of job, so he left her, and a few weeks later, José Marino caught her on the rebound. As for Albina and Teresa, many rumors were flying around Quivilca.

"How about a game of craps?" Marino responded with impudence to Machuca's repeated questions. "Winner takes the girl, what do you say?"

"That's it! Craps! Craps! But let's all bet on it," argued Baldazari.

A circle formed around the counter. Everyone, including Benites, was smashed. Marino was shaking the dice and yelling, "Who's the boss?" and he gave them a toss, counting aloud and pointing at them and then at his friends, "One, two, three, four! You're the boss!" It was Benites's turn to play.

"But, what are we betting on?" asked Benites, dice in hand.

"Just throw 'em!" Baldazari said. "Didn't you hear? We're playing for the Rosada girl!"

"No way, man!" said Benites, more disturbed than drunk. "Play craps for a woman! Ya' don't do that. Let's bet a drink instead." But unanimous rebukes, insults, and zingers strangled his timid scruples, and he started to gamble.

"Bravo! Drinks are on him! The prize for taking your turn!"

Commissioner Baldazari won the game of craps and the stakes: the Rosada girl. He ordered a round of champagne, and Machuca came up to him, saying, "What a pretty little *chola* you're gonna eat tonight, commissioner. She's got haunches like this . . ."

The bookkeeper, while saying this, opened his arms into a circle and made a gluttonous, repugnant expression. The commissioner's eyes also threw off sparks, remembering the Rosada girl.

"Where's she living these days?" he asked Machuca. "I haven't seen her in a while."

"Near the La Poza. Let's have someone go get her right now!"

"No way, man! Not now. It's daytime. People could see us."

"People? What people! All the Indians are working! Send for her right away!"

"But, come on. It was a joke. You think Marino's going to let go of the *chola*? If he was leaving for good, sure, but he's only going to Colca for a few days . . ."

"What does that matter? What has been won has been won. Play stupid all you want! That woman is like opium! Personally I like that it's outrageous! Send for her! You're the commissioner, the boss! Oh, you're such a drag. And the rest of you, fools! Come on!"

"And you think she's going to come?"

"Of course."

"Who does she live with?"

"With her sisters, who are delectable too."

Baldazari stood there thinking and cracking his horsewhip. A few minutes later, Marino and Baldazari walked out the door.

"Go on, Cucho," Marino said to his nephew. "Go to the Rosadas' and tell Graciela to come here, to the store. Tell her I'm waiting for her, because I'm leaving soon, and if she asks who I'm with, don't tell her who's here. Say I'm alone, all by myself. You hear?"

"Yes, Uncle."

"Don't forget! Tell her I'm alone, that there's no one in the store. Leave the horse. Tie it to the foot of the display case. Get a move on! Off you go and get back here right away . . ."

Cucho tied the end of the horse's rope around the foot of the display case and left to do as he was told.

"Move it! Move it!" Marino and Baldazari kept saying.

José Marino often heaped praise on anyone who might be of use to him somewhere down the line. His servility to the commissioner had no limits.

Marino would even assist him in his romantic affairs. They'd go out after dusk to make rounds through the workers' camps and mining sites, accompanied by an officer, and sometimes Baldazari would end up staying in the shack of some laborers with the wife, daughter, or mother that he found in the middle of the night. The officer would return alone to the commissioner's office, and Marino, alone to his general store. Why the merchant's praise of the commissioner? There were plenty of reasons.

At present, the merchant was about to depart, and he'd asked the commissioner to keep an eye on the store, since Zavala usually looked after it but would be on vacation. Moreover, the commissioner was now consuming a wide array of items in the store, and he was instructing the others to do the same. Three in the afternoon and Marino had already sold many bottles—vermouth, cognac, and whisky. But these were ephemeral and rather petty motivations. There were, however, more notorious reasons and they were the most serious of all.

Commissioner Baldazari was Marino's right-hand man in all matters contracting, the point man for the throng of Indians, and U.S. Mining's management too. When Marino couldn't get anywhere with a worker, who was denying his debts, refusing to accept a miserable salary or to work a graveyard shift or a holiday, Marino would turn to the commissioner, who'd get that laborer to cave, by jailing him overnight and using his "leverage" (torture proper to Peruvian prisons) or the crack of his horsewhip. Additionally, when Marino was unable to obtain from Taik and Weiss these or those advantages or facilities, any favor or benefit, Marino would turn to Baldazari and the latter would intervene with the clout and might of his authority, obtaining from the patrons all that Marino desired. Therefore, it wasn't strange at all that the merchant was ready to hand over his darling to the commissioner, ipso facto and in public.

Not long afterward, Graciela appeared from around the corner, joined by Cucho. The men in the store quickly hid, and only Marino went to the door, trying to mask his drunkenness.

"Come on in," he said affectionately to Graciela. "I'm leaving soon. Come on in. I've called you because I'm leaving soon."

"I thought you were just gonna leave," Graciela said shyly, "without even saying good-bye."

A sudden giggle erupted in the store and all the guests appeared out of nowhere in front of Graciela. Blushing and shocked, she stepped back against the wall, once they surrounded her, reaching out their hands, hugging her, or caressing her chin.

"Sit down. Sit down," said Marino, splitting his sides in laughter. "It's a farewell party. What did you expect! These friends of mine. Our *patrones*! Our great, dear commissioner! Sit down! Sit down! What will you have to drink?"

They closed the door, but not completely, and from outside Cucho took the horse's rope, sitting down on the stoop to wait.

It started to snow. Countless people came to purchase something in the store, but left without daring to enter. An Indian woman with a painful, desperate expression came running.

"Is your uncle here?" she asked Cucho, trying to catch her breath.

"Yeah, he's in there. Why?"

"I need some laudanum. I've got no time, my mom's about to die."

"Go on in, if you want."

"But for all I know he's got guests . . . ?"

"He's with several men, but go on in if you'd like."

The woman hesitated and stopped at the door to wait. Growing anguish painted her face. Cucho, without removing the rope from the horse, amused himself by drawing the national coat of arms with his red-tipped pencil on a sheet from his school notebook. The woman paced back and forth, desperate yet reluctant to enter the store. She peered inside to see what was going on, listened momentarily, and started to pace again.

"Who's in there?" she asked Cucho.

"The commissioner."

"Who else?"

"The bookkeeper, the engineer, the professor, the gringos . . . They're good and drunk. They're drinking champagne."

"But I hear a woman! . . ."

"Graciela."

"The Rosada girl?"

"Yeah. My uncle sent me to bring her here 'cause he's leaving soon."

"Oh my God! When will they ever leave? When will they ever leave?" said the woman, and she began to groan.

"Why are you crying?" Cucho asked.

"My mom's about to die, and Don José is with people . . ."

"If you want, I'll call my uncle over, so he can sell it to you . . ."

"But he might get angry . . ."

Cucho peeked inside and timidly called, "Uncle Pepe! . . ."

The orgy was reaching its peak. From the store a confusing clamor poured forth, mixed with laughter, shrieks, and a nauseating stench. Cucho called several times. Finally, José Marino came to the door.

"What do you want, goddamn it?" he said, irritated with his nephew.

When Cucho saw that his uncle was drunk and angry, he jumped back in fear, and the woman stepped to the side as well.

"She wants you to sell her some laudanum," Cucho mumbled from a distance.

"Laudanum, you've got to be fuckin' kidding me!" Marino groaned, furiously lunging at his nephew to give him a good slap upside his head, which sent him to the ground.

"God damn it!" shouted the merchant, kicking him with his toes. "You idiot! Always naggin' me for something!"

Some bystanders came to defend Cucho, and the woman seeking the laudanum begged Marino on her knees.

"Don't hit him, *taita*!" she pleaded. "It's true, he did it for me, because I told him to. Hit me instead, if you want! Hit me instead, if you want! . . ."

Several boot heels fell upon the woman. Blind with rage and booze, José Marino kept beating her, until the commissioner came out and pulled him away.

"What do we have here, my dear Marino?" he said, grabbing him under the armpits.

"Forgive me, commissioner!" Marino replied, humbly. "A thousand times, forgive me!"

Both men entered the store. Cucho was lying in the snow, bloody and sobbing. The woman, rising to her feet next to Cucho, also wept in pain.

"Just because you called him, he hits you. Just for that! And me too, just because I came for the remedy! . . ."

"Chana! Chana!" an Indian boy came running, tears dripping down his face. "Mom is dead! Come on! She just died!"

Chana, the Indian woman, took off running, followed by the boy.

After being spooked, Marino's horse had fled, and so, while he was drying his tears and blood, Chuco went to fetch him, since he knew very well that, if the horse got away, "his ass would no longer be his," as his uncle liked to say when he threatened to whip him. He returned, fortunately, with the animal, and he sat back down at the door of the general store, which remained ajar. He crouched down and peered inside. What was happening in there now?

José Marino was conversing behind the door, in secret and cup in hand, with Mr. Taik, the U.S. Mining manager.

"But, I saw it with my own eyes," he said to him, in an insinuating and flattering tone.

"You are very kind, but that's dangerous," argued the flushed, smiley manager.

"Yes, yes, yes, Mr. Taik, you just decide. I know what I'm saying. Rubio's sick in the head. She (they were talking about Rubio's wife) doesn't love him. On top of it, she's hot for you. I've seen her."

"But, Mr. Marino," the manager kept smiling, "Rubio could find out . . ."

"I assure you that he won't, Mr. Taik. Cross my heart and hope to die." Marino drank his glass and added, decidedly, "Do you want me to take Rubio on an excursion out of Quivilca, so that you might seize the day?"

"Well, we shall see. We shall see. Thanks very much. You're very kind . . ."

"Speaking of you, Mr. Taik, you know I can't spare a thing. I'm your very modest, very humble, and very poor friend, maybe the last in line, but a true friend willing to help you even if it means my life. Your poor servant, Mr. Taik. Your poor friend!"

Marino bowed low.

At that moment, from the other end of the store, Mr. Weiss was calling to the merchant.

"Marino! Another round of champagne!"

José Marino flew to serve the glasses.

By then, Graciela had gotten drunk. José Marino, her lover, had given her a strange mysterious cocktail to drink, which he himself had secretly prepared, and just one glass had completely inebriated her.

"Astonishing! Astonishing!" the commissioner, in a low voice, said to Marino on the side "You are a wonder! She's already two sheets to the wind."

"And to think," replied Marino, boastfully, "and to think that I added just a bit of the green stuff. Otherwise, she would've keeled over a while ago." He put his arm around Baldazari, adding, "You deserve this, Commissioner. Anything for you. I'm not talking about a cocktail! I'm talking about a woman! For you, my life! Believe me."

In spasms produced by the alcohol, Graciela was singing and crying for no reason at all. She suddenly stood up, started to dance alone, while everyone clapped amid laughs and catcalls.

"I'm a poor wretch!" Graciela was saying, with a glass in her hand, swaying back and forth now without her shawl. "Don José! Come here! What are you to me? Please! 'Cause I'm nothin' but a poor girl . . ."

The laughter and shouting grew. Marino stood at the commissioner's side.

"You see?" Marino said to Graciela, as if to a blind woman, and loud enough so everyone could hear. "Here's the commissioner, the real authority, the greatest man in Quivilca, after our bosses, Mr. Taik and Mr. Weiss. You see him here, with us?"

"Yup. I see 'em," Graciela said, her eyes drooping with drunkenness, squinting at the commissioner. "Yup. The commissioner. There he is . . ."

"Good. So the commissioner is going to be responsible for you while I'm gone. You understand? He'll look after you. He'll take my place in everything and for everything." Marino, while saying this, made mocking faces and added, "You'd better obey him as if he was me. You hear? You hear me, Graciela?"

"Yup," Graciela responded, her voice raspy, her eyes almost shut. "Okay . . . that's fine . . ."

She started to sway back and forth, about to fall, and Machuca let out a hoot. Marino motioned for him to shut up and winked at Baldazari, indicating that the fruit was ripe for the picking. Everyone else, in chorus, was saying to Baldazari, "Now, Commissioner! Just go for it! Just go for it!"

The commissioner limited himself to laughing and drinking, while Graciela, who'd been holding herself up on the display case, went to sit down.

"Don José!" she cried out. "Come over next to me! Come over here!"

José Marino motioned Baldazari over to the Rosada girl. Baldazari, as was his answer to any question, continued to drink. There were few instances when Baldazari completely reached a state of intoxication, and this was no exception, for while he had served himself many rounds of champagne, he was merely buzzed, whereas everyone else was drunk out of their minds. Rubio was shouting to Taik about international politics, and, on the other side, Zavala, Benites, and Weiss were interlocked in a group hug. Marino and Baldazari kept circling Graciela, who put her arms around Marino, but quickly he slipped away from her and put Baldazari in his place, between Graciela's arms. She realized what happened and abruptly pulled away from the commissioner.

"Kiss the good commissioner!" Marino angrily ordered.

"No!" she replied energetically, as if she was waking up.

"Leave her alone!" Baldazari said to Marino, but the labor contractor was already irate.

"I said kiss the good commissioner, Graciela!"

"No! Not that! Never, Don José!"

"So you're not going to kiss him, eh? Not going to do as I say? You wait one minute!" growled the merchant, and he went to mix her another cocktail.

As night fell, they closed the door all the way, and the general store sunk into complete darkness. Except for Benites, who'd fallen asleep, all the guests experienced Graciela's body, one after another. First Marino, and then Baldazari, had generously offered the young girl to their friends. The first ones to taste the spoils, naturally, were the bosses, Mr. Taik and Mr. Weiss. The other men entered afterward, by order of social class and economic rank: Commissioner Baldazari, Machuca the bookkeeper, Rubio the engineer, and then Professor Zavala. Out of modesty, politeness, or perhaps it was refinement, José Marino went last. He took his turn in the middle of a diabolical ruckus and, in the dark, uttered words, interjections, and shouts of hair-raising abjection and vice. During the horrifying act, Marino continued an appalling conversation with his accomplices, while a muted, stifled snore was the only sign of life coming from Graciela, until he let out one final macabre squawk.

When they lit the lamps of the store, there were bottles and broken glasses on the countertop, champagne spilled on the floor, pieces of torn fabric scattered at random, and gaunt faces beaded with sweat. One bloodstain after another blackened the cuffs and collars of their shirts. Marino brought over some water in a basin for everyone to wash their hands. While they stood in a circle cleaning up, a gunshot rang out, sending the basin in the air. Laughter parted the lips of the commissioner, who had pulled the trigger.

"Got to test my men!" Baldazari said, holstering his revolver. "But look at the way you're shakin' in your boots."

Leónides Benites awoke.

"Where's Graciela?" he asked, wiping the sleep from his eyes. "Did she leave yet?"

"Mr. Baldazari, she needs to be woken up," said Taik, cleaning the lenses of his glasses. "Seems she ought to return to her ranch now. It's getting late."

"Yes, yes, yes," the commissioner said seriously. "She must be woken up—you, Marino, you're always the man!"

"Ah!" exclaimed the merchant. "This is gonna be hard. The only remedy for that cocktail is sleep."

"But, in any case," Rubio argued, "we can't just leave her here lying on the ground . . . Don't you agree, Mr. Taik?"

"Oh, well, yes," said the manager, between puffs on his pipe.

Benites approached Graciela, followed by everyone else. There was the Rosada girl, lying on the floor, motionless, rumpled, with her skirt in disarray and still pulled up above her waist. They called to her and poked at her body, but she showed no sign of coming to—even when they brought her a candle, kept calling her, and moved it back and forth. Nothing. She just stayed there, still, and while everyone else just waited in silence, Marino put his ear to her chest.

"Shit!" the merchant exclaimed, as he rose to his feet. "She's dead!"

"Dead?" asked the others, in shock. "Quit your nonsense! No way!"

"She is," Graciela's lover replied in a carefree tone. "She's dead. We've had our fun."

"Okay, so, if anyone asks," Taik whispered severely, "I never said this. You hear? Not a word! Someone has to take her home and tell her sisters she's had a heart attack and that they should let her get some sleep. Tomorrow, when they find her dead, everything will be fine . . ."

All those present consented, and the deed was done.

At ten o'clock that night, José Marino got on his horse and left for Colca. Graciela was buried the day after. At the front of the funeral procession was the commissioner of Quivilca, accompanied by Zavala, Rubio, Machuca, and Benites. Marino's nephew, Cucho, watched on from a distance.

All the men who'd been at the store returned from the cemetery with certain ease, in the midst of an inconsequential conversation. Only Leónides Benites was lost in thought, feeling the weight of Graciela's death and prickled by regret. In his conscience, the land surveyor knew that she hadn't died of natural causes. True, he didn't see anything that happened to her in the dark, since he'd passed out, but he suspected everything, even if it was only in an obscure, dubious way. Once he was back from the burial, Benites locked himself in his room, regretting the event at the store—an emotion he wasn't used to feeling and found repulsive on principle. He stretched out on his bed to think and fell asleep.

That afternoon, Teresa and Albina, the dead girl's two sisters, showed up crying at Mr. Taik's office, accompanied by two other Indian women who, like the Rosadas, were also *chicha* vendors. Albina and Teresa requested a meeting with the boss, and, after a short wait, they were introduced to the Yankee, who from time to time was joined by his compatriot and assistant manager, Mr. Weiss. Both men puffed their pipes.

"What can I do for you?" Mr. Taik asked in a dry tone.

We've come here," Teresa said in tears, "because everyone in Quivilca is sayin' that Graciela was killed and didn't die of natural causes. They say it's 'cause someone got her drunk at the store, that's why, and that you should bring them to justice. How can they just kill a poor woman like that and no one does anythin' about it?"

Her sobs, which prohibited her from continuing, irritated Taik.

"Who's saying that?"

"Everyone, everyone . . ."

"Have you gone to the commissioner to file a complaint?"

"*Sí, patrón.*[49] He says that it's just gossip, but that's not true."

"Well, if that's what he said, then why did you come here? And why do you still believe such rubbish? Quit being stupid and go home. Death is death, and everything else is useless nonsense and sniffling," he retorted, getting ready to walk out too. "Off you go," he added paternally in a protective tone, sucking on his pipe and pacing back and forth. "Don't make a mountain out of a molehill. Get going now. No time for sermons and hogwash. Off you go."

Filled with dignity and despotism, the two bosses showed the Rosada girls to the door; Teresa and Albina had dried their tears but were irate.

"It's just because you're the bosses!" they shouted. "That's why you do what you want and kick us out—we came to file a complaint! They killed Graciela! Killed her! Killed her!"

An assistant came to lead them out by force, and the two girls walked away protesting and weeping, followed by other *chicha* vendors, protesting and weeping too. [JM]

Paco Yunque

When Paco Yunque and his mother arrived at the door of the school, the children were playing in the yard. His mother let him go and he ran along. Paco slowly stepped into the yard, with his first book, notebook, and pencil. He was scared, because this was the first time he'd seen a school, and he'd never seen so many children together before.

Several students his size went up to him, and Paco, who was timid, backed up against the wall and blushed. Those kids were so smart! So uninhibited! As if they were in their own homes. They were shouting, running, busting their guts in laughter, jumping around, and jabbing one another. It was a mess.

Paco was also stunned because in the country he'd never heard so many people's voices talking all at once. He'd heard as many as four or five people speaking at the same time. There was his father, his mother, Don José, Anselmo the gimp, and Tomasa, but this was no longer the sound of people. It was some other kind of sound instead—a very different kind. This school thing sure was a terrible racket, and Paco's ears were ringing.

A fat blond boy dressed in white was talking to him. Another kid, smaller than him, going hoarse, and wearing a red shirt, started talking to him too. From different groups the students split off and came to see Paco and ask him questions, but he couldn't hear anything over everyone's shouting. A tan-skinned boy, with a round face and a green jacket cinched around his waist, grabbed Paco by the arm and tried to drag him away, but Paco resisted. The boy grabbed him again, this time with more force, so Paco stepped closer to the wall and blushed some more. Just then the bell rang, and they all went into the classrooms.

Two boys—the Zumiga brothers—each took one of Paco's hands and led him into the first-grade classroom. At first Paco didn't want to follow but decided otherwise when he saw everyone else doing the same. He entered the room and grew pale. Everything suddenly fell silent, and this silence frightened Paco. The Zumigas were pulling at him, one on each side, then they suddenly let go and left him alone.

The teacher came in. All the children were standing up, with their right hand raised to their temples, saluting in silence with perfect posture.

Without letting go of his book, notebook or pencil, Paco stood in the middle of the room, between the first row of student desks and the teacher's desk. His head was whirling. Children. Yellow walls. Mobs of children. Shouting. Silence. A bunch of chairs. The teacher. There, all by himself, standing up, in the school. He wanted to cry. The teacher took him by the hand and showed him to a desk in the front row next to a boy his size.

"What's your name?" the teacher asked.

"Paco," he replied, with a warbling voice.

"And your last name? State your full name."

"Paco Yunque."

"Very well."

The teacher returned to his desk and, after casting a very serious gaze over all the students, spoke like a soldier.

"Be seated!"

A clatter of desks, and all the students were seated.

The teacher also sat down and wrote in his books for several moments. Paco Yunque was still holding his book, notebook, and pencil.

"Put your things in your desk," said the boy next to him, "like I did."

Paco Yunque remained in a daze and paid him no attention. His classmate took his books from him and put them in the desk.

"My name is Paco too," he said to him happily. "Paco Fariña. Don't feel bad. We're going to play some chess. Yours are the black pieces. My aunt Susana bought it for me. Where's your family?"

Paco Yunque didn't respond. That other Paco was annoying him. Surely all the other children were like this one: talkative, happy, and unafraid to be at school. Why were they like that? And why was Paco Yunque so scared? He surreptitiously looked at the teacher, the teacher's desk, the wall behind it, and the ceiling. He also looked out the corner of his eye, through the window, at the yard now empty and silent. The sun was shining outside. Every now and then, sounds from other classrooms and noises from wagons on the street could be heard. It was so strange to be in school! Again, Paco Yunque started to fall into a daze. He thought about his house and his mom.

"What time will we go home?" he asked Paco Fariña.

"At eleven o'clock. Where's your house?"

"That way."

"Is it far?"

"Yeah . . . No . . ."

Paco Yunque didn't know the name of his street, because it had been only a few days since they brought him from the country, and he didn't know the city yet.

Sounds of a wagon came in from the yard, and at the door Humberto appeared, the son of Mr. Dorian Grieve, an Englishman, employer of the Yunques, manager of Peruvian Rail Corporation, and mayor of the town. They'd had Paco come from the countryside so he could join Humberto at school and play with him, as they were the same age. Though, since Humberto was usually late to school and since this was Paco's first day, Mrs. Grieve had other plans.

"Take Paco to school already," she said to his mother. "He can't be late for the first day. Starting tomorrow you'll wait for Humberto to get up and bathe them together."

"Late again today?" the teacher said, when he saw Humberto Grieve.

"I overslept." Humberto replied, with complete self-assurance.

"Well," said the teacher, "let this be the last time. Take your seat."

Humberto Grieve scanned the room to see where Paco Yunque was sitting. When he found him, he went over to him.

"Come over to my desk with me," he ordered.

"No. The teacher put him here," Paco Fariña said to Humberto Grieve.

"What do you care?" Grieve snapped, dragging Yunque by the arm.

"Señor!" Fariña shouted, "Grieve's taking Paco Yunque to his desk."

"Let's just see!" said the teacher as he stopped writing and turned around. "Silence! What's going on over there?"

"Grieve took Paco Yunque to his desk," Fariña repeated.

"That's right," Grieve said, now seated at his desk with Yunque, "because Paco Yunque is my boy. That's why."

"Very well," said the teacher, as he already knew this, adding, "but I placed him with Paco Fariña so that he pays better attention to the explanations. Let him return to his place."

The students silently stared at the teacher, Humberto Grieve, and Paco Yunque. Fariña went and took Paco Yunque by the hand and tried to return him to his desk, but Grieve grabbed Yunque by the other arm and wouldn't let go.

"Grieve!" the teacher exclaimed. "What's this?"

"No," yelled Grieve, red with anger, "I want Yunque to stay with me."

"I said, leave him alone."

"No, señor."

"What do you mean, no?"

"No."

"Grieve! Grieve!" screamed the outraged teacher in a threatening tone.

Humberto Grieve had lowered his eyes and was clinging to the arm of Yunque, who was confused and let Fariña and Grieve tug at him like rope. Now he was more afraid of Humberto than the teacher, the other students, and the school itself. Why was Paco Yunque afraid of Humberto Grieve? Why did this Humberto Grieve often hit Paco Yunque?

The teacher went up to Yunque, took him by the arm, and led him to Fariña's desk. Grieve started to cry and bang his stool furiously. More footsteps were heard in the yard and another student, Antonio Gesdres, the son of a stonemason, appeared at the classroom door. "Why are you late?" the teacher asked.

"I went to buy bread for breakfast."

"Why didn't you go earlier?"

"I was getting my little brother up, and Mom is sick and Dad went to work."

"Well," said the teacher very seriously, "Stop right there, and spend an hour in time-out."

He pointed to the corner, near the blackboard.

"Grieve was late too," Paco Fariña said, rising to his feet.

"He's lying," Grieve immediately replied. "I wasn't late."

"Yes he was! Yes he was!" the students said in unison. "Grieve was late!"

"Shh! Silence!" said the teacher angrily, and all the children were silent. The teacher paced back and forth in thought.

"Grieve was late," Fariña whispered to Yunque, "and he didn't get punished, because his dad has money. He's late every day. You live in his house, right? Is it true that you're his boy?"

"I live with my mom," he replied.

"In Humberto Grieve's house?"

"It's a very nice house. The master and his lady are there. My mom's there, and I'm there with my mom."

From his stool on the far side of the room, Grieve was glaring at Yunque, and he showed him his fists for having let himself be led back to Fariña's desk. Paco Yunque didn't know what to do. That boy, Humberto, was going hit him again, because he didn't stay at his desk. When school lets out, Humberto would give him a shove and a good kick to the shin. That boy, Humberto, was bad and hit him every chance he got: on the street, in the hall, on the stairs, and also in the kitchen, in front of his mom and the master's lady too. Now he was going to hit him, since he was showing him his fists and staring with the whites of his eyes.

"I'm going over to Humberto's desk," Yunque said to Fariña.

"Don't go," Fariña replied. "Don't be silly. The teacher is going to punish you."

Fariña turned to look at Grieve, who showed his fists to him too, mumbling I don't know what behind the teacher's back.

"Señor!" Fariña shouted. "Over there, Grieve is showing me his fists."

"Silence! Attention!" teacher said. "Today we're going to talk about fish, and then we're going to do a writing assignment in our notebooks, and then you'll give them to me for review. I want to see who does the best assignment, and the winner will make honor roll. Did you hear me loud and clear? We're going to do the same thing we did last week. Exactly the same. Everyone must pay close attention and carefully copy the assignment I'm going to write on the chalkboard. Do you understand?"

"Yes," the students responded in unison.

"Very well," said the teacher. "So now we're going to talk about fish."

Several children wanted to speak. The teacher told one of the Zumigas to go ahead.

"Señor," said Zumiga, "on the beach there was lots of sand. One day we were digging and found a fish that was half-alive, so we took it to our house, but it died on the way . . ."

"Señor," said Grieve, "I've caught lots of fish and taken them to my house and dropped them in my living room, and none of them died."

"But . . . do you leave them in a tank with water?" the teacher asked.

"No. They're out in the open, near the furniture."

All the students started to laugh.

"That's a lie," said a wiry, little boy, "'cause if a fish is out of the water, it will die in no time."

"No it won't," said Humberto Grieve, "'cause in my room they don't die, 'cause my living room is fancy, and my daddy told me to bring home some fish and drop them on the floor near the chairs."

Paco Fariña was dying of laughter. The Zumiga brothers were too. The fat blond boy in a white jacket, and the other round-faced boy in the green, were roaring in laughter as well. What a riot Grieve is! Fish on the living room floor! Near the furniture! As if they were birds! Grieve had told a whopper. All the kids were shouting at once, exploding with laughter, "Hahahahaha! He's lying! Hahaha! Liar! Liar!"

Humberto Grieve grew angry, because they didn't believe what he'd said. He recalled that he once brought home two fish and left them in the living room for several days. When he moved them, they moved. He wasn't sure if they stayed alive for long or died right away, but more than anything he wanted everyone to believe what he was saying.

"Sure! 'Cause my daddy has money," he said to one of Zumigas over the laughter, "and he told me he's gonna have all the fish from the sea brought to my house—just for me—so I can play with them in my big living room."

"There now! There now! said the teacher, raising his voice. "Silence!

Grieve surely doesn't remember well. Because fish die when . . ." and the kids added in unison, "they're taken out of the water."

"That's right," said the teacher.

"Because mommy fish are in the water and when kid fish are taken out, they don't have their moms," the wiry pale boy said.

"No, no, no!" said the teacher. "Fish die out of water because they can't breathe. They get the air that's in the water, and when they're taken out, they cannot absorb the air outside."

"Because it's like they're already dead," another boy suggested.

"My dad can give them air at my house," Humberto insisted, "'cause he's got a ton of money and can buy anything."

"My dad has money too," the boy dressed in green said.

"My dad too," said another boy.

All the kids said that their dads had a lot of money. Paco Yunque didn't say anything and was thinking about the fish that would die out of water.

"Doesn't your dad have money?" Fariña asked Yunque.

Paco Yunque reflected and recalled once having seen his mom with a few pesetas in her hand.

"My mom has lots of money too," Yunque said to Fariña.

"How much?" Fariña asked.

"Like four pesetas."

"Paco Yunque says that his mom has lots of money too," Fariña shouted to the teacher.

"That's a lie!" Grieve replied. "Yunque's lying. His mom is my mom's servant, and she hasn't got a thing."

The teacher took the chalk and wrote on the board with his back to the students.

Taking advantage of the fact that the teacher wasn't watching, Humberto Grieve jumped over and pulled Yunque's hair, before racing back to his desk. Yunque started to cry.

"What's this?" said the teacher, turning around to see what was happening.

"Grieve pulled his hair," Fariña said.

"I did not," contested Grieve. It wasn't me. I haven't left my seat."

"Come now, come now!" the teacher said. "Be quite, Paco Yunque! Silence!"

He continued to write on the chalkboard, and then he asked Grieve, "If a fish is taken out of the water, what happens to it?

"It goes to live in my living room," replied Grieve.

Again the children laughed at him. That Humberto didn't know squat.

He didn't think about anything but his house and living room, his dad and money—always talking nonsense.

"Let's see, you, Paco Yunque," said the teacher, "what happens to a fish, if it's taken out of the water?"

"Fish die out of water because they have no air," whimpered Paco Yunque, repeating what the teacher had said.

"That's right!" exclaimed the teacher. "Very good," he added and continued to write on the chalkboard.

Meanwhile, since the teacher wasn't looking, Grieve went and gave Fariña a good punch in the mouth and quickly returned to his desk. Rather than crying like Yunque, Fariña decided to do something about it.

"Señor!" he yelled, "Humberto Grieve just smacked me!"

"He did! He did!" said all the children at once.

A tremendous ruckus arose in the classroom.

"Silence!" yelled the teacher, slamming his fist on his desk.

The room fell into complete silence and each student sat still and stared seriously at the teacher. Oh, the things that Humberto would do. You've already seen for yourselves what was going on there! Now, you'll have to see what the teacher is going to do, since he was seeing red! And it was all Humberto Greive's fault!

"What kind of mess is this?" the teacher asked Fariña.

"Humberto Grieve punched me in the face," Paco Fariña said, his eyes glowing in rage, "and I never did anything to him."

"Is that true, Grieve?"

"No," said Humberto, "I didn't hit him."

The teacher looked at all the students, trying to pick one out. Which of the two was telling the truth? Fariña or Grieve?

"Who saw it?" the teacher asked Fariña.

"Everyone! Paco Yunque saw it too."

"Is that true, what Paco Fariña says?" the teacher asked Yunque.

Paco Yunque looked at Humberto and didn't dare respond, because if he did, that boy would've beat him up on his way out. Yunque didn't say anything and lowered his head.

"Yunque's not saying anything," Fariña said, "because Humberto hits him, because he's Grieve's boy and lives in his house."

"Who else has seen what Fariña is talking about?" the teacher asked the other students.

"I did, señor! I did! I did!"

"So then, it's true, Grieve," the teacher said, "that you hit Fariña?"

"No, señor! I didn't hit him."

"Mind your lying, Grieve. A decent boy like you ought not to lie!"

"I didn't hit him."

"Well. I believe you. I know that you never lie, but be more careful in the future."

The teacher began to pace back and forth in thought, and all the students were circumspect, sitting up straight on their stools. Paco Fariña was groaning in a low voice as if he was about to cry.

"Humberto doesn't get punished," he said, "just 'cause his dad is rich. Well I'm gonna' tell my mom on him."

"What are you saying?" asked the teacher, angrily stomping his foot in front of Fariña. "Humberto is a good student. He never lies. He doesn't bother anyone. That's why I don't punish him. Here, all children are equal, whether their families are rich or poor. Even rich kids get punished. Given what you're saying about Grieve's father, I'll have to put you in time-out for two hours. You hear me?"

Paco Fariña put his head down. Paco Yunque did too. Both knew that Humberto was going to beat them up and that he was a liar. The teacher walked up to the chalkboard and started to write again.

"Why didn't you tell the teacher that Humberto hit me?"

"Because he'll beat me up."

"So why don't you tell your mom?"

"Because if I tell her, she'll hit me too, and the master's lady will get mad."

While the teacher was at the chalkboard, Humberto started doodling in his notebook. Paco Yunque was thinking about his mom. Then he remembered the master's lady and her boy Humberto. Would they beat him up when he got home? He was looking at the other children, and they weren't hitting him or Fariña or anyone else. No one else wanted to drag him to any other desk, like that boy Humberto did. Why did Humberto treat him like this? Yunque would tell his mom right away, and if that boy hit him, he'd tell the teacher. But the teacher wouldn't do anything to Humberto. So he decided to speak with Fariña.

"Does Humberto hit you too?" he asked.

"Hit me? How's he going to hit me? I'll smack him silly and make him bleed. You'll see! Just wait and see! And I'll tell my mom! And my dad will come and smack Grieve and his dad too, and everyone else as well!"

Paco Yunque was frightened to hear what Paco Fariña was saying. Was he really going to hit Humberto? And was his dad going to come and hit Grieve's dad? Paco Yunque didn't want to believe it, because no one would hit Humberto. If Fariña hits him, the *patrón* would come and hit Fariña and Fariña's father too. The *patrón* would hit everyone, because everyone is afraid of him. Because Mr. Grieve would speak very seriously and give everyone orders. And men and women would come to his house who were very afraid and always obey the master and his lady. For all intents and purposes, Mr. Grieve could do more than the teacher and everyone else.

Paco Yunque looked at the teacher writing on the board. Who was this teacher? Why was he so serious and scary? He continued to look at him. The teacher was the same as his dad or Grieve's dad; that is, he looked like other men who'd come to the house and speak with the master. His neck was red and his nose seemed to drip like a turkey's wattle.[50] His shoes would squeaky-squeak when he walked too much.

Yunque started to grow irritated. What time would he get to go home? But Humberto was going to smack him on his way out of school, and Yunque's mom would say to Humberto, "No, child. Don't hit my Paquito. Don't act up." But that's all she'd say, and Paco's leg would be red from Humberto's kick, and he'd start to cry, because no one ever did anything to Humberto, and because the master and his lady loved their son Humberto very much. Paco Yunque felt bad because Humberto always beat him up. Everyone, everyone, everyone was afraid of Humberto and his parents: Venancio with her apron and María who washes the chamber pots. Yesterday a chamber pot broke into three pieces. Would the master also hit Yunque's dad? All this stuff with the master and Humberto was just terrible. Paco wanted to cry. When would the teacher stop writing on the board?

"Well," said the teacher, when he finally stopped, "there's the assignment, all written out. Now, take out your notebooks and copy what's on the board. Copy it exactly as it appears."

"In our notebooks?" Paco Yunque asked timidly.

"Yes, in your notebooks," replied the teacher. "Do you know how to write?"

"Yes. My dad showed me in the country."

"Good. So then, everyone, start copying."

The children took out their notebooks and started copying the assignment their teacher had written on the board.

"There's no rush," he said. "Write slowly, so that you don't make a mistake."

"Is the writing assignment about fish?" Grieve asked.

"Yes. Now, get copying everyone."

The room fell into silence. Only the sound of pencils could be heard.

The teacher sat at his desk and started to write in his notebook too. Rather than doing his assignment, Humberto went back to doodling and filled his notebook with drawings of fish, dolls, and squares.

"Have you finished yet?" the teacher stood up and asked, after a while had passed. "Good. Be sure to write your names clearly."

Then the recess bell rang, and again the children cheered and ran into the schoolyard. Paco Yunque had done a good job on his assignment, and he went outside with his book, notebook, and pencil. As soon as he got to the yard, Humberto came and grabbed him.

"Come over here for a chicken fight."[51]

He pushed him aside and made him drop his book, notebook, and pencil. Yunque did as Grieve ordered, but he was blushing and embarrassed that the other kids could see how that boy was shaking him down. Yunque wanted to cry.

Paco Fariña, the Zumigas, and other children surrounded Humberto Grieve and Paco Yunque. The wiry, pale-faced boy picked up Yunque's book, notebook, and pencil, but Humberto knocked them out of his hands.

"Leave them alone!" he said. "Stay out of this! Yunque's my boy."

Humberto Grieve took Paco Yunque's things into the classroom and placed them in his own desk. Then, he returned to the yard to play with him. He grabbed him by the scruff of his neck, made him bend at the waist and walk on all fours.

"Stay still," Grieve ordered. "Don't move until I say so."

Humberto stepped back a ways, then came running, and leapt over Yunque, pressing on his back and giving him a sharp kick in the butt. He stepped back again, then jumped on Yunque a second time and gave him another kick. For a long while Humberto kept playing this game with Paco Yunque. Twenty times he jumped; twenty times he kicked.

Suddenly weeping could be heard. It was Yunque, crying from the clouts of that boy Humberto. Then Paco Fariña left the circle formed by the other children, and he stepped in front of Grieve.

"No! I'm not going to let you jump on Paco Yunque!" he shouted.

"Would you look who it is!" Grieve replied. "Paco Fariña! Come here so I can give you a smack!"

But Fariña did not move; he stayed firm in front of Grieve.

"Just because he's your boy you hit him and jump on him and make him cry!" Fariña said. "Do it again and see what happens!"

The Zumiga brothers put their arms around Paco Yunque, told him not to cry, and consoled him.

"Why do you let him jump on you and kick you like that?" they said. "Hit him! Fight back! Why do you give in? Don't be a dummy! Shut up! Quit crying! We're going home now!"

Paco Yunque was still crying and now choking on his tears. A crowd of kids formed around him, and another crowd around Grieve and Fariña.

Grieve gave Fariña one heck of a shove and knocked him to the ground. Then came a bigger student from the second grade to defend Fariña by giving Grieve a kick to the shin. And another student, from the third grade, bigger than everyone else, defended Grieve by socking the second-grader good. A storm of right hooks and dropkicks rained down on countless boys. It was a mess.

The bell rang, and the children returned to the classroom. The Zumiga brothers carried Paco Yunque on their shoulders. There was a ruckus in the first-grade classroom when the teacher walked in. Everyone quieted down. The teacher stared at them seriously.

"Be seated!" he said with the serious voice of a soldier.

A clatter of desks, and all the students were seated.

Then the teacher sat down at his desk to call roll and have each student hand in the writing assignment on the topic of fish. While receiving the assignments, he started to read them, and write their grades in one of his books.

Humberto went to Yunque's desk and gave him his book, notebook, and pencil, but he had already snatched the notebook page where Yunque had done his work and signed his name. When the teacher called Humberto, he went and handed in Paco Yunque's assignment as if it was his own. And when the teacher called Paco Yunque, he started looking through his notebook for the page where he'd done the assignment, but he couldn't find it.

"Did you lose it?" asked the teacher, "or didn't you do it in the first place?"

Paco Yunque didn't know what had happened to that notebook page, and since he was so embarrassed, he stayed quiet and lowered his head.

"Very well," the teacher said, and he gave Paco Yunque an F.

Then the rest of the students handed in their assignments. When the teacher had finished looking at them, the school principal entered the room. The teacher and the students respectfully stood up. The principal glared at the students.

"Be seated!" he said to them, and then asked the teacher, "Do you know who the best student of your class is? Are your weekly assignments ready to be graded?"

"Yes, Principal," said the teacher. "They've just finished. The highest grade was achieved by Humberto Grieve."

"Where is his assignment?"

"It's right here."

The teacher flipped through all the students' papers and found the assignment signed by Humberto Grieve. He gave it to the principal, who stood there staring at it for quite a while.

"Very nice," the principal said with satisfaction.

He went to the teacher's desk and scrutinized the students. Then he spoke with his slightly hoarse but still animated voice.

"Out of all the assignments you've done so far," he said, "the best yet is Humberto Grieve's. So this boy is going to be inducted into the Honor Society this week, as the top student of the first grade. Grieve, step up here."

The children anxiously watched Humberto, who rose to his feet, and strutted to the teacher's desk with perfect posture, proud as could be.

"Well done, Humberto Grieve," said the principal, shaking his hand. "Congratulations. You're a model student. Very well done." The principal then turned to the other students and said, "You all follow Humberto's example. You should be good students like him. Study and apply yourselves like him. Be serious, formal, and good students like him. And if you do, you'll all receive a reward at the end of the year, and you too will make honor roll. Let's see if by next week there's another student who has does an assignment as well as Humberto has today. I hope there is."

The principal stood there quietly for a moment. The students were thinking and staring at Humberto Grieve with admiration. Grieve is great! What an assignment he did! That thing was excellent! His was the best! And showing up for class late and all! Kicking everyone's butt! And look at him now! Shaking hands with the principal! Humberto Grieve, the best in the first grade!

The principal said good-bye to the teacher, waved to the students, who said good-bye to him, and he left.

"Be seated!" the teacher said.

A clatter of desks, and all the students were seated.

"Go to your seat," the teacher ordered Grieve.

Humberto Grieve happily returned to his desk, and as he walked by Paco Fariña, he stuck his tongue. The teacher sat down at his desk and started to write in one of his books.

"Look at the teacher," Fariña whispered Yunque. "He's putting your name in his book, 'cause you didn't hand in your assignment. Look at him!

He's going to give you detention, and you won't be able to go home! Why did you tear up your notebook? Where did you put your assignment?"

Paco Yunque didn't respond and remained there with his head hanging low.

"Come on!" Fariña continued to say. "Answer me! Why don't you answer? What did you do with your assignment?"

Paco Fariña bent down to look at Paco Yunque's face, and he saw that he was crying. "Let it go," he consoled him. "Don't cry. Let it go. Don't feel bad. Let's play with my chessboard. Yours are the black pieces. Let it go. You can have my chessboard. Don't be a dummy. Quit crying!"

But Paco Yunque remained doubled over in tears.

[*Apuntes del Hombre* (Lima), vol. 1, July 1951]   [JM]

From *Brothers Colacho*

ACT 1
Scene 1

> *Radiant afternoon in the Andean village of Taque. Inside the general
> store of brothers* ACIDAL *and* MORDEL COLACHO. *Upstage, a door
> opens to an alley, where straw and clay houses appear between the
> bushes. Upstage left, a small door on the side leads to the kitchen.
> Downstage right, thrown on the floor, sheep skins and an afghan: the two
> homeowners' sole bed. Center stage, parallel to the road and audience,
> a short dilapidated counter. On the walls, shelves with items of basic
> necessity and bottles. The sum of the collection is miserable, rampant.*
>
> *It's Sunday. Countless peasants shuffle through the alley—men,
> women, drunks, rabble-rousers; other people sing and play the
> squeezebox.* ACIDAL *is busy arranging merchandise on the shelves to
> attract his clientele. He's a fat, dumpy, sweaty, rosy-cheeked man. His
> black bristly hair seems untouched by a comb. His clothes are poor
> and tattered, his shirt, dirty, without a collar or visible cuffs. He wears
> sandals.*
>
> ACIDAL *and* MORDEL, *mestizos of indigenous and Spanish blood,
> originally serfs, currently work in stonemasonry and ambitiously desire
> to become merchants, investing the few pesos they saved from their day's
> wages.* ACIDAL *is nearly forty years old.*

First Movement

ACIDAL (*still working, he hawks his goods to passersby*): Fine, nice, and
cheap! Cigarettes with yellow-tipped filters! Salt and dried peppers!
Kerchiefs of silk! Two-headed sardines! Golden lumps of sugar!

GIRL (*at the door to the store*): Do ya' have any black thread, patrón?

ACIDAL: Come right in, come right in! How much do ya' want?

GIRL: A forty-weight spool. What's it go for? (*enters*).

ACIDAL: Is that all you're looking for? Can't I offer ya' somethin' else?
Aniline? Matches? Soap?

GIRL: What I'm lookin' for, patrón, is some black thread . . .

ACIDAL: But, child, soap or black thread, it's all the same. When clothes
are tattered, instead of mending 'em you've got to give 'em a good

439

wash, scrubbing 'em with lots of soap, and then they come out shinin' like new. I'll sell ya' a bar of soap that'll make you scream! (*shows her the soap*).

GIRL: I'm in a rush. Since ya' don't have black thread . . . (*leaves*).

ACIDAL: Don't leave. I've also got green gumdrops, shortening, pills for toothaches, pains, hemorrhoids, and bad dreams . . . (*from the front door, to the passersby*) Kids! Lovers! Accordion players! Singers! . . . We've got rum, tobacco, coca leaves from Huayambo, limestone in powder! . . . (*Two* BOYS *stop in front of* ACIDAL; *one plays his accordion, and the other dances an indigenous jig while clapping.*) What a bash they're sure to bring! Come right in! What're ya' drinkin'?

Second Movement

ACIDAL, *the two* BOYS.

FIRST BOY: Lord be with ya', patrón. How 'bout a drink? (*counting his coins*).

ACIDAL: But, of course, man! How much ya' lookin' for?

SECOND BOY: Let's see, patrón, how 'bout a discount for your poor boys!

ACIDAL (*bottle in hand*): Fifty cents for the bottle, with stopper and all. And what rum it is! With just one shot, you'll be dreamin' of hogs in hats!

FIRST BOY: Pricey, patrón.

SECOND BOY: What do ya' say, patrón?

ACIDAL: Fifty cents for the bottle. But so that you always come back and shop here, as a special gift from me to you, I'm gonna stick on it a piece of colored paper with my name. (*On a scrap of colored paper, he writes something with a pencil and sticks it on the bottle.*) There ya' go! Take it with you! . . . Even though my business is going under! . . . (*The* BOYS, *disconcerted by* ACIDAL's *cynicism, remain pensive, while* ACIDAL *interprets their stupor as stupidity.*) You still don't get it? The bottle, for all my clients, costs fifty cents . . .

BOTH BOYS: Fifty cents.

ACIDAL: Right, so that you always come and shop here, I'm giving you, along with the bottle, a special gift: a piece of colored paper with my name. You understand? (*turns his back to them, to organize other shelves*) You see, it's all very simple.

FIRST BOY (*taking advantage of the fact that* ACIDAL *isn't looking, grabs*

another bottle from the counter and hands it to his friend): Simple as
can be, patrón. May God reward you. (SECOND BOY *struggles to hide
the palmed bottle.*)

ACIDAL (*still with his back to them*): Here, no one robs or gets robbed, my
friends. We Colachos are poor, but we're honorable.

FIRST BOY (*helping the other* BOY *get the bottle into his pocket*): That's
what I say: honesty's the best policy!

SECOND BOY: And God is watchin' us all!

ACIDAL: And then, there's that adage that goes, "Nobody dies without
paying his dues." (*Right then, a bottle slips out of his hands and he
catches it midflight.*) Whoops! (*The* SECOND BOY *pockets the other
bottle.*) It got away from me! Damn bottle! Slipped right through my
fingers!

SECOND BOY: Would you look at that! Sassy little thing!

FIRST BOY (*paying*): Thank God patrón was sharp! 'Cause if he
wasn't! . . .

ACIDAL: So what's the deal! Are ya' finally happy? A bottle of 399,934
proof rum! Especially for . . . What line of work you in? (*receives the
payment, and the* FIRST BOY *takes the bottle with the colored piece of
paper*).

FIRST BOY: We're shepherds, patrón.

ACIDAL (*wiping down the countertop*): Exactly, my rum is specially
for shepherds. In the inventories of Saint Peter and Saint Paul, the
animals, in particular the oxen, are drawn back by the smell of my
rum. With this rum, there won't be a sheep that wanders off or a wolf
that snatches him . . .

MORDEL COLACHO *hurries into the store, upset;* MORDEL *is* ACIDAL's
*twin brother, with whom he shares an astonishing resemblance,
physically and morally; his clothes are as poor as* ACIDAL's.

Third Movement

ACIDAL, MORDEL, *minus the two* BOYS.

MORDEL (*taking off his hat, wiping the sweat from his forehead*): Ugh! I'm
sweatin' like a pig! How are sales?

ACIDAL: Couldn't be worse.

MORDEL (*opens the drawer under the counter and counts the money*): How much have ya' made since I left this morning? (*The two* BOYS *go off dancing.*)

ACIDAL: 3.95. The whole morning!

MORDEL: Only 3.95, all morning?

ACIDAL: People aren't even stoppin' at the door. I don't know how we're gonna pay Tuco!

MORDEL: To hell with Tuco![52] We'll pay him when we can.

ACIDAL: The old man is furious about his rooms. Chepa was just here, says her sister Tomasa heard Tuco yesterday sayin' he's gonna evict us . . .

MORDEL (*devouring some crackers*): I could eat a horse.

ACIDAL: You're gonna finish the box of crackers like that! You see how broke we are and you start devouring what little there is in the store . . .

MORDEL: And who ate the three potatoes I left in the big pan last night? (*throwing the crackers in his brother's face*) Here! Eat 'em yourself! Enjoy . . .

Pause. MORDEL *angrily paces back and forth in the store.* ACIDAL *continues to organize the shelves. Shortly,* MORDEL *grabs a glass and drinks water from a large pitcher on the end of the counter.*

ACIDAL: And now you're drinking the holy water! You've got some nerve!

MORDEL (*surprised*): What! . . . What day is today?

ACIDAL: Wednesday plus Thursday. Didn't you realize it's Sunday?

MORDEL: Sunday . . . Sunday! And at noon the pitcher is still brimming with holy water! . . .

ACIDAL: Now you see! And who's traveled miles to Cleta's well, fetchin' that holy water this morning? Did you go?

MORDEL: You really haven't sold even one cup all morning? (ACIDAL *doesn't reply.*) The priest probably already knows and has prohibited them from buying it from us! . . .

ACIDAL: What's more, Old Lady Romasinda denied me the breadcrumbs again.

MORDEL: No doubt 'cause you didn't know how to ask for them.

ACIDAL: Sure! You can ask your neighbor for a piece of bread, once, twice, three times, under any pretext at all, but not every day and for months on end.

MORDEL: Why not?

ACIDAL: 'Cause they're sure to realize the bread's for eating.

MORDEL: Didn't you tell her again that you need the crumbs to mix with spit and cover a boil?

ACIDAL: Yeah, but she said that boil's a real pain in the butt, and she left me empty-handed.

VOICES (*on alert in the street*): Peira! Peira! . . . Here comes Peira! . . .

(*Some pedestrians flee; the* COLACHOS *turn white.*)

ACIDAL: We've got to close the door! . . .

But it's too late. At the door to the store appears PEIRA, *a terrible rebel and the best tailor in town. He's drunk, wearing a top hat and frock coat, but with a T-shirt under it. Around his waist a red rope is tied, and one of its ends drags on the ground and disappears down the street. When they see him, the* COLACHOS *are scared stiff.*

Fourth Movement

ACIDAL, MORDEL, PEIRA, *and, shortly thereafter, a* WOMAN *and two* CHILDREN.

PEIRA (*at the door, with his forefinger militarily tracing a curve around the store*): Everywhere! Set fire everywhere! (*addressing an invisible crowd of followers*) You can begin underneath the counter! It'd be more strategic! Got the matches? Hurry up! What're ya' waitin' for? . . . (*advances to the center of the store, as if he were the ultimate owner of the situation*) Fed by the oil and alcohol in the store, flames just might explode right off the bat and rise over the hats of the passersby, toward the houses across the way, and then they might light up the bell tower, the balcony of the parish, the church, the house of the priest's girlfriend, the counsel, and they might finally go out, with mild, nearly rustic radiance all along the joists of the shacks on the outskirts. What's more important than anything is . . . One moment! . . . Let's see here . . . Let's see . . . Hmm! . . . Yes! We'd manage to achieve our objective in a less onerous way for the revolution, if the fire begins in the kitchen of the store . . . (*with resolve he heads toward the kitchen*) Come on now! Follow me! . . .

His wife appears in the store, holding the end of the rope tied to his waist. The WOMAN *is followed by* CHILDREN *from the town, who are laughing hysterically.*

WOMAN: Jughead! The judge recognized his frock coat and he's comin' for you, says he didn't give ya' his coat so you'd wear it, but so you'd clean it. (*laughter of the* CHILDREN).

PEIRA (*continuing his bellicose reflections*): Beware of us! The merciless! The hour is grave! I am no doubt a man, and as such, I have, underneath this frock that the judge gave me to mend, a human heart sensitive to the disasters of others; but, beware of us, the revolution has nothing to do with hearts or frocks. (*addressing the crowd*) What? What is it you're after? . . . Oh, how I know, señores! I comprehend your holy civil outrage! Break your own trail! Fire it up! Sack it! Murder! Rape! . . . (*He interrupts himself with a burp, but immediately, in a gesture of resolve, leans on the counter.*)

WOMAN (*pulling the end of the rope with all her might*): Jughead! Be careful! You're going to throw up on the judge's suit! (*laughter of the* CHILDREN).

PEIRA (*who has stumbled back and leans on his wife*): This poor wife of mine! Uncivilized creature! A waist without a womb! An empty head! . . .

WOMAN (*cries*): I'm ashamed of you, Jughead! . . .

PEIRA: What do you want from me, woman?

WOMAN: We're going home. You're the joke of this town, a mean drunk[53] (*weeps twice as hard, and the* CHILDREN *burst into laughter*).

PEIRA: You wretch, listen to me: in my capacity as supreme chief, statesman, and soldier, of the northern, central, and northeastern provinces, I simply can't entrust you with my plans . . .

ACIDAL: Give 'em a chair. He's gonna fall! (MORDEL *moves, but doesn't get one.*)

PEIRA (*to his wife*): I have my secrets. What's more, you'd be incapable of comprehending even an iota of my elevated mission. You'd just keep censuring me, instead of applauding and encouraging me. (ACIDAL *signals mysteriously to* MORDEL.)

WOMAN: Why did I ever let you put on clients' clothes? Last week it was the captain's pants.

PEIRA: Well, Senda my dear, tell me, to lay this to rest: how much is nine times nine? Answer me! Or, even more simply: how much is nine times seven? Come on!

WOMAN: Always with your questions. You're well aware I don't even know the letters of my name.

PEIRA (*to the* COLACHOS): You see? You see?

WOMAN: What do numbers have to do with the bender you're on!

PEIRA: Have you no shame, Senda? If you're so ignorant and obtuse that you don't even know how much nine times seven is—which is common knowledge even to a schoolboy—then what gives you the right to stand up and pass judgment on me? A woman who doesn't know anything about anything and that, nonetheless, decides to give me lessons about what I should or shouldn't do! . . . This much is evident! . . . All joking aside! . . . Let's move on to something else! . . . (*the* WOMAN *is completely ashamed and lowers her head, while the tailor says in an apocalyptic tone to the* COLACHOS) Here we are, finally, at the day of days! The city will be completely devastated. Psh! . . . That's nothing! . . . It's all in vain! . . . All pleas are useless! . You shall succumb! I regret it, but it's unavoidable. (*the* WOMAN *drops the rope and walks into the street, humiliated and defeated, and* PEIRA *says to her*) Get out of here, woman! Only when you've learned what seven times nine is, will you know whether I'm right or wrong to put on clients' cloths. Off with you!

The WOMAN *leaves, amid the silence of the* CHILDREN, *who look at her surprised.*

ACIDAL (*pleading*): Peira, please! . . .
PEIRA (*inexorable*): Useless, I said! Consideration for no one!
ACIDAL: Señor Peira, at least let us keep the money from the sales!
PEIRA (*vengeful*): Ah-hah! . . . That you use to strip the people of their last grains and animals! Scoundrels! The punishment will be terrible! A tooth for a tooth, an eye for an eye!
ACIDAL (*hands together*): The fabric, Peira! Compassion!
PEIRA (*suddenly starts staggering with barbarous steps toward the door to the store, shouting*): Beware of us! The matches! Without delay! The matches! What're ya' waiting for? . . . (*He exits; the* CHILDREN *follow him, forming a circle around him and making an awful ruckus.*)

Fifth Movement

ACIDAL, MORDEL.

ACIDAL (*exhausted*): We're in the clear!
MORDEL: And now? What do we do now?
ACIDAL (*going to the door to look out on the street*): Wait! It looks like he's comin' back! . . . No . . . He's turned the corner . . . The cops are on his

tail . . . (MORDEL *also goes to look.*) They caught him! Now they got him! (*voices and racing in the street*).

MORDEL: Yes, yes! They're haulin' him away, over there, takin' him in!

ACIDAL: Whoa, man! What a scare! (*Both continue for an instant with their eyes on the street scene.*) They should've stuck him behind bars long ago! Thief! Killer!

MORDEL: You get scared and start shakin' in the face of that scarecrow.[54]

ACIDAL: Me? Shakin'?

MORDEL: It's a wonder you didn't piss your pants.

ACIDAL: Mordel, would you please! Anyway, I'm the only one around here who looks after the few knickknacks we have. You wouldn't have given a crap if they'd lit the store on fire.

MORDEL: Who? Who was going to light the store on fire?

ACIDAL: What do you mean, who? Peira!

MORDEL: Peira! Are you that? . . .

ACIDAL: Shakin', shakin'! You're the coward, since you were too scared to protest.

MORDEL: But were you gonna believe the words of a drunk?

ACIDAL: You didn't even offer him a chair. If you want to know everything, I'll tell you. In the back of his pants, Peira was carrying a gun this big! I saw it.

MORDEL: It must be the judge's.

ACIDAL: The judge's gun! Why must it be the judge's gun?

MORDEL: Come on! Whose frock coat was he wearing?

ACIDAL: The frock was the judge's, but the pants were not. Peira's pants were Peira's. And to be specific, the gun that was hanging from his pants . . . (*A* YOUNGSTER *comes running into the store, with several envelopes in hand.*)

YOUNGSTER: Acidal and Mordel Colacho? A letter from the president of the Regional Counsel.

He delivers an envelope to MORDEL *and leaves.* MORDEL *anxiously opens the envelope and* ACIDAL *approaches to look on. Both men avidly read the card.* MORDEL *turns to* ACIDAL *with his eyes popping out, and they look at each other, silent, stupefied.*

MORDEL (*rereading portions of the card*): ". . . to Señores Acidal and Mordel Colacho . . . to dine . . . Silverio Frutos . . . President of the Regional Counsel . . ." (*again turning to* ACIDAL, *in a shout*) Brother! . . .

ACIDAL (*rereads the card in his mind, and then*): But . . . this can't . . . this can't be! It must . . . must have been an error . . .

MORDEL (*pacing triumphantly, beside himself*): Finally! After so much hard work and suffering! An invitation from the president of the Regional Counsel! Our ticket in! Our ticket in to the salons! High society! Finally! A couple of peasants, mingling with celebrities!

ACIDAL (*keeping his eyes on the card, as if dumbfounded*): ". . . has the honor . . ." (*turning to* MORDEL) He says that he has the honor . . .

MORDEL: But obviously! He has the honor! What do you think?

ACIDAL (*suddenly*): What time is it?

MORDEL (*in a state of uncontainable nervousness*): What time is it? I don't even know! (*lets out a convulsive cackle*) Let us dine! Señores Acidal and Mordel Colacho! (*another cackle*) Amazing! Truly amazing!

ACIDAL (*consulting an enormous pocket watch*): Twelve twenty. The invitation is for one in the afternoon. There's no time left!

MORDEL: For what? There's no time left for what?

ACIDAL: Wouldn't we need to respond before going? How do these things work?

MORDEL: You'll have to go alone. I'll stay here to watch the store. Go ahead and start getting dressed. Where's the pink shirt with green polka dots? Is it clean? (*starts looking for it*)

ACIDAL: Mordo, you go! You can stand a hard collar better than me! It chokes me like a noose.

MORDEL (*furious*): Fine! You don't want to go?

ACIDAL (*pleading*): Mordito, for God's sake, you go!

MORDEL (*tosses clothes in the trunk*): This one won't let you move an inch. We're gonna miss this godsend, this opportunity to enter high society, and it'll be all your fault!

ACIDAL: But I don't know how to sit among the elite. It's embarrassing. They give you a fork and a whole slew of knives . . .

MORDEL: Where's some nice paper, so we can send a response before the meal starts?

ACIDAL: Is this how you're supposed reply to invitations? (*Both look for paper.*) I thought that after the meal you send a thank you note.

MORDEL: Before! In high society, thank 'em before the meal. Here, write. I once saw Pilar do it, that one-eyed woman. (ACIDAL *gets ready to write.*) Use your best cursive. Clear. Nice and neat. Close those Os all the way! Cross your Ts! And in black ink! . . . (*takes more clothes out of the trunk*).

ACIDAL (*suddenly remembering something*): Oh, man! . . . There's a template for cards over there in the first-grade schoolbook . . . (*Among the packages, he pulls out and blows the dust off a little book, unbound, and looks for a page.*) Impressive! Like a bull in a china shop!

MORDEL (*brushing off his clothes*): Template my ass! It's already twelve thirty! What time are you gonna get dressed! . . .

ACIDAL (*who has found the page with the template*): Here it is. The example is exactly the same . . . (*suddenly annoyed, his eyes fixed on the page of the book*) Come have a look at this! . . . When the devil lurks in the orchard! . . .

MORDEL: Hurry up! What's wrong?

ACIDAL: Here, a word's been smudged, and ya' can't tell what it says.

MORDEL: Where? Must be the sleep in your eyes.

ACIDAL (*reads and shows his brother the page*): "We have the . . ." Look at that. It's smudged. (*scratches the page with his fingernail*) It's a . . . Seems like they might have pissed on it . . . Can't see . . .

MORDEL (*taking his turn at scratching the page*): Hold on . . . Hold on . . .

ACIDAL: I think the rats have gotten to it . . .

MORDEL: The paper is gonna tear. Fix it however you can.

ACIDAL: What it should say there is: honor . . ."We have the honor of thanking you . . ." Doesn't it seem to you that the word the rats pissed on is "honor"? Look.

MORDEL: "Honor," without a doubt.

ACIDAL: For sure. It's "honor" all right (*begins to copy the template*).

MORDEL: Have you shaved? (*looks closely at his face*) Well, you've got to comb your hair . . . (*goes and brings the comb and combs his brother's hair, while the latter writes the card with the utmost care*). Time is flying, don't move your head.

ACIDAL (*leaning over*): How do ya' spell "honor"?

MORDEL: "Honor," without an H.

ACIDAL: I know that, but with one or two Ns? (*breaks it into syllables, accenting the "-nor" of "honor"*) Hon-nnnor! After the first O, only one N, I think. Ooon-nnnor . . . Yeah, that's it.

MORDEL: "Honor" is spelled with just one N, of course! But add two or three so that they don't go thinkin' we're stingy. I told you to quit movin' your head.

ACIDAL (*writing*): With three . . . Ns. There it is . . .

MORDEL (*combing his brother's hair jubilantly*): The Flores are going to burst with envy! Acidal and Mordel Colacho! Acidal Colacho, a guest of the president of the Regional Counsel! At your service! (*He's finished combing his brother's hair and now paces, giving him advice.*)

Don't speak too much at the table. Be very serious and respectful to everyone. Remember, you're going to have the honor of eating with the family of the president of the Regional Counsel, with the governor, the professors—the upper crust of Taque. Our entire fate rests on this meal! The key is to enter high society, and the rest will come on its own: fortune, honors . . . (*delirious*) Good-bye, workingman's life! That's all she wrote! Ole Tuco, paid at last! Doña Ubalda, paid as well! The doors of commerce are opening for us, and this time they're opening all the way!

ACIDAL (*closing the letter of response*): All set. How are we going to send it? Who'll take it?

MORDEL: I'm going to see Fidel. (*Takes the envelope and walks through the room.*) In the meantime, you get dressed.

ACIDAL: Hey! I'm not going to the lunch! You are! (*By himself,* ACIDAL *leaves the door to the street ajar, examines the clothes he's supposed to wear and, in a corner of the store, unbuttons the three-quarter length coat, but then refuses.*) No! Now's the time to put my foot down! Let him go! Let him get dressed! . . . (*sits down on a stool, resting his head in his hands, then raises his eyes and considers the stiff collar; walks up to it and tries it on, groaning*). Figures! A collar purchased for both of us that doesn't fit either! . . . (*Pauses, suddenly,* ACIDAL *turns serious and looks himself over, from head to toe, meditates. Then he takes a few stately steps, solemnly turns on his heels, moves his head with arrogance, looks straight ahead with dignity, blinks as if in a dream, puts his hands in his coat pockets, sucking in his gut, mumbles a few pleasantries, and polishes himself.*) Yes . . . Now I believe it . . . I understand perfectly. (*turning his face to one side, fine and elegant*) You were saying, señora? Perhaps . . . It's very likely . . . In the afternoons . . . Do you think so? (*stands there thinking, with force*) No! I'm not going! I'm not and I won't!

MORDEL (*comes back running*): Okay! Okay! What's going on? You're still not dressed? (ACIDAL *sits down and hides his face between his hands.*) Man, don't be such a lout! Just think, you're gonna shake hands with celebrities! Tomorrow, if we need a recommendation, a guarantee, a bond, any kind of credit for that matter, they'll give it to us right away. The governor is surely going to be at the lunch. If Tuco wants to press charges against us, the governor won't be able to stick us in the slammer, once he's seen that you were the guest of the president of the Regional Counsel. (ACIDAL *uncovers his face and stares straight at* MORDEL.) He'll play dumb, because he'll be afraid to rock the boat, to wrong a friend of the president of the Regional Counsel. That's how good luck comes: from wealthy friends. (*Without saying anything,* ACIDAL *again starts unbuttoning his coat and changing his clothes.*) Tuco himself will be there, and once he realizes you're among the guests, he won't do anything to us. You'll see! Don't you think so too?

ACIDAL (*dressing, gritting his teeth*): Look at the clock! What time is it? And give me the tie.

MORDEL: You've got enough time I think. It's . . . twenty to one! Just as long as you arrive at one on the dot! (*giving more advice*) Don't be afraid. Don't sell yourself short. If they ask about me, tell 'em that I'm . . . Tell 'em, in this tone, (*acting refined*) "that I'm a tad congested, but it's nothing too serious." (*combs him*) Be sure to speak of important things. Smile only from time to time, without opening your mouth too wide, like the sacristan.

ACIDAL (*putting on the stiff collar*): If this thing is too tight, I'm not going to respond. They'll surely see me suffocating and everything will go down the drain.

MORDEL: Try to get as close as you can to the governor. Remember what Chepa told you about Tuco. Otherwise, either we're off to prison or we'll be shinin' his kitchen floor.

ACIDAL (*exploding with rage*): Where have you put my hat?

MORDEL (*bringing the hat*): Here it is. (ACIDAL, *with hat in hand, crosses himself;* MORDEL *does the same and the two of them, excited, whisper a short prayer.*) Before you leave, pray to Our Mother of Perpetual Help. Pray! Pray to her with all your heart! (*Imprisoned by a combination of distressing anxiety and resentment for his brother,* ACIDAL *prays to the image.*) Confide in her and you shall see!

ACIDAL (*stuffed up, sweating more than ever*): Well . . . I should get goin' now . . . (*takes a few indecisive steps*).

MORDEL: Where do you put the napkin when you eat? Remember where it's supposed to go?

ACIDAL (*mechanically*): The napkin? Keep it in your left hand. No, in your right.

MORDEL: No, man! You put in on your chest, like a bib—and don't forget it.

ACIDAL (*without daring to move his head*): All right, on my chest, I'm out of here (*two more indecisive steps*).

MORDEL: Walk a bit here first, so I can see you. Move your head around.

ACIDAL (*taking another step and sweating buckets*): I don't know if

I'm gonna be able to handle this. My Adam's apple is completely squashed!

MORDEL: Do your best, brother.

ACIDAL (*decided*): See you soon (*leaving*).

MORDEL (*suddenly*): Hey! Hey! Dry off the sweat!

ACIDAL (*stopping at the door to the store, swallowing his pain*): Be quiet! Quit riding me!

MORDEL: Your nose is dripping. Wipe it with a handkerchief.

ACIDAL: Leave me alone, Mordel! Please!

MORDEL (*sticking a pocket mirror in front of his eyes*): Look! Look! You knucklehead!

ACIDAL: I couldn't care less. Leave me alone!

MORDEL: Excellent! By God! Here we go! Don't start crying! (*a momentary embrace*).

ACIDAL (*almost groaning*): I'd give anything to get out of this lunch!

MORDEL: I know, little brother. But it's necessary! (ACIDAL *turns his face and pats the sweat.*) No pain, no gain!

ACIDAL (*resigned*): Well then, I'm off. It's getting late (*about to leave*).

MORDEL: Wait! Wait! It would be good for you to rehearse a bit, so you really know what you're gonna do. Let's see! Walk. Step forward. With dignity! Stand up straight! (ACIDAL *painstakingly performs the movement.*) That's it! That's it! You can stick one hand in your pants pocket, the left one, there ya' go. Don't stick it in too deep, they say that's antihygienic. Very good, very good. Now say "Good afternoon, señora." Come on! A greeting . . . Suppose you find yourself in the courtyard with a servant of the president of the Regional Counsel. I'm the servant and I greet you. (MORDEL *greets* ACIDAL, *with infinite humility.*) Good afta'noon, señor." So, how are you gonna reply? Come on! Reply!

ACIDAL (*showing off, dryly, disparagingly, without looking at the servant*): Good-day.

MORDEL: Magnificent! And if you find yourself with a professor? I'm Professor Talón and I walk within a certain distance of you. What would you do? How would you say good-bye to me? (*They play out the scenario.*)

ACIDAL (*removes his hat, bows, smiles, his voice saccharine, servile*): Farewell, Professor.

MORDEL: Tremendous! Terrific! Is the stiff collar still botherin' you?

ACIDAL (*heroically*): My neck is in a vice! But, wearin' a stiff collar is better than diggin' my own grave! Or havin' to go to the slammer! See ya' soon. (*He leaves the store.*)

MORDEL (*following a few steps behind*): Good, my little brother! Good! While you're at the lunch, may God's merciful eyes fall upon you! (*reaching the door, he opens it all the way and shouts in a triumphant expression*) Fine, nice, and cheap! Handkerchiefs nearly of silk! Two-headed sardines! We've got lard! Pills for toothaches, pain, hemorrhoids, and even for bad dreams!

CURTAIN

Scene 2

Ten years later. One afternoon, in the great general store of ACIDAL *and* MORDEL COLACHO, *at the gold mines of the Cotarca Corporation, in Cotarca, province of Taque. A long counter runs from the footlights to the end downstage. On the shelves and a portion of the counter, merchandise: provisions and textiles. Upstage, a window, through it, snow-capped mountains. Stage right, two doors open to the street; stage left, behind the counter, a door to the back room.*

MORDEL *appears in profile to the audience, downstage left, behind the counter; he's seated at a small but comfortable and elegant desk, browsing through his accounting books. His clothes and manners are those of a day laborer transformed into a merchant. Behind the counter,* NOVO, *ten years old, washes a case of bottles. Stage right, center,* OROCIO, *the shop assistant—about thirty years old—beats and folds textiles and dusts items on the shelves.* MORDEL *keeps casting gazes of severe vigilance at* OROCIO *and* NOVO. *Pause. Enter* ACIDAL. *His clothes and manners are also those of a newly moneyed laborer.*

First Movement

ACIDAL: Mordel, I'm on my way out. There's nothing else you have to tell me?

MORDEL: Not really. Have a good trip.

ACIDAL (*in* MORDEL's *ear*): So, going back to what we were talking about before, don't forget to visit the bosses and people of certain repute in Cotarca. Remember: all that we've become, we owe to the high society.

MORDEL: And you don't forget to take care of things in Taque.

ACIDAL: Of course. It's my constant concern.

MORDEL: Wear something nice, but not too expensive.

ACIDAL: Aside from this, convince yourself: politics is not a must.

MORDEL: That will require some meditation.

ACIDAL: Write to me. Keep me up-to-date, mainly regarding what Tenedy says (*hugs him*).

MORDEL: You got it. Good-bye, brother.

ACIDAL: Good-bye. Tell our friends I say good-bye.

MORDEL: Go with God. Have a good trip.

ACIDAL (*approaching* MORDEL *again*): For the last time, reflect on your candidacy. If we decide to get into politics, God only knows where we'll end up, with the help of Heaven.

MORDEL: We'll see. Everything depends on Cotarca.

ACIDAL: And I won't grow tired of urging you: in your free time, study, read, learn, in a word, cultivate yourself. See you soon! (*exits*).

MORDEL: Have a good trip. Go with God. (*returns to his books, pause, suddenly, to* NOVO) Give me one of the bottles you've washed. (*Because he's hurried*, NOVO *fumbles the bottles and breaks three of them*; MORDEL *lunges at him.*) What kind of hands do you have, you animal! (NOVO *steps back in terror.*) All you know how to do is break things! I'll grind down your ribs, boy! Pick up that broken glass, and make the floor sparkle. (NOVO *picks up the broken glass, and* MORDEL *smacks him*; NOVO *starts crying.*) Did you get it all? Keep washin' the bottles. And careful you don't break any more of 'em. (*As he walks by* NOVO, MORDEL *plunges his hands in* NOVO's *pocket.*) What do we have here? (NOVO *is paralyzed.*) Don't you move . . . (*removing a piece of candy from his pocket*). Where did you get this? (NOVO *bursts into tears.*) Thief! You know how much a piece of candy costs us? Even one? (*grabs him by the ear, yanks him to his feet, making him writhe in pain*) You punk!

OROCIO: That's enough, patrón. Give him a break, he's got no mom!

MORDEL: He's got no mom, but he's got two dads instead of one, since all he eats comes out of the pockets of my brother and me. (*to* NOVO) Wash the bottles, you slacker, if you don't want me to make you work in the mines and with a stick of dynamite send your bones to kingdom come! (NOVO *resumes his job.*)

Second Movement

> *Same characters as previous movement, plus the* WOMAN.

WOMAN (*entering the store*): Good afternoon, patrón.

MORDEL: Ah, Old Lady Rimalda! How many eggs have you brought me?

WOMAN (*putting a batch of eggs on the counter*): Two weeks' worth from the black hen and one from the two chickens. Count 'em up, patrón. (MORDEL *counts the eggs.*) And also tell me how many I brought you in all and how much I'll get for 'em, 'cause I wanna take a few things from your store.

MORDEL: Fourteen. At three for a half. (*shuffles some papers*) I'm gonna tell you . . . (*on the side, he writes some numbers on a piece of paper*). Here it is . . . On the third you brought me eight; on the twelfth, sixteen; and today, fourteen . . . Let's have a look-see . . . (*starts to add them up*). Look closely, Rimalda, so that you don't go thinkin' I'm pulling one over on you . . .

WOMAN: Hail Mary, Mother of God, patrón!

> MORDEL *has put the three amounts on the piece of paper, in a vertical column. He adds in front of the woman's eyes, reciting the operation aloud.*

MORDEL: Four and six is ten; ten and eight, eighteen. I leave the eight and carry the one . . . (*pauses in thought*) Actually . . . (*looking affectionately at the woman*) What am I doing carryin' anything of yours, ya' ole coot! I'm not gonna carry this one so that you keep bringin' me your eggs. Come on! Look at how good I am to you! I couldn't think of carryin' away anything of yours . . .

WOMAN (*confused*): May God reward you, patrón, for not carryin' anything of mine.

MORDEL: Even if he doesn't reward me, Rimalda! I simply couldn't take anything from a nice ole lady like you. (*continues the operation*) We were saying, four and six is ten; ten and eight, eighteen. I leave eight and don't carry anything. One and one is two. Twenty-eight eggs in all. I owe you for twenty-eight eggs (*disconcerted*, OROCIO *looks at his employer*).

WOMAN: So be it, patrón.

MORDEL (*taking some coins from a drawer*): Twenty-eight eggs times 4.5 cents is 35 cents. Here you go, Rimalda, your 35 cents.

WOMAN: Thanks a million, patrón. God will reward you.

MORDEL: Don't thank me. I'm just doing my job. (*shows her the paper*) Have a look. Don't you agree? There's no one cheatin' anyone here. (OROCIO *turns to his employer.*)

WOMAN: Hail Mary, Mother of God, patrón!

MORDEL (*patting her shoulder*): Good ole Rimalda! You don't know your numbers, I know. What do you want from the store? Some fabric? Salt?

WOMAN: A bundle of fabric, patrón. I don't know if you could give it to me for the eggs.

MORDEL: A bundle of fabric it is. Orocio, give Rimalda a 35-cent bundle of fabric.

OROCIO: Right away, patrón.

MORDEL: Novo, grab these eggs. (NOVO *runs to grab them.*) And don't forget to keep bringing me your eggs, Rimalda! Every week!

WOMAN: Yes, patrón. You can count on the eggs (*after it's handed to her, she puts on the counter the money that* MORDEL *gave her, as payment for the fabric, and she leaves*). Good-bye, patrón. See ya' next week.

MORDEL (*returning to his books*): Go with God, woman! (*pauses, to* OROCIO) Did ya' count how many boxes of matches came in the five packages that just arrived?

Third Movement

Same characters as previous movement, minus the WOMAN.

OROCIO (*going to consult the paper*): Not yet, patrón. Here are the counts, to add them up.

MORDEL: How many boxes have come in each package? Tell me, one by one, before adding them together.

OROCIO (*consulting his notes*): In one there were twenty-five, in another fifteen, in another seventeen, in another twenty-six, and in another twenty-four.

MORDEL (*makes sure the shop assistant is adding correctly*): Good. Now, add 'em up. Count out loud, so I can head you.

OROCIO (*adding his column of five amounts*): five and five is ten; and seven, seventeen; and six, twenty-three; and four, twenty-seven. Drop the seven and carry the two—

MORDEL (*stopping him*): Hold it right there! You're not carryin' away anything, my little friend. (*glares at* NOVO) What kind of manners are these, takin' merchandise that doesn't belong to you. Here you're nothing but my assistant, and you don't have the right to carry away anything from the store (*again glares at* NOVO).

OROCIO (*confused*): Patrón, it's just to get the sum, so I can carry the two, not for anything else.

MORDEL (*snatching the pencil to do it himself*): All right, all right! I know my people all too well.

OROCIO: I haven't taken anything from the store.

MORDEL: Silence! . . . (*again glares at* NOVO). We shall see . . . (*doing the operation aloud*) five and five is ten; and seven, seventeen; and six, twenty-three; and four, twenty-seven. I drop the seven and carry the two—

OROCIO (*interrupting*): See, patrón, to get the sum, you carry the two as well . . .

MORDEL: Yes, I know! I can't just carry the two, I can carry away as many boxes as I please, since I'm the store owner! What kind of manners are those!

Fourth Movement

> *Same characters as previous movement, plus* TENEDY, *a creolized man from the United States, manager of the Cotarca Corporation. He enters from the right, smoking a long pipe, and speaks with a dry authoritative voice.*

TENEDY: Good day, Mordel.

MORDEL (*startled*): Mr. Tenedy, a very good day to you.

> TENEDY *turns toward the street, and through a door on the right, waves to someone the audience can't see.*

TENEDY: Who's that going around singing? Hey! Hey! You!

> *A faint, sad, indigenous song is heard in the distance, sung by a man.* MORDEL *remains silent in the back, keen to the actions and words of* TENEDY, *who returns from the other side of the street, giving an order.*

TENEDY: Guard!

VOICE OF THE GUARD: Sir!

> *A* GUARD *appears on the right and gives* TENEDY *a soldier's salute.*

Same characters as previous movement, plus the GUARD.

TENEDY (*to the* GUARD): Do you hear that song lingering through the camp?

GUARD: Yes, sir, it's a worker from Taque.

TENEDY: I know that. For a long while that worker's passed his time singing the tunes of Taque—a sure sign he misses his family after so many years from his homeland. One of these days he'll escape. Keep an eye on him, soldier (*returns to the middle of the store*).

GUARD: Sir, yes, sir. Understood (*salutes and exits*).

TENEDY: Mordel, the company needs fifty more laborers, today. Damn Indians keep escaping from the mines. In the shafts there aren't but a few workers from Taque. Do me a favor and replace at least the ones who fled or died last month.

MORDEL: Mr. Tenedy, Acidal just left for Taque. If only we'd known . . . I'll send him a wire immediately. Immediately! Although, as you're aware, people don't want to come here anymore. They say it's very—

TENEDY: And the governor, what's he doing? What good are his soldiers? Don Mordel, I'm tired of these pea brains. The company needs fifty workers, and you guys are going to bring them here, come hell or high water.

MORDEL: Mr. Tenedy, we will do everything we can—

TENEDY: Don't you tell me that. Tell me categorically that those workers will come. It's urgent. By the . . . the end of the month. And no postponing!

MORDEL: Mr. Tenedy, those workers will come, no matter what, by the end of the month.

TENEDY: All fifty of them. Not one less.

MORDEL: All fifty, Mr. Tenedy. Not one less. I'll send Acidal a telegram this very minute.

TENEDY (*about to leave*): All right. Anything new around here?

MORDEL: Nothing.

TENEDY: Good.

TENEDY *exits, but suddenly stops at the door. A young, frail* WORKER, *sickly looking, bumps into* TENEDY *at the entrance.*

Sixth Movement

Same characters as previous movement, plus the WORKER.

WORKER (*falling to his knees before* TENEDY, *who is terrified*): Patrón! . . .

TENEDY: Shirker! Where are you coming from? When did you get back? Stand up and respond.

WORKER (*standing up, without raising his head, his arms, crossed, with a pleading voice, barely perceptible*): Forgive me! Sick. My back! I didn't escape! . . .

TENEDY (*in a booming shout*): Speak up! (*The* WORKER *collapses as if struck by a bolt of lightning, convulses, and lies stiff.*)

MORDEL (*approaches the* WORKER *and moves him with the tip of his shoe*): Hey there, Huato! Get up! What's the matter?

TENEDY: Inferior race, rotten! Even just a shout is enough to kill 'em.

MORDEL (*continues to kick the man's head with the tip of his shoe*): Get up, Huato! (*and as* HUATO *shows no sign of life,* MORDEL *crouches down to examine him and listens to his heartbeat, then, standing up, to* TENEDY) I don't think he's breathing, Mr. Tenedy.

TENEDY: He's one of the eight that escaped more than a month ago.

Seventh Movement

Same characters as previous movement, plus the SOLDIERS.

CAPTAIN: Mr. Tenedy, good afternoon.

TENEDY (*to the* CAPTAIN): I've had it. Take him away and see what's wrong with him. (*exits*)

CAPTAIN: Yes, sir. (*two soldiers enter*) Take him to the infirmary—No, one moment . . .

MORDEL: I don't know what happened to him.

CAPTAIN (*examines the* WORKER *for himself*): What's going on? He's stiff, seems to be . . .

MORDEL: He suddenly fell, when the patrón was talking to him. I don't think he's breathin'.

CAPTAIN: He's dead, Mordel! The poor Indian! (*The* SOLDIERS *also examine the* WORKER.)

MORDEL: What do you want! One more down! And one less in the mine! We're history! . . .

SOLDIER: He's not breathin', patrón. There's no breath.

CAPTAIN: Take him to the morgue. If he doesn't come back to life by tomorrow morning, bury him behind the dump. (*The* SOLDIERS *carry away the* WORKER'*s body.*)

MORDEL: Simply out of fear, that Indian! Doesn't take more than that!

CAPTAIN: Some people are like this: doctors call them cardiacs or something like that.

An indigenous MAN *and* WOMAN *appear stage right.*

Eighth Movement

Same characters as previous movement, plus the MAN *and* WOMAN *minus the* WORKER *and the* SOLDIERS. *The* MAN *and* WOMAN *remove their hats with great humility.*

MAN AND WOMAN: Hail Mary, Mother of God, patrón!

MORDEL: Hello there, folks! Finally, you've decided. Come right up.

The CAPTAIN *goes behind the counter and serves himself a glass of whiskey, still talking about* HUATO, *the worker.*

CAPTAIN: Well, patrón! In the end, that Indian's a good spade, but drunk as only he can get!

MAN (*stopping with his wife to admire some colored kerchiefs hanging at the door*): These are nice, patrón! Green, maroon, white!

MORDEL: Orocio, get the colored pitchers. (OROCIO *follows his order;* MORDEL, *to the couple*) Do ya' like the maroon ones? Come on in! What's new in the world?

MAN (*advancing, followed by his wife*): You tell me, patrón.

MORDEL (*holding up the colored pitcher to the light*): Look how precious this is! Look how gorgeous! Do ya' see the hens in hats painted on it?

The CAPTAIN *lets out a giggle which he immediately stifles.* OROCIO *also strives to contain his hilarity. On the side,* MORDEL *threatens him.*

MORDEL: You dog, laughing like that!

MAN AND WOMAN (*observing the pitchers in wonder*): Patrón, it's precious! . . .

MORDEL: Aren't they truly precious? In this larger one, there are golden trees with soldiers on the leaves. Look how wonderful! Come close!

Closer! . . . (*the* CAPTAIN *continues to laugh to himself, and since the* MAN *and* WOMAN *don't dare touch the pitchers,* MORDEL *says to them*) Hold it for yourself! Right here! Nice and firm!

MAN (*with the pitcher in hand, intimidated*): Patrón . . . patrón . . .

CAPTAIN AND MORDEL (*to the* MAN): Don't be afraid, man! You can even walk around with it. (*The* MAN, *however, doesn't dare make the slightest movement.*)

MAN (*suddenly terrified*): Patrón, take it back! I'm gonna drop it!

MORDEL (*grabbing him by the arm and making him take a few steps*): Come on! Come on! . . . Walk! That's it. Careful you don't trip. See? Nothing will happen. (*While the* MAN *walks with the pitcher in his hands, the* WOMAN *anxiously follows him with her eyes.*)

CAPTAIN: You can also turn and keep walking. (*to* MORDEL) Mordel, you're a genius!

Toward the end of the store, the MAN *is completely immobile, with the pitcher raised to the height of his chest. The* WOMAN *has immediately gone to his side, hurrying to his aid in the event of an accident.*

MORDEL: So what do ya' say? Like the one you've got there? Or do ya' want a different one?

MAN: Must cost a ton, patrón!

MORDEL: But, tell me. Do ya' like that one you've got there. Tell it to me straight.

MAN: Yeah, this one, patrón. But—

MORDEL: I'll give it to you for your wheat field at Gorán. What's the difference? Take it home! (*resigned*) What are we gonna do! (*The* MAN *and* WOMAN *appear to have misunderstood so greatly that they deem the proposal flattering.*) This is how I am: all that I have, I give to my clients . . . (MORDEL *starts wrapping the pitcher in paper.*)

CAPTAIN (*pretending to find* MORDEL's *generosity scandalous, interrupts*): Don Mordel! Are you seriously going to give them a blue pitcher for nothing but a wheat field?

MORDEL: That's right, captain. Now ya' see: I can't help myself; it's just the way I am!

CAPTAIN (*stops* MORDEL *from wrapping the pitcher*): No! Don't do it! This is madness! (*raising the pitcher in front of everyone's eyes*) A pitcher as precious as this! It looks like an ostensory! For a measly field of wheat!

MORDEL: Misery, my captain, will be the end of me. It doesn't matter! (*to *the* MAN *and* WOMAN, *whose jaws have dropped*) What do ya' say? Do we have a deal?

MAN (*indecisive*): Patrón, I mean, what can I say!

CAPTAIN: Mordel, I resent you!

MORDEL: Why, Captain? Why do you resent me?

CAPTAIN: You know that for quite some time I've had my eye on that blue pitcher, and now, instead of selling it to me, you'd rather give it away to these Indians, for a simple wheat field. That's not how you treat a friend!

MORDEL: Oh, Captain! In the stockroom I've got another one that I'll sell to you and you alone. I promise (*handshake*). You have my word!

CAPTAIN (*to the* MAN *and* WOMAN): There you have it, folks! Take it home! It's all yours!

MORDEL: Orocio, pack up this pitcher. (*to the* CAPTAIN) Now I know that in business I'm the one who loses. But, Captain, such is life . . .

MAN (*runs up to kiss* MORDEL's *hand*): My dear patrón, God will reward you! (*The* WOMAN *also kisses* MORDEL's *hand, and the* CAPTAIN *stifles a laugh and drinks his whiskey.*)

MORDEL: Last night I dreamed of eggs: the sign of robbery. Who cares!

CAPTAIN (*into* MORDEL's *ear*): Pinch me, man! . . .

MORDEL (*loudly*): Captain, it's a deal: one measly wheat field isn't worth as much as a pitcher blue as Heaven, but if I'm gonna talk the talk, I'd better walk the walk. No skin off my back.

CAPTAIN: That's your call.

MORDEL: Hurry up, Orocio. A splendid pitcher only landowners have in their houses! Right?

CAPTAIN: Landowners, and priests too. They also have pitches blue as Heaven! Isn't that right?

MORDEL: It is! Priests, of course, but, priests, ya' know, priests are priests.

CAPTAIN: I completely agree.

MORDEL: Here's your pitcher, young man. Hold it nice and tight. Careful you don't drop it.

The MAN *raises the pitcher to the height of his eyes and carries it the way a priest lifts the consecrated host.*

CAPTAIN: Mind where you stick those hoofs of yours, so you don't trip.

MORDEL (*leading the* MAN *by the arm to the door, more slowly*): Come on

... Step-by-step ... This way ... Little by little ... That's it ... That's it ... (*The* WOMAN *follows her husband's every step, and* MORDEL *abruptly stops the* MAN.) When are ya' gonna turn over the field?

MAN: Whenever you want.

MORDEL: How many months along is the wheat?

MAN: Planted on All Saints Day. And it's not long before Carnival ...

MORDEL: Good. I'll have a look sometime this week. Anyways, the land is mine now. Agreed?

MAN: Patrón, the land is yours.

MORDEL: Good. (*releases the* MAN's *arm and nudges him from behind toward the street*) Go with God, my good fellow! Give my best to Challa. (*The couple leaves, the* MAN *in front, slowly, with the pitcher raised up; the* WOMAN, *spotting him from behind.*)

CAPTAIN (*suddenly looking into the distance, on the street*): Mr. Tenedy! Mr. Tenedy's looking for me! (*In a gulp he finishes his whiskey and hurries away stage right.*)

Ninth Movement

Same characters as previous movement, minus the CAPTAIN, MAN, *and* WOMAN.

MORDEL (*turning to his assistant, who's still arranging the merchandise*): Orocio!

OROCIO: Patrón.

MORDEL: Come here.

OROCIO (*coming*): Yes, sir.

MORDEL (*at his desk*): Where's Novo?

OROCIO: In the back room.

MORDEL (*severe, quietly*): Why do you set a bad example for him?

OROCIO: I'm not setting any kind of example.

MORDEL: What did ya' do, not a minute ago, when you were addin' up the matchboxes?

OROCIO: Patrón, I didn't do anything.

MORDEL: Do ya' know what it means for a dummy like him to see you, the shop assistant, carry two or more packages away, right from under the store owner's nose? Do ya' know what a bad example you're settin' so that one day Novo too will wanna take whatever he feels like, under the pretext that he's gonna do this or this with the merchandise? Answer me!

OROCIO: Patrón, that's very different . . .

MORDEL: Little kids must not be taught, in jest or for any other reason, to carry away anything that doesn't belong to 'em.

OROCIO: It was just to add them up. 'Cause that's what I always say when adding.

MORDEL: No! I'm telling you: not for any reason. Did ya' hear me?

OROCIO: Loud and clear, patrón. I won't do it again.

MORDEL: Never! Don't let it happen again! When Novo is here and you have to add something, don't sing the operation out loud. Do it in your head or go hide somewhere and do it. Novo doesn't know how to add or anything about the words we use for addition. All he hears is that you're carryin' away my matchboxes.

OROCIO: Patrón, when you order me to add out loud, then what?

MORDEL: When I order you to do it . . . When I order you to do it . . . Well, then . . . instead of saying "I carry the two or three or four" or whatever the number, you say, "Patrón, you carry the two or three or four," and so on and so forth.

OROCIO: Very well, patrón.

MORDEL: Except if the boxes or merchandise that you're addin' up don't belong to me, but to a client or anyone else. In that case, you can carry whatever your little heart desires. I could give a shit. Understood?

OROCIO: Loud and clear.

MORDEL (*getting ready to write, aloud*): Novo, come here!

VOICE OF NOVO: Be right there, Uncle. (NOVO *comes.*)

MORDEL: Take this letter to the telegraph. On the double! And keep on the balls of your feet so the soles of your shoes don't wear down.

NOVO: Okay, Uncle (*exits with the letter*).

MORDEL (*thumbing through his accounting book, to* OROCIO): Check your notebook to see how many Indians died in the mines last month and how many escaped.

OROCIO (*consulting a notebook*): Right away, patrón.

MORDEL: Mr. Tenedy is asking for fifty. I presume the figure is not exact.

OROCIO (*reading from his notebook*): Escaped, twenty-seven; dead, nineteen. Total, forty-six.

MORDEL: Give or take, that's the number: fifty . . . Hmm! . . . And the month before?

OROCIO (*reading*): Escaped, thirteen; dead twenty-eight. Total, forty-one.

MORDEL: Each time, more of 'em escape and fewer die. Strange indeed . . .

From *Brothers Colacho* 463

Tenth Movement

Same characters as previous movement, plus TENEDY.

TENEDY (*returning, in a good mood*): Mordel, give me a whiskey.

MORDEL: Comin' right up, Mr. Tenedy.

TENEDY: The soldiers just nabbed twelve Indians.

MORDEL: Fugitives?

TENEDY: Yes, twelve of the fugitives from last month. Join me, Mordel: another round.

MORDEL: Gladly.

TENEDY: The Indians said there's a lot of fugitives roaming around Parahuac. Cheers!

MORDEL: Cheers, Mr. Tenedy.

TENEDY: Tonight, the soldiers are going to look for them.

MORDEL: I'd already told the captain that the Indians have come down to Parahuac.

TENEDY: Anyways, we still need more workers. As many as possible.

MORDEL: I've just sent the telegram to Acidal.

TENEDY: How does the governor in Taque treat you guys? Please speak candidly. Does he lend you the facilities necessary for corralling the Indians?

MORDEL: Mr. Tenedy, the governor is all ours. Acidal is completely satisfied with his support.

TENEDY: You know very well that the Cotarca Corporation got Calpo that position to have the infantry behind us in matters relating to human resources . . .

MORDEL: I know perfectly well.

TENEDY: So, if Calpo doesn't behave himself with you two, tell me right away. I'll immediately contact our headquarters and they'll replace him on the spot.

MORDEL: Mr. Tenedy, I repeat: Acidal assures me that Calpo is giving him all sorts of facilities.

TENEDY: You think your brother can get us the fifty laborers we need by the end of the month?

MORDEL: I'm sure of it.

TENEDY: Good. And, Mordel, what do you know about politics? What does Acidal tell you?

MORDEL: About politics, Mr. Tenedy, nothing new.

TENEDY (*secretly*): It appears that your brother's candidacy is going to meet certain challenges.

MORDEL: That's what I keep telling them.

TENEDY: The sole act of day-to-day living with the people and politicians of Taque creates a crowd of envy and jealousy around him.

MORDEL: I loathe politics, Acidal would love to become a parliament member. It's his decision.

TENEDY: A member of parliament! Acidal may think our company would make a killing if he were a member of parliament, but I don't.

MORDEL: He's a child when it comes to these things.

TENEDY: The Cotarca Corporation has no need for members of parliament. We'll be satisfied when we have the president of Peru on the take.

MORDEL: Naturally.

TENEDY (*pensive*): Our trade union's interests in the U.S. are far too great.

MORDEL: I understand perfectly well.

TENEDY: To protect those interests, a parliament member won't do. Anyways, to cut to the chase, our company will recommend your brother's candidacy to the government, provided that he'd accept it (*finishes his whiskey*).

MORDEL: Thank you kindly, Mr. Tenedy. We owe everything to you.

TENEDY (*mysteriously*): Mordel, it occurs to me that one day the Cotarca Corporation might call on you to enter the world of politics. There will be time to talk about that . . .

MORDEL (*smiling, not understanding*): Mr. Tenedy, Me . . . politics . . .

TENEDY: Not so fast. That's still a ways away.

MORDEL: It would be the worst punishment you could give me. Politics frightens me, it—

TENEDY: We'll just see about that. Business is business, Mordel, and you, first and foremost, are a businessman.

MORDEL: I prefer my shop, where I can sell the Indians my salt, my cotton drill . . .

TENEDY (*handshake, about to leave*): Mr. Edison has said that the individual's worst flaw is his reluctance to change professions. At least give it a try. A great man may be hiding even in the most obscure creature.

MORDEL: See you soon, Mr. Tenedy.

TENEDY (*at the door*): Edison is really something!

TENEDY *exits.* MORDEL *laughs to himself.* OROCIO *faces a crate of bottles on the counter, at the other end of the store.*

OROCIO: Patrón, how many bottles of water do I add to each bottle of rum? Two to one, right?

MORDEL: Shush! You animal! They'd better not hear you! Make it three to one!

OROCIO: Very well, patrón. My bad.

Enter a WORKER *in rags, coming forth painfully, like a sleepwalker or a zombie.*

Eleventh Movement

MORDEL, OROCIO, *the* WORKER.

MORDEL (*to the* WORKER): Now what do *you* want?

WORKER (*timidly, almost in secret*): Patrón, I wanna give you my four pesos (*holds out some bills to him*).

MORDEL: Give me four pesos . . . What are you talkin' about?

WORKER: I've brought four pesos for you, patrón.

MORDEL *stares at the* WORKER *from his feet on up, and the* WORKER *lowers his eyes, continuing to hold out the bills.*

MORDEL (*suddenly on the defensive*): Get out of here, you hoodlum. I don't need your pesos.

WORKER: Oh, Patroncito! Please! Accept my gift!

MORDEL: I don't accept gifts from anyone. (*Grabs him by the arm and pushes him toward the door on the right*) Get out of here! Get out of here! If you don't want to see me angry . . .

The WORKER *has been kicked out and* MORDEL, *from the door, observes him with a strange discomfort.*

VOICE OF THE WORKER (*pleading*): Don't be mean, patrón. Accept my pesos!

MORDEL: I said, get out of here!

As the WORKER *goes out of view,* MORDEL *quickly returns to his desk. After a moment, he gives a sideways glance at the street.*

VOICE OF THE WORKER (*like that of a beggar*): Hail Mary, Mother of God, patrón! Four pesos! I'm givin' 'em to you! . . .

MORDEL *again looks away from the* WORKER *and nervously returns to his papers, while the voice of the* WORKER *continues his monotonous, tearful pleas.*

VOICE OF THE WORKER: Don't be mean, patrón! My four pesos! For you! They're for you! They're for you!

CURTAIN FALLS SLOWLY

END OF ACT 1

[1932–34]   [JM]

Letters

TO NÉSTOR P. VALLEJO

Nice, October 27, 1929

My Dear Little Brother Néstor,

After a trip through the principle capitals of Europe, I'm writing these lines from Nice, on the eve of my return to Paris. I imagine that you and Víctor must have received some postcards I sent from several countries.

It's very likely that I'll return to Peru this coming year. Before that, I'm going to publish four books on topics and aspects derived from my experience and life spent over the seven years of my absence from America.

I've suffered so much, yet at the same time I've learned a great deal and tremendously benefited from my pain. However, or rather, therefore, it seems that I must return to America to fight and work publicly for my country. I've suffered, I repeat, and nonetheless before God I feel youthful, strong, and full of hope.

Give my best to your wife, and may you both receive my most heartfelt affection.

I've significantly changed: in my morals, behavior, mindset, and even physically. People arriving from Peru say I'm not even the shadow of the man I used to be.

Write to me always and give me some news on your situation and where you're living. I'll address my future letters there.

Kind, warm regards from your brother who's dying to see you.

César

[JM]

TO JOSÉ CARLOS MARIÁTEGUI

Vienna, October 17, 1929

Dear Comrade,

Commandant Julio Guerrero, whom you undoubtedly know from his writings on Europe, has just published a book of memoirs about the Germany of 1914–23. It seems to me that this book reveals unforeseen aspects of German politics during those years, since, as an eyewitness at the events he recounts, Guerrero exposes a great deal between the lines and highlights many assumptions about the process in question.

While talking with him about his work, I obtained a few chapters that I've decided to share with you, hoping you publish them in *Amauta*, if you find them suitable. Later on we will send you a copy of the entire book so that you see just how well it fits within the spirit of your press and whether or not it's publishable.

Fraternal regards from your comrade.

César Vallejo   [JM]

TO GERARDO DIEGO

Paris, January 6, 1930

Dear Gerardo,

Again I thank you and Bergamín for your continued interest in a new edition of my book, *Trilce*. I find your advice most tactful and kind, with regard to the conditions in which the Spanish edition is to be made. Following your prudent insinuations, I authorize you to draw up the contract with Compañía Iberoamericana de Publicaciones. I am sure that you will handle it as though it were your own.

As the basis of the contract, it seems to me that we could request an edition of 2,000 copies in all. Accepting the form of royalties, it would be suitable to request an advance of 1,000 pesetas, since Alberti was advanced 500 pesetas for 1,500 copies. This is all I can say, as a starting point for the contract. If it's not possible to get a 1,000 peseta advance for 2,000 copies, the only option would be to accept the highest offer you can get and, if possible, accept the terms used in Alberti's deal. I entrust you with my rights and guarantee that no matter the conditions of this forthcoming edition, I hereby approve them and hold the copyright in full and without limitations.

Regarding foreign rights, reserved for Peru, I'm not interested. The reason is simple: if I'm not there to control the sales, they could cheat me out of everything. I know my countrymen.

Naturally, I'd like the book to have a prologue by you and Bergamín. That would be a great honor for me, aside from the conveniences of such a preface, and would add prestige to the book in the marketplace. I thank you both in advance for the prologue.

As Larrea must have written to you, I'm thinking of going to Peru sometime soon, perhaps only for a few weeks, which is why I ask that you settle this matter as soon as possible. I'm especially interested in negotiating and signing the contract immediately. With regard to when I will receive the advance, I would expect it upon delivery of the manuscript, as you yourself were thinking.

Since I've never written to Bergamín before, as I didn't know his address, I do so now.

Looking forward to news from you and, reiterating my appreciation, cordial regards from your friend and comrade.

César Vallejo

11 avenue de l'Ópera—Paris   [JM]

TO GERARDO DIEGO

Madrid, January 27, 1932

Dear Gerardo,

I just sent you a telegram, begging you to add 300 pesetas to your kind loan of 1,000. My wife left for Paris on Wednesday, and she tells me that the money she took with her to straighten out her matters isn't enough, since the woman to whom my wife sent 1,000 francs in October so that she make a payment hasn't made it. Before we settle our matters, my wife needs to make that payment, and we were not prepared here for what that woman has done. And, a shopkeeper who owed my wife two payments currently isn't in Paris. For all these reasons, I've come back to bother you, dear brother Gerardo, and it pains me to do so, because of how generous you've been to me. I apologize and appreciate it greatly.

Juan's address is not in Boulogne-sur-Mer, but rather in Boulogne-sur-Seine, according to what he tells me in a letter I've just received. If you had it wrong, see that you update it. His letter is short and he promised to write again, saying that, for the moment, he's not thinking of coming to Madrid.

Lorca has been very kind to me, and we went to see Camila Quiroga, regarding my comedy, without any success. She finds it out of style. We're going to check out another theater. Also Lorca tells me very rightly that several passages of the comedy must be edited before I offer it to another theater. I'm no good at those things for the public—it's evident. Only economic necessity obliges me. Were it not for that, I'd naturally make a different sort of comedy.

What are you working on now? As for me, nothing. Why write, if there are no publishers? All we can do is write and keep the manuscript under lock and key. Don't forget to respond.

Fraternal regards,

César   [JM]

TO JUAN LARREA

Madrid, January 29, 1932

Dear Juan,

My wife has already written to say you've been to see her. I really appreciate that. I know, for now, you've settled in Paris for a good while. I'm not sure what to say, except that after all I think you've done the right thing. Madrid is an intolerable place to live. In passing it's passable and even charming, but to do something and as a place to live, one doesn't live or do anything. You know it better than I.

I'm dying to give you a hug and hear about you and your trip to America. It's not just a brotherly interest, but a neighborly curiosity to peer into your new life, spirit, and eyes. When will we see each other? I can't guarantee anything, unless you come to Madrid. There are so many and such fickle contingencies, a few economic and many others political. Financial weakness, as you already know, is and always has been my strength. As for politics, I've been drawn by the weight of things themselves, and it's not been in my hands to avoid it. You understand me, Juan. One lives and life penetrates in ways that, almost always, take us by surprise. However, I don't think politics has totally killed the man I was before. I've changed, for sure, but perhaps I'm also the same. I share a life between sociopolitical unrest and my inner, personal, introspective unrest.

What do you want, brother! We'll talk about all these things, relating them to you and your life and to me and mine. When can I go to Paris? My wife ought to be giving me news soon that will help me see more clearly in this respect. I'll write to you at length about this soon.

During my stay in Madrid, which is already approaching a year, I've been able to note that your name is planted—clear, landmarked, solid— amid the Spanish literary hustle and bustle. This, you'll understand, has struck my attention, in the first place because you hardly publish anything and second because, so published, just as you've contributed to Diego's magazines, it seems strange that your things are liked and applauded by numbskull yokels and the *Western Review*. It's extraordinary! It turns out that what you might call the Spanish *elite* has admiration and almost religious respect for your work. When someone says "Larrea," another responds, raising his hand, "Hey! Stop it with that already!" Thus, in light of this I believe you're a sacred object not to be discussed. Thankfully, the majority of your admirers are young and quite young indeed, which is of course very comforting.

In any case, as you probably suspect, I would've preferred to find in my hands writings from you of a less literary and more vital nature. And naturally, given the life you always take to when you're here—retracted in furious, centripetal, nebular concentration and promophobia—I've found that no one who talks about you as a person also eats and breathes and suffers like a man, or loves and resolves and rises up and ponders. Nobody, except Gerardo, when he's come to Madrid, only once in a blue moon.

What does your wife say of Peru? Have you gone up to Titicaca? Have you met by chance some brother of mine in Lima? And the Mores?

Here, in Madrid, there are only a few things I like: the sun, which is unwavering, like the pope; Valencian-style rice (which, I'll say in passing, they're making very badly now); the famous eels, which you introduced me to so many years ago; elevators in houses and the village peace in which one lives. As you'll see, this is a very small thing, beside the boredom of Madrid, its emptiness and village air.

As for the Spanish Revolution, you must be very much in the current of all that: of the new King Niceto I, of General Azaña's dictatorship and (this is serious) Spain's terrible poverty. I hope that you'll write to me as soon as possible and extensively.

In every way you help my wife, I'll be thankful to you.

Best wishes to yours and my love to the baby. Greetings to the great Riquelme. And for you a tight brotherly embrace.

César

Write to section 466.   [MLR]

Notebooks

The mercy and compassion of men for men. If at a man's moment of death, all the mercy of all the men were mustered up to keep him from dying, that man wouldn't die.

* * *

The pure and unadapted one who bumps into the world of farce and sleight of hand.

* * *

The actor who one day stopped being himself in order to be one of the characters that he used to act out onstage.

* * *

I've seen three workers collaborate and make a screw: that's the socialism of production. I've seen four share a table and some bread: that's the socialism of consumption.

* * *

Religious crooks, upon rebirth, are all born godless.

* * *

A new poetic: to transport Picasso's aesthetic to the poem. To address nothing but strictly poetic beauty, without logic or coherence or reason. Like when Picasso paints a man and, for reasons of harmony in line and color, instead of making a nose for him, he makes in its place a box or a stairway or a glass or an orange.

* * *

For souls of the absolute, death is an everlasting disgrace—a disgrace seen from here, from there, from the world, from the heavens, from the moment and from the future and from the past. For materialistic beings, it's just a disgrace seen from this world: like being poor, falling, making a fool of oneself, etc.

* * *

I want my life to be sprinkled evenly over each and every number (forty-four kilos) of my weight.

* * *

The two social classes of Moscow are looking for something: one by night; the other by day.

* * *

The revolutionary intellectual who, under a pseudonym, secretly contributes to reactionary magazines.

* * *

Bolshevism is humanism in action. The same can be said of revolutionism or communism, which are humanisms in action, that is, the humanistic idea and feeling and ideal, completed by humanistic action and technique which that ideal incarnates.

* * *

My yard is two yards long; my pound weighs a ton.

* * *

He who today walks by the tragedy of the worker unaffected is not a poet. Paul Valéry, Maeterlinck, they are not.

* * *

The man who was born old and died young: aging backward.

* * *

Laughter from tickling and laughter from moral joy: Rabelais.

* * *

The eyes accustomed to the cinema and the eyes accustomed to distance.

* * *

Intellectuals are rebels, but not revolutionaries.

* * *

Her gaze is the size inside a violin just when its sound is dying in the distance.

* * *

The death of a person is not, as is believed, a disgrace. Disgrace is something else.

* * *

Love frees me in the sense that I *am able to* stop loving. The person I love should give me the freedom to be able to abhor her at any moment.

* * *

Aviation in the air, in the water, and in the spirit. Its laws in each of the three cases are different. The spirit flies when it's heavy and sinks deeper into itself. The heavier the spirit, the higher and farther it flies.

* * *

I love plants for their root and not their flower.

* * *

The dog that in the end never let anyone come close to treat the wound of his owner. The latter, naturally, died.

* * *

Nature creates the eternity of Substance. Art creates the eternity of Form.

* * *

No one dies except after having done something interesting. This guy or that one has done something interesting, provided he dies right now.

* * *

The arts (painting, poetry, etc.) are not just these. There are also the arts of eating, drinking, walking: every act is an art. The slippery slope toward dadaism.

* * *

My bitterness falls on Thursday.

* * *

The same street that unfolds there leads here.

* * *

Artistically, *socialism* is not the same as *humanism*.

* * *

Can one speak of spiritual liberation while the social and material revolution hasn't been brought about, and while one lives within the material and moral atmosphere of production and bourgeois relations of the economy?

* * *

Surrealists seek the liberation of the spirit before and even independent of the abolition of bourgeois-class conditions.

* * *

The bourgeois psychology of a communist and the communist psychology of a bourgeois.

* * *

The old owner of a painting, expropriated by the Soviet, has ended up becoming the preserver of that painting: right of individual property, possession, and alienation. How curious.

* * *

Collectivism in Russia eschews certain individual ways of life and, at once, originates other individual ways. People eat all day long in Moscow, that is, *not everyone eats* at the same time. *Not everyone rests* the same day, according to the new calendar.

* * *

There's revolution in literature (which isn't necessarily revolution in politics): Proust, Giraudoux, Morand, Stravinsky, Picasso; and then there's revolution in politics: Prokofiev, Barbusse, Diego Rivera. The latter is a revolution of themes and, sometimes, is accompanied by technique. The former is of technique and, sometimes, is accompanied by themes. In Russia one only knows or, at least, prefers, the thematic revolution. In Paris, the technical revolution. These are the differences between revolutionaries and reactionaries, between the avant-garde and the rearguard, etc.

* * *

Someone copies the trademark of a car, and the copier is sued and pays punitive damages. Someone copies a poem and nothing happens.

* * *

Does art come before the technique of production or follow it as its reflection?

* * *

Humankind suddenly finds itself facing a problem (the worker) that, containing all the other problems (human, moral, artistic, etc.), is frightening, since it can't be resolved with reason or consciousness, without abdicating the classist rights of the bourgeoisie. This is when bourgeois thought evades reason and consciousness and plunges into the unconscious, into superreason, and the Freudian libido, because it doesn't have the courage to use its reason fairly to resolve the giant problem of the worker, which would bring about solutions to all other universal problems.

* * *

Everything comes down to this: what's the biggest and most acute problem of our time? Indisputably, it's the social problem, the worker. Why don't intellectuals resolve it?

* * *

The only one who tells the truth is the liar.

* * *

When I read, it seems like I see myself in a mirror.

* * *

Has it stopped raining? The month of May is the biggest drag in the world.

* * *

My eyeglasses have stopped (like a clock).

* * *

Espinoza seems disguised to himself, as Espinoza.

* * *

I am well aware that right now someone is eating out my heart.

* * *

I've got the urge to write a note to everyone, saying, "That's great!"

* * *

He says, Get serious so they do what you ask them to. And I tell him, They'll do it not because I get serious, but because what I ask of them is fair.

* * *

A theoretical and practical cold has set in.

* * *

I wrote a line where I spoke about an adjective that was sprouting grass. A number of years later, in Paris, I saw on a headstone in the Montparnasse cemetery an adjective covered with grass. Prophesy of poetry.

* * *

The portrait of every person is always found in the private room.

* * *

The advantage of the cinema is that we see the artists face-to-face, while they don't see us.

* * *

The instinct to labor is, chronologically and hierarchically, the first of all, prior to the instincts of sex and survival. At birth the first thing a child does is put forth effort (groan, movement, gesture) to thwart the ache, pain, or discomfort. This can be called the instinct to fight for one's life (the instinct to work), the foundation for a new aesthetic: the *aesthetic of labor.*

* * *

Everyone is a hero at something.

* * *

My simple anarchy, my great pain composed of joy.

* * *

Write a poem: "Gentlemen: I have the honor of telling you that I am just fine . . ." and then communicate the state of my affairs and everything else.

* * *

A peddler hawks his goods—popular eloquence and the spirit of the street fair. A scene to address in *Vestiare*.

* * *

Pierre the metropolitan, successor of the patriarch Thakou and current head of the Russian Orthodox Church, is in harmony with the Soviet. The emigrant Russian priests have been put under the authority of the Constantinople patriarch. A kind of schism in the heart of the Russian Church.

* * *

Little prince Paul, when taken to a military parade, given that he was the inheritor of the throne, let out blood-curdling shouts upon seeing the soldiers, the horses, the tanks, etc.

* * *

A new theatrical aesthetic: a piece in which the author cohabits—he, his family, and his relatives—with the characters he has created, who take part in his daily life, his interests, and passions. It's hard to tell or easy to confuse the theatrical characters with living people in reality.

* * *

Upon hearing Beethoven, a woman and a man cry before the greatness of that music. And I say to them, but it's you who in your heart have this greatness.

* * *

A new aesthetic: short poems, of varied form, about evocative and anticipatory moments, like *L'Opérateur* in the cinema of Vertov.

* * *

Everyone runs from his own thought. He who comes down the stairs, steps onto a train, walks through the street, etc., anything makes him run from his thought.

* * *

The spot or place or landscape or way of the world, through which no one has ventured and where nothing has happened.

* * *

Everyone holds a hidden gun to me.

* * *

The man who never cried in the eighty years of his life.

* * *

Spain's incomprehension of South American writers who, out of fear, did not dare to be Indo-American but almost completely Spanish (Rubén Darío, et al.). Lorca is Andalusian. Why don't I have the right to be Peruvian? Why are they going to tell me that they don't understand me in Spain? And me, while an Austrian or Englishman will understand the purebred turns of Lorca and Co.

* * *

One must not deceive people by saying that in the work of art there's only the economic. No. One must state clearly that the contents of the work are many—economic, moral, sentimental, etc.—but that, at times like these, it's compulsory to *insist* on the economic, because the whole solution to the problem of humanity resides therein.

* * *

There's revolutionary Russian literature and revolutionary literature that combats from within the capitalist world. The objectives, work methods, techniques, means of expression, and social materials vary one to the next. No one has yet made this distinction with the Marxist critique.

* * *

Gide would like the revolution not to end with the disappearance of misery. "If it ends with that," he says, "it would be a measly thing. The revolution must end endowing humanity with great happiness." Gide is wrong. The revolution must end not only with great happiness but with a great humanity made of *happiness and of pain and everything else*. The thing is that Gide, a wealthy man, doesn't know what a superior source of humanity not having anything to eat is.

* * *

The revolutionary writer erroneously thinks that there's a need for proletarian art, considering that the worker is a pure worker, which is untrue, because the worker also has something of a bourgeois in him. The worker breathes bourgeois air and is more imbued with bourgeois spirit than we would suspect. This is very important in order to conceive of proletarian art or art of the masses.

* * *

Careful with the human substance of poetry!

* * *

The most eloquent case of social solidarity is to see several workers lifting a giant stone.

* * *

Everything always starts at the beginning.   [JM]

BOOK FIVE 1936–1938

Articles and Chronicles

RECENT DISCOVERIES IN THE LAND OF THE INCAS[1]

The National Museum of Lima has long directed important projects of archaeological exploration in different regions of Peru. After unveiling the structure of the celebrated fortress of Sajsawamán in the city of Cuzco (legendary capital of the Inca Empire), they've just discovered several megalithic constructions in the Chokechaka basin connected underground to the base of the archaeological site on the eastern edge of that citadel.

They are large foundations, walls, terraces, doors, ramps, and galleries of the palace of Incan nobility and vestiges of temples, chapels, stadia, and gardens of the imperial court, scattered among hills and embankments and often carved into the rock itself.

In his report addressed to the Ministry of Education, Luis Valcárcel provides a detailed inventory of the ruins, which includes ornamental treasures. As in all works of the Incas, the architecture we are dealing with contains various styles, linked by the one essential feature of its construction material: stone.

According to the old theogonic legend of the Incas, the supreme God, Viracocha, created man and his descendants alike, not out of soil but stone. The Incas left their thoughts, their deepest feelings, and also their socioeconomic activities, their fears, their lives, and their fate imprinted on stone.

To understand the universal and immortal meaning of a culture like this, nothing can be more useful than the contemplation and study of its megalithic constructions, spread from the highest lake in the world, Titicaca—on the border between Peru and Bolivia—all the way to San Agustín, Colombia.

Right from the start, the stones of Chokechaka offer us an idea of eternity. One feels that these constructions have been made by giants and immortal men. The buildings surrounding the fortifications cease to highlight the usual urban style, only to acquire the architectonic dimension and weight of true conglomerations of polyhedral stones spellbound by nature. Never has a city or fortress from antiquity left us such a geologic sort of abode (to put it this way). The Roman and Babylonian Empires built their palaces with bricks and mortar, or mediocre stone and mud. Each Incan palace has been erected with gigantic blocks of basalt porphyry, without any mixture to hold them together, when the rock core hasn't been hollowed out, as the case is for the dwellings at Chokechaka.

Here, as in many other great Incan cities, one discovers walls still intact measuring thirty feet in length, twenty in height, and six in width, formed by only three or four stones. Their seam is so perfect and junctures so exact as to invite the suspicion that a single, rocky, one-of-a-kind unit had been excavated whole and transported from some fabled quarry. Their harmonious placement so tight fitting as to prohibit a sword blade from passing through, as Prescott says, adds to the perfection of this direct carving of the Incan constructions. When unions of stones are even more subtle, they could be mistaken for lines of decorative drawings.

In Sapiantana, one great rock among the many, "the only seat," as the Indians call it, dominates the Chokechaka riverbank, forming the center of the city's neighborhoods, and from that height it must have towered over the residences lining the two shores of the river. No vestige of construction has been uncovered; only this high point that even today resembles something of an unnamable, untamable god and may well have been the object of pantheist worship.

In his wise observations on these excavations, Valcárcel calls attention to the extraordinary beauty of the landscape that brings out the spectacle of the unearthed ruins. It's an astonishing place during any season of the year. The countryside is always of a gentle, tropical green, in a spectrum of mild hues, but is full of this life and color with which only the soul of America nourishes its vegetation, its humans and their human endeavors. The lesson of history is found here: since the most remote periods of world prehistory, all or almost all the monuments of human genius have budded and blossomed—in Egypt as in America, in the Indies as in Greece—surrounded by peaceful wilderness, on the banks of long silent rivers, amid dense, lush vegetation, under sweet and high clear skies.

Another no less disconcerting and admirable miracle of those constructions is the transportation of stone blocks from very distant quarries, entailing the crossing of torrential rivers, forests, and ravines, and raising them up to multiple floors and terraces of their palaces. The Incas didn't know of any mechanically powered traction procedure or device: the wheel was yet unknown; animal power, utilized by the old civilizations for this kind of labor, was likewise foreign to them. The great mammals, the ox and the horse, among others, didn't exist in pre-Columbian America. Therefore one can attribute these wonders of urban planning only to human strength, the arms and shoulders of humans and the virtues of audacity, cooperation, and tenacity characteristic of this race—a fact that becomes even more surprising when one sees Incan cities like Machu Picchu set upon extremely high cordillera crests.

Finally, the excavations of Chokechaka demonstrate a knowledge, rare and surprising for the period, possessed by the Incas with regard to the facilitation of leisure in their cities. Scientists today have begun to study the physical and chemical properties that haven't been established yet. The formula of such great work grounded on the balance of liquids and properties of certain metals remains an impenetrable mystery, as does the Inca's knowledge of prophylaxis and medicine, moving wise Americans and Europeans to bow in admiration and curiosity, with the hopes of finding the cardinal laws that the scientific foundations of our civilization fall short of discerning and shorter of formulating.

[*Beaux-Arts* (Paris), no. 165, February 28, 1936]   [JM]

THE ANDES AND PERU[2]

An excellent French exploration and research team departed to the Upper Amazon a few weeks ago. Scientific circles of Paris showed the utmost interest in these projects that will help those still virgin regions of South America be known. The soil, flora, fauna, and the mysterious life of the Jivaroans are the object of these studies, whose results will expand the data of several current branches of sociology and ethnography or just maybe formulate offshoots of new fields. In the Oriente territory of Ecuador, five hundred kilometers east of the capital, Quito, the team has begun its research and, circumstances and scientific interest permitting, will then head up the Río Marañón toward northern Peru, widening the scope of its study.

We wish to call attention to the European scientific centers' incalculable interest, which, if piqued, could be directed at another South American region: the Peruvian sierra. This eternally snowcapped Andean region, with its western buttresses resting on the distant hills of the Pacific coast, was the cradle of countless admirable pre-Columbian civilizations of which the Inca was summum. However, what science knows of this area is poor, vague, confusing, or (what's worse) entwined with strands of literary smoke in fantastic tales that aren't seriously grounded in reality.

Like the Amazon rain forest, the Peruvian sierra has given rise to a bountiful, motley, and arbitrary bibliography. The lover of the Far West, between rubberneck and interloper or tropical zoology and botany aficionado, including journalists eager to pounce on sensational headlines, past the novelist whose fertile imagination in fables anesthetizes even insomniacs—this entire swarm of mystifiers has consciously or unconsciously waxed legendary over the course of centuries, without making any deep-reaching, authentic contact, and our ignorance of this region lives on, at least in ethnography and the natural sciences.

Following the period of Spanish domination, European expeditions through the land of the Incas have been strictly concerned with archaeology, and in this regard the research carried out by museums of Berlin, London, Copenhagen, New York, and Madrid contains comprehensive conclusions that can be used as a base for American prehistoric science. Contrary to that, the geognostic, sociological, and geographic expeditions have been few and far between.

Great difficulties clearly explain this gap: the distance between continents and, especially, the absence of communications in the Peruvian cordillera and among diverse landmarks of its extensive expanse, inter alia. The splendid network of roads from the Incan period has vanished. The only way to reach the high planes is by flying, and no one has *attempted* that, so to speak.

It would be valuable to overcome these difficulties, considering the wealth of scientific and artistic knowledge waiting to be extracted from the land, climate, and folklore of the indigenous populations—even their superstitions and magic. We must be careful not to wear too skeptical or disdainful a smile, since science and art have constantly drunk from the wells of embryonic arts and sciences of primitive peoples, when they haven't reestablished verbatim and outright validated exhumed formulas from countries considered barbaric or savage.

At the presentation, General Perrier, a member of the institute backing the expedition to Ecuador, spoke of "reductant" Indians. "In conclusion," he said, "we hope our knowledge of the Jivaroans will no longer be limited to their renowned ability to mummify enemies' severed heads." To this we add that life in the Peruvian Andes should also be studied and known from an angle more penetrating and serious than the picturesque, squalid, and fantastic.

[*L'Amerique* (Paris), no. 390, June 21, 1936]   [JM]

MAN AND GOD IN INCAN SCULPTURE[3]

How many centuries passed from the time man had the first notion of God until he had the first notion of himself? For it's true that before discovering in his consciousness his own image, independent of other beings, he discovered the image of the Being of beings. This temporal priority of one idea over another is best reflected by the evolution of visual arts among primitive peoples perhaps than by any other expression of the human spirit. Although precise dates demarcating successive periods have yet to be established, the development of Incan sculpture offers us suggestions of lively historical interest for comparative study with visual arts.

An exclusively religious character predominates in the earliest prehistoric Incan sculpture, where, as in other early Indo-American statuary—Mayan and Aztec, inter alia—the human is never treated as an autonomous aesthetic entity, the image of God being the constant subject matter that takes on multiple forms of polytheism. When a human appears in the monoliths, masks, gravestones, and bas-reliefs, the feat is performed by a limb of the divinity's body, from which one or another attribute is incarnated allegorically or symbolically. Therefore, the visual intervention has a cabalistic value equal or equivalent to that of zoomorphic signs.

Man appears in the role and semblance of a priest, and here the figure—so barely human and so very religious—is stylized to such an extent that one would be more likely to call it an idol instead of a human being. Sculpture would still need to pass through many long phases in search of other thematic conceptions before it could represent everyday social life—this being the first step toward the discovery of man-the-motif, considered in flesh and bone, independent of all links to the theogonic world.

The people of Egypt and, especially, Rome have certainly left us monuments—the pyramids, the arcs of triumph—of extraordinary value with regard to the visual revelation of the spirit in the municipal, constructive order of these peoples. Among the Incas, the sculptural and monumental expressions of the same genre reveal this spirit of social organization and administration through visual media of the most direct inspiration and with a surprising expressive power. Numerous sculptures in stone and bas-reliefs in porphyry recently discovered in the regions of Cuzco and Puno translate the ceremonies, rites, and customs of the epoch through scenes of verism with a host of impressive details. There, the strokes depicting people are too indistinct and exaggerated for one to discern concrete individual figures, and yet they abound with harmony and an aura hardly equaled (in this aspect) by the Phoenicians and Greeks.

Although social life, in that sky, has stopped revealing itself as a flood of mythological concerns, it still unveils its cosmogonic interests peculiar to that period through religious evolution of the people. Thus, many sculptures—especially those of Tiahuanaco—often incorporate signs that refer to the relations of order and hierarchy of the planetary systems with the realist play of human relations. Examples of this art include the celebrated door of Chavín and the Stone of the Sun, called Kalasasaya.

A much broader arc of centuries would be required for this process of ideological and representative differentiation to humanize the figure of man more radically, bringing about the period in which figures of individuals are made patent in sculpture along with collective representations definitively emancipated from gods and stars. Statues of high magistrates and captains of the Tahuantinsuyo appear crowned, undoubtedly with theocratic emblems relating to the principle of authority, but at once they're radically liberated from all supernatural demeanor. Many of the sculptures discovered in Pikillajta belong to this cycle. Professor Valcárcel, director of the Museo Nacional de Lima, interprets them in these terms: "The forty surrounding sculptures, of the *champi* (scepter, symbolizing authority), the sea-snail shell (war horn, military signal), and of the *mulli* (conch, symbolizing a divine sect), represent the submission of the diverse nations of the Tahuantinsuyo to the political, military, and religious strength of the Incas."

These sculptures concisely announce the proximity of an art in which man would finally be treated as he is, for himself, detached from all framework beyond his own environment and exonerated of all contents not belonging to his own individual matter. We find this art flourishing in the civilizations of the Pacific coast, and more particularly in the Mochica or Chimú sculpture of northwestern Peru. Are we to deduce that portraiture existed in Incan sculpture?

In truth, numerous Chimú heads manifest a very marked portrait-like character. Each is a different psychophysiological case, expressing a different soul, with different feelings and passions. On the other hand, this psychophysiology of the character responds to such reiterated explorations and studies of a single model that we can recognize a sort of realism quite akin to that of modern European aesthetics.

This art marks the high point of Incan sculpture. As a result of political and social events that took place in the country, did this art evolve into a more accentuated individualization of the model? Could it have suddenly stopped upon the arrival of the Spanish? Could it have agonized slowly, without external causes, by consuming itself socially and physically? One gets lost in conjectures. It falls to sociologists and historians of art to respond to these questions, such as, why and how would a feudal-collectivist (and not communist) society give birth to an art of individualist tendencies as liberal as that of Chimú sculpture?

[*Beaux Arts* (Paris), September 11, 1936]   [JM]

THE GREAT CULTURAL LESSONS
OF THE SPANISH CIVIL WAR

Paris, February 1937

The turn of politics certainly doesn't depend on what intellectuals say or do, no matter how much they'd like to place its deep social foundations in the hands of banks, large estates, and industrial cartels (cavemen and brutes of the ages)—natural enemies and judges of the intelligentsia. It's useless for encyclopedists to rise up and blaspheme medieval society: the kingship, clergy, and nobility have been ready to suck the blood of the masses for the past hundred years. Hugo's apostrophes won't sway Thiers's spirit to stop or, at least, mitigate his ferocious repression of the commune; over the heads of Pushkin, Gogol, Dostoevsky, and Tolstoy, the tzarist torture machines operate as usual, without encountering any obstacles; André Gide's profession of communist faith, of course, was completely ignored when the time came for Laval to plot with Mussolini and facilitate his conquest of Ethiopia, or when it was Blum's turn to covertly recognize that conquest; and on the day that Ortega y Gasset, Benavente, Marañón, Menéndez Pidal, and Machado joined in a single cry of liberty to defend the republic of Spain, Franco, Hitler, and Mussolini ordered the execution of thousands of women and children in the streets of Irún, Badajoz, and Madrid. The phenomenon is always the same.

Let's not kid ourselves. There are writers on the left who close their eyes to experience and reality and overestimate the intellectual's immediate political influence, attributing to his slightest public action a repercussion that they simply don't have. Today more than ever, the social mechanism that champions industrial technique operates without deference to the consensus of spirit, personified by the artist, writer, or thinker. Someone has said, in this regard, that we're witnessing the empire of barbarity on culture, citing the dictators' persecution of Einstein, Mann, Renn, Ludwig, and Reinhart in Berlin. With the difference, one would add, that the same doesn't occur in *democratic* countries. This is debatable, if we look at the following two examples: the French Academy asked Laval's government to keep its hands off Italy as it invaded Ethiopia, and this is just what Laval did; however, afterward Romain Rolland, Langevin, Rivet, and Gide asked the government of the Front Populaire not to sit on its hands while Italy and Germany invaded Spain, and good old Blum let them have their way. What does this mean? Precisely that, in the cases of Ethiopia and Spain, French politics, working as it has, before heeding the inspiration of intellectuals, has followed the dictates of prevailing financial oligarchies. The reality is none other. The only thing that differs from Germany to France is the manner: there, brutal, terrorist; here, indirect, respectful.

But the jurisdiction of thought has its revenge. If the protest cries out loud and clear, and the expression of combat in the flesh truly explodes against the coagulated powers of the economy, then the timeless inflection of an idea from a speech, article, message, or manifestation could be a petard that falls into the guts of the people and explodes into certain incontrovertible outcomes on the day we least expect it. It's by thinking and constructing, without expecting immediate explosive miracles from their present work, and by devoting the maximum spiritual strength and dignity necessary for the social interpretation of contemporary problems—like Rousseau, Hugo, and Pushkin did—that they exercise influence and have a bearing on the ulterior process of history. And it's especially important for the intellectual to translate the popular aspirations in the most authentic and direct way, worrying less about the immediate (I'm not saying demagogic) effect of their actions and more about their resonance and efficacy in the social dialectic, since the latter, in the long run, laughs off hurdles of all kinds, including economic ones, when a social *leap* is ripe for the taking.

Furthermore, the intellectual can even abstain from rising up—not without acknowledging the social ignominies of his surroundings—with practical, tangible acts against ignominies, if he prefers to create a work that bears seeds and ferments that are intrinsically revolutionary due to their material and essential play with the human medium. Hence, Shakespeare, Goethe, Balzac, Michelangelo. When the intellectual's public conduct contains a maximum degree of ideological irradiation, along with the vivid, vivacious gesture of protest and combat, it's pointless to say that the case has been made for a true archetype and model thinker.

I've pondered this at a meeting in Paris, while listening to the great writers of the Spanish Republic: Rafael Alberti, José Bergamín, María Teresa León, and Max Aub. Examples of this type of perfect intellectual, in addition to other eminent comrades like Ramón Sender, Serrano Plaja, and Cernuda, actually fight in the trenches of Madrid on one hand, while on the other they translate—and with such inner fire! with such historic loyalty! with such a social vision of our times!—the length of this throbbing, human, universal, Spanish gash over which the world leans to look, as if in a mirror, suddenly overwhelmed by stupor, passion, hope. And after hearing them, I've decided that, among the other goods the Spanish people's victory over fascism will bring is proof to foreign intellectuals that, although creating an intrinsically revolutionary work in the silence and seclusion of a study is a beautiful and transcendent act, creation is even more revolutionary when it's done in the heat of battle by pulling it from life's hottest and deepest pits.

[*Repertorio Americano* (San José, Costa Rica), no. 796, March 27, 1937]   [JM]

POPULAR STATEMENTS OF THE SPANISH CIVIL WAR

Paris, March 1937

So many new statements of human greatness and civil foresight have burst from the war's atrocious fallowness into the soul of the Spanish people! Never has history seen a war more deeply seeded in the agitated essence of the people and never, as a result thereof, have the forms of epopoeia been renovated—if not substituted—by actions more stunning and unexpected.

For the first time, the cause of a war is not the cause of a nation, but the direct, immediate expression of the people's interest and historical instinct, manifested out in the open and off the cuff. For the first time a war is waged by the spontaneous will of the people, who've replaced soldiers to march for themselves, without State coercion, captains, military training, weapons, or kepis, running to confront the enemy and dying for a clearly defined cause, divested of official nebulae that nearly defy utterance. Thus, with the people in charge of their own fight, one understands from their situation that in this fight they feel human heartbeats of popular authenticity and an extraordinary, germinal scope that has no precedents.

The European media—even on the right—has registered cases of unparalleled heroism with remarkable human disinterest, consummated individually and collectively by the militia of the republic. But there are other actions whose heroism no longer resides in an episodic rage, visible in special circumstances of war, but rather in other obscure struggles, as fecund as they are anonymous and impersonal.

"The world was stunned," says Miguel González, metallurgist from

Madrid, "by the feat of Antonio Coll, spontaneously, chest to chest, facing seven enemy tanks by himself and destroying them in triumph. Cases like Coll's appear frequently on the different battlefronts. It's just that, in most cases, no one knows the names of the heroes and, what's more, no one cares too much about them. In this war, Comrade," González adds, "everyone does what he can, without concern for glory."

And as I ask him to try to point out some outstanding cases of bravery, reported particularly on the Madrid front, González smiles and says to me, "Heroes, feats—they no longer exist. Look: it's raining mortars on the line of Guadalajara, which our side's just taken. A team of sappers has sprung out to dig new trenches under fire. Who gave the order? No one. In those circumstances, a commander would've wanted to call for reinforcements, but with pickax in hand, the sappers go flying, blown to shreds by enemy mortars. The order now comes from command to dig, and another team picks up, still under fire, where the last one left off. How many volunteers have died? How many heroes? Comrade, they're counted by the thousands in the army of the people. Either they're all heroes, or there are no heroes left."

There's certainly been talk of the "unknown soldier," the anonymous hero of all wars, but the heroism of duty is different; it generally consists of defying danger by following a higher order that appears in the eyes of he who carries it out, vested with an authority that embodies the technical reasons of victory and a principle of cold, unavoidable, and fatal necessity. On the tomb under the Arc de Triomphe, the French soldier proclaims, "A supreme law rules the mechanics of the body and soul in the trench: duty." The deepest and sharpest drama of the soldier in 1914, the tragedy that concentrates and summarizes all the dilemmas of fate, doesn't emanate from the pain and danger of combat but from the drama of duty—the tragedy of its inexorability. At the critical hours of danger, the combatant no longer knows why he fights. One problem and one concern seize him: to do his duty, avoiding pain and death however he can. Thus, he channels his fearlessness toward mounting the greatest offensive with the smallest sacrifice. Taught during or resulting from early instruction, this is the soldier's code of conduct.

The heroism of the soldier of the Spanish people, on the contrary, comes from an instinctive, impassioned, direct drive of human being. It's a reflexive, core action, comparable to something he'd do to defend his individual life in common circumstances. A man who counters an attack on his person certainly doesn't act to follow the order of duty to self-preservation; he does so on an unthinking impulse and even on the fringe of all conscious and reasoned ethics.

The first months of the Spanish Civil War reflected this instinctual accent, throbbing with pristine, popular purity, which made Malraux exclaim, "At this instant at least, a revolution has been pure forever." Men and women hit the roads of Somosierra and Extremadura in delirious movement, from the chaos of ancient exploitation, to face the rebels. A state of grace—we may call it just this—few times bestowed upon any people in history and indeed quite explainable in the Spaniards' sensible, direct, and almost Adamic nature, created the possibility for them to accurately receive at the outset the royal objectives of the fascist insurrection: ending in Spain what few rights had recently been won by the working classes, to globally extend the empire of power at the service of the organized reaction. In response to the mere announcement of the actual aggression against their dearest and fondest interests, the popular masses' counter doesn't wait for the government's ever-dawdling bureaucratic initiative, or even the harangues and appeals of the press and parties of the people, or anything else that might rouse in them the notion and feeling of *duty*; instead they take to the street in a whirlwind, demand weapons, and head to the frontline, dragging directorial boards and official sectors in tow, which have traditionally been responsible for taking initiative in these sorts of conflicts.

In this regard, one may cite the ancient Spartan agoras and, perhaps, the Roman elections, the revolutionary wars of 1789 in France and 1917 in Russia. But let's be clear. At the origin of the Greeks' most popular expeditions, certain psychological and special political factors detracted a collective frenzy from the wartime movement. At the head, there's always some great man, a legislator, tribune, or general, since the decision of the people to go to war is habitually the result of debates, indictments really, but laid out with this dialectical, academic rigor, proper to Apollonian society. (The Dionysian was always banished from the republic.) As for the Roman crowds, the popular tribunes' eloquence always kept them domesticated under lock and key in the anteroom of the Forum, where they wouldn't ruin their appetite for plunder with perspective. As for the wars of France and Russia, we must recall that they rose to the impelling cries of the Marats and the Lenins, in the climate created beforehand by Jacobians and Bolsheviki.

In the Spain of 1936, at the origin of the people's warring thrust, one doesn't find any man of stature, any orator, general, or organizer; the workers who embark to capture the barracks of La Montaña or Atarazanas have never attended a tribune's speeches in the plazas, nor do they emerge from conspiratorial catacomb tongues burned in the mouths of enlightened men, whose resonance was lit with the sacred spark by the soul of the masses, nor are they seduced by the regressive, zoological ration of plunder and gastronomical revenge. During the first few weeks of the conflict, Largo Caballero, Azaña, and Prieto lose all prominence in the tremendous turmoil of the people; the military chiefs are revealed as the traders and murderers of the people; and among the army's lowest ranks, ever loyal to the government, the figures of the obscure, undecorated republican captains of the future await their moment. Hence, Bloch has claimed to have witnessed in Barcelona, Madrid, Valencia how the workers, after taking a barracks or a rebel palace, would indifferently stroll past the wardrobes, coffers, vaults, and pantries of the powerful, seized by a social emotion of victory.

From these viewpoints, popular Spanish epopoeia stands alone in history. It reveals the capacity of common people, driven by their own means and civic inspirations, to defend their rights: In a matter of months they subdue a vast military insurrection; halt two powerful, allied foreign invasions; create a revolutionary, public order, a structure, its economy, on new foundations; form a great army of the people from head to toe; and step to the frontlines of civilization to defend imperiled democracy worldwide with blood never before equaled in purity and ardor. And this entire miracle—one must insist—they consummate with their own collective, sovereign work, sufficed by itself and its incontrovertible becoming.

[*César Vallejo o Hispanoamérica en la Cruz de Su Razón* (Córdoba, Argentina: Universidad Nacional de Córdoba, 1957), 167–75]　　　　　　　　　　　　　[JM]

THE WRITER'S RESPONSIBILITY

Barcelona, July 1937

I bear greetings from my comrades to the Spanish people, who fight with supernatural devotion and vocation unprecedented in history and astonishing to the world. You're aware that Peru, like other countries in America, is living under the domination of an implacable dictatorship: this dictatorship has reached new extremes. On the streets of Lima or any Peruvian city it's now prohibited to speak about the Spanish Republic. The writers have organized an enormous campaign in the most remote regions and garnered the government's condemnation.

Along with this greeting from our writers, I bear greetings from Peru's working masses. Contrary to what you may imagine (that our country drags an old chain of ignorance and obscurity), the masses have perceived at the outset that the cause of republican Spain is the cause of the world. What is the meaning, you ask, of the swiftness with which the masses of Peru and the rest of the world have directed so much effort toward Spain? The explanation is clear: people who've suffered repression, tyranny, a dominating class' control, powerful for centuries, acquire this swiftness out of an extraordinary aspiration: long-standing pain and social oppression punish and refine man's instinct of freedom in favor of the freedom of the world, until it crystallizes in liberating action. Thus, the working masses of America fight alongside the working masses of Spain. American governments wrongly try to stop it, and despite their obstructions, detentions, and persecutions, the masses are certainly organizing support for Spain.

In the Spanish fighters, my comrades, Ibero-Americans see a cause that's all the more common insofar as we proceed from the same race and, especially, the same history, and I inflect this not with that familiar racial pride, but human pride, for one historical coincidence has placed the American people so close to the fate of Mother Spain. America sees Spain fulfilling its historical destiny, and this continuity consists in the fact that it's fallen to Spain to be the creator of continents; she pulled one continent out of the same thin air that today she pulls the world.

Over the course of these debates, my comrades, I've watched every delegate come from his respective country with a gravelly voice, like a herald of revolutionary life; but to my understanding there's a point that's barely been touched upon which turns out to be one of the gravest and should've been treated with greater diligence, namely, the writer's responsibility with regard to History and, especially, the most serious moments of History. This poor aspect of the writer's professional awareness has been addressed admirably by Dutch writer Grao.

Let's speak briefly about that responsibility, for I believe that, now more than ever, free writers are wont to determine the circumstance with the people, make their intelligence reach the people's, and shatter the secular barrier between intelligence and the people, between spirit and matter. As we know, these barriers were created by the ruling classes prior to the monarchy's control. Therefore, fellow writers of the Second International Antifascist Congress, I deem it necessary, not for the spirit to go to matter, as any writer of the ruling class would say, but for matter to draw near the spirit of intelligence, horizontally not vertically, man to man.

Jesus said, "My kingdom is not of this world." I believe the time has come for the awareness of the revolutionary writer to be synthesized in a formula that will replace the former by saying, "My kingdom is of this world, but also of the other."

Unfortunately, awareness of professional responsibility lacks self-confidence among most writers of the world. These are the ones who side with fascism because they're blind to their historical action; but on our side we have the best thinkers, qualitatively. The proof is that writers of the greatest intrinsic courage have come to this congress to manifest their support of the Spanish people. Further proof of the writer's unawareness of his responsibility is that, through these difficult times, most writers keep quiet in response to the ruling governments' persecutions; nobody utters a word against them, and this is a very convenient attitude. At these violent hours when the police and armed forces are threatening lives, writers must raise their voices and have the courage to protest that tyranny.

One of the most notable comrades said we should demand the International Workers to place more pressure on the masses so that they express their protest against the attitudes of their respective governments and so that they take to the street, with the goal of supporting republican Spain's undeniable right to defend itself against foreign invasion.

We're the ones responsible for what happens in the world, because we have the most formidable weapon—the word. Archimedes said, "Give me a lever, the right word, and the right material, and I will move the world." Since we possess that lever, our pen, it's our job to move the world with our weapon.

Naturally, the problem breaks down to the type of person a writer is and what interests he has, because we're not mobilizing our pens, we're not standing up to the governments, the opposing press, the so-called neutral writers. In most cases, we're not heroic; we have no spirit of sacrifice. Charlot said, "We writers feel a shame so terrible it makes us lower our heads, and it's the shame of being writers." Our time has come to assume this role courageously no matter how propitious or detrimental the government may be.

I'm abusing the short time that we have here. This congress hasn't convened to discuss problems of professional technique, but we have come with an objective. We've come on a professional mission that consists in realizing the raw material that each writer-creator has—direct contact with Spanish reality—which today more than ever can bear ripe fruit.

For revolutionary writers like us, a man of culture is one who contributes individually and socially to the development of the collective, in free terrain, concordance, harmony, and with justice for common and individual progress.

When we learned how the Fifth Regiment had saved the artistic treasures found in the palace of the Duque de Alba at the price of one fatality, some intellectuals might have wondered, "Could the concept of culture be diffused to the point that man must be the slave of what he's made by sacrificing his life for a sculpture or painting?" For us, the concept of culture is something else: we believe that museums are perishable works of man's greater capacity, and we want—within this radius of artistic vision, of this almost absurd ideal—this tragic contingency of the Spanish people to happen the other way around.

In the midst of a battle that frees the Spanish people and the world as a whole, let the museums and subjects portrayed in those paintings receive such a breath of vitality that they too become soldiers on the side of humanity. We must realize our mission here and, when we return to our countries, we mustn't forget the situation of this fight of the Spanish people but rather mobilize the spirits, the masses, in favor of the Spanish Republic.

One more word, and I will finish. This congress is called the Congress for the Defense of Culture, but it's unlikely that the intellectuals of the world will agree. A few years ago, this topic was the matter of a most interesting discussion to see whether a man is cultured or not. One English writer said, "The cultured man is an honorable man who meticulously fulfills his duties, his friendships, etc., even when he's completely ignorant, incompetent, and doesn't know how to appreciate a symphony by Beethoven." A French man said, "For us a cultured man is one who has specialized in a field, and in that field has made a discovery to benefit humanity, even if he's dishonest and dishonorable."

We must clearly understand our task. When we return to our countries we mustn't forget the Spanish combatants. Everyone must mobilize support of republican Spain. How emotional it is in literary circles and among workers to wait for news, books, pamphlets, and placards from Spain! And yet what a joy it is to greet those messages and their heralds!

I propose that a propaganda campaign be organized by intellectuals: legal Spain can take pride in its artists and writers, since all true artists have placed themselves at its disposal. South America awaits you! America hopes that you transmit the voice of Spain, that you incite the Committees of Aid and the groups of intellectuals that fight for Spain in South America.

The names of Spanish poets, young and old, ring with familiarity. There is even a cult of Machado. And the masses know who Rafael Alberti is, and Bergamín, León Felipe, Prados, Altolaguirre, Cernuda, Aleixandre, Serrano Plaja, Rafael Diestre, Miguel Hernández, Gil Albert, Aparicio, Herrera Petere. In the land of Rubén Darío and José Asunción Silva, of Herrera Reissig, Enrique Banchs, and our dear Pablo Neruda, the poets of

Spain were never more praised than they are today. And here, between tears and smiles, I open my burning South American heart, my Spanish heart that's never felt more Spanish: for the famous Antonio Machado now up there in age, I salute the tradition of Spain, and, in memory of Federico García Lorca, I renew the protest of all South America against the limitless crime of fascism!

[*El Mono Azul* (Madrid), no. 4, 1939] [JM]

From *Human Poems*

Today I would like to be happy willingly,
to be happy and behave leafy with questions,
by temperament to open wide my room, like a mad man,
and to demand, in short,
reclined on my physical trust,
only to see if they would like,
only to see if they would like to try my spontaneous position,
to demand, I keep saying,
why they hit me like this so much in my soul.

For I would like in substance to be happy,
to proceed without cane, laic humility, or black jackass.
Thus the sensations of this world,
the subjunctive songs,
the pencil that I lost in my cavity
and my beloved organs for crying.

Persuadable brother, comrade,
father through greatness, mortal son,
friend and opponent, immense document of Darwin:
at what hour, then, will they come with my portrait?
At the delights? Perhaps around delight shrouded?
Earlier? Who knows, at the disputations?

At the misericordias, comrade,
fellow man in rejection and observation, neighbor
in whose enormous neck rises and lowers,
naked, without thread, my hope . . .
[1937]   [CE]

_____

POEM TO BE READ AND SUNG

I know there is a person
who looks for me in her hand, day and night,
finding me, every minute, in her shoes.
Doesn't she know that the night is buried
with spurs behind the kitchen?

I know there is a person composed of my parts,
who I make whole when my waist
gallops off on its punctual little stone.
Doesn't she know that the coin
imprinted with her effigy will not return to her coffer?

I know the day,
but the sun has escaped me;
I know the universal act she performed in her bed
with alien courage and that tepid water, whose
superficial frequency is a mine.
Is that person, perhaps, so small
that even her own feet step on her?

A cat is the boundary between her and me,
right at the edge of its measure of water.
I see her on the street corners, her robe
opening and closing, formerly an inquiring palm tree . . .
What can she do but change weeping?

But she looks and looks for me. What a story!
[September 7, 1937]   [CE]

———————

The tip of man,
the petty mockery of shrinking
after smoking his universal ash;
tip yielding to secret snails,
tip one grasps wearing gloves,
tip Monday restrained with six bridles,
tip emerging from listening to his soul.

Otherwise,
the soldiers could have been fine rain
and neither square gunpowder, returning from their brave follies,
nor deadly bananas; only
a bit of sideburn on the silhouette.
Otherwise, walking fathers-in-law,
brothers-in-law on a sonorous mission,
sons-in-law by the most unpleasant route of a rubber,

all the equine grace walking
can flash resplendently!

Oh to think geometrically against the light!
Oh not to die lowly
from majesty so swift and so fragrant!
Oh not to sing; barely
to write and to write with a little stick
or with the edge of a restless ear!

Pencil chord, deafest eardrum,
stirrut[4] in robust halves
and to eat by heart choice meat,
ham, if there is no meat,
and a piece of cheese with female worms,
males worms and dead worms.

September 14, 1937

[CE]

––––––––––––––

My chest wants and does not want its color,
through whose rough paths I go, I cry with a stick,
try to be happy, cry in my hand,
remember, write
and rivet a tear into my cheekbone.

Evil wants its red, good its red reddened
by the suspended ax,
by the trot of the wing flying on foot,
and man does not want, sensitively
does not want this;
he does not want to be lying down
in his soul, horn throbs in his temples,
the bimanous, the very brutish, the very philosophical.

Thus, I am almost not, I collapse
from the plow with which I succor my soul
and almost, in proportion, almost exalt myself.
To know why this dog dogs life,
why I cry, why,
big-browed, inept, fickle, I was born

screaming;
to know it, to comprehend it
to the sound of a competent alphabet
would be to suffer for an ingrate.

And no! No! No! Neither scheme, nor ornament!
Anguish, yes, with a yes firm and frenetic,
coriaceous, rapacious, want and does not want, sky and pecker;
anguish, yes, with all my zipper.
Struggle between two sobs, theft of a sole chance,
painless path on which I endure in clogs
the velocity of walking blind.

September 22, 1937   [CE]

———————

I stayed on to warm up the ink in which I drown
and to listen to my alternative cavern,
tactile nights, abstracted days.

The unknown shuddered in my tonsil
and I creaked for an annual melancholy,
solar nights, lunar days, Parisian sunsets.

And still, this very day, at dusk
I digest the most sacred certainties,
maternal nights, great-granddaughter days,
bicolored, voluptuous, urgent, lovely.

And yet
I arrive, I reach myself in a two-seated plane
under the domestic morning and the mist
which emerged eternally from an instant.

And still,
even now,
at the tail of the comet in which I have earned
my happy and doctoral bacillus,
behold that warm, listener, male earth, sun and male moon,
incognito I cross the cemetery,
head off to the left, splitting
the grass with a pair of hendecasyllables,

tombal years, infinitary liters,
ink, pen, bricks and forgiveness.

    September 24, 1937 [CE]

    The peace, the wausp,[5] the shoe heel, the slopes,
the dead one, the deciliters, the owl,
the places, the ringworm, the sarcophagi, the glass, the brunettes,
the ignorance, the kettle, the altar boy,
the drops, the oblivion,
the potentate, the cousins, the archangels, the needle,
the priests, the ebony, the rebuff,
the part, the type, the stupor, the soul . . .

    Flexible, saffroned, external, neat,
portable, old, thirteen, blood-smeared,
those photographed, ready, tumescent,
those linked, long, beribboned, perfidious . . .

    Burning, comparing,
living, raging,
striking, analyzing, hearing, shuddering,
dying, standing firm, succeeding, weeping . . .

    After, these, here,
after, above,
perhaps, while, behind, so much, so never,
below, by chance, distant,
always, that one, tomorrow, how much,
how much! . . .

    The horrible, the sumptuous, the slowest,
the august, the fruitless,
the ominous, the convulsive, the wet, the fatal,
the whole, the purest, the lugubrious,
the bitter, the satanic, the tactile, the profound . . .

    September 25, 1937 [CE]

Confidence in glasses, *not* in the eye;
in the staircase, never in the step;
in the wing, *not* in the bird
and in yourself alone, in yourself alone, in yourself alone.

Confidence in wickedness, *not* in the wicked;
in the glass, but never in the liquor;
in the corpse, not in the man
and in yourself alone, in yourself alone, in yourself alone.

Confidence in many, but no longer in one;
in the riverbed, never in the current;
in pants, not in legs
and in yourself alone, in yourself alone, in yourself alone.

Confidence in the window, not in the door;
in the mother, but not in the nine months;
in destiny, not in the gold die,
and in yourself alone, in yourself alone, in yourself alone.

October 5, 1937   [CE]

———————

Alfonso:[6] you are looking at me, I see,
from the implacable plane where
the lineal always, the lineal nevers, dwell
(That night, you slept, between your dream
and my dream, on rue de Riboutté)
Palpably,
your unforgettable cholo hears you walk
in Paris, he feels you go silent on the phone
and it is your last act's turn on the wire
to test its weight, to drink
to the depths, to me, to you.

I still
buy "du vin, du lait, comptant les sous"
under my overcoat, so that my soul will not see me,
under my overcoat that one, dear Alfonso,
and under the simple ray of my compound temple;
I still suffer, and you, not now, never again, brother!
(I have been told that in your centuries of pain,

beloved being,[7]
beloved to be,
you made zeros of wood. Is that true?)

In the "boîte de nuit," where you played tangos,
your indignant child playing out his heart,
escorting yourself, crying
for yourself and for your enormous resemblance to your shadow,
Monsieur Fourgat, the owner, has aged.
To let him know? To tell him about it? No more,
Alfonso; that's it, not now!

Hôtel des Écoles is open as always
and they still buy tangerines;
but I suffer, like I say,
sweetly, remembering
what we both suffered, in both of our deaths,
in the opening of the double tomb,
of that other tomb with your being,
and of this mahogany one with your to be;
I suffer, drinking a glass of you, Silva,
a glass to straighten me out, as we used to say,
and afterward, we'll see what happens . . .

This is the other toast, among three,
solemn, diverse
in wine, in world, in glass, the one that we raised
more than once to the body
and, less than once, to the mind.
Today is even more different;
today I suffer bitterly sweet,
I drink your blood as to Christ the hard,
I eat your bone as to Christ the soft,
because I love you, two by two, Alfonso,
and could almost say so, eternally.

October 9, 1937 [CE]

Chances are, I'm another; walking, at dawn, another who proceeds
around a long disk, an elastic disk:
a mortal, figurative, audacious diaphragm.
Chances are, I remember while waiting, I annotate marble
where scarlet index, and where bronze cot,
an absent, spurious, enraged fox.
Chances are, a man after all,
my shoulders anointed with indigo misericordia,
chances are, I say to myself, beyond there is nothing.

The sea gives me the disk, referring it,
with a certain dry margin, to my throat;
nothing, truly, more acidic, sweeter, more Kantian!
But somebody else's sweat, but a serum
or tempest of meekness,
decaying or rising—that, never!

Lying down, slender, I exhume myself,
smashing my way into the tumefied mixture,
without legs, without adult clay, nor weapons,
a needle stuck in the great atom . . .
No! Never! Never yesterday! Never later!

Hence this satanic tuber,
this moral plesiosaurian molar
and these posthumous suspicions,
this index, this bed, these tickets.

October 21, 1937   [CE]

THE BOOK OF NATURE

Professor of sobbing—I said to a tree—
staff of quicksilver, rumorous
linden, at the bank of the Marne, a good student
is reading in your deck of cards, in your dead foliage,
between the evident water and the false sun,
his three of hearts, his queen of diamonds.

Rector of the chapters of heaven,
of the burning fly, of the manual calm there is in asses;
rector of deep ignorance, a bad student
is reading in your deck of cards, in your dead foliage,

the hunger for reason that maddens him
and the thirst for dementia that drives him mad.

Technician of shouts, conscious tree, strong,
fluvial, double, solar, double, fanatic,
connoisseur of cardinal roses, totally
embedded, until drawing blood, in stingers, a student
is reading in your deck of cards, in your dead foliage,
his precocious, telluric, volcanic, king of spades.

Oh professor, from having been so ignorant!
oh rector, from trembling so much in the air!
oh technician, from so much bending over!
Oh linden, oh murmurous staff by the Marne!

    October 21, 1937   [CE]

The anger that breaks the man into children,
that breaks the child into equal birds,
and the bird, afterward, into little eggs;
the anger of the poor
has one oil against two vinegars.

The anger that breaks the tree into leaves,
the leaf into unequal buds
and the bud, into telescopic grooves;
the anger of the poor
has two rivers against many seas.

The anger that breaks goodness into doubts,
doubt, into three similar arcs
and the arc, then, into unforeseeable tombs;
the anger of the poor
has one sword against two daggers.

The anger that breaks the soul into bodies,
the body into dissimilar organs
and the organ, into octave thoughts;
the anger of the poor
has one central fire against two craters.

    October 26, 1937   [CE]

INTENSITY AND HEIGHT

I want to write, but out comes foam,
I want to say so much and I mire;
there is no spoken cipher which is not a sum,
there is no written pyramid, without a core.

I want to write, but I feel like a puma;
I want to laurel myself, but I stew in onions.
There is no spoken coughv,[8] which doesn't come to brume,
there is no god nor son of god, without progression.

For that, then, let's go eat grass,
the flesh of sobs, the fruit of wails,
our melancholy soul canned.

Let's go! Let's go! I'm struck;
let's go drink that already drunk,
raven, let's go fecundate your mate.

October 27, 1937   [CE]

———————

GUITAR

The pleasure of suffering, of hating, dyes
my throat with plastic venoms,
but the bristle that implants its magic order,
its taurine grandeur, between the first string
and the sixth
and the mendacious eighth, suffers them all.

The pleasure of suffering . . . Who? whom?
who, the molars? whom society,
the carbides of rage in the gums?
How to be
and to be here, without angering one's neighbor?

You are worthier than my number, man alone,
and worthier than all the dictionary,
with its prose in poetry,
its poetry in prose,
are your eagle display,
your tiger machinery, bland fellow man.

The pleasure of suffering,
of hoping for hope at the table,
Sunday with all its languages
Saturday with Chinese, Belgian hours,
the week, with two hockers.

The pleasure of waiting in slippers,
of waiting cringing behind a line,
of waiting empowered with a sick pintle;[9]
the pleasure of suffering: hard left by a female
dead with a stone on her waist
and dead between the string and the guitar,
crying the days and singing the months.

    October 28, 1937   [CE]

THE NINE MONSTERS

AND, unfortunately,
pain grows in the world all the time,
grows thirty minutes a second, step by step,
and the nature of the pain, is twice the pain
and the condition of the martyrdom, carnivorous, voracious,
is twice the pain
and the function of the purest grass, twice
the pain
and the good of being, our dolor doubled.

Never, human men,
was there so much pain in the chest, in the lapel, in the wallet,
in the glass, in the butcher's shop, in arithmetic!
Never so much painful affection,
never did the distance charge so close,
never did the fire ever
play better its role of dead cold!
Never, Mr. Minister of Health, was health
more mortal,
did the migraine extract so much forehead from the forehead!
Did the cabinet have in its drawer, pain,
the heart, in its drawer, pain,
the lizard, in its drawer, pain.

    Misfortune grows, brother men,
faster than the machine, at ten machines and grows
with Rousseau's livestock, with our beards;
evil grows for reasons we know not
and is a flood with its own liquids,
its own mud and its own solid cloud!
Suffering inverts positions, it acts
in that the aqueous humor is vertical
to the pavement,
the eye is seen and this ear heard,
and this ear sounds nine strokes at the hour
of lightning, and nine guffaws
at the hour of wheat, and nine female sounds
at the hour of weeping, and nine canticles
at the hour of hunger, and nine thunderclaps
and nine lashes, minus a scream.

    The pain grabs us, brother men,
from behind, in profile,
and drives us wild in the movies,
nails us to the gramophones,
unnails us in bed, falls perpendicularly
onto our tickets, our letters,
and it is very serious to suffer, one might pray . . .
For as a result
of the pain, there are some
who are born, others grow, others die,
and others who are born and do not die, others
who die, without having been born, and others
who neither are born nor die (the majority)
And likewise as a result
of suffering, I am sad
up to my head, and sadder down to my ankle,
from seeing bread, crucified, the turnip,
bloodied,
the onion, crying,
cereal, in general, flour,
salt, made dust, water, fleeing,
wine, an ecce-homo,
such pallid snow, such an arduent[10] sun!

How, human brothers,
not to tell you that I can no longer stand it and
can no longer stand so much drawer,
so much minute, so much
lizard and so much
inversion, so much distance and so much thirst for thirst!
Mr. Minister of Health: what to do?
Ah! unfortunately, human men,
there is, brothers, much too much to do.

    November 3, 1937   [CE]

———————

A man walks by with a baguette on his shoulder
Am I going to write, after that, about my double?

Another sits, scratches, extracts a louse from his armpit, kills it
How dare one speak about psychoanalysis?

Another has entered my chest with a stick in hand
To talk then about Socrates with the doctor?

A cripple passes by holding a child's hand
After that I'm going to read André Breton?

Another trembles from cold, coughs, spits blood
Will it ever be possible to allude to the deep Self?

Another searches in the much for bones, rinds
How to write, after that, about the infinite?

A bricklayer falls from a roof, dies and no longer eats lunch
To innovate, then, the trope, the metaphor?

A merchant cheats a customer out of a gram
To speak, after that, about the fourth dimension?

A banker falsifies his balance sheet
With what face to cry in the theater?

An outcast sleeps with his foot behind his back
To speak, after that, to anyone about Picasso?

Someone goes to a burial sobbing
How then become a member of the Academy?

Someone cleans a rifle in his kitchen
How dare one speak about the beyond?

Someone passes by counting with his fingers
How speak of the non-self without screaming?

November 5, 1937   [CE]

THE SOUL THAT SUFFERED FROM BEING ITS BODY

You suffer from an endocrine gland, it's obvious,
or, perhaps,
suffer from me, from my tacit, start sagacity.
Your endure the diaphanous anthropoid, over there, nearby,
where the tenebrous darkness is.
You revolve around the sun, grabbing on to your soul,
extending your corporal Juans
and adjusting your collar; that's obvious.
You know what aches you,
what leaps on your rump,
what descends through you by rope to the ground.
You, poor man, you live; don't deny it,
if you die; don't deny it,
if you die from your age, ay, and from your epoch.
And, even if you cry, you drink,
and, even if you bleed, you nourish your hybrid eyetooth,
your wistful candle and your private parts.
You suffer, you endure and again you suffer horribly,
miserable ape,
Darwin's lad,
bailiff spying on me, most atrocious microbe.
And you know this so well,
that you ignore it, bursting into tears.
You, then, were born; that
too is obvious at a distance, poor devil and shut up,
and you put up with the street fate gave you
and you question your navel: where? how?

My friend, you are completely,
up to your hair, in the year thirty-eight,
Nicolas or Santiago, someone or other,

either with yourself or with your abortion or with
me
and captive in your enormous freedom,
dragged on by your autonomous Hercules . . .
But if you calculate on your fingers up to two,
it's worse; don't deny it, little brother.

   You say no? You say yes, but no?
Poor ape! . . . Gimme your paw! . . . No. Your hand, I meant.
To your health! Keep suffering!
      November 9, 1937   [CE]

   Let the millionaire walk naked, stark naked!
Disgrace for whoever builds his deathbed with treasures!
A world for whoever greets;
an armchair for whoever sows in the sky;
weeping for whoever finishes what he makes, keeping the beginnings;
let the spur-wearer walk;
no duration for that wall on which another wall is not growing;
give to the wretched all his wretchedness,
bread, to whoever laughs;
let the triumphs lose, the doctors die;
let there be milk in blood;
let a candle be added to the sun,
eight hundred to twenty;
let eternity pass under the bridges!
Scorn whoever gets dressed,
crown feet with hands, fit them in their size;
let my self sit next to me!
To weep having fit in that womb,
blessed be whoever observes air in the air,
many years of nail for the hammer stroke;
strip the naked,
make the cape put on pants,
let copper gleam at the expense of its plates,
majesty for whoever falls from the clay into the universe,
let the mouths weep, the looks moan,
prevent steel from enduring,

thread for the portable horizons,
twelve cities for the stone path,
a sphere for whoever plays with his shadow;
a day made of one hour, for the husband and wife;
a mother for the plow in praise of soil,
seal liquids with two seals,
let the mouthful call roll,
let the descendants be,
let the quail be,
let the race of the poplar and the tree be;
contrary to circular expectations, let the sea defeat his son
and weeping the gray hair;
leave the asps alone, fellow men,
furrow the flame with seven logs,
live,
raise the height,
lower the deepage deeper,
let the wave accompany its impulse walking,
the crypt's truce succeed!
May we die;
wash your skeleton daily;
pay no attention to me,
a lame bird for the despot and his soul;
a dreadful stain, for whoever goes it alone;
sparrows for the astronomer, for the sparrow, for the aviator!
Give off rain, beam sun,
keep an eye on Jupiter, on the thief of your gold idols,
copy your writing in three notebooks,
learn from the married when they speak, and
from the solitary, when they are silent;
give the sweethearts something to eat,
the devil in your hands something to drink,
fight for justice with your nape,
make yourselves equal,
let the oak be fulfilled,
let the leopard between two oaks be fulfilled,
let us be,
let us be here,
feel how water navigates the oceans,
nourish yourselves,

let the error be conceived, since I am weeping,
accept, while goats and their young climb the crags;
make God break the habit of being a man,
grow . . . !
They are calling me. I'll be back.

  November 19, 1937   [CE]

  The fact is the place where I put on
my pants, is a house where
I take off my shirt out loud
and where I have a floor, a soul, a map of my Spain.
Just now I was speaking
about me with myself, and placing
on top of a little book a huge loaf
and I have, then, made the transfer, I've transferred,
desiring to hum a little, the right
side of life to the left side;
later, I've washed all of me, my belly,
vigorously, with dignity;
I've turned around to see what soils itself,
I've scraped what takes me so near
and have neatly arranged the map that
was nodding or weeping, I don't know.

  My house, unfortunately, is a house,
a floor fortunately, where with its
inscription my beloved little spoon lives,
my dear now unlettered skeleton,
the razor, a permanent cigar.
Truthfully, when I think
about what life is,
I can't help expressing it to Georgette,
to be able to eat something agreeable and go out,
for the afternoon, to buy a good newspaper,
to save a day for when there isn't one,
a night too, for when there is
(as one says in Peru—my apologies);
in the same way, I suffer with great care,

in order to not shout or weep, now that our eyes
have, independently of one, their poverties,
I mean, their occupation, something
that slips from the soul and falls to the soul.

    Having crossed
fifteen years; after, fifteen, and, before, fifteen,
one feels, really, a little stupid,
it's natural, on the other hand, what can one do!
And what to stop doing, that's even worse?
Only to live, only to become
what one is among millions
of loaves, among thousands of wines, among hundreds of mouths,
between the sun and its beam, a moonbeam
and among the Mass, the bread, the wine and my soul.

    Today is Sunday and, for this reason,
the idea comes to my head, the weeping to my chest
and to my throat, like a big lump.
Today is Sunday, and this fact
is many centuries old; otherwise,
it would be, perhaps, Monday, and the idea would come to my heart,
the weeping, to my brain
and to my throat, a dreadful urge to drown
what I now feel,
like a man that I am and who has suffered.
    November 21, 1937   [CE]

———————

    In short, I have nothing with which to express my life, except my death.

    And, after everything, at the end of graded nature and of the sparrow in bloc, I sleep, hand in hand with my shadow.

    And, upon descending from the venerable act and from the other moan, I repose thinking about the inexorable march of time.

    Why the rope, then, if air is so simple? What is the chain for, if iron exists on its own?

    César Vallejo, the accent with which you love, the language with which you write, the light wind with which you hear, only know of you through your throat.

César Vallejo, prostrate yourself, therefore, with vague pride, with a nuptial bed of ornamental asps and hexagonal echoes.

Return to the corporeal honeycomb, to beauty; aromatize the blossomed corks, close both grottoes to the enraged anthropoid; mend, finally, your unpleasant stag; feel sorry for yourself.

For there is nothing denser than the hate in a passive voice, no stingier udder than love!

For I'm no longer able to walk, except on two harps!

For you no longer know me, unless instrumentally, longwindedly, I follow you!

For I no longer issue worms, but briefs!

For I now implicate you so much, you almost become sharp!

For I now carry some timid vegetables and others that are fierce!

So the affection that ruptures at night in my bronchia, was brought during the day by occult deans and, if I wake up pale, it's because of my work; and, if I go to sleep red, because of my worker. This explains, equally, this weariness of mine and these spoils, my famous uncles. This explains, finally, this tear that I toast to the happiness of men.

César Vallejo, it's hard
to believe that your relatives are so late,
knowing that I walk a captive,
knowing that you lie free!
Flashy and rotten luck!
César Vallejo, I hate you with tenderness!

November 25, 1937   [CE]

THE WRETCHED

The day is about to come; wind
up your arm, look for yourself under
the mattress, stand once more
on your head, so as to walk straight.
The day is about to come, put on your coat.

The day is about to come; grip
your large intestine tightly in your hand, reflect,
before meditating, for it is horrible
when misfortune befalls one
and one's tooth falls out completely.

You have to eat, but, I tell myself,
do not grieve, for grief and graveside
sobbing do not belong to the poor;
patch yourself, remember,
trust in your white thread, smoke, call roll
on your chain and keep it behind your portrait.
The day is about to come, put on your soul.

The day is about to come; they go by,
they've opened up an eye in the hotel,
lashing it, beating it with one of your mirrors . . .
You're trembling? It is the remote state of the forehead
and the recent nation of the stomach.
They're still snoring . . . What a universe is stolen by this snore!
What state your pores are in, on judging it!
With so many twos, ay! how alone you are!
The day is about to come, put on your dream.

The day is about to come, I repeat
through the oral organ of your silence
and it is urgent to take the left with hunger
and to take the right with thirst; in any case,
abstain from being poor among the rich,
poke
your cold, for my warmth is one with it, beloved victim.
The day is about to come, put on your body.

The day is about to come;
the morning, the sea, the meteor, go
in pursuit of your weariness, with banners,
and, because of your classic pride, the hyenas
count their steps in time with the ass,
the female baker thinks about you,
the butcher thinks about you, palpating
the cleaver in which the steel
and the iron and the metal are prisoners; never forget
that during Mass there are no friends.
The day is about to come, put on your sun.

The day is coming; double
your breath, triple
your rancorous goodness
and scorn fear, connections and affectation,
for you, as one can observe in your crotch, the evil one
being aie! immortal,
have dreamed tonight that you were living
on nothing and dying from everything . . .

[End of November–First week of December 1937]   [CE]

SERMON ON DEATH

And, finally, passing now into the domain of death,
which acts as squadron, former bracket,
paragraph and key, huge hand and dieresis,
for what the Assyrian desk? for what the Christian pulpit,
the intense tug of Vandal furniture
or, even less, this proparoxytonic retreat?

Is it in order to end,
tomorrow, as a prototype of phallic display,
as diabetes and in a white chamber pot,
as a geometric face, as a dead man,
that sermon and almonds become necessary,
that there are literally too many potatoes
and this watery specter in which gold blazes
and in which the price of snow burns?
Is it for this, that we die so much?
Only to die,
must we die each instant?
And the paragraph that I write?
And the deistic bracket that I raise on high?
And the squadron in which my helmet failed?
And the key which fits all doors?
And the forensic dieresis, the hand,
my potato and my flesh and my contradiction under the bedsheet?

Out of my mind, out of my wolvum,[11] out of
my lamb, out of my sensible horsessence!
Desk, yes, my whole life long; pulpit,
likewise, my whole death long!
Sermon on barbarism: these papers;
proparoxytonic retreat: this skin.

In this way, cognitive, auriferous, thick-armed,
I will defend my catch in two moments,
with my voice and also with my larynx,
and of the physical smell with which I pray
and of the instinct for immobility with which I walk,
I will be proud while I'm alive—it must be said;
my horseflies will swell with pride,
because, at the center, I am, and to the right,
likewise, and, to the left, equally.

  December 8, 1937   [CE]

From *Spain, Take This Cup from Me*

I. HYMN TO THE VOLUNTEERS FOR THE REPUBLIC

Spanish volunteer, civilian-fighter
of veritable bones, when your heart marches to die,
when it marches to kill with its worldwide
agony, I don't know truly
what to do, where to place myself; I run, write, applaud,
weep, glimpse, destroy, they extinguish, I say
to my chest that it should end, to the good, that it should come,
and I want to ruin myself;
I bare my impersonal forehead until touching
the vessel of blood, I stop,
my size is checked by those famous architectural falls
with which the animal that honors me honors itself;
my instincts flow back to their ropes,
joy smokes before my tomb
and, again, without knowing what to do, without anything, leave me,
from my blank stone, leave me,
alone,
quadrumane, closer, much more distant,
since your long ecstatic moment won't fit between my hands,
I swirl my tininess costumed in greatness
against your double-edged speed!

One fertile, attentive, clear, diurnal day
—oh biennial, those lugubrious semesters of begging,
through which the gunpowder went biting its elbows!
oh hard sorrow and harder flints!
oh bits champed by the people!
One day the people struck their captive match, prayed with anger
and supremely full, circular,
closed their birthday with elective hands;
the despots were already dragging padlock
and in the padlock, their dead bacteria . . .

Battles? No! Passions. And passions preceded
by aches with bars of hopes,

by aches of the people with hopes of men!
Death and passion for peace, of common people!
Death and passion for war among olive trees, let's get it straight!
Thus in your breath the winds change atmospheric needles
and in your chest the tombs change key,
your frontal rising to the first power of martyrdom.

    The world exclaims: "Merely Spanish matters!" And it's true. Consider,
on balance, point-blank,
Calderón, asleep on the tail of a dead amphibian,
or Cervantes, saying: "My kingdom is of this world, but
also of the next one": point and edge in two roles!
Contemplate Goya, on his knees and praying before a mirror,
Coll, the paladin in whose Cartesian assault
a simple walk had the sweat of a cloud,
or Quevedo, that instantaneous grandfather of the dynamiters,
or Cajal, devoured by his tiny infinite, or even
Teresa, a woman, dying because she was not dying,
or Lina Odena, in conflict with Teresa on more than one point . . .
(Every act or brilliant voice comes from the people
and goes toward them, directly or conveyed
by incessant filaments, by the rosy smoke
of bitter watchwords which failed)
Thus your child, civilian-fighter, thus your anemic child,
stirred by a motionless stone,
sacrifices herself, wanders off,
decays upward and through her incombustible flame rises,
rises to the weak,
distributing spains to the bulls,
bulls to the doves . . .

    Proletarian who dies of universe, in what frantic harmony
your grandeur will end, your extreme poverty, your propelling whirlpool,
your methodical violence, your theoretical and practical chaos, your
    Dantesque
hunger, so very Spanish, to love, even treacherously, your enemy!
Liberator wrapped in shackles,
without whose effort extension would still be today without handles,
nails would wander headless,
the day, ancient, slow, reddened,
our beloved skulls, unburied!

Peasant fallen with your green foliage for man,
with the social inflection of your little finger,
with your ox that remains, with your physics,
likewise with your word tied to a stick
and your rented sky
and with clay inserted into your fatigue
and with that under your fingernail, walking!
Agricultural
builders, civilian and military,
of a busy, swarming eternity: it was written
that you would create the light, half-closing
your eyes in death;
that, at the cruel fall of your mouths,
abundance will come on seven platters, everything
in the world will be suddenly gold
and the gold,
fabulous beggars for your own secretion of blood,
and the gold itself will then be of gold!

All men will love each other
and will eat holding the corners of your sad handkerchiefs
and will drink in the name
of your ill-fated throats!
They will rest walking at the edge of this course,
they will sob thinking of your orbits, fortunate
they will be and to the sound
of your atrocious, burgeoned, inborn return,
they will adjust their chores tomorrow, the figures they've dreamt and
    sung!

The same shoes will fit whoever climbs
without trails to his body
and whoever descends to the form of his soul!
Entwining each other the mutes will speak, the paralyzed will walk!
The blind, now returning, will see
and throbbing the deaf will hear!
The ignorant will know, the wise will not!
Kisses will be given that you could not give!
Only death will die! The ant
will bring morsels of bread to the elephant chained
to his brutal gentleness; aborted children

will be born again perfect, spatial
and all men will work,
all men will beget,
all men will understand!

    Worker, our savior and redeemer,
forgive us, brother, our debts!
As a drum says in its roll, in its adagios:
what an ephemeral never, your back!
what a changing always, your profile!

    Italian volunteer, among whose animals of battle
an Abyssinian lion is limping!
Soviet volunteer, marching at the head of your universal chest!
Volunteers from the south, from the north, from the east
and you, the westerner, closing the funereal song of the dawn!
Known soldier, whose name
flies by in the sound of an embrace!
Fighter who the earth raised, arming you
with dust,
shoeing you with positive magnets,
your personal beliefs in force,
distinct in character, your ferule intimate,
complexion immediate,
your language moving about your shoulders
and your soul crowned with cobblestones!
Volunteer bound by your cold,
temperate or torrid zone,
heroes in the round,
victim in a column of conquerors:
in Spain, in Madrid, the command is
to kill, volunteers who fight for life!

    Because in Spain they kill, others kill
the child, his toy that stops working,
radiant mother Rosenda,
old Adam who talked out loud with his horse
and the dog that slept on the stairs.
They kill the book, they fire at its auxiliary verbs,
at its defenseless first page!
They kill the exact case of the statue,

the sage, his cane, his colleague,
the neighborhood barber next door—maybe he cut me,
but a good man and, then, unlucky;
the beggar who yesterday was singing out in front,
the nurse who today passed by crying,
the priest burdened with the stubborn height of his knees . . .

    Volunteers,
for life, for the good ones, kill
death, kill the evil ones!
Do it for the freedom of all,
of the exploited and the exploiter,
for a painless peace—I glimpse it
when I sleep at the foot of my forehead
and even more when I go around shouting—
and do it, I keep saying,
for the illiterate to whom I write,
for the barefoot genius and his lamb,
for the fallen comrades,
their ashes clasped to the corpse of a road!

    So that you,
volunteers for Spain and for the world, would come,
I dreamt that I was good, and it was to see
your blood, volunteers . . .
Since then there's been much chest, much anxiety,
many camels old enough to pray.
Today good on your behalf marches in flames,
reptiles with immanent eyelashes follow you affectionately
and, at two steps, one step,
the direction of the water coursing to see its limit before it burns.

          [CE]

III

    He used to write with his big finger in the air:
"Long live all combanions! Pedro Rojas,"[12]
from Miranda de Ebro, father and man,
husband and man, railroad-worker and man,
father and more man, Pedro and his two deaths.

Wind paper, he was killed: pass on!
Flesh pen, he was killed: pass on!
Advise all combanions quick!

Stick on which they have hanged his log,
he was killed;
he was killed at the base of his big finger!
They have killed, in one blow, Pedro, Rojas!

Long live all combanions
written at the head of his air!
Let them live with this buzzard b in Pedro's
and in Rojas's
and in the hero's and in the martyr's guts!

Searching him, dead, they surprised
in his body a great body, for
the soul of the world,
and in his jacket a dead spoon.

Pedro too used to eat
among the creatures of his flesh, to clean up, to paint
the table and to live sweetly
as a representative of everyone.
And this spoon was in his jacket,
awake or else when he slept, always,
dead alive spoon, this one and its symbols.
Advise all combanions quick!
Long live all combanions at the base of this spoon forever!

He was killed, they forced him to die,
Pedro, Rojas, the worker, the man, the one
who was born a wee baby, looking at the sky,
and who afterward grew up, blushed
and fought with his cells, his nos, his yets, his hungers, his pieces.
He was killed softly
in his wife's hair, Juana Vásquez by name,
at the hour of fire, in the year of the gunshot,
and when he was already close to everything.

Pedro Rojas, thus, after being dead,
got up, kissed his blood-smeared casket,
wept for Spain

and again wrote with his finger in the air:
"Long live all combanions! Pedro Rojas."
His corpse was full of world.

    November 7, 1937   [CE]

IV

    The beggars fight for Spain,
begging in Paris, in Rome, in Prague
thus authenticating, with an imploring, Gothic hand,
the Apostles' feet, in London, in New York, in Mexico City.
The mendicants fight satanically begging
God for Santander,
the combat in which no longer is anyone defeated.
They deliver themselves to
the old suffering, they glut their fury at the foot of the individual,
by weeping social lead,
and they attack with moans, these beggars,
killing by merely being beggars.

    Pleas of the infantry,
in which the weapon pleads from the metal up,
and wrath pleads, this side of the wrathful gunpowder.
Tacit squadrons which fire
their meekness, with mortal cadence,
from a doorway, from themselves, ay, from themselves.
Potential fighters
without socks when shoeing thunder,
satanic, numerical,
dragging their titles of strength,
crumb under belt,
double-caliber rifle: blood and blood.
The poet hails armed suffering!

    October 23, 1937   [CE]

VIII

Back here,
Ramón Collar,
your family carries on from rope to rope,
one after another,

while you visit, you, out there, at the hour of seven swords, in Madrid,
at the Madrid front.

Ramón Collar, ox-driver
and solder even son-in-law of his father-in-law,
husband, son bordering the old Son of Man!
Ramón of sorrow, you, brave Collar,
paladin of Madrid and by sheer balls; Ramonete,
back here,
your folks think a lot about your combed hair!

Anxious, quick to cry, during the tear!
And during the drums, they walk; they speak
before your ox, during the earth!

Ramón! Collar! To you! If you are wounded,
don't act up when you succumb; restrain yourself!
Back here,
your capacity for cruelty is in little boxes;
back here,
your dark trousers, after a while,
finally know how to walk in utter solitude, how to wear out;
back here,
Ramón, your father-in-law, the old man,
loses you each time he encounters his daughter!

I tell you that back here they've eaten your flesh,
without realizing it,
your chest, without realizing it,
your foot;
but they all brood over your steps crowned with dust!

They've prayed to God,
back here;
they've sat on your bed, talking loudly
between your solitude and your little things;
I don't know who has taken over your plow, don't know who
went after you, nor who returned from your horse!

Back here, Ramón Collar, at last, your friend!
Greetings, man of God, kill and write!
    September 10, 1937   [CE]

X. WINTER DURING THE BATTLE FOR TERUEL

Water falls from washed revolvers!
Precisely
it is the metallic grace of the water,
in the nocturnal afternoon in Aragón,
in spite of the constructed grass,
the burning vegetables, the industrial plants.

Precisely
it is the serene branch of Chemistry,
the branch of explosives in one hair,
the branch of automobiles in frequencies and good-byes.

This is how man responds, as well, to death,
this is how he looks forward and listens sideways,
this is how water, contrary to blood, is made of water,
this is how fire, the opposite of ash, smooths its frozen ruminants.

Who goes there, under the snow? Are they killing? No.
Precisely
it is life wagging along, with its second rope.

And war is utter horror, it incites,
it makes one long, eye-filled;
war entombs, fells,
makes one make an odd anthropoid leap!
You smell it, companion, perfectly,
upon stepping
distractedly on your arm among the corpses;
you see it, for you touched your testicles, blushing intensely;
you hear it in your natural soldier's mouth.

Let's go, then, companion;
your alerted shadow awaits us,
your quartered shadow awaits us,
noon captain, night common soldier . . .
That is why, on referring to this agony,
I withdraw from myself shouting wildly:
Down with my corpse! . . . And sob.

[CE]

From *Spain, Take This Cup from Me*　531

XII. MASS

At the end of the battle,
the combatant dead, a man approached him
and said to him: "Don't die; I love you so much!"
But the corpse, alas! kept on dying.

Two more came up to him and repeated:
"Don't leave us! Be brave! Come back to life!"
But the corpse, alas! kept on dying.

Twenty, a hundred, a thousand, five hundred thousand appeared,
crying out: "So much love, and no power against death!"
But the corpse, alas! kept on dying.

Millions of individuals surrounded him,
with a common plea: "Don't leave us, brother!"
But the corpse, alas! kept on dying.

Then, all the inhabitants of the earth
surrounded him; the corpse looked at them sadly, deeply moved;
he got up slowly,
embraced the first man; started to walk . . .

     November 10, 1937   [CE]

XV. SPAIN, TAKE THIS CUP FROM ME

Children of the world,
if Spain falls—I mean, it's just a thought—
it her forearm
falls downward from the sky seized,
in a halter, by two terrestrial plates;
children, what an age of concave temples!
how early in the sun what I was telling you!
how quickly in your chest the ancient noise!
how old your 2 in the notebook!

Children of the world, mother
Spain is with her belly on her back;
our teacher is with her ferules,
she appears as mother and teacher,
cross and wood, because she gave your height,
vertigo and division and addition, children;
she is with herself, legal parents!

If she falls—I mean, it's just a thought—if Spain
falls, from the earth downward,
children, how you will stop growing!
how the year will punish the month!
how you will never have more than ten teeth,
how the diphthong will remain in downstroke, the gold star in tears!
How the little lamb will stay
tied by its leg to the great inkwell!
How you'll descend the steps of the alphabet
to the letter in which pain was born!

Children,
sons of fighters, meanwhile,
lower your voice, for right at this moment Spain is distributing
her energy among the animal kingdom,
little flowers, comets, and men.
Lower your voice, for she
shudders convulsively, not knowing
what to do, and she has in her hand
the talking skull, chattering away,
the skull, the one with a braid,
the skull, the one with life!

Lower your voice, I tell you;
lower your voice, the song of the syllables, the wail
of matter and the faint murmur of the pyramids, and even
that of your temples which walk with two stones!
Lower your breathing, and if
the forearm comes down,
if the ferules sound, if it is night,
if the sky fits between two terrestrial limbos,
if there is noise in the creaking of doors,
if I am late,
if you do not see anyone, if the blunt pencils
frighten you, if mother
Spain falls—I mean, it's just a thought—
go out, children of the world, go look for her! . . .

[CE]

From *The Tired Stone*

ACT 1
Scene 1

The scene displays several megalithic walls, forming part of a bastion under construction at the Sajsawaman fortress. Porticoes, corridors, stairways. Some trapezoidal windows already finished, others incomplete. At the base of the walls, loose blocks of different sizes, thick pikes, large handbarrows, and other materials and tools of the stonemasons. Cyclopean atmosphere. Before the program begins, the curtain is already raised, and the decoration is, therefore, visible to the audience. When the bell rings, all the lights of the theater go off and complete darkness and silence reign. Dawn slowly reaches the largest of the blocks that are loose at the base of the walls, leaving the rest of the stage in darkness. When the brightness of day floods the scene, TOLPOR *appears seated at the base of the lit block, with his elbows resting on his knees and his face in his hands, sunken in deliberation. Approaching footsteps of a crowd echo around the scene. Out of the rhythmic tumultuous noise of these footsteps, the Hymn to the Sun is recited without interruption, while stonecutters and stonemasons hurry to work, with their tools in hand. Positioned across the scene, they sing the hymn in an unwavering chorus, while the sun rises behind the walls of the bastion.* TOLPOR *raises his head and rubs his eyes.*

QUECHUAS (*finishing the song, they greet one another*): Ama sua! Ama llulla! Ama kella! . . .[13] (*They surround the giant stone and try to move it with ropes and poles.*)

QUECHUA 1 (*from high on one of the walls*): Mama Rock! Beautiful stone! Another day illuminates your tiredness! Another day we're going to lift you. Will you arise? Will you finally give in to our pikes and champis? . . .[14] (*anxiously staring at the fatigued block*).

QUECHUA 2 (*from high on one of the walls*): It's useless. The Pissaj quarries have bloated guts, just like sterile women.

QUECHUA 3 (*below*): The stones of Pissaj lactate curdled milk, their earthly gaze distorted. From the time they leap from the quarry, to their placement in the fortresses, they put an end to everything—

blood, tears, many a life lost, smashed by their implacable fateful weight.

QUECHUA 4 (*below*): The stones of Pissaj are the most beautiful in the reign!

QUECHUA 5, 6, 7, 8, *and* 9 *from high on the walls, at once.*

QUECHUA 5: Telluric block, arise!

QUECHUA 6: Wretched basalt, get up!

QUECHUA 7: Lugubrious rock!

QUECHUA 8: Whole stone, proud as you are! Stone stone! Basalt grain chosen for the great spokes of simple agglutinations! Give in! Give in!

QUECHUA 9: What's wrong, Mama Rock? What's come over you? Perhaps you're sleeping? In pain? Who knows? Does it ache? Are you dreaming? . . . (*all await the stone's response again*). Answer me! . . . (*pause*).

TOLPOR (*from atop the highest wall*): Workers of the stone! Builders of palaces, citadels, and temples! Two mysterious birds have sung last night in the branches of my pepper tree: the one-winged bird and the . . .

VOICE (*anxiously interrupting*): And the apterous bird?

TOLPOR: Yes. The bird with no wings (*surprised voices and movements*). When the stars took leave, the pepper tree, unmoving as it was, began to rustle and twist, as if the tips of its leaves were writhing.

QUECHUA 10: That's what all plants do when they're sprouting.

TOLPOR: I got out of bed, looked through the keyhole of the door . . .

QUECHUA 11: Wickedness! The secrets of a tree are sacred!

TOLPOR: Seated on a lower branch—

VARIOUS (*lively*): The bird with no wings? The apterous bird?

TOLPOR: No. The bird with only one wing. A delicate little creature, but at once, god-awfully ugly! Its neck was arched toward my hut, as though it were spying on me. A shudder ran through my body. I gasped and returned to bed in horror.

VARIOUS: Beware! Violent defeats! Oh, the wretched wars!

TOLPOR: But there I was, about to leave the doorway, when I heard that mangy bird let out a long, deep, raspy caw . . . (*murmurs, excitement*).

QUECHUA 12: Before the Inca Pachacutec died, they heard the same bird cawing from the rooftop of the palace at Kassana.

VARIOUS: May Viracocha protect his people.

TOLPOR: The pepper tree then began to bellow, like it does when a storm is close. And I sensed the bird leave the branches . . .

QUECHUA 13: The flight of those birds can't be heard: it's as quiet and imperceptible as the flight of the soul when it passes from the branch of life to the branch of death.

TOLPOR: Shortly thereafter, a song—this time it was a song and no longer a caw—a song wandered off through the night. Where did that song go?

QUECHUA 14: The song of the apterous bird is the voice of fetuses still in their mothers' wombs.

QUECHUA 15: It's the voice of accursed pumas.

QUECHUA 16: It's the voice of plants that weep for humans.

TOLPOR: Good workers of the stone, architects of the greatest fortresses in the Tahuantinsuyo! There's no song sweeter or sadder than that of the wingless bird!

QUECHUA 17: Enough! Get back to work! The designs of fate don't depend on man, and neither do birdsongs.

TOLPOR (*comes down from the wall and, with a mysterious air, looks firmly at the tired stone*): It vanished along with the bird. What's happened? I don't know. (*The others, intrigued, leave* TOLPOR *alone, who turns around to face the stone, as if looking for something.*) It came right from the pepper tree and stopped here, no doubt about it . . .

QUECHUA 17: What stopped here, next to the stone?

TOLPOR (*with exaltation*): The wingless bird is here! Under the tired stone! (*They laugh;* TOLPOR *raises his voice and invokes the block.*) Weary pebble! Where is it? Did it leave? Are you hiding it? Could it be hiding beneath your mass? (*With both hands he pushes the stone and shouts, infuriated.*) Say jusca![15] Mama Rock! Where is it? Have you swallowed it? (*He pushes against it again with all his might.*)

ALL (*with sudden astonishment*): Oh! Oh! Oh! It moved! It moved!

An infinitely sad song comes from the other side of the wall. QUECHUAS *stop to listen.*

TOLPOR (*with his stunned upward gaze*): There it is! . . .

The song comes closer and becomes clearer: it's the ARCHITECT, *foreman of the workers at the fortress, who comes singing. When they see him,* TOLPOR *and the other workers hurry up and try to move the block in a vast, collective effort.*

ALL (*shocked, to the* ARCHITECT *who descends a stairway between two walls*): It's moved! The tired stone has moved!

ARCHITECT: No killing! No lying! No being lazy!

QUECHUAS: The tired stone has moved!

ARCHITECT: Good. The Inca had expressed his desire to attend the lifting. But before that, I wish to see it move for myself. Let's go. Champis! Pikes! Picks!

The curtain starts descending amid the bustle of QUECHUAS *bracing the block.*

Scene 2

As the curtain rises, center stage, total darkness, a SERVANT *squats facing the audience, on the first step of a stairway under the stage lights parallel to the audience. A clay jug with a flat base and two handles rests on the ground in front of the* SERVANT, *who sings an aria in Quechua, interjecting recitations.*

SERVANT (*after a chorus, he recites*): The rains have begun. Priests scour the color of new serpents, the uncertain future, and the mortality of the year. May Viracocha smile upon his race! May the land produce the stalk that gives shade and freshness, the seed that feeds and begets, the flower that blooms for the tabernacles, cradles, and tombs! . . . (*The* SERVANT *sings and, again, recites.*) The great celebration of the Situa is upon us. The ten doors of the ten temples shall open up wide. To the rhythm of ribbon-wrapped drums, the ñustas shall dance their way into womanhood, and from the dry, salty deserts of the south, new mitimaes shall come, bearing mysterious animals with smooth long tails! . . . (*The* SERVANT *sings, then stands up, raising his arms and the jug to the height of his face.*) Lord Sun! Father of the world! This is the cup of Kaura! . . . (*in ecstasy, facing the sky*). What will fall into my ñusta's clay cup today? . . . Yesterday it was a bug, the kind that with a soothing buzz guide the blind who live in the jungle. How did this insect make it all the way here alive? It's a miracle! Another day, a drop of blood fell from a condor flying at high altitudes. Today . . . (*eagerly putting his ear to the mouth of the jug*) what will fall? I hear a sigh inside! . . . No! . . . (*petrified*) A root! . . . A root! . . . A root with new shoots! Into the cup two roots have fallen!

The SERVANT *quickly places the jug on his head, turns his back to the audience, climbs the stairway, and disappears into the deep darkness of the scene.*

CURTAIN

Scene 3

In the Uyurqut Palace, a rectangular chamber, completely made of polished stone. Carved into the walls, four ornamental monoliths. All around, stone benches covered with feline pelts and alpaca wool cushions. On the floor, carpets and more animal skins. Right center, a door. In the wall upstage, windows open to the sky. KAURA *is sitting on the floor, on a jaguar skin, stage right. Two young* LADIES *stand and hold a small portable weft on which the ñusta weaves a sling. At the base of each monolith, an elderly* AMAUTA, *seated, consults ancient characters in smooth, wide banana leaves. Silence.*

AMAUTA 1: During the reign of Sinchi Roca, the Chosen Women of Acllawassi wove a sash out of wool from alpacas of Hatun for the heir apparent. On the sash, dyed in bright vegetable ink, all the animals of the kingdom appeared, each species in its own climate and landscape. But the precision of feathers and shadows cast on the lines of pelts was especially disconcerting. If you stared at the wonderful sash, your eyes would strangely look away . . . And so, as the heir to the throne examined it, trying to grasp its most minute details, he shed tears of blood and went blind . . .

Through the door to the right, the SERVANT *from the previous scene enters, carrying a giant jug on his head. The* AMAUTAS *and the* LADIES *turn toward him and follow him with their eyes. Only* KAURA *doesn't look at him, immersed in her weaving and reflections. The* SERVANT *walks through the chamber, ritually, slowly, and stops at the* AMAUTA, *who was speaking, placing the jug on the floor in front of the elderly man. Then he walks toward the same door and leaves in silence. Pause.*

AMAUTA 1: Unancha yawarpa! . . .[16]
AMAUTA 2 (*turning over a leaf*): The waists of the kings are rung by the people's rivers of sorrow.
AMAUTA 3: On the waists of princes all circles fit—all except one.

AMAUTA 1: Speaking of the blind: what a strange condition! Strange I say! Sibylline! One day the sun will shine in the soul of the blind and will never rise again from behind the Andes!

KAURA (*happy, carefree, examining her weave*): It looks like a slingshot way off target! Frog green, huayruro red, cinnabar, again a green and the gold of unpanned sands!

AMAUTA 4: Ñusta, remember that green on green makes for a disastrous oracle!

KAURA: Some time ago, Sajta, my cousin, who's from the Yungas, went outside one morning to hunt in the forest with her friends. Once they got into the thicket, she was the first to shoot her slingshot. The dead body of a young peasant was found a few feet away with a contusion in his forehead. His hair was still warm.

AMAUTA 3: In my mind, a murder worthy of a symbol!

KAURA: Since then, around her neck Sajta wears a tuft of hair from the Quechua involuntarily put to death by her hand, to bring piety to her life for that disgrace.

AMAUTA 1: Chanca astronomers claim that it's not good to fall in love with a corpse.

KAURA: The poor thing! He was a young man from the village, a young herder.

AMAUTA 4 (*immersed in another reflection*): One question has seized me for some time now. Out of the thirteen sins that a commoner can commit, adultery is registered in fourth place and loving a woman of nobility in seventh place, and yet the sin of adultery is punished with death by fire, while the other, death by freezing. Oh, enigma of the laws!

KAURA (*starts laughing*): Venerable amautas, love is a mysterious beast who rests its paws on four black stones: the stone of the cradle, the short-lived, startled stone of the mouth, the great stone of the chest, and the long stone of the tomb. Do you understand?

AMAUTAS 1–4: Words of great wisdom! (*enter* RUNTO KASKA).

RUNTO KASKA: Ama sua! Ama llulla! Ama kella!

KAURA: Runto Kaska, welcome.

AMAUTAS *resume their silent reading.*

RUNTO KASKA: Princess, the Inca is going to attend the raising of the tired stone tonight at Sajsawaman. The kolla[17] will also be there and wishes for you to join her entourage.

From *The Tired Stone*   539

KAURA: Kind messenger, our kolla is indulgent.

RUNTO KASKA: The most beautiful ñusta in the empire, in her own right, forms part of the Court of the Incas. On your forehead Viracocha has lit a rainbow, and the race of the sun pursues its new destiny under that arc . . .

KAURA (*rising to her feet, ill-tempered*): Runto Kaska!

RUNTO KASKA: Never in the reign have there been eyes like yours! Tunneling eyes! Bridging eyes!

KAURA (*looking through a window, gasps, terrified*): The koyllur! The koyllur, in the middle of the day!

RUNTO KASKA: Quite the contrary, a promising omen!

KAURA (*below, leaning, complaining*): In autumn, no one knows what his midday presence shall pronounce!

RUNTO KASKA: May the eastern dolmens rest in our favor! May the southern stars cross the tutelary tombs! (*silence,* RUNTO KASKA *whispers*). Kaura! (*she doesn't respond, pause*).

KAURA (*without looking up, in an exasperated plea*): Runto Kaska! Enough!

RUNTO KASKA (*getting ready to leave, also pleading*): Princess! . . . (*The ñusta, still leaning over, doesn't respond;* RUNTO KASKA *gets up and leaves.*)

AMAUTA 3 (*reading, in a deep voice*): Beyond the door, there's a road. Beyond the lips, there's silence! Beyond the wings, there's flight! . . . (KAURA, *taciturn, returns to her weft, takes a seat, and weaves.*)

AMAUTA 2 (*reading, in a deep voice*): Sadder than footsteps are the feet! Further than death is life! Greater the pain of being loved than the pain of loving!

AMAUTA 1 *stands up, takes the jug in both hands and carries it away stage right. The remaining* AMAUTAS, *two* LADIES, *and* KAURA *watch him leave, with utter concentration and seriousness.*

CURTAIN

Scene 4

The bell rings, house lights turn off, and before the curtain is raised, the sound of working en masse is heard on the stage: smashing of rocks with picks, hurried footsteps, unclear voices. Then, a distant drum roll.

Exclamations: "The Inca! The imperial entourage! The calli-sapas! The yellow princesses!" The noise of the work ceases. A female choir, coming close, intones the haylli, and the curtain is slowly raised, revealing a second section of the bastions under construction at Sajsawaman. A half-built semicircular wall, with a corridor or portico to the side, second-level left. The wall, facing the audience, gives way downstage to a sort of rotunda, with exits on both side of the stage. A CROWD *of workers with their eyes raised to the sky, submerged in mystical ecstasy, on their knees and facing the left-hand corridor, hear the invisible female choir. A profound silence then takes over the stage.*

CROWD (*standing, applauds the emperor*): Payta Yuyarina![18] Soul of light! Standard of the Aurora! Almighty Lloque! (CROWD *falls silent again, and the* QUECHUAS, *absorbed, look toward the door to the left.*)

QUECHUA 1 (*in a raised voice, as in an invocation*): Say kusca! Mama Rock! Tired stone! How many years resting in the patient embankment! How many years have crowds been swarming around you, trying to lift you up!

CROWD (*in unison*): All in vain! All in vain!

QUECHUA 2: They've stirred you by beating you good; they've begged you; they've even wept over you!

CROWD: All in vain! All in vain!

QUECHUA 3: They've called you in booming shouts, pushing you from all sides, pulling you even with ropes!

CROWD: All in vain! All in vain!

QUECHUA 4: The floodwaters turned the earth you rest on and dragged it away, but you stayed right where you are, motionless!

CROWD: Like a stone! Like a stone!

QUECHUA 5: From far away, when searching for their flocks, the herders would gaze upon you with frightful piety at dusk, as if staring at gravestones.

CROWD: All in vain! All in vain!

QUECHUA 6: The vultures and owls would perch on your chest at night; by day, the warbles from the trees and the grunts of the burrows would coo through your mysterious silence—your tenacious material indolence!

CROWD: All in vain! All in vain!

QUECHUA 7 (*in a startled shout*): Viracocha! They're raising it! They're raising it!

The CROWD *watches the raising of the stone, with a mixture of stupor and terror. The female choir intones the itu. Suddenly, a booming crash is heard on the side of the left corridor, and the entire fortress shakes. The* CROWD *lets out a shriek, followed by a deadly silence. And then, shouts of panic and calls for help. The* CROWD *runs in all directions, terrified.*

VOICES: It fell! It fell! The stone of Pissaj! The stone—

From the crowd emerge princes, dignitaries of the court, and some sipakoyas, who've fainted, held up by the townsfolk. TOLPOR *comes from the left, holding* KAURA *in his arms, blacking out, pallid.* TOLPOR *anxiously examines her face.*

TOLPOR: Water! . . . Water! . . . She's not breathing! . . . (*He stops at center stage, takes a few more steps, then stops again, calling her with anguish.*) Ñusta! Princess! Tonapa Camaj![19]

TOLPOR *listens to her heartbeat.* KAURA *slowly regains consciousness, sits up with difficulty, and as her eyes meet his, she's in shock; then, she smiles at the stonemason and caresses his hair.* TOLPOR *is stunned and lowers his head, just when* RUNTO KASKA *rushes in from stage left.*

RUNTO KASKA: Kaura! Kaura!

A whirlwind of people from the right close in on KAURA *and* RUNTO KASKA. TOLPOR, *as if under a spell, ardently holds his gaze on the princess.*

CURTAIN

Scene 5

At the Koricancha portico. Numerous Quechuas, either standing barefoot or kneeling in a show of adoration, cross in front of the Temple of the Sun. Some people enter or exit it. There are children walking hand-in-hand with young villacs, carrying high stalks of maize. An elderly piruc walks out of the temple, at the head of a small ayllu—rural women, children, and adolescents, from whose knees dangle flowers and sonorous copper piruros.[20] At the base of a pilaster, on the left side of the portico, two YOUNG LADIES *set coca leaves on fire in a human skull producing an odorous smoke.* TOLPOR *appears on the left, distracted, his gaze lost in the distance. Groups of people pull away from him, with a mixture of piety and repulsion, because he hadn't removed his shoes at the sacred place.*

ELDERLY MAN (*severely*): Go in the temple. Correct your misdeed. (TOLPOR *falls to his knees at the base of the pilaster and loses himself in reflection.*)

TOLPOR (*snapping out of his introspection, jubilantly, to the* YOUNG LADIES): My antara, beautiful virgins, is made of thirteen pipes. (*The* YOUNG LADIES *turn toward him, smiling.*) They're fastened with a web of tendons that once belonged to a gigantic colla, killed by my father, like a slinger of the Inca, in the celebrated battle of Jonday.

YOUNG LADY 1: Do you know how to play the antara?

TOLPOR: I can make it say whatever I please. When I play, it stays around my neck like a beautiful braid of pita fiber. And when I'm not playing it, I store it in a frog-skin pouch, inlaid with valerian, Angel's trumpet, and other vilca herbs, which terrified seers rub against their bodies.

YOUNG LADY 2: Where do you live? What's your name?

TOLPOR: I'm Tolpor, the stonemason.

YOUNG LADY 2: What ayllu are you from?

TOLPOR: The Taucasquis. I live in the slums of Hurin-Cuzco, near the palace of Yucay.

YOUNG LADY 1: And your family?

TOLPOR: My mother and my sister. My father died of the evil wind, taken away while passing by the tomb of an adulteress. And you?

YOUNG LADY 2: We're mitimaes from the mountain. Where do you work?

TOLPOR: In the summertime I water the oasis and grottoes of leisure at Yucay; in the fall, I work on the fortress and aqueducts.

YOUNG LADY 2: Why don't you enter the temple?

TOLPOR: Why? Because, first, I'm going to have an ablution in the Huatanay.[21]

YOUNG LADIES 1 AND 2 (*overwhelmed*): Oh! . . . Don't touch us! Get away! (*They hold on to each other, withdrawing, leaving* TOLPOR *alone.*)

TOLPOR: Beautiful mitimaes, ladies of the mountains, do you know what love is? Have you ever loved? Run away from me, but hear me out.

YOUNG LADY 1: Love? . . . Love, they say, is born in the shade of blooming palm trees.

YOUNG LADY 2: Love comes in the crops of the northern condors. It's a little blue stone that cures the illness of distance.

From *The Tired Stone* 543

TOLPOR (*laughing like a boy*): Strangers, love doesn't come from plants or animals. Love—all love and all lovers of plants, animals, and stars— all love in the world is born in the breast of humans. I know so from experience. My love, the love that bore me this afternoon I've dreamed of for so many suns, moons, and seasons, while playing the reeds of my antara. (*The* YOUNG LADIES *laugh childishly.*)

YOUNG LADY 1: And where is your girlfriend? Who is she?

TOLPOR: My girlfriend is a ñusta! A terrified ñusta! She has caressed my hair.

YOUNG LADIES 1 AND 2 (*spellbound*): A ñusta! . . . She's a ñusta! . . . More impiety! More blasphemy! Get away! Stains! Go! Go!

They leave him. Some people walking by stop and observe the scene. TOLPOR, *sharply fallen into shadow, removes his shoes and, downcast, enters the Koricancha.*

CURTAIN

Scene 6

Evening at an intersection in Chokechaka. Center stage, a stone dolmen in the shape of a serpent. Around it, groves. AUQUIS *and* SIPACOYAS *celebrate* KAURA's *coming of age, presided over by* UYURQUI *and* MAMA PAYO. *In front of the dolmen, the attendees are seated in two rows, back-to-back—in pairs—on two long wooden benches, covered with grass and placed from one to the other end of the stage. In the back, behind the dolmen, the parents of* KAURA *are seated on the high, thick trunk of a recently chopped tree, still covered with leaves and branches. A procession of virgins, dressed in red, stand at the side of each attendant, holding in one hand a glass and in the other a branch of blooming white cotton. Dressed with multicolor feathers and garlands of flowers,* KAURA *is standing between her parents, facing the audience.* UYURQUI *and* MAMA PAYO *hold her hands. An unseen choir of children intones the ritual song of the quipuchika, and when it ends, a long, profound silence reigns. Then, the virgins extend the glasses to the attendees who participate in the ceremonial libation. Another pause.*

AUQUI 1: In the ancient quipuchikas, if I'm not mistaken, they didn't drink spirits made from bark. Foreign invasions from the deep south, long before its unity had been secured, introduced the reign to the liquor of the maddening stalk mash. During quipuchikas particularly, celebrating a girl's entrance to womanhood meant drinking maize chicha, strong and downright bitter. The nubile virgin would often get drunk, and the words she'd say in the trance of inebriation would be used by her parents as the key to reading her future.

UYURQUI: What a barbarian, heathen tradition!

AUIQUI 2: Certainly not all the ayllus of the empire celebrate this ritual in the same way.

VARIOUS: No. That's for sure.

AUQUI 3: In the region of the eastern forests, the virgin undresses and is wrapped in banana leaves and put to sleep in a wild glade of the woods. The beasts come at the scent of new blood, until the tender flesh is ready . . .

VARIOUS SIPACOYAS: Good God of the Water! Floods! Mudslides! Storms!

AUQUI 2: Silently, the elastic bear cub licks her thighs, while she sleeps in a hopeful position, but the old jaguars take turns providing her an impenetrable wall of defense.

UYURQUI: I know that custom. It's remarkable!

AUQUI 2: Rarely is the virgin attacked by some famished puma or one that's in rut, and even more rarely is she abandoned by her feline guard, since a wound from a human or animal in recently blossomed flesh foretells of sterility and prenuptial death.

AUQUI 3: In certain Porus ayllus, the virgin decants a pitcher of lime juice into two basalt cups and pours them onto her father's head, which mustn't become shiny. The slightest amount of oil in the hair signals a death-filled marriage deprived of offspring.

SIPACOYA 1: Among the Watallas and the Maules,[22] epithalamic vows aren't made on the day the girl enters womanhood, but on her wedding day.

SIPACOYA 2: The ayllus of hunters in the northern cordilleras attribute the omen of adultery to the hooting of the owl on the day she comes of age.

UYURQUI: Speaking of this, the symbolism of the wanderer from early this morning won't stop piquing my curiosity.

MAMA PAYO: A strange vision. That makes me nervous.

UYURQUI: I know, naturally, if that stranger was crying, we'd need to be concerned for Kaura. If he was singing, it'd be something else altogether . . .

MAMA PATO (to KAURA, *tenderly*): What might this splinter in the trunk be?

UYURQUI: Could it have been a herder of sacred flocks searching for a lost alpaca? (*Those present shrug their shoulders in unison.*) Was it a tired chasqui who, trudging uphill burdened with some sad message, stopped to get his bearings in the early morning light? (*Those present shrug their shoulders.*) I was sleeping or perhaps dreaming. Suddenly, the voice of a strange song—let's call it a song—it made me shudder. The glow of dawn appeared, and a blurry shadow was stuck to the wall alongside the road . . . I called out, "Who are you?" I asked, "Who's singing or crying in the penumbra of dawn?"

AUQUI 4: No one knows if he was singing! No one knows if he was crying!

AUQUI 3: Was it still nighttime? Or had day already come?

MAMA PAYO: It was between sky and sky. How can we specify?

AUQUI 5: So in the end, who was it? Did he say?

UYURQUI: I've asked the oracle, but he didn't know. Could it have been a guard from the neighboring imperial palace just as day was rising over the valley, who was dreaming of the people and homeland he'd left, one afternoon, yoked to the Armies of the Sun? . . . (*Those present shrug their shoulders.*) Again he started to sing . . . or cry, so again I called out . . . I said, "At least tell me if you're singing or crying!"

SIPACOYA 3: Brutal uncertainty! No one knows it he was singing! No one knows if he was crying!

SIPACOYA 4: Perhaps it was an escaped mitimae who had suffered the torment of the laws . . .

UYURQUI (*interrupting*): And before day came and night left, there he was, the mysterious one. Suddenly possessed by irrepressible unrest, I shouted, "Get out of here! You'd better leave! Day is already breaking. The sun might grow angry if it sees you, and from places tainted by your plants weeds could grow that will rot the walls of Cuzco and turn the kingdom into swamps, the coraquenques[23] will die, the Huatanay will dry, the fields will burn, rust will devour the granaries, and, in chacus to come, instead of the Inti's alpacas, black condors will arrive with chaos and darkness in their talons! . . . Get out of here, right now! Your voice—be it a cry or a song—is poisonous like the blood of aborted children (*long silence*).

AUQUI 6: Nobody cries while singing. Nobody sings while crying. It purely and simply must have been a song.

EVERYONE (*raising their glasses to toast*): A song! A song! A song! To the virgin! To her wedding! To her offspring! (*they drink*)

AUQUI 7 (*the oldest of those present, standing, priestly, in a spell*): Hymn to the Blood! . . .

EVERYONE (*standing, in chorus*): Viracocha, beginning of the seeds!

AUQUI 7: May the married couple beget healthy, vigorous ayllus; may the women give birth to organized, flourishing reigns!

EVERYONE: Viracocha, beginning of the testes and the womb!

AUQUI 7: May the offspring grow, breathe, work, think, love, procreate, and perish!

EVERYONE: Viracocha, beginning of the head of the body, end of the feet of the soul!

Profound pause of unction. KAURA *steps forth, agile, smiling, and stops in front of the dolmen, still facing the audience. The spellbound* AUQUI *approaches her and, placing his hands on her head—both leaning over, looking at the ground—makes an invocation in a raised voice at the dolmen. Those present, standing, looking, listen to the monolith.*

AUQUI: Guardian Pebble, Father of the Dust, Grandfather of the Stone, God of the Home! Behold the new virgin that this couple is offering you! (*short silence*) Is her sign a morning star, a giant quiet river, a beard of grain, a mammal? . . . Where will she place her mind—in her silence? Where will she find the path—in her thicket? Where, for her womb, child of the children?

Short silence. An AUQUI *and a* SIPACOYA *hold hands, and, forming an arch, she with her back to the dolmen, he with his eyes fixed on the stone, disappear into the grove.*

VOICE OF MAN 1 (*invisible*): Nubile girl, I'll give you the door to your house!

VOICE OF WOMAN 1 (*invisible*): Don't open or close it: leave it ajar, woman! (*Another couple leaves in the same way as the previous.*)

VOICE OF MAN 2 (*invisible*): I will give you a lantern of clay!

VOICE OF WOMAN 2: Light it before the eyes of others, but blow it out before the eyes of your lover! (*Another couple leaves.*)

VOICE OF MAN 3: I will give you a feather bed!

VOICE OF WOMAN 3: Lie down on it, but don't fall asleep! (*Another couple leaves.*)

VOICE OF MAN 4: I'll admire the health and beauty of your offspring!

The VOICE OF WOMAN 4 *is weeping. Astonishment and emotion in the characters that remain onstage. The spellbound* AUQUI *raises his eyes.*

Everyone looks around anxiously. A rustling of wind comes from the grove, grows, howls.

AUQUI 7: It's the wind! The sign of the virgin is the wind! (*From the grove the couples return, and all begin an epithalamic dance, singing around the dolmen and* KAURA; *they stop.*) Night is falling! Evil shadows lie in wait! Dance, sing, and force them out with your sound and motion!

They keep dancing and singing. Little by little, the couples disperse and disappear from the stage, where, in the end, only KAURA *and* RUNTO KASTA *are left, in the growing darkness of night. Pause.*

RUNTO KASKA (*from a corner, between the trees, timidly, panting*): Kaura! . . . (KAURA *stands still next to the dolmen and smiles, leaning over.* RUNTO KASKA *approaches.*) Kaura! . . .

KAURA (*radiantly*): The dancing of the wind stirs my breast.

RUNTO KASKA: Your voice is new, Kaura! Your eyes, they're new! . . . Why are you laughing like that?

KAURA: At dawn, I too heard that singing or crying.

RUNTO KASKA: You heard it too?

KAURA (*hiding her face and tearing apart some of the leaves that adorn her*): Father wonders if it was a song or a cry, but I know it was a song that was crying and a cry that was singing.

RUNTO KASKA: Does this vision worry you, Kaura, on the day you enter womanhood?

KAURA: It wasn't a vision. It was a rapturous voice. I'm not nervous: it's left an ineffable ringing in my ears.

RUNTO KASKA (*with adoration*): Kaura! . . . You're strange! . . . A new halo appears above your head. You look milder to me . . . More . . . Your face burns with its familiar flame, but—

KAURA (*about to leave*): I wanted to be alone . . .

RUNTO KASKA (*holding her back*): Look at me, Kaura! Look at me! (*He cups her face and looks at her directly.*)

KAURA: My terror has ended! When night fell, I was afraid. When day broke, I was still afraid . . .

RUNTO KASKA (*anxiously, passionately*): Your eyes are more eyelike! Your mouth is more mouthlike!

KAURA: As a shadow passed, as a light passed, I was afraid . . .

RUNTO KASKA: There is another forehead on your forehead!

KAURA: When Mother was sleeping, I was so afraid! When Father was speaking, I was so afraid!

RUNTO KASKA: At the base of your neck, there lies a road whose ends blend in, on the right and on the left, to your hair!

KAURA: As I saw a sapling sprout in a seedbed, my heart fluttered; as I saw a little bug die in the sun, my heart fluttered . . .

RUNTO KASKA: There's a breath within your breath! There's a breath within your breasts! A breath on your thighs! A breath in your sides!

KAURA: I once heard a vicuña grazing, and I screamed; another time, I heard a stone rustling on the road, and I screamed . . .

RUNTO KASKA: Are your hands cut off from your voice, finger by finger? And where are you going? Kaura, your waistline shows traces of another waist!

MAMA PAYO (*appearing in the forum*): It's not good, my dear, to be alone with the dolmen on the day you enter womanhood.

RUNTO KASKA (*saying good-bye*): Mama Payo, Kaura . . . May Viracocha protect his people.

MAMA PAYO: Today the souls of our forebears cross beneath the guardian stone unnoticed, on tiptoe, and even if the beings of this world who loved deeply exhale generous perfumes in the nubile virgin's presence, there are also people whom hatred planted in the soil that seize her with infernal spells. Come, let's go. Prudence.

MAMA PAYO *takes her by the arm, leads her though the forum. Pause.* TOLPOR *appears, with anguish, in search of* KAURA; *he listens, turns around, waits . . . Silence and solitude. Then he traces his footsteps and leaves, pensively, sadly, slowly.*

CURTAIN

ACT 2

Scene 1

The hut of TOLPOR, *evening, in the slums of Cuzco. Stage right, a door open to the street.* OKAWA *is busy tattooing wooden bowls with a red-hot burin, humming softly and talking to herself while she works. A small hearth burns at her side.*

OKAWA (*looking at the drawing she just finished on a plate*): Deer head, true lines! As if it's looking at a mysterious country in the distance. Over there! . . . (*takes another plate and sings, after a moment, contemplating it aloud*). What a strange yellow! Neither sweet oca, nor bitter mashua![24] The wild chest of a vicuña! . . . Not that either. I'd say . . . I'd say, tamarind spirits. Or, rather, the color of a dusty road traveled by no one under the sun . . . Next! (*grabs another plate and sings*).

VOICE OF MAMA CUSSI (*from backstage*): Hurry up, Okawa!

OKAWA (*talking to herself*): So many plates, and for what? An extra plate, so says the proverb, is the mouth of the departed who doesn't eat. (*raising her voice*) Mother, what are the plates like that the Virgins of the Sun dine on?

VOICE OF MAMA CUSSI: Some are white, purple, lapis lazuli . . . Tattooed in the center with mysterious shapes.

OKAWA (*to herself*): And the plate for meat is black and has no shapes.

VOICE OF MAMA CUSSI: See if the foreigner is coming, Okawa. (OKAWA *goes running to the front door and peers into the street.*)

OKAWA (*returning to her work*): Still no sign.

VOICE OF MAMA CUSSI: Did you finish? What are you doing?

OKAWA: The last one. It's the last one . . . (*then, daydreaming, to herself*) And the plate for the milk is a sheet of gold. On the border, priestly figures of mahogany are set in. (*stopping her work, pensively*) Guayaba with the color of chirimoya, apple-scented lime—how might these be served on the plate that no one's ever seen before? . . . (*She stays there for a moment, thinking, and then laboriously resumes her work, mumbling.*) And in how many cups . . . The virgins don't know what cups are. They drink from *keros*. Bare *keros*, without engravings, without colors: sad keros . . . (*Silence, then* OKAWA *suddenly screams, raising her eyes to the sky, dropping the plate she was working on in a crash.*) Mother! Mother! The imperial pumas!

MAMA CUSSI (*rushing from the back*): Did you hear them? Did you hear them too?

OKAWA: Shhh! . . . (*both of them listen;* TOLPOR *comes from the back and listens;* OKAWA, *overwhelmed again*) Do you hear? Do you hear?

MAMA CUSSI: Yes! Yes! . . . (*again, they listen*)

TOLPOR (*fatally*): Finally! Tomorrow! At the crack of dawn! . . . (OKAWA *runs to the door that opens to the street and anxiously looks out.*)

MAMA CUSSI (*impatiently*): The foreigner hasn't come yet. What's going on?

TOLPOR (*stationary, bleakly*): The war will be long. About ten moons or so—not counting the two it will take to get there and another two it will take to come back.

MAMA CUSSI: Okawa, are you coming?

OKAWA (*leaving the doorway*): People are passing by. Many people. There are boys with the same live branches as always in their hands.

Groups of men and women can be seen crossing the street in a great bustle. MAMA CUSSI, OKAWA, *and* TOLPOR *look outside.*

MAMA CUSSI: Be patient. He'll come.

OKAWA: A huaraca! A huaraca is passing by! . . . Another! And another! . . . Look! All the mothers! One is running with a silver llauto[25] in her hands.

TOLPOR: Tambos and camps will start filling up by dawn. I shall leave! Saddened! Bleeding! Poisoned! (*paces back and forth*).

OKAWA (*without looking away from the street*): Sandals! Green belts! More sandals! (*to* TOLPOR) And where are yours?

TOLPOR: Sallcupar has them. The cotton ones.

MAMA CUSSI: The leather ones and the woolen ones have been hanging from the roof since yesterday, awaiting the sign of wayward bird droppings.

TOLPOR: To love a princess, what a strange evil, a strange notion, a strange feeling!

MAMA CUSSI: Don't lose your patience. Keep calm. You'll leave all healed, and when you return, the blade of your battle-ax will replace your dead father's guardian sickle above the front door of the house . . .

An elderly man, with the face and air of a foreigner, a little drum hanging from his belt, appears in the doorway.

OKAWA: Pucutu! Pucutur![26] The foreigner!

FOREIGNER: The equinox withdraws. Twilight lingers upon the hills.

MAMA CUSSI: The Army of the Sun departs tomorrow.

TOLPOR: Yes. The slingers and axmen, by night; the archers, lancers, and war beasts, by day. (*All move toward center stage.*)

FOREIGNER (*gazing up at the sky*): One size has been given to each sky. And each ayllu has its sky and each king and each man.

TOLPOR: Except me, foreigner, my head has lost its sky—it's skyless.

FOREIGNER: There are skies as large and glamorous as thrones, and others small as puquios.[27]

MAMA CUSSI (*with fervor*): The sky of the Tahuantinsuyo is incommensurable!

FOREIGNER: The sky of the Tahuantinsuyo . . . Now I believe you. But, have you seen? Despite the grunting imperial pumas that announce the expedition, people show no enthusiasm in the streets. The Rainbow has passed through Cusipata; a group of teenaged soldiers was carrying it, followed by a mob . . .

TOLPOR: The town has been indifferent?

FOREIGNER: Strangely indifferent. They neither cheer nor applaud. The women and children, appearing at the doors, beheld the standard coldly. Some elderly folk have crossed the road and given the warriors a few swigs of chicha to drink, some hominy to eat . . .

MAMA CUSSI: The campaign is far away; the punas, craggy, hazardous . . .

FOREIGNER: A shadowy silence wherever you listen. As the members of this future expedition vanished beyond Hanai-Cuzco, one old woman began to weep.

MAMA CUSSI: The race of Manco is invincible!

FOREIGNER (*changing his tone*): Back to that: as for this young man's situation (*speaking of* TOLPOR), I don't hide my surprise when I see among the ayllu one man's crime—loving a ñusta, coya,[28] or sipacoya. Among the Shiras,[29] it's permitted: the Sunlight itself once slept with a virgin of the cloud, and the humble potters impregnate the daughters of high priests.

MAMA CUSSI: That's what I'm saying: my son is as much a man as any prince. The pain of my womb, when I delivered him, rose to my womanly hips. As for the princess, to be convinced that she's nothing more than a woman, let's just see who she accepts and who she denies.

FOREIGNER: Just between us, even old Viracocha begets countless lives in the glacial flesh of lizards and iguanas. Not to mention anything of his heat with girls of no rank or breed at all.

TOLPOR: In any case, foreigner, what say you? By watching me leave, what will you be able to find in my footsteps that could clear up in the amauta's presence what's clouded to my own mother? How and why does whoever loves love whomever is loved? Unfortunately, with or without his wise appearance, Sallcupar will never know.

FOREIGNER (*taking* TOLPOR *by the hand, he exits the front door onto the street*): Come on, follow me. The amauta awaits us.

CURTAIN

Scene 2

In the meeting room of the house of the amauta, SALLCUPAR. *Twilight. Silence.*

VOICE OF SALLCUPAR (*droning on*): A constant image reaches the peaks of his thoughts: the image of the ñusta! One constant note keeps ringing in his ears! . . . Tolpor walks among the masses as if he were carried on the wings of that voice and by that image's beams of light! A shadow is on his trail: the remorse for loving a princess—for loving a ñusta! (*pause*) There's a place in the world where man will never step foot. What place is that? Where can it be found? There's a law to be discovered for all the good fortune of this world! What law? Where is it? How can its whereabouts be verified? Mysteries! Mysteries! Mysteries!

Silence. Suddenly, a ray of westerly sunlight enters and a small torch lights up, center stage right; from the other side a second ray reaches center stage and another torch lights up; and then a third torch, on the left. Once the room is aglow, its severe schematic decoration becomes visible. A circular series of trapezoidal windows open to the sky. The torches that have just been lit hang over three broad, truncated columns, made of white tree trunks, rising just a bit higher than a man. The room continues on but disappears stage left; where it falls out of view, the soffit holds up a giant copper disk hanging halfway to the ground, like a bell. SALLCUPAR *is sitting on the ground under the disk with his profile to the audience, looking stage left. Pause. In the distance, a small drum starts tapping, slowly, rhythmically, monotonously.*

WHITE CHASQUI (*on the right, with a black pouch*): No killing! No lying! No being lazy! (*stops alongside the torch center stage, leaning toward* SALLCUPAR, *with his profile to the audience*). A road . . . In my pouch I bring a road. A piece of the road, discovered in the corner of a prison.
SALLCUPAR (*without turning around*): You must be lying. Could it be a jaguar claw, filed and shined in the shape of a knife?

WHITE CHASQUI: I left at daybreak and arrived at nightfall, Father. What else could I bring you but a road?

SALLCUPAR: Could it be a little bone in the shape of a tiara or something of that sort?

WHITE CHASQUI: It's no weapon or special power. I've walked, grown tired, and continued to walk again, so what else could I bring you, Father, but a road?

SALLCUPAR: Blow out the torch so I may see. Is it a road?

The WHITE CHASQUI *blows out the torch in the center, and* SALLCUPAR *covers his eyes with both hands. Pause. All that can be heard is the drum in the distance. A* BLACK CHASQUI *comes rushing from the right and stops next to the torch on that side.* SALLCUPAR *uncovers his eyes, looking again stage left.*

SALLCUPAR: Above the masses on the high pepper trees that surround the Intipampa, one can manage to distinguish the terraced slope of Mount Huanacaure,[30] Salkamarca[31] Tower, and some of the smaller walls of temples and palaces. The crowd of people shrieks, and a sudden rumble is heard. Is it the archers, just an arrow shot away, stepping forth in the imperial march?

BLACK CHASQUI: No. It's not the imperial archers, Father. It's a young man who's crossing the city at a fast and anxious pace . . . (*The little drum's tapping grows closer.*)

SALLCUPAR: Blow out the torch so I may hear. Are those his footsteps? . . . (*the* BLACK CHASQUI *blows out the torch on the right, and the drum immediately stops tapping; a deep silence*) A note . . . An image . . . A shadow . . . A giant shadow. And, while he cuts through the city, the dimensions of the world and life itself fight out their fate, like birds of prey . . . (*silence, then a sharp, painful shriek from the left*; SALLCUPAR, *suddenly standing up, without looking away from that side of the stage*) Who's that? . . . Who's there? . . .

DISTANT VOICE (*singing, desolate, on the left, decrescendo*): The distance . . . The distance . . . The distance . . .

BLACK CHASQUI: The distance between fire and ash.

WHITE CHASQUI: The distance between eye and gaze.

DISTANT VOICE: Neither one distance nor the other. Only the distance between the tiny pebble and the vast mountain made of pebbles. Only the distance between the king's crown and the humblest heel of his servants.

SALLCUPAR (*addressing the voice*): Well then, speak. I'm listening. Where are you coming from like this, and where are you going? What law compels you to depart from our laws? What sign forms its body by stirring or by resting? (*short silence, heavy footsteps approach*).

WHITE CHASQUI: The distance between bodies walks without moving forever (*lights the center torch again and removes it from the column, places the column on the ground and lays the torch on its side, as if it were next to a corpse*).

BLACK CHASQUI: The distance between souls walks without moving, at the pace of a caged beast (*relights the torch on the right and leaves on that side; when the footsteps coming from this side are about to reach the stage from the right,* SALLCUPAR *exits stage left*).

FOREIGNER (*without the drum, on the left*): Chasqui! Messenger!

WHITE CHASQUI (*going forth to meet him*): May Viracocha protect his people!

FOREIGNER: What kind of custom is this? Greeting a stranger who arrives at a dwelling by walking out just as he walks in?

WHITE CHASQUI: Among the Quechuas, Father, beings and things meet one another in profile: vegetables by vibrating, plants by standing still, humans by walking. (*bowing*) Ama sua! Ama llulla! Ama kella!

FOREIGNER: Was the amauta waiting for me?

WHITE CHASQUI: The amauta was waiting for a foreigner.

FOREIGNER: I am the foreigner.

WHITE CHASQUI: Your greeting? Your farewell? Your route?

FOREIGNER: From the land of the giant looms and waterfalls. Farmhand by trade. Healthy children, eight of them in all. I've been in Cuzco for seven solstices now.

WHITE CHASQUI: May the temples lack shade beneath the solar light of noon! (*bows and exits stage left; the* FOREIGNER, *alone, looks around in curiosity*).

SALLCUPAR (*on the right*): May the temples lack shade beneath the solar light of noon!

FOREIGNER: The infallible Sallcupar: receive my bones so that with them you may build a hearth and in its glow see whether malice, interest, or pretense drives my words . . .

SALLCUPAR (*urgently*): How has this servant conceived of such passion?

FORIEGNER: Here I have my report from abroad: it was not he who went to her, nor she to him . . .

SALLCUPAR: How many times have you seen the princess?

FOREIGNER: Many times. Up close, from afar.

SALLCUPAR: Have you ever spoken to her?

FOREIGNER: Very few times. But in passing, yes.

SALLCUPAR: And does she know that the serf is in love with her?

FOREIGNER: She doesn't suspect a thing. She barely remembers that he exists or that she's seen him before. Do you know her?

SALLCUPAR: I know her as much as you do. Listen up: the human body has two vertical halves, a profound abyss separates them, and yet one hand is closer than the other to the foot on the same side.

FOREIGNER: A brilliant aphorism, Sallcupar!

SALLCUPAR: Very well, on the ladder of our social hierarchy, as on the ladder of the human organism, there's the foot and the hand, the ayllu and the nobility; and this, transferred to the domain of love, means that there is the vicinity and union of the man of the ayllu with the woman of the ayllu, flush with the soil, and, above, the vicinity and union of the prince and the ñusta, of the auqui and the coya . . .

FOREIGNER: It's the sacred law of the Quechuas.

SALLCUPAR: By infringing upon it, Tolpor is inspired and moved by the supay![32]

FOREIGNER (*looking stage left*): He comes in a cold sweat, as agitated as can be, mortally pale.

SALLCUPAR: He spent most of yesterday lying down.

FOREIGNER: His eyes frighten me, beneath that flat forehead of his, without a ridge, as if it were made of a mysterious fang.

SALLCUPAR: By any chance does he rub his body with living bugs?

FOREIGNER: At times, a portentous world possesses him. To the questions posed to him, he gives disjointed, meaningless answers.

SALLCUPAR (*looking in the same direction*): Yesterday he was seen with foam coming from the corners of his mouth, and he was stretching his arms and legs for moments, as would a dying man on his deathbed.

FOREIGNER: When he was walking by, the skin of the drum emitted something like the hissing of one boa that coils around another.

SALLCUPAR: No one knows the origin of his line. Some say that his forebears came from an eastern country, beyond Pacaretambu, the dwelling that cracks with dawn, the place of the four dimensions; other people say that they came from some remote empire, where light has its nocturnal bed. This deplorable uncertainty that, heading into the past, reaches the future!

FOREIGNER: The rocks of his house exhale a harsh mineral scent at night.

SALLCUPAR (*after looking through the windows at the sky*): Call him! Call him! Crowned with reptiles, the experience of man has the breast of the dove! . . . (*The* FOREIGNER *leaves to the left.*) What can I say to him? Out of what clay might I mold my advice? The wide green tunic adorns the amauta's body; the seven-color crest covers the heroes' heads; the blue clothing, with threads of aloe in the shape of twinkling insects, adorns the meek and mild arabicus; the cape of speckled bat skins majestically falls upon the shoulders of the Inca; and the graceful refined skirts, embroidered with polychrome fringe, is voluptuously cinched around the waists of the Virgins of the Sun . . . Nonetheless, there are outfits that don't look good on anyone and that nobody wears at all; likewise there are passions that don't fit in any rationale, which cannot be forgiven. Not in the least! (*growing excited*) Viracocha, axis of the world! Depth of the water! Height of the flame! From the silver temple walls release a reflection of light for my brain!

TOLPOR *enters stage left, with a nightmarish expression on his face; he comes to a halt at the entrance of the scene, fixing his stunned eyes to* SALLCUPAR, *who wraps him in a long, compassionate gaze. Pause.*

TOLPOR (*whispering*): A tortoise . . . When I was crossing through Hurin-Cuzco, I saw some children crushing a tortoise with their slings.

SALLCUPAR (*softly, relaxed*): Enter, come in . . . (TOLPOR *steps forth.*) Have a look around you, without fear or suspicion. (TOLPOR *looks around.*) This is the Mansion of Ideas. Here, things are clear, precise; their edges, sharp, defined. (TOLPOR *swims through the foggy darkness.*) In this house our pupils reach maximum dilation. (*while* TOLPOR *is looking out one of the windows*) That window faces the volcanic land of Sumpe. Now night has fallen and nothing can been seen anymore. (*pointing to the other windows*) The rest of them—

TOLPOR (*looking through one of them*): Who's passing through that one? (*anxiously takes a few steps toward the window*).

SALLCUPAR: Through that one pass the stubborn livestock that leave. And through this one (*pointing to another window*), the counted livestock that return.

TOLPOR (*suddenly, looking though a fourth window, captivated*): What do I see!? . . . It's her abode. Over there, that light! (*covers his eyes with his hand*).

SALLCUPAR: Indeed, it is. I've already told you: here the pupils manage to see . . . (TOLPOR *lets out a moan*; SALLCUPAR, *in another tone*) The foreigner claims that everything has been beyond your control and also beyond hers.

TOLPOR (*weeping*): Rawa! . . . Wiru! . . .[33] Tender shoot! . . . Little root! . . .

SALLCUPAR: The torch of bark is burning, the ostrich marrow torch made of wausa[34] is burning too (*indicates which one is burning next to the column that's fallen to the ground*)—terrible liquor of the double essence!

TOLPOR (*with sudden, savage rebelliousness*): No! It's not a mistake or a crime or a sin! (*The torch stage left goes out.*)

SALLCUPAR: The river is flowing upstream! Mudslides! Floods!

TOLPOR (*looking through the window, as if in ecstasy*): Beautiful ñusta! . . . Place your face before my eyes one more time. There you are! You return! . . . The burning footprints of your steps are small lagoons; your scent is musky; one after another your movements are linked together like a downpour's pearls; your fire's embers are soaked! Tunkuy! Tunkuy![35] Confluence! Coalescence! Nuptials! Fire! Fire and water, mixed together! (*The torch stage right goes out.*)

SALLCUPAR: After the freeze, one cob from the crop remained on its stalk, and it's just fallen off. (*with sudden severity*) Be gone, blasphemer! Far away from here!

TOLPOR (*backing away from the window*): Father, a strange silence reigns outside. I'm afraid.

SALLCUPAR: Those two lanterns have gone out: that one, with your breath; and this one, with hers . . . (*a deep, extended silence*).

FOREIGNER (*coming from the left*): Amauta, a bad omen! In the trunk of the tree, poisonous ants have made a nest!

A deadly silence. TOLPOR, *finally, dismally, quietly exits right.* SALLCUPAR *and the* FORIEGNER *remain there, bowing.*

SALLCUPAR (*once* TOLPOR *has left*): The stone is the substance of universal life. The Inti is the Stone God, the Quechuas are the stone men, animals and plants are made of stone, and even the stones themselves, pure stone!

FOREIGNER (*relighting the torch stage right*): No one must walk into the shade: fourth wisdom of the Shiras.

SALLCUPAR: Sometimes, an entire city is buried in a stone! Another stone contains the sunshine, and another, an echo, and another the odor of life's urine, and another the odor of death's sulfur.

FOREIGNER (*relighting the torch stage left*): No one must stay in the shade: fifth wisdom of the Shiras.

SALLCUPAR: Certain chalky stones watch over the borders of the land and distribute water to towns.

FOREIGNER: In the ravines of my land there are pensive, millennial spinner stones, spinning night and day for the ayllu.

SALLCUPAR: There's a diabolic stone over there! A round stone! One of those stones in which certain deadly birds roost! I've fathomed in him and in me (for the study of one's neighbor is incomplete, if it's not met by the study of oneself); I've fathomed in him and in me: he's a goner! It's his fiery passion of the underworld: only the devil himself will be able to put it out! (*makes an expression that shows he's finished*).

FOREIGNER (*straightening the center column and placing the third torch against it*): May Viracocha protect his race! (*A sharp ringing comes from the copper disk.*)

SALLCUPAR (*placing his ear against the disk*): The doors have creaked. Did you hear them?

FOREIGNER: It was a bell. I heard it.

SALLCUPAR: Bells are doors that close, foreigner. Deaf night! Adversities! Ama sua! Ama llulla! Ama kella!

FOREIGNER: Merciful little stones! Green blades of grass! Guardian crickets! . . . (*leaves stage left, a pause, then a* RED CHASQUI *crosses from right to left, carrying* TOLPOR's *sandals, raised in V-formation*).

SALLCUPAR (*lamenting*): The seven rebel vipers delight in the one hand that knows not what the other hand does!

CURTAIN

[JM]

Letters

TO JUAN LUIS VELÁSQUEZ

Paris, June 13, 1936
Dear Juan Luis,

Why don't you give me your address? In the two letters you've written to me from Peru, you kept saying you'd write at length, giving me your address so I can reply, but haven't, which is why I'm sending you this letter via Dolores, whom I ask to deliver it as soon as possible.

For too long you've deprived me of reliable reports on what's happening there. I hardly receive the same old pages from the government and the reaction, which I know don't accurately reflect what's transpiring in Peru. The Left no longer exists in Paris. That being said, I'm at a complete loss for information to form an impression—much less an idea—of the present moment, particularly with regard to the upcoming elections. Given what you say in your note, a National Front seems possible, or at least so say certain government sources. But under what conditions and with whom? I suppose that by the time you receive this, the electoral field will already have been established, at least for the presidential candidacy and the formation of a National Front. Will the elections be in September, or, as rumor has it, will they be postponed?

Please take a moment to update me as soon as you receive this letter. I beg you, likewise, to ask about my brother Néstor in Lima and to give him word of the possibility of my return to Peru. Speak with the Trujillanos, as they might know him. It's of great interest to me that you see him. Tell him I wrote to him but didn't receive his response.

The truth is I'd like to return to Peru as soon as possible, but I can't foresee the means and a *climate* conducive to taking such a trip or, if it were possible, the diverse objectives of my return. Essentially, what would I do there? With what funds will I travel? How would I stay afloat in Lima? And more seriously, what projects will I work on? From here, it's certainly impossible to figure this out, and I can't make a decision, without a base of probable calculations. It seems like you could help me gauge the situation, since you're in the middle of it. In any case, I get the impression that my return largely depends on how the upcoming elections will tilt on the scale of national politics. This is why I so anxiously await news from you about the elections. If I don't hear from you, it will be understood that nothing of interest or magnitude is happening there that could be susceptible to influencing the matter of my trip. Naturally, I'd like you to write me no matter what. Please! Don't fall into silence.

I don't know if I'm going to Spain. It depends on how things unfold on one and the other side of the Pyrenees. Of course, if I go, I'll let you know, or Dolores will tell you.

And you still haven't told me anything about you. Tell me what you're doing, what you're going to do. I'm not attaching a contribution because you haven't told me what kind of magazine yours is going to be . . . Do you know what I mean? I look forward to seeing the first issue, so I can see some guidelines and send you things of my own and from other people.

Neither you nor Dolores has told me anything about Igor, nor about the second girl. In Peru? In Madrid? Her letter is as laconic and telegraphic as yours. You guys are terrible. Georgette sends her affectionate memories and I, warm regards from the brother you know.

César   [JM]

TO JUAN LARREA

Paris, October 28, 1936
Dear Juan,
Excuse me for only now responding to your letter from the south of France. We're so absorbed in Spain that our entire souls aren't enough!

Your telegram doesn't mention your projects, your spiritual state, your points of view, or the play you and I and everyone else argued about. Here we work a lot, and not always at what we'd like to, on account of our foreigner status. And none of us is satisfied with this, and we'd just as soon fly to the battlefront itself. Never have I measured my human smallness as I do now. Never have I been so aware of how little an individual can do alone. This crushes me. Of course, at moments like this, each person has his role, no matter how humble, and our gears must shift and submit to the collective cog, in accordance with the total necessities of the cause. This consideration, however, doesn't manage to harness our spontaneous fits.

We want to know how you and yours are doing. Where are you? What kind of luck have you run into during that turmoil? Now we know that we were fortunate to have you and Guite and the babies here, on the eve of the uprising. We were so terribly worried, since we'd not received news from you. What a joy it was when Lipchitz told us you were in France!

Write to me at greater length, and you'll see how this agony for our dear friends disappears! But the cause of the people is sacred and will triumph today, tomorrow, or the day after—but triumph it will. Viva España! Viva the Popular Front!

Affectionate regards from Georgette for Guite, you and the kids, and for you, brother Juan, my most human regards.

César   [JM]

TO JUAN LARREA

Paris, January 22, 1937
Dear Juan,

I went back to Spain, then on to Brussels, and yesterday returned. This cause and the bug Georgette caught have prohibited me from sending you my New Year's greetings, to wish the best for you and us. I don't know why, but I think this year is going to bear more fruit than the previous ones. Things are budding all over the place. Don't you sense that too?

I've come back from Spain with a great affirmation of faith and hope in the triumph of the people. There's a remarkable power in humans and the atmosphere. No one accepts or even entertains the possibility of defeat. From the revolutionary point of view, the steps they've taken are even more flattering. We'll speak about this soon enough.

Bergamín is still in Paris. I saw him at the embassy ten days ago. We spoke about you. He tells me that he's waiting for news from you. It doesn't seem like he'll be leaving Paris, and I think that you could get ahold of him there. Speaking of news, I can tell you that the activities of publishers in Spain are for now utterly relegated to the Civil War, and those that aren't have already fizzled out. We'll have to wait until the drama of dust concludes. Write to me, in any case, about what you think you'll do. Isn't it about time for you to get out of there, after making arrangements with Bergamín? My sense is that the war is going to last many more months. One must reflect on that. Write to me about it.

Neruda and Delia have been here for several weeks. Neruda says he's going to Chile to appeal in the matter of his position, but I don't think his trip is set in stone.

Georgette and I send Guite and the children our best memories and affection, and counting on your lengthy letter to come, my warmest regards aimed straight for your heart.

Your brother,

César

Bergamín is still at the same hotel.   [JM]

TO JUAN LARREA

Paris, June 11, 1937

Dear Juan,

Forgive me for only recently replying to your letters. The delay was due to the fact that I wanted to send you the possibly practical result of certain interviews I've recently had with the director of the Bellas Artes in Spain, Renau, who was just here. Unfortunately, he left yesterday without finalizing anything with me. As you'll suspect, the matter at hand was propaganda in America, which he gives the importance that, in reality, it deserves. Of course, we spoke about you. He was the one who told me about your situation, upset that he hasn't taken you up yet on your offer to collaborate. He spoke very highly of you, and I think he's willing to address your case rather soon. That's how it's transpired. Renau is returning to Paris next Thursday. Maybe then we'll put an end to the gravity of the matter. I'll let you know.

Renau seemed to be a most intelligent, honorable man, magnificently oriented in the matters that fall to him. He's given me, aside from other things, the sense that he doesn't bumble about in useless verbiage and knows better how to work than how to speak. We'll see what can be done. In any case, he inspires great confidence in me. He left along with Bergamín, who's going to organize the Congress of Writers and return to Paris only after it's been held. Has he written to you? Has he mentioned his trip? The word is that the congress will be on July second. I suppose that they'll soon inform us officially. I haven't received a letter yet.

I find your article (the one you sent) magnificent, but you didn't include your signature or type your name. From personal experience I know that this kind of article arouses moderate interest in the American press, among the right readers, but, except on rare occasions, they won't publish anonymous articles. Since your name has weight there, I'd suggest you sign it, provided you have no personal reasons not to. In any case, I'll do as you say, but answer me as soon as you can so that the article gets sent immediately. I believe the tone you've given it is first rate, particularly for the op-ed section—of which there are many in America—regarding liberal ideas. That's why it seemed like a gem for the American press. The fire and sincerity you've given it will bear fruit. I'm sure.

You promised me another one for the bulletin. I hope you set aside time to do it and that you send it to me soon. You can even make it a tad shorter than the last.

I don't think Renau has heard anything about you in Valencia. He said it was not here that your matter had been resolved. I thought you'd be interested to know that, so as to familiarize yourself with what Navarro Tomás could've done, in view of your letter, which I found very good. I think he'll reply. Keep me posted. I'm returning the copy you sent me.

Regarding the other *friends*, nothing to speak of. You already know how life slips by. It's admirable. As always, I live most withdrawn from that environment. It's better this way.

Finally, if we go to the congress, once we're there we could put something together, on every level. In the meantime, patience. What else is there!

I almost forgot to tell you that Calderón's thing was to inform me of a telegram from Lima for me. They asked me to choose between the government, with all that it desires, and my ideas. Naturally, I opted for my ideas. The result: for now I'm prohibited from returning to Peru. How about that!

Affectionate memories from Georgette and me for Guite and the kids. Until my next letter and looking forward to yours, all best regards from your brother.

César   [JM]

TO LUIS JOSÉ DE ORBEGOSO

Paris, March 15, 1938

Dear Distinguished Friend,

A terrible *surmenage* has laid me up in bed for the past two weeks, and the doctors don't know yet how long I'll continue like this. I need a lengthy treatment, and finding myself without the resources to continue with it, I have thought of you, Luis José, my close friend from the start, to ask for your help and support. In the name of our long-standing and unshakable friendship, I allow myself to hope that my dear friend of so many years will stretch out his hand, as new evidence of that noble, generous, familiar spirit that has always inspired him.

Many thanks in advance, with heartfelt regards, from your solid, un-wavering friend.

César Vallejo

César Vallejo
Poste Restante—Bureau no. 43
rue de Rennes
Paris (6èsme)   [JM]

Notebooks

March 29, 1938

Whatever the case may be that I must defend before God, beyond death, I have a counsel for the defense: God.

NOTES

INTRODUCTION

1 Vallejo wrote in Castilian Spanish. In this book the terms "Castilian" and "Spanish" are used interchangeably to refer to *la lenga castellana*.

2 Puccinelli 2002, xxv. The following selections and introductory remarks constitute close readings of the *Obras completas* published by PUCP, edited and with introductions by Ricardo Silva-Santisteban, Cecilia Moreano, Manuel Miguel de Priego, Jesús Cabel, Jorge Puccinelli, and Rosario Valdivia Paz-Soldán; as well as the *Obras completas* published by Editora Perú, edited with extensive commentary by Ricardo González Vigil and Jorge Puccinelli. In this introduction, I rely on their work heavily, translate their commentary sporadically, and, with gratitude, occasionally paraphrase their ideas.

3 The Vallejo children from oldest to youngest were María Jesús, Victor Clemente, Francisco Cleofé, Manuel María, Augusto José, María Encarnación, Manuel Natividad, Néstor de Paula, María Águeda, Victoria Natividad, Miguel Ambrosio, and César Abraham.

4 Monguío's commentary on the 1940 census has offered excellent data to help us understand the living conditions of La Libertad at the time when Vallejo lived there. See *Censo nacional de población de 1940*, vol. 3, *Departamentos Lambayeque, Libertad, Ancash* (Lima: Ministerio de Hacienda y Comercio, Dirección Nacional de Estadística, 1947), 3, 8, 10, 4, 22, 24, 70.

5 Luis Monguío 1952, 16.

6 Hart 2007, in Eshleman 2007, 689.

7 Eshleman and Rubia Barcia 1980, xxi.

8 Ciro Alegría is best known for his novel *El mundo es ancho y ajeno* (1941) and as a figurehead (next to José María Arguedas) of the Peruvian indigenist movement.

9 To commemorate the passing, Vallejo wrote the elegy "To My Dead Brother," which he first published in the magazine *Cultura Infantil* in August 1917, only to then rework it as "To My Brother Miguel" and place it in the section "Songs of Home" of the book *The Black Heralds*.

10 Clemente Palma, note to Vallejo, *Variedades*, September 22, 1917.

11 See XVIII, XXIII, XXVIII, LII, LVIII, and LXV, *Trilce*, in Ortega 2002; "Más allá de la vida y la muerte," *Escalas*, in Silva-Santisteban and Moreano 1999, 34–47; and "Lánguidamente su licor," in De Priego 2002, 508.

12 Of the dedicated copy sent to his father, only the following fragment remains: "Father: with my dusty heart covered with the dust of life, I place in your hands my first book of poems; read it, like you used to read your old papers from those distant years when you ran the government of your town" (Espejo Asturrizaga 1989, 96).

13 See I, II, XVIII, XX, XL, L, LVIII, and LXI of *Trilce* and "Northeastern Wall," "Antarctic Wall," "Eastern Wall," and "Doublewide Wall" in *Escalas*, in Silva-Santisteban and Moreano 1999.

14 Hart 2007, 691, 700.

15 Prior to 1923, he went by the name Alfonso Silva-Santisteban.

16 Known to his friends as "el Chino Gálvez," Julio Gálvez Orrego was prohibited from fighting in the Spanish civil war, so he worked in a hospital until being captured, executed, and buried in a mass grave by Francoist forces.

17 Eshleman and Rubia Barcia 1980, xxiv.

18 Alfonso de Silva to Carlos Raygada, in *110 Cartas y una sola angustia: Cartas de Alfonso de Silva a Carlos Raygada* (Lima: Mejía Baca, 1975), 241.

19 See Rosa Alarco, *Alfonso de Silva: Biografía* (Havana: Casa de las Américas, 1981).

20 *El Norte* released its first volume on February 1, 1923, funded by Juan Vega, uncle of the Spelucín brothers. The masthead consisted of Alcides Spelucín, Antenor Orrego, Federico Esquerre, Franscico Xandóval, Belisario Spelucín, Francisco Spelucín, and Leoncio Muñoz.

21 See Puccinelli's synthesis (2002), on which I heavily draw in the following.

22 Published first in *L'Amerique Latine* and then in *El Norte* (Trujillo), March 12, 1924.

23 See "Against Professional Secrets: On Pablo Abril de Vivero," *Variedades* (Lima), May 7, 1927.

24 See "Spain in the International Exhibit of Paris, *Mundial* (Lima), October 23, 1925.

25 Vallejo to Pablo Abril de Vivero, October 19, 1924, in Cabel 2002, 86–87.

26 See also Vallejo to De Vivero, November 8, 1924, ibid., 91.

27 The masthead of *Mundial* in 1925 was made up of Andrés Avelino Aramburú, José Chioino, Luis Alberto Sánchez, Edgardo Rebagliati, Alejandro Belaunde, Humberto del Aguila, and the artists Jorge Vinatea Reinoso and Jorge Holguín Lavalle.

28 Puccinelli 2002, xxxviii.

29 Alejandro Peralta was a central component of the Orkopata cultural movement, from which some of the premiere indigenist documents emerged: *Boletín Kuntur* and *Vórtice* (Sicuani), *Atusparia* (Huaraz), *Chiripu* and *Waraka* (Arequipa), *Inty* (Huancayo), *La Sierra* and *La Región* (Lima), *Puna* (Ayaviri), and *Boletín Titikaka* (Puno), fostered by the magazine *Amauta* by José Carlos Mariátegui.

30 Cabel 2002, xxviii.

31 See Juan Domingo Córdoba Vargas's *César Vallejo del Perú profundo y sacrificado* (Lima: Jaime Campodonico, 1995).

32 See Hart 2007, in Eshleman 2007, 694.

33 As for the remaining authors that Vallejo mentions in his articles, there is still not enough evidence to specify them with certainty. It is believed that most of those present were part of the RAPP (Russian Association of Proletarian Writers), an extremely radical and exclusive organization.

34 Vallejo, "The Passion of Charles Chaplin," *Mundial*, March 9, 1928, in Puccinelli 2002, 560–62.

35 Ibid.

36 See Vallejo, "The Economic Meaning of Traffic," *Mundial*, April 5, 1929.

37 Vallejo, "Las lecciones del marxismo," *Variedades*, January 19, 1929, in Puccinelli 2002, 684–86.

38 César Vallejo, "El cinema: Rusia inaugura una nueva era en la pantalla," *Rusia en 1931*, in *Ensayos y Reportajes Completos*, ed. Manuel Miguel de Priego (Lima: PUCP, 2002), 152, 156.

39 See César Vallejo "The State of Spanish Literature," *Favorables-París-Poemas*, vol. 1 (Paris: Renacimiento, 1926).

40 Meneses 1994, 38.

41 See Henri Barbusse, *Elevación*, trans. César Vallejo (Madrid: Ulises, 1931); and Marcel Aymé, *La calle sin nombre*, trans. César Vallejo (Madrid: Cenit: 1931).

42 See César Vallejo, "The New North American Poetry," *El Comercio*, July 30, 1929.

43 See Philippart de Vallejo 1978, 40.

44 Theodore Dreiser traveled to the Soviet Union in 1927, John Dos Passos in 1928, Langston Hughes in 1932–33, John Steinbeck in 1949, and Pablo Neruda in 1949, inter alia.

45 Priego 2002, lxxi.

46 See César Vallejo, *Rusia ante el segundo plan quinquenal*, in *Ensayos y reportajes completos*, ed. Manuel Miguel de Priego (Lima: PUCP, 2002), 364.

47 See Vallejo to Gerardo Diego, January 27, 1932, in Cabel 2002, 413–14.

48 See Eshleman and Rubia Barcia 1980, xxv.

49 See Hart 2007, 696.

50 See "Black Stone on a White Stone," "It was Sunday in the clear ears of my jackass," "Today I like life much less," "Epistle to the Passerby," "Telluric and Magnetic," "The miners came out of the mine," "Considering coldly," and "Idle on a Stone."

51 Vallejo to Juan Larrea, October 28, 1936, in Cabel 2002, 448–49.

52 See "Popular Statements of the Spanish Civil War," an article Vallejo wrote in March 1937 (Larrea 1957, 167–75).

53 Eshleman and Rubia Barcia 1980, xxvi.

54 For a more complete description of the event and its cultural significance, see Manuel Aznar, Maria Campillo, Montse Gutiérrez, and Fructuós Moncunill, "El Segundo Congreso Internacional de Escritores para la Defensa de la Cultura (Valencia–Madrid–Barcelona–Paris)," La Universitat Autónoma de Barcelona, accessed August 9, 2014, http://ddd.uab .cat/pub/expbib/2007/exili/aznar.asp.html.

55 This speech was transcribed and published in *El Mono Azul* (Madrid), no. 4, 1939.

56 See More 1968.

57 Eshleman and Rubia Barcia 1980.

58 Vallejo to Luis José de Orbegoso, March 15, 1938, in Cabel 2002, 468.

59 Eshleman and Rubia Barcia 1980, xxvii.

60 The epitaph can be translated as "I have snowed so much / so that you sleep / Georgette." The widow's hair has turned white as snow from the pain she has endured to bury her husband.

61 See Hart and Cornejo Polar 2002, as well as David Sobrevilla, *Introducción bibliográfica a César Vallejo* (Lima: Amaru, 1995).

62 Vallejo, *El romanticismo en la poesía castellana*, in Puccinelli 2002, 31–32, reprod. in Puccinelli 2002, anexos.

63 Ibid., 46–47.

64 See González Vigil 1991, 1:xix.

65 Efraín Kristal, introd. to Eshleman 2007, 11.

66 The 1922 publications include *The Waste Land* by T. S. Eliot, *Ulysses* by James Joyce, *The Enormous Room* by e. e. Cummings, *Most Interesting Preface* by Mario de Andrade, *20 Poems to Be Read on the Tram* by Oliverio Girondo, *My Sister, Life* by Boris Pasternak, *The Marine Cemetery* by Paul Verlain, *The Beautiful and the Damned* by F. Scott Fitzgerald, *The Hairy Ape* by Eugene O'Neil, and *The Death of Tarelkin* by Alexksandr Sukhovo-Kobylin, produced at the Meyerhold Theatre that year.

67 Julio Ortega, introd. to *Trilce* (Madrid: Cátedra, 1991), 9.

68 Ferrari, introd. to *Trilce* (Eshleman 1992, xxvii).

69 *Wind Choir*, or *Coro de vientos*, can be rendered several ways. A *coro* is both a "choir" and a "chorus," and *vientos* may refer to "winds" but also "woodwinds."

70 See Vallejo, "Muro antártico," *Escalas*, in Silva-Santisteban and Moreano 1999, 16, 18.

71 Silva-Santisteban and Moreano 1999, xxi.

72 Ibid., xxi–xxii.

73 See Vallejo, "El otro imperialismo," *Hacia el reino de los sciris*, ibid., 187.

74 See Vallejo, "La paz de Túpac Yupanqui," ibid., 202.

75 Puccinelli 2002, xvii.

76 See Vallejo to Ricardo Vegas García, May 15, 1926, in Cabel 2002, 173.

77 See Cabel 2002, 434–35.

78 Vallejo to Luis José de Orbegoso, *Oiga* (Lima), March 9, 1992, 54–60.

79 See Silva-Santisteban's introduction in Silva-Santisteban and Moreano 1999, xxvii.

80 See Emma Goldman's *My Disillusionment in Russia* (New York: Doubleday, Page, 1923) and *My Further Disillusionment in Russia* (New York: Doubleday, Page, 1924).

81 For Kolbasiev's position, see "Artist's Facing Politics," *Mundial*, December 31, 1927.

82 An earlier version of this summary first appeared in Mulligan 2011, 9–12.

83 See *Aphorisms* (Vallejo 2002).

84 César Vallejo, *The Final Judgment* (Lima: PUCP, 1979).

85 Some scenes started to appear in *Letras peruanas* (1956), thanks to Jorge Puccinelli.

86 See Vallejo, poem LVI of *Trilce*, in Silva-Santisteban 1997, 109.

87 See Escobar 1973, 213–40.

88 González Vigil 1991, 1:xxxiv–xxxv.

89 See César Vallejo, *España, aparte de mi esta cáliz*, ed. Alan Smith Soto (Madrid: Árdora, 2012).

90 See Silva-Santisteban's introduction to *Poesía completa* 1997, 4:9.

91 Ibid., 15–16.

92 Eshleman and Rubia Barcia 1980, xxvi.

93 See Silva-Santisteban 1997, 13.

94 See González Vigil 1991, 736.

95 Ibid., 742.

96 See Higgins 1970, 334.

97 See Oviedo 1982, 310.

98 See Hopkins Rodriguez 1993, 278.

99 "The Incas, Revived," written in January 1935, published posthumously in *Aula Vallejo*, nos. 11–13 (1972–74), repr. in Puccinelli 2002, 935–44.

100 Eleazar Boloña, "Saycuscca-Rumi: Tradición cusqueña," *El Perú Ilustrado* (Lima), no. 62 (July 1888), in Silva-Santisteban and Moreano 1999, 214–18; *Ollantay: Edición crítica de la obra anónima quechua*, ed. Julio Calvo Pérez (Cuzco: Bartolome de las Casas, 1998); Vladimir Kirshon, *Rel's'y Gudyat* (Moscow, 1931).

101 See Hopkins Rodriguez, 1993, 291.

BOOK ONE

1 August Wilhelm Schlegel (1767–1845) and his brother, Karl Wilhelm Friedrich Schlegel (1772–1829).

2 See Gustave Le Bon, *The Psychology of Revolution*, trans. Bernard Miall (London: Fisher Unwin, 1913).

3 The passages on Espronceda and Zorrilla have been extracted from "Crítica de romanticismo," the most extensive portion of the thesis. Cesar Vallejo, *El romanticismo en la poesía castellana*, reprod. in Puccinelli 2002, 34–47.

4 See José Martí's prologue to Juan Antonio Bonalde's poem, "El poema del Niagara," New York, 1882, reprod. in José Martí's *Con los pobres de la tierra* (Caracas: Fundación Ayacucho, 1991), 53–65.

5 See José de Espronceda, *Obras poéticas*, ed. Juan Eugenio Hartzenbusch and Antonio Ferrer del Río (Paris: Laloux Hijo y Guillot, 1870), 155.

6 See the prologue to Espronceda's *El diablo mundo: Poema* (Madrid: Gaspar y Roig, 1852), iv.

7 See Salvador Camacho Roldán's introduction to *Poesías de Gregório Gutiérrez González* (Paris: Librería de Garnier Hermanos, 1888), iv.

8 Tirso de Molina, pseudonym of Brother Gabriel Téllez (1579–1648), Spanish Baroque dramatist to whom the creation of the *Don Juan* myth is often attributed, as represented in his comedy *El burlador de Sevilla*, completed around 1615–20.

9 Alphonse de Lamartine (1790–1869), poet, politician, and key figure in the creation of the Second Republic; and Alfred de Musset (1810–1857), dramatist, poet, and novelist.

10 See Alberto Rodriguez de Lista y Arragón's essay "Poesías de D. José Zorrilla," in *Artículos críticos y literarios* (Palma: Imprenta y Librería de Estévan Trias, 1840), 270.

11 **Aristarchuses of the world** In the Spanish we read *los aristarcos*, where *aristarco* makes reference to the great Greek critic Aristarchus of Samos. Although it is not a common phrase, in Spanish an *aristarco* is a critic who is understood but excessively severe. To communicate the idiomatic sense of the phrase, we have added "of the world."

12 See Camacho Roldán, introd. to *Poesías*, iii–iv.

13 **corequenque** "A fabulous bird, which according to the Incans was discovered on a small lake at the foot of snow-covered Vilcanota. The Incans carefully extracted two feathers from its wings, which their sovereign then displayed as his insignia of supreme authority. The word is probably based on *curiquingue* (caracara)" (Eshleman 2007, 621).

14 **La Grama . . . La Ramada** "La Grama is a rural horse track outside Trujillo, and La Ramada its sole grandstand. Apparently it had ceased to be active in Vallejo's time, becoming a sad, dilapidated place" (Eshleman 2007, 622).

15 *tahuashando* "A neologism based on the Quechuan word *tahua* (four). José Cerna-Bazán, author of *Sujeto a cambio: De las relaciones del texto y a sociedad en la escritura de César Vallejo*, has often wondered about this word, so he asked his father, José Diego Cerna López (who, as part of his work, was often in the La Libertad area of the Peruvian sierra in the 1930s). His father told him: "Ah, yes, that word was used, or is still used, I should say, when we would arrive at an observation point, especially at a crossroads, with our mules, and we would look around to see if anyone else was coming down the road. Cerna-Bazán mentions that when he read to his father Vallejo's line using the word, the latter said, 'Sure, that's it—Vallejo is saying that this person is *tahuashando*'" (Eshleman 2007, 622).

16 **yaraví** "A song in which indigenous and Spanish melodic elements have been fused. The word is a hybrid in tonality as well as spirit and appears to derive from the Incan *harawi*, which was adapted for religious hymns from the time of the conquest until the eighteenth century" (Eshleman 2007, 622).

17 **Quenaing** "A neologism based on *quena*, the term for a five-holed Quechuan flute (which once accompanied the *yaravís*)" (Eshleman 2007, 622).

18 **the Pallas** "Beautifully adorned young women who perform group dances that were originally part of the religious festivals in Cuzco" (Eshleman 2007, 622).

19 *caja* **from Tayanga** "The *caja* is a musical instrument combining a kind of drum with a ditch reed (from which *quenas* can be made). Tayanga is a northern Peruvian town specializing in the fabrication of *cajas*" (Eshleman 2007, 622). In modern Peruvian Spanish, the instrument is more commonly called a *cajón*.

20 *huaino* "The most well-known and representative indigenous dance of Peru, with happy, flirtatious movements (and sometimes words)" (Eshleman 2007, 622).

21 **coricanchas** "The Coricancha was the great Temple of the Sun in Cuzco; using the Incan walls as a base, the Spanish conquistadors built the cathedral of Santo Domingo. In the poem's fourth stanza, Vallejo suggests that the Coricancha of the Sun rises up against the cathedral" (Eshleman 2007, 622).

22 **Brahacmanic** "Vallejo has placed an 'ac' in the middle of the Spanish *brahmanico* (Brahmanic) to form the word *brahacmanicos*. Ferrari conjectures that the poet may have confused the spelling of the word with *dracma* (drachma). González Vigil does not comment" (Eshleman 2007, 623).

23 **kick our poor sponge** *Estiraremos la rodilla* (literally, will we stretch our knees) is a play

on *estirar la pata* (literally, 'to stretch the foot' but in slang meaning 'to kick the bucket,' die). I have adjusted the English accordingly" (Eshleman 2007, 623).

24 **Januneid** (title) "The Spanish 'Enereida' is a neologism fusing *enero* (January) and *Eneida* (Aeneid). The English version matches it" (Eshleman 2007, 623).

25 **Epexegesis** (title) "Thought by some scholars to be a neologism, the word *espergesia* actually exists in Spanish. It is a rhetorical term that means 'using a surplus of words for a fuller and more embellished declaration.' This definition is to be found in the *Diccionario de autoridades de la Real Academia Española*, in the first edition, 1732. The word I have chosen in an attempt to match it in English is defined as follows (in *Webster's New International Dictionary*): 'Provision of additional explanation or definition; that which is added for elucidation'" (Eshleman 2007, 623).

26 Vallejo does not seem to be quoting anyone here, but rather indicating his own imagined dialogue with the recently deceased Valdelomar, in which he appears to be writing through Valdelomar's poem "El hermano ausente en la cena de pascua . . ." See Abraham Valdelomar, *Poesía y estética* (Lima: Universo, 1971), 39.

27 **not knotting a shameless note** In the Spanish, Vallejo offers the following wordplay: *a fuerza de sin y sin y sin metí un sinvergüenza*. The ludic element foreshadows the aesthetic we see in *Trilce*, where phonetic cohesion often receives priority over semantic clarity. A literal translation that ignores the phonetic wordplay could be "by dint of without and without and without I stuck in a shameless person or thing."

28 **the count** "el Conde [de Lemos]," pseudonym of Abraham Valdelomar.

29 **Korriskoso** Vallejo's nickname among his bohemian friends in Trujillo.

BOOK TWO

1 **Who's making all that racket** "Espejo writes that while Vallejo was in the Trujillo jail, inmates were taken outside to use the latrines four times a day. There the guards would coarsely urge them to hurry up (123). The first two stanzas of poem L indicate that this is not gratuitous but quite pertinent information. Looking at the first stanza of this opening poem, it would seem that the racket-makers are the wardens and guards, and that the 'islands' are the inmates' turds. For a study of the construction of this poem, see "A Translational Understanding of *Trilce #I*" in my collection of essays *Companion Spider* (Wesleyan University Press, 2002)" (Eshleman 2007, 626).

2 **guano** "The dried excrement of seabirds, found mixed with bones and feathers on certain Peruvian coastal islands, was widely used as fertilizer. Guano workers visited the mainland ports and cities on their days off, and Vallejo would have been able to observe them not just in Trujillo but also in the vicinity of the jail" (Eshleman 2007, 626).

3 **fecapital** "Based on *tesoro* (treasure), the word *tesórea* has provoked differing interpretations. Giovanni Meo Zilio identifies it as a neologism incorporating the latter part of *estercórea* (excrement), influenced by the guano references in the stanza (as well as by the 'islands' in the first)" (Eshleman 2007, 626).

4 **ponk** "The Spanish *calabrina*, meaning 'an intolerable, intense stench,' is archaic. If I had used the word *stench*, the translation would reflect the common Spanish word *hedor*—thus the necessity, in such cases, of finding archaic English words (or expressions) for their Spanish equivalents" (Eshleman 2007, 626).

5 **muzzled** "The Spanish *abozaleada* is based on *abozalada* (muzzled), with an *-ear* infinitive ending substituted for the standard *-ar* ending. Meo Zilio considers the word to be a neologism" (Eshleman 2007, 626).

6 **nighttime fog** The Spanish word *relente* refers to dew or fog that appears in the night or to the bright glare of the sun, reflected or not, that forces onlookers to advert their gaze.

The sense of repulsion is strong here, but the notion that "noon" contains the fog from the night before seems coherent with the pump that "backwashes" time.

7 **songsing** Vallejo verbalizes the noun *canción*, probably following the morphology of *cantar* (to sing).

8 **What calls all that puts on hedge us** The very idiosyncratic line reads thusly in the Spanish: *¿Qué se llama cuanto heriza nos?* In the beginning of the expression we find the odd phrase *qué se llama* instead of the expected *cómo se llama* (what does one call). Moreover, according to Meo Zilio, *heriza nos* shows a psychological impulse of *herir* (to wound) and thus grafts the image of the *herida* (wound) onto the word; the syntactic inversion of the position of *nos* is added to the viewable effect of prosthesis, aimed at concentrating the shuddering action of *erizar* (to bristle) upon the passive subject of *nos* (1993, 253–54). Larrea suggests that the attachment of the *h* to *erizar* "evokes the presence of various expressions of bristling [raising hairs on end]: horrendous, horrible, horrify and horripilate" (in González Vigil 1991, 231). To account for the neologism, the phrase *to put on edge* has been modified with *hedge* to evoke the spiny hedgehog (i.e., the bristling), and the syntactical inversion has likewise been recreated.

9 **Thesame . . . namE** The word *Lomismo* is a contraction of *lo mismo* (the same). The capitalization of the final *e* in "namE" imitates Vallejo's *nombrE*.

10 **three-pwronged** Martos and Villanueva define *trifurcas* from "*trifurcado* (trifurcated): Of three opposing branches or arms (*R.A.*, 1925)" (1989, 60). Meo Zilio determines the presence of apocope: "'trifurcas' for 'trifurcados': [based on an] analogical pattern and a psychological impulse of 'trifulca' [rompus, row, squabble] + 'trifurcas' [trifurcates]" (1993, 257). We have attempted to evoke the sense of dispute homophonically by highlighting the *wrong* in *prong*.

11 **embitternessed** In the Spanish, *amargurada* is a neologism that Vallejo prefers over *amargada* (embittered).

12 In characteristic Vallejo fashion, the writer here swaps the *g* for a *j* to get *aljidas*; hence, we use *aljid* rather than *algid*.

13 **two dose up on mother** In the Spanish, *dosificarse en madre* draws attention to *dos* (two), evoking the sense of *double-dosing* or *overdosing*.

14 **otilian** Vallejo coins the adjective *otilianas* after one of his early lovers, Otilia, perhaps modeling it morphologically after *cristalinas* (crystalline).

15 **At this our** In the Spanish, Vallejo separates *Ahora* (now) to read *A hora*, which hints at *a la hora* (at the time, or hour). *At this our* attempts to replicate the homophonic play in the Spanish.

16 **on the nightstand of so much what'll become of me** In the phrase *el velador de tánto qué será de mí*, the nightstand is qualified with the exclamation, "what will become of me," "what will be of me," or "how will I end up." In step with *Trilce V*, where Vallejo substantivizes the exclamation "ohs de ayes," this syntactic torsion is upending.

17 **all readies truth** "The first two words in the Spanish, *todo avía verdad*, play off *todavía* (yet, still, nevertheless), while the second word sounds like a past tense of *haber* (to have)" (Eshleman 2007, 628).

18 **I transasfixiate** "*Envetarse* is a rare verb that has at least two meanings, both of which may be operative here with *enveto*. In Ecuador, it means 'to dominate'; according to Eduardo Neale-Silva, Vallejo uses it in this sense in a 1927 article, 'El arco de triunfo' (The arch of triumph), in speaking of *un fornido mozo en actitud de envetar un toro* (a husky youth getting ready to subdue a bull). The use of *toroso* (torose, taurine) in the third stanza supports this meaning. However, in Peru the word also means 'to become asphyxiated by the poisonous emanations from the veins of a mine,' and given the context of 'Bolivarian asperities'

(rugged landscapes in which mines might very well exist), this meaning also seems pertinent (though I notice that by using the verb actively, Vallejo reverses its passive usage as a mining term)" (Eshleman 2007, 628).

19 **How whales go dutch with doves** In the line *Cómo escotan las ballenas a palomas*, at least two meanings can be noted, as González Vigil (1991, 251) observes, the first pertaining to the adjustment of size, as in tailoring; the second, to the payment for someone else's share in the cost of something. Others have suggested that *escotan* is a typographical error for *escolatan* (escort), though the former seems more plausible than the latter.

20 **How we saddlebow** In the phrase *cómo arzonamos*, one can perceive the verbalization of the noun *arzón* (saddlebow, saddle frame), that is, the arch piece of the saddle. As a neologism at the hand of Vallejo, we may, with Meo Zilio, associate the neologism, "by opposition, to *desarzonar* [to buck off, to throw], semantically meaning *cabalgamos* [to ride on horseback], with the face directed backwards, towards the monotonous haunches (of the horse)" (1993, 280).

21 **smears on the soothing salfe** González Vigil claims that it means *untar* (to anoint) or *pringar*, (to grease or oil, with ointment) (1991, 252), which is confirmed by Martos and Villanueva (1989, 90), who cite the definition in the *Diccionario de la Real Academia 1925*. Furthermore, *misturas* are not only "wildflowers," as one may suspect, but also products made from them, such as infusions and tinctures, which rings homophonically from *misturas* (mixtures), possibly imitating a rural speech pattern. Moreover, that Vallejo uses *misturas* instead of *mixturas* leads us to consider it akin to the antiquated form *salfe* over the modern *salve* (*OED*, compact ed., vol. 2, s.v. "salfe"). So at the end of the poem, the patient is now seated in a bed and he *empavona tranquilas misturas*; he smears on his body, in a feeble attempt to save his own a life, a salve that he cannot even pronounce correctly, emphasizing the futility of his action.

22 **daughterloin** "By adding a silent 'h' to *ijar* (loin, or flank), Vallejo strongly evokes *hija* (daughter, or child)" (Eshleman 2007, 629).

23 **ovulatable** "That which can be ovulated. According to Ferrari, the word *ovulandas* is based on the verb *ovular* (to ovulate), using 'the adjectival ending of a passive Latin conjugation.'" (Eshleman 2007, 630).

24 **bromined slides** In the phrase *bromurados declives* we find the neologism *bromurados*, where Vallejo seems to have fused *bromuro* (bromide) with *amurallado* (walled, fortified). It is our sense that the neologism results in a meaning of "vein" or "streak," running through the "slides" that the mother and child cross.

25 **stunted adulthood of man** The line *mayoría inválida de hombre* encapsulates a major idea to which Vallejo returns time and again through *Trilce* and other works as well: the idea of reaching one's potential. As Martos and Villanueva point out, by the end of the poem the narrator "is not even left with the image of his mother; he is in search of a 'terciario brazo': be it the Beloved or any other human being who may symbolize protection, tutelage, help. He is an adult, but is also disabled [*inválido*]. He is an imploring man-child" (1989, 125). Ferrari perceives an "obsession with the mother and with the feeling of mutilation that awakens the consciousness of adulthood in the poet . . . The final line, which is an extension of 'Dios' and 'Desnudo en barro' in *Los heraldos negros*, clarifies the sense of the whole poem. It is the outcry of the orphan, the mutilated, one-armed heart, which looks for the third protective presence, the mother perhaps, the new mother (1997, 122, 124). For Escobar, at the end of the poem, "this action of affective interest is projected upon the 'donde' and 'cuando' (i.e., space and time) of the man who is suffering a *mayoría inválida de hombre*, whose full human condition, despite being an adult, is cut off and damaged" (1973, 105–6). Most English translations render this line as "invalid majority of man"; however,

mayoría is not only "majority" but the state of being a *mayor* (adult), that is, adulthood. The sense of coming up short, of not reaching completion, the repeating odd number throughout *Trilce* here takes the form of an adulthood that exists only as a horizon.

26 **with an itty bit of silyba and dirt** Vallejo prefers *saliba* over *saliva*, as a way to evoke the language of the little girl shining the shoes of her convicted father. A similar gesture is made at the end of the poem, where the sound of spitting is evoked graphically.

27 **Chess bishops upthrust to stick** The Spanish phrase is semantically and phonetically complex: *Alfan alfiles a adherirse*. The assonance of this line is, at the very least, disconcerting in any translation, but the semantic elements are even more troublesome. The verb *alfar* seems to describe the action of a horse "that lifts the front quarter too high, without bending the hocks or lowering the haunches, while galloping or during other violent exercises (*R.A.*, 1939)" (in Martos and Villanueva 1989, 151). As for *alfiles*, or *alfil* in the singular, by way of Hispanic Arabic roots, it refers to the *chess bishop*; though a second meaning, pointed out by Larrea, is that of an *omen* (1978, 791). Neale-Silva, on the other hand, claims "it is the result of a euphonic play on the verb 'alfar': *alfan alfiles*. In this way it is a neologism, which might well have been suggested by the weeds of the *Geraniaceae* species, called *alfileres* or *alfilerillos*" (1975, 68).

28 **carabel snorts, without amerecanizing** In the Spanish, the word is correctly spelled *carabela*; however, Vallejo substitutes a 'v' for a 'b' to get *caravela*—a phonetic play he returns to throughout *Trilce*. Similarly, in the verb *ameracanizar*, which would normally be spelled *americanizar*, he has preferred an *a* over the *i* and thereby evokes the word *mera* (mere). González Vigil notes that Ferrari "believes it is an error from the first two editions, instead of "carabela", considering that Vallejo is alluding to the 'instruments of the invasion of European powers'' . . . , but liberating the morphological suggestion (evident in other languages: Portuguese and Galician, *caravela*, Italian, *caravella*, French, *caravelle* . . .)" (1991, 288). The word *caravelas* has been preserved by González Vigil (ibid), Merino (1996b, 261), Silva-Santisteban (1997, 67), Martos and Villanueva (1989, 150), Hernández Novás (1988, 136), Ortega (2002, 138); however, the change to *carabelas* has been made by Larrea (1978) and Ferrari (1968) (cf. González Vigil, 1991, 289). As González Vigil observes, many specialists think that *americanizar* (following the 1922 and 1930 editions) is "an error for 'americanizar', linking the caravels with the discovery and conquest of America. We prefer to preserve 'ameracanizar'" (1991, 288–89). The 1922 and 1930 editions have also been respected by Merino (1996b, 261), Ortega (2002, 138), Martos and Villanueva (1989, 150); contrary to this, the change to *americanizar* is made by Silva-Santisteban (1997, 67) and Hernández Novás (1988, 136).

29 **imnazaled** Meo Zilio describes *ennazala* as a lexical neologism that does not follow the pattern by which the ending *-izar* is appended, in the way that *nasal* becomes *nasalizar*, that *vocal* becomes *vocalizar*, that *labial* becomes *labializar*, and so on (1993, 249). This neologism breaks that pattern but, in so doing, it is performative in the sense that it contains onomatopoeic elements, since one must produce a nasal sound to speak it. And for this reason, we have preferred the prefix "im-" to produce a similar effect.

30 **when innanimous gryphion only reports / blundered mute-due crusades** The end of this stanza is wrought with neologisms, thereby problematizing the translation considerably. To begin, Meo Zilio breaks down *inánima* into *in-* + *anima* (soul) and suggests that the formation is based on an analogical pattern with *magnánima* (magnanimous) + *inánime* (inanimate); he also reminds us that Vallejo's creation may have been an echo of Herrera y Reissig's neologism: "Fausta embriaguez la *inanima*" in the poem "Ciles Alucinadas" (1993, 252). As for *gifalda*, there appears to be a fusion of *grifalto* (griffin), that is, the mythological figure that is half eagle and half lion, and the *grifa*, that is, the cursive

letter, so called after Sebastian Gryphius (1492–1556), the printmaker and book dealer who produced a wealth of works in gothic script. Finally, the word *callanda*, also a neologism, seems to describe "what should be silenced" (267).

31 **Viandry** "An archaic word that refers to food. It is also a medieval term for the tax or provisions given to a monarch by a town, as he and his entourage pass through. . . . As a verb, *yantar* used to be a common word meaning 'to eat.' While it would be out of common usage for most Spanish speakers today, it may still be in use in remote sierra areas of Peru" (Eshleman 2007, 632).

32 **degllusion** "Vallejo alters *deglución* (deglutition, swallowing), evoking *ilusión* (illusion) to form *deglusión*" (Eshleman 2007, 632).

33 **vigrant** Meo Zilio suggests that *vagoroso* (*vago* + *-roso*) is based on an analogical pattern with *vaporoso* (vaporous) and a psychological impulse of *vagaroso* (vagrant) + *vigoroso* (vigorous) (1993, 276). Neale-Silva interprets the neologism based on *vagaroso* (vagrant) and *vigoroso* (vigorous) (1975, 153). We prefer "vigrant" as a way to extend the neologistic use by applying Neale-Silva's insight into the sense of "vigor."

34 **all sweetnessed-up** González Vigil sees a neologism stemming from *dulzor* (sweetness) and the suffix *-ada* of a qualifying adjective (1991, 302).

35 **Hope between cotton bawls** The phrase *entre algodones* (literally, between cottons) is used in the expression *criar entre algodones* (to coddle, pamper); however, in the context of the poem, the image of the cottons or cotton balls is made explicit at the end, where the now-bloodstained, gauzelike material is opened up. The translation relies on the homophony of *bawls* and *balls* to evoke both meanings.

36 **hell-bent on winning** "*A las ganadas* is a northern Peruvianism" (Eshleman 2007, 633).

37 **ammoniafies** "The Spanish *amoniácase* is *amoníaco* (ammoniac, ammonia) turned into a verb. While we have a verb in English (ammonify), I do not use it, since none exists in Spanish" (Eshleman 2007, 633).

38 **neverthelessez** "The Spanish *todaviiza* is the adverb *todavía* (yet, still, nevertheless,— and, in old Spanish, always) extended/warped into a verb. A few lines later, another adverb, *aunes* (evens), is treated as a plural noun" (Eshleman 2007, 633).

39 **iridesends** Martos and Villanueva suggest the word is derived "from *iridiscente* (iridescent), what shows or reflects the color of the iris (*R.A.* 1925)" (1989, 248), an interpretation with which Meo Zilio agrees, though he suggests that the psychological drive behind the formation is in the *suavizar* and that, semantically, the construction refers to "that which may illuminate (like a rainbow) the Mondays of reason'" (1993, 280).

40 **Samain would say** "Vallejo quotes from the first two lines of 'L'automne,' by Albert Samain (1856–1900), which, translated by Juan Ramón Jiménez, was included in *La poesía francesa moderna* (1913), edited by Díez-Canedo and Fortún. This is the book that introduced Vallejo to French Symbolist poetry. Among the poets included were Nerval, Baudelaire, Gautier, Corbière, Laforgue, Rimbaud, Verlaine, Mallarmé, Jammes, Maeterlinck, and Claudel." The first stanza of "L'automne" is as follows: "Comme dans un préau d'hospice ou de prison, / L'air est calme et d'une tristesse contenue; / Et chaque feuille d'or tombe, l'heure venue, / Ainsi qu'un souvenir, lente, sur le gazon" (Eshleman 2007, 635).

41 *La Prensa* "Daily Lima newspaper (1903–1984)" (Eshleman 2007, 635), to which Vallejo contributed an article in 1919.

42 **empatrolled** "The Spanish *empatrullado* is a neologism based on *patrullado* (patrolled)" (Eshleman 2007, 635).

43 **stripshredding** "The Spanish *se harapan* is a neologism based on *harapo* (rag) and possibly *arroparse* (to clothe oneself, wrap up). Since the *desnudos* (nudes) in the line above are probably pinups the prisoners have tacked to the wall, I attempt to create a word that

inverts *arroparse* so as to evoke 'stripping' by turning one's clothes into rags" (Eshleman 2007, 635).

44 **bubblish** The Spanish *bullosas* is a neologism, possibly based on *bullir* (to boil, bubble) or *bullicioso* (bustling, boisterous).

45 **ill-paved oxident** The word *oxidente* has attracted the attention of many. Meo Zilio considers it a "phonetic-graphical neologism" that receives the CC=X substitution of signs, noting "'oxidente' for 'occidente' based on an analogical pattern and a psychological impulse of *óxido* (rust, oxide), given the presence of the prior 'mal asfalto' as well" (1993, 250). González Vigil recalls that the neologism *oxidente* was "already used in 'Los arrieros' of *Los heraldos negros*" (1991, 381). The word "has two meanings," according to Estela dos Santos, "one from *óxido* which is joined to *mal asfaltado*; it is something damaged, oxidized, and the other, from *occidente* (west) linked to the 'muebles hindúes'; that is, the 'east'" (in Larrea 1961, 44).

46 **dizmal** Vallejo substitutes homophones *b/v* in *torbo* with reference to *torvo* (fierce, grim, irate, and terrible to the sight).

47 **tori** "Round moldings (torus, in the singular), not to be confused with Shinto temple gateways! In the same line as *tondos*, *repulgos* could be translated as architectural 'borders' or as 'pie endings.' I opted for the latter" (Eshleman 2007, 636).

48 **axling** "*Ejando* is *eje* (axle) turned into a verb" (Eshleman 2007, 636).

49 **reveilles champing** "This mysterious phrase, *tascar dianas*, might also be translated as 'dianas scotching' or even more dramatically, 'bull's-eyes crunching.' It appears, however, to play off *tocar dianas* (to sound reveille), which would eliminate the other two denotations of 'Diana.' *Tascar* means 'to scotch or swingle flax,' as well as 'to nibble, browse, or champ' (as in 'to champ against the bit'). . . . Perhaps the sensation here is that of trumpet blasts trying to break the constraints of reveille and reach the dead mother (to awake the dead)" (Eshleman 2007, 636).

50 **humblest** "According to Meo Zilio (and to Antenor Orrego before him), with *humildóse* Vallejo has taken an archaic verb, *humildarse*, and substituted it for the current *humillarse*. Meo Zilio quotes Orrego: 'When he says *humildarse* instead of *humillarse* reviving an archaism in the language, the habitual semantic cap has been broken and the word has been transformed, now signifying tenderness and loving reverence. The father does not lower and humiliate himself before his wife [see stanza 4], he exalts his love and gives it a tender reverence *humbling himself* 'until less than half a man, / until being the youngest child that you had.' I am not aware of such a distinction in English, though the difference between *to humble* and *to humiliate* may be close (the former implying self-abasement without the loss of respect, the latter always implying ignominy). The translation problem is that to render *humildóse* as *humble* does not, as such, sound a difference with *humiliate*" (Eshleman 2007, 636).

51 **my paletot / a / t / f / u / l / m / a / s / T** In the Spanish, *a toda asta* is the phrase the reader expects, but Vallejo elides the second *a* and thereby phonetically and graphically fuses *toda* and *asta* into *todasta*, which problematizes the English construction, where such fusion can only be hinted at by my omitting an *l* from *at full mast*.

52 **sub- / merge** In the 1922 edition of *Trilce* the lines of this poem were broken as is reflected in the present translation. In editions subsequent to the first, it was sometimes treated as a prose poem, and the lines were not broken deliberately. Critics, like Meo Zilio, have even offered analyses on the neologisms formed by the enjambments in the 1922 edition.

53 **Barrancos** Toponym, a present-day district of Lima; in Vallejo's time, Barranco was not formerly part of the city proper, but was a popular area to go on excursions and swimming in the Pacific Ocean.

54 **horizontifying** According to Meo Zilio, this neologism is based on *horizontal* (horizontal) and *electrizante* (electrifying), evoking the meaning, "what produces or likens horizon" (1993, 271).·

55 **whippt** The Spanish word is traditionally spelled *flagelados* (whipped, lashed), with a *g*. Vallejo's "flajelados" has been considered accepted usage by González Vigil (1991, 397); Ortega thinks the altered spelling may be "deliberate" (2002, 329). The slight neologism is likewise reprinted by Merino (1996b, 318) and Silva-Santisteban (1997, 129), while on the other hand, *flagelados* has been reprinted by Hernández Nóvas (1988, 191). The present text offers *whippt* as a translation of the alteration.

56 *antara* A type of Andean flute, pan flute.

57 **for ever and never** In the Spanish, *por siempre jamás* contains a similar inherent contradiction.

58 **scope out** It is not clear what Vallejo means by *arcenan*. Given the context, it appears to express the act of "looking," perhaps with hints of "scoping," given the phonetic proximity of *arcenar* to *arsenal*.

59 **carabids** While the Spanish word *cárabos* might also be translated as some sort of an "owl," which would seem appropriate given the context of being watched over, the ground beetle "carabid" seems like a better fit, since these are insectivorous, which seems to rhyme thematically with the psychological cannibalism that goes on between Palomino and the other inmates.

60 **porcelained** Vallejo coins the adjective *aporcelandas*, which appears to derive from *porcelana* (porcelain). The word here seems to give the "soul" and "pituitaries" of the narrator's friend a sense of fragility.

61 **bronzemongery** The Spanish word *broncería* refers to a collection of bronze pieces. A close rendering in English is "ironmongery," though, for our translation, we have preferred to incorporate "bronze," since this substance contains strong cultural connotations (i.e., *la raza de bronce*) and because we know that the provisional title of *Trilce*—written during the same period as *Scales*—was *Cráneos de bronce*.

62 **edgility** Vallejo uses the neologism *aristaje*, forming an abstract noun by applying the ending -*aje* to the noun *arista* (edge). While this word formation is perfectly in agreement with Spanish morphology, it is not recognized by the *Diccionario Real de la Academia Española* (*DRAE*).

63 **hexagonned** Vallejo coins the word *exagonados*. Instead of using the adjectival form (either *hexagonal* or *exagonal*) he imparts a new verbal emphasis on the word by adding the ending -*ado*, giving the function of a passive participle employed as an adjective.

64 **personage whose goatee seemed to be dripping** Vallejo characterizes the man as a *personaje de biscotelas chorreantes*. *Biscotela* is very light semisweet bread, often served to accompany coffee or tea. The poet appears to be making a homophonic play by replacing *bigotes* with *biscotelas*. We have veered away from the text to conserve the clarity of the image.

65 *Savage Lore* The Spanish title *Fabla salvage* seems to play off the polysemy of *fabla*, which refers to the conventional imitation of Old Spanish. A *fabla* is a *fábula* (fable), but also refers to *habla* (speech), which is why translating the title as *Savage Fable* or *Savage Tale* is less appropriate than employing *Savage Lore*, allowing us to evoke the morphological structure of folklore and the oral tradition.

66 It's not entirely clear what Vallejo means by "*pulucha*," which he places in quotation marks in the original. Since the word is not capitalized, it is unlikely the name of the animal. Given the context, it could refer to a fabled ominous being in the realm of highland superstition.

67 *cholo, -a* This Castilian word refers to a person of European and indigenous blood.

68 *yerba santas*, also *hierbasantas* Vallejo is most likely referring to the plant *Piper auritum*.

69 **sling's throw** Vallejo uses the expression *tiro de honda*. An *honda* refers to the pre-Hispanic weapon *warak'a*. Idiomatically, the expression likens "a stone's throw" as a measurement based on the distance a stone can travel as propelled by human strength. To preserve this rich meaning, we've modified the idiomatic expression in English here and throughout these selections.

70 Vallejo refers to Balta's ancestors as *carne de surco*, literally, "flesh of [the] furrow," which, similar to *carne de canon* (cannon fodder), appears to refer to people socially destined to a life as peasants.

71 **triptolemic** The invention *triptolémico*, which had already been used by Ruben Darío in his poem "Salutación del optimista"—"y el rumor de espigas que inició la labor tripto-lémica"—is an adjective that alludes to Triptolemus, who was taught the art of agriculture by Demeter, and who in turn taught the Greeks to farm. Vallejo seems to use it as a synonym of *agricultural*.

72 **vertexilar** In the Spanish, *verticilar*, a neologism in adjective form derived from *vértice* (vertex, apex).

73 *jalca* [*hallka*] Quechua, village or hamlet in an inhospitable region.

74 **sharecropper** Vallejo uses the regionalism *alpartidario*, which refers to a rural farmer who works land owned by someone else, both of whom receive equal shares of the harvest.

75 Gastón Roger (pseudonym of Ezequiel Balarezo Pinillos and chronicler of *La Prensa* in Lima) published this letter in the evening edition of that newspaper on December 29, 1920.

76 Carlos C. Godoy was Vallejo's attorney in the Santiago de Chuco case. While it is unclear what credentials he had, we have decided to translate "Dr." as "Esq." to specify his profession.

77 **swept under the rug** In the Spanish, Vallejo writes *ha vuelto al tapete negro*. The meaning appears to be that the case has been deliberately forgotten.

78 This letter was originally typewritten on stationary from the Odessa Hotel of Paris.

79 **eternalfather** In the Spanish we read *padretérnica*, apparently an invention of Vallejo or an archaism. If we take the word as a neologism, we see *padre* (father) and *etérnico*, which would seem to represent the old sage of the extant tradition that Vallejo is criticizing.

80 **clarinate** In the Spanish, Vallejo uses the verb *clarinee*, which seems be a fusion of *clarinete* (clarinet) and *clarear* (to clarify).

81 Luis Ángel Firpo (1894–1960), legendary Argentine boxer, is best remembered for being the first Latin American challenger of the world heavyweight title. In 1923, in what many have called the greatest boxing match in history, Firpo knocked Jack Dempsey out of the ring. Despite losing the match, he garnered fame across Latin America and the world.

BOOK THREE

1 See "Chinese Bolshevist Admits Instigation of Legation Outrage," *Straits Times*, June 26, 1925.

2 Vallejo here takes a tongue-in-cheek shot at his friend Corpus Barga. The pun "the Barga outweighs the Corpus" plays off the Latin meaning of *corpus* (body), insinuating that Barga's evaluation of Hernández lacked body, that is, lacked substance.

3 **Michelangelic** In the Spanish, *miguelangélicos*.

4 **suck a yucca** In the Spanish, Vallejo explains that these believers *echan una buena yuca a los demás*, literally, that they "throw a good yucca at everyone else"; but the meaning of the action is to demean, to discard, to diminish, not unlike "throwing rotten tomatoes." Rather than losing the image of the yucca, we have adapted the expression at the risk of vulgarity.

5 **arguing with an adversary** It is not completely clear what Vallejo means by *hostilano*, a word that does not show up in the *DRAE*. However, we notice the presence of *hostil* (hostile) and suspect that Vallejo was referring to a hostile person, which would make *conversando* into the action of an argument.

6 Cf. Luis. Astrana Marín, "Los nuevos vates del más allá," *El Imparcial*, October 20, 1925.

7 Ibid.; "Las escuelas literarias: Ultraístas y creacionistas; La desaprensión de Vicente Huidobro," *El Imparcial*, 1918.

8 **columbeid adventures** Vallejo writes *aventuras colónidas* in reference to the literary magazine *Colónida*, which had been founded by Abraham Valdelomar. The publication attacked the prevailing elitist aesthetics of Lima and proposed a reconsideration of the possibilities for new poetic modalities. Based on the name "Colón" (Columbus), it has been suggested that the neologism refers to a sequel to the literature of Columbus, perhaps following the analogical pattern of Virgil's *Eneida* (*Aeneid*).

9 *il n'y a rien a fáire* French, there's nothing to do.

10 The original version of this article has been lost. It was published in an Italian journal edited by Palmiro Macchiavello and then retranslated to Spanish by Jorge Puccinelli. The present translation is based on the Spanish.

11 **Aymara** A native of the Peruvian-Bolivian high plateau.

12 *huaco* Prehispanic ceramic piece depicting an Andean face. Its utilitarian use is for drinking *chicha* or as a recipient of other liquids. It is a word from a language predating Quechua.

13 Vallejo interchanges spellings of "Shiris" and "Sciris," both of which refer to the pre-Columbian people of Ecuador. Throughout these translations, we respect these orthographical inconsistencies.

14 Daniel Alomía Robles (1871–1942), Peruvian composer and ethnomusicologist. His 1913 song "El condor pasa" was a hit the melody of which was adapted by American musicians Simon and Garfunkel into "El condor pasa (If I could)" on the 1970 album *Bridge over Troubled Water*.

15 Heitor Villa-Lobos (1887–1959), Brazilian composer who successfully incorporated Brazilian folklore melodies into classical music.

16 *quena* Quechua, Andean pan flute.

17 *chalumeau* A recorder-like woodwind instrument with a mouthpiece similar to that of a clarinet.

18 It is unclear what Vallejo means by *vela verde*, or whether Hugo makes a direct reference to Napoleon as either a green candle or sail (another valid translation of *vela*) in any of his poems.

19 Vallejo mistakes Oscar Wilde's nationality for English when it was Irish.

20 Cf. Andrea Solario's painting, *Salome with the Head of Saint John the Baptist*.

21 Cf. Bernardino Luini's painting, *Salome Receiving the Head of Saint John the Baptist*.

22 Cf. Gian Francesco Barbieri di Guerchin's painting *Salome Receiving the Head of Saint John the Baptist*.

23 The reference here appears to be made to Ludwig van Beethoven's Symphony no. 6 in F Major, Op. 68, which in German was also called *Pastoral-Sinfonie*; however, we should also point out that the allusion may be to Ralph Vaughn Williams's Symphony no. 3, which was completed and performed in 1922.

24 Raymond Radiguet (1903–23) was a French author of poetry, two novels, and a play. He died of typhoid at the age of twenty.

25 **radio broadcasting** In the Spanish, Vallejo uses the term *radismo*, which appears to be

formed from the word "radio." The context of inventions likewise supports the meaning of "radio broadcasting."

26 *surmenage* French, extreme fatigue, a breakdown.

27 Vallejo had probably read Boris Pilnyak's *L'année nue*, as translated by Louise Desormonts and Louis Bernstein (Paris: Gallimard, 1926).

28 **the Tramp** In the Spanish, Vallejo refers to Chaplin's famous character as "Charlot," the name he was often called in France, where Vallejo saw Chaplin's films. In the United States, this character was called "the Tramp." Throughout these translations, we have rendered Charlot as the Tramp and have adapted any derived words (*charlotismo/trampism*) accordingly.

29 *ècran* French, screen.

30 James Joseph "Gene" Tunney (1897–1978) was a professional American boxer who defeated Jack Dempsey in 1926 and then in 1927 in what has been called the Long Count Fight. Harry "The Black Panther" Wills (1889–1958), also a professional American boxer, trained from 1920 to 1926, trying to secure a title shot against Dempsey, to no avail.

31 *godillots* French, boots.

32 It's unclear where Vallejo has obtained this quote.

33 **VAPP** Founded in 1921, the organization was renamed RAPP (Russian Association of Proletarian Writers) in 1928.

34 Georgi Valentinovich Plekhanov (1856–1918).

35 Nikolai Ivanovich Bukharin (1888–1938).

36 *robe de chambre* French, bathrobe.

37 Section 11 of Marx's *Theses on Feuerbach*. Translation from the German provided by Foreign Languages, Moscow, reprinted in *Marx and Engels: Basic Writings on Politics and Philosophy*, ed. Lewis S. Feuer (New York: Anchor Books, 1959), 245.

38 The passage from Marx appears in the preface to the second edition of *Capital: A Critique of Political Economy*. The translation from the German is by Samuel Moore and Edward Aveling, based on the third edition of the original German text, reprinted in Feuer, *Marx and Engels*, 146.

39 **this-sided** In the Spanish, we find the word *terrestres*, literally translated as "terrestrial," "earthly," or "worldly," but I sense that Vallejo is applying a Spanish translation of Marxist lingo, namely, of the concept of *Diesseitigkeit*, which can be translated from the German as "worldliness" or, as seems more accurate, as "this-sideness."

40 "Jesus answered, 'My kingdom is not of this world. If My kingdom were of this world, then My servants would be fighting so that I would not be handed over to the Jews; but as it is, My kingdom is not of this realm.'" John 18:36 (New American Standard Bible).

41 Max Eastman (1883–1969). We have translated Vallejo's Spanish version of the English.

42 These passages have been excerpted from a longer text by the same title, "La function revolucionaria del pensamiento," in Priego 2002, 369–75.

43 Probably Jean-François Millet (1814–75), French painter, known for his realistic portrayal of rural peasants.

44 *pompier* French, pompous.

45 Robert Fulton (1765–1815), American engineer credited with developing the first commercial steamboat.

46 **muse** In the Spanish, *numen*, literally translated as "numen," can refer to what is perceptible to the mind but not the senses; however, the phrase *numen poético* is more appropriately rendered as "poetic inspiration." In view of the latter, a nonliteral translation has been preferred.

47 This probably comes from *Cement* by Fyodor Gladkov. See the English translation by A. S. Arthur and C. Ashleigh (Evanston, Ill: Northwestern University Press, 1994).

48 **abracadabrant** Adjective coined by Vallejo, in Spanish *abracadabrante*, meaning pompously clever.

49 **Maurrasian** Maurras-like, in the style of Charles Maurras (1868–1952), French writer, poet, and political theorist.

50 Vallejo translates these passages from the French to the Spanish. The English translations are based on Vallejo's Spanish version. For more, see the pamphlet *Un cadavre*. André Breton, Georges Ribemont-Dessaignes, and Jacques Prévert (Paris: "Du Cadavre," 1924).

51 Georges Courteline (1858–1929), dramatist and novelist, whose work, for the surrealists, would surely have seemed outmoded.

52 *désaxée* French, literally, imbalanced; figuratively, a madman, lunatic.

53 *déraciné* French, rootless, ungrounded.

54 *izba* Traditional Russian countryside home, similar to a log cabin.

55 *sur commande* French, made to order.

56 *au dessus de la mêlée* French, over the [noise of the] tussle.

57 *marchand de tableaux* French, art dealer.

58 *drôles* French, weird, odd.

59 *pas intéressants* French, uninteresting.

60 The reference is likely to Laval's large-scale investment, between August 1927 and June 1930, of around 50 million francs, all of which was not his own but was backed by several financiers and banking institutions.

61 From Émile Zola's open letter to the president of the republic, "J'accuse . . . !" (*L'aurore*, no. 87, January 13, 1898), Vallejo translates from the French, "Mon devoir est de paler, je ne veux pas être complice."

62 This translation is selected from a longer article by the same title.

63 **Against Professional Secrets** In the Spanish, the phrase appears in the singular, *el secreto professional*, and refers to the confidentiality between doctor and patient or attorney and client. In this sense, as a position against this oath of confidentiality, the title of the work could be translated as *Breach of Confidentiality*. Yet, *el secreto profesional* is also *un secreto de la profesión*, that is, a trade secret kept by the master technicians, the initiated members of an exclusive professional order. In this context, the title becomes an allusion to *Le secret profesionnel* (1922) by French surrealist Jean Cocteau, who lays out his concept of the poet-as-angel and establishes a set of prerequisites that one must meet to enter the circle of the initiated.

64 **Poker-faced** An alternate version of this text—"Un extraño procedimiento criminal" (One strange criminal court proceeding)—presents a more expository version, geared toward magazine publication. At this place in the text, Vallejo cuts out the exposition to achieve a more literary result. The splice, however, is not a clean one. In the longer version, the court scene is *confuso* (confusing) because of the waves of gasps and voices, whereas in the shorter version, that confusion is not mentioned. The term "poker-faced" does not translate the language of the poem but rather salvages the image of the criminal, through a reading of both versions.

65 **circuit** The word *periplan* appears to be the verbal neologism *periplar*, based on the masculine noun *periplo*, which refers to a trip, often returning to the point of departure, such as a round-trip. Likewise, it may also refer to a spiritual journey, and in ancient geography it signified circumnavigation. The poet assigns a noun the function of an intransitive verb. Semantically, this simply means "the statues that are spread throughout the plaza, from

one end to the other, walking all around it like people." The noun "circuit" has been chosen to replicate this function.

66 **leapfrog** The phrase *un juego de dulce de hierro*—literally, "a game of iron candy"—is apparently a colloquial expression for a children's game. Due to the unconfirmed nature of the expression, the name of a children's game recognizable to English language readers has been preferred.

67 **scrawny** González Vigil's 1991 edition reads *flavo y dulce*, repeating *flavo* (tawny), whereas Priego's (2002) version reads *flaco* (skinny, slim, thin). Thus, either choice here sends the translation in a different direction. The difficulty resides in the fact that Vallejo is renowned for making slight (graphical and phonetic) alterations. Whether this is a deliberate alteration made by the poet himself or a typographical error in Priego's version is another question. In the present volume—aware of the risk of reproducing an error—I have opted to follow Priego and translate *flaco*, since I believe that if this risk could preserve the complexity and subtlety of the original, then it is worth taking. In this way, *flaco* becomes "scrawny."

68 **A half-baked sun** The expression *un sol a medias* plays off *media luna* (half moon), but an action that occurs *a medias* occurs incompletely. Moreover, *a medias* exceeds the realm of the incomplete. It also refers to what is shoddy, not done well. I have highlighted the connotative meaning with "half-baked."

69 **Out of his cocoon** The Spanish here is riddled with symbolic meaning. Vallejo evokes the *pavo* (turkey) and *pavo real* (peacock) in his sister Nativa's voice: "Miguel me ha echado al pavo. A su pavo." It is important to remember that Miguel, the poet's brother, died in 1915, affecting the young Vallejo, who would eulogize him in several poems of *The Black Heralds* and *Trilce*. In Spanish the *pavo* appears in the phrase *la edad del pavo* that refers to the age of awkwardness in a young person's life as he or she enters the teenage years. In this light, it might be interpreted as "Miguel has thrown me into adolescence" (i.e., by dying at an early age and leaving me to fend for myself). Another line emerges from the interpretation of this expression as a play on *echarle gindes al pavo* (to throw [morello] cherries at the turkey), semantically "to embarrass." In this sense, it could mean "what was supposed to embarrass Miguel, embarrassed me instead." Translating the image of the turkey or the peacock here is virtually impossible, since the symbolism is—if not lost—then grossly deformed. The phrase used here—"kicked me out of the cocoon"—attempts to account for the idea of loss and the consequential hardship that the poet and his sister endured, while keeping the image in the realm of the animal kingdom.

70 **Sajsahuamán** [*Saqsaywaman*] Quechua, Incan archaeological enclosure in Cuzco that, due to its zigzag design, appears to have been a place of worship dedicated to lightning. Literally, "speckled eagle."

71 **Intipampa** Quechua, place of worship dedicated to the sun god, literally, "plane of the sun."

72 *rumancha* Most likely not Quechua. In this context it seems to allude to the slingers (*honderos*), the soldiers who led the battalions. The sling is an instrument woven from wool that is used to throw small stones long distances.

73 *suntupáucar* [*sunturpawkar*] Quechua, design of an insignia or crest. Its literal meaning is "circular garden."

74 *queschuar* [*q'eswa*] Quechua, braided rope. According to the context, it appears to refer to a bundle of cords interwoven with straw and vegetal fibers, carried by the combatants.

75 *guayacán* [*wayaqa*] Quechua, sack, bag, rucksack. Compact mesh made of this resistant thread, designed to carry heavy objects.

76 *apusquepay* [*apuqhepay*] Quechua, bodyguard, literally, "he who goes behind the leader."

77 *chicha* Castilian word that replaces the Quechua *akha*, which refers to maize beer.

78 **oca** [*oqa*] Quechua, Andean tuber, *Oxalis tuberosa*.

79 **hailli**, also **haylli** [*haylli*] Quechua, pre-Hispanic poetic form that exalts military victories.

80 **Hanai-Cuzco** [Hanan-Qosqo] Quechua, the center of the northern zone of the city of Cuzco, or Upper Cuzco.

81 Cusipata is the square in front of the Coricancha, or Temple of the Sun, in Cuzco. It means "Place of Rejoicing." Vallejo translated it to Spanish, "Plaza de la Alegría," as opposed to the more common "Plaza del Regocijo." We've preferred to translate the proper name back to Quechua.

82 **mitimae** [*mitmaq*] Quechua, a group of displaced individuals, driven from one place to inhabit another; outsider, foreigner.

83 **chasqui** [*chaski*] Quechua, messenger, pre-Hispanic courier.

84 **Maule** Name of a region and of a Chilean river.

85 **huaraca** [*warak'a*] Quechua, sling or rigging woven with woolen thread, used to launch stones.

86 **llacta-camayoc** [*llaqtakamayoq*] Quechua, authority of a people.

87 **chacu** [*chaqo*] Quechua, collective celebration where men surround packs of wild animals to catch them alive. A literal translation would be a "hunt."

88 **alco** [*alqo*] Quechua, dog.

89 **llanques** Probably in a dialect from northern Peru: footwear, sandals; in the Quechua of Cuzco the word would be *usuta*.

90 **Patasca** Castilian, a stew typical of the mestizaje in Andean-Hispanic cuisine, made with such ingredients as pork, *mote*, and wheat, among others.

91 **masato** Fermented beverage made from yucca.

92 **mate, poto** These were pitchers and cups for beverages made from dried-out gourds, in contrast to the *q'ero*, which was made from clay.

93 **molle** [*mulli*] Tree native to the Andes. Among other things, it is used to make *chicha* and a dye for wool.

94 **charqui** [*ch'arki*] Quechua, dried, salted meat, originally, that of alpaca or llama.

95 **olluco** [*ulluku*] Quechua, Andean tuber, *Ullucus tuberosus*.

96 **pirca** [*pirqa*] Quechua, wall.

97 **amauta** [*hamut'aq*] Quechua, thinker, philosopher; individual gifted with great intelligence and knowledge.

98 **antun-apu** This may derive from the Quechua *hatun apu*, or principal leader. An *apu* is the concrete representation of a patron deity (hills, mountains, rocks, rivers, etc.). Among mortals it may refer to leaders or commanders. It is unclear what Vallejo means by *antun* in this construction.

99 **curaca** [*kuraka*] Quechua, authority of a pre-Hispanic community.

100 **Inti** Quechua, sun, Incan deity.

101 **Raymi** Quechua, collective, communal celebration. According to the context, it appears to refer to the verb *raymay*: to trim the branches, to prune.

102 **ñusta** Quechua, Incan princess.

103 **quipu** [*khipu*] Quechua, memory encoded in knots and cords of different colors and sizes. Pre-Hispanic mnemonic system.

104 **Coricancha** [*qorikancha*] Quechua, golden premises, Temple of the Sun. Place of worship in Cuzco.

105 **malaqui** [*mallki*] Quechua, mummy of the ancestors. Note that in the original, Vallejo translates the word to Spanish immediately following the Quechua.

106 **yllapa** [*illapa*] Quechua, lightning, deity.

107 **ayllo**, also **ayllu** [*ayllu*] Quechua, community, region; family, lineage.

108 **Collahuata** [*Qollawa*] Quechua, ethnic group of southern Peru, in the Arequipa region.

109 **Chuco** According to the context, it appears to refer to inhabitants of northern Peru, such as those from Huamachuco.

110 **Hurin-Cuzco** [*Urin Qosqo*] Quechua, outskirts or southern region of the city of Cuzco.

111 *lliclla* [*lliklla*] Quechua, blanket, feminine outfit.

112 **Viracocha** [*Wiraqocha*] Quechua, patriarch of the founding gods of the Andean world. Name of one of the Incan emperors.

113 *tambo* [*tanpu*] Quechua, lodging or shelter for travelers.

114 **Aclla-Huasi** [Aqlla Wasi] Quechua, premises of the selected princesses. This was the place where the Incan princesses lived, who were devoted to spiritual work and other tasks like the production of woven clothes for the Inca or the preparation of *chicha* for ceremonies and rites.

115 **Tahuantinsuyo** [*Tawantisuyu*] Quechua, the four domains or regions that formed the Incan Empire, the center of which was Cuzco.

116 *auqui* [*awki*] Quechua, guardian deity in the form of a mountain or river. Prince or inheriting offspring of the Inca.

117 **Yunga** [*yunka*] Quechua, region made up of the Andean valleys and jungle.

118 *rumay-pachaca*, also *rumay-pachacca* According to the context, it appears to refer to a priest or officiant of a pre-Inca Chimú culture.

119 **Chanca** Andean ethnic group.

120 *aravicu*, also *arabicu* [*harawiku*] Quechua, poet, troubadour.

121 *sipacoya*, also *sipakoya* [*sipas qoya*] Quechua, maiden, princess, noninheriting noble female in the court of the Inca.

122 *vilca* [*willka*] Quechua, sacred object or plant.

123 *huaraco* [derived from *warachiku*] Quechua, ceremony, ritual celebration of training for future warriors.

124 *quipuchica*, also *quipuchika* According to the context, it appears to refer to the training ceremony for future princesses or women of the court.

125 *villac* [derived from *willaq uma*] Quechua, reporter or officiant of ceremonies.

126 *coyllur*, also *koyllur* [*qoyllur*] Quechua, star.

127 **Situa** Quechua, windy season, prior to the first rainfall (August and September).

128 *aclla* [*aqlla*] Quechua, a chosen princess who formed part of the Inca's imperial entourage. In this case, it refers to a "chosen princess."

129 **Kalasasaya** According to the context, it appears to refer to an observatory. In Bolivia, Kalasasaya is a temple from the pre-Incan culture of Tiawanaku.

130 *piruc* According to the context, the expression appears to refer to an Incan officiant or servant.

131 *ytu*, also *itu* Quechua, according to the context, it appears to refer to a hymn or prayer.

132 *huaca* [*waka*] Quechua, sacred place or sanctuary, deity.

133 *chuño* [*ch'uño*] Quechua, dehydrated potato.

134 **thorniest thorn of the patch** In the Spanish, Vallejo has *el mochuelo más mochuelo de los mochuelos*, where the noun *mochuelo* is literally a "small owl," but figuratively it refers to a complicated matter that no one wants to handle. We have endeavored to evoke this figurative sense with the image of the thorn.

135 *Tovarishchi* Russian transliteration, comrades.

136 *Kotoryi chas* Russian transliteration, What time is it?

137 **akeists** It's unclear what Vallejo means with the word *akeistas*, as it appears in *The River Flows between Two Shores*, or the slight variant, *atkeistas*, as it appears in *Moscow vs. Moscow*, an earlier version of the same play.

138 **bygoners** In the Spanish we read *anteistas*, a word that appears to be an invention of Vallejo. From *ante-* we interpret the meaning of "before" or "prior," making the word itself describe a proponent of the past.

139 See *I milioni di arlecchino*, ballet by Italian composer Riccardo Drigo (1846–1930).

140 *étonnés* French, stunned, amazed.

141 *congé* French, leave, notice.

142 *sur-le-champ* French, on the spot.

143 **deliteraturizing** In the Spanish, Vallejo coins the term *desliteraturizándose* with the meaning of ridding oneself of literature.

BOOK FOUR

1 **navehall** "Vallejo misspells *ombligo* (navel) as *hombligo* (playing off *hombre*—man). There is a temptation to mistranslate the English as "humbilicus cord, but I have resisted this, since the speaker would have lost his umbilicus cord long ago" (Eshleman 2007, 646).

2 **calcarid** "The Spanish *calcárida* appears to be a neologism based on *calcáreo* (calcareous) and *árida* (arid)" (Eshleman 2007, 647).

3 **stallion louse** "As an adjective *padre* (father) is a common augmentative for almost everything, e.g. *una vida padre* (a great life), *un automóvil padre* (a great car). Here we have tried to translate the act of the lowest parasite being ironically elevated to a role of seminal importance" (Eshleman 2007, 647).

4 **they can jerk me off!** "In answer to our query about *me las pelan!* Larrea wrote to Barcía: 'In our Hispanicamerican group in Montparnasse in 1926, we often sang a kind of ballad, thanks to a good Mexican friend, which had a refrain which went: *Pélame la pinga* (Peel my foreskin down). I would say that this is the origin of that line of Vallejo's. That he puts it in the plural surprises me—perhaps he does that out of modesty! It would translate something like *me la menean*' (they jack me off)" (Eshleman 2007, 650).

5 **aerent** "The Spanish *airente* appears to be a neologism based on *aire* (air), to which an *-ente* suffix has been attached, a common suffix but not one normally attached to the word *aire*. In the same line, *amarillura* derives from *amarillo* (yellow) but is not of normal or frequent usage. Near the end of the same line, *trístidos*, based on *triste* (sad), appears to be a neologism; *-idos* is normally not attached to that word. Last, *tristes* could either be a plural noun of the adjective *triste* or the word for a sad song (which would have no translation). We interpret it as the former" (Eshleman 2007, 650).

6 Kliment Yefremovich Voroshilov (1881–1969), Soviet military and political leader who played a key role in the Great Purge of the 1930s and took over as head of state in the wake of Stalin's death.

7 Alexei Ivanovich Rykov (1881–1938), Russian Bolshevik revolutionary and politician, premier of Russia and the Soviet Union.

8 The title Vallejo offers is *"Leninismo teórico y práctico,"* though it is not completely clear what work he is referencing. It could be *Concerning Questions of Leninism* (1926).

9 *midinette* French, sales clerk or, in the familiar sense, a listless girl.

10 **Great Square** Vallejo refers to the location as the "Gran Plaza," literally the "Great Plaza." He is probably referring to Red Square.

11 **Central Committee for Breastfeeding** In the Spanish, the "Comité Central de las Gotas de Leche," literally, the "Central Committee of Drops of Milk."

12 Vallejo mistranslates the title of Vladimir Kirshon's play *Rel'sy gudyat* as *El brillo de los rieles* (The Glow of the Rails).

13 Kirshon actually coauthored *Red Rust* with Andrei Vasilyevich Uspenski (1927).

14 *Pas de vedettes* French, meaning, there are no celebrities.

15 See *Au-delà du Marxisme* (Brussels: L'Églantine, 1927). See also *Beyond Marxism*, trans. Peter Dodge (The Hague: Nijhoff, 1966).

16 Cf. *Nibelungenlied* (*The Song of the Nibelungs*), written in Middle High German, reinterpreted by Richard Wagner in his *Der Ring des Nibelungen* (*The Ring of the Nibelung*), circa 1874.

17 **kombinat** Transliteration from the Russian, industrial complex or works, as in steelworks.

18 **deconstructionist** With slight poetic license, Vallejo prefers *criticista* over *crítica*, to avoid the meaning of a "dire moment" and emphasize the opposition between the processes of breaking down and building up, as seen in the two films he discusses. The term "deconstructionist" is used without any intention of implying the postmodern theory of deconstructionism.

19 *Isvestia* Daily broadsheet newspaper in Russia, founded in 1917.

20 *refoulé* French, repressed.

21 **vertebralize** Vallejo coins the verb *vertebralizar*, from the noun *vértebra* (vertebra), apparently with a meaning of "to structure with vertebrae," that is, to give it a backbone.

22 **wheeled are the wheels that wheel** Vallejo plays with the double meaning of the noun *rueda* (wheel) and the verb *rodar* (to roll, to turn). The lexical redundancy is deliberate in the original.

23 See *Los de abajo*, by Mariano Azuela, first published in 1915, and in English translation as *The Underdogs*, by Segio Wiasman (New York: Penguin, 2008).

24 See "His Excellency the Governor" (1905), in *Works by Leonid Andreyev*, trans. Maurice Magnus (London: Daniel, 1921).

25 See *Konets Sankt-Peterburga*, 1927 silent film by Vsevelod Pudovkin and hinge of the revolutionary trilogy that includes *Mother* (1926) and *Storm over Asia* (1928).

26 Fay's quote is an English back translation rendered from Vallejo's Spanish.

27 *poncifs* French, clichés, banalities.

28 *Le Populaire* Socialist daily newspaper in French, principal outlet of the French Section of Workers' International. Founded in 1918, directed by León Blum.

29 *au relenti* French, meaning at half speed, slowly.

30 **multanimous** Vallejo coins the word *multánime* by substituting the prefix *multi-* for *uni-*, following the pattern of *unánime* (unanimous).

31 Probably Giraudoux's play *Siegfried*, written in 1928, based on his novel *Seigfried et le Limousin*.

32 *boutades* French, jokes.

33 **Theater of Art** is a translation from Vallejo's Spanish rendering of "Teatro del Arte."

34 *paccarina* [derived from *paqariy* (to dawn, to create, to be born)] Quechua, place of origin of individuals, animals, plants, and so on.

35 *calli-sapa* According to Teodoro Meneses, this refers to "singers with very high-pitched voices." See Teatro *completo* (Lima: PUCP, 1999), 3:108. We, in turn, see the possibility of Castilian-Quechua fusion, in which the Quechua augmentative *sapa* appears to be affixed to the Castilian noun *calle* (street), spelled with an *i* in Vallejo's intuition, which would allow us to see the *calli-sapa* as someone who walks in front of the entourage and announces its imminent presence.

36 *chulpa* [*chullpa* Quechua, sarcophagus, sepulcher of Andean forebears.

37 *huara* [*wara*] Quechua, long pants, men's garment.

38 Omissions in Vallejo's text are replicated here.

39 **creatrice racial euphoria** The Spanish reads *euforia racial creatriz*. The word *creatriz* is a Hispanicization of the French singular feminine adjective *créatrice*, the Spanish equivalent of which is *creadora*. We let Vallejo's French be felt in the English translation.

40 See Ephraim George Squier, *Peru Illustrated; or, Incidents of Travel and Exploration in the Land of the Incas* (1877; repr., Whitefish, MO: Kessinger, 2010); and Marquis de Nadaillac, *Prehistoric America*, trans. N. N. D'Anvers (1893; repr., Whitefish, MO: Kessinger, 2007).

41 ***kero*** [*q'ero*] Quechua, ceremonial cup.

42 ***aribalo*** Used for rituals, it was a ceremonial cup in which *chicha* was prepared or transported. The word doesn't appear to be in Quechua.

43 ***quechuar*** [qeswar] In this context, it refers to the wood of a tree native to the Peruvian Amazon. The Quechuar are an ethnic group of the region. The word may derive from *qeswar*, which is a type of jute or rope woven from vegetal fibers.

44 ***taita*** [*tayta*] Quechua, term used to address an older person, literally, "father."

45 ***humita*** [*humint'a*] Quechua, steamed sweet-corn cake.

46 See Samuel Smiles, *Self-Help* (London: Partridge, 1859).

47 **rat-scented recollection** The construction *recuerdo roedor* (literally, "a rodent memory") refers metaphorically to a morally suspect memory of one's own action.

48 ***encomendero*** This Spanish word is used to refer to the person charged by the Spanish Crown to establish a system of tributary labor in a region of Latin America.

49 ***patrón*** This noun is used to refer to an employer in a broad sense of the word. The plural form is *patrones*.

50 **turkey's wattle** Vallejo doesn't seem to use *moco de pavo* in its idiomatic sense of "uselessness."

51 **chicken fight** It's unclear what the children's game *melo* entailed.

52 **To hell with Tuco!** In the Spanish we read, *¡Qué Tuco ni cuatro gatos negros!* This colloquial expression, centered around the figure of "four black cats," appears to communicate a sense of dismissal, on account of the subject's lack of importance to the speaker.

53 **mean drunk** The phrase *tener diablos azules* (to have blue demons) is a Peruvianism referring to angry behavior induced by alcohol consumption.

54 **in the face of that scarecrow** In the Spanish, *por quítame allá esas pajas*, a regional expression, which also appears in *Trilce*, means "for no reason at all."

BOOK FIVE

1 This English version of "Recent Discoveries in the Land of the Incas" is based on a retranslation to the Spanish by Jorge Puccinelli Villanueva from the French version by Georgette Philippart. The Spanish original has been lost.

2 This English version of "The Andes and Peru" is based on a retranslation to the Spanish by Jorge Puccinelli Villanueva from the French version by Georgette Philippart. The Spanish original has been lost.

3 The English version of "Man and God in Incan Sculpture" is a retranslation from the Spanish by Juan Larrea from the French version by Georgette Philippart.

4 **stirrut** "In 'Village Scene' (in *The Black Heralds*), the bell and voice context led me to a translation of *dondoneo* as 'dronedongs.' Here in a situation that is both abstract and erotic, a different version seems called for. The neologism here strongly evokes a play on *contoneo* (strut); so by adding an 'ir' to *strut* (drawing forth *stir* and *rut*), I hope to match the strangeness of the original" (Eshleman 2007, 652).

5 **wausp** "The Spanish word *avispa* (wasp) appears to have been intentionally misspelled as *abispa*, once again a distortion that registers visually but not as a sound. The point of this may be, in Vallejo's mind, to point out the arbitrariness of spelling in writing what is heard—and too, perhaps, to reinforce a feeling that language itself is highly unstable, especially in charged meditation, and may, like Dalí's melting watches, give way at any moment" (Eshleman 2007, 653–54).

6 **Alfonso** "Alfonso de Silva was a Peruvian musician whom Vallejo met in Paris in 1923. Along with this extraordinary elegy, Vallejo appears to have written a second poem referring to the death of Silva, 'Piensan los viejos asnos' (Old Asses Thinking)" (Eshleman 2007, 655).

7 **beloved being** "The Spanish *amado sér* (beloved being) and *amado estar* (beloved to be) cannot be fully translated (without interpretation, which would distort the meaning of the original), since *ser* ('to be,' as a verb) is not the same thing as *estar* ('to be,' as a verb). If the two verbs are matched, the meaning distinction in English is more or less 'to be' versus 'to exist,' since *ser* is less time-bound and temporary than *estar*. However, Vallejo has turned *ser* into a noun by placing an accent over the 'e,' and in doing so seems to be stressing that which is or is idealized to always be, versus that which has potential to be. To translate *estar* here as 'existence' would be to lose the noun-verb relationship clearly established in Vallejo's handling of the Spanish. Notice that the 'double tomb' referred to in line 34 is not merely a 'tomb' with Silva's 'being,' but a 'mahogany one' with his 'to be,' which emphasizes the abstractness associated with *sér* and the materiality associated with *estar*" (Eshleman 2007, 655).

8 **coughv** "The Spanish *toz* appears to be a neologism, combing *tos* (cough) with *voz* (voice)" (Eshleman 2007, 655).

9 **pintle** "We have been unable to find the word *poña* in any Spanish dictionary. According to Barcia, the word exists in the Spanish Galician language and was perhaps used as a euphemism by Vallejo's grandfathers. Its equivalence in Spanish is *porra*, which literally means a 'strong stick' but figuratively, and when spoken as an exclamation, is a polite euphemism for *polla* (cock, slang for penis). *Mala poña* also suggests a parallelism with common Spanish expressions like *mala roña* (awful mange) and *mala saña* (terrible hatred). For the 1978 edition of *the Complete Posthumous Poetry*, Barcia and I decided on 'boner' as a translation, but today this strikes me as too direct and not obscure enough. So I have chosen *pintle*, literally, a 'pivot pin,' which is also obsolete and vulgar slang for *penis*. The speaker in this stanza seems to have been responding to sexual frustration with considerable ambivalence, so I hope that the play on 'hard left' (*zurdazo*)—to be left with an erection as well as to be hit with a left-handed blow—in the following line will help reinforce Vallejo's meaning in English" (Eshleman 2007, 656).

10 **arduent** "The Spanish *ardío* appears to be a metaplasm derived from *ardiente* (ardent) and *arduo* (arduous). It is possible that the word *ardido* (intrepid, angry) also figures into the construction. It is also possible that Vallejo meant *árido* (arid)" (Eshleman 2007, 657).

11 **wolvum** "The Spanish *lovo* (which plays off *loco*, 'crazy') appears to be an intentional misspelling of *lobo* (wolf), a usage that González vigil understands as a way to link the word to *ovo* (egg, or ovum). I agree and have tried to approximate this construction in English" (Eshleman 2007, 660).

12 **Pedro Rojas** "Appears to be a fictitious character, a symbol of the humblest and most oppressed human beings. He has just learned to write a little, and hearing *vivan* as *viban* and *avisa* as *abisa*, misspells the words. We pick up the misspellings by using 'combanions' in place of 'companions'" (Eshleman 2007, 665).

13 *Ama sua! Ama llulla! Ama kella!* According to Andean indigenists, this was the national greeting or motto in the time of the Incas; other scholars believe it an indigenist invention attributed to the Incas. Literally, it means, "no thief, no liar, no slacker." Vallejo translates it to Spanish as *no matar, no mentir, no estar ociosos* (no killing, no lying, no being lazy).

14 *champi* [*chanpi*] Quechua, tool made with a metal alloy.

15 *say jusca*, also *say kusca* [*sayk'usqa*] Quechua, tired, exhausted.

16 *unancha yawarpa* [derived from *unanchay* (to symbolize) and *yawar* (blood)] Quechua, according to the context, it appears to allude to situations related to the royal bloodline.

17 *kolla*, also *colla* [*qoya*] Quechua, Incan princess, women of high Incan stock or royal lineage.

18 **Payta Yuyarina** Given the context, the expression seems to refer to the Incan emperor. Literally, it means "The Unforgettable One," "The one who must always be kept in the memory."

19 **Tonapa Camaj** [*Tonapa Kamaq*] Quechua, according to the context, the expression appears to allude to the princess as the "Generator" or "Mother of Tonapa," a god of the Andean high plateau.

20 *piruro* [*phiruru*] Quechua, a disk, small wheel akin to a rattle.

21 **Huatanay** River that traverses the city of Cuzco.

22 **Poru**, **Watalla**, and **Maule** According to the context, these term appear to allude to ethnic groups conquered by the Incas.

23 *coraquenque* Not a Quechua term, this refers to a bird and is a recurring figure in the indigenist imagination.

24 *mashua* Probably a dialect of northern Peru. Andean tuber, *Tropaeolum tuberosum*. According to the context, the allusion seems to be to its color.

25 *llauto* [*llawt'u*] Quechua, royal emblem belonging to the Inca.

26 **Pucutu! Pucutur!** According to the context, this seems to be a proper name.

27 *puquio* [*pukyu*] Quechua, natural spring.

28 *coya* [qoya] Quechua, wife, female partner, or woman at the service of the Inca.

29 **Shira** According to the context, it appears to allude to an Andean ethnic group.

30 **Huanacaure** [*wanakawri*] Quechua, name of a sacred guardian mountain of Cuzco.

31 **Salkamarca** Quechua, name of a canton of Cuzco.

32 *supay* Quechua, demon, evil.

33 *Rawa! . . . Wiru!* Quechua, *wiru* is the stalk of the maize plant and, in this context, *rawa* appears to refer to its root.

34 *wausa* [*wawsa*] Quechua, literally, "semen." According to the context, it appears to allude to a type of wax or sperm used for candles.

35 **Tunkuy! Tunkuy!** Quechua, an expression used to bring about the beginning of a competition or battle.

SELECTED BIBLIOGRAPHY

Vallejo's works are listed by their title first, followed by the name of the editor(s) cited in the text.

Works by Vallejo

POETRY

España, aparta de mí este cáliz. Edited by Juan Larrea and Alan Smith. Madrid: Árdora, 2012.

España, aparta de mi este cáliz. Prologue by Juan Larrea. Drawing by Pablo Picasso. Edited by Manuel Altlaguirre. Ediciones Literarias del Comisariado. Ejército del Este ([Barcelona?]: Montserrat Monastery), 1939.

Los heraldos negros. Lima: Souza Ferreira, 1918.

Obra poética completa. Edited by Américo Ferrari. Lima: Mancloa, 1968.

Obras completas. Vol. 1, Obra poética. Edited by Ricardo González Vigil. Lima: Centenario, 1991.

Poemas humanos (1923–1938). Epilogue by Luis Alberto Sánchez and Jean Cassou. Bio-bibliographical note by Raúl Porras Barrenechea. Edited by Georgette de Vallejo and Raúl Porras Barrenechea. Paris: Les Editions des Presses Modernes, Au Palais Royal, 1939.

Poesía completa. Edited by Antonio Merino. Madrid: Akal, 1996b.

Poesía completa. Edited by Juan Larrea. Barcelona: Barral, 1978.

Poesía completa. Edited by Raúl Hernández Novás. Havana: Arte y Literatura Casa de las Américas, 1988.

Poesía completa I–IV. Edited by Ricardo Silva-Santisteban. Lima: PUCP, 1997.

Trilce. Edited with critical commentary by Julio Ortega. Madrid: Catedra, 2002.

Trilce. Prologue by Antenor Orrego. Lima: Talleres Tipográficos de la Penitenciaría, 1922.

Trilce. Prologue by José Bergamín. "Salutation" (poem) by Gerardo Diego. Madrid: Compañía Iberoamericana de Publicaciones, 1930.

NARRATIVES

Escalas. Lima: Talleres Tipográficos de la Penitenciaría, 1923.

Escalas melografiadas. Edited by Claude Couffon. Arequipa: UNAS, 1994.

Fabla salvaje. Prologue by Pedro Barrantes Castro. La Novela Peruana, May 16, 1923.

Hacia el reino de los sciris. Nuestro Tiempo, January, March, May 1944.

Narrativa completa. Edited by Antonio Merino. Madrid: Akal, 1996a.

Narrativa completa. Edited by Ricardo Silva-Santisteban and Cecilia Moreano. Lima: PUCP, 1999.

Novelas: Tungsteno, Fabla salvaje, Escalas melografías. Lima: Hora del Hombre, 1948.

Novelas y cuentos completos. Edited by Georgette de Vallejo. Lima: Moncloa, 1967.

Paco Yunque. Apuntes del Hombre 1 (July 1951).

El tungsteno. Madrid: Cenit, 1930.

El tungsteno (novela proletaria). Lima: Fondo de Cultura Popular, 1965.

Tungsteno y Paco Yunque. Lima: Baca y Villa Nueva, 1957.

PLAYS

Moscú contra Moscú. In Letras peruanas, no. 6 (1952): 37–38, and no. 7 (1952): 81, 108. Edited by Jorge Puccinelli. Translated by Li Carrillo and Georgette de Vallejo.

La piedra cansada: Tres actos y quince cuadros. Edited by Washington Delgado. Visión del
    Perú 4 (July 1969): 283–321.
Piezas y escritos sobre teatro. Preliminary note and translation by Carlos Garayar. Revista
    Peruana de Cultura 2, no. 1 (1982): 107–161.
Piezas y escritos sobre teatro de Vallejo. In Podestá, César Vallejo, su estética teatral, 163–313.
Teatro completo I–II. Edited and translated by Enrique Ballón Aguirre. Lima: PUCP, Fondo
    Editorial, 1979.
Teatro completo I–III. Edited by Ricardo Silva-Santisteban and Cecilia Moreano. Lima: PUCP,
    1999.

ARTICLES, CHRONICLES, REPORTS, AND OTHER PROSE
Artículos y crónicas (1918–1939) desde Europa. Edited by Jorge Puccinelli. Lima: Banco de
    Crédito, 1997.
Artículos y crónicas completos I–II. Edited by Jorge Puccinelli. Lima: PUCP, 2002.
César Vallejo: Crónicas de poeta. Edited by Manuel Ruano. Caracas: Biblioteca Ayacucho,
    1996.
César Vallejo en El Comercio. Edited by Aurelio Miro Quesada S. Lima: Edición de El
    Comercio, 1992.
Crónicas I–II. Edited by Enrique Aguirre Ballón. Mexico City: Dirección General de
    Publicaciones, Universidad Nacional Autónoma de México, 1984.
La cultura peruana: Crónicas. Edited and translated by Enrique Aguirre Ballón. Lima: Mosca
    Azul, 1987.
Ensayos y reportajes completos. Edited by Manuel Miguel de Priego. Lima: PUCP, 2002.
Rusia ante el segundo plan quinquenal. Edited by Georgette de Vallejo. Lima: Graf. Labor,
    1965.
Rusia en 1931: Reflexiones al pie del Kremlin. Madrid: Ulises, 1931.
Traducciones completas. Edited by Rosario Valdivia Paz-Soldán. Lima: PUCP, 2002.

LETTERS
Cartas: 114 de César Vallejo a Pablo Abril de Vivero, 37 de Pablo Abril de Vivero a César
    Vallejo. Prologue by Manuel Castañón. Lima: Mejía Baca, 1975.
César Vallejo: A lo mejor soy otro . . . 27 nuevas cartas. Lima: Villanueva, 1998.
César Vallejo a Pablo Abril: En el drama de su espistolario. Edited by Manuel Castañón.
    Valencia: Universidad de Carabobo, 1960.
César Vallejo cartas a Pablo Abril: Un documento humano conmovedor. Edited by Manuel
    Castañón. Buenos Aires: Alonso, 1971.
Correspondencia completa. Edited by Jesús Cabel. Lima: PUCP, 2002.
Epistolario general. Edited by Manuel Castañón. Valencia: Pretextos, 1982.

Works on Vallejo
Abril, Xavier. Exégesis trílcica. Lima: Gráfica Labor, 1980.
Ballón, Aguirre E. Cesar Vallejo: Ideólogo y político. Lima: Intercampus, 1986.
———. Poetología y escritura: Las crónicas de César Vallejo. Mexico City: Dirección General
    de Publicaciones, Universidad Nacional Autónoma de México, 1985.
———. Vallejo como paradigma: Un caso especial de escritura. Lima: Instituto Nacional de
    Cultura, 1974.
Clayton, Michelle. Poetry in Pieces: César Vallejo and Lyric Modernity. Berkeley: University of
    California Press, 2011.
Escobar, Alberto. Cómo leer a Vallejo. Lima: Villanueva, 1973.

Eshleman, Clayton. Companion Spider: Essays. New York: Wesleyan University Press, 2002.

Espejo Asturrizaga, Juan. César Vallejo: Itinerario del hombre, 1892–1923. Lima: Seglusa, 1989.

Ferrari, Américo. Figura para abolirse. Trujillo, Perú: SEA, 1991.

———. El universo poético de César Vallejo. Lima: Heraldo, 1997.

Flores, Ángel, ed. Aproximaciones a César Vallejo. Long Island City: Las Americas, 1971.

Franco, Jean. César Vallejo: The Dialectics of Poetry and Silence. Cambridge: Cambridge University Press, 1976.

González Montes, Antonio. Escalas hacia la modernización narrativa. Lima: Fondo Editorial Universidad Nacional Mayor de San Marcos, 2002.

González Vigil, Ricardo. César Vallejo. Lima: Editorial Brasa, 1995.

———. Claves para leer a César Vallejo. Lima: San Marcos, 2009.

———. Leamos juntos a Vallejo. Lima: Banco Central de Reserva del Perú, Fondo Editorial, 1988.

Granados, Pedro. Poéticas y utopías en la poesía de César Vallejo. Lima: PUCP, Fondo Editorial, 2004.

Gutiérrez, Gustavo, and William Rowe. Vallejo: El acto y la palabra. Lima: Fondo Editorial del Congreso del Peru, 2010.

Hart, Stephen. "A Chronology of Vallejo's Life and Works." In Eshleman 2007, 689–704.

———. Religión, política y ciencia·en la obra de César Vallejo. London: Tamesis, 1987.

———. Stumbling between 46 Stars: Essays on César Vallejo. London: Centre of César Vallejo Studies, 2007.

Hart, Stephen, and Jorge Cornejo Polar. César Vallejo: A Critical Bibliography of Research. London: Boydell and Brewer, 2002.

Higgins, James. César Vallejo en su poesía. Lima: Seglusa, 1989.

———. The Conflict of Personality in César Vallejo's "Poemas Humanos." N.p., 1966.

———. Los nueve monstruos de César Vallejo: Una tentativa de interpretación. Bogotá: Universidad de los Andes, 1967.

———. Visión del hombre y de la vida en las últimas obras poéticas de César Vallejo. Mexico City: Siglo XXI, 1970.

Hopkins Rodriguez, Eduardo. "Análisis de La piedra cansada de César Vallejo." In Intensidad y altura de César Vallejo, ed. Ricardo González Vigil, 265–319. Lima: PUCP, 1993.

Larrea, Juan. Aula Vallejo, nos. 1–13. Córdoba, Argentina: Dirección General de Publicidad, 1961–74.

———. César Vallejo o Hispanoamérica en la cruz de su razón. Córdoba: Universidad Nacional de Córdoba, 1957.

———. César Vallejo y el surrealismo. Madrid: Corazón, 1976.

Martos, Marco, and Elsa Villanueva. Las palabras de Trilce. Lima: Seglusa, 1989.

Meo Zilio, Giovanni. Estudios hispanoamericanos: Temas lingüísticos y de crítica semántica. Rome: Bulzoni, 1993.

Monguío, Luis. César Vallejo: Vida y obra. New York: Perú Nuevo, 1952.

More, Ernesto. Vallejo, en la encrucijada del drama peruana. Lima: Bendezú, 1968.

Neale-Silva, Eduardo. César Vallejo en su fáce trílcica. Madison, WI: Madison University Press, 1975.

Orrego, Antenor. Mi encuentro con César Vallejo. Bogotá: Tercer Mundo, 1989.

Orrillo, Winston. César Vallejo: Periodista paradigmático. Lima: UNMSM Fondo Editorial, 1998.

Ortega, Julio. César Vallejo. Madrid: Taurus, 1975.

———. La teoría poética de César Vallejo. Providence: Del Sol, 1986.

Oviedo, José M. César Vallejo. Lima: Visión Peruana, 1987.

———. Escrito al margen. Mexico City: Premìa, 1987.

Paoli, Roberto. El lenguaje conceptista de César Vallejo. Buenos Aires: Instituto de Cooperación Iberoamericana de Buenos Aires, 1988.

———. Mapas anatómicos de César Vallejo. Firenze: Casa Editrice d'Anna, 1981.

———. La poesía de César Vallejo a la luz de sus variantes. Fasano di Puglia: Schena, 1972.

Philippart de Vallejo, Georgette. ¡Allá ellos, allá ellos, allá ellos! Lima: Zalvac, 1978.

Podestá, Guido. César Vallejo, su estética teatral. Minneapolis: Institute for the Study of Ideologies and Literature, 1985.

Yurkievich, Saúl. Fundadores de la nueva poseía latinoamericana. Barcelona: Barral Editores S.A., 1971.

———. Valoración de Vallejo. Resistencia: Departamento de Letras, Escuela de Humanidades, Universidad Nacional del Nordeste, 1958.

Articles on Vallejo

Aguirre, Enrique Ballón. "César Vallejo en viaje a Rusia." Hispamérica 6, no. 18 (1977): 3–30.

Bruzual, Alejandro. "Los viajes de César Vallejo a la Unión Soviética: La dialéctica del vaso de agua." A Contra Corriente: Una Revista de Historia Social y Literatura de América Latina 4, no. 1 (2006): 23–39.

Cárdenas, Miguel Ángel. "La otra pluma del poeta." El Comercio 24 (May 2008): 2B.

Chirinos, Eduardo. "Vallejo y los elefantes: Sobre la peculiar zoología vallejiana." El Dominical. Suppl. of El Comercio, November 2, 2007.

Escribano, Pedro. "Vallejo era inocente." La República, April 18, 2008.

Estrada, Francisco. "Ricardo González Vigil: Vallejo es muy difícil, y el crítico debe explicarlo." Peru 21, November 5, 2005.

Gonzales, Ulises. "Todo Vallejo en inglés: Clayton Eshleman, traductor de 'The Complete Poetry of César Vallejo.'" Sunday suppl. of El Comercio, December 4, 2006.

González Montes, Antonio. "La narrativa de César Vallejo." In Intensidad y altura de César Vallejo, edited by Ricardo González Vigil, 221–64. Lima: PUCP, 1993.

González Vigil, Ricardo. "El humor en la poesía de Vallejo." El Comercio, June 7, 2010.

Hart, Stephen. "Was César Vallejo Guilty as Charged?" Latin American Literary Review 26, no. 51 (1998): 79–89.

Higgins, James. "La orfandad del hombre en los Poemas Humanos de Cesar Vallejo." Revista Iberoamericana 34, no. 66 (1968): 299–311.

Kirstal, Efrain. "Review of Tungsten." Harvard Book Review 11–12 (Winter–Spring 1989): 20.

Lévano, César. "Vallejo: Las cartas perseguidas." La Primera, March 18, 2012.

López Soría, José Ignacio. "El no-saber como actitud existencial de César Vallejo." Amaru 5 (January–March 1968): 91–92. Reproduced by Ángel Flores in 1971.

Lora, Juan José. "El dadaísmo: Sus representantes en el Perú." La Crónica, June 20, 1921.

Machaca Escobar, César. "El poeta del dolor humano." Los Andes (Puno), May 16, 2010.

Mendoza C, Raúl A. "Los días y las noches de Vallejo en París." La República, September 25, 2011.

Meneses, Carlos. "1931, en vida y obra de Vallejo." Vallejo: Su tiempo y su obra. Actas de Coloquio Internacional. Universidad de Lima. (August 25–28, 1994): 38.

Oviedo, J. M., and Keith A. McDuffie. "Polémica sobre César Vallejo." Revista Iberoamericana 42, no. 96 (1976): 593–600.

Oviedo, José Miguel. "Vallejo cincuenta años después." Hispania 72, no. 1 (1989): 9–12.

Oviedo, Perez T. R. "La imagen diagonal: De lo cinematico en Cesar Vallejo." Anales de Literatura Hispanoamericana 32 (2003): 53–70.

Rowe, William. "La lectura del tiempo en Trilce." Cuadernos Hispanoamericanos: Homenaje a César Vallejo 1, no. 454–55 (1988): 297–304.

Villanes Cairo, Carlos. "Vallejo y la despiadada pobreza." La República March 26, 2011.

Zavaleta, Carlos Eduardo. "Apuntes sobre su prosa: Vallejo en la narrativa peruana actual." Expreso, January 3, 2005.

Works by Vallejo in English Translation

After So Many Words: Fragments from Four Poems. Translated by Clayton Eshleman. Madison, WI: Tiramisu, 1988.

Against Professional Secrets. Translated by Joseph Mulligan. New York: Roof Books, 2011.

Aphorisms. Translated by Stephen Kessler. Los Angeles: Green Integer 52, 2002.

Autopsy on Surrealism. Translated by Richard Schaaf. Willimantic, CT: Curbstone, 1982.

Battles in Spain: Five Unpublished Poems. Translated by Clayton Eshleman and José Rubia Barcia. Santa Barbara, CA: Black Sparrow, 1978.

The Black Heralds. Translated by Richard Schaaf and Kathleen Ross. Pittsburgh, PA: Latin American Literary Review Press, 1990.

Cesar Vallejo, a Selection of His Poetry. Translated by James Higgins. Wolfeboro, NH: Cairns, 1988.

Complete Later Poems, 1923–1938. Translated by Michael Smith and Valentino Gianuzzi. Saint Paul: Plum Books, 2005.

The Complete Poetry: A Bilingual Edition; César Vallejo. Edited and translated by Clayton Eshleman. Berkeley: University of California Press, 2007.

The Complete Posthumous Poetry. Translated by Clayton Eshleman and José Rubia Barcia. Berkeley: University of California Press, 1980.

Four Poems of Cesar Vallejo. Translated by Thomas Merton. New York: Pax, 1960.

The Mayakovsky Case. Translated by Richard Schaaf. Willimantic, CT: Curbstone, 1982.

Palms and Guitar. Translated by J. C. R. Green. Portree, Isle of Skye: Aquila/Phaethon, 1982.

Paris, October 1936. Translated by Clayton Eshleman and Barcia J. Rubia. Binghamton, NY: Bellevue, 1978.

Selected Poems. Translated by H. R. Hays and Louis Hammer. Old Chatham, NY: Sachem, 1981.

Selected Poems. Translated by Stephen Hart. Bristol: Bristol Classical, 2000.

Selected Poems [of] César Vallejo. Translated by Edward Dorn and Gordon Brotherston. Harmondsworth: Penguin, 1976.

Seven Poems. Translated by José Hierro and Clayton Eshleman. Reno, NV: Morris, 1967.

Spain, Take This Chalice from Me (and Other Poems). Translated by Margaret S. Peden. New York: Penguin Books, 2008.

Telluric and Magnetic: A Sift of Thirteen Poems. Translated by Clayton Eshleman. Toronto: Letters Bookshop, 2005.

Trilce. Translated by Clayton Eshleman. Introduction by Américo Ferrari. Middletown: Wesleyan University Press, 1992.

Trilce. Translated by David Smith. Introduction by Fernando Alegría. New York: Grossman, 1973.

Trilce. Translated by Rebecca Seiferle. Edited by Stanley Moss. Riverdale-on-Hudson, NY: Sheep Meadow, 1992.

Tungsten. Translated by Robert Mezey. Syracuse: Syracuse University Press, 1988.

lvii, 207, 333–36. *See also* Leningrad; *The Rails are Humming*

Koricancha. *See* Coricancha

labor, xxxiv, xlix, 3, 49, 331, 353, 360–61; aesthetic of, lix, 357–58, 478; collective, xxxiii, xxxvi, lxviii, 257, 275, 387, 486; forced, lii, 283, 457–59, 464–66; manual, lxi, 22, 236–37, 239, 250–51, 343, 346, 364–66, 398–99

Lake Titicaca, 389, 397, 472, 485

Larrea, Juan, xxv, xxvii, xxxviii, xlix, li, lxv, 299–301, 469, 471–72, 561–54

leap: Marxist, 358, 362, 372; in nature, l, 156; in society, 156, 189, 337, 492

Leningrad: article from, 381–83; meeting in, xxix–xxx, lv, lvii, 207, 333–36; trip through, xxxiii

Leninism, 334; ductility of, 345; inorganic, 209

Lenin, Vladimir, xxxiv, lx, 135, 160, 180–83, 197, 199, 226, 246–47, 264, 368, 382–83

liberalism, 129–30

Lima, xlvi, li, lii, 18, 92, 114–16, 472, 496; departure from, xxvi, xlviii; funds from, 298; magazines of, xviii, xxii, xxvi, xxxiii, 301, 312; National Museum of, 485–87, 490; possible return to, 560, 564; residence in, xix–xxi, 39–40, 42, 303

Lipatov, Boris Viktorovich, xxx, lv, 334. *See also* Leningrad

Liszt, Franz, lvi, 363–64

loan: from Pablo Abril, 308; from Gerardo Diego, 470; from Juan Larrea, 300–301

Lorca, Federico García, xxxv, xxxvii, 470, 480, 500

Lunacharsky, Anatoly, liv, lvi–lvii, 182, 334, 360–61

madness: as aesthetic, 175–77; as illness, xlvi–xlvii, xlviii, 85–92, 109–12, 233–36

Madrid: at the battlefront of, xxxviii, 491–96, 526, 530; correspondence from, xxvii; law studies, xxiv, xxvi; letters from, 299, 470–72; publications in, xliv, xlviii, lii–liii, 385–86, 398–90, 496–500; stays in, xxviii–xxxv, xxxvii, 139–41

Maeterlinck, Maurice, xxiii, 34, 121–23, 474. See also *The Blue Bird*; theater

Mansiche, xx, 19, 114

Marañón, Río (river), 81, 83, 230, 487

Mariátegui, José Carlos: letters to, 302, 468; in Lima, 39; style of, xxiv. See also *Amauta*; indigenism

marxism: dialectics, xlvi; exploitation of, xxxii, 350; ideology, xxiii, l, 355, 367–69; Lunacharsky on, lvii; shortcomings of, 339; surrealism's adoption of, lviii, 203–5

Marx, Karl: dialectic of, 196–97, 213–14, 321, 335, 357 (*see also* Heraclitus of Ephesus); essential developments of, xxxii–xxxiii, 355, 372–74; exploitation of, 203, 266, 283, 367–69; on life as experiment, 207; on literature, 181; loyalty to, lxv; on technique of production, 383–84

Mayakovsky, Vladimir, xxix, xxxiii, lvii, 173, 201, 207–310, 334, 354–55

Montmartre, xxiii, 146, 168

Montparnasse, xxiii, xli, 122–23, 190, 294, 478

Moscow: dramatization of, xxxvii, lx, lxii, 245–93; kolkoz outside of, lxi; lodging in, 333, 336; with Mayakovky in, 207–10; trips to, xxviii–xxix, xxxiii–xxxv, liv, lvi, 310–12, 347, 380–81, 385–87; uprisings in, 130

nihilism, 202, 256, 274, 389

Orbegoso, Luis José, xl, li, 564–65

orphanhood, xx, xxvi, xlv, xlvi, lxiv, 58, 60, 71–72, 86, 291–93, 297, 410

Orrego, Antenor, xviii, xx, xxii, xxiv, xliv, 116–17, 171

Palma, Clemente, xix, 39

Paris, 317–18, 323, 328; death in, 320; fashion of, 131–32; letters from, 119–20, 294–98, 300–312; move to, xxiii–xxiv, xlviii, lviii, 117–18; published in, lxiv; residence in, xxii, xxv–xxxiv, xxxvii, xl–xli, xlix, lxxiii; theater scene of, 121–22

Pasternak, Boris, xxix, lii, 201, 207, 334

pessimism, 4, 203, 369

Phillippart, Georgette, xxviii, xxxii–xxxviii, xli– lii, lxiv, lxxii–lxxiii, 517, 561–62, 564

Picasso, Pablo, lxv, 135, 154–56, 176, 186, 191–93, 210–11, 473, 476, 513

ABOUT THE AUTHOR

César Vallejo (1892–1938) was born in the Peruvian Andes and, after publishing some of the most radical Latin American poetry of the twentieth century, moved to Europe, where he diversified his writing practice to encompass theater, fiction, and reportage. As an outspoken critic of the European avant-garde, Vallejo stands as one of the most authentic and multifaceted creators to write in the Castilian language.

ABOUT THE EDITOR

Joseph Mulligan is a writer, poet, translator, and scholar whose work has focused on experimental literatures across the Americas and Western Europe. He has translated *Against Professional Secrets* by César Vallejo (2001) and Gustavo Faverón's novel *The Antiquarian* (2014). His translations of Sahrawi poetry appeared in *Poems for the Millennium, vol. 4: The University of California Book of North African Poetry* (2013), and his translations of Jorge Eduardo Eielson's poems appeared in *Asymmetries: Anthology of Peruvian Poetry* (2015). With Mario Domínguez Parra, he has coedited and cotranslated into Spanish a selection of poems and essays by Pierre Joris, *Mawqif* (2015). He lives in Rochester, New York.